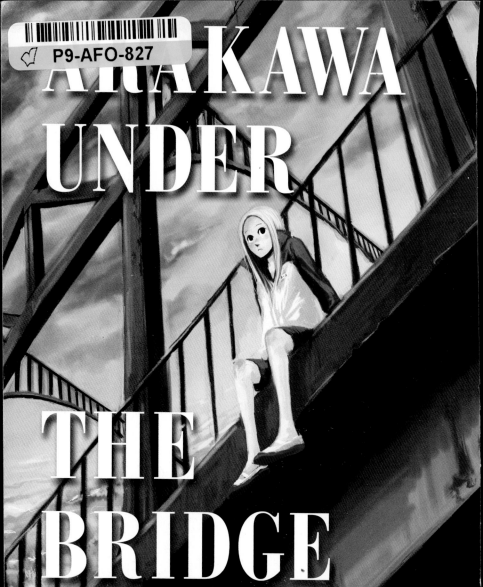

ARAKAWA UNDER THE BRIDGE 1

Hikaru Nakamura

CONTENTS

ORANGES

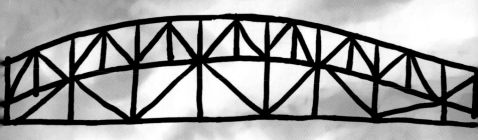

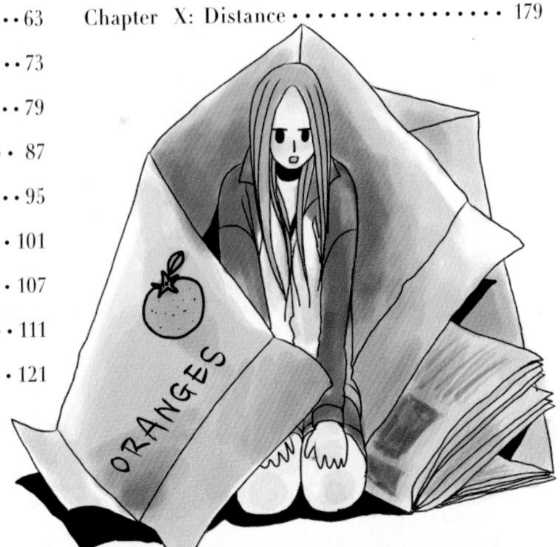

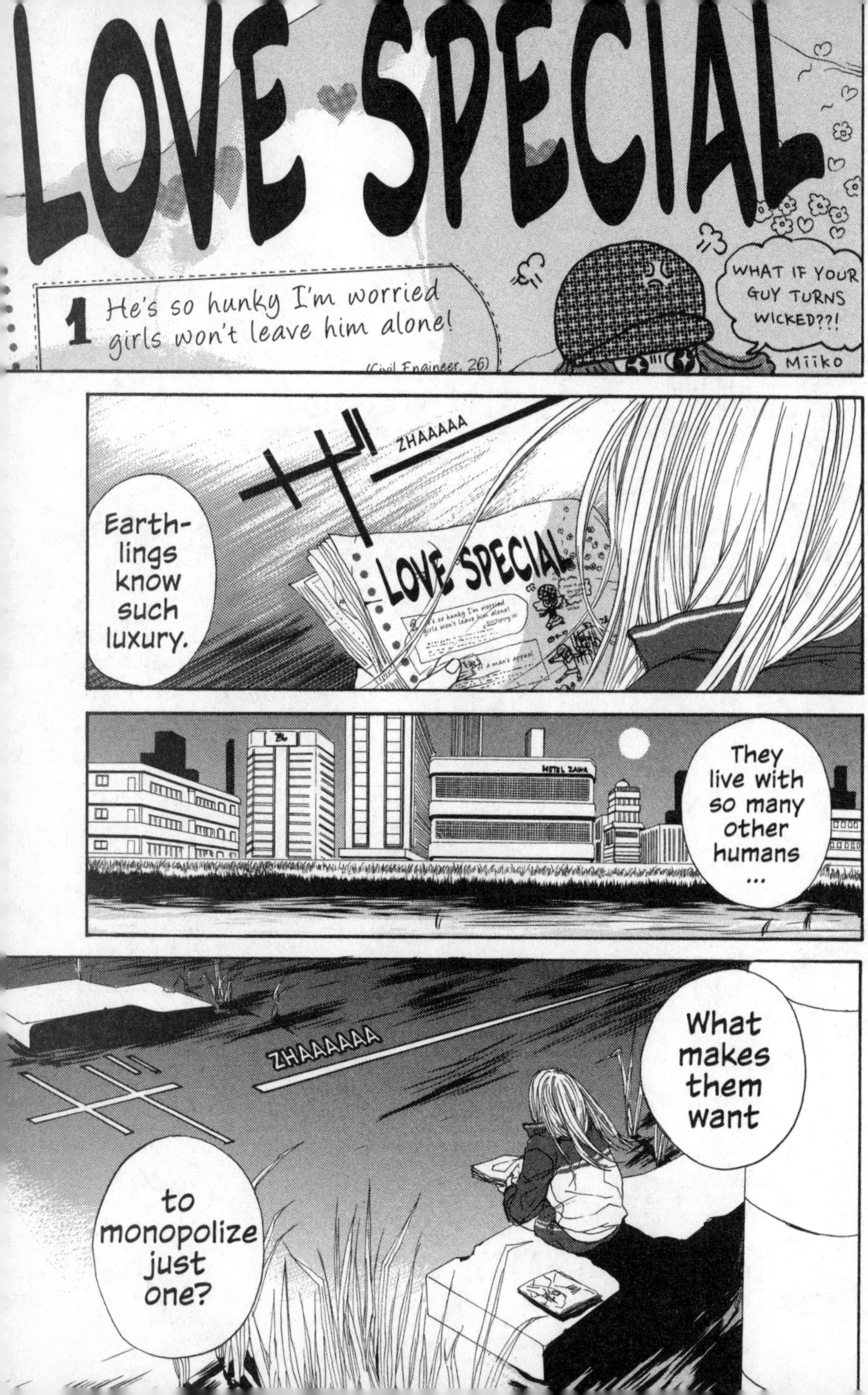
LOVE SPECIAL
WHAT IF YOUR GUY TURNS WICKED??!
Miiko
1 He's so hunky I'm worried girls won't leave him alone!
(Civil Engineer, 26)
ZHAAAAA
Earth-lings know such luxury.
LOVE SPECIAL
They live with so many other humans ...
What makes them want
ZHAAAAAA
to monopolize just one?

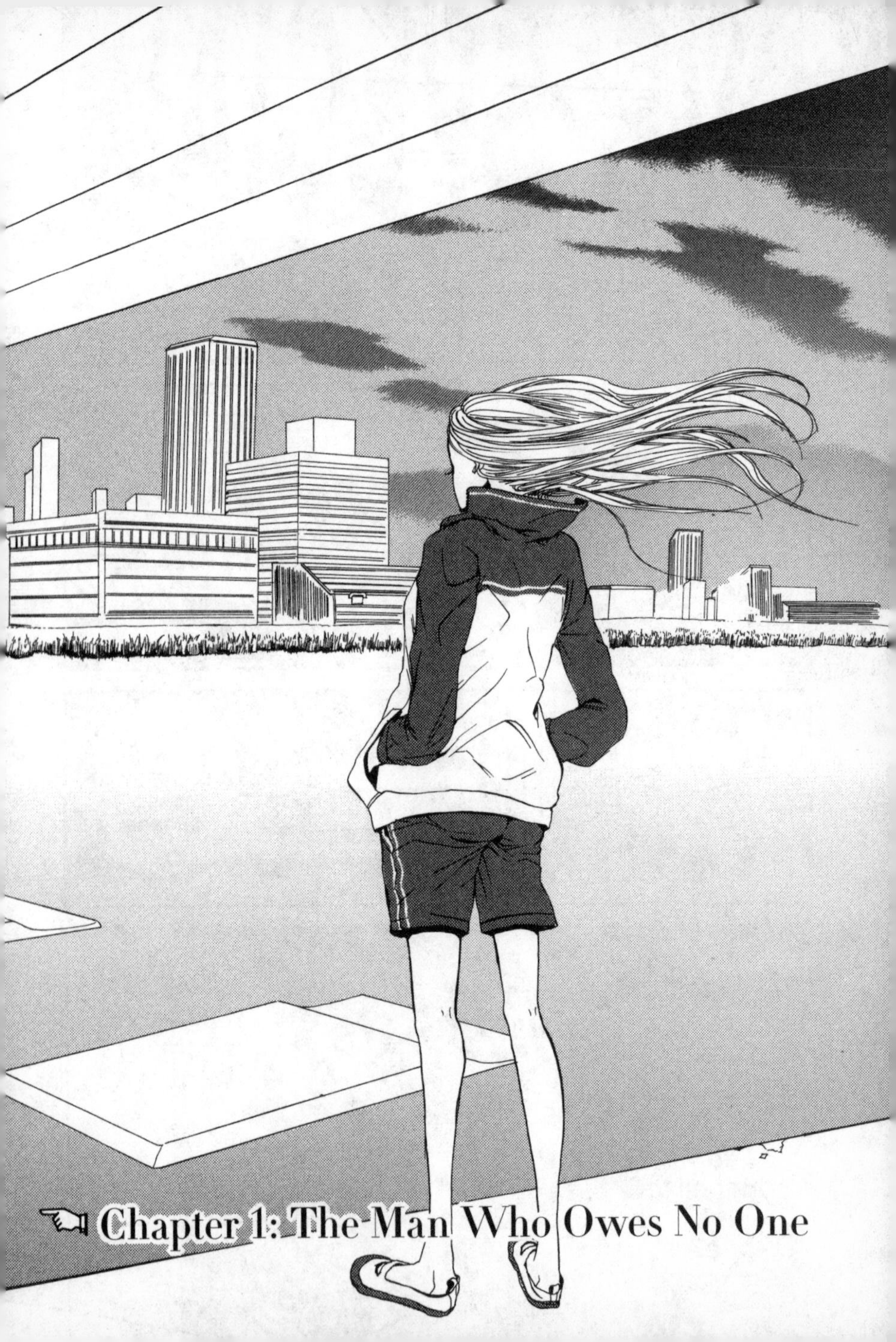

☜ Chapter 1: The Man Who Owes No One

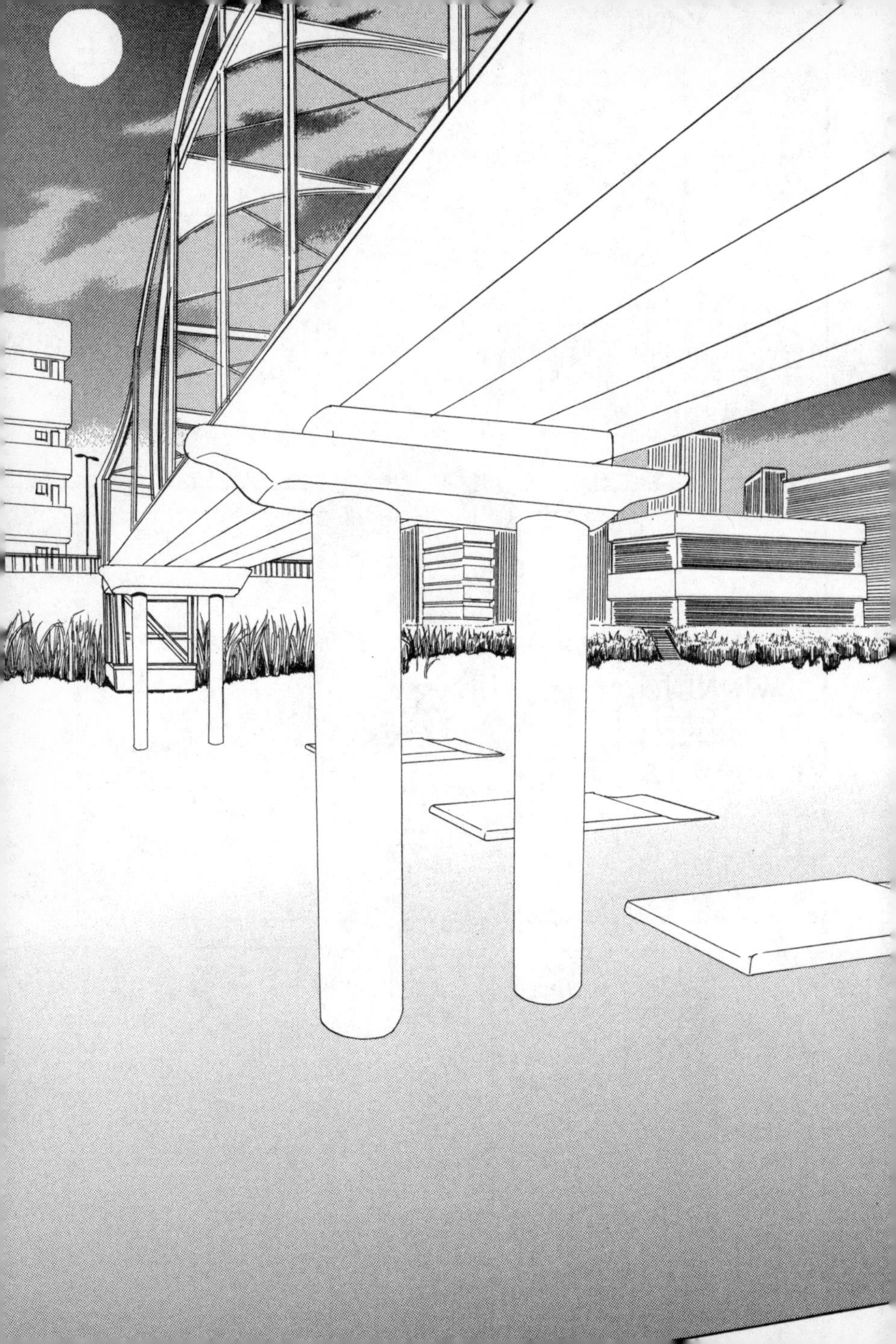

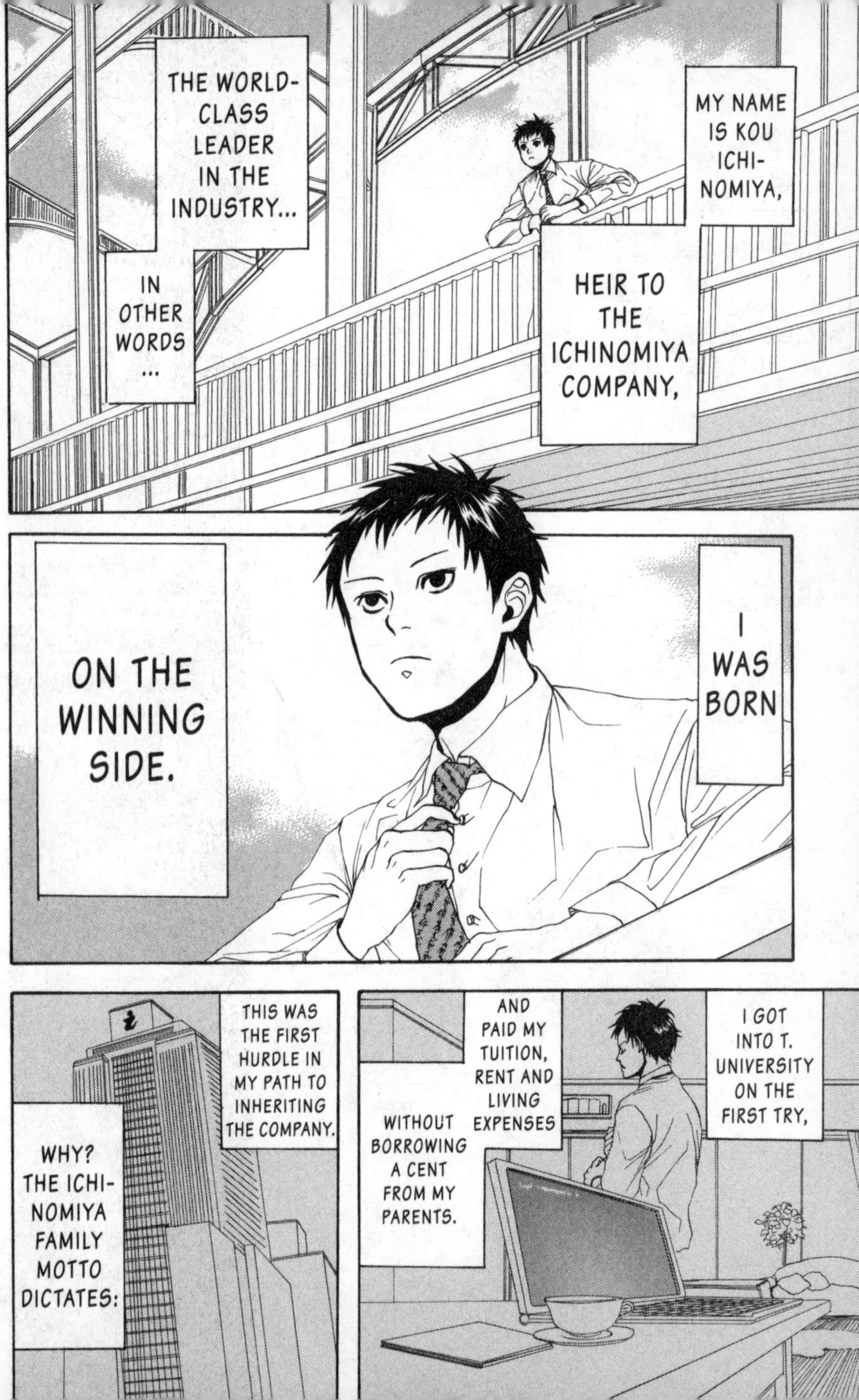
MY NAME IS KOU ICHI-NOMIYA,
HEIR TO THE ICHINOMIYA COMPANY,
THE WORLD-CLASS LEADER IN THE INDUSTRY...
IN OTHER WORDS ...
I WAS BORN
ON THE WINNING SIDE.
I GOT INTO T. UNIVERSITY ON THE FIRST TRY,
AND PAID MY TUITION, RENT AND LIVING EXPENSES
WITHOUT BORROWING A CENT FROM MY PARENTS.
THIS WAS THE FIRST HURDLE IN MY PATH TO INHERITING THE COMPANY.
WHY? THE ICHI-NOMIYA FAMILY MOTTO DICTATES:

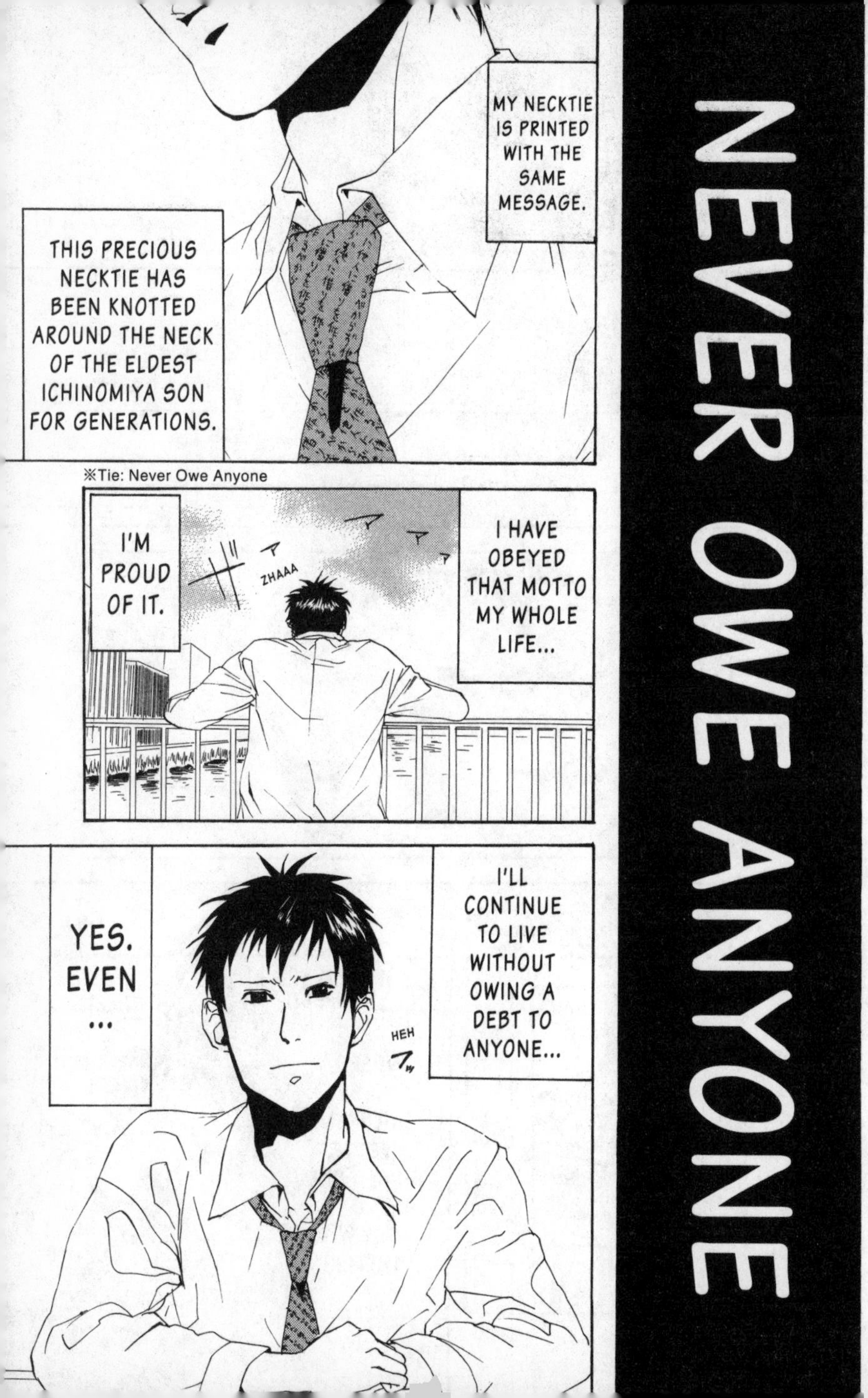
NEVER OWE ANYONE
MY NECKTIE IS PRINTED WITH THE SAME MESSAGE.
THIS PRECIOUS NECKTIE HAS BEEN KNOTTED AROUND THE NECK OF THE ELDEST ICHINOMIYA SON FOR GENERATIONS.
※Tie: Never Owe Anyone
I HAVE OBEYED THAT MOTTO MY WHOLE LIFE...
ZHAAA
I'M PROUD OF IT.
I'LL CONTINUE TO LIVE WITHOUT OWING A DEBT TO ANYONE...
HEH
YES. EVEN ...

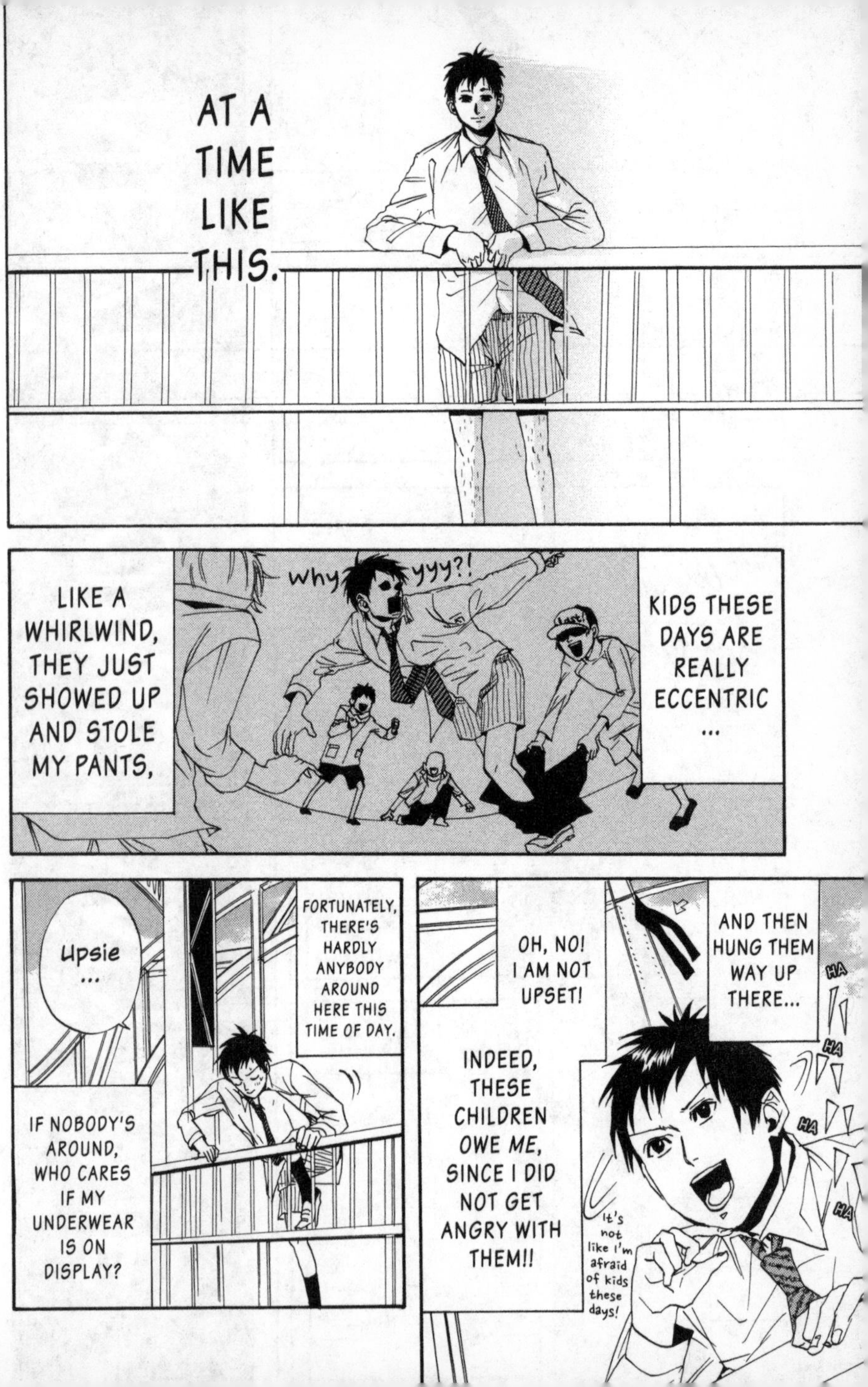
AT A TIME LIKE THIS.
KIDS THESE DAYS ARE REALLY ECCENTRIC ...
why yyy?!
LIKE A WHIRLWIND, THEY JUST SHOWED UP AND STOLE MY PANTS,
AND THEN HUNG THEM WAY UP THERE...
HA
HA
HA
HA
OH, NO! I AM NOT UPSET!
INDEED, THESE CHILDREN OWE ME, SINCE I DID NOT GET ANGRY WITH THEM!!
It's not like I'm afraid of kids these days!
FORTUNATELY, THERE'S HARDLY ANYBODY AROUND HERE THIS TIME OF DAY.
Upsie ...
IF NOBODY'S AROUND, WHO CARES IF MY UNDERWEAR IS ON DISPLAY?

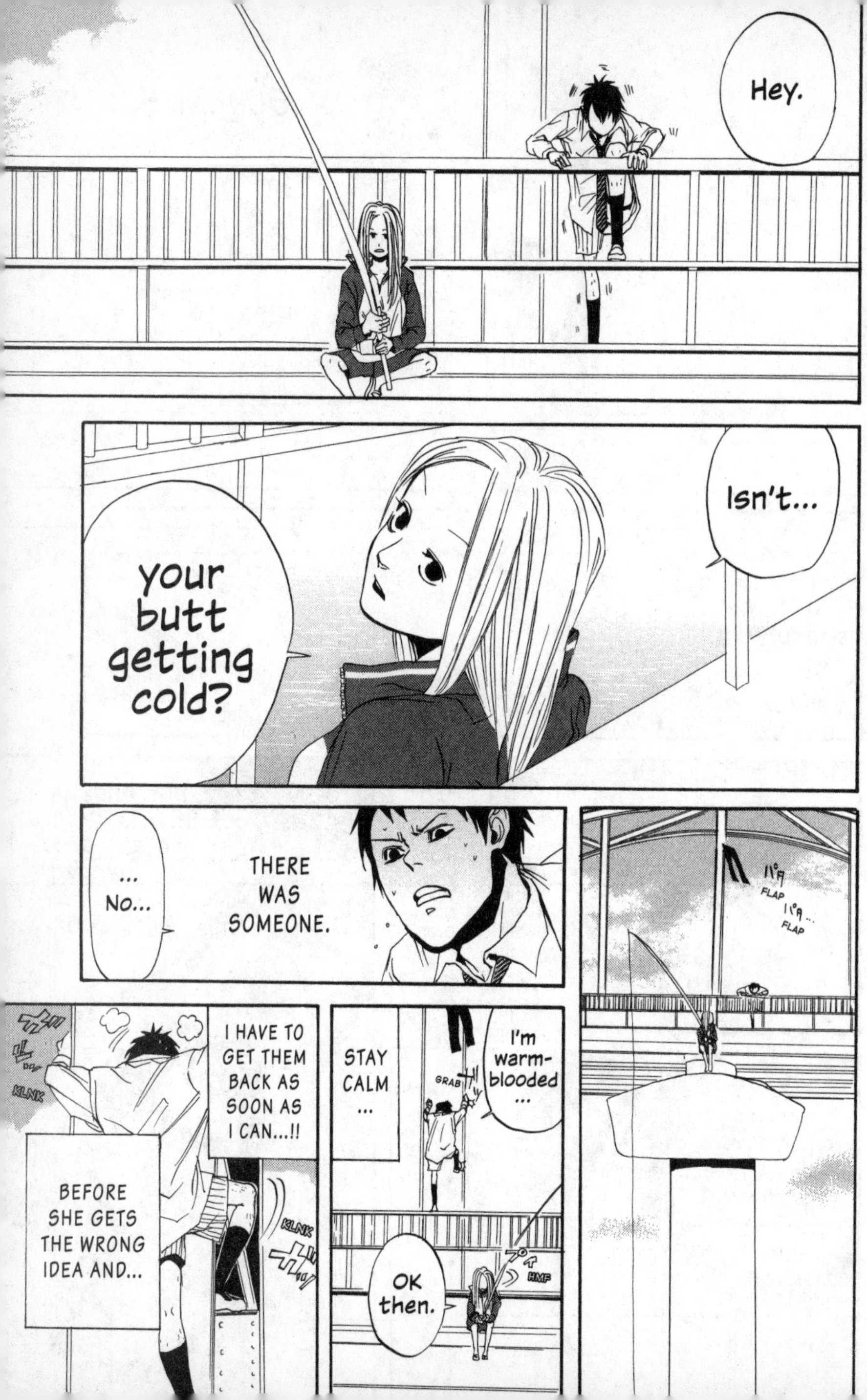

Hey.
Isn't...
your butt getting cold?
パタ
FLAP
パタ..
FLAP
THERE WAS SOMEONE.
... No...
I'm warm-blooded ...
GRAB
STAY CALM ...
HMF
OK then.
I HAVE TO GET THEM BACK AS SOON AS I CAN...!!
KLNK
BEFORE SHE GETS THE WRONG IDEA AND...
KLNK

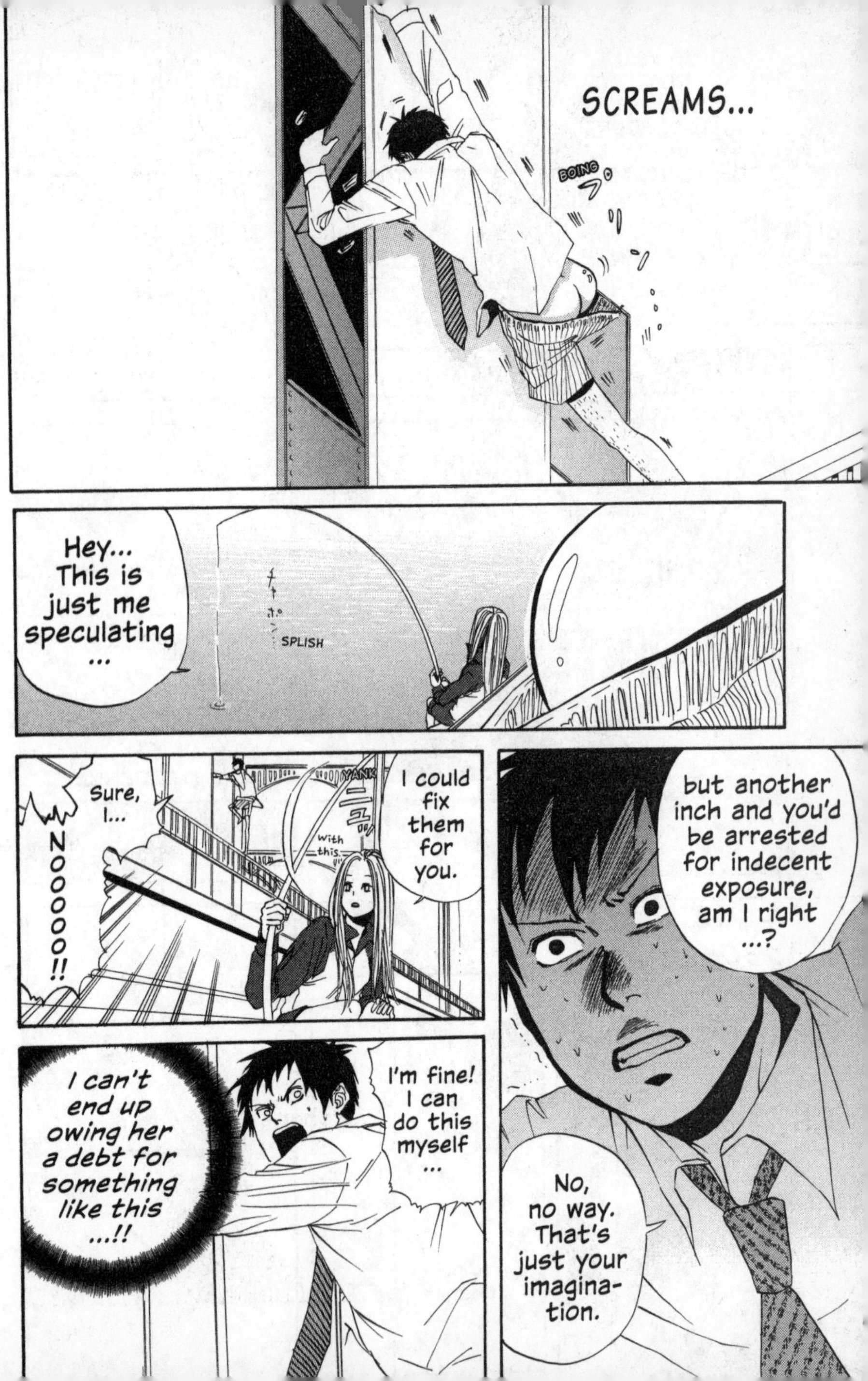
SCREAMS...
BOING
Hey... This is just me speculating ...
SPLISH
but another inch and you'd be arrested for indecent exposure, am I right ...?
No, no way. That's just your imagination.
I could fix them for you.
YANK
With this.
Sure, I...
NOOOOOO!!
I'm fine! I can do this myself ...
I can't end up owing her a debt for something like this ...!!

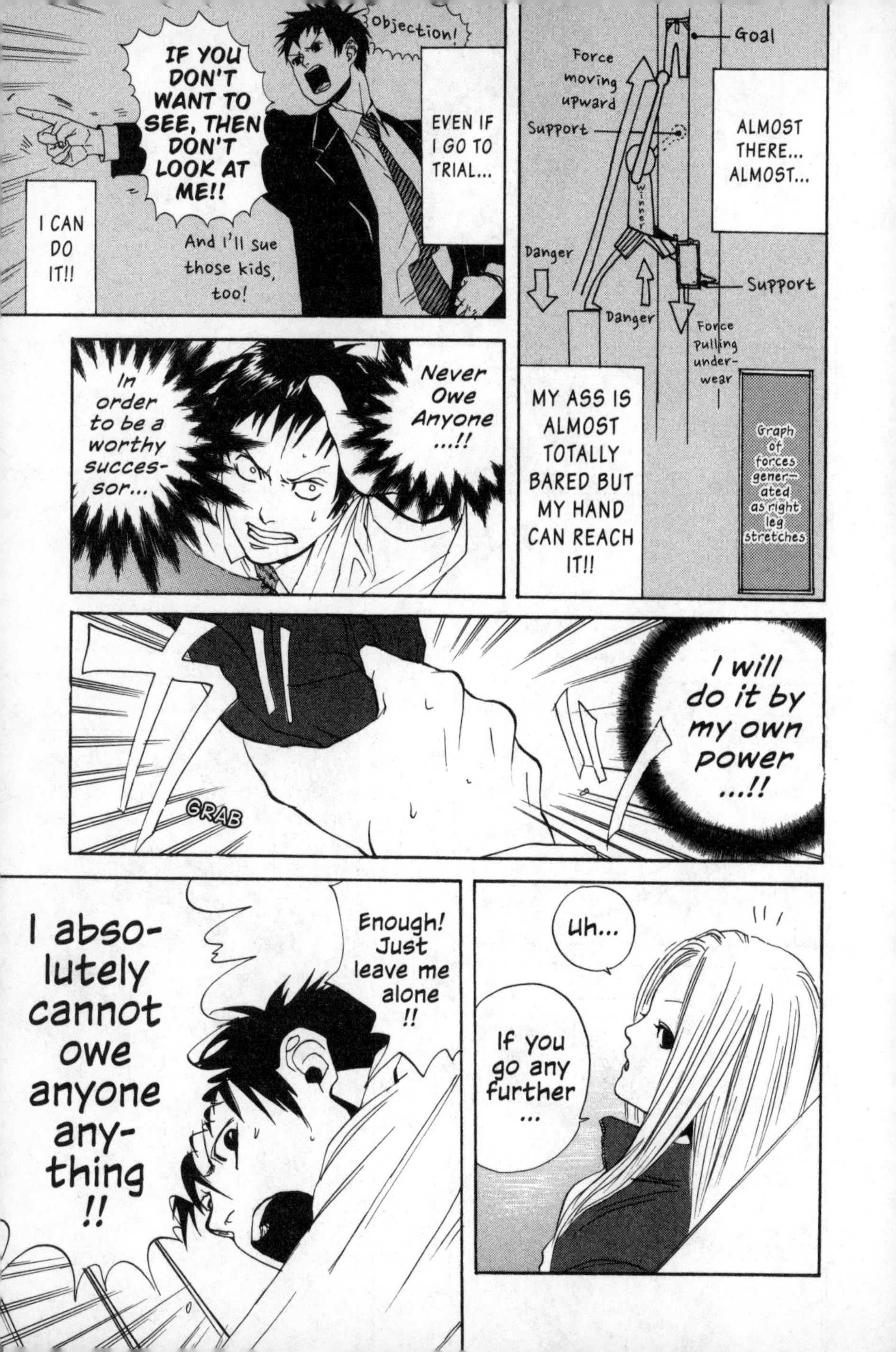
ALMOST THERE... ALMOST...
Goal
Force moving upward
Support
Winner
Danger
Support
Danger
Force pulling underwear
Graph of forces generated as right leg stretches
MY ASS IS ALMOST TOTALLY BARED BUT MY HAND CAN REACH IT!!
Objection!
EVEN IF I GO TO TRIAL...
IF YOU DON'T WANT TO SEE, THEN DON'T LOOK AT ME!!
And I'll sue those kids, too!
I CAN DO IT!!
Never Owe Anyone ...!!
In order to be a worthy successor...
I will do it by my own power ...!!
GRAB
Uh...
If you go any further ...
Enough! Just leave me alone !!
I absolutely cannot owe anyone anything !!

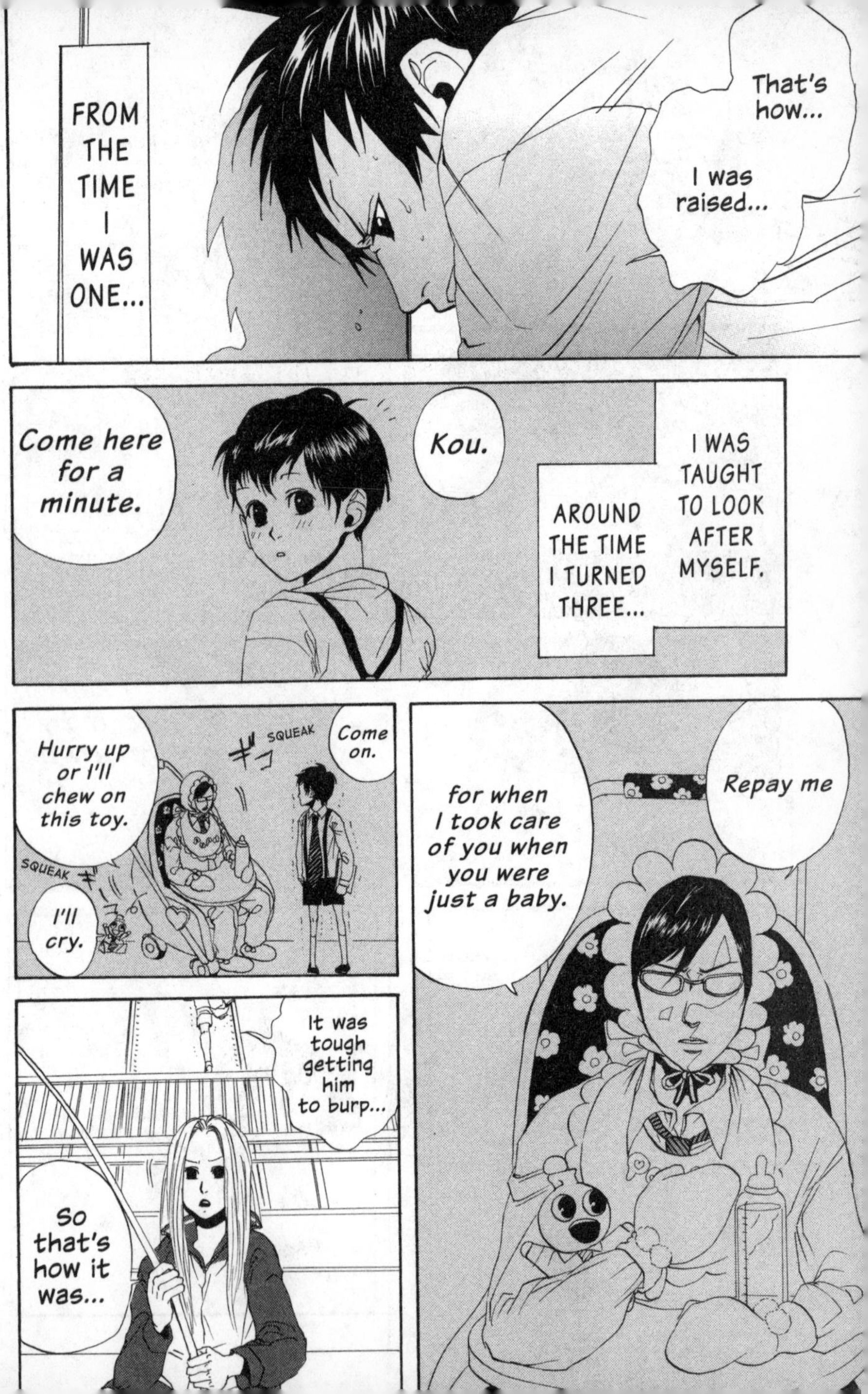
That's how...
I was raised...
FROM THE TIME I WAS ONE...
AROUND THE TIME I TURNED THREE... I WAS TAUGHT TO LOOK AFTER MYSELF.
Kou.
Come here for a minute.
Repay me
for when I took care of you when you were just a baby.
Come on.
SQUEAK
Hurry up or I'll chew on this toy.
SQUEAK
I'll cry.
It was tough getting him to burp...
So that's how it was...

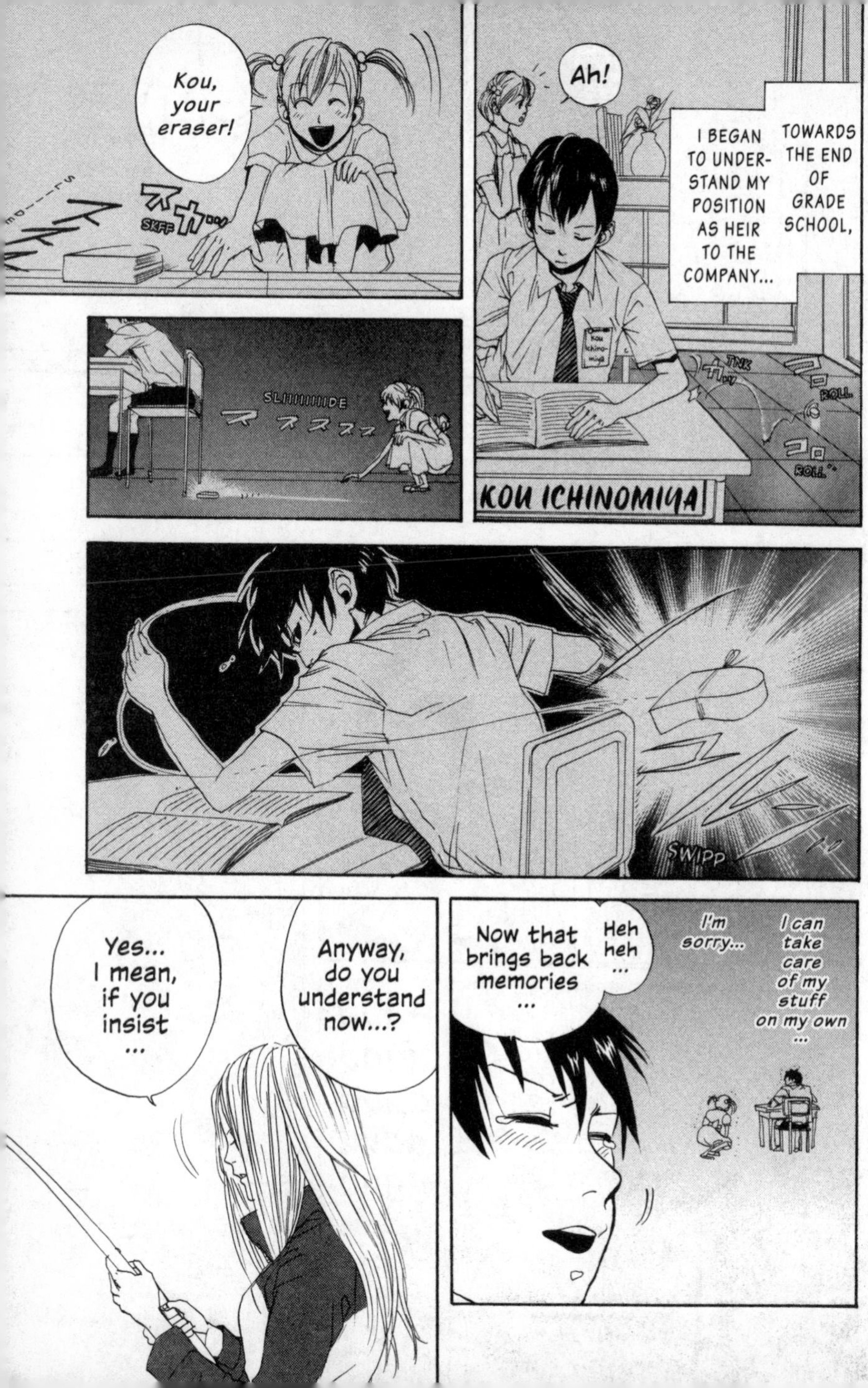

TOWARDS THE END OF GRADE SCHOOL,
I BEGAN TO UNDERSTAND MY POSITION AS HEIR TO THE COMPANY...
Ah!
TNK
ROLL
ROLL
KOU ICHINOMIYA
Kou, your eraser!
SKFF
SLIIIIIIIDE
SWIPP
I can take care of my stuff on my own...
I'm sorry...
Heh heh...
Now that brings back memories...
Anyway, do you understand now...?
Yes... I mean, if you insist...

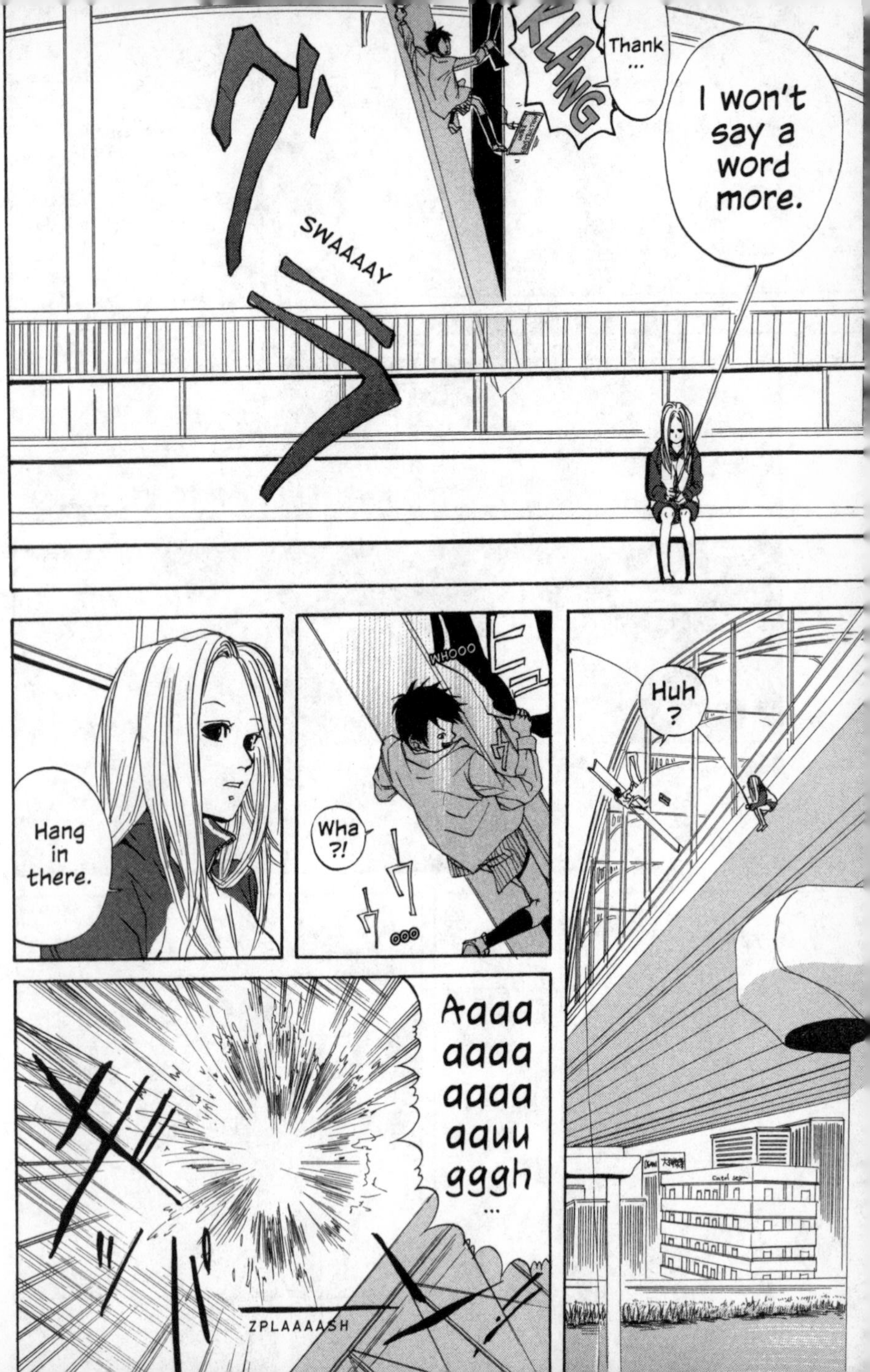
I won't say a word more.
Thank ...
KLANG
SWAAAAY
Huh?
WHOOO
Wha?!
Hang in there.
Aaaaaaaaaaaaaauugggh...
ZPLAAAASH

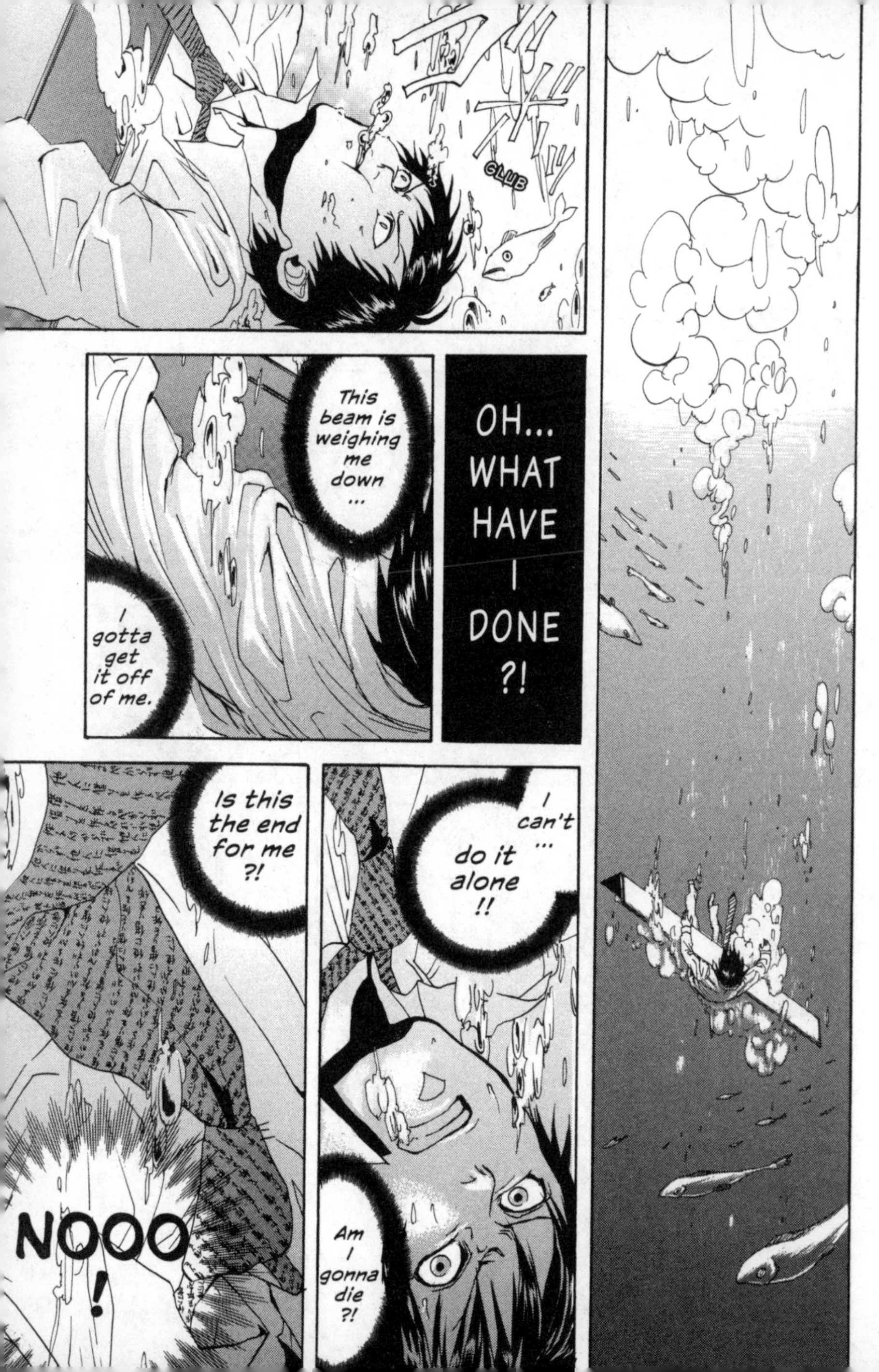
GLUB
OH... WHAT HAVE I DONE?!
This beam is weighing me down...
I gotta get it off of me.
I can't... do it alone!!
Am I gonna die?!
Is this the end for me?!
NOOO!

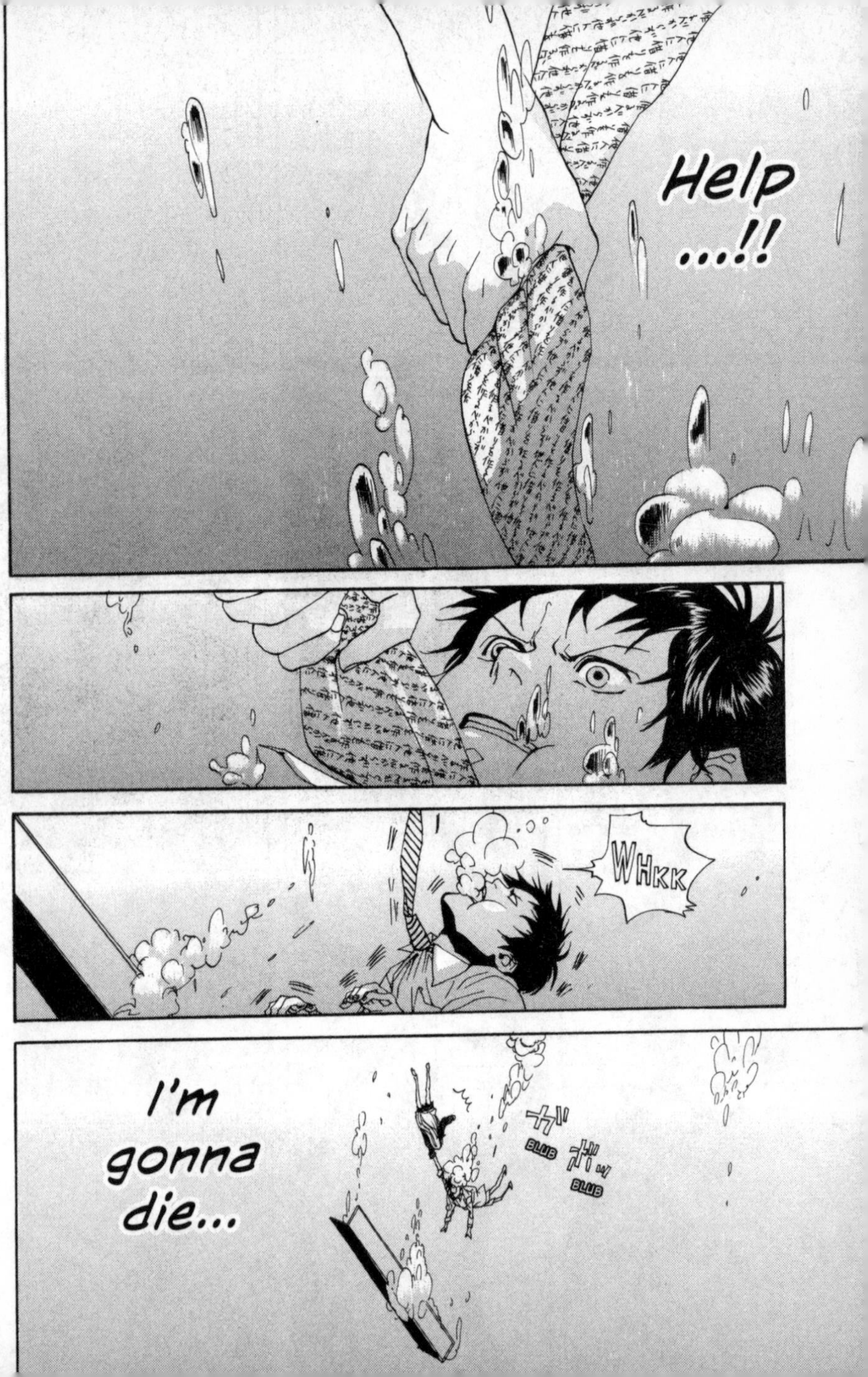
Help ...!!
WHKK
I'm gonna die...
BLUB
BLUB

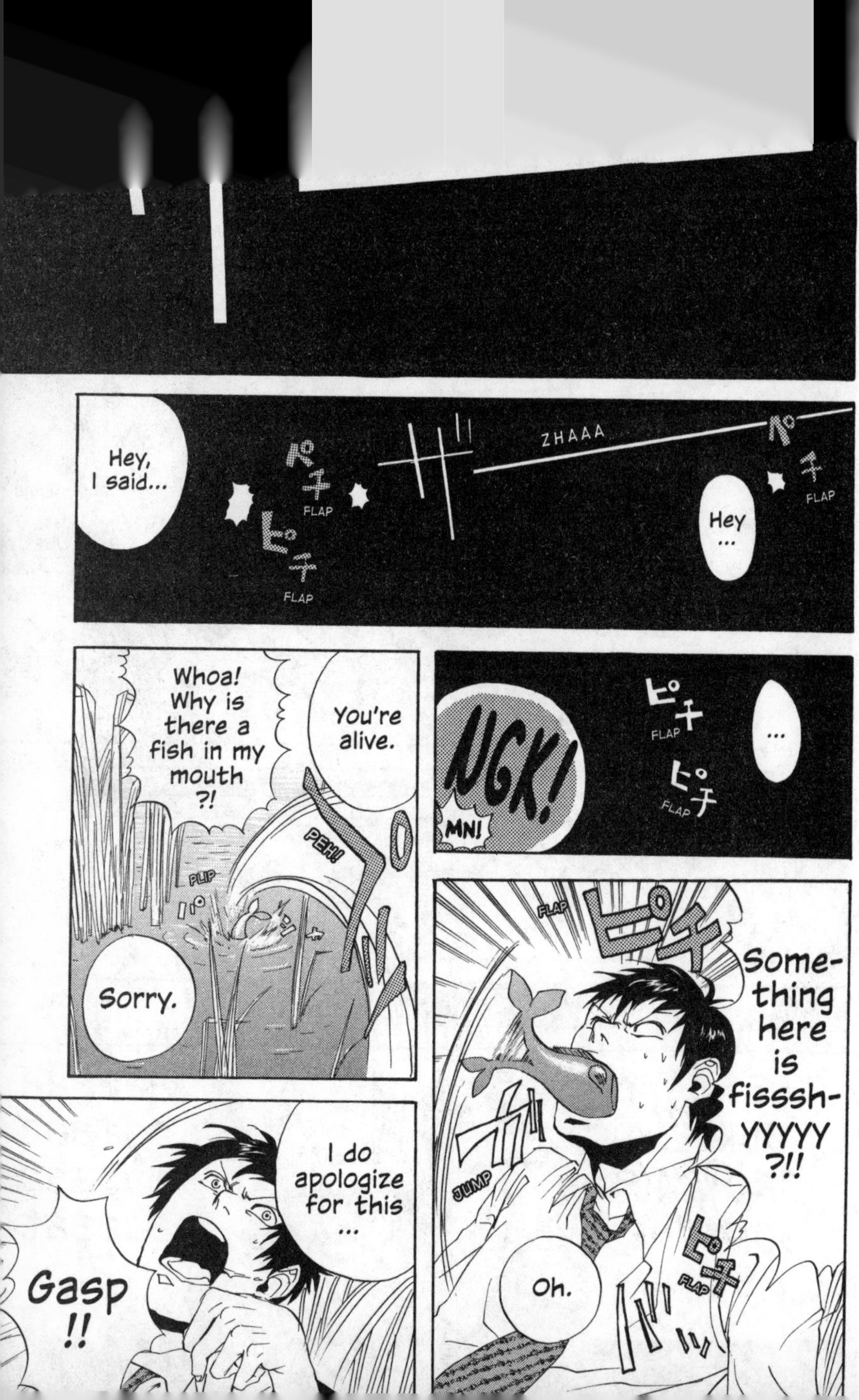

FLAP
Hey ...
ZHAAA
FLAP
FLAP
Hey, I said...
FLAP
FLAP
...
NGK!
MN!
You're alive.
Whoa! Why is there a fish in my mouth ?!
PEH!
PLIP
Sorry.
FLAP
Something here is fisssh-YYYYY ?!!
JUMP
FLAP
Oh.
I do apologize for this ...
Gasp !!

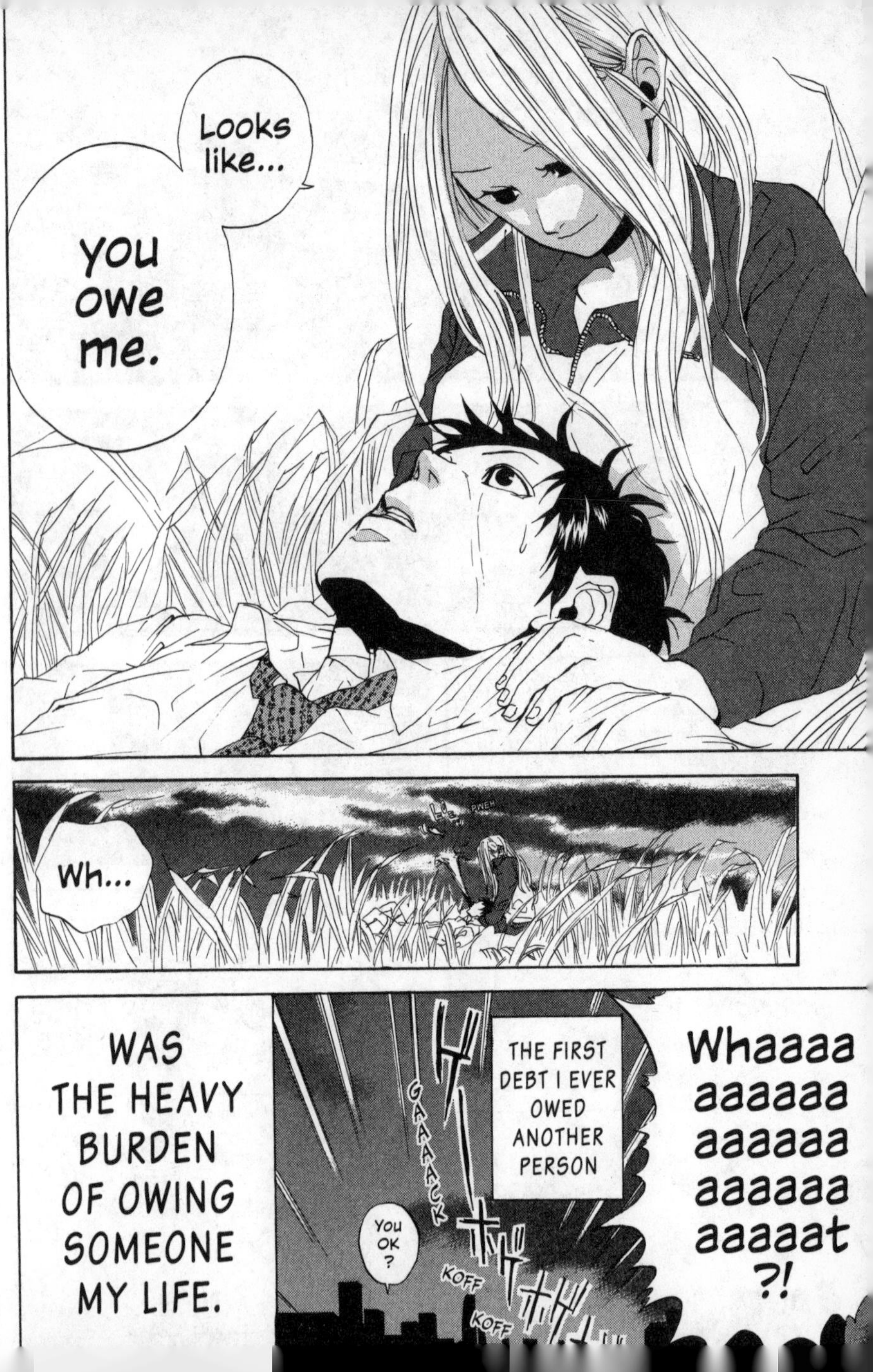
Looks like...
you owe me.
PWEH
Wh...
Whaaaaaaaaaaaaaaaaaaaaaaaaaaaat?!
THE FIRST DEBT I EVER OWED ANOTHER PERSON
GAAAACK
You OK?
KOFF
KOFF
WAS THE HEAVY BURDEN OF OWING SOMEONE MY LIFE.

☜ Chapter 2: Under the Big Star Bridge

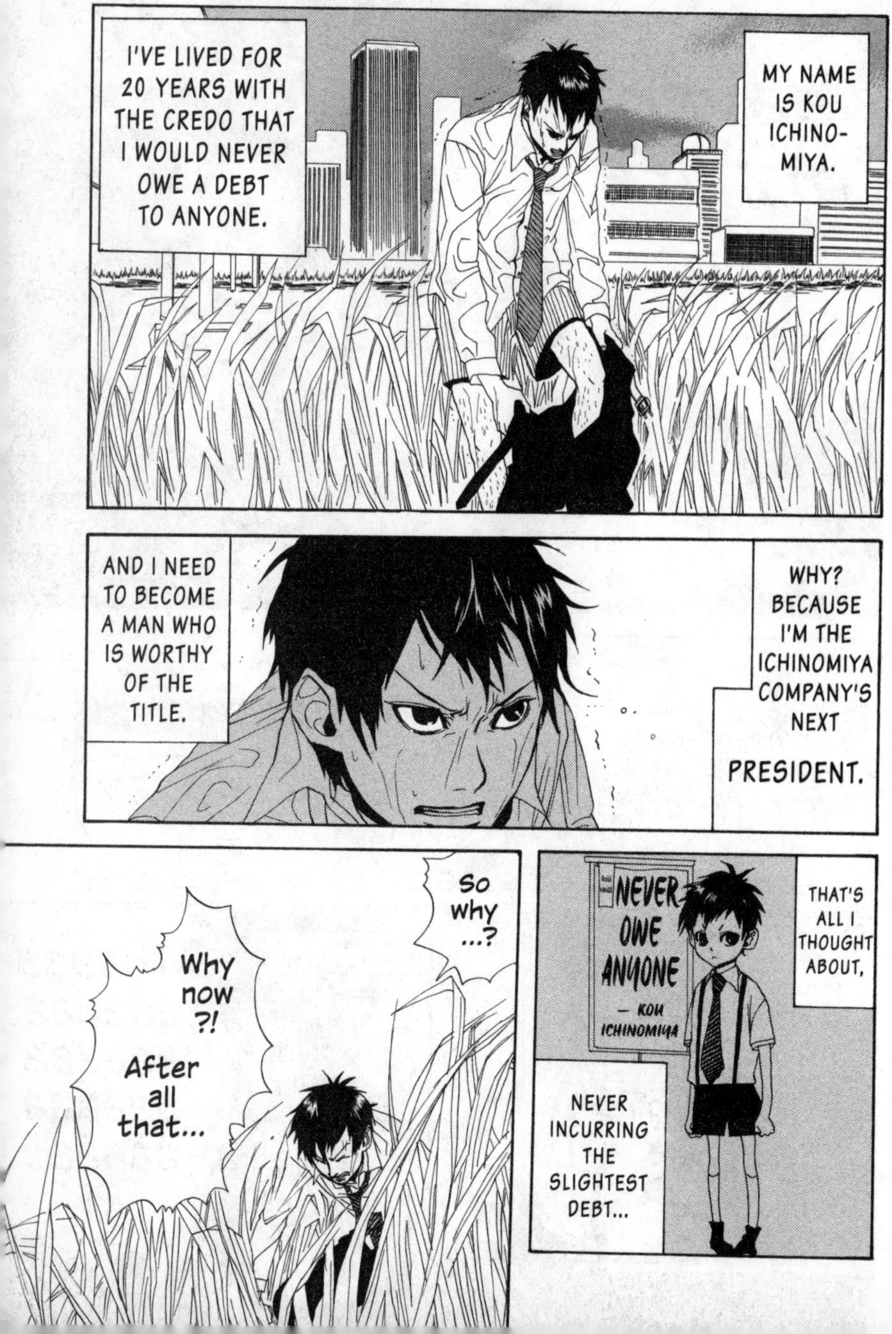
MY NAME IS KOU ICHINOMIYA.
I'VE LIVED FOR 20 YEARS WITH THE CREDO THAT I WOULD NEVER OWE A DEBT TO ANYONE.
WHY? BECAUSE I'M THE ICHINOMIYA COMPANY'S NEXT PRESIDENT.
AND I NEED TO BECOME A MAN WHO IS WORTHY OF THE TITLE.
NEVER OWE ANYONE
— KOU ICHINOMIYA
THAT'S ALL I THOUGHT ABOUT,
NEVER INCURRING THE SLIGHTEST DEBT...
So why ...?
Why now ?!
After all that...

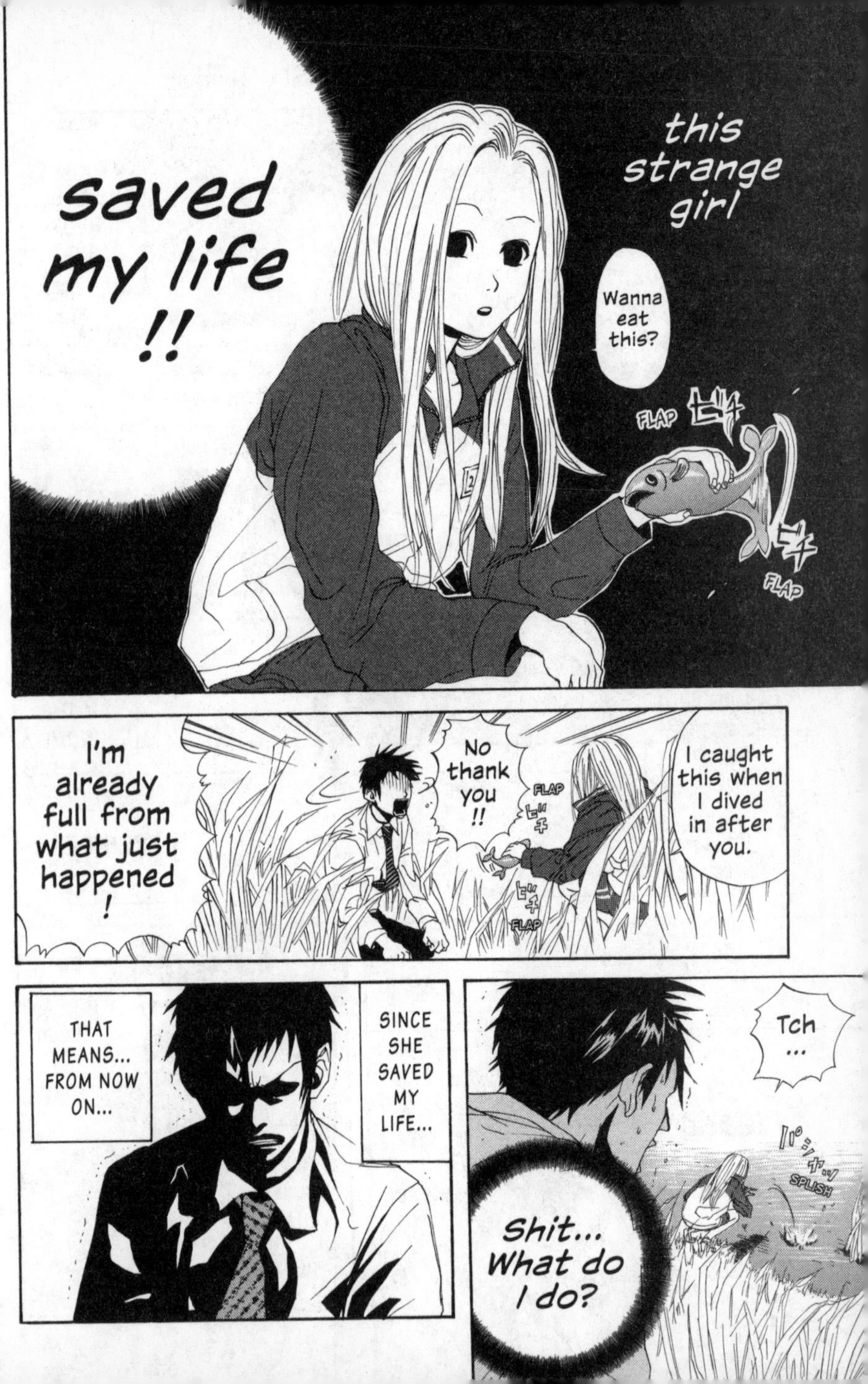
this strange girl
Wanna eat this?
FLAP
FLAP
saved my life !!
I caught this when I dived in after you.
FLAP
FLAP
No thank you !!
I'm already full from what just happened !
Tch ...
SPLISH
Shit... What do I do?
SINCE SHE SAVED MY LIFE...
THAT MEANS... FROM NOW ON...

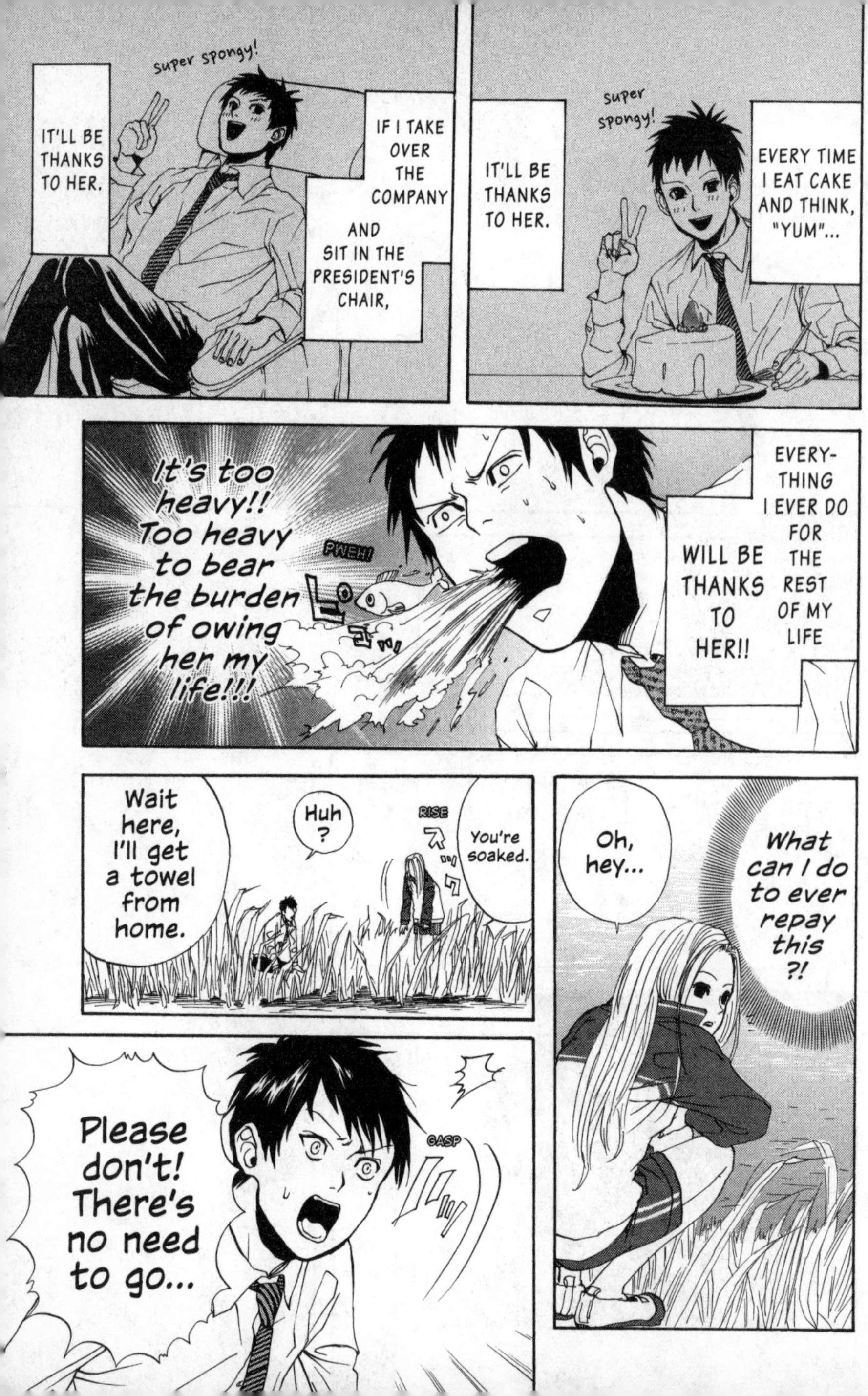

Super spongy!
EVERY TIME I EAT CAKE AND THINK, "YUM"...
IT'LL BE THANKS TO HER.
IF I TAKE OVER THE COMPANY
AND SIT IN THE PRESIDENT'S CHAIR,
Super spongy!
IT'LL BE THANKS TO HER.
EVERY-THING I EVER DO FOR THE REST OF MY LIFE
WILL BE THANKS TO HER!!
PWEH!
It's too heavy!! Too heavy to bear the burden of owing her my life!!!
What can I do to ever repay this?!
Oh, hey...
You're soaked.
RISE
Huh?
Wait here, I'll get a towel from home.
GASP
Please don't! There's no need to go...

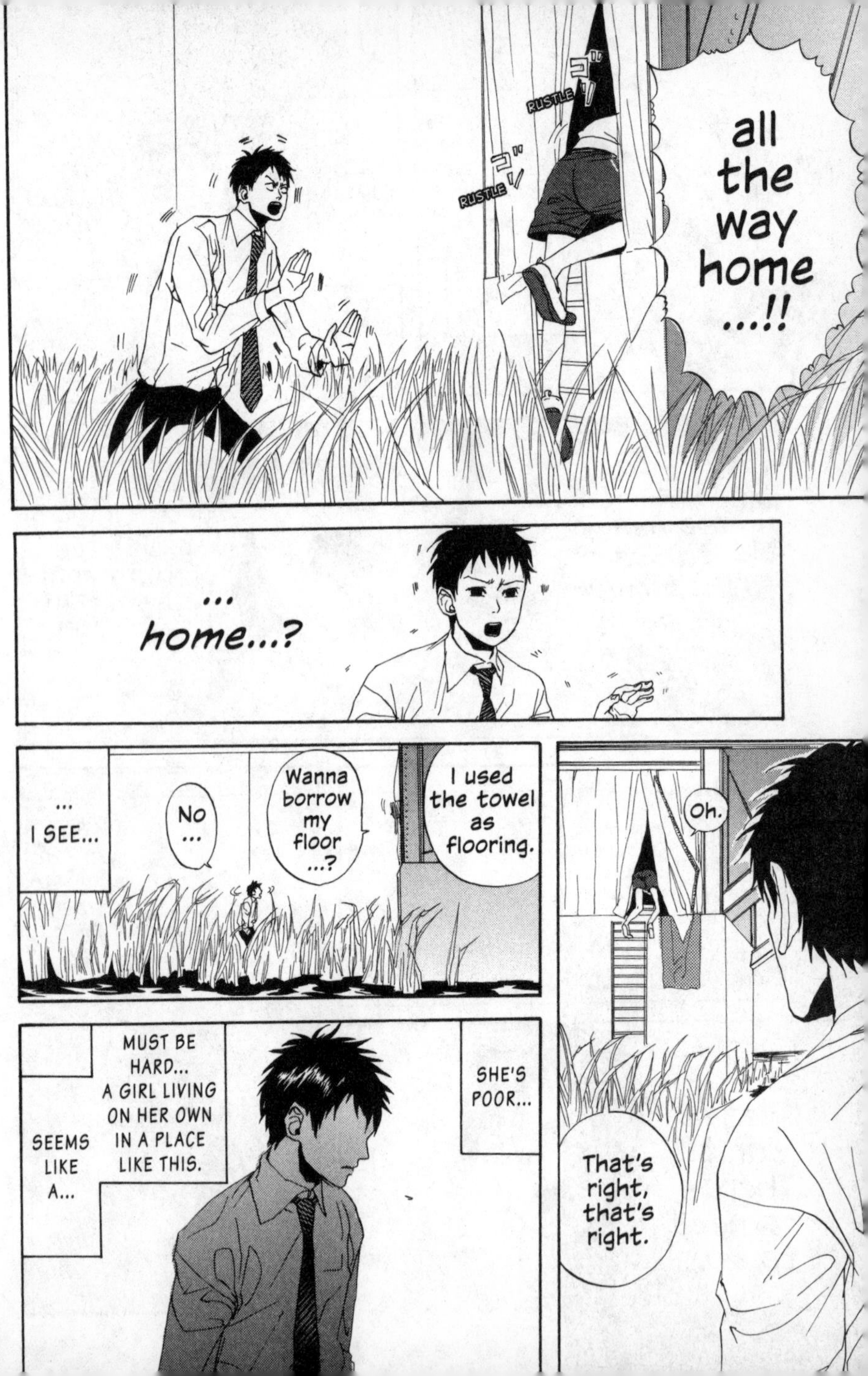
all the way home ...!!
RUSTLE
RUSTLE
... home...?
Oh.
That's right, that's right.
I used the towel as flooring.
Wanna borrow my floor ...?
No ...
... I SEE...
SHE'S POOR...
MUST BE HARD... A GIRL LIVING ON HER OWN IN A PLACE LIKE THIS.
SEEMS LIKE A...

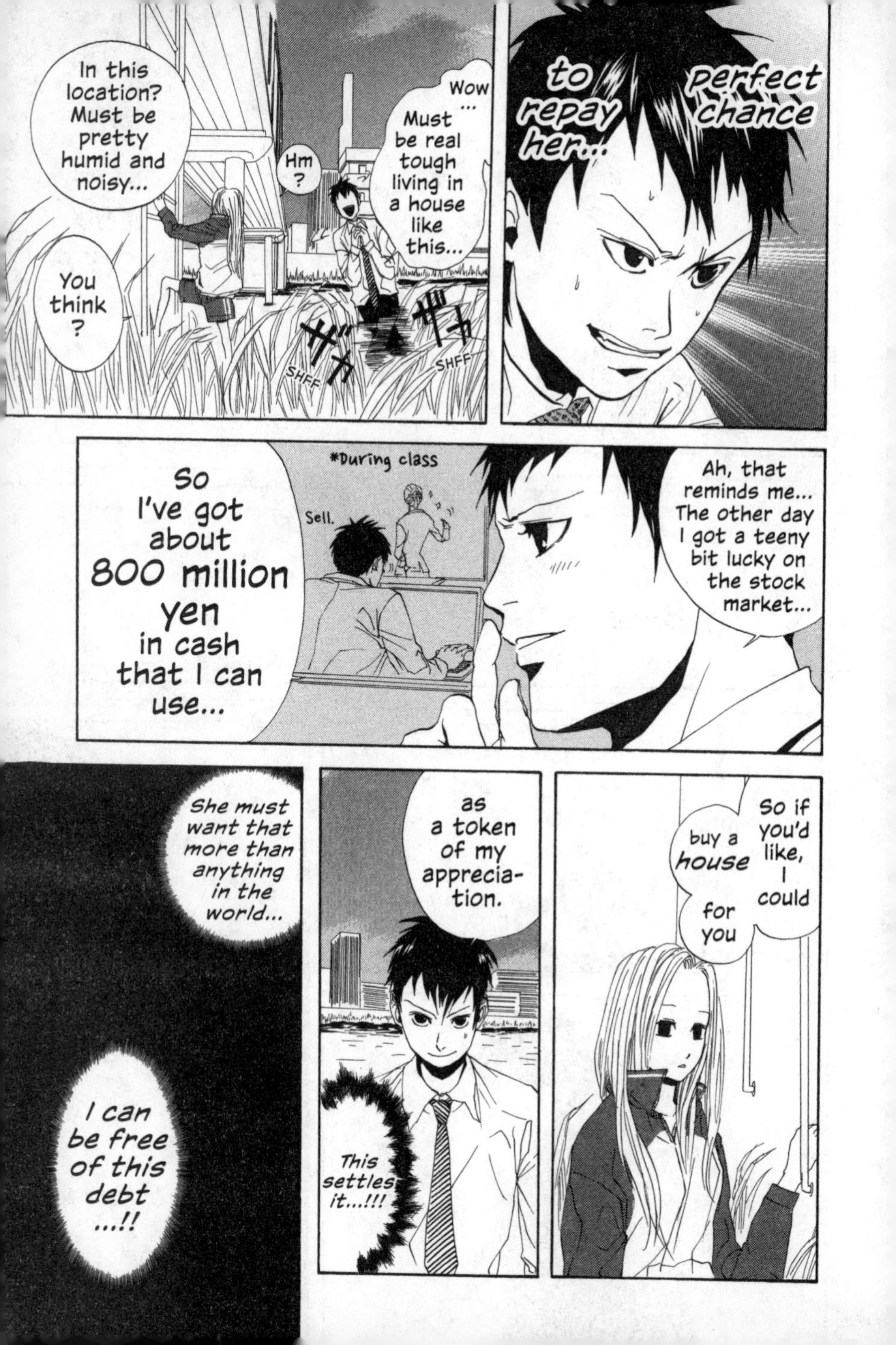
perfect chance
to repay her...
Wow ... Must be real tough living in a house like this...
Hm ?
In this location? Must be pretty humid and noisy...
You think ?
SHFF
SHFF
Ah, that reminds me... The other day I got a teeny bit lucky on the stock market...
*During class
Sell.
So I've got about 800 million yen in cash that I can use...
So if you'd like, I could
buy a house for you
as a token of my apprecia-tion.
This settles it...!!!
She must want that more than anything in the world...
I can be free of this debt ...!!

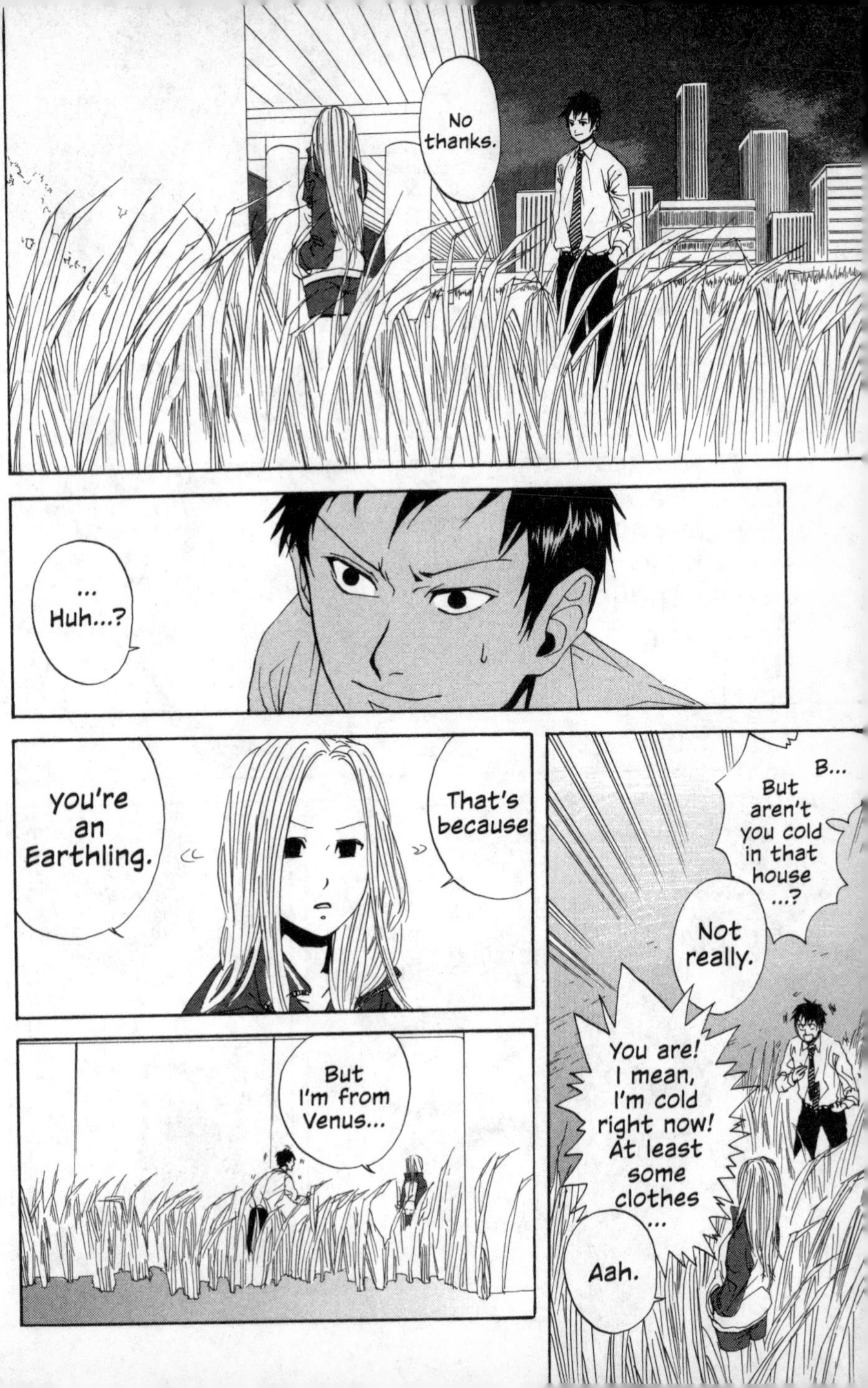
No thanks.
... Huh...?
B... But aren't you cold in that house ...?
Not really.
You are! I mean, I'm cold right now! At least some clothes ...
Aah.
That's because
you're an Earthling.
But I'm from Venus...

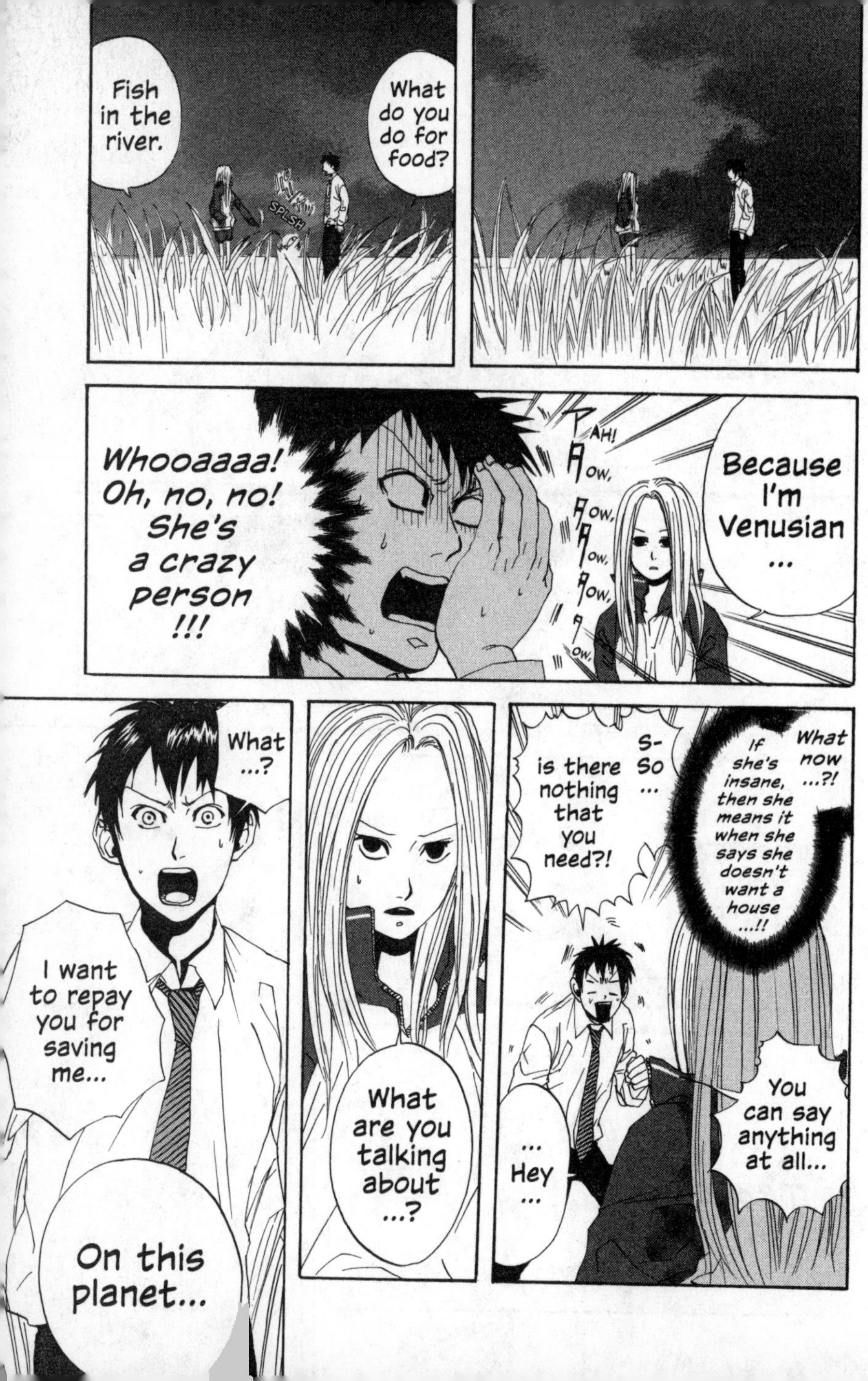
What do you do for food?
Fish in the river.
SPLSH
Because I'm Venusian ...
AH! OW, OW, OW, OW, OW.
Whooaaaa! Oh, no, no! She's a crazy person !!!
What now ...?!
If she's insane, then she means it when she says she doesn't want a house ...!!
S- So ...
is there nothing that you need?!
You can say anything at all...
... Hey ...
What are you talking about ...?
What ...?
I want to repay you for saving me...
On this planet...

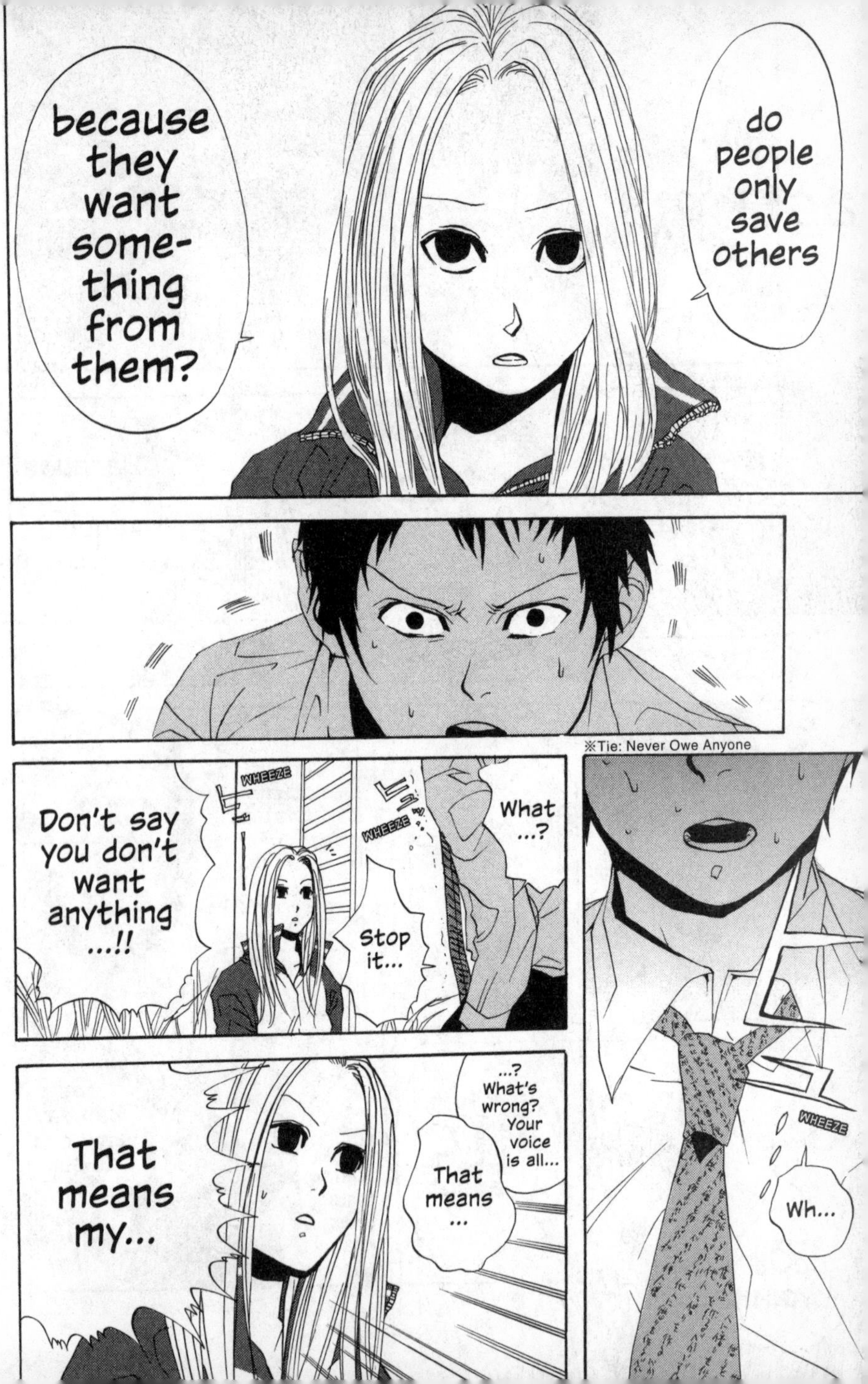
do people only save others
because they want some-thing from them?
※Tie: Never Owe Anyone
WHEEZE
Wh...
What ...?
WHEEZE
Stop it...
WHEEZE
Don't say you don't want anything ...!!
...? What's wrong? Your voice is all...
That means ...
That means my...

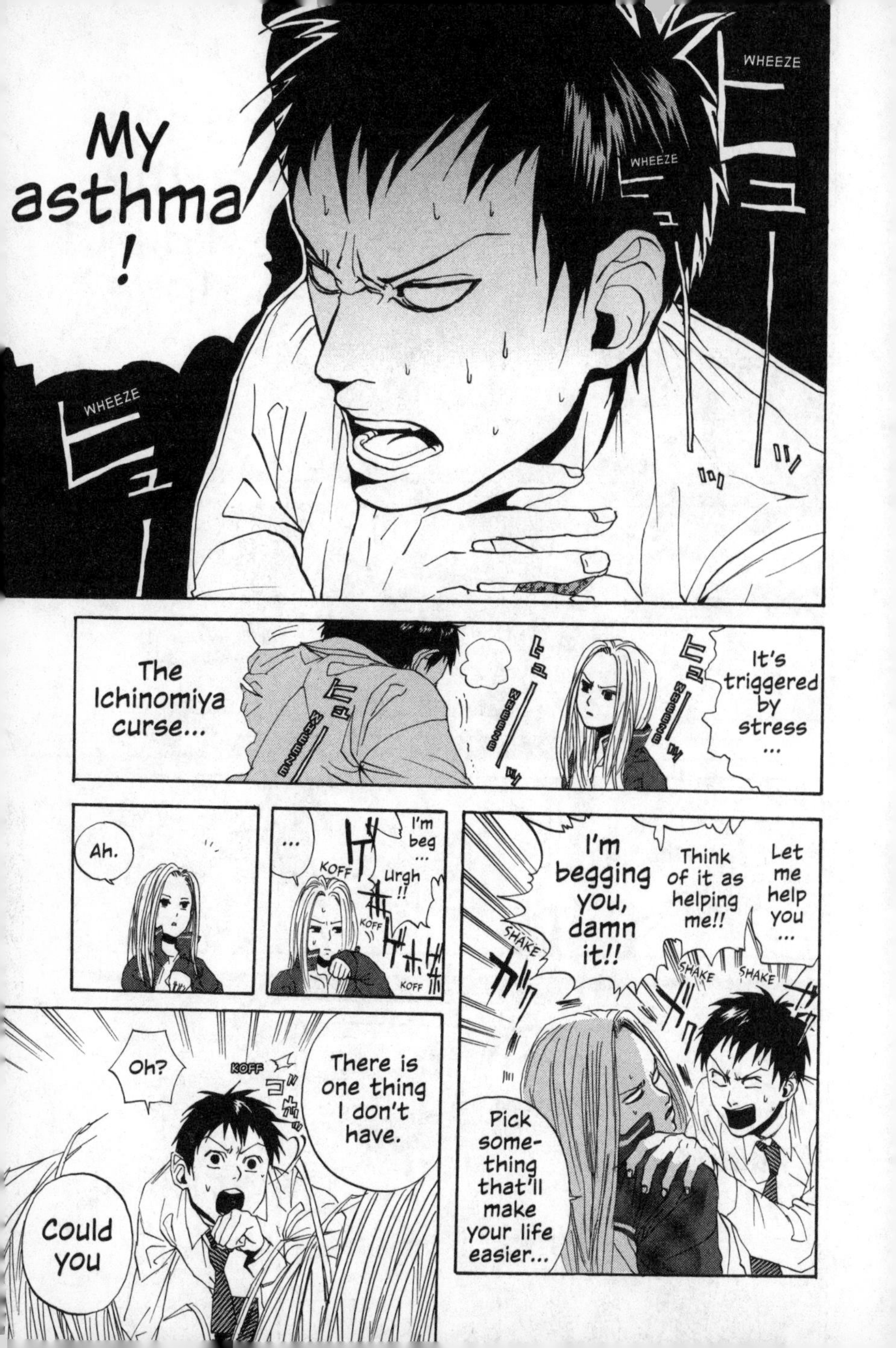
WHEEZE
WHEEZE
My asthma!
WHEEZE
It's triggered by stress...
WHEEZE
WHEEZE
The Ichinomiya curse...
Let me help you...
Think of it as helping me!!
I'm begging you, damn it!!
SHAKE
SHAKE
SHAKE
Pick something that'll make your life easier...
I'm beg... urgh!!
KOFF
KOFF
KOFF
...
Ah.
There is one thing I don't have.
KOFF
Oh?
Could you

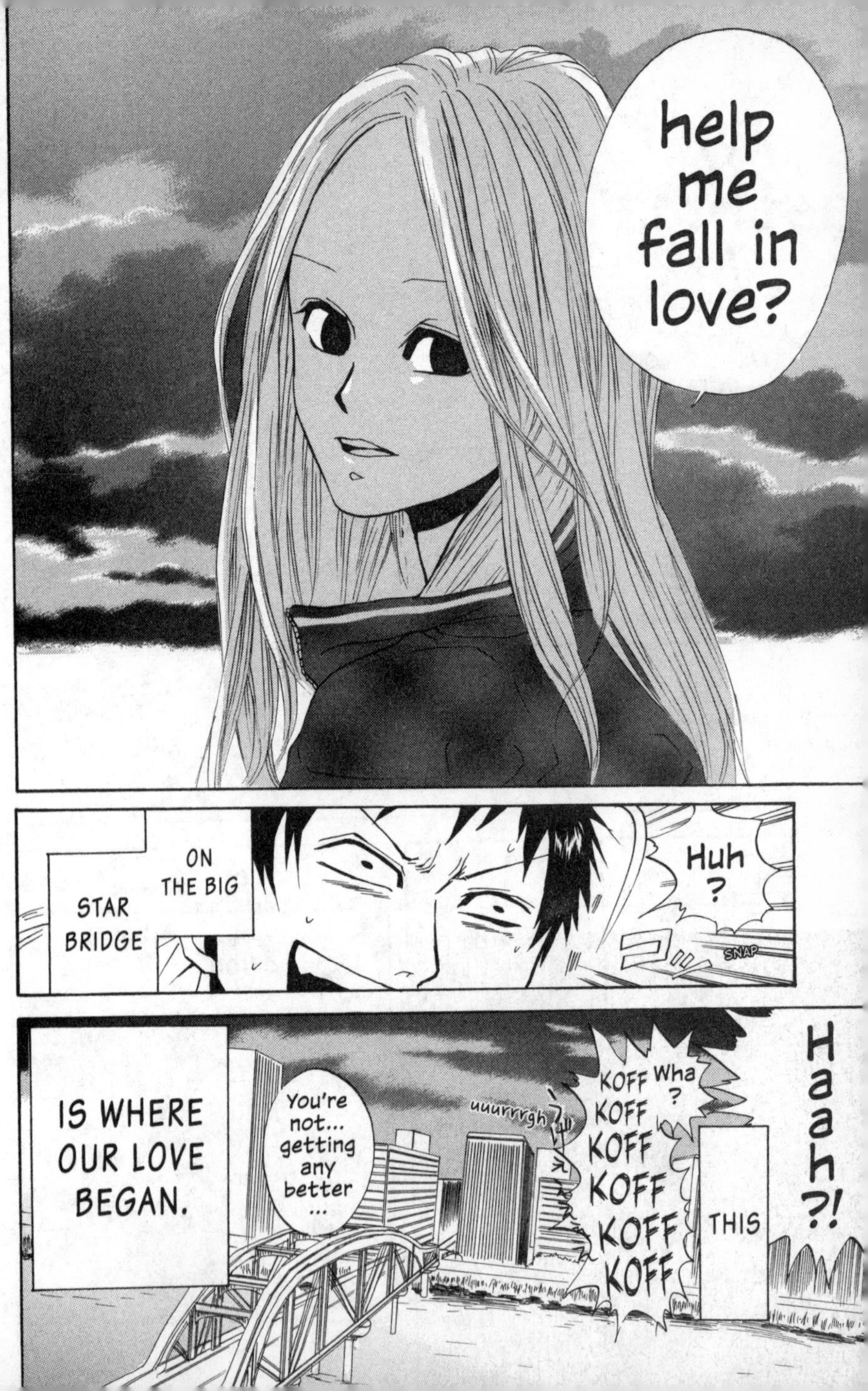
help me fall in love?
Huh ?
SNAP
ON THE BIG
STAR BRIDGE
Haah?!
THIS
Wha ?
KOFF KOFF KOFF KOFF KOFF KOFF
uuurrrgh
You're not... getting any better ...
IS WHERE OUR LOVE BEGAN.

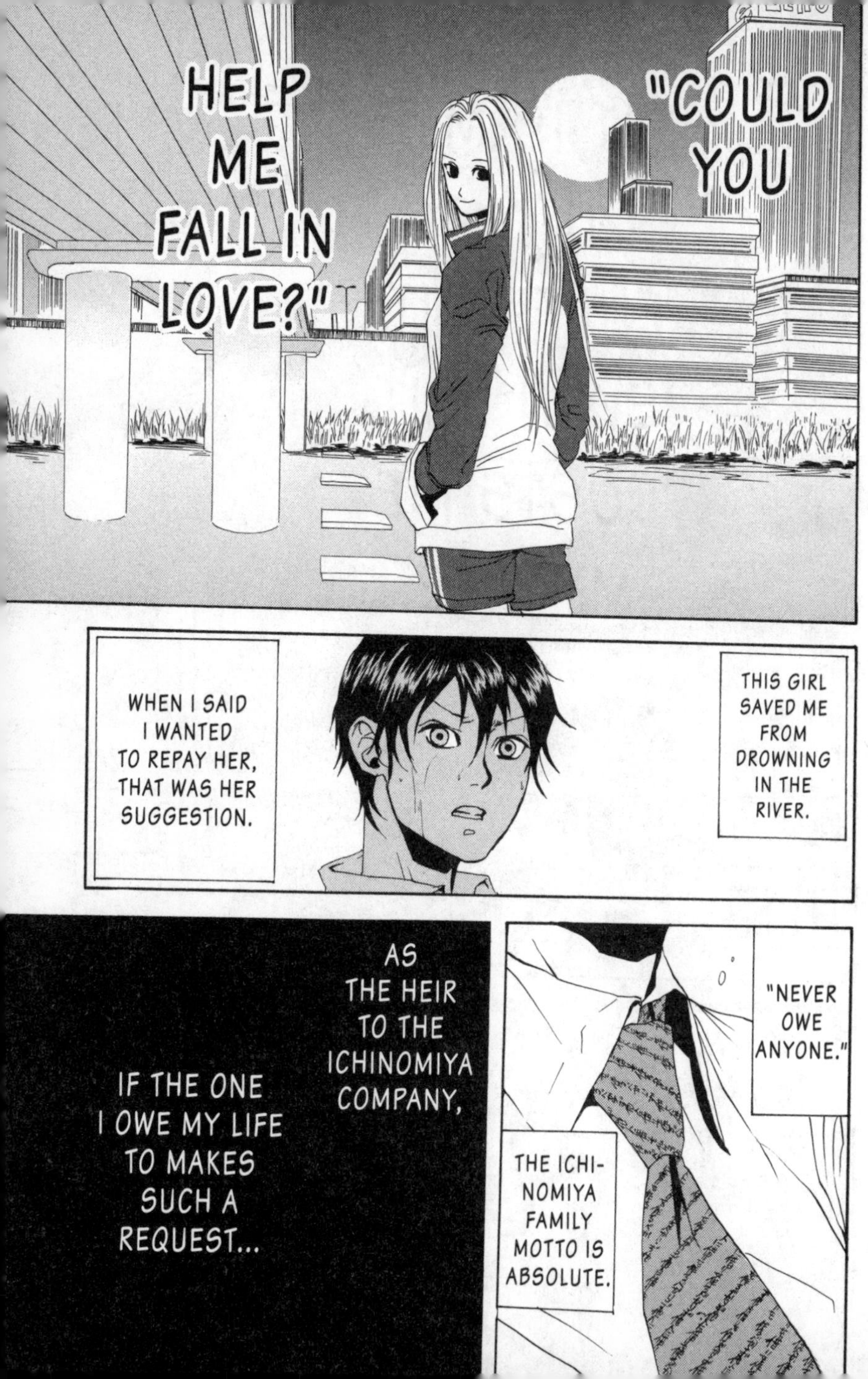
"COULD YOU
HELP ME FALL IN LOVE?"
THIS GIRL SAVED ME FROM DROWNING IN THE RIVER.
WHEN I SAID I WANTED TO REPAY HER, THAT WAS HER SUGGESTION.
"NEVER OWE ANYONE."
THE ICHI-NOMIYA FAMILY MOTTO IS ABSOLUTE.
AS THE HEIR TO THE ICHINOMIYA COMPANY,
IF THE ONE I OWE MY LIFE TO MAKES SUCH A REQUEST...

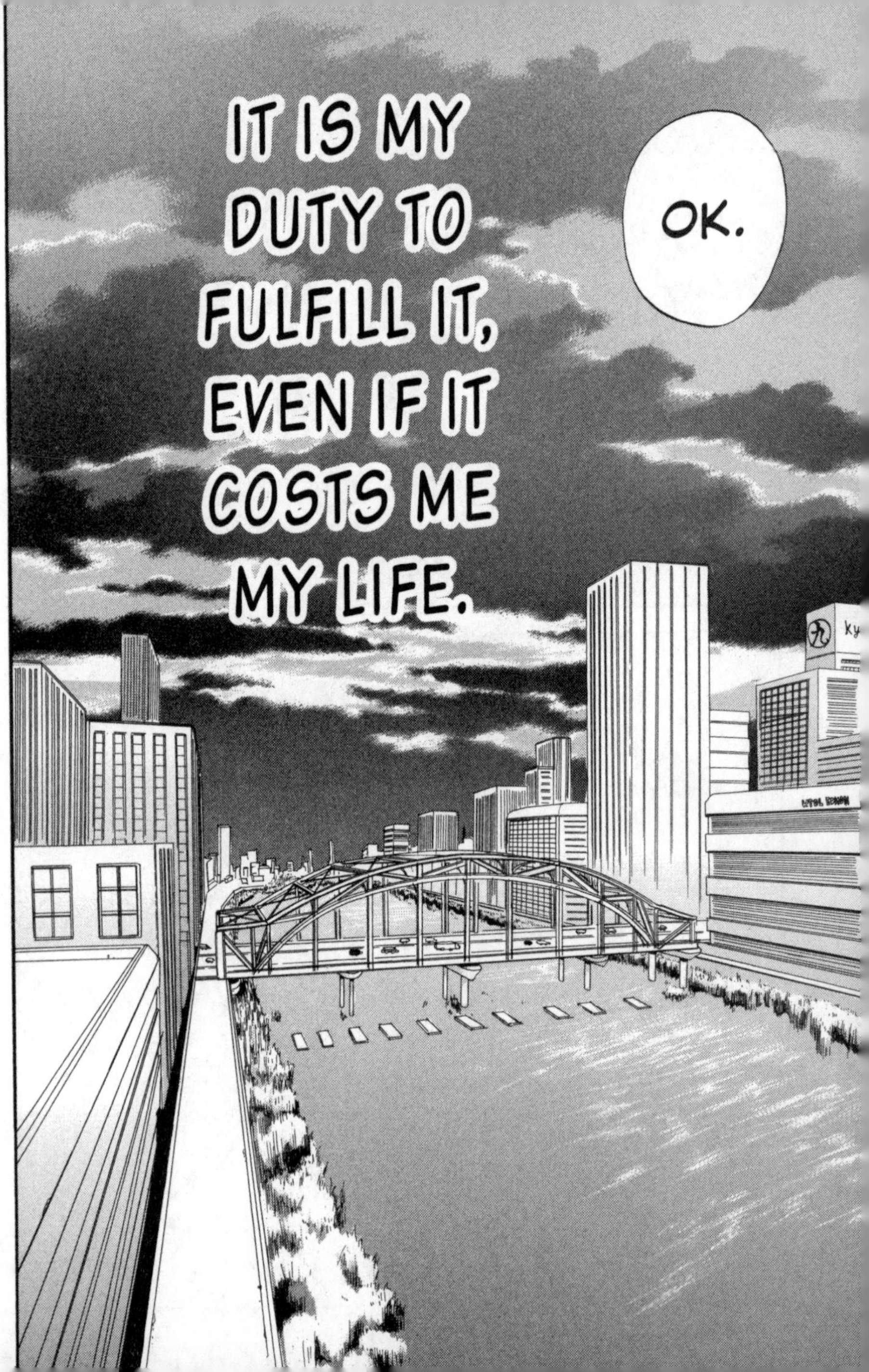
OK.
IT IS MY DUTY TO FULFILL IT, EVEN IF IT COSTS ME MY LIFE.

☜ Chapter 3: Positive Thinking

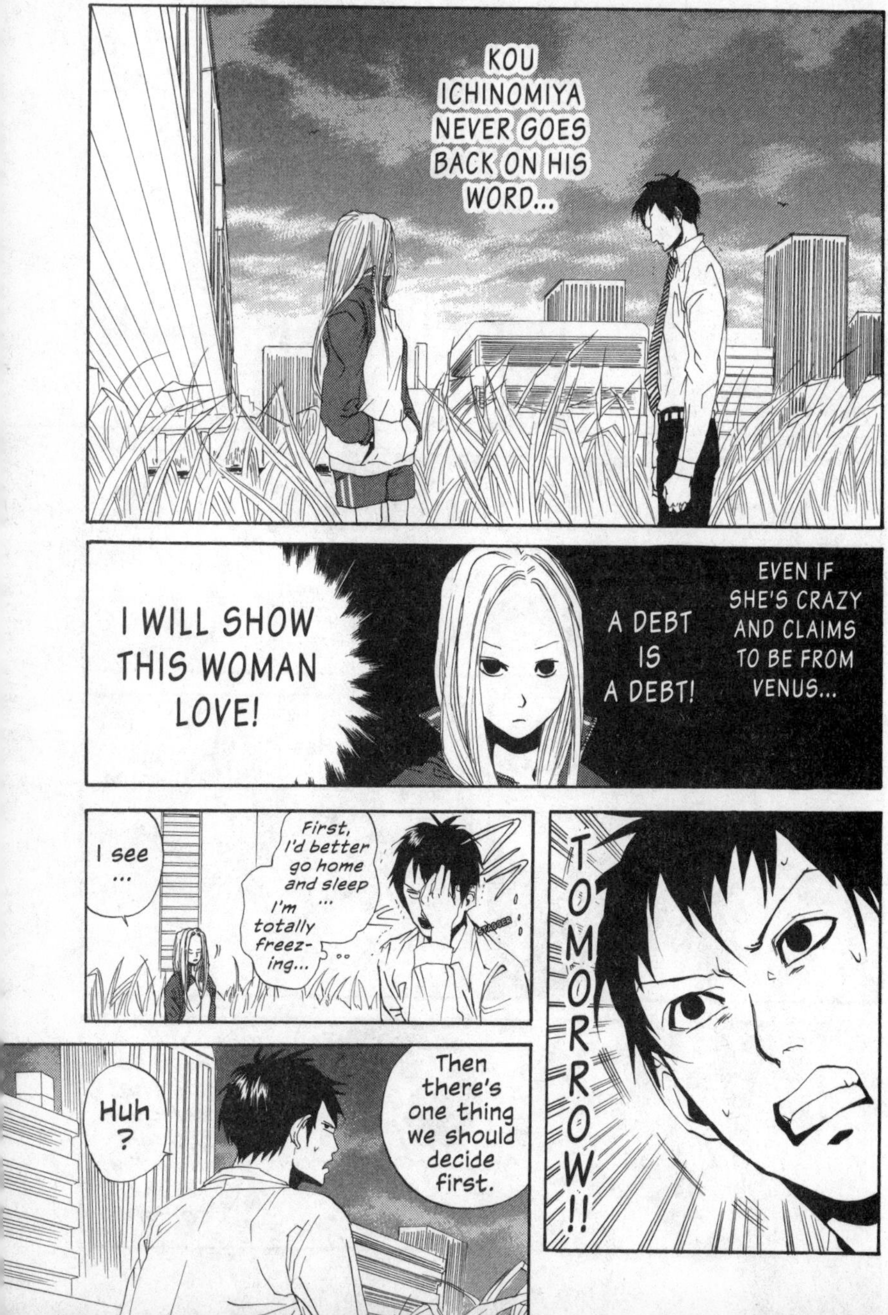
KOU ICHINOMIYA NEVER GOES BACK ON HIS WORD...
EVEN IF SHE'S CRAZY AND CLAIMS TO BE FROM VENUS...
A DEBT IS A DEBT!
I WILL SHOW THIS WOMAN LOVE!
TOMORROW!!
First, I'd better go home and sleep ...
I'm totally freez-ing...
STAGGER
I see ...
Then there's one thing we should decide first.
Huh ?

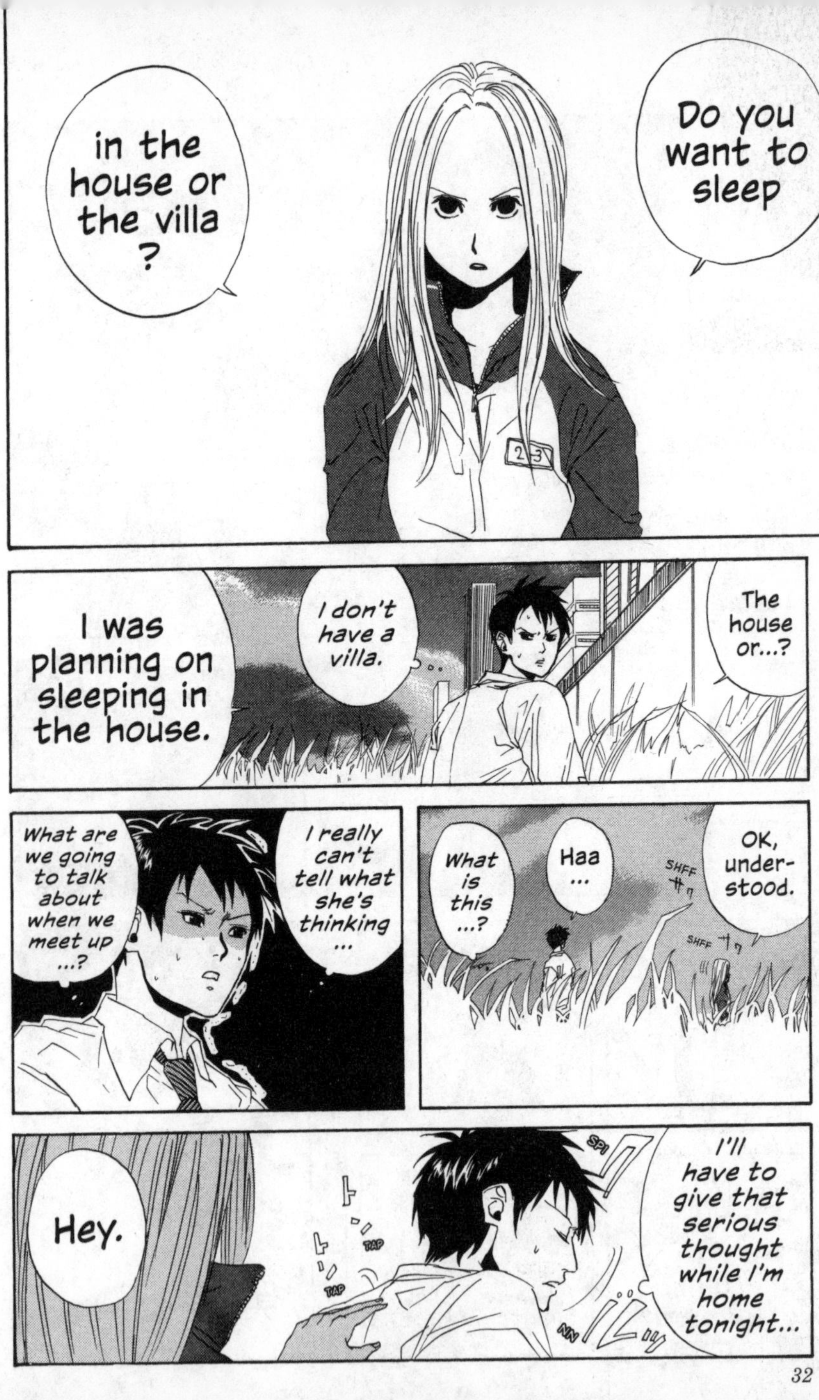
Do you want to sleep
in the house or the villa ?
The house or...?
I don't have a villa.
I was planning on sleeping in the house.
OK, under-stood.
SHFF
Haa ...
SHFF
What is this ...?
I really can't tell what she's thinking ...
What are we going to talk about when we meet up ...?
I'll have to give that serious thought while I'm home tonight...
SPI
NN
TAP
TAP
Hey.

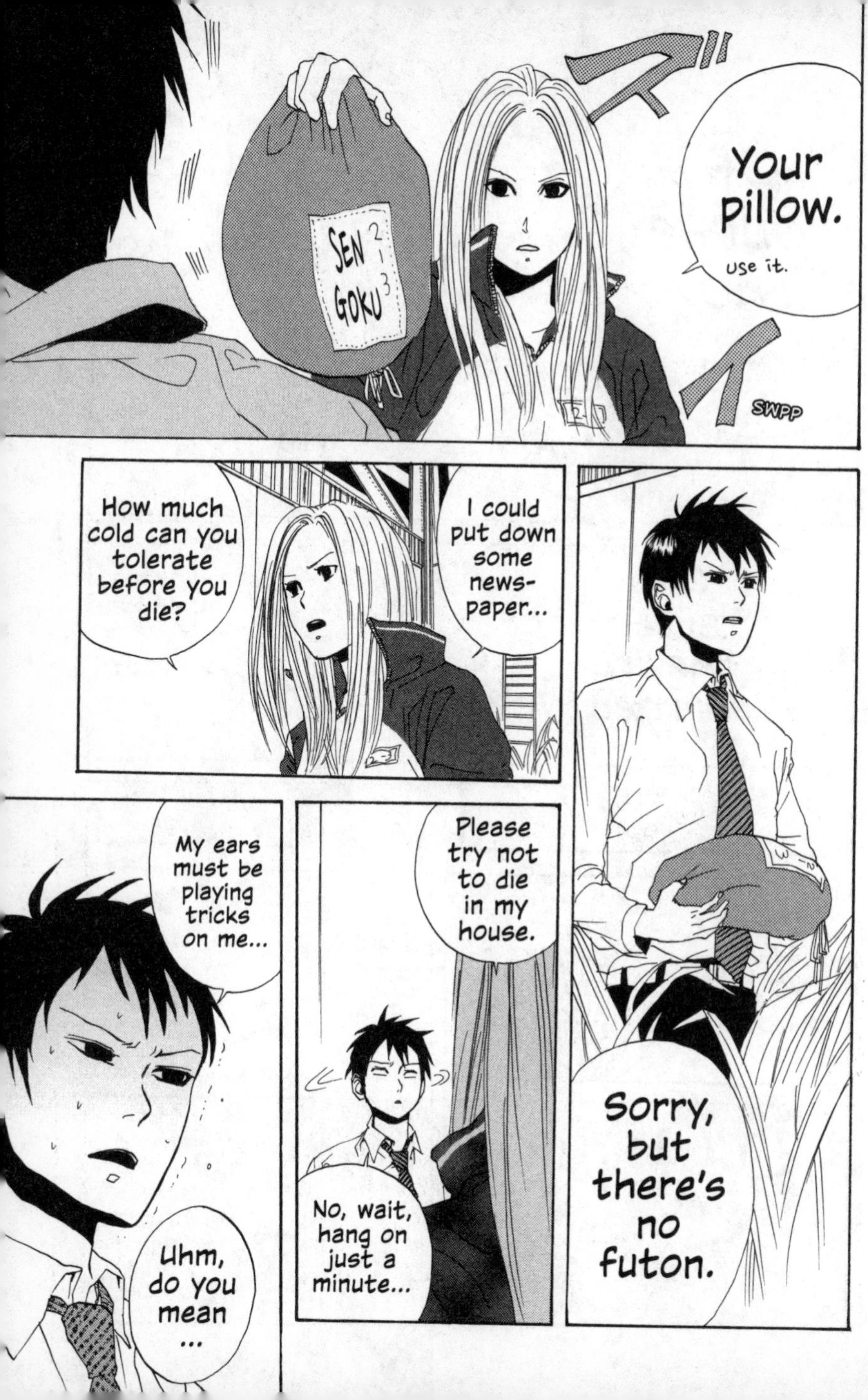
Your pillow.
use it.
SEN GOKU 2 1 3
SWPP
Sorry, but there's no futon.
I could put down some news-paper...
How much cold can you tolerate before you die?
Please try not to die in my house.
No, wait, hang on just a minute...
My ears must be playing tricks on me...
Uhm, do you mean ...

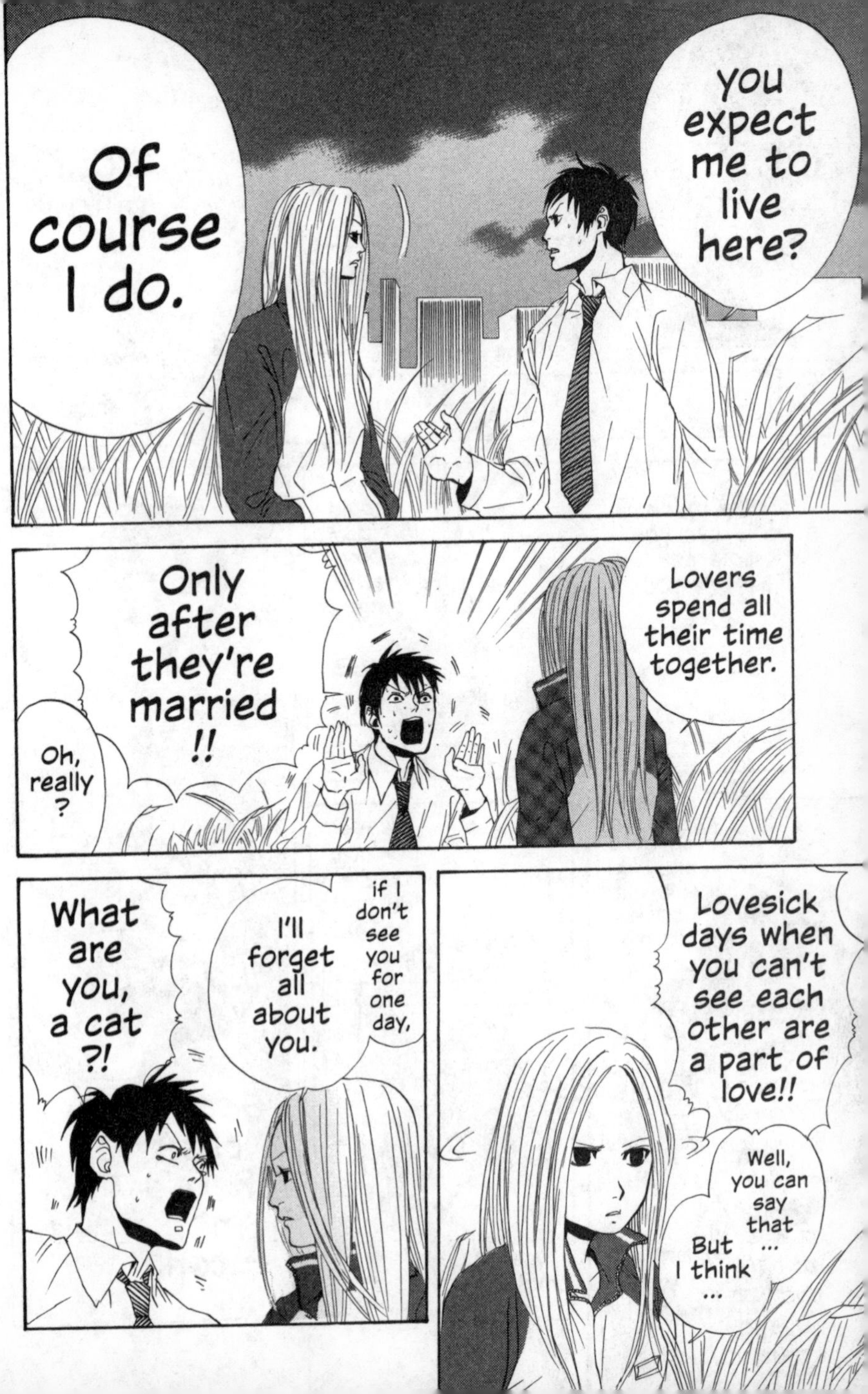
you expect me to live here?
Of course I do.
Lovers spend all their time together.
Only after they're married!!
Oh, really?
Lovesick days when you can't see each other are a part of love!!
Well, you can say that ...
But I think ...
if I don't see you for one day,
I'll forget all about you.
What are you, a cat?!

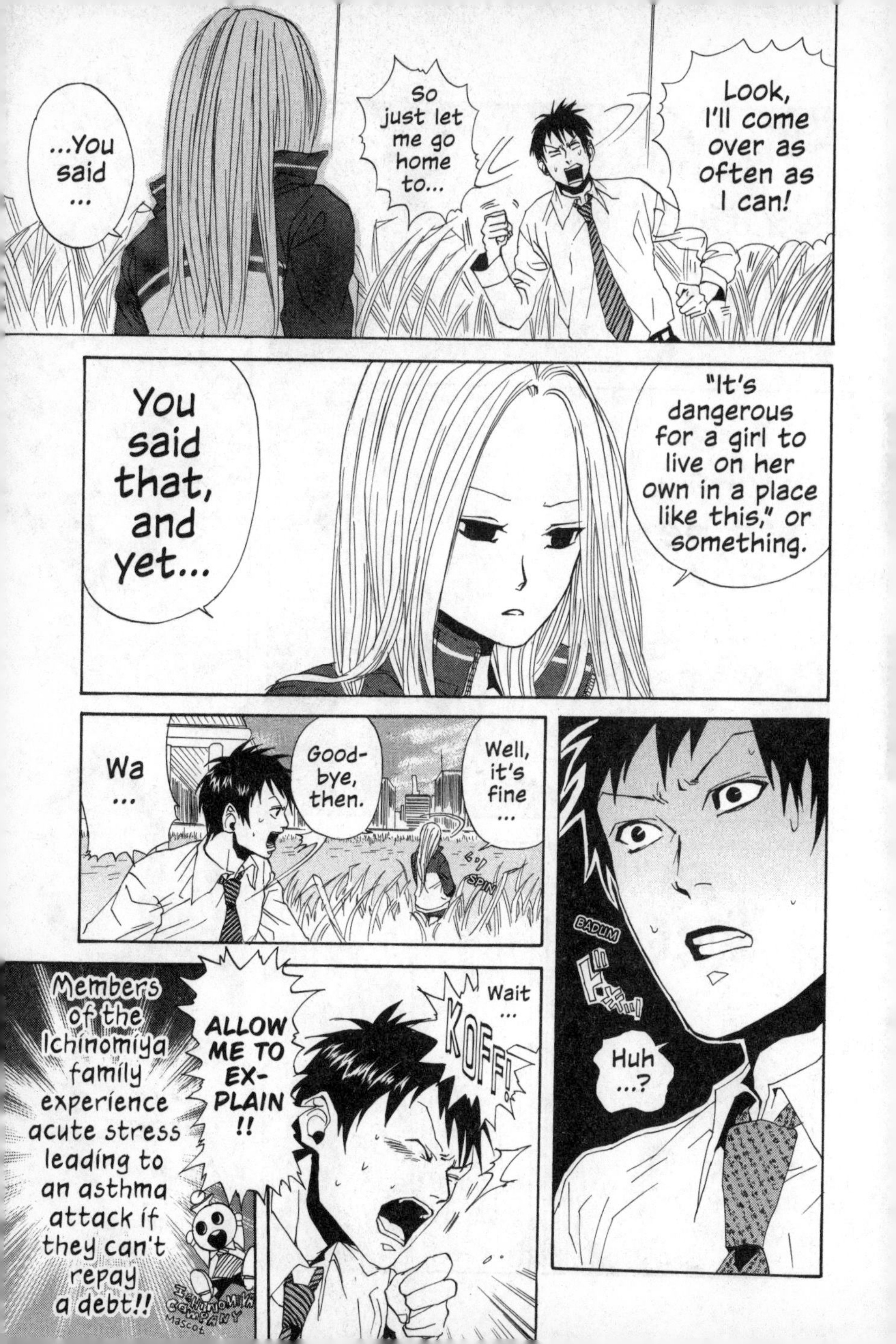
Look, I'll come over as often as I can!
So just let me go home to...
...You said ...
"It's dangerous for a girl to live on her own in a place like this," or something.
You said that, and yet...
BADUM
Huh ...?
Well, it's fine ...
SPIN
Good-bye, then.
Wa ...
Wait ...
KOFF!
ALLOW ME TO EX-PLAIN !!
Members of the Ichinomiya family experience acute stress leading to an asthma attack if they can't repay a debt!!
Ichinomiya Company Mascot

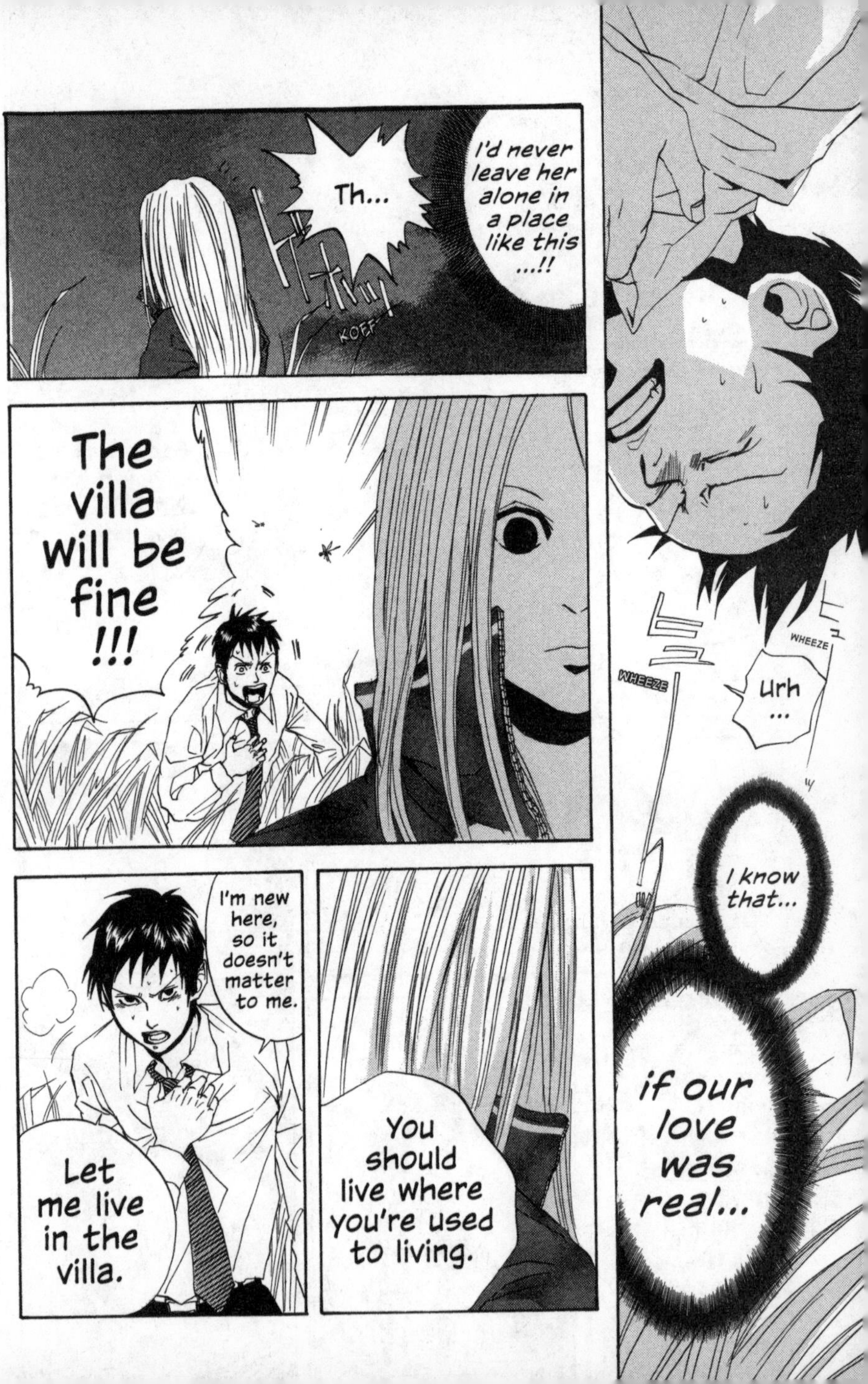
WHEEZE
Urh ...
WHEEZE
I know that...
if our love was real...
I'd never leave her alone in a place like this ...!!
Th...
KOFF
The villa will be fine !!!
You should live where you're used to living.
I'm new here, so it doesn't matter to me.
Let me live in the villa.

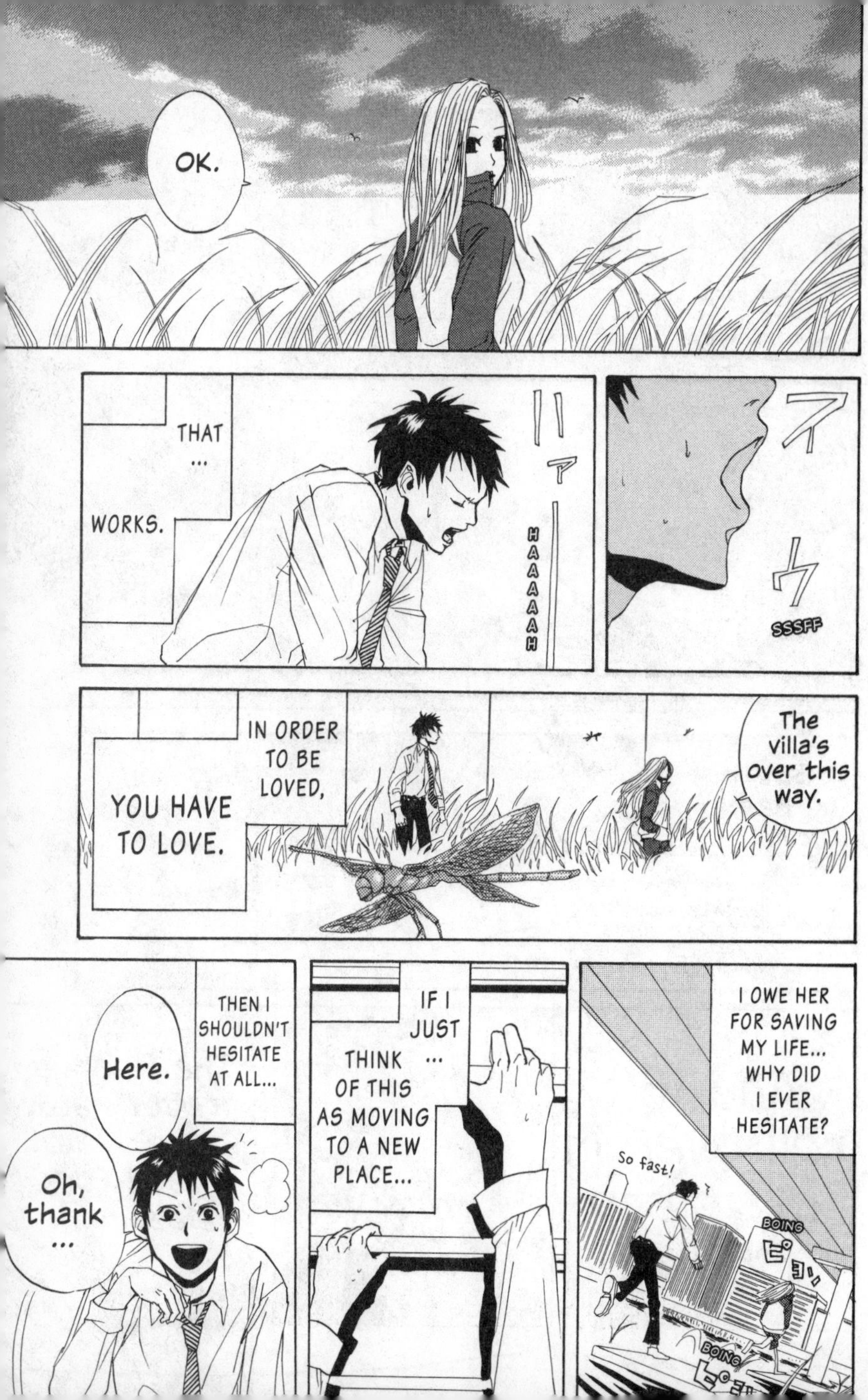

OK.
スゥ
SSSFF
ハァー
HAAAAAAH
THAT ... WORKS.
The villa's over this way.
IN ORDER TO BE LOVED,
YOU HAVE TO LOVE.
I OWE HER FOR SAVING MY LIFE... WHY DID I EVER HESITATE?
So fast!
BOING
ピョン
BOING
IF I JUST ...
THINK OF THIS AS MOVING TO A NEW PLACE...
THEN I SHOULDN'T HESITATE AT ALL...
Here.
Oh, thank ...

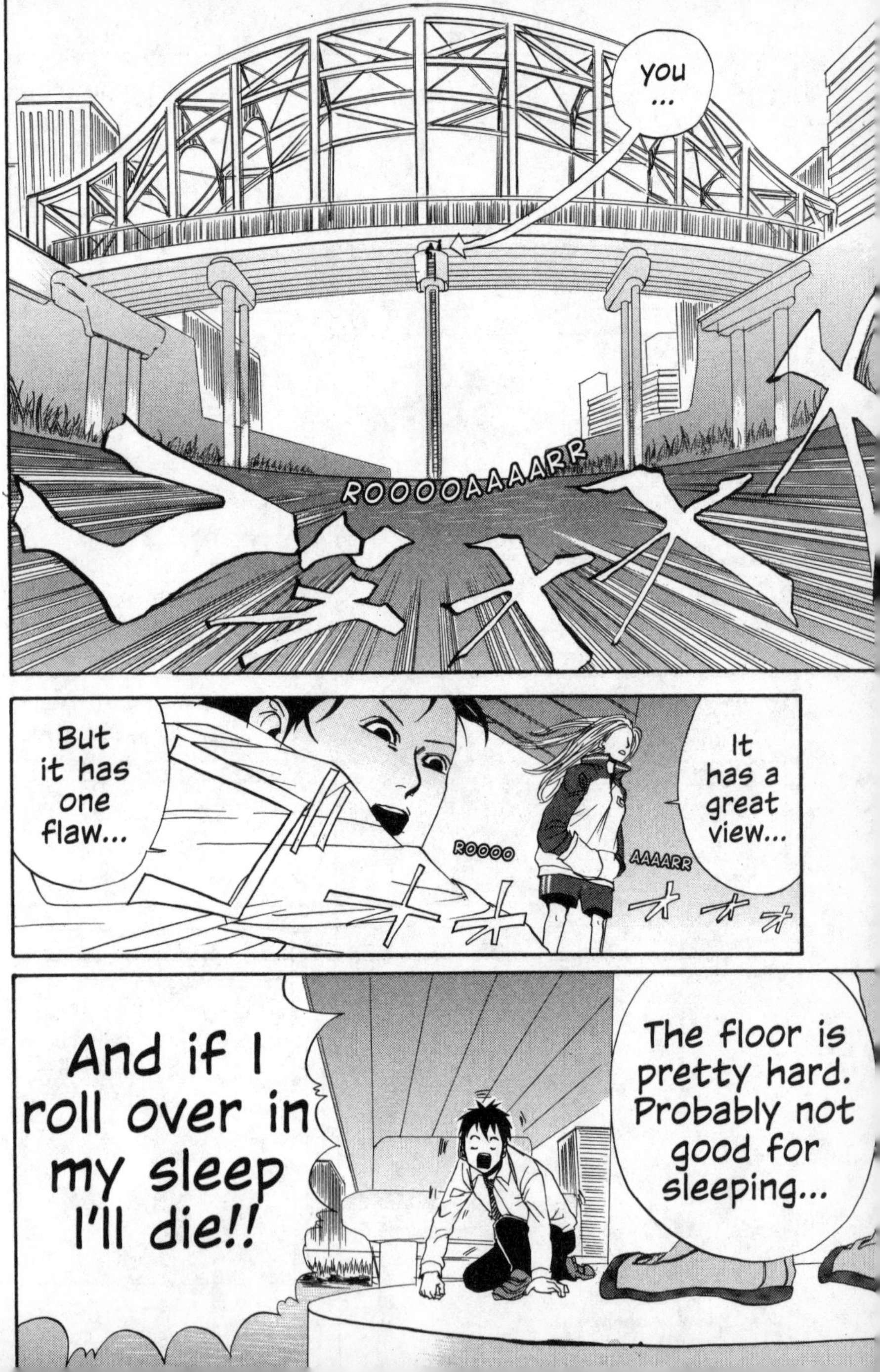
you ...
ROOOOAAAARR
It has a great view...
ROOOO
AAAARR
But it has one flaw...
The floor is pretty hard. Probably not good for sleeping...
And if I roll over in my sleep I'll die!!

☜ Chapter 4: Green Green

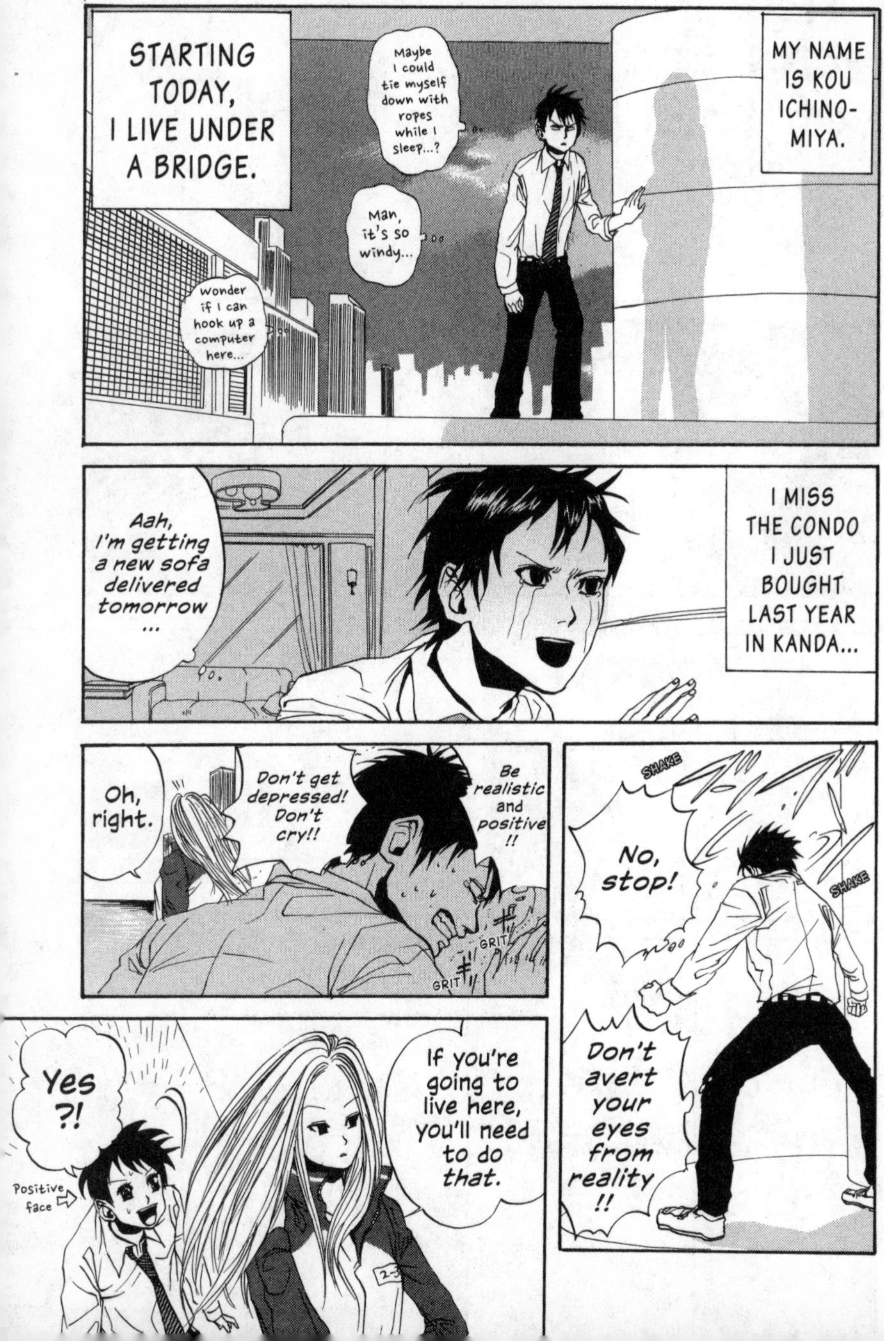
MY NAME IS KOU ICHINO-MIYA.
Maybe I could tie myself down with ropes while I sleep...?
STARTING TODAY, I LIVE UNDER A BRIDGE.
Man, it's so windy...
wonder if I can hook up a computer here...
I MISS THE CONDO I JUST BOUGHT LAST YEAR IN KANDA...
Aah, I'm getting a new sofa delivered tomorrow ...
SHAKE
No, stop!
SHAKE
Don't avert your eyes from reality !!
Be realistic and positive !!
Don't get depressed! Don't cry!!
Oh, right.
GRIT
GRIT
If you're going to live here, you'll need to do that.
Yes ?!
Positive face

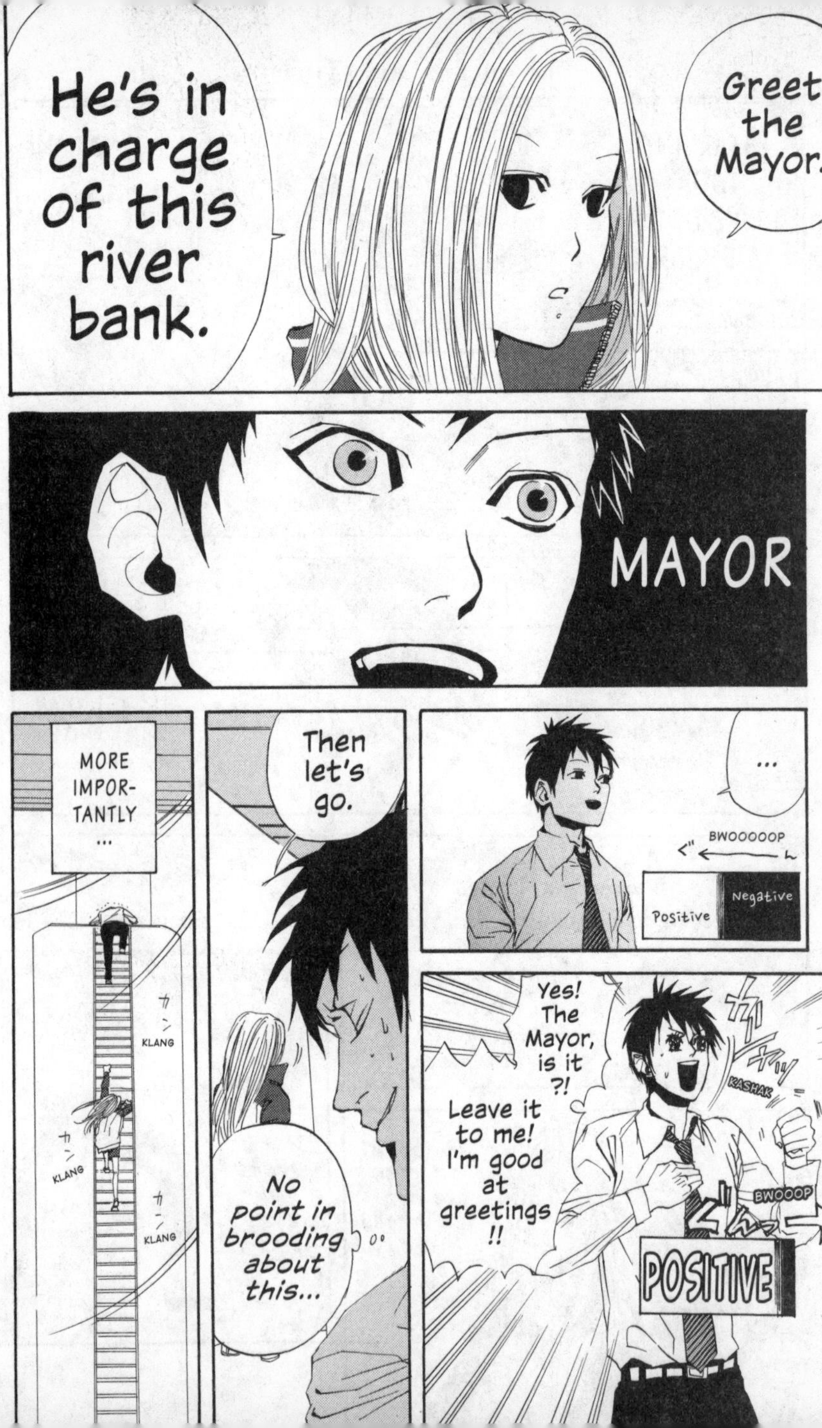
Greet the Mayor.
He's in charge of this river bank.
MAYOR
...
BWOOOOOP
Negative
Positive
Yes! The Mayor, is it ?!
Leave it to me! I'm good at greetings !!
KASHAK
BWOOOP
POSITIVE
Then let's go.
No point in brooding about this...
MORE IMPOR-TANTLY ...
KLANG
KLANG
KLANG

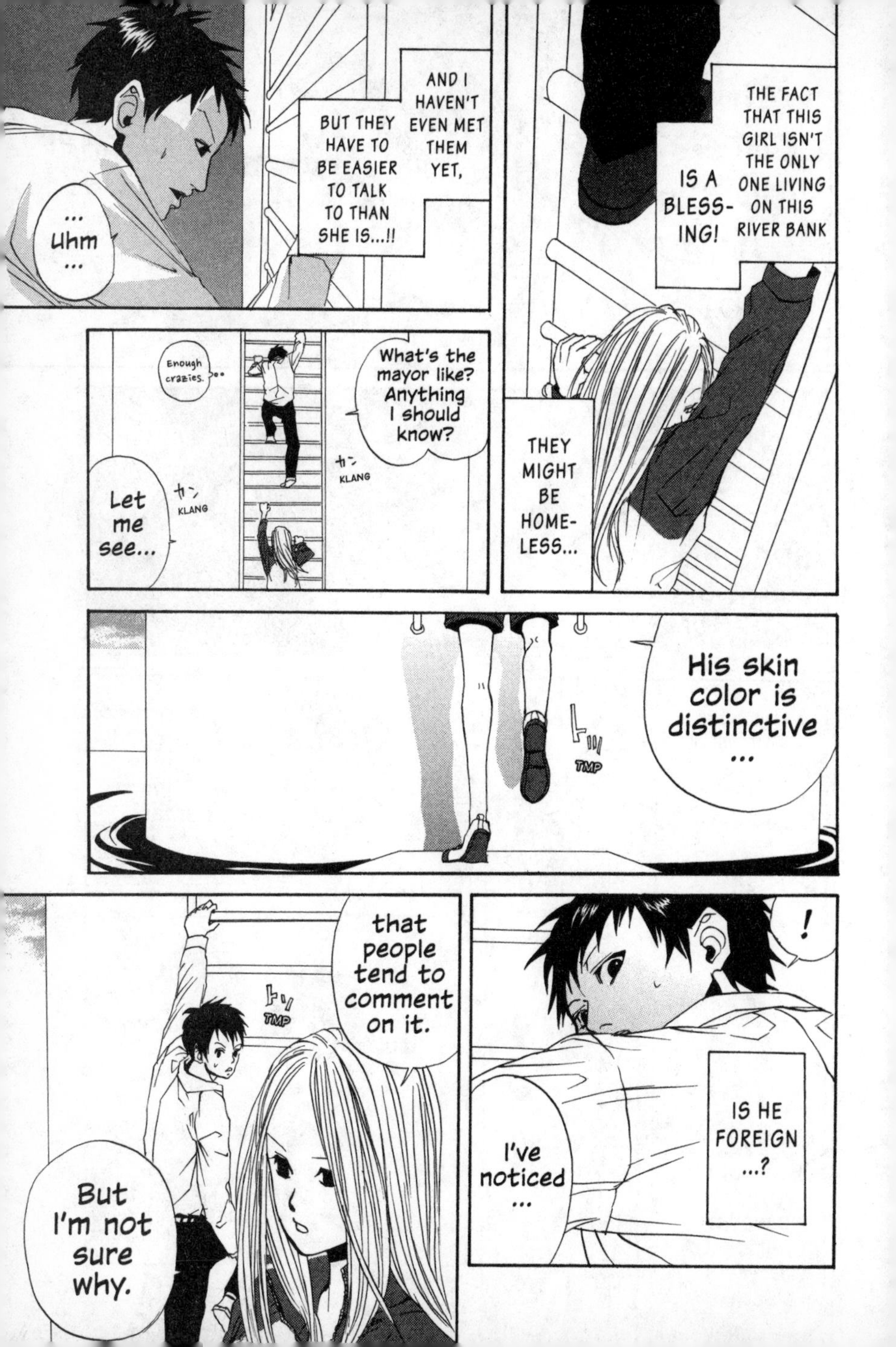
THE FACT THAT THIS GIRL ISN'T THE ONLY ONE LIVING ON THIS RIVER BANK
IS A BLESS-ING!
THEY MIGHT BE HOME-LESS...
AND I HAVEN'T EVEN MET THEM YET,
BUT THEY HAVE TO BE EASIER TO TALK TO THAN SHE IS...!!
...Uhm...
What's the mayor like? Anything I should know?
KLANG
Enough crazies...
KLANG
Let me see...
His skin color is distinctive...
TMP
!
IS HE FOREIGN...?
I've noticed...
that people tend to comment on it.
TMP
But I'm not sure why.

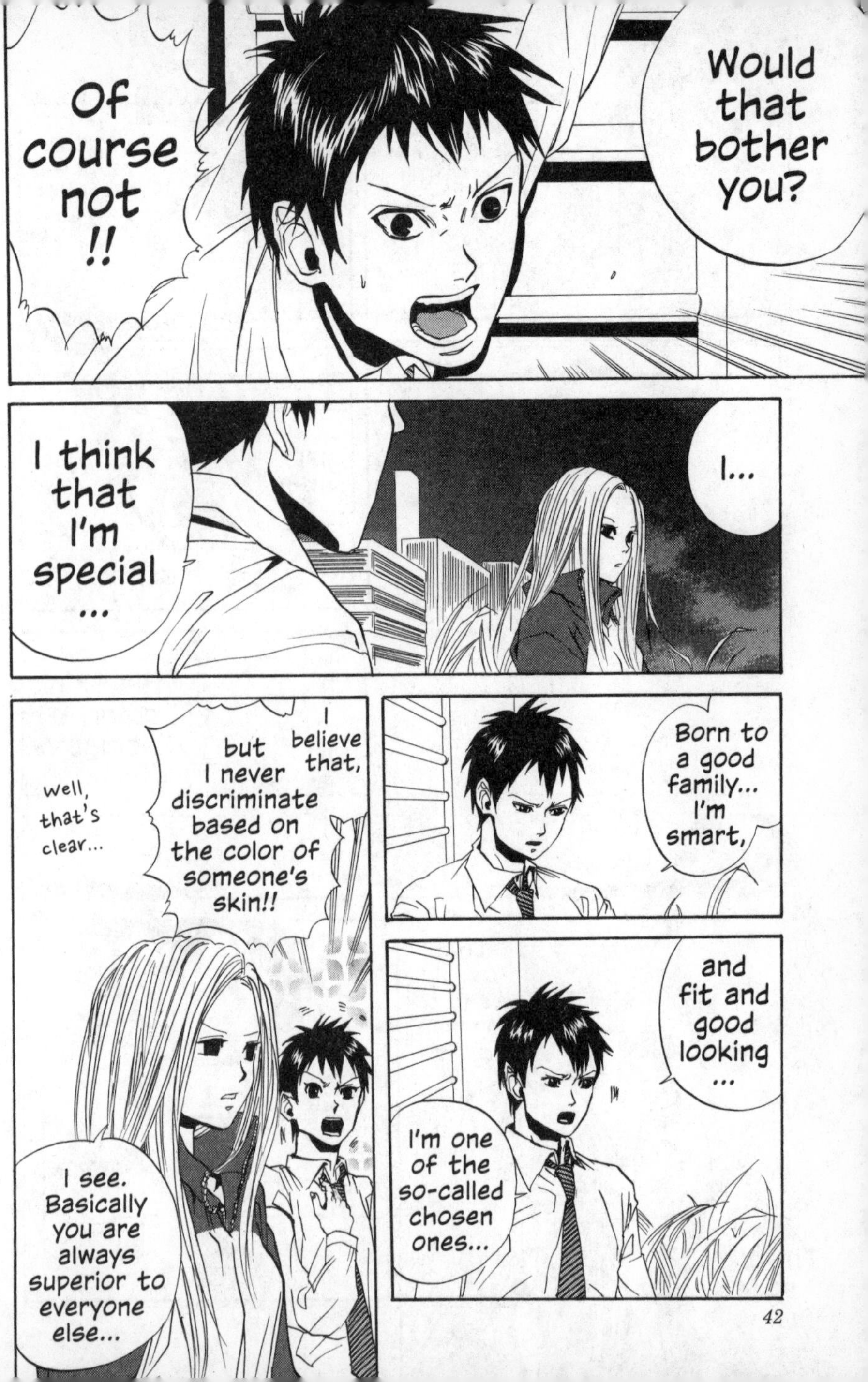
Would that bother you?
Of course not !!
I...
I think that I'm special ...
Born to a good family... I'm smart,
and fit and good looking ...
I'm one of the so-called chosen ones...
I believe that, but I never discriminate based on the color of someone's skin!!
well, that's clear...
I see. Basically you are always superior to everyone else...

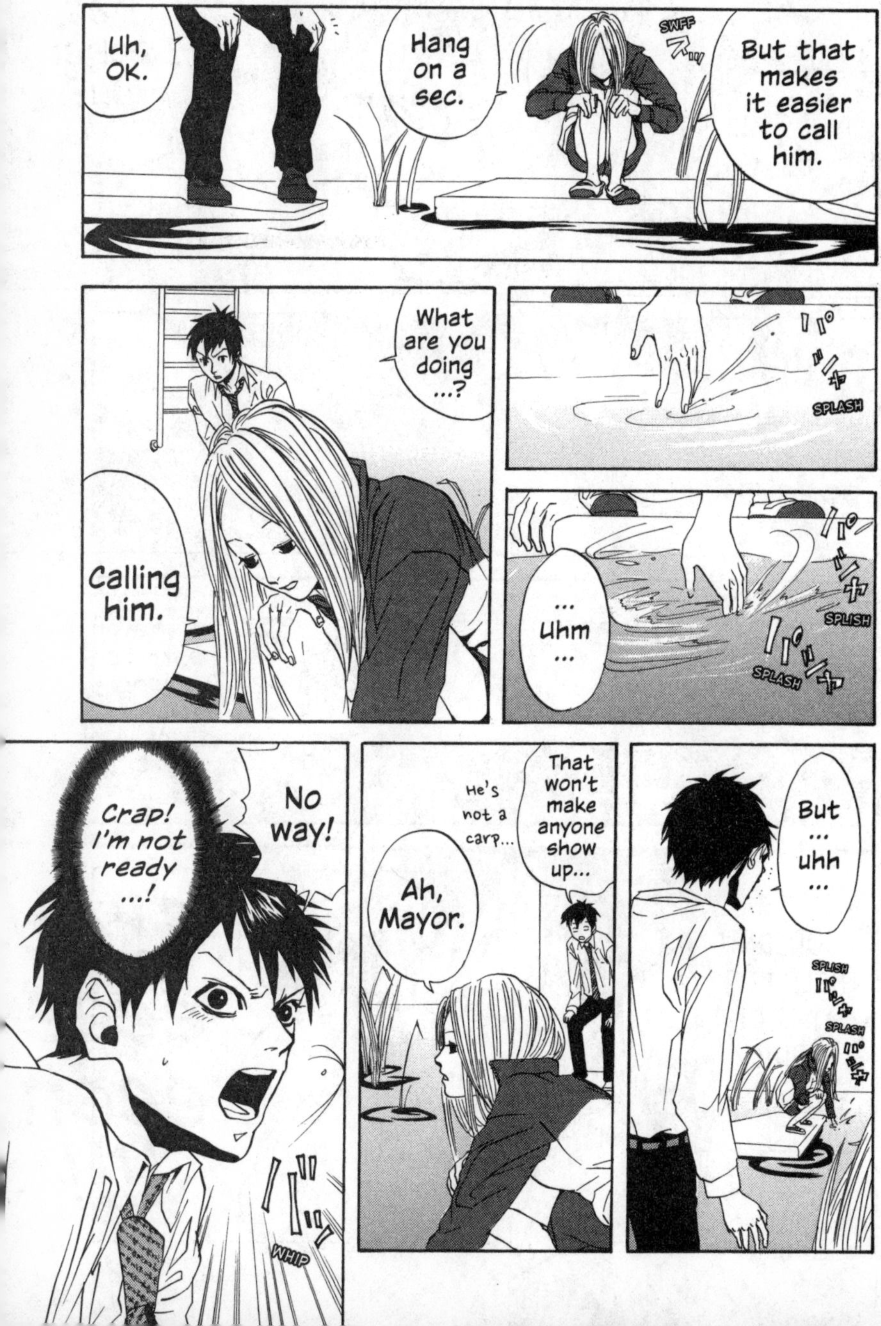
But that makes it easier to call him.
SWFF
Hang on a sec.
Uh, OK.
SPLASH
SPLISH
SPLASH
... Uhm ...
What are you doing ...?
Calling him.
But ... uhh ...
SPLISH
SPLASH
That won't make anyone show up...
He's not a carp...
Ah, Mayor.
No way!
Crap! I'm not ready ...!
WHIP

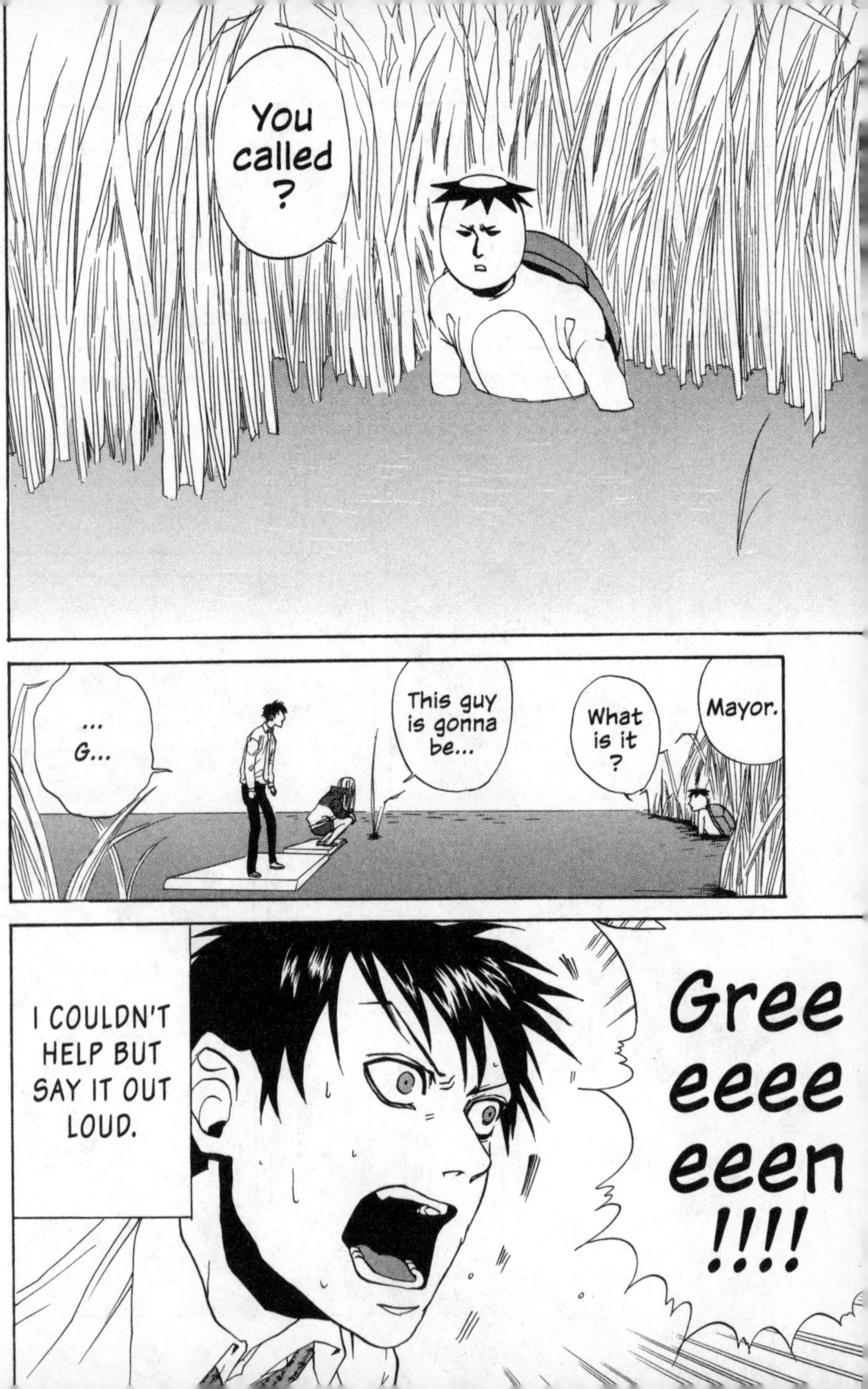
You called?
Mayor.
What is it?
This guy is gonna be...
... G...
Greeeeeeeeen!!!!
I COULDN'T HELP BUT SAY IT OUT LOUD.

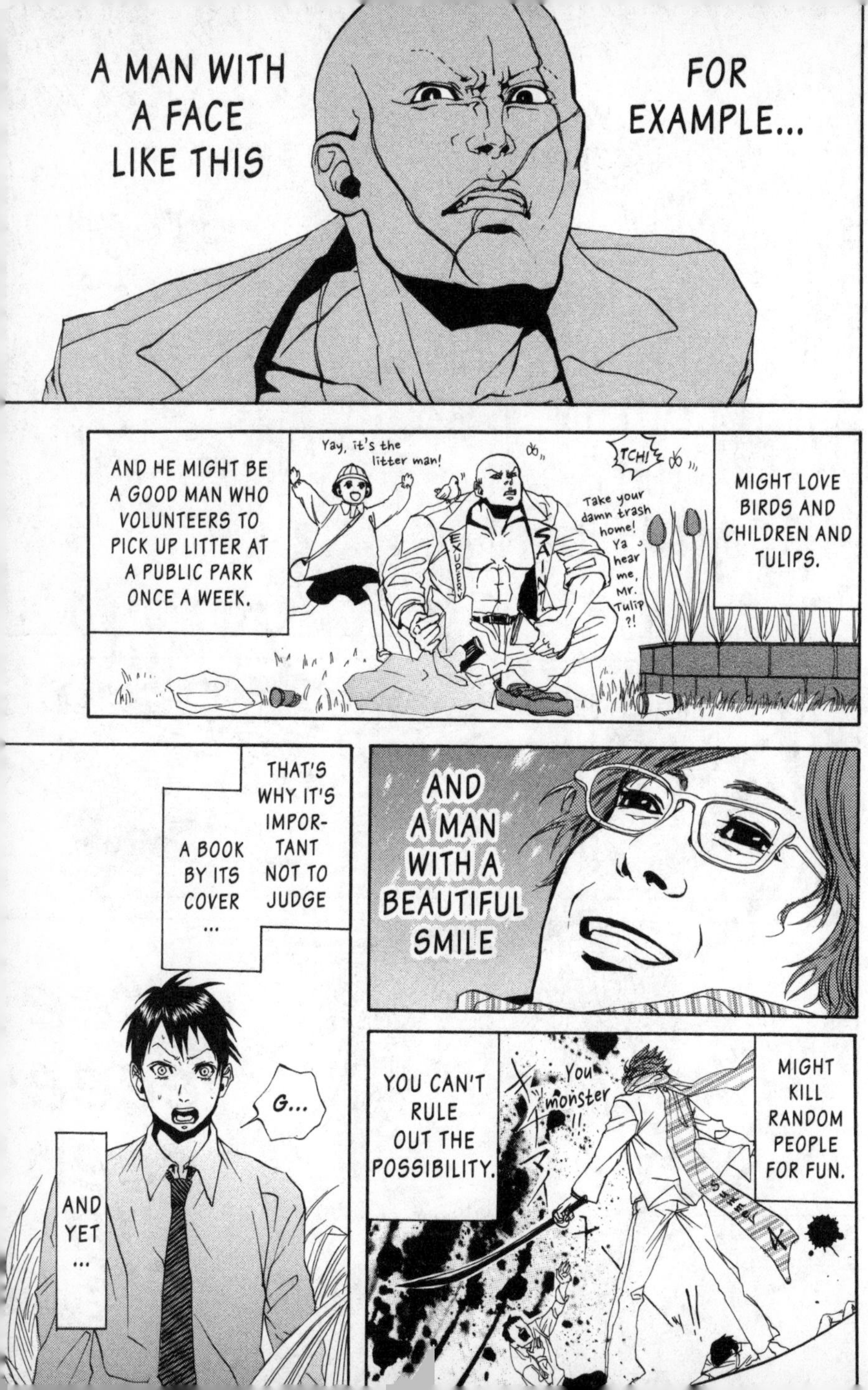

FOR EXAMPLE...
A MAN WITH A FACE LIKE THIS
MIGHT LOVE BIRDS AND CHILDREN AND TULIPS.
TCH!
Take your damn trash home! Ya hear me, Mr. Tulip?!
Yay, it's the litter man!
AND HE MIGHT BE A GOOD MAN WHO VOLUNTEERS TO PICK UP LITTER AT A PUBLIC PARK ONCE A WEEK.
AND A MAN WITH A BEAUTIFUL SMILE
MIGHT KILL RANDOM PEOPLE FOR FUN.
You monster!!
YOU CAN'T RULE OUT THE POSSIBILITY.
THAT'S WHY IT'S IMPOR-TANT NOT TO JUDGE
A BOOK BY ITS COVER...
G...
AND YET...

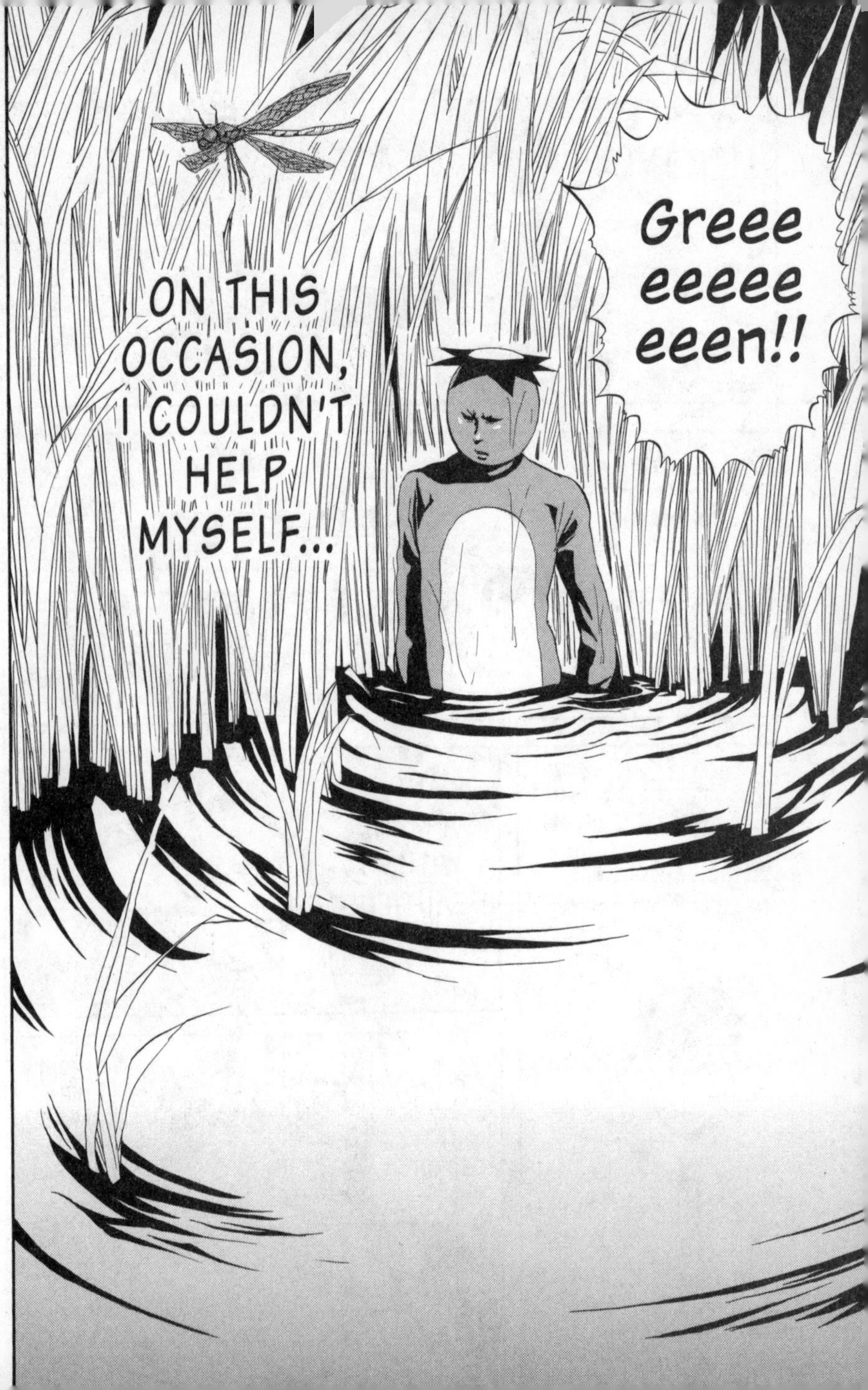
Greee eeeee eeen!!
ON THIS OCCASION, I COULDN'T HELP MYSELF...

☜ Chapter 5: The Inside

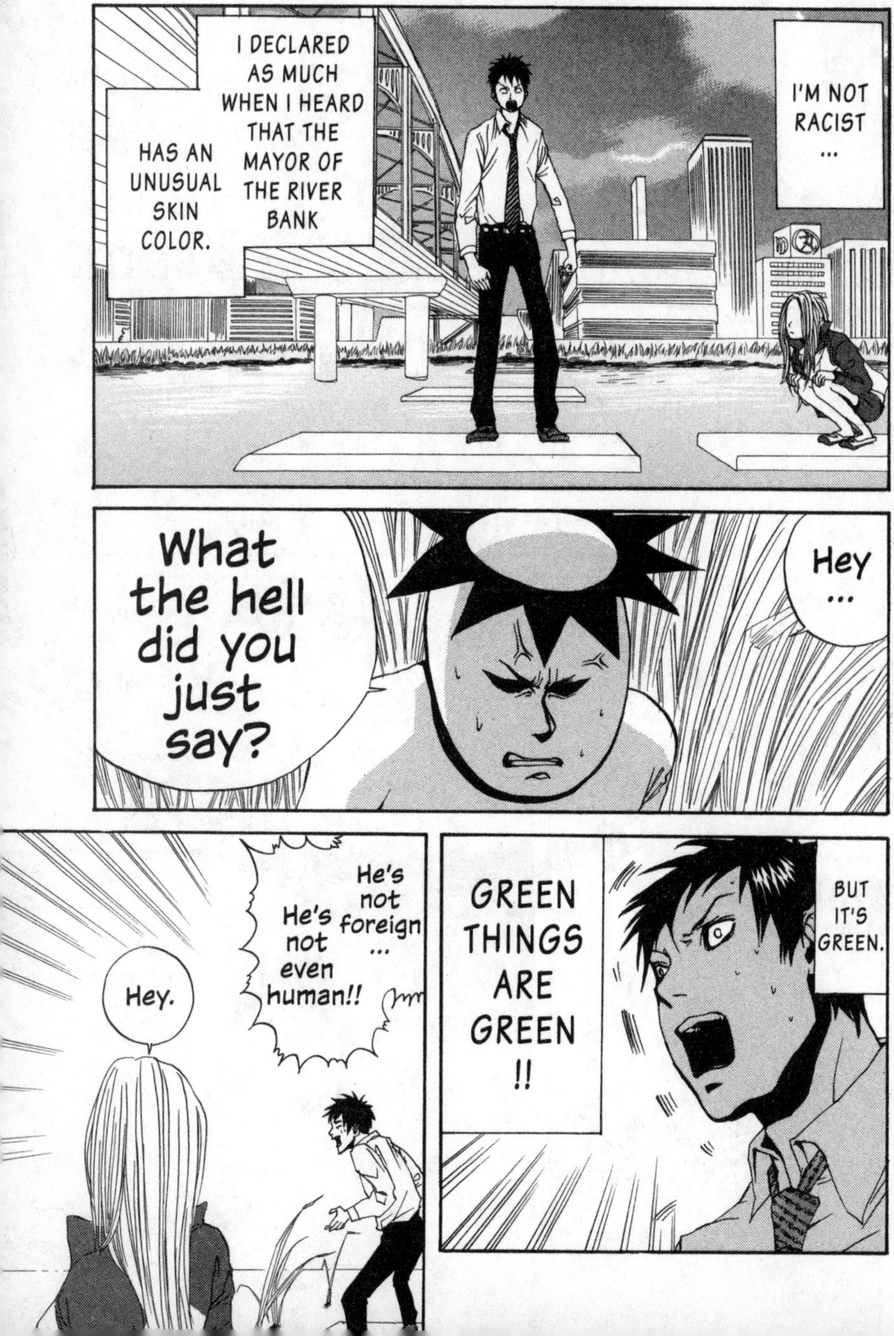

I'M NOT RACIST ...
I DECLARED AS MUCH WHEN I HEARD THAT THE MAYOR OF THE RIVER BANK
HAS AN UNUSUAL SKIN COLOR.
Hey ...
What the hell did you just say?
BUT IT'S GREEN.
GREEN THINGS ARE GREEN !!
He's not foreign ...
He's not even human!!
Hey.

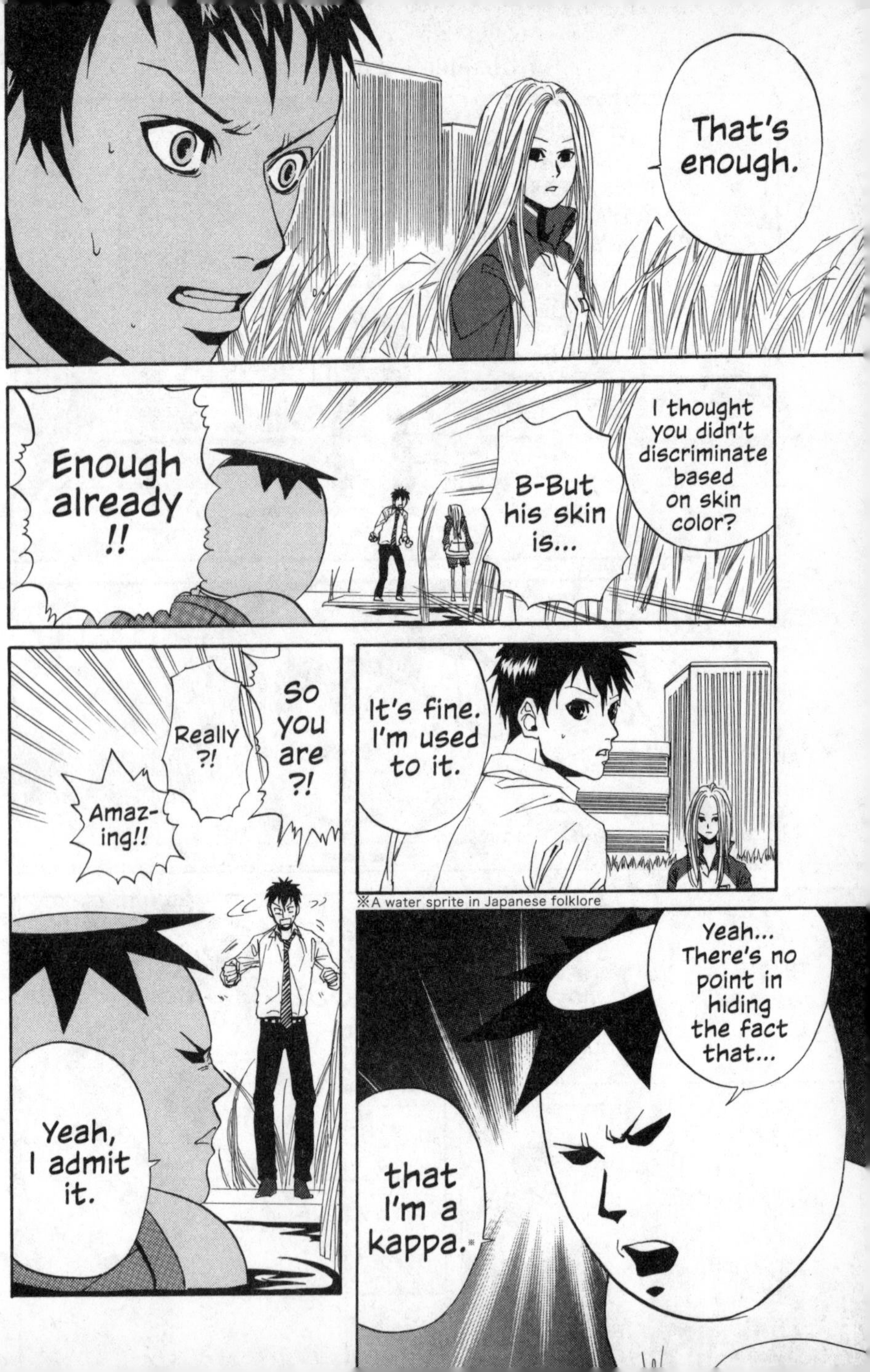
That's enough.
I thought you didn't discriminate based on skin color?
B-But his skin is...
Enough already !!
It's fine. I'm used to it.
So you are ?!
Really ?!
Amazing!!
Yeah... There's no point in hiding the fact that...
that I'm a kappa.※
Yeah, I admit it.
※A water sprite in Japanese folklore

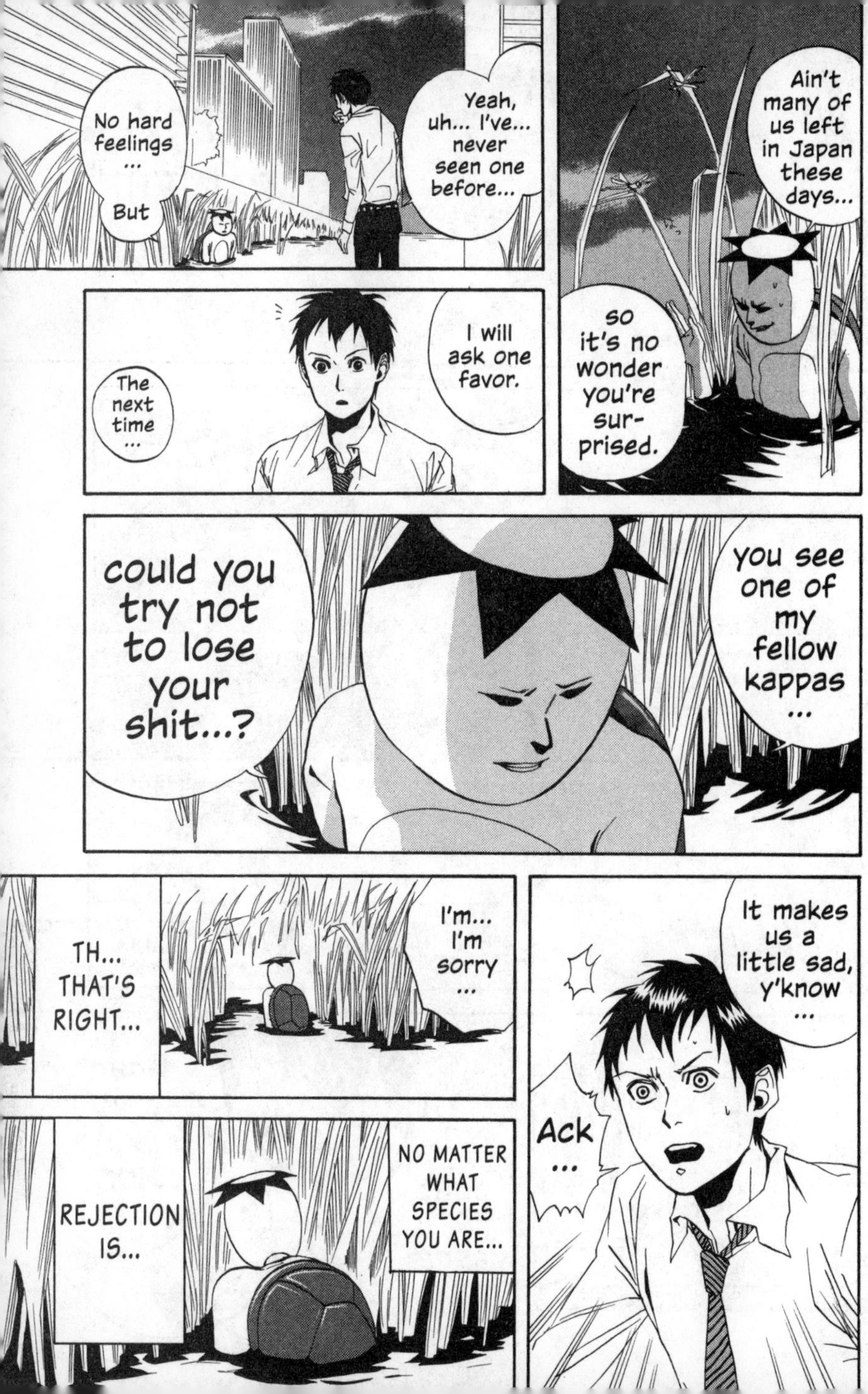

Ain't many of us left in Japan these days...
so it's no wonder you're sur-prised.
Yeah, uh... I've... never seen one before...
No hard feelings ...
But
I will ask one favor.
The next time ...
you see one of my fellow kappas ...
could you try not to lose your shit...?
It makes us a little sad, y'know ...
Ack ...
I'm... I'm sorry ...
TH... THAT'S RIGHT...
NO MATTER WHAT SPECIES YOU ARE...
REJECTION IS...

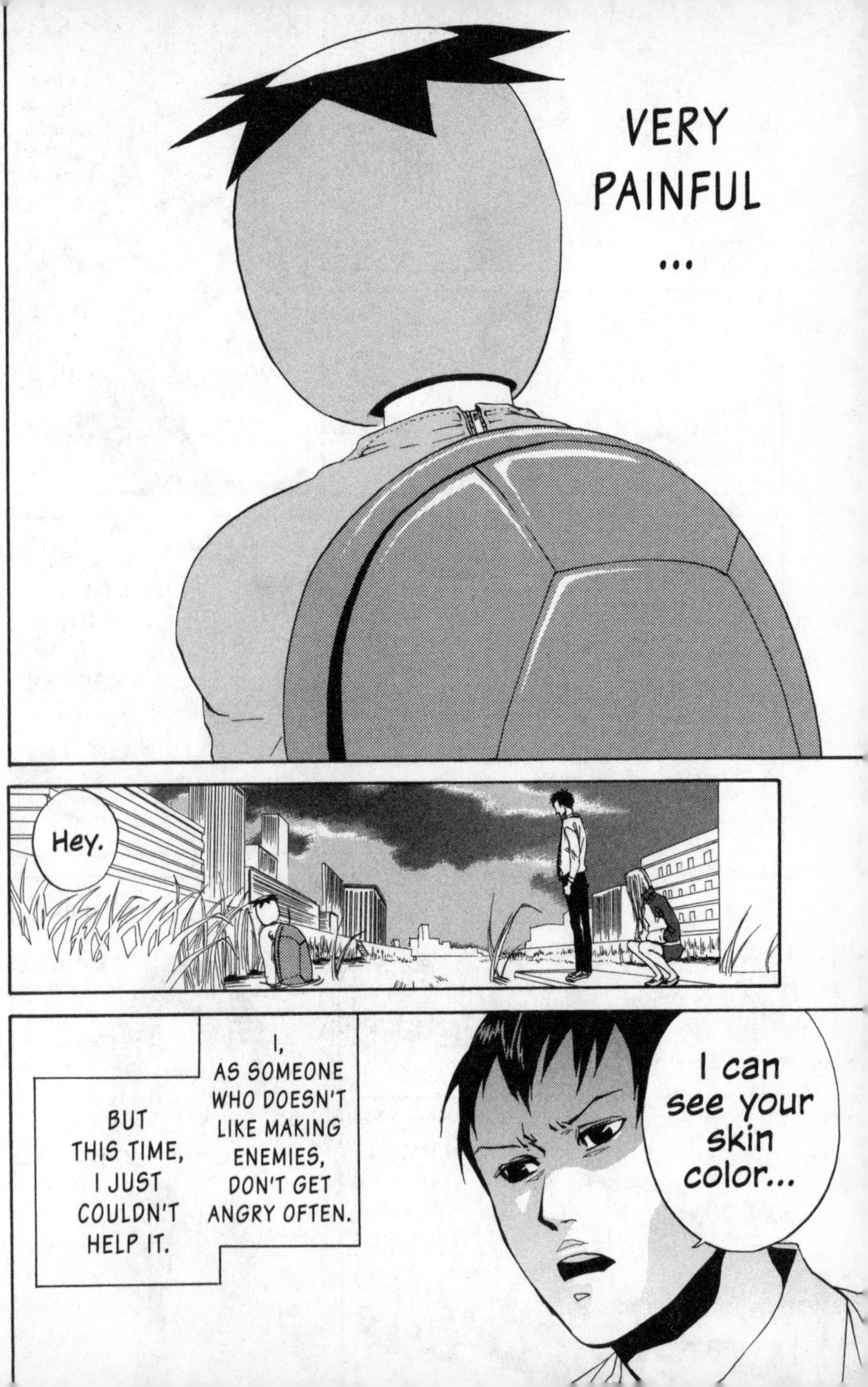
VERY PAINFUL ...
Hey.
I can see your skin color...
I, AS SOMEONE WHO DOESN'T LIKE MAKING ENEMIES, DON'T GET ANGRY OFTEN.
BUT THIS TIME, I JUST COULDN'T HELP IT.

☜ Chapter 6: Truth

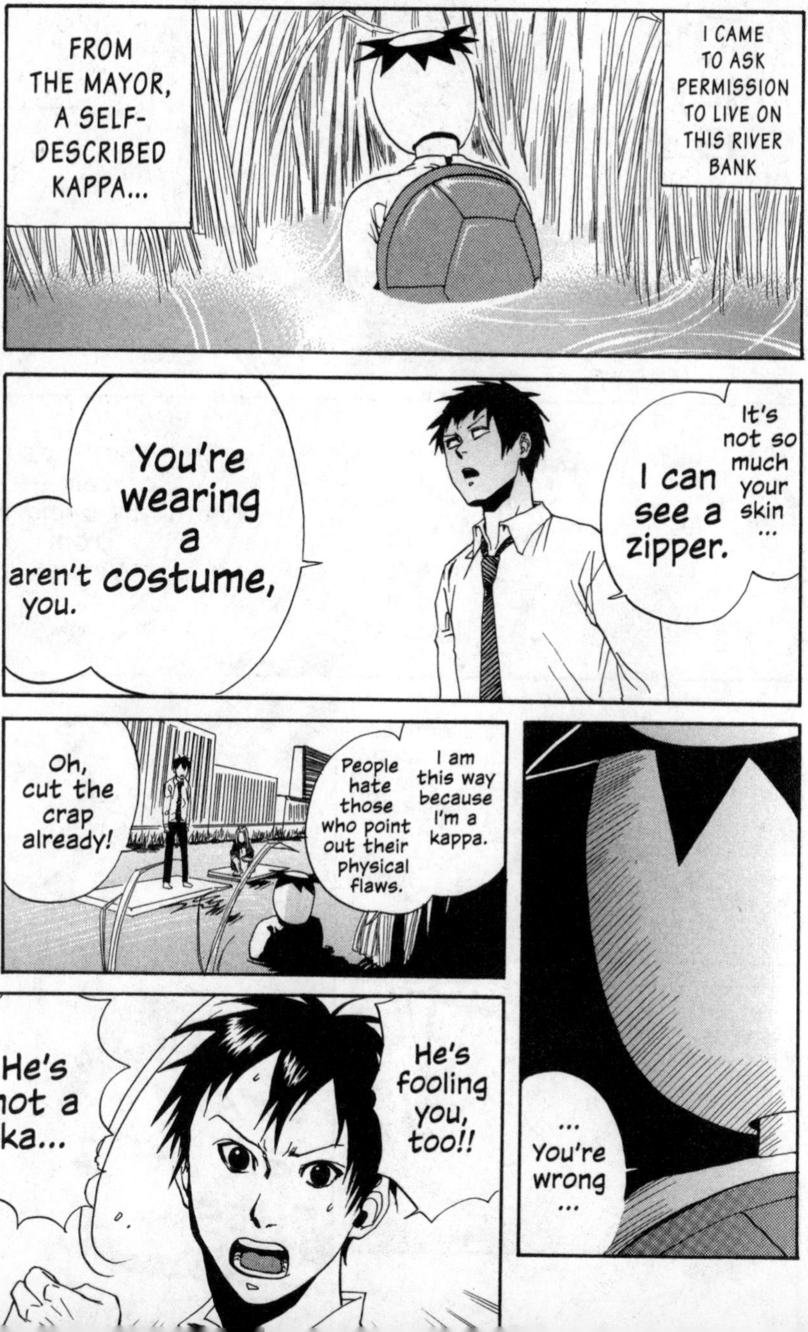
I CAME TO ASK PERMISSION TO LIVE ON THIS RIVER BANK
FROM THE MAYOR, A SELF-DESCRIBED KAPPA...
It's not so much your skin ... I can see a zipper.
You're wearing a costume, aren't you.
... You're wrong ...
I am this way because I'm a kappa.
People hate those who point out their physical flaws.
Oh, cut the crap already!
He's fooling you, too!!
He's not a ka...

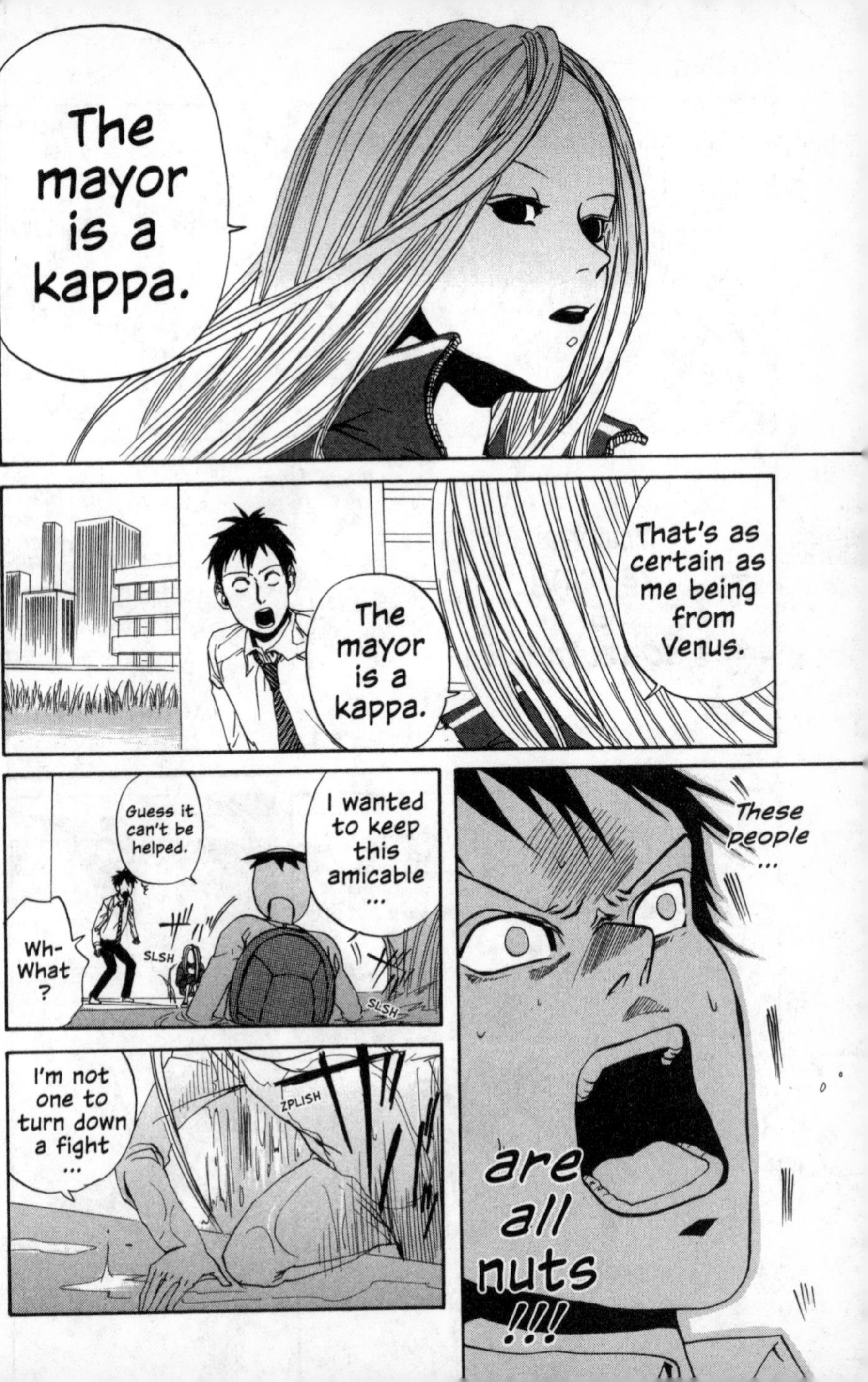
The mayor is a kappa.
That's as certain as me being from Venus.
The mayor is a kappa.
These people ...
are all nuts !!!
I wanted to keep this amicable ...
Guess it can't be helped.
SLSH
Wh- What ?
SLSH
ZPLISH
I'm not one to turn down a fight ...

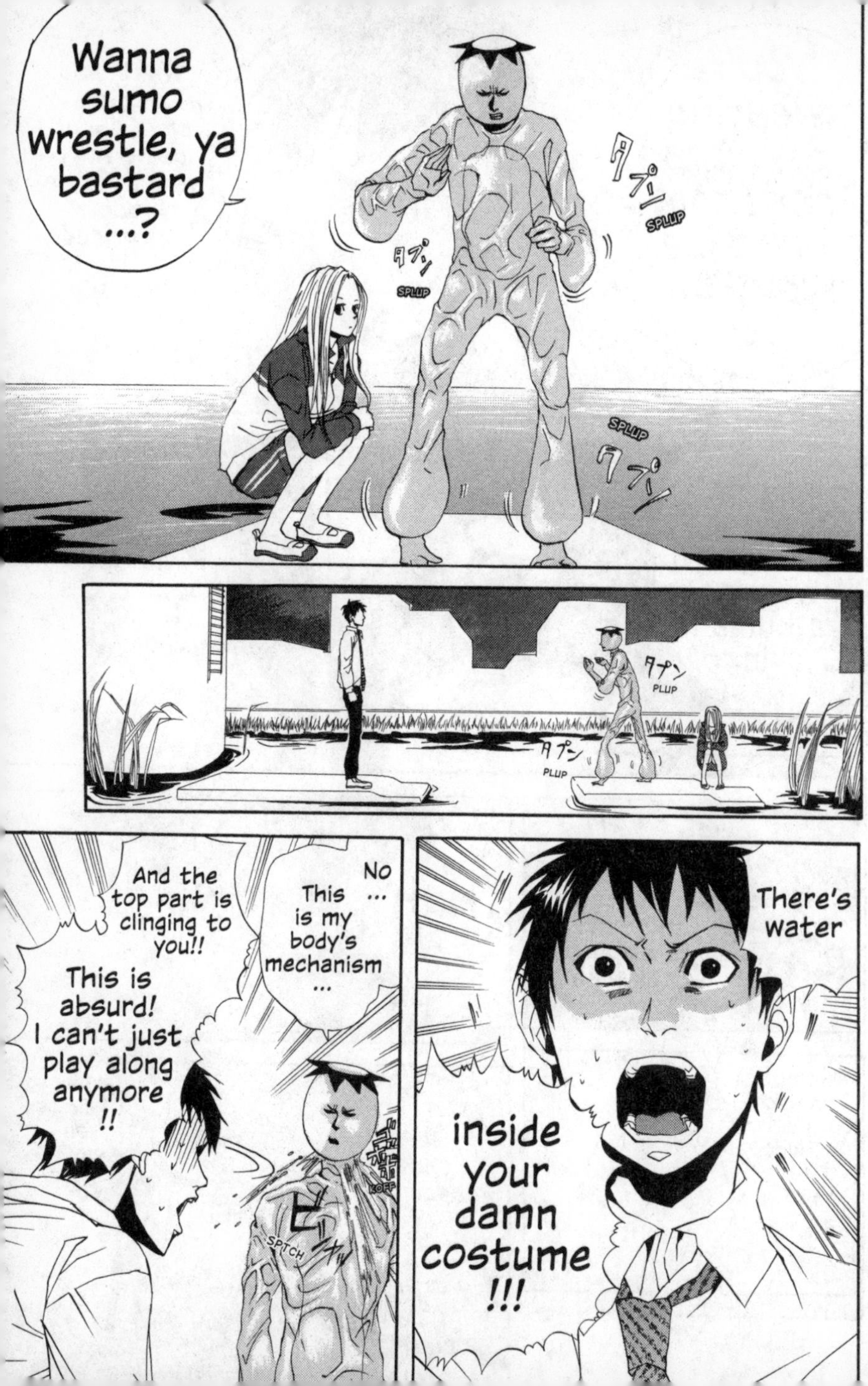
タプン
SPLUP
Wanna sumo wrestle, ya bastard ...?
タプン
SPLUP
SPLUP
タプン
タプン
PLUP
タプン
PLUP
There's water
inside your damn costume !!!
No ... This is my body's mechanism ...
And the top part is clinging to you!!
This is absurd! I can't just play along anymore !!
KOFF
SPTCH

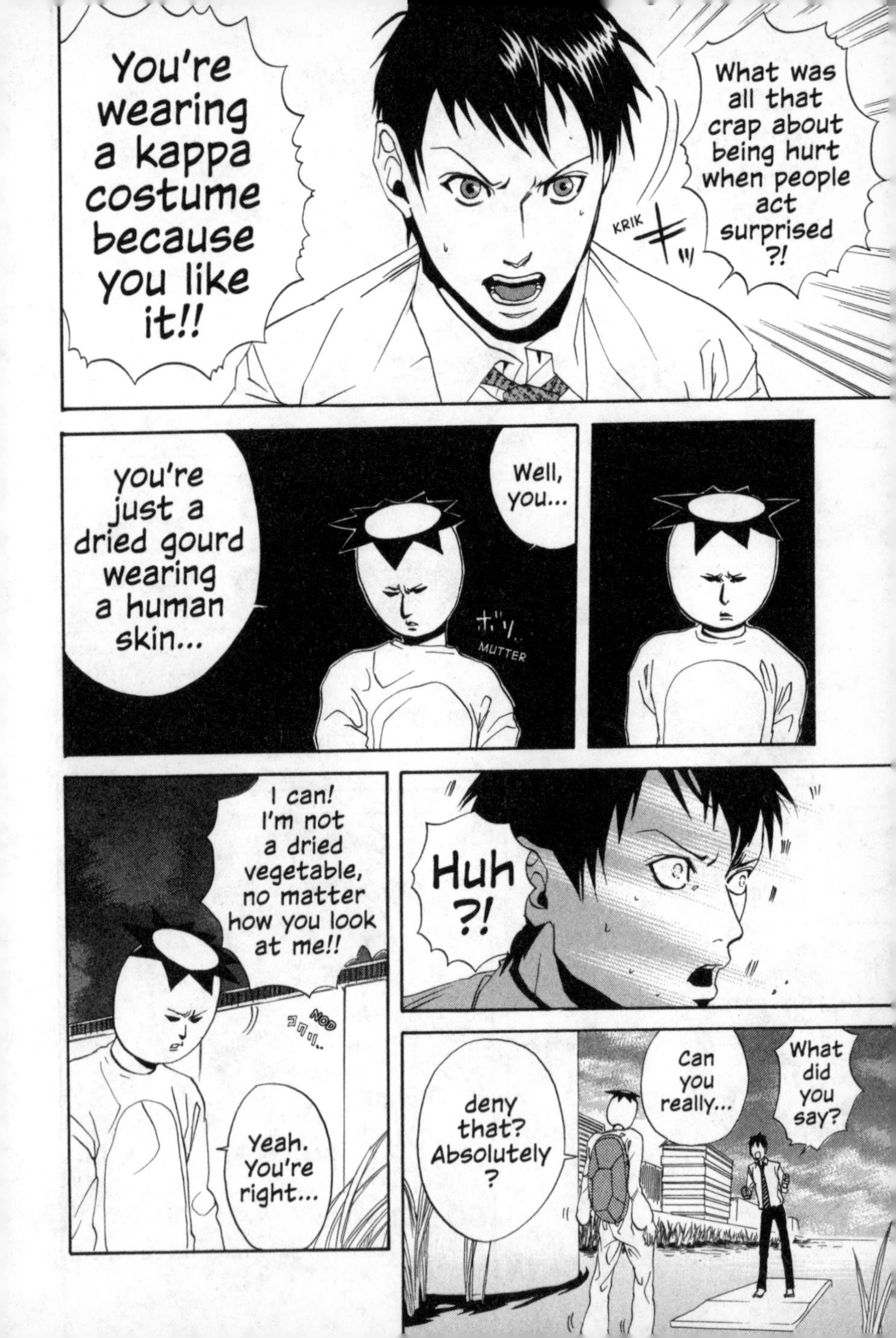
What was all that crap about being hurt when people act surprised?!
KRIK
You're wearing a kappa costume because you like it!!
Well, you...
you're just a dried gourd wearing a human skin...
MUTTER
Huh?!
What did you say?
Can you really...
deny that? Absolutely?
I can! I'm not a dried vegetable, no matter how you look at me!!
NOD
Yeah. You're right...

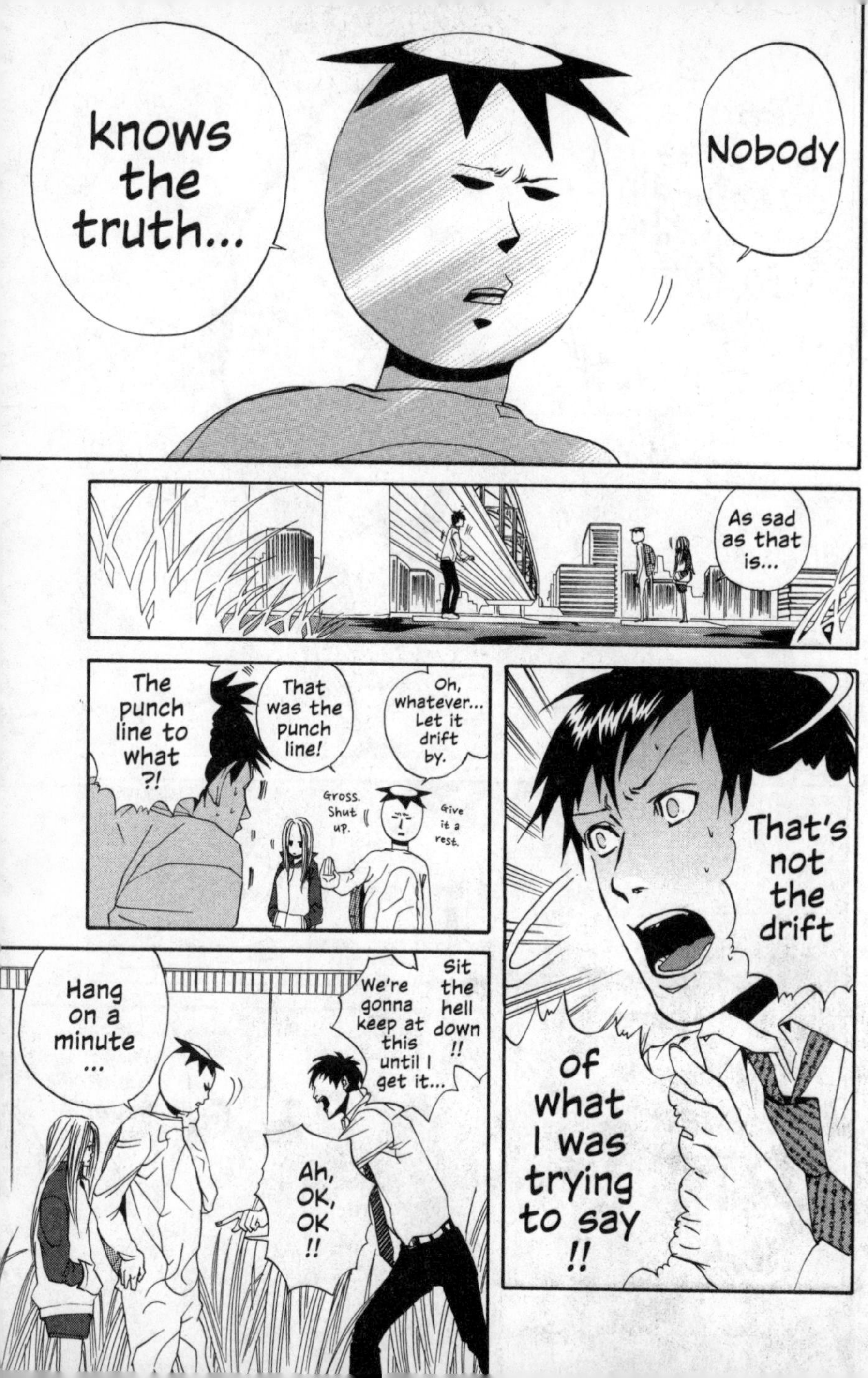
Nobody
knows the truth...
As sad as that is...
That's not the drift
of what I was trying to say !!
Oh, whatever... Let it drift by.
That was the punch line!
The punch line to what ?!
Give it a rest.
Gross. Shut up.
Sit the hell down !!
We're gonna keep at this until I get it...
Hang on a minute ...
Ah, OK, OK !!

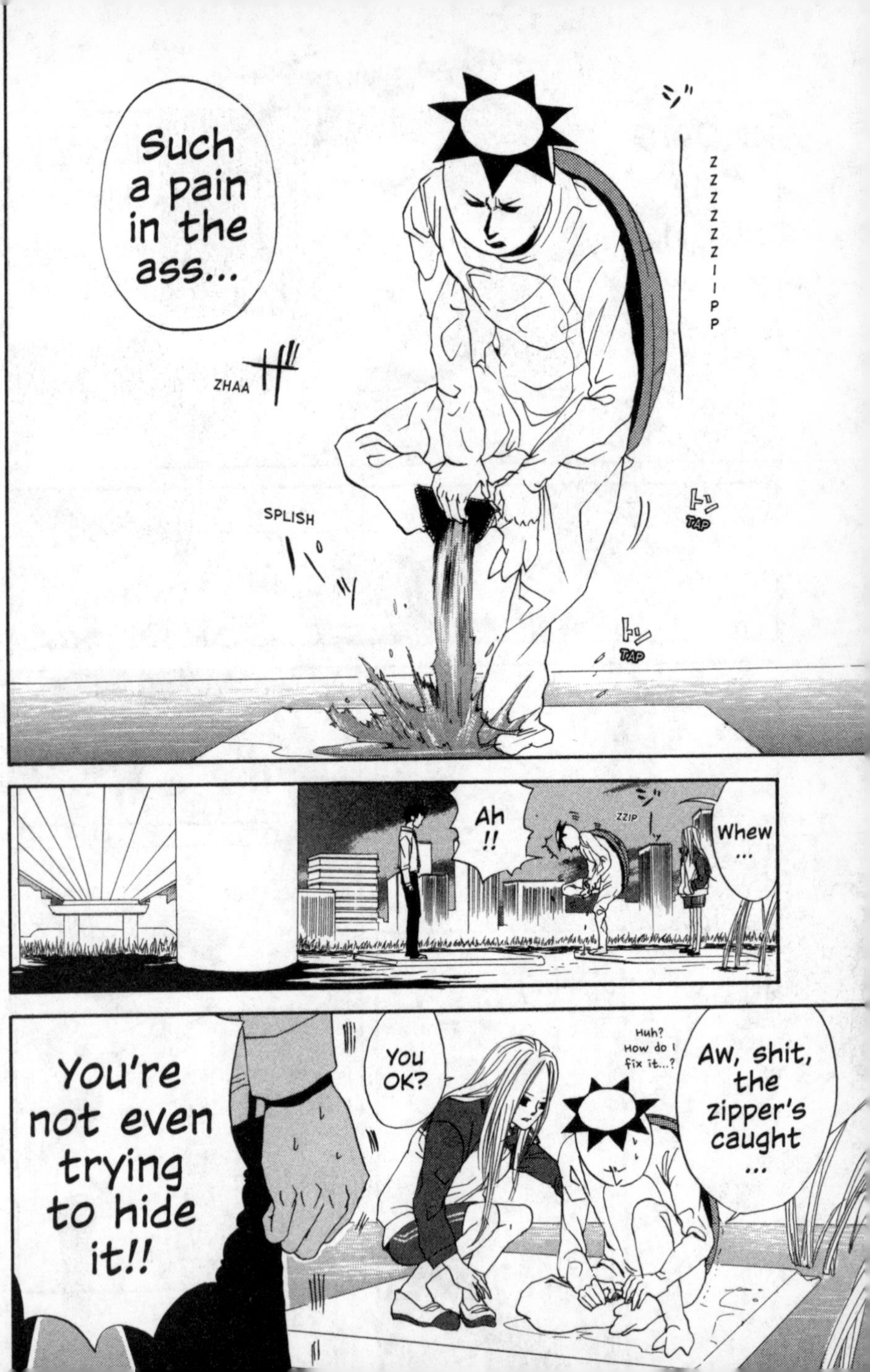
ZZZZZZIIPP
Such a pain in the ass...
ZHAA
TAP
SPLISH
TAP
Whew ...
ZZIP
Ah !!
Aw, shit, the zipper's caught ...
Huh? How do I fix it...?
You OK?
You're not even trying to hide it!!

☜ Chapter 7: Rec Under the Bridge

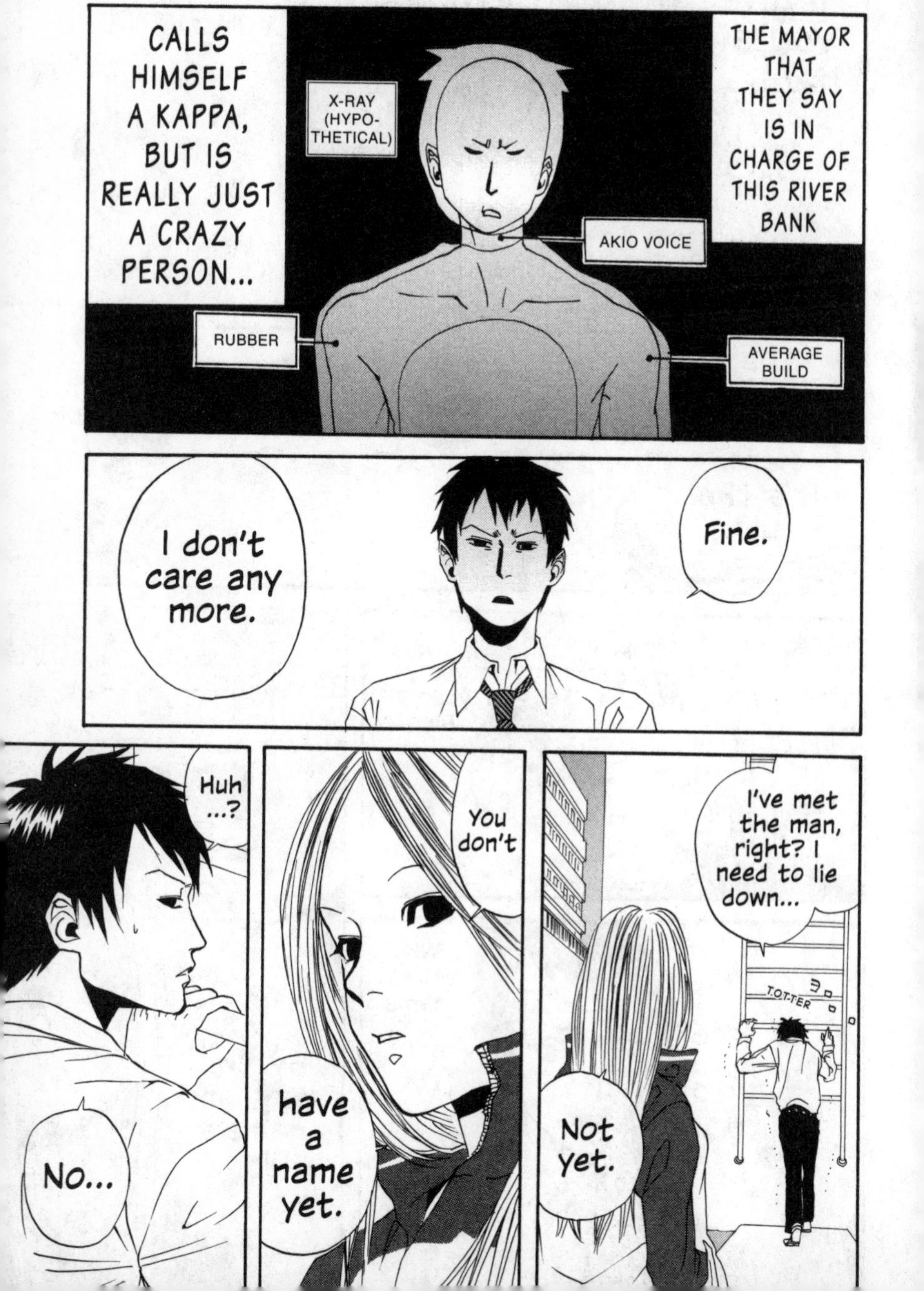
THE MAYOR THAT THEY SAY IS IN CHARGE OF THIS RIVER BANK
X-RAY (HYPO-THETICAL)
AKIO VOICE
CALLS HIMSELF A KAPPA, BUT IS REALLY JUST A CRAZY PERSON...
AVERAGE BUILD
RUBBER
Fine.
I don't care any more.
I've met the man, right? I need to lie down...
T.OT.TER
Not yet.
You don't
have a name yet.
Huh ...?
No...

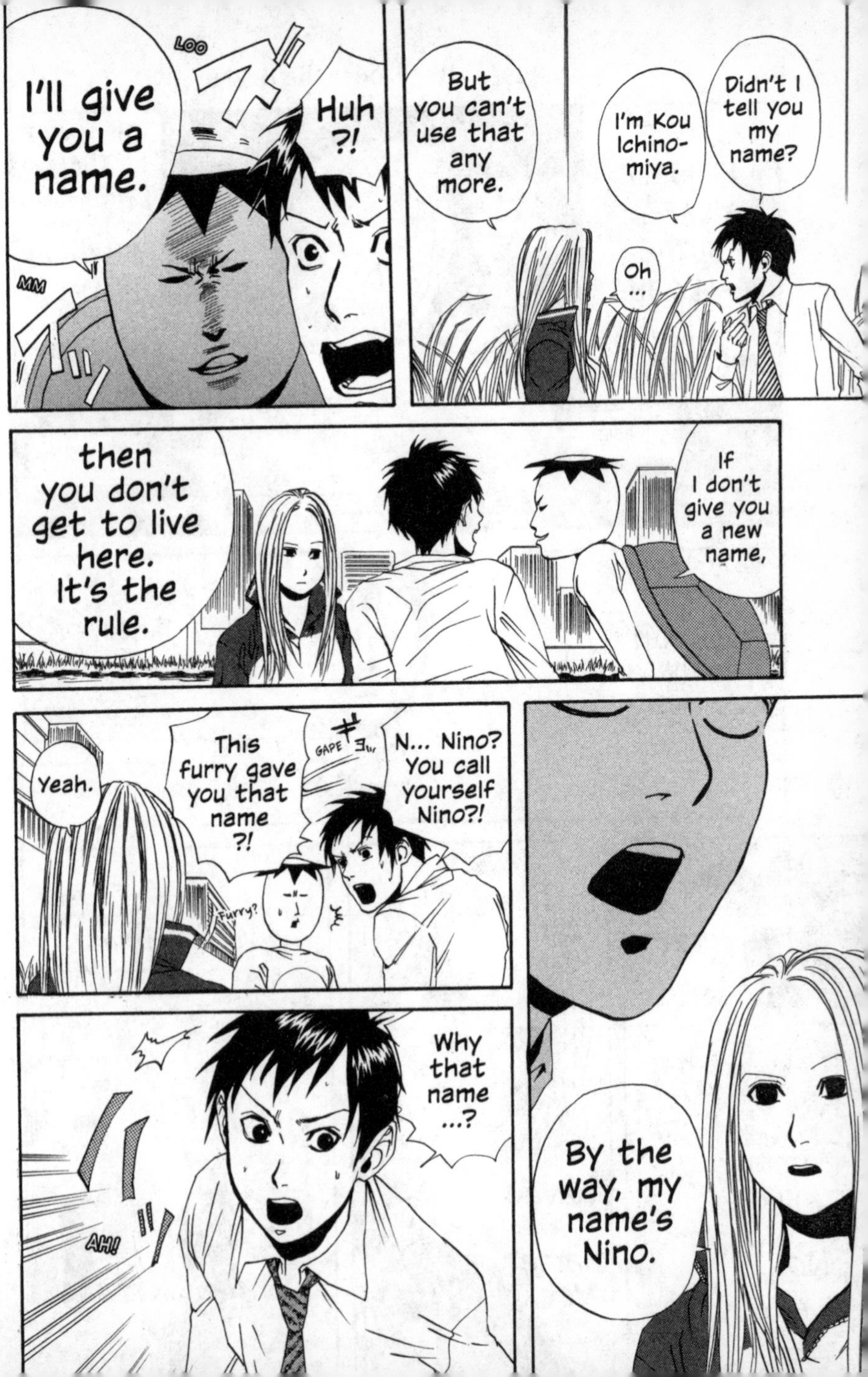
Didn't I tell you my name?
I'm Kou Ichino-miya.
Oh ...
But you can't use that any more.
Huh ?!
LOO
I'll give you a name.
MM
If I don't give you a new name,
then you don't get to live here. It's the rule.
By the way, my name's Nino.
N... Nino? You call yourself Nino?!
GAPE
This furry gave you that name ?!
Yeah.
Furry?
Why that name ...?
AH!

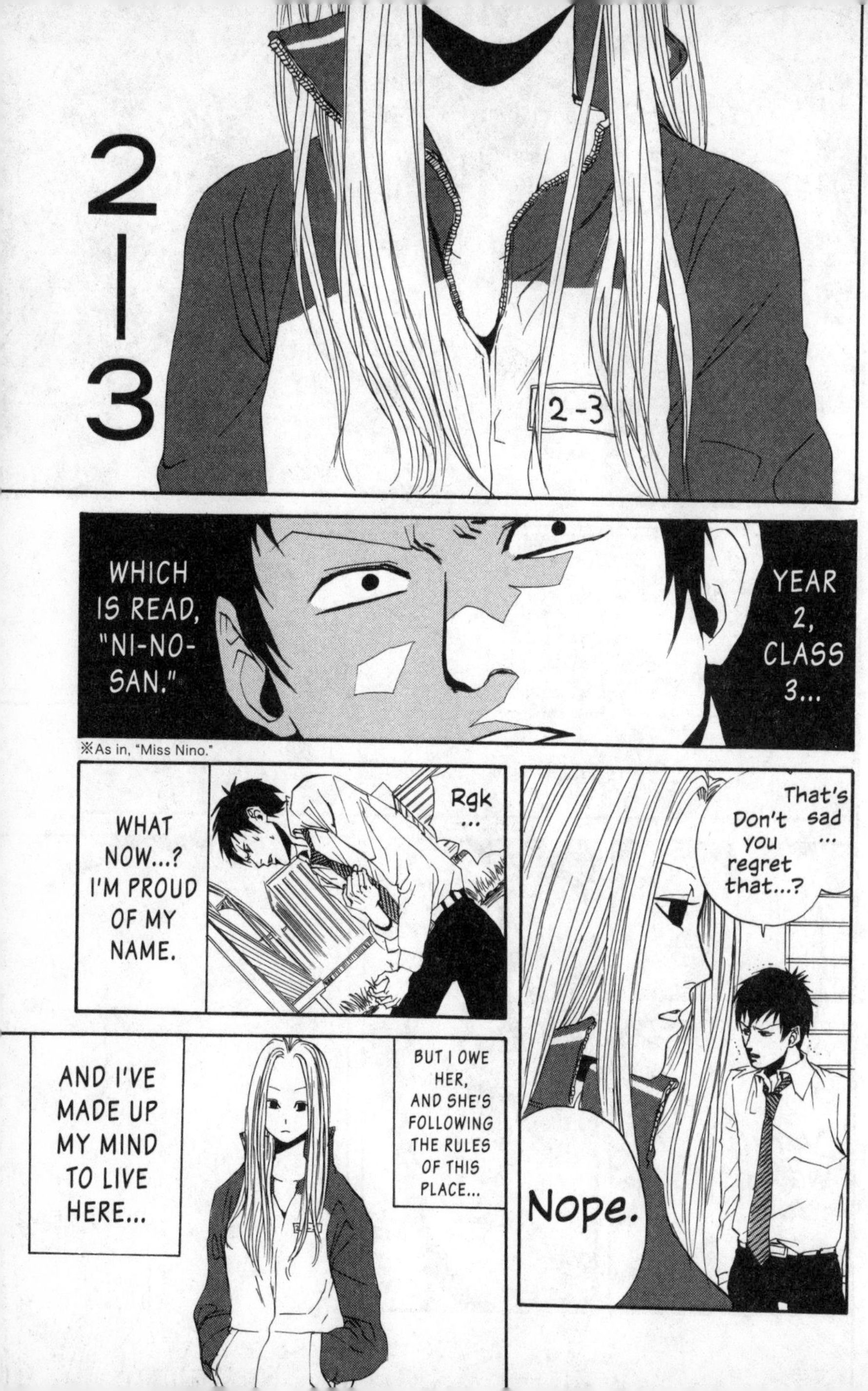
2
|
3
2-3
YEAR 2, CLASS 3...
WHICH IS READ, "NI-NO-SAN."
That's sad...
Don't you regret that...?
Nope.
Rgk...
WHAT NOW...? I'M PROUD OF MY NAME.
BUT I OWE HER, AND SHE'S FOLLOWING THE RULES OF THIS PLACE...
AND I'VE MADE UP MY MIND TO LIVE HERE...
※As in, "Miss Nino."

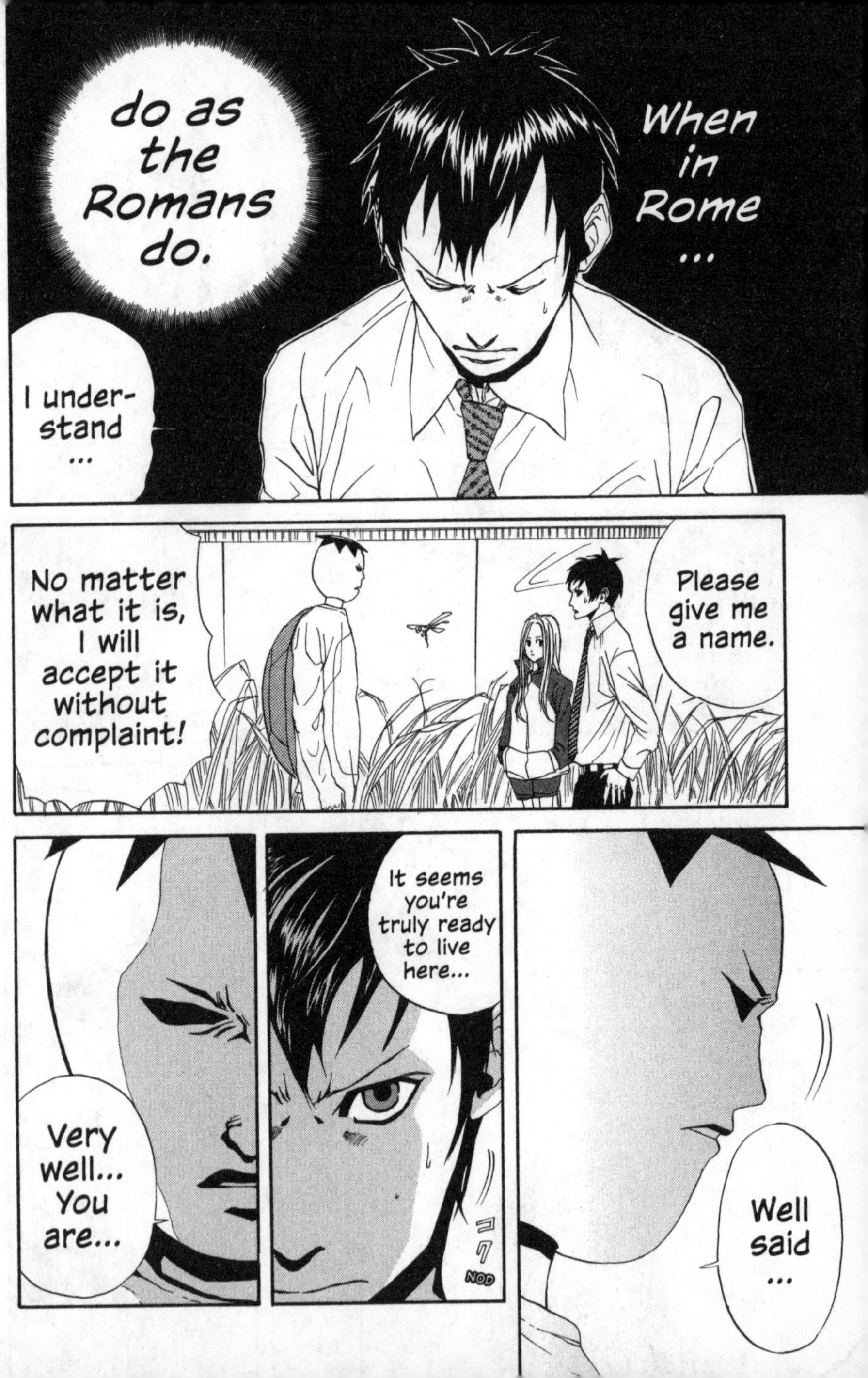
When in Rome ...
do as the Romans do.
I under-stand ...
Please give me a name.
No matter what it is, I will accept it without complaint!
Well said ...
It seems you're truly ready to live here...
コク
NOD
Very well... You are...

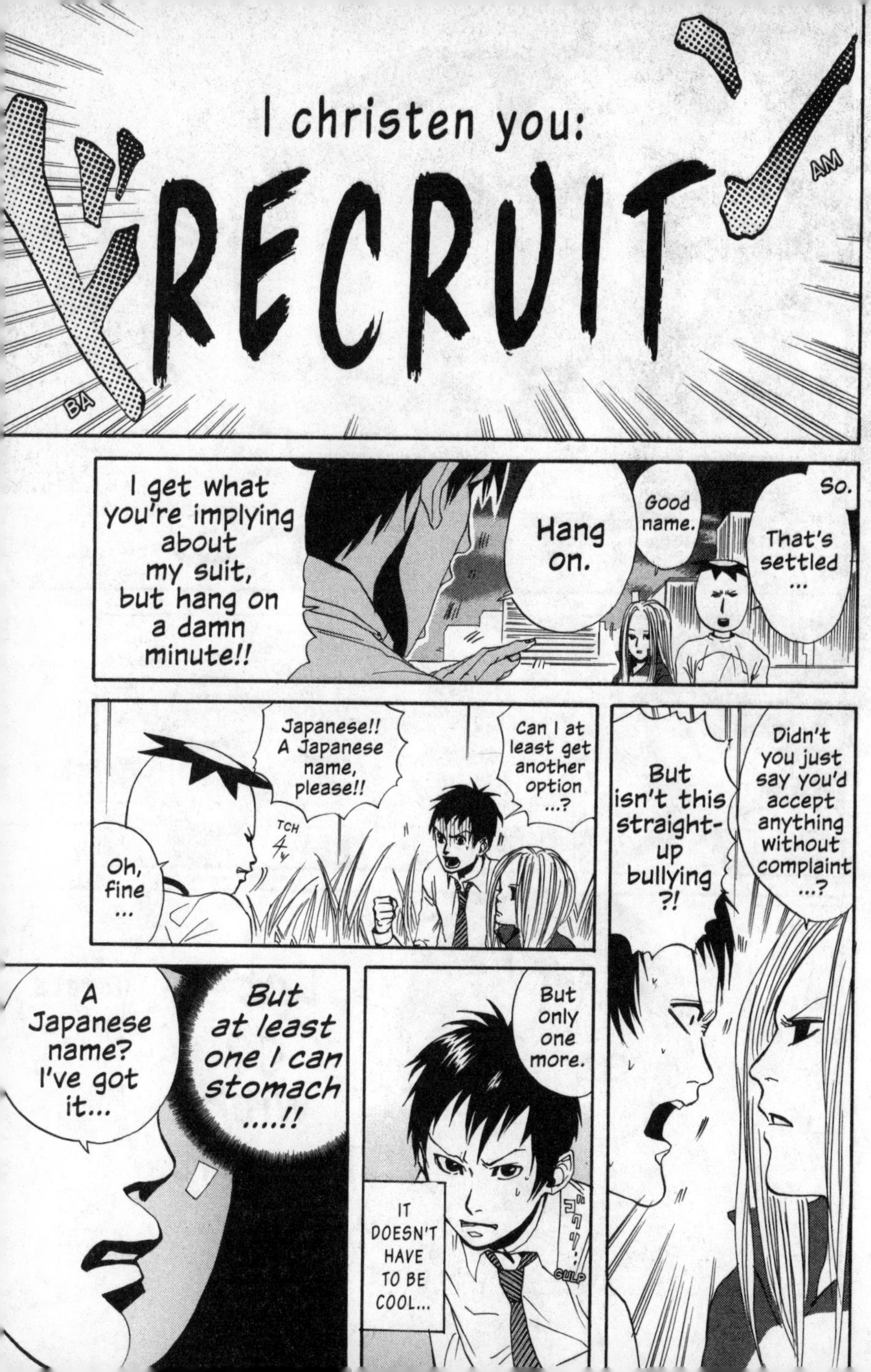
I christen you:
RECRUIT
BA
AM
So. That's settled...
Good name.
Hang on.
I get what you're implying about my suit, but hang on a damn minute!!
Didn't you just say you'd accept anything without complaint...?
But isn't this straight-up bullying?!
Can I at least get another option...?
Japanese!! A Japanese name, please!!
TCH
Oh, fine...
But only one more.
IT DOESN'T HAVE TO BE COOL...
GULP
But at least one I can stomach.....!!
A Japanese name? I've got it...

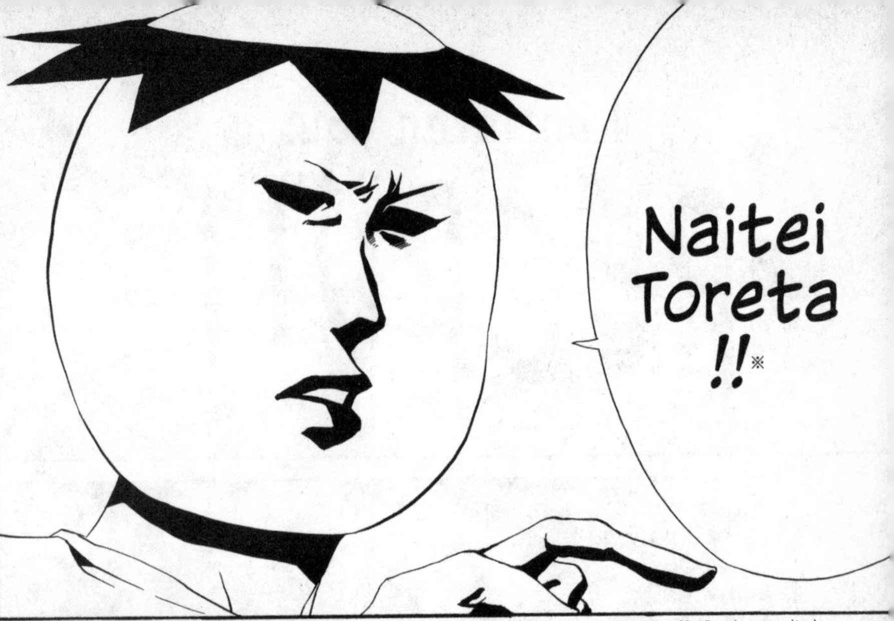

Naitei Toreta !!※

※ Literally, "I got a job offer," as in, recruited.

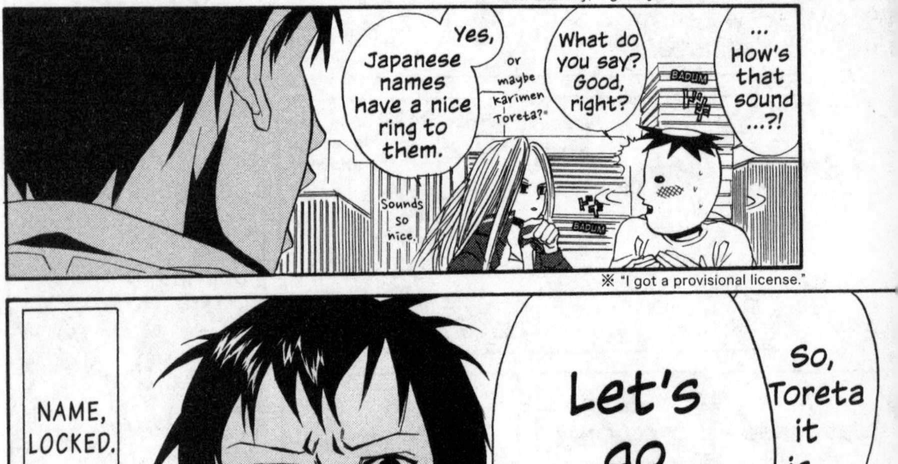

... How's that sound ...?!
BADUM
What do you say? Good, right?
or maybe Karimen Toreta?※
Yes, Japanese names have a nice ring to them.
Sounds so nice.
BADUM

※ "I got a provisional license."

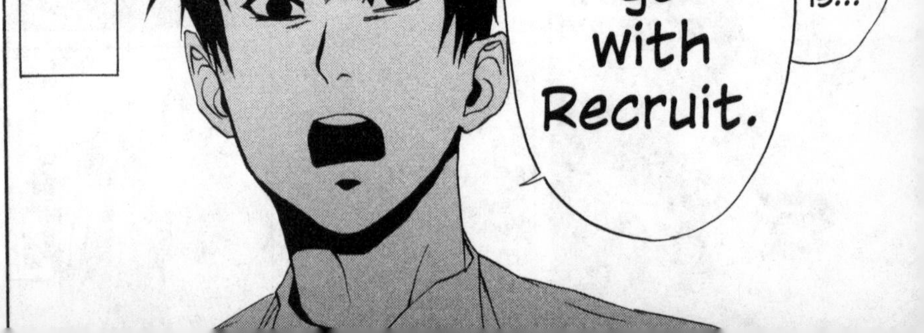

So, Toreta it is...
Let's go with Recruit.
NAME, LOCKED.

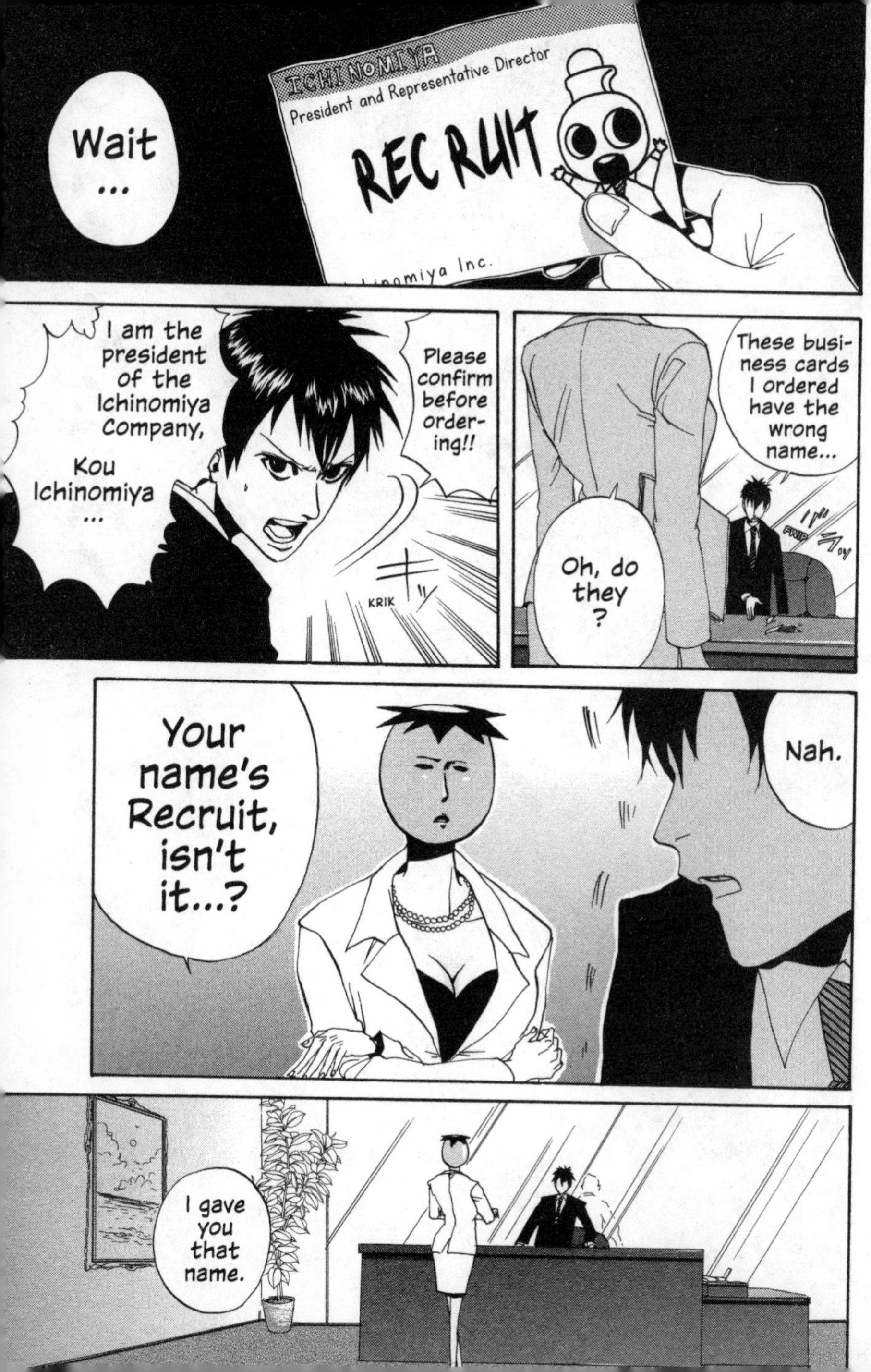

ICHI NOMIYA
President and Representative Director
RECRUIT
inomiya Inc.
Wait ...
These busi-ness cards I ordered have the wrong name...
FWIP
Oh, do they ?
Please confirm before order-ing!!
I am the president of the Ichinomiya Company,
Kou Ichinomiya ...
KRIK
Nah.
Your name's Recruit, isn't it...?
I gave you that name.

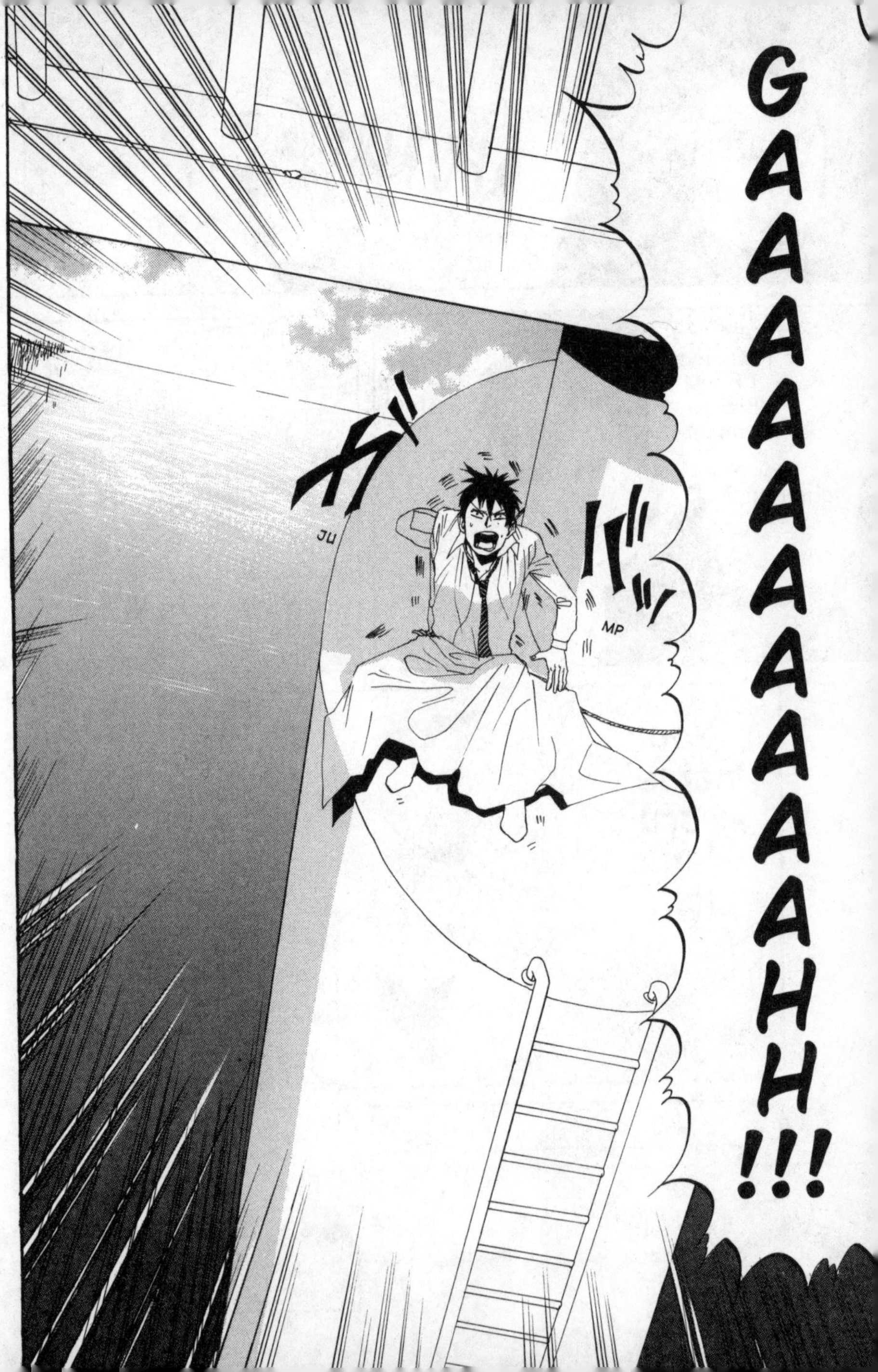
GAAAAAAAAAAAAHH!!!
JU
MP

☜ Chapter 8: A Place of Repose

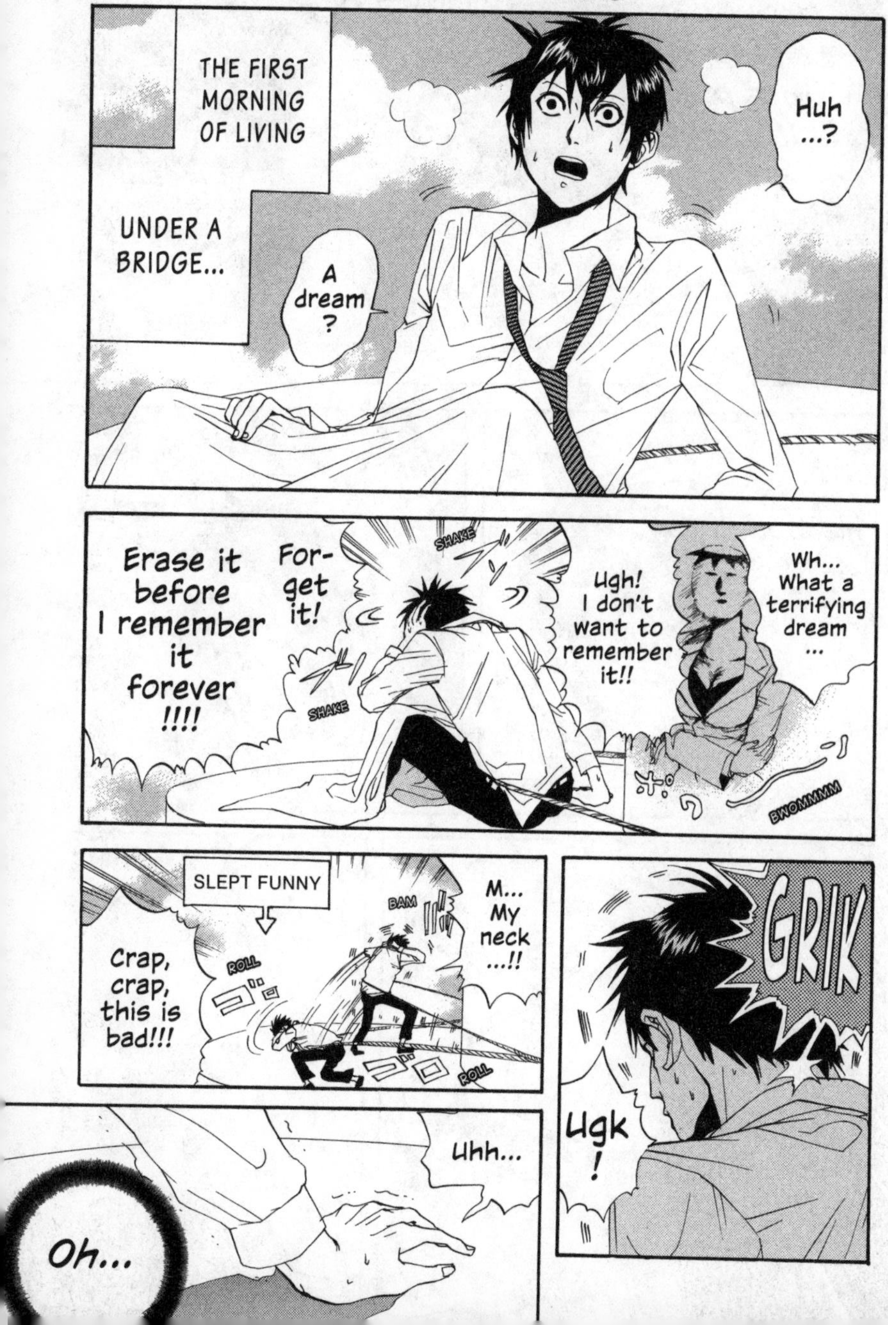
Huh ...?
THE FIRST MORNING OF LIVING
UNDER A BRIDGE...
A dream ?
Wh... What a terrifying dream ...
Ugh! I don't want to remember it!!
SHAKE
For-get it!
Erase it before I remember it forever !!!!
SHAKE
BWOMMMM
GRIK
Ugk !
M... My neck ...!!
BAM
SLEPT FUNNY
Crap, crap, this is bad!!!
ROLL
ROLL
Uhh...
Oh...

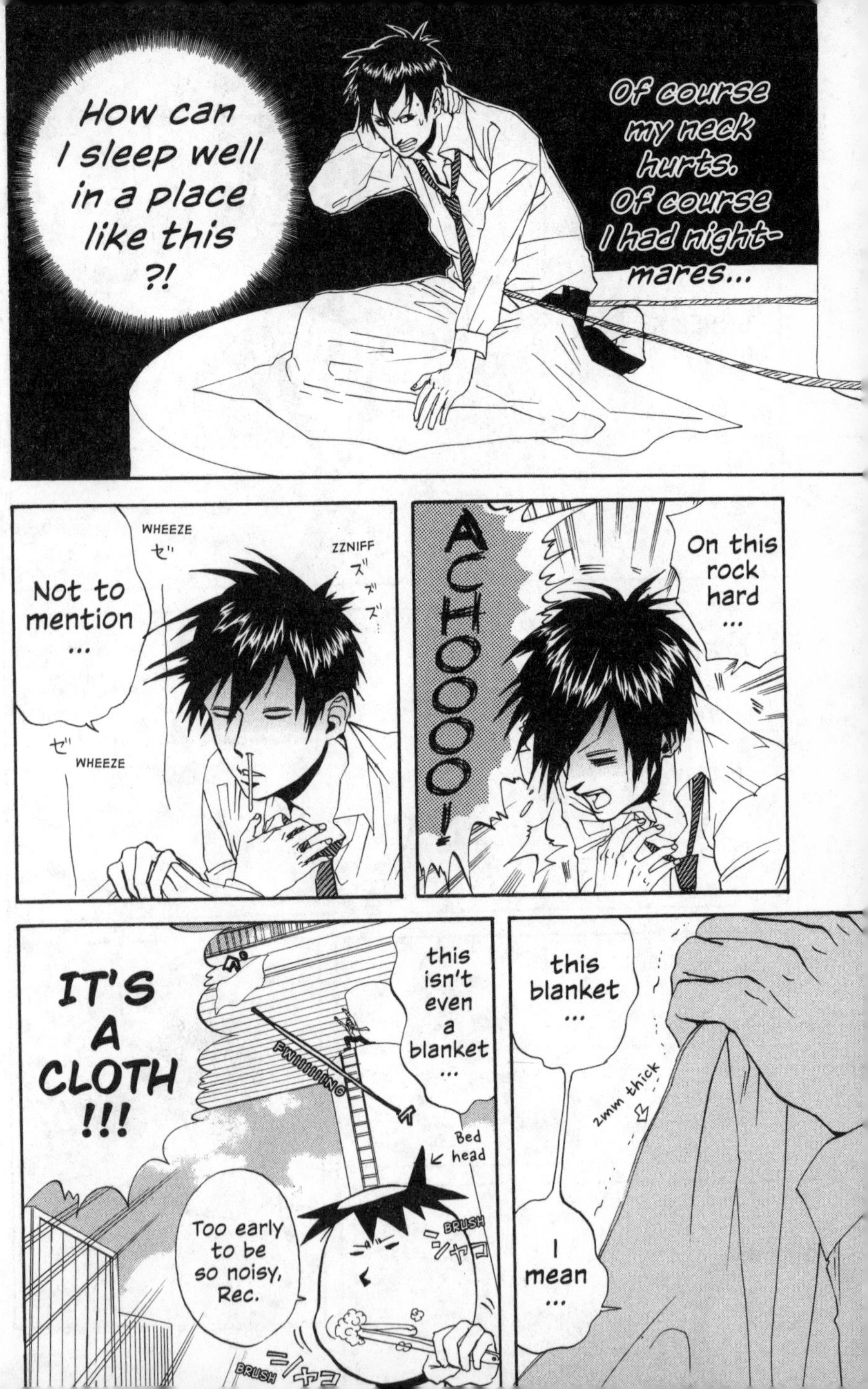
Of course my neck hurts. Of course I had night-mares...
How can I sleep well in a place like this ?!
On this rock hard ...
ACHOOOOO!
ZZNIFF ズズズ
WHEEZE ゼ
Not to mention ...
ゼ WHEEZE
this blanket ...
2mm thick
I mean ...
this isn't even a blanket ...
IT'S A CLOTH !!!
FWIIIIIING
Bed head
BRUSH シャコ
Too early to be so noisy, Rec.
BRUSH シャコ

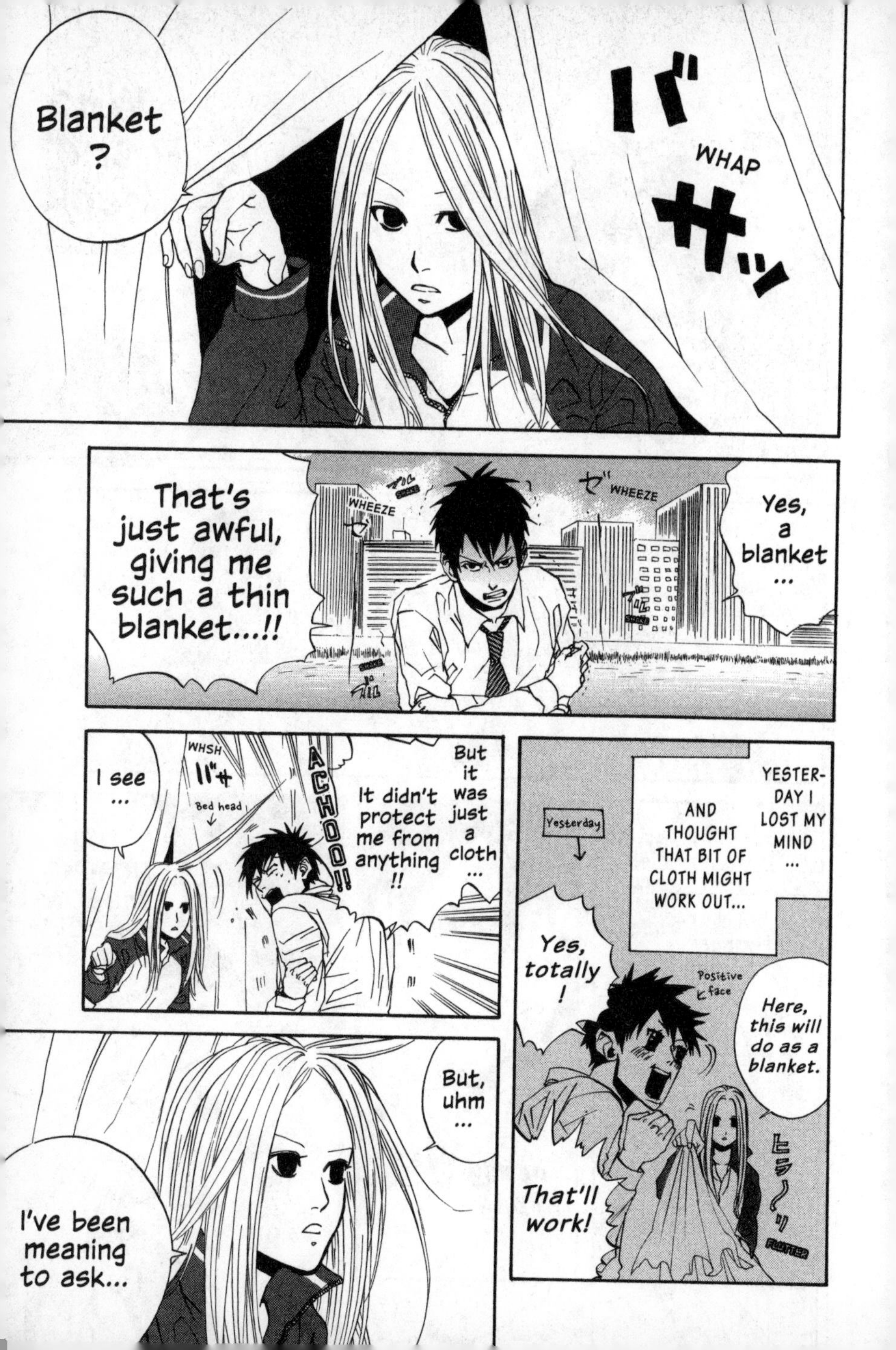
WHAP
Blanket ?
WHEEZE
Yes, a blanket ...
WHEEZE
That's just awful, giving me such a thin blanket...!!
YESTER-DAY I LOST MY MIND ...
AND THOUGHT THAT BIT OF CLOTH MIGHT WORK OUT...
Yesterday
Here, this will do as a blanket.
Positive face
Yes, totally !
That'll work!
FLUTTER
But it was just a cloth ...
It didn't protect me from anything !!
ACHOO!!
WHSH
Bed head
I see ...
But, uhm ...
I've been meaning to ask...

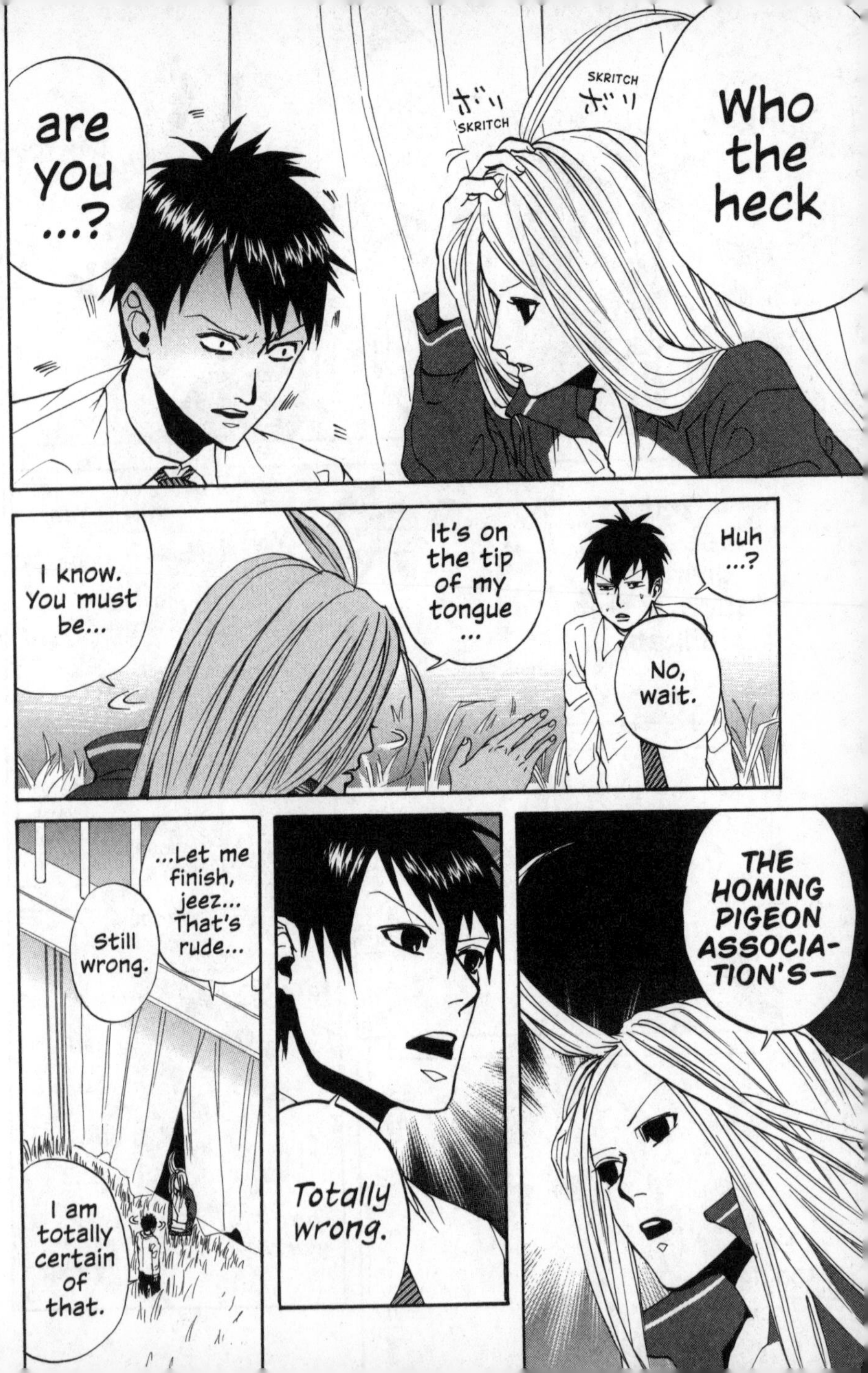
Who the heck
ボリ
SKRITCH
ボリ
SKRITCH
are you ...?
Huh ...?
No, wait.
It's on the tip of my tongue ...
I know. You must be...
THE HOMING PIGEON ASSOCIA-TION'S—
Totally wrong.
...Let me finish, jeez... That's rude...
Still wrong.
I am totally certain of that.

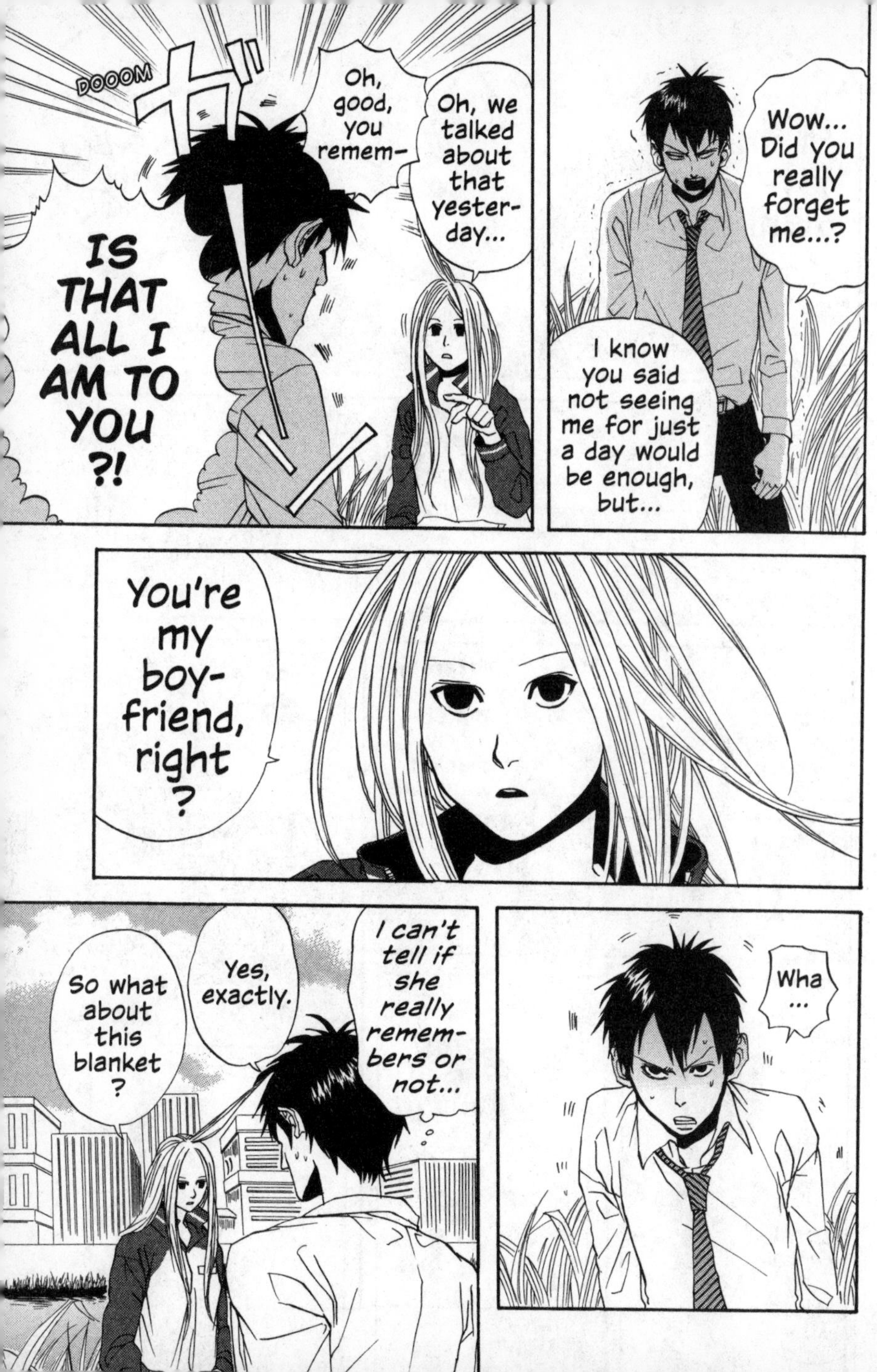
Wow... Did you really forget me...?
I know you said not seeing me for just a day would be enough, but...
Oh, we talked about that yesterday...
Oh, good, you remem-
DOOOM
IS THAT ALL I AM TO YOU ?!
You're my boyfriend, right ?
Wha ...
I can't tell if she really remembers or not...
Yes, exactly.
So what about this blanket ?

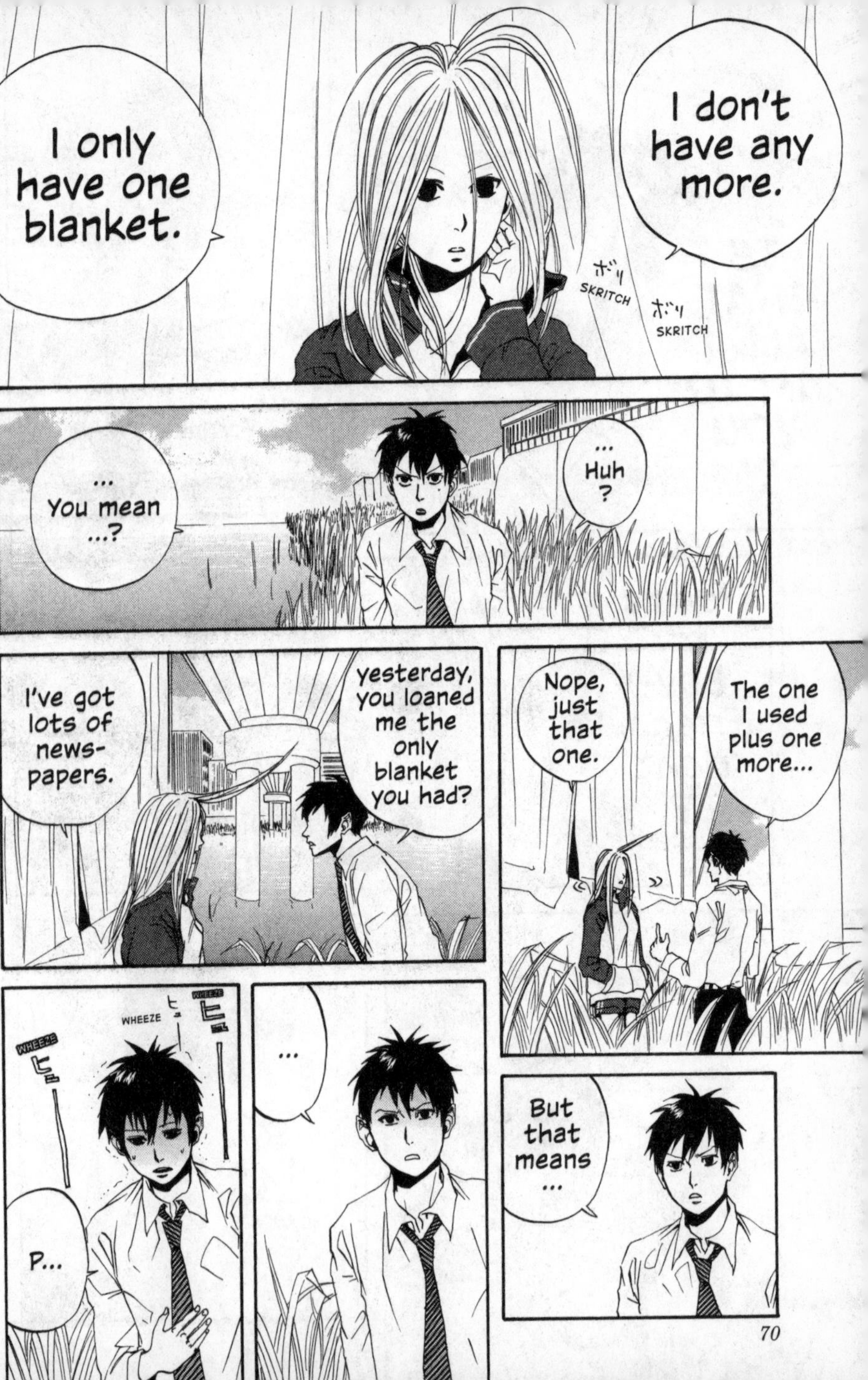
I don't have any more.
I only have one blanket.
ボリ SKRITCH
ボリ SKRITCH
... Huh?
... You mean ...?
The one I used plus one more...
Nope, just that one.
yesterday, you loaned me the only blanket you had?
I've got lots of news-papers.
But that means ...
...
ヒュ WHEEZE
ヒュ WHEEZE
ヒュ WHEEZE
P...

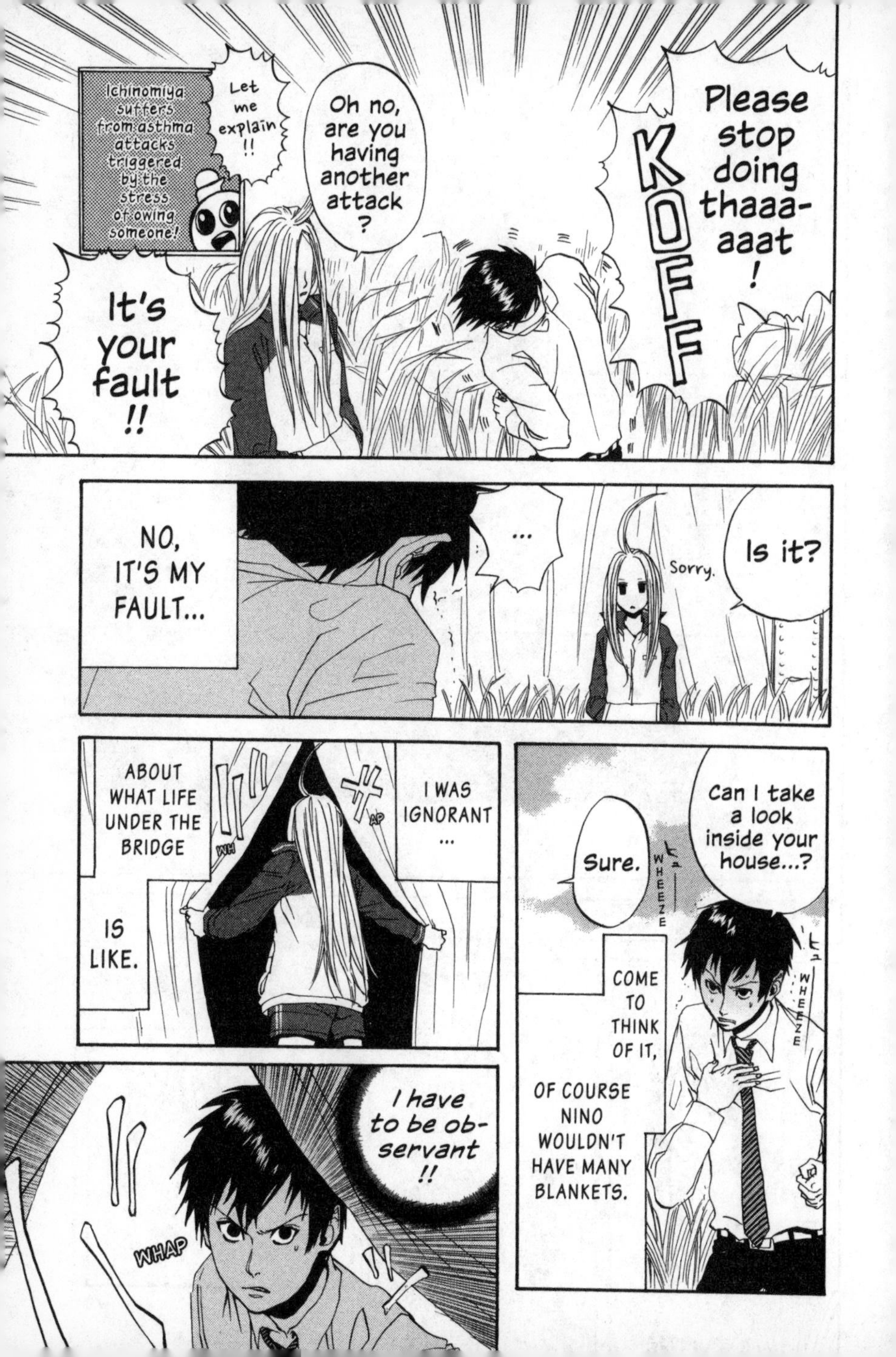

Please stop doing thaaa-aaat!
KOFF
Oh no, are you having another attack?
Let me explain!!
Ichinomiya suffers from asthma attacks triggered by the stress of owing someone!
It's your fault!!
Is it?
Sorry.
...
NO, IT'S MY FAULT...
Can I take a look inside your house...?
WHEEZE
Sure.
WHEEZE
COME TO THINK OF IT,
OF COURSE NINO WOULDN'T HAVE MANY BLANKETS.
I WAS IGNORANT ...
AP
WH
ABOUT WHAT LIFE UNDER THE BRIDGE
IS LIKE.
I have to be ob-servant!!
WHAP

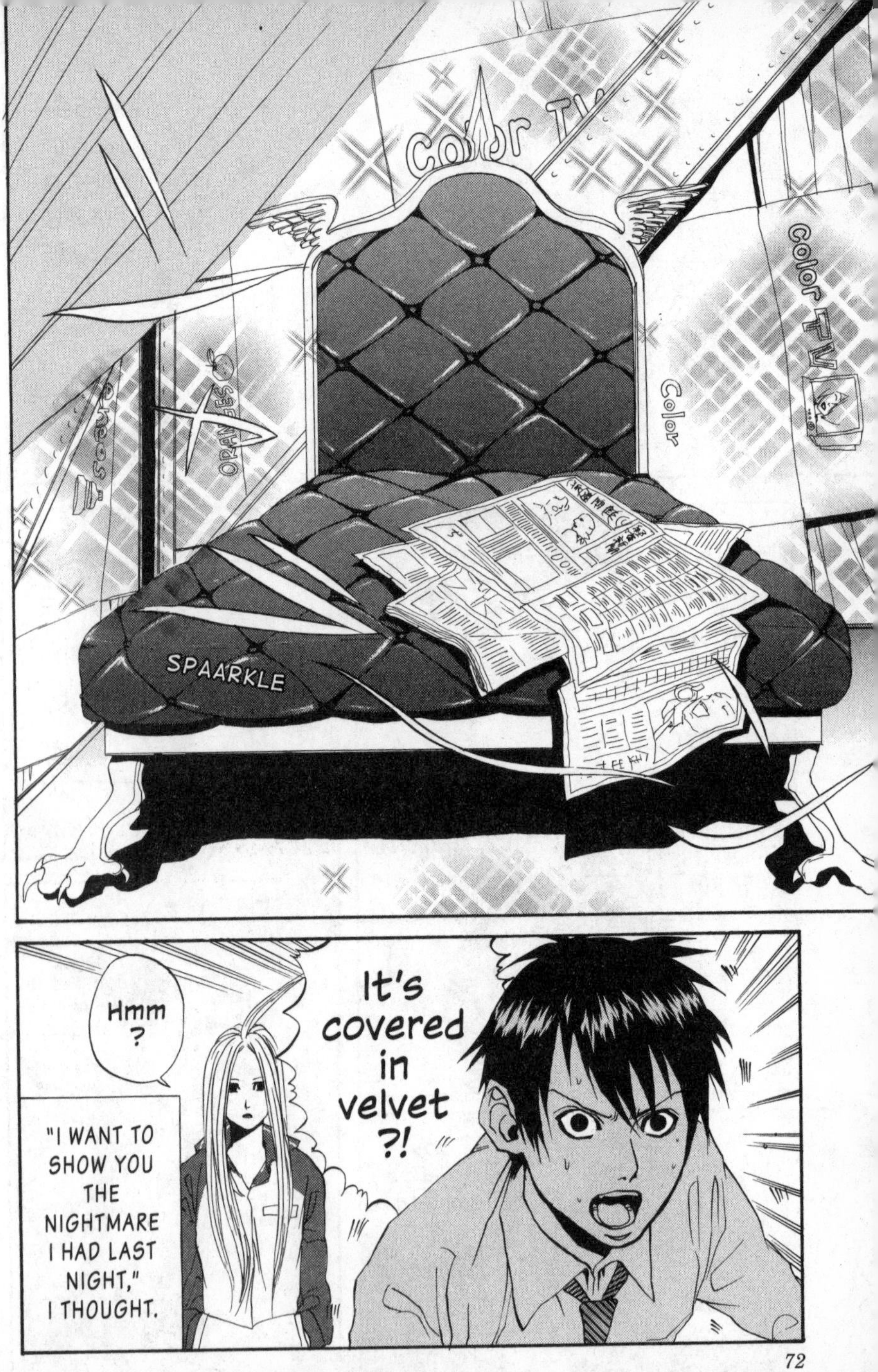
SPAARKLE
It's covered in velvet ?!
Hmm ?
"I WANT TO SHOW YOU THE NIGHTMARE I HAD LAST NIGHT," I THOUGHT.

Chapter 9: Go

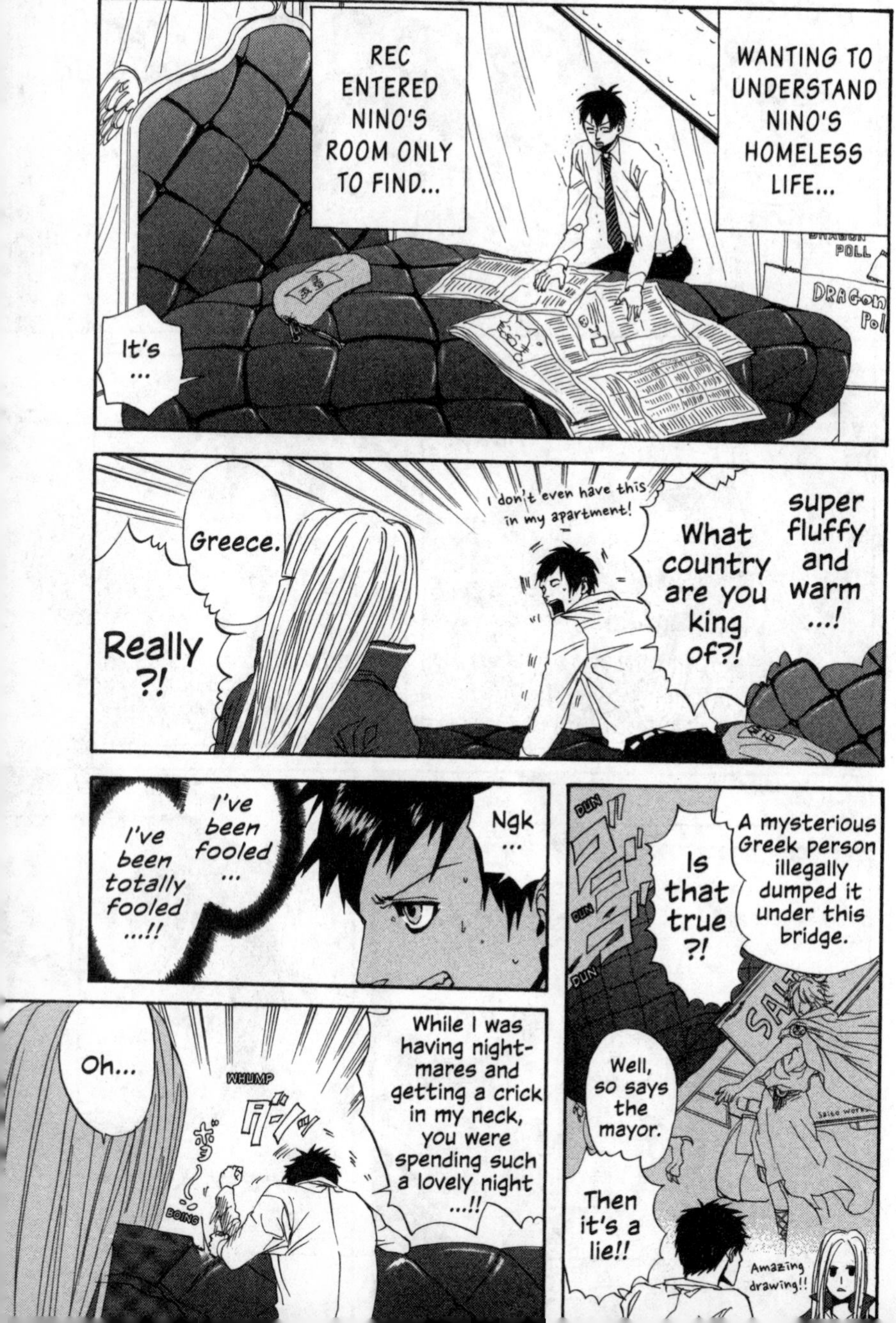
WANTING TO UNDERSTAND NINO'S HOMELESS LIFE...
REC ENTERED NINO'S ROOM ONLY TO FIND...
DRAGON POLL
It's ...
super fluffy and warm ...!
What country are you king of?!
I don't even have this in my apartment!
Greece.
Really ?!
A mysterious Greek person illegally dumped it under this bridge.
Is that true ?!
DUN
DUN
DUN
Well, so says the mayor.
Then it's a lie!!
Amazing drawing!!
Ngk ...
I've been fooled ...
I've been totally fooled ...!!
While I was having night-mares and getting a crick in my neck, you were spending such a lovely night ...!!
WHUMP
BOING
Oh...

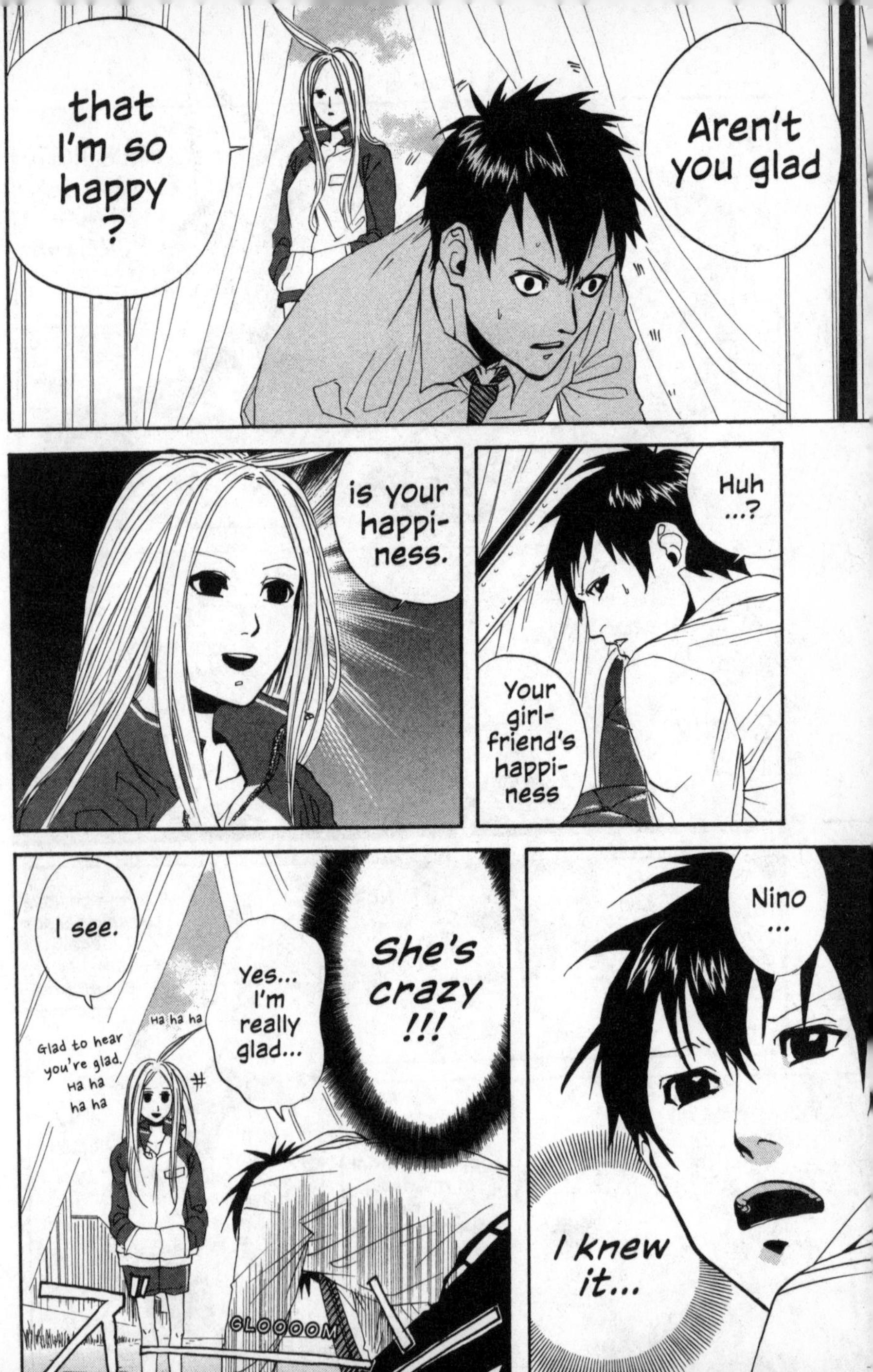
Aren't you glad
that I'm so happy ?
Huh ...?
Your girl-friend's happi-ness
is your happi-ness.
Nino ...
I knew it...
She's crazy !!!
Yes... I'm really glad...
Ha ha ha
I see.
Glad to hear you're glad. Ha ha ha ha
GLOOOOOM

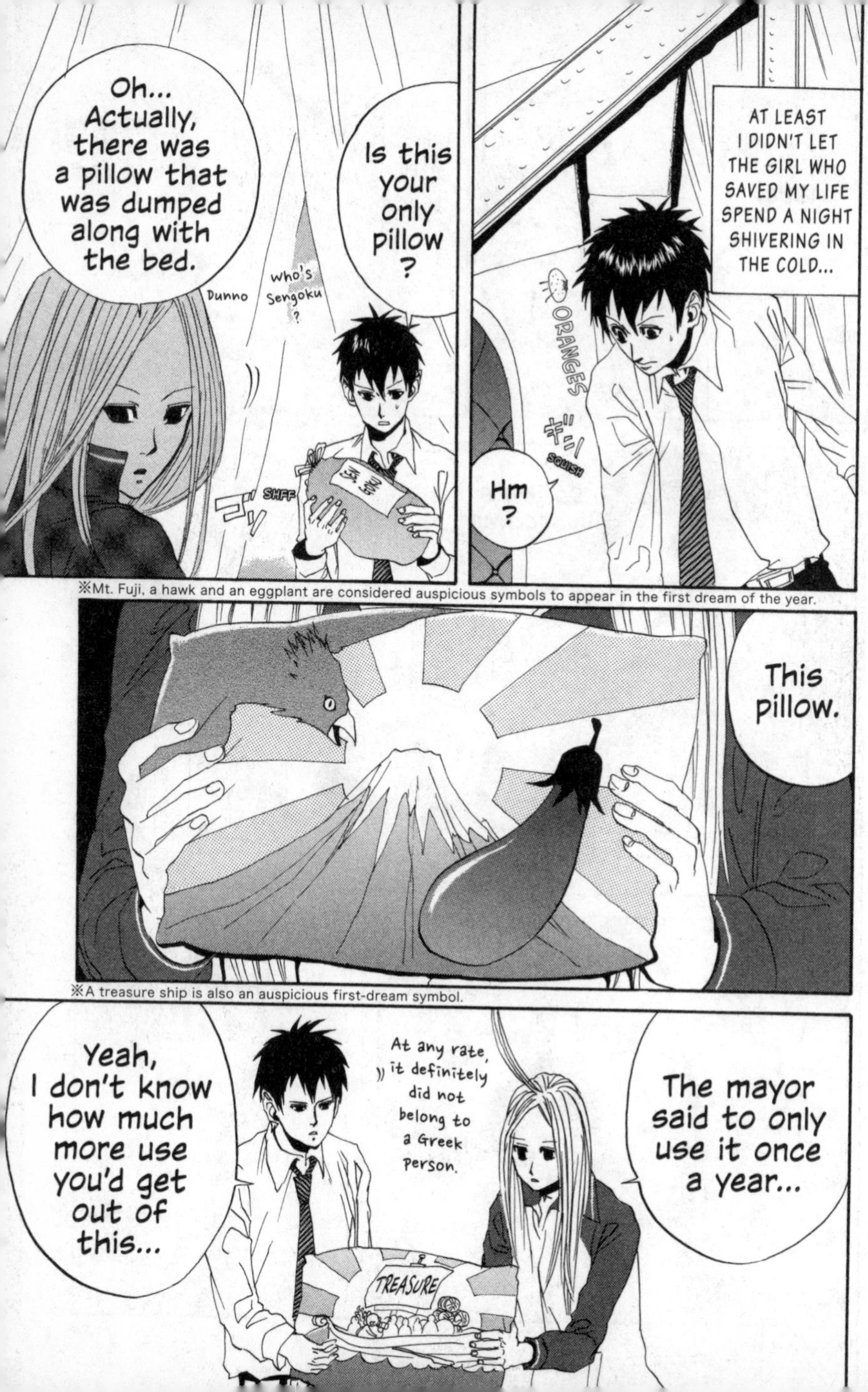
AT LEAST I DIDN'T LET THE GIRL WHO SAVED MY LIFE SPEND A NIGHT SHIVERING IN THE COLD...
ORANGES
SQUISH
Hm?
Is this your only pillow?
Oh... Actually, there was a pillow that was dumped along with the bed.
who's Sengoku?
Dunno
SHFF
This pillow.
The mayor said to only use it once a year...
Yeah, I don't know how much more use you'd get out of this...
At any rate, it definitely did not belong to a Greek person.
TREASURE
※Mt. Fuji, a hawk and an eggplant are considered auspicious symbols to appear in the first dream of the year.

※A treasure ship is also an auspicious first-dream symbol.

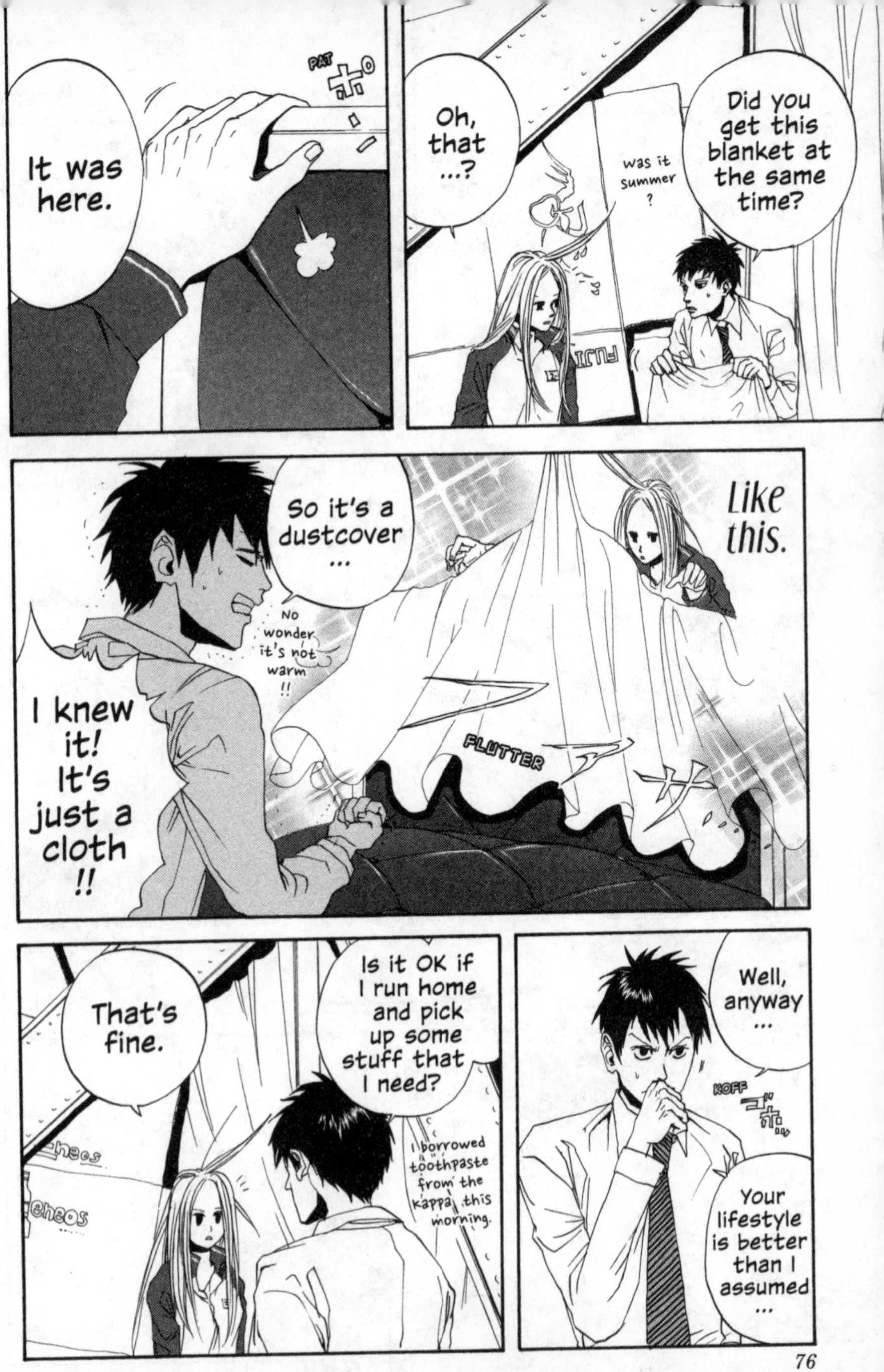
Did you get this blanket at the same time?
Was it summer?
Oh, that ...?
PAT
It was here.
Like this.
So it's a dustcover ...
No wonder it's not warm !!
FLUTTER
I knew it! It's just a cloth !!
Well, anyway ...
KOFF
Your lifestyle is better than I assumed ...
Is it OK if I run home and pick up some stuff that I need?
I borrowed toothpaste from the kappa this morning.
That's fine.

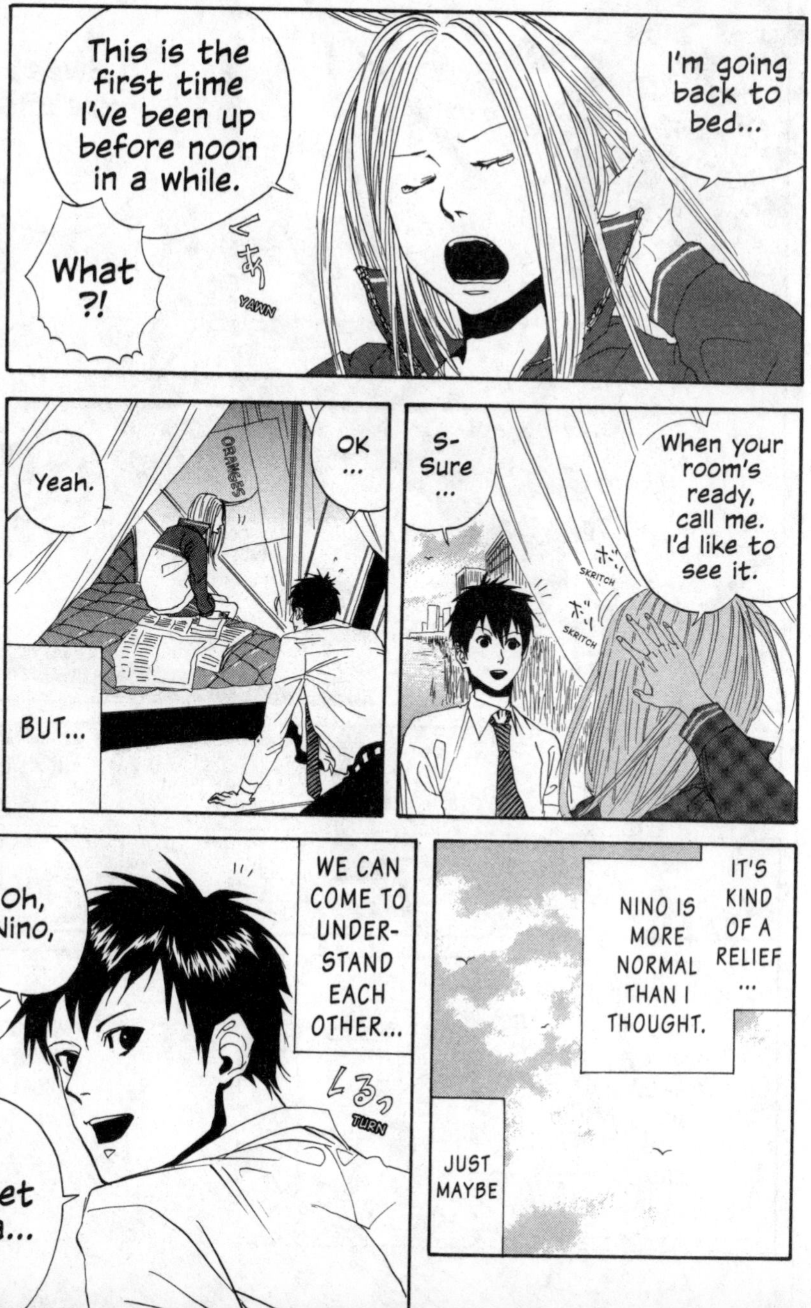
I'm going back to bed...
This is the first time I've been up before noon in a while.
YAWN
What ?!
When your room's ready, call me. I'd like to see it.
SKRITCH
SKRITCH
S- Sure ...
OK ...
ORANGES
Yeah.
BUT...
IT'S KIND OF A RELIEF ...
NINO IS MORE NORMAL THAN I THOUGHT.
JUST MAYBE
WE CAN COME TO UNDER- STAND EACH OTHER...
Oh, Nino,
TURN
sweet drea...

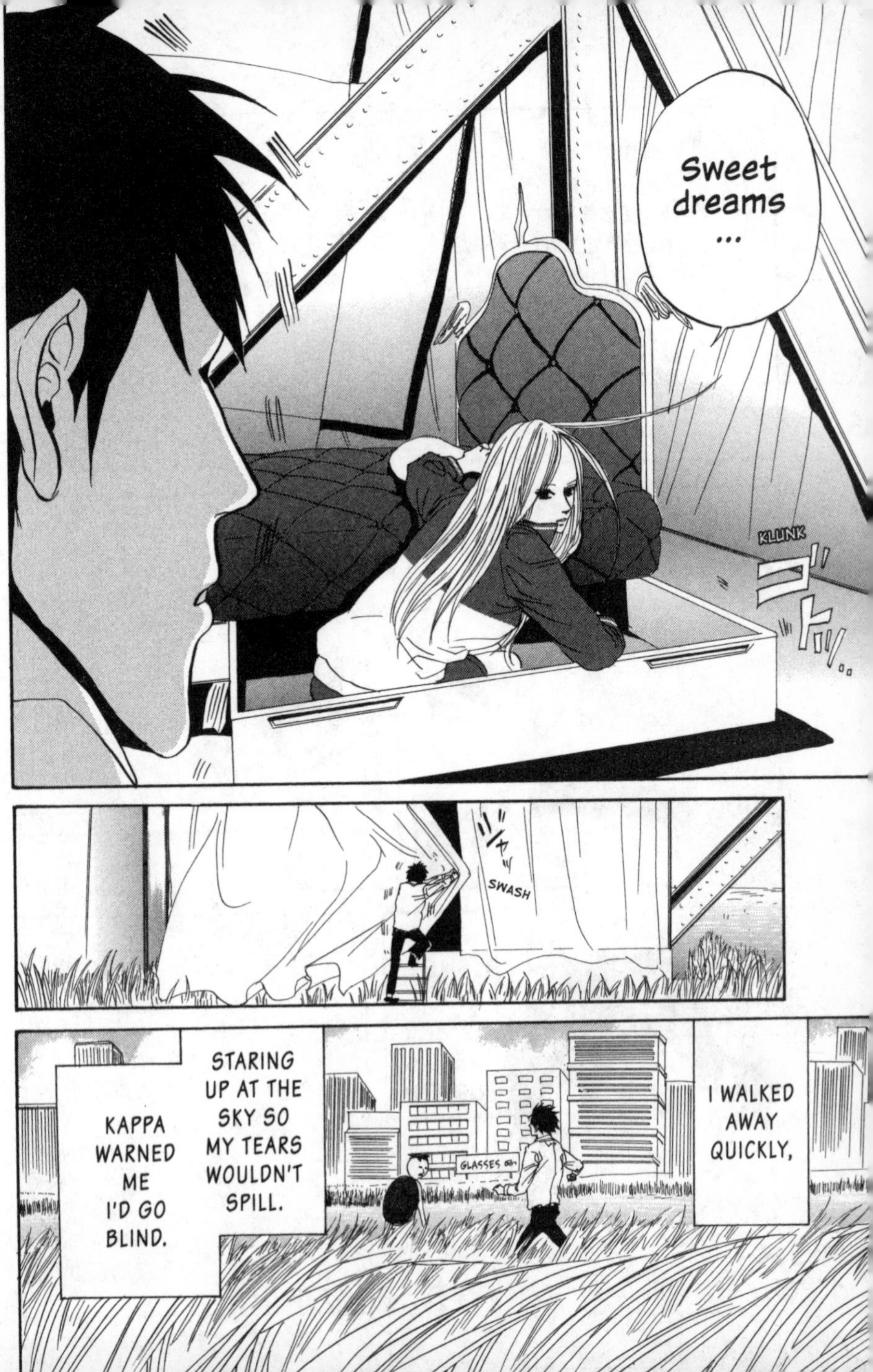
Sweet dreams ...
KLUNK
SWASH
I WALKED AWAY QUICKLY,
STARING UP AT THE SKY SO MY TEARS WOULDN'T SPILL.
GLASSES
KAPPA WARNED ME I'D GO BLIND.

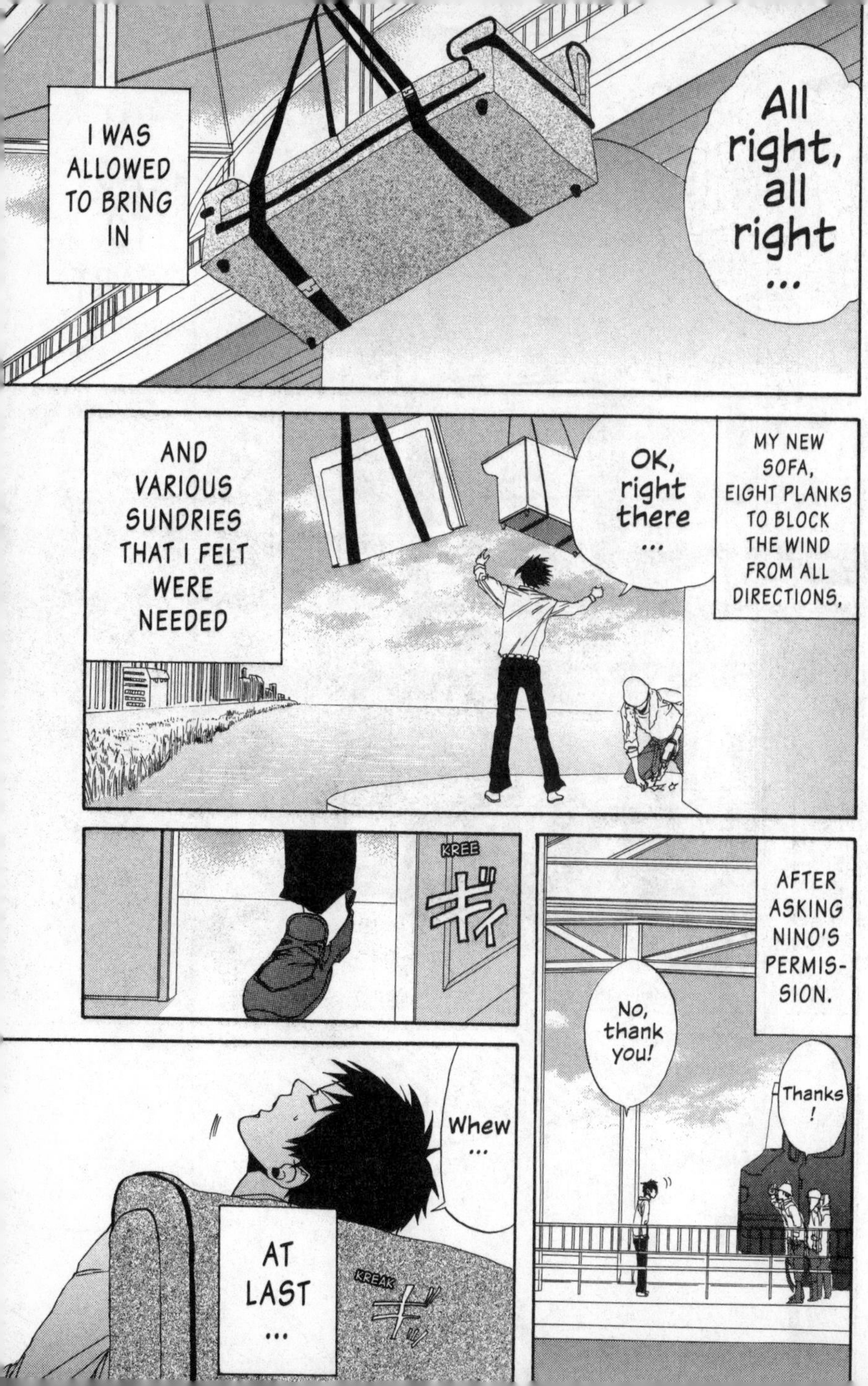
All right, all right ...
I WAS ALLOWED TO BRING IN
MY NEW SOFA, EIGHT PLANKS TO BLOCK THE WIND FROM ALL DIRECTIONS,
OK, right there ...
AND VARIOUS SUNDRIES THAT I FELT WERE NEEDED
AFTER ASKING NINO'S PERMISSION.
Thanks!
No, thank you!
KREE
ギィ
Whew ...
AT LAST ...
KREAK

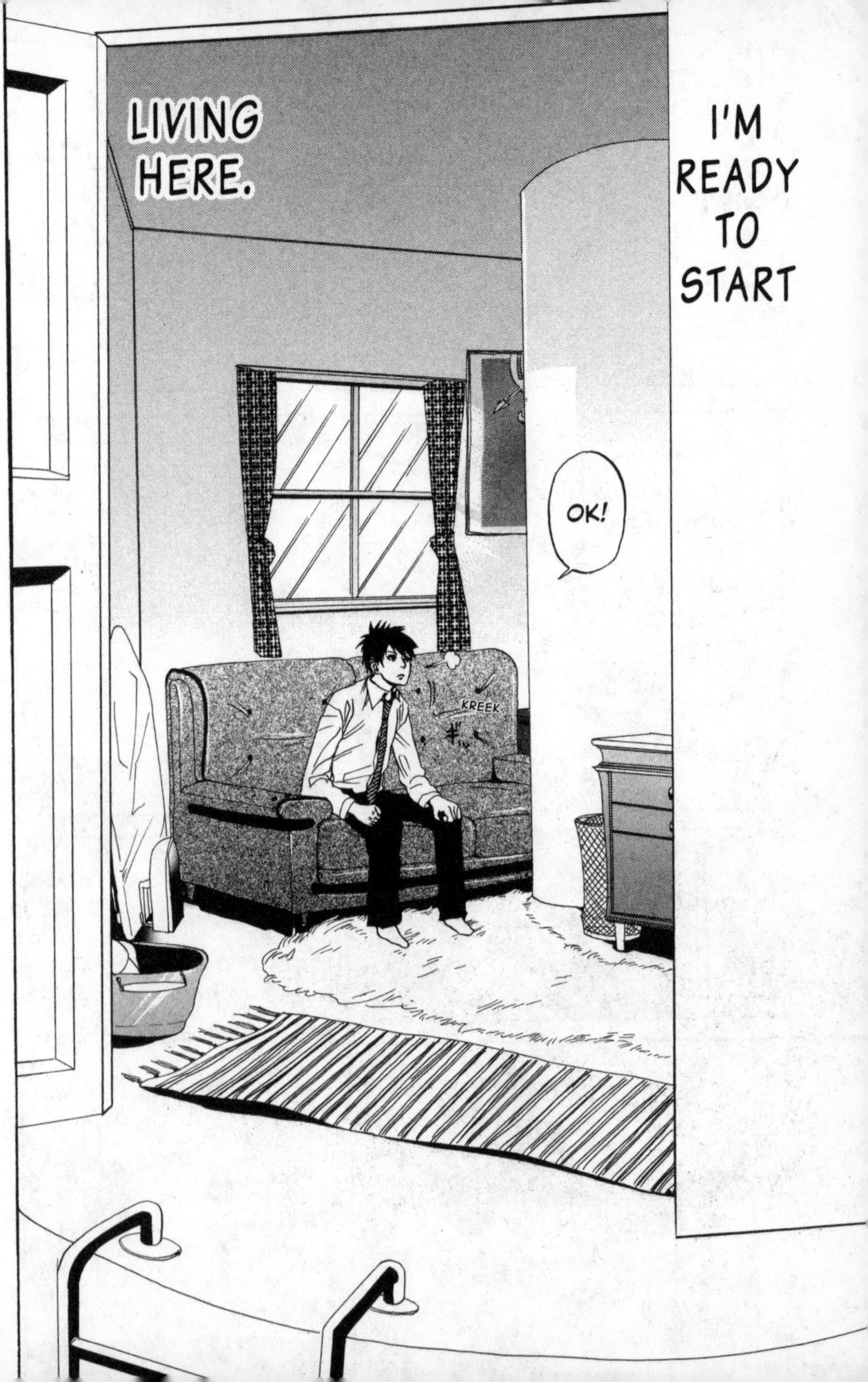
I'M READY TO START
LIVING HERE.
OK!
KREEK

Chapter 10: New Life

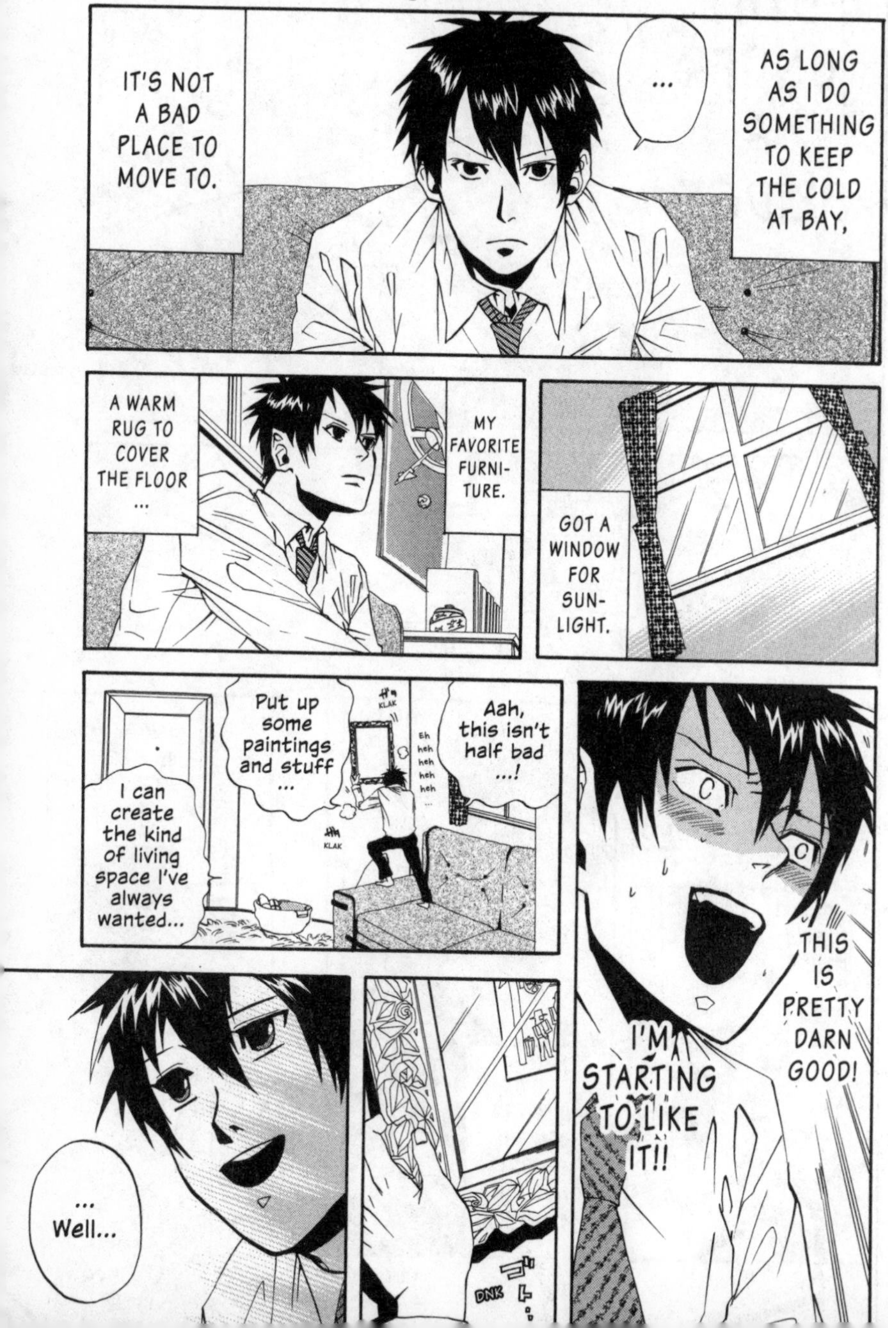
AS LONG AS I DO SOMETHING TO KEEP THE COLD AT BAY,
...
IT'S NOT A BAD PLACE TO MOVE TO.
GOT A WINDOW FOR SUNLIGHT.
MY FAVORITE FURNITURE.
A WARM RUG TO COVER THE FLOOR ...
THIS IS PRETTY DARN GOOD!
I'M STARTING TO LIKE IT!!
Aah, this isn't half bad ...!
KLAK
Eh heh heh heh heh ...
Put up some paintings and stuff ...
I can create the kind of living space I've always wanted...
KLAK
DNK
... Well...

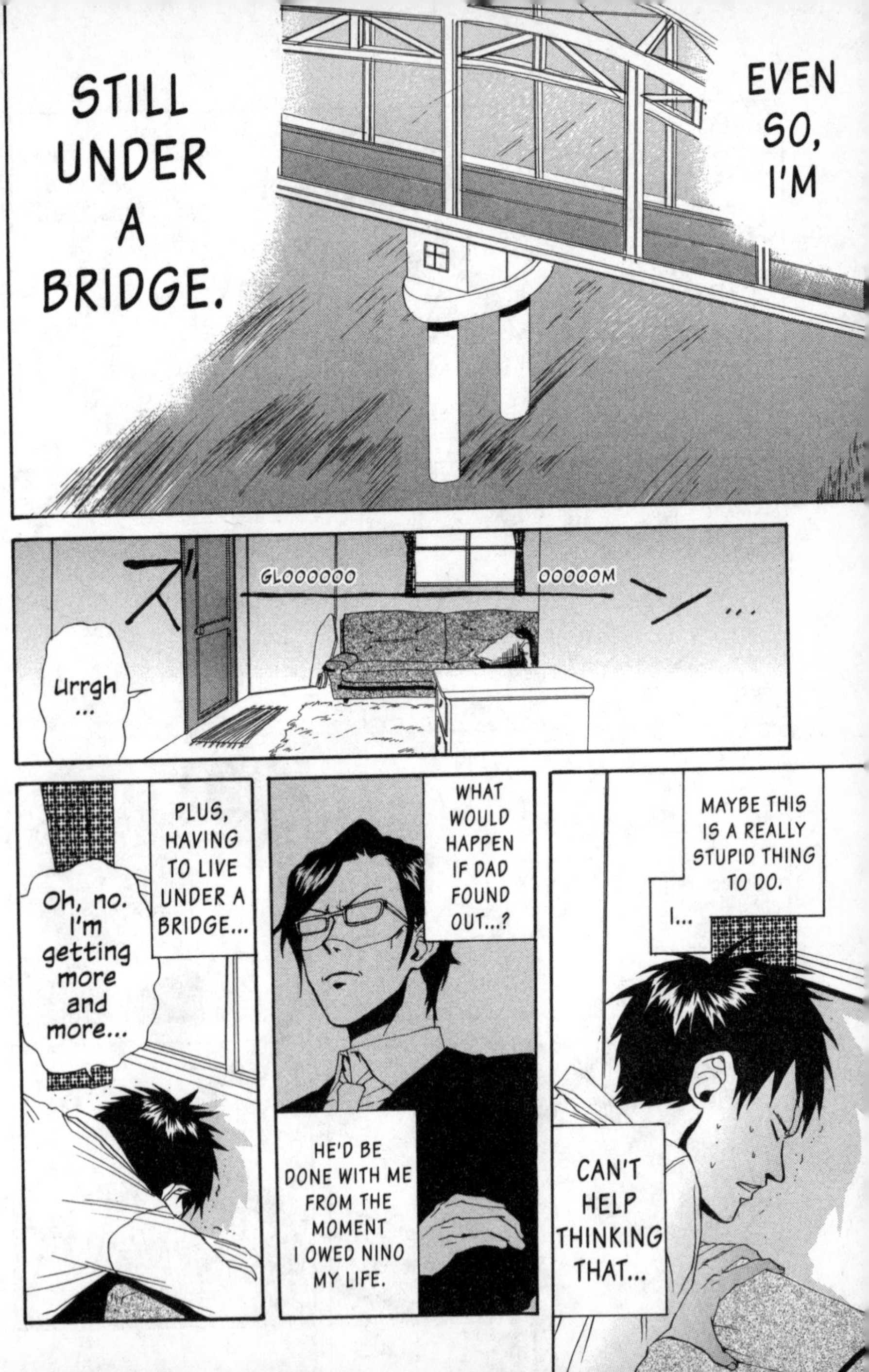

EVEN SO, I'M
STILL UNDER A BRIDGE.
ズ
GLOOOOOO
OOOOOM
ン...
Urrgh ...
MAYBE THIS IS A REALLY STUPID THING TO DO.
I...
CAN'T HELP THINKING THAT...
WHAT WOULD HAPPEN IF DAD FOUND OUT...?
HE'D BE DONE WITH ME FROM THE MOMENT I OWED NINO MY LIFE.
PLUS, HAVING TO LIVE UNDER A BRIDGE...
Oh, no. I'm getting more and more...

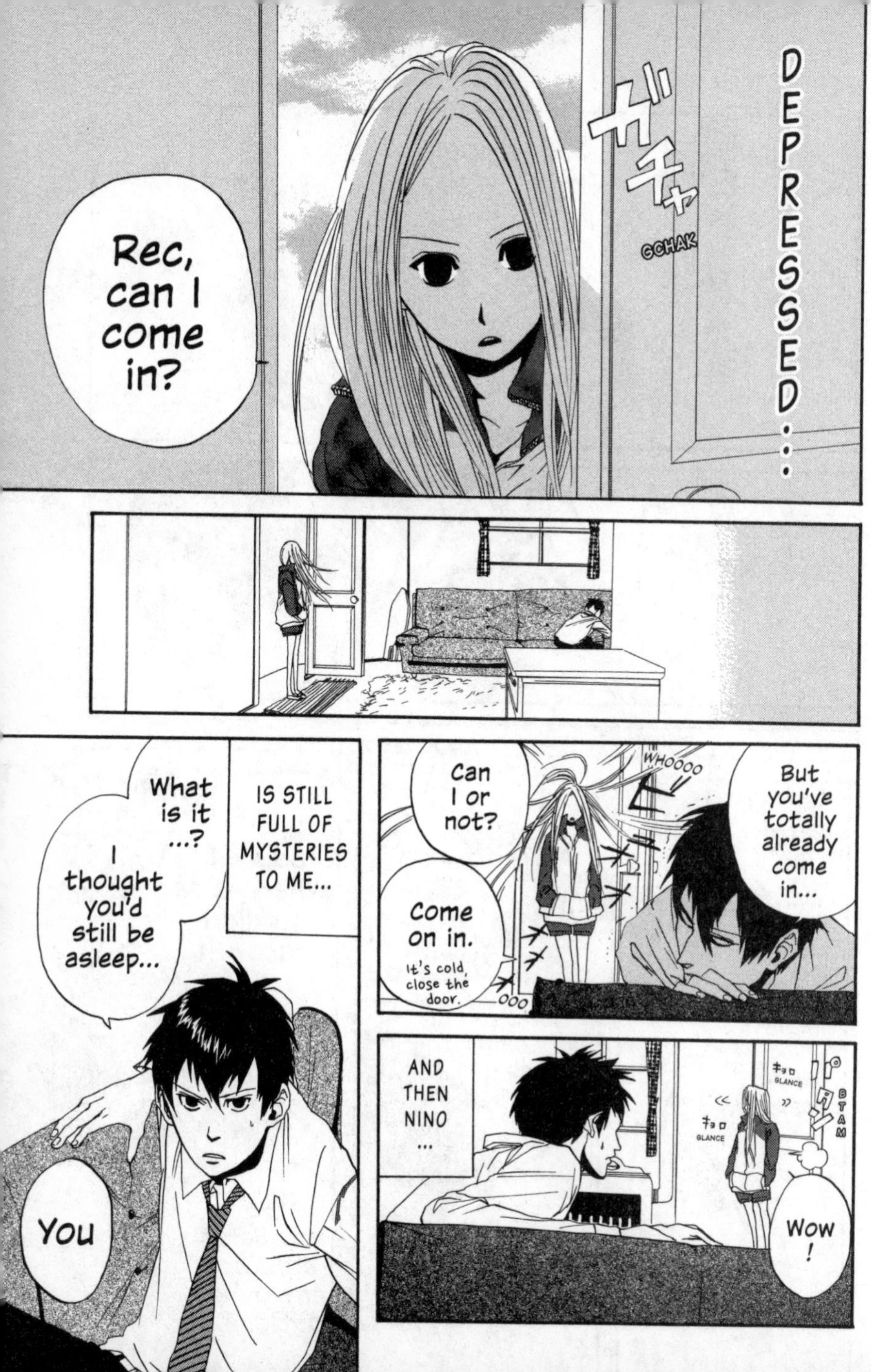
DEPRESSED...
ガチャ
GCHAK
Rec, can I come in?
But you've totally already come in...
WHOOOO
Can I or not?
Come on in.
It's cold, close the door.
BTAM
キョロ
GLANCE
キョロ
GLANCE
Wow!
AND THEN NINO ...
IS STILL FULL OF MYSTERIES TO ME...
What is it ...? I thought you'd still be asleep...
You

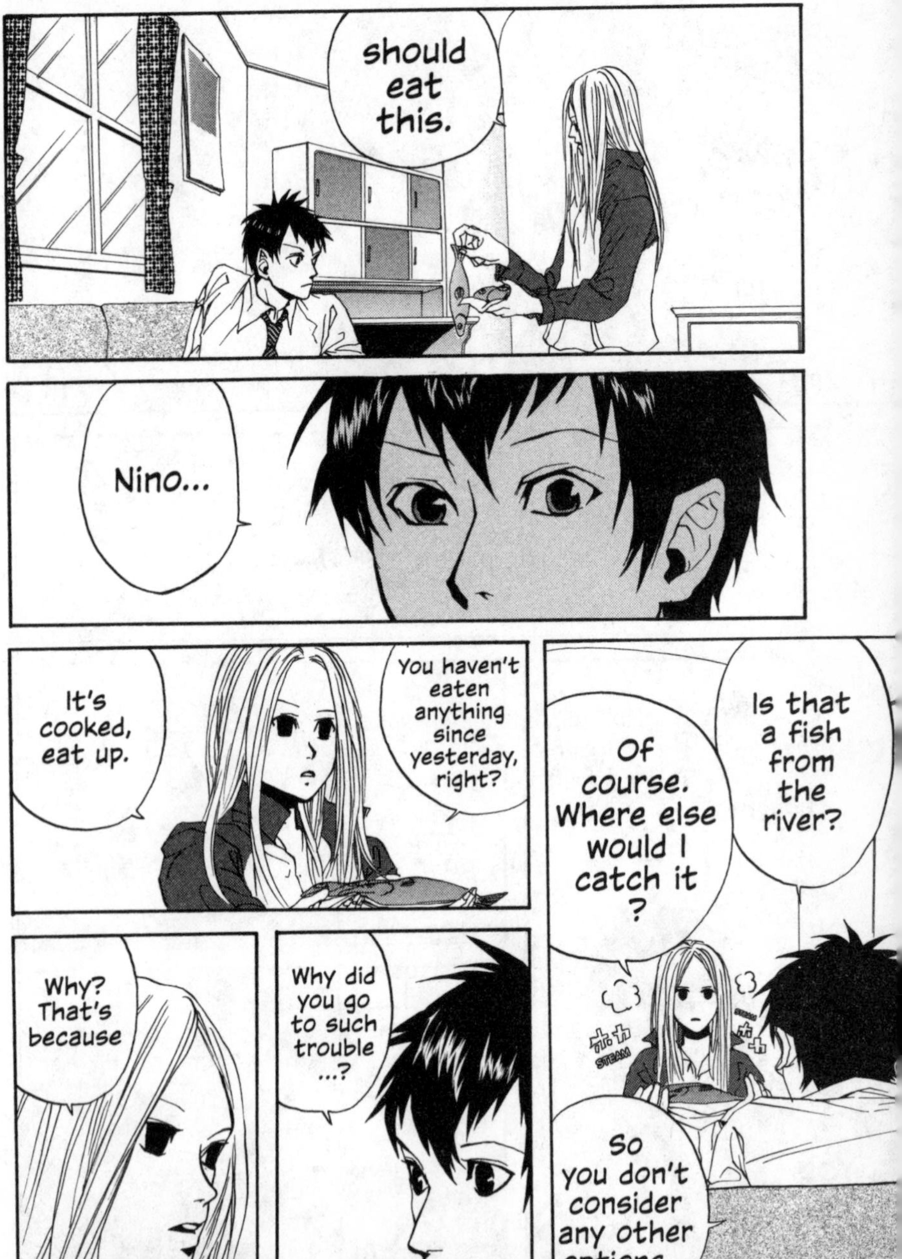
should eat this.
Nino...
Is that a fish from the river?
Of course. Where else would I catch it?
STEAM
STEAM
So you don't consider any other options...
You haven't eaten anything since yesterday, right?
It's cooked, eat up.
Why did you go to such trouble...?
Why? That's because

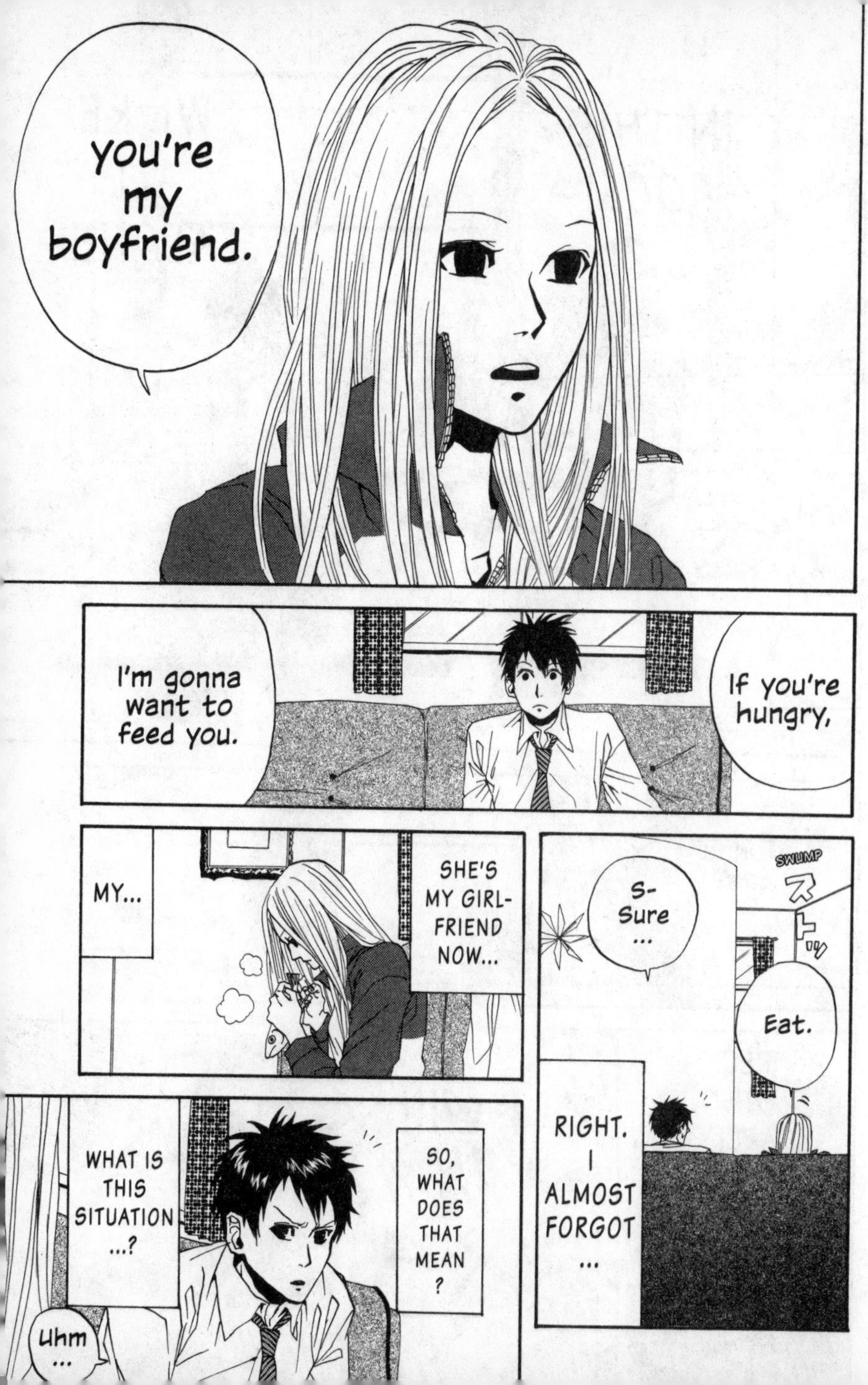
you're my boyfriend.
If you're hungry,
I'm gonna want to feed you.
SWUMP
ストッ
S- Sure ...
Eat.
RIGHT. I ALMOST FORGOT ...
SHE'S MY GIRL-FRIEND NOW...
MY...
SO, WHAT DOES THAT MEAN ?
WHAT IS THIS SITUATION ...?
uhm ...

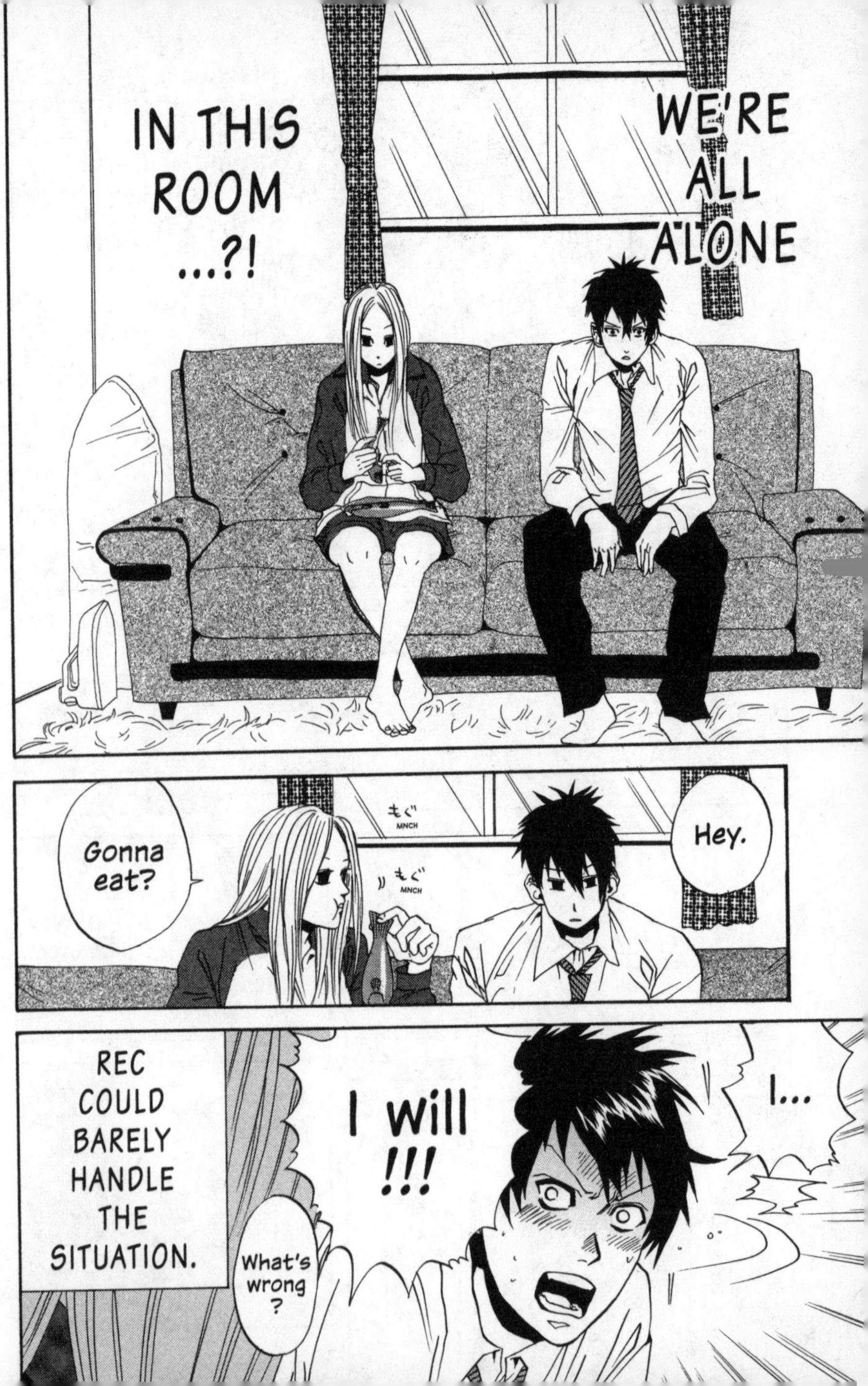
WE'RE ALL ALONE
IN THIS ROOM ...?!
Hey.
もぐ MNCH
もぐ MNCH
Gonna eat?
I...
I Will !!!
What's wrong ?
REC COULD BARELY HANDLE THE SITUATION.

☜ Chapter 11: Spending Time Together

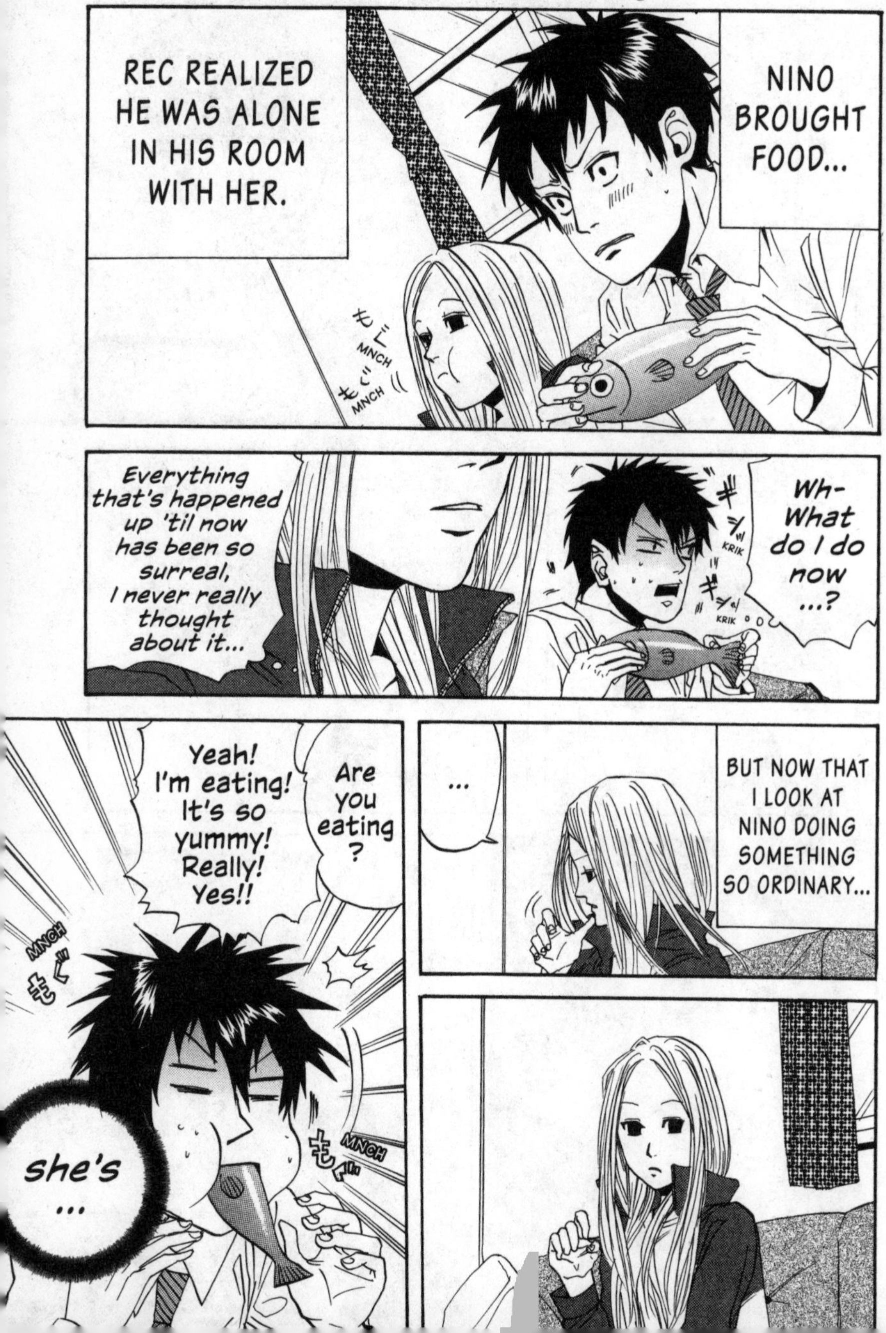
NINO BROUGHT FOOD...
REC REALIZED HE WAS ALONE IN HIS ROOM WITH HER.
もぐ MNCH
もぐ MNCH
Wh- What do I do now ...?
ギシ KRIK
ギシ KRIK
Everything that's happened up 'til now has been so surreal, I never really thought about it...
BUT NOW THAT I LOOK AT NINO DOING SOMETHING SO ORDINARY...
...
Are you eating ?
Yeah! I'm eating! It's so yummy! Really! Yes!!
MNCH もぐ
もぐ MNCH
she's ...

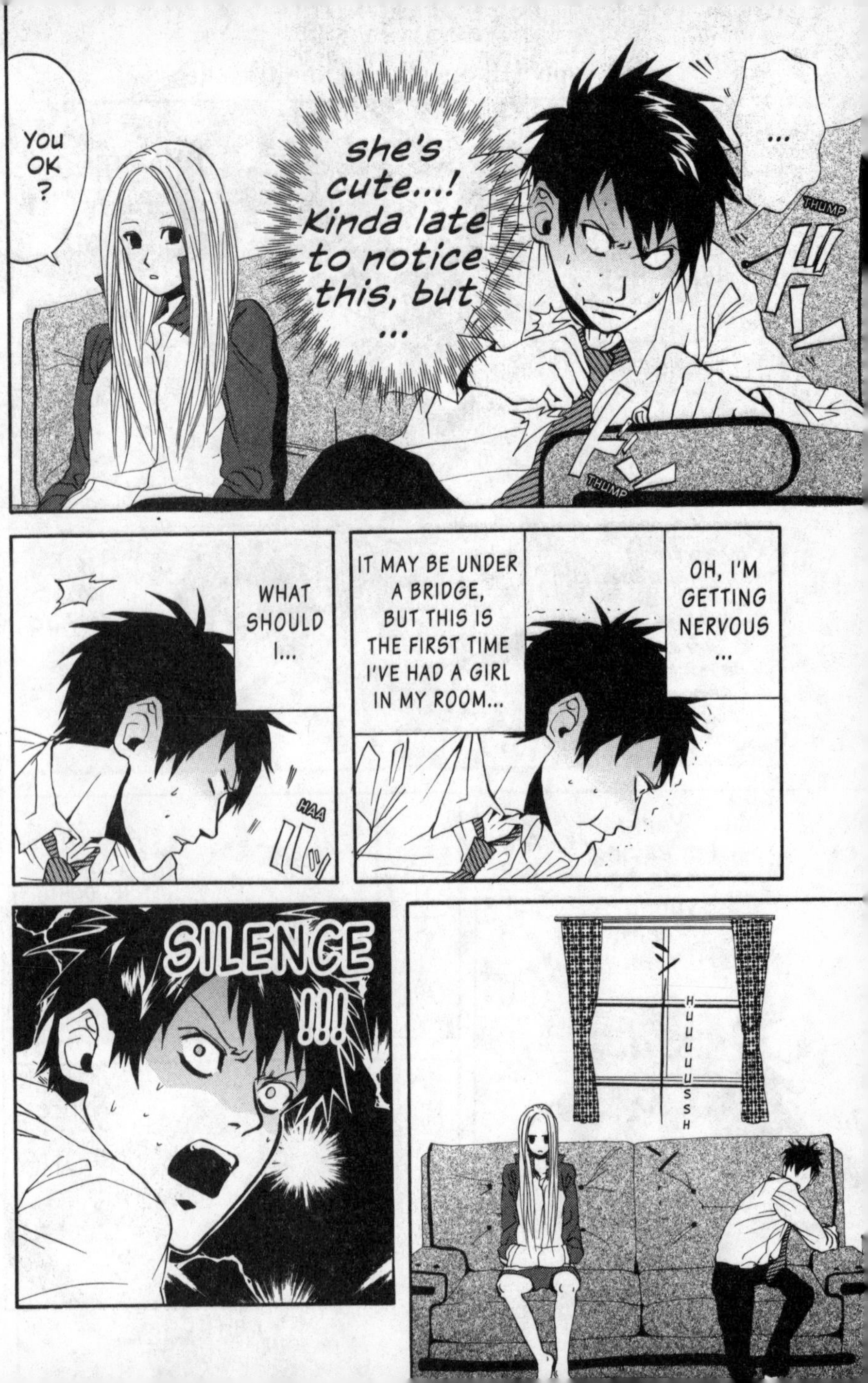
...
THUMP
THUMP
she's cute...! Kinda late to notice this, but ...
You OK ?
OH, I'M GETTING NERVOUS ...
IT MAY BE UNDER A BRIDGE, BUT THIS IS THE FIRST TIME I'VE HAD A GIRL IN MY ROOM...
WHAT SHOULD I...
HAA
HUUUUUSSH
SILENCE !!!

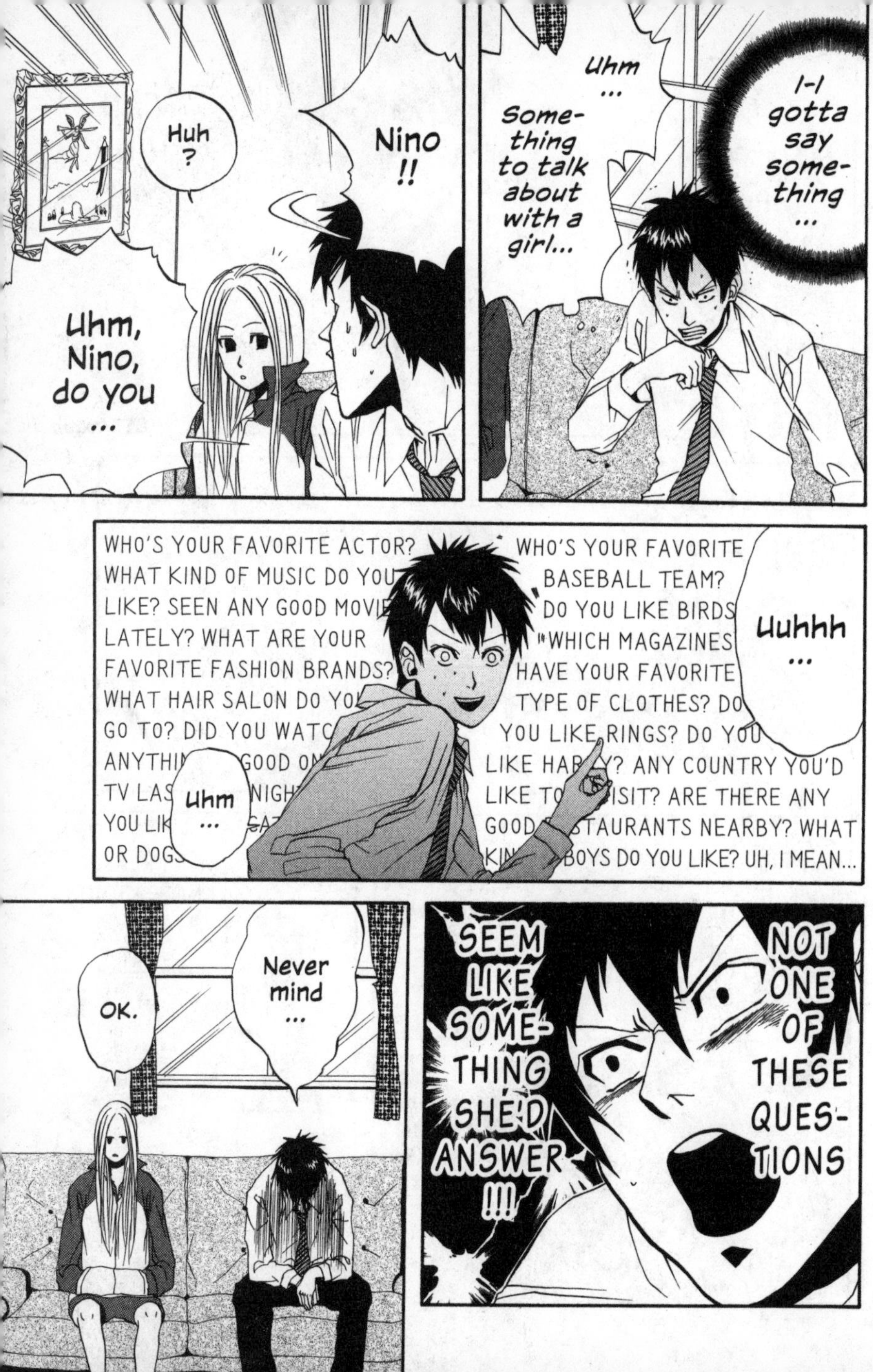
I-I gotta say something ...
Uhm ... Something to talk about with a girl...
Nino !!
Huh ?
Uhm, Nino, do you ...
Uhhh ...
WHO'S YOUR FAVORITE BASEBALL TEAM? DO YOU LIKE BIRDS WHICH MAGAZINES HAVE YOUR FAVORITE TYPE OF CLOTHES? DO YOU LIKE RINGS? DO YOU LIKE HA Y? ANY COUNTRY YOU'D LIKE TO ISIT? ARE THERE ANY GOOD STAURANTS NEARBY? WHAT KIN BOYS DO YOU LIKE? UH, I MEAN...
WHO'S YOUR FAVORITE ACTOR? WHAT KIND OF MUSIC DO YOU LIKE? SEEN ANY GOOD MOVIE LATELY? WHAT ARE YOUR FAVORITE FASHION BRANDS? WHAT HAIR SALON DO YO GO TO? DID YOU WATC ANYTHIN GOOD ON TV LAS NIGH YOU LIK AT OR DOGS
Uhm ...
NOT ONE OF THESE QUESTIONS SEEM LIKE SOMETHING SHE'D ANSWER !!!
Never mind ...
OK.

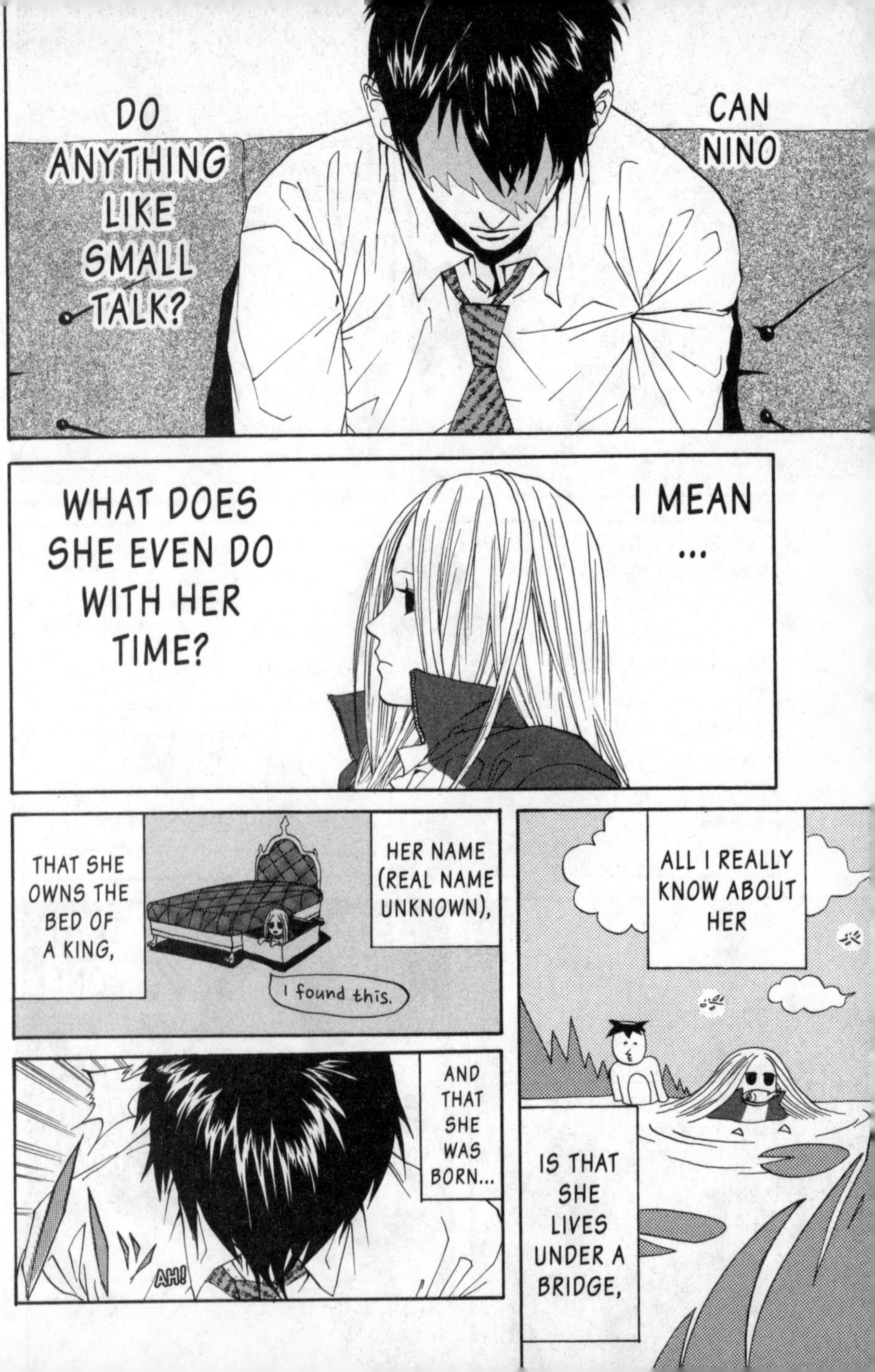
CAN NINO
DO ANYTHING LIKE SMALL TALK?
I MEAN ...
WHAT DOES SHE EVEN DO WITH HER TIME?
ALL I REALLY KNOW ABOUT HER
IS THAT SHE LIVES UNDER A BRIDGE,
HER NAME (REAL NAME UNKNOWN),
THAT SHE OWNS THE BED OF A KING,
I found this.
AND THAT SHE WAS BORN...
AH!

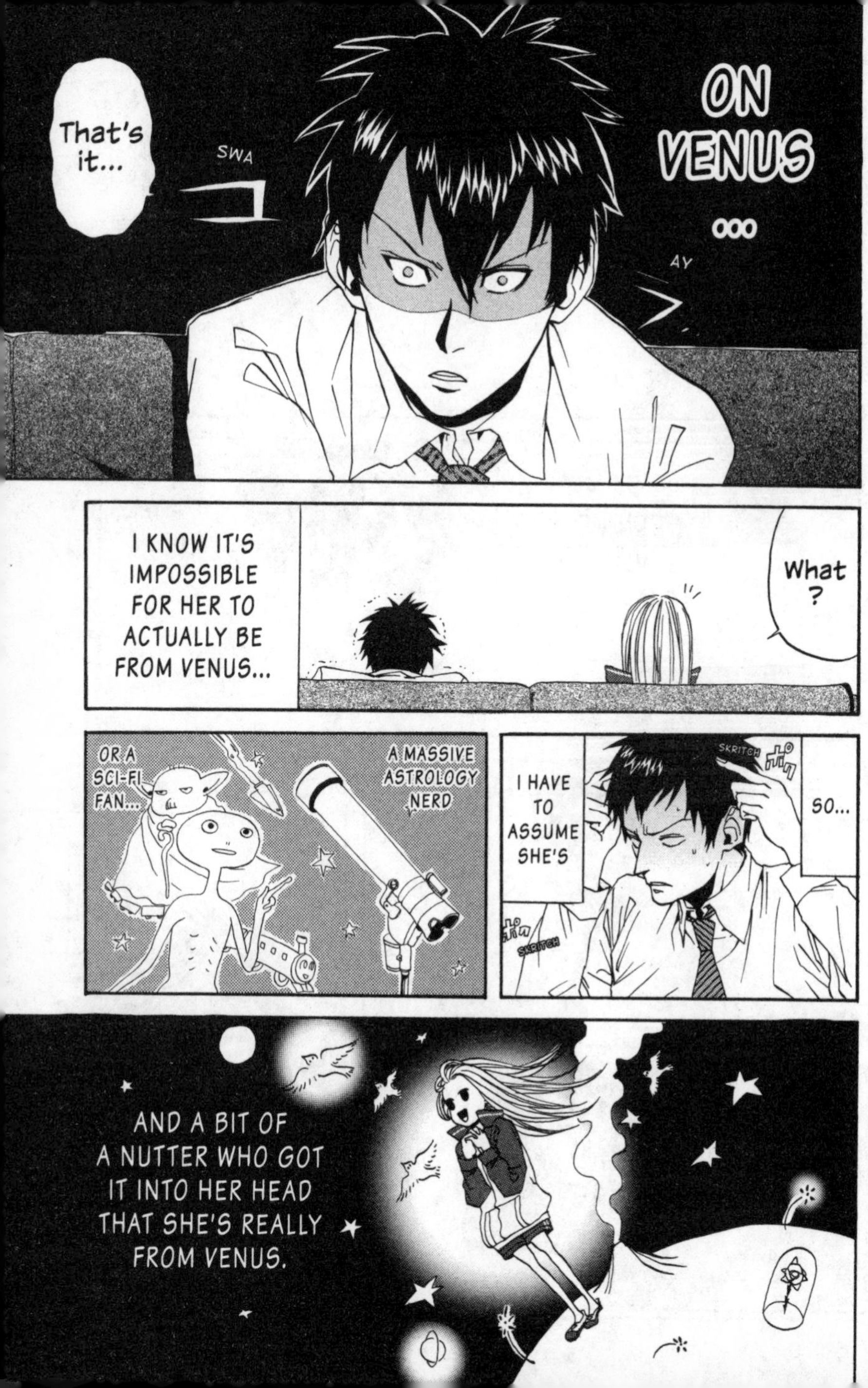
ON VENUS ...
That's it...
SWA
AY
What?
I KNOW IT'S IMPOSSIBLE FOR HER TO ACTUALLY BE FROM VENUS...
SO...
SKRITCH
I HAVE TO ASSUME SHE'S
SKRITCH
A MASSIVE ASTROLOGY NERD
OR A SCI-FI FAN...
AND A BIT OF A NUTTER WHO GOT IT INTO HER HEAD THAT SHE'S REALLY FROM VENUS.

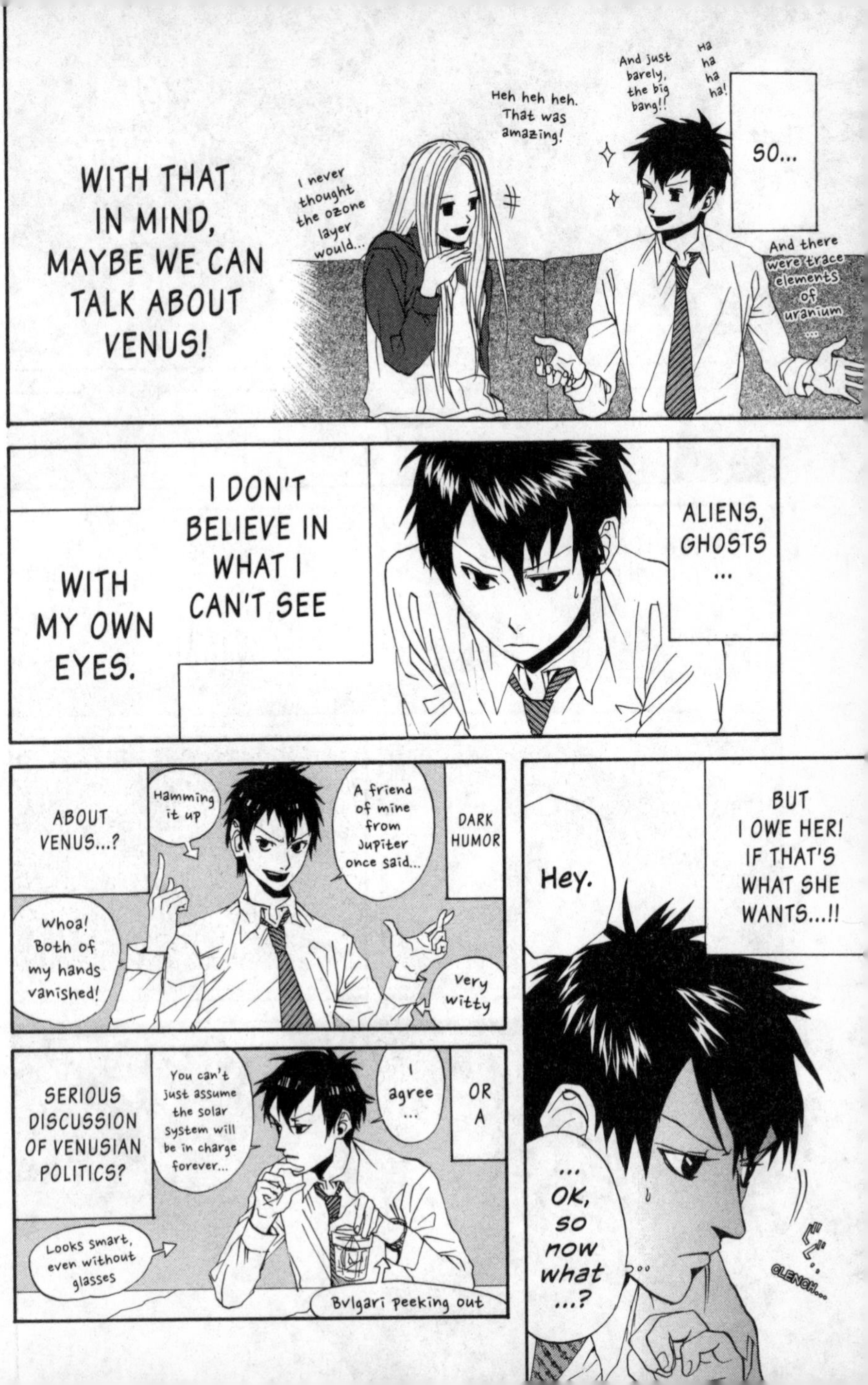
Ha ha ha ha!
SO...
And just barely, the big bang!!
Heh heh heh. That was amazing!
And there were trace elements of uranium ...
I never thought the ozone layer would...
WITH THAT IN MIND, MAYBE WE CAN TALK ABOUT VENUS!
ALIENS, GHOSTS ...
I DON'T BELIEVE IN WHAT I CAN'T SEE
WITH MY OWN EYES.
BUT I OWE HER! IF THAT'S WHAT SHE WANTS...!!
Hey.
CLENCH...
... OK, so now what ...?
DARK HUMOR
A friend of mine from Jupiter once said...
Hamming it up
ABOUT VENUS...?
Whoa! Both of my hands vanished!
Very witty
OR A
I agree ...
You can't just assume the solar system will be in charge forever...
SERIOUS DISCUSSION OF VENUSIAN POLITICS?
Looks smart, even without glasses
Bvlgari peeking out

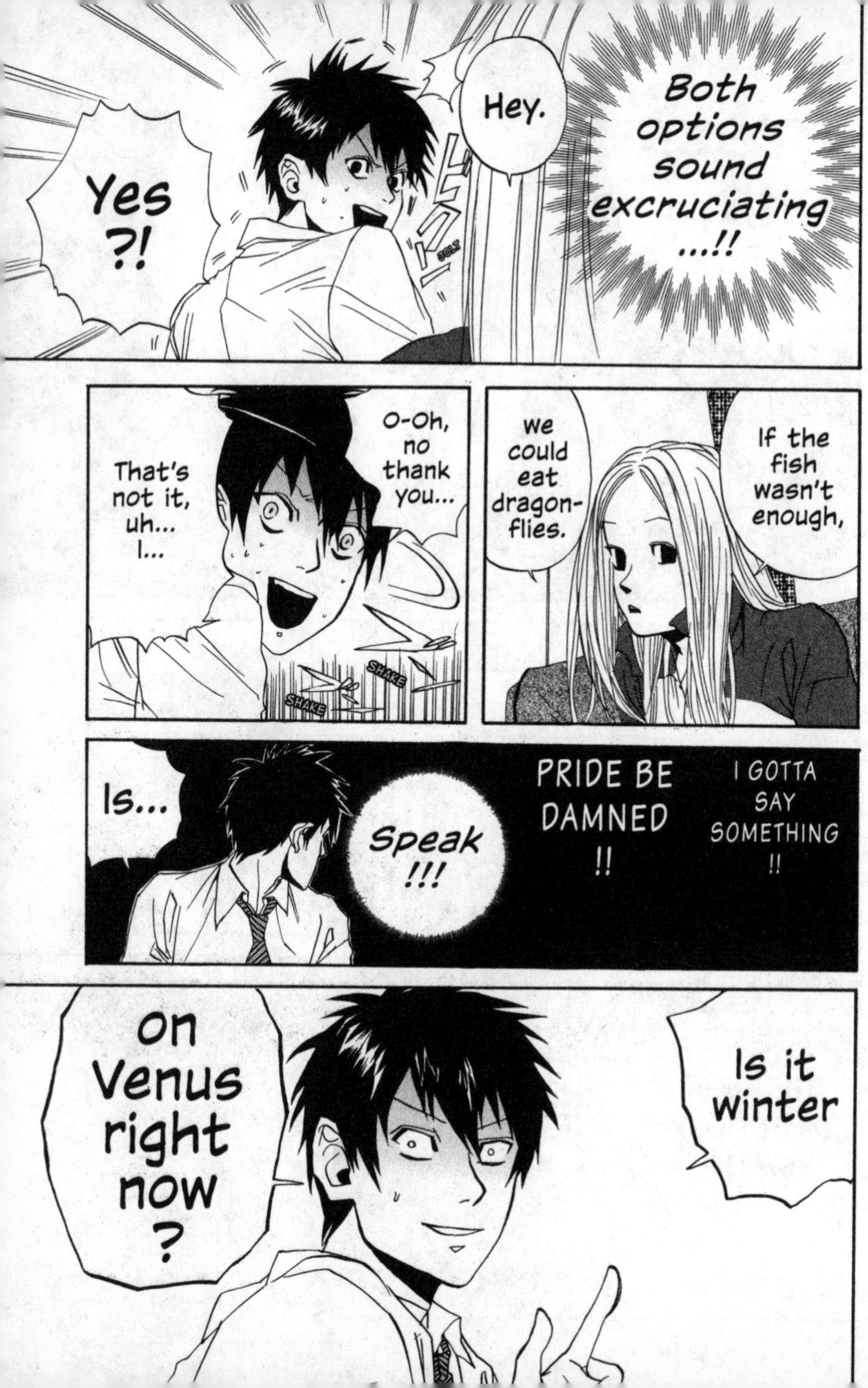
Both options sound excruciating ...!!
Hey.
JOLT
Yes ?!
If the fish wasn't enough,
we could eat dragonflies.
O-Oh, no thank you...
That's not it, uh... I...
SHAKE
SHAKE
I GOTTA SAY SOMETHING !!
PRIDE BE DAMNED !!
Speak !!!
Is...
Is it winter
on Venus right now ?

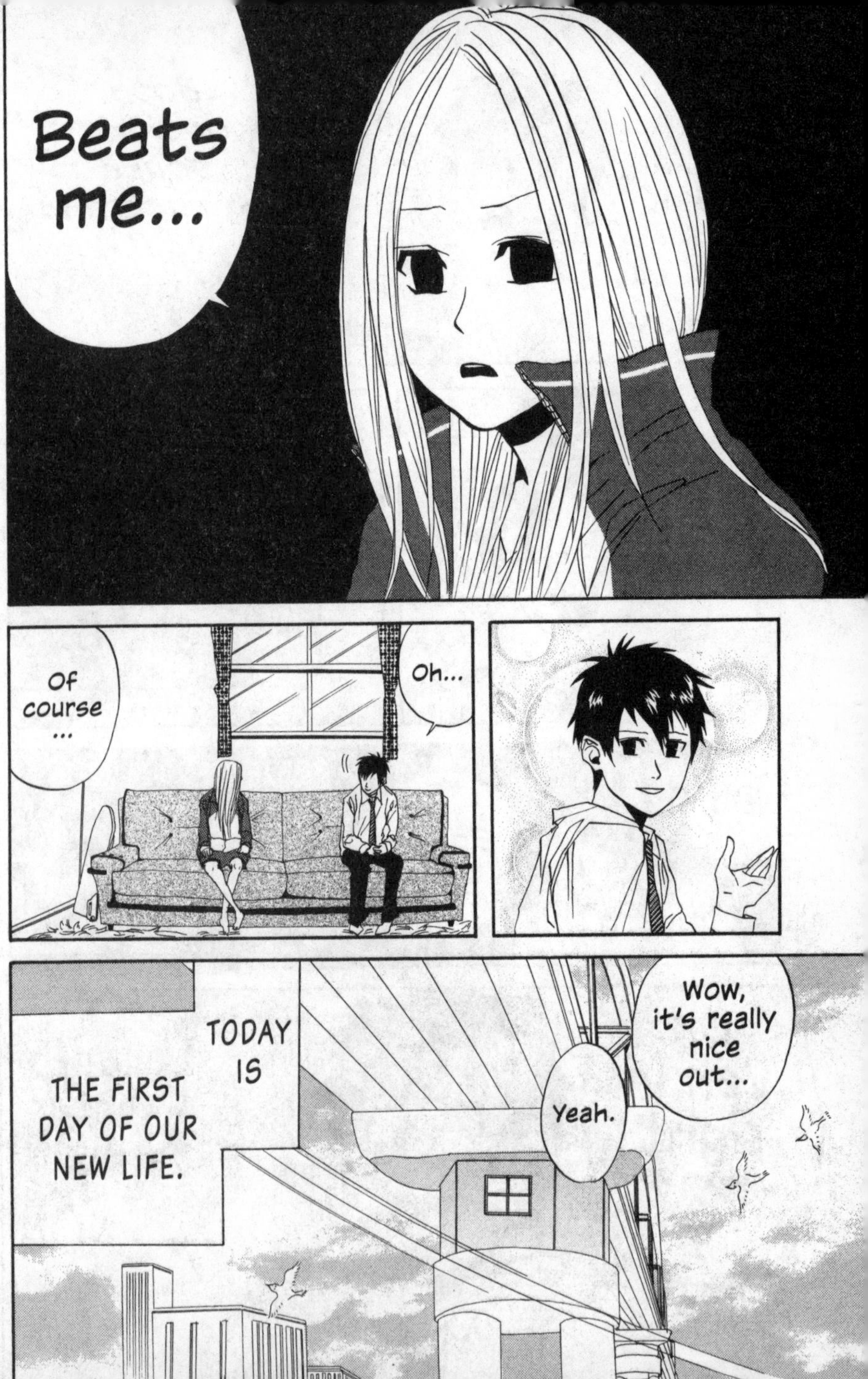
Beats me...
Oh...
Of course ...
Wow, it's really nice out...
Yeah.
TODAY IS
THE FIRST DAY OF OUR NEW LIFE.

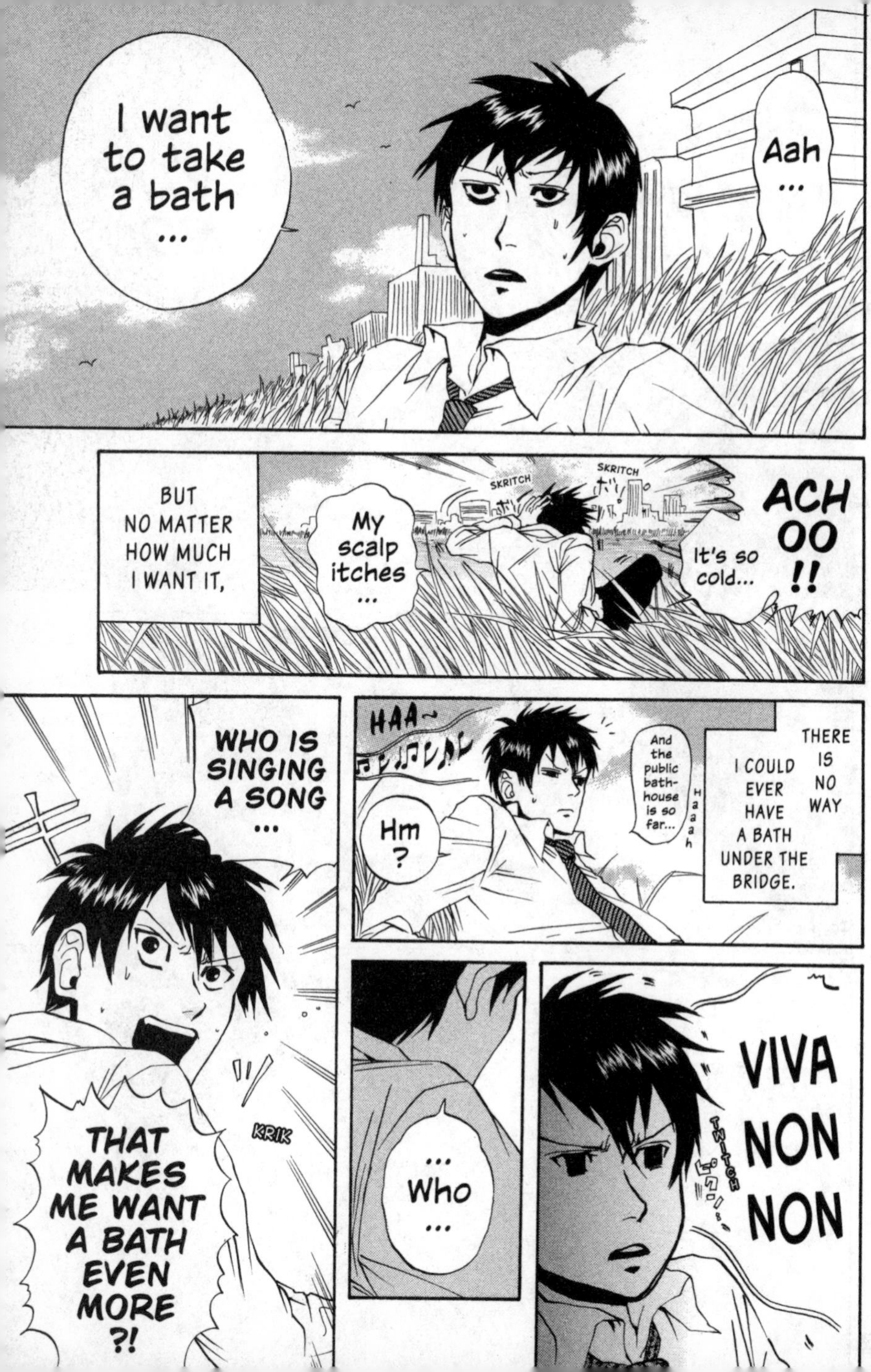

Aah ...
I want to take a bath ...
ACHOO !!
It's so cold...
SKRITCH
SKRITCH
My scalp itches ...
BUT NO MATTER HOW MUCH I WANT IT,
THERE IS NO WAY I COULD EVER HAVE A BATH UNDER THE BRIDGE.
Haaah
And the public bathhouse is so far...
Hm ?
HAA~
VIVA NON NON NON
TWITCH
... Who ...
WHO IS SINGING A SONG ...
KRIK
THAT MAKES ME WANT A BATH EVEN MORE ?!

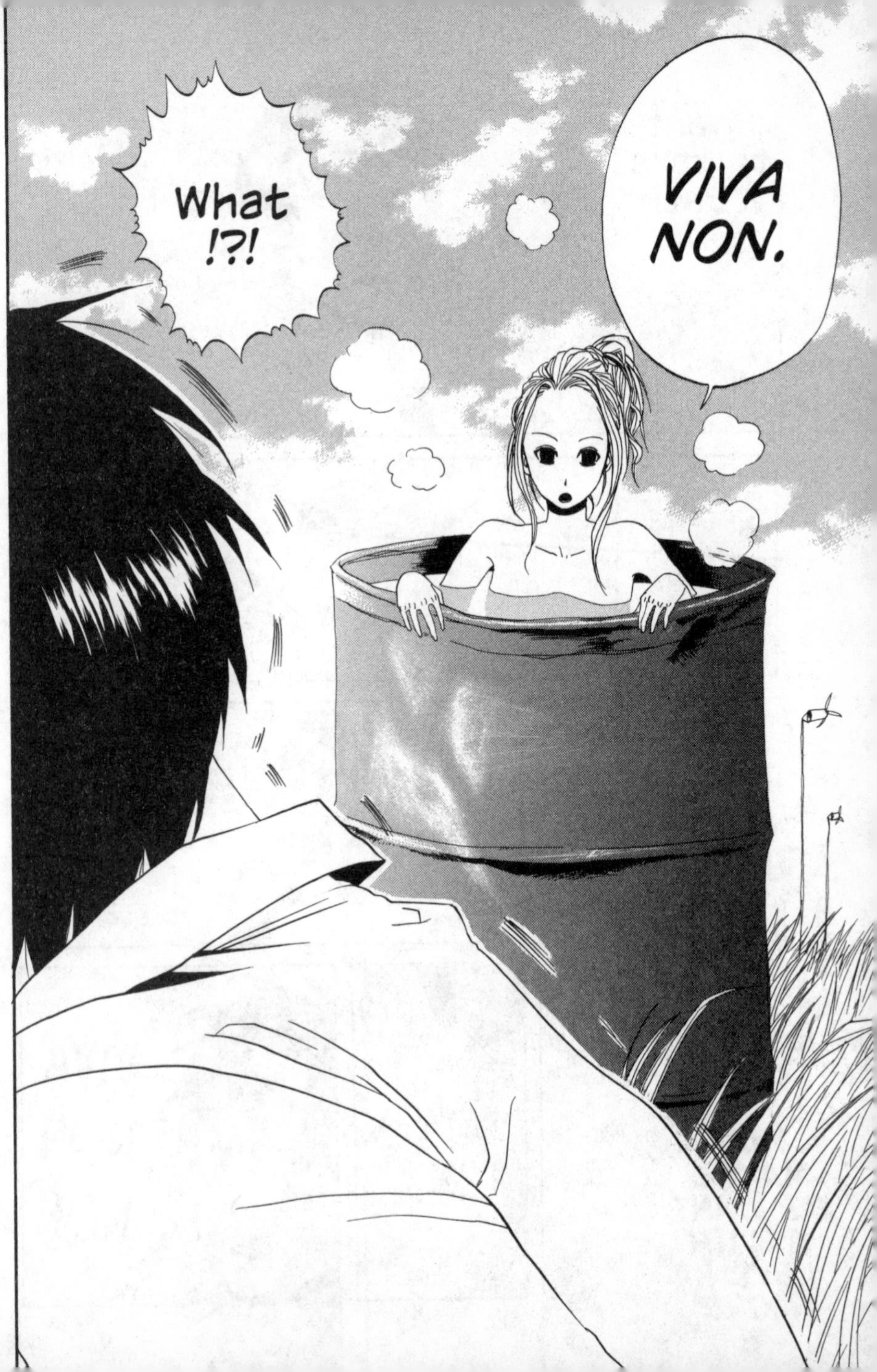
VIVA NON.
What !?!

☜ Chapter 12: Leaving the Bath

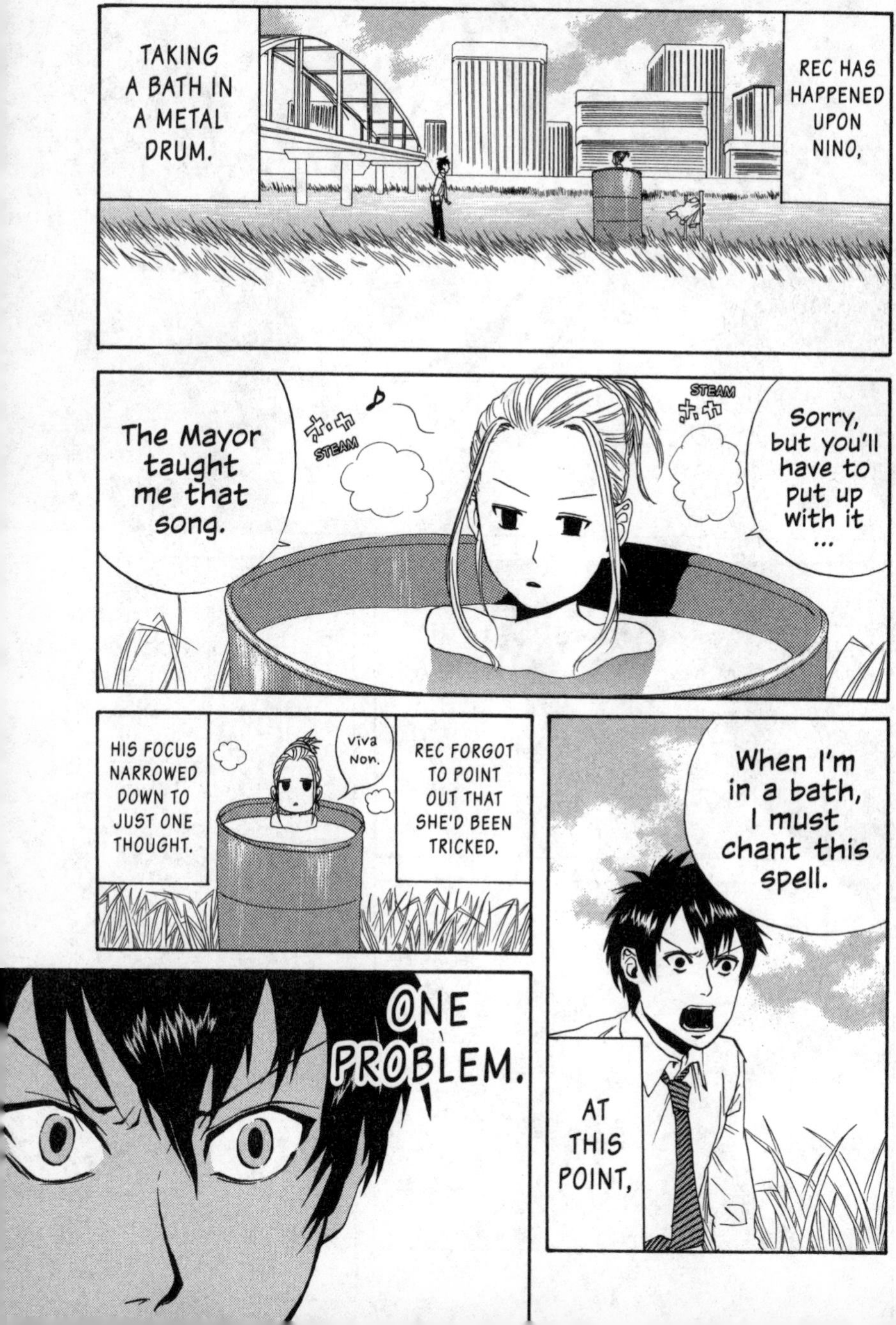
REC HAS HAPPENED UPON NINO,
TAKING A BATH IN A METAL DRUM.
STEAM
Sorry, but you'll have to put up with it ...
STEAM
The Mayor taught me that song.
When I'm in a bath, I must chant this spell.
AT THIS POINT,
REC FORGOT TO POINT OUT THAT SHE'D BEEN TRICKED.
Viva Non.
HIS FOCUS NARROWED DOWN TO JUST ONE THOUGHT.
ONE PROBLEM.

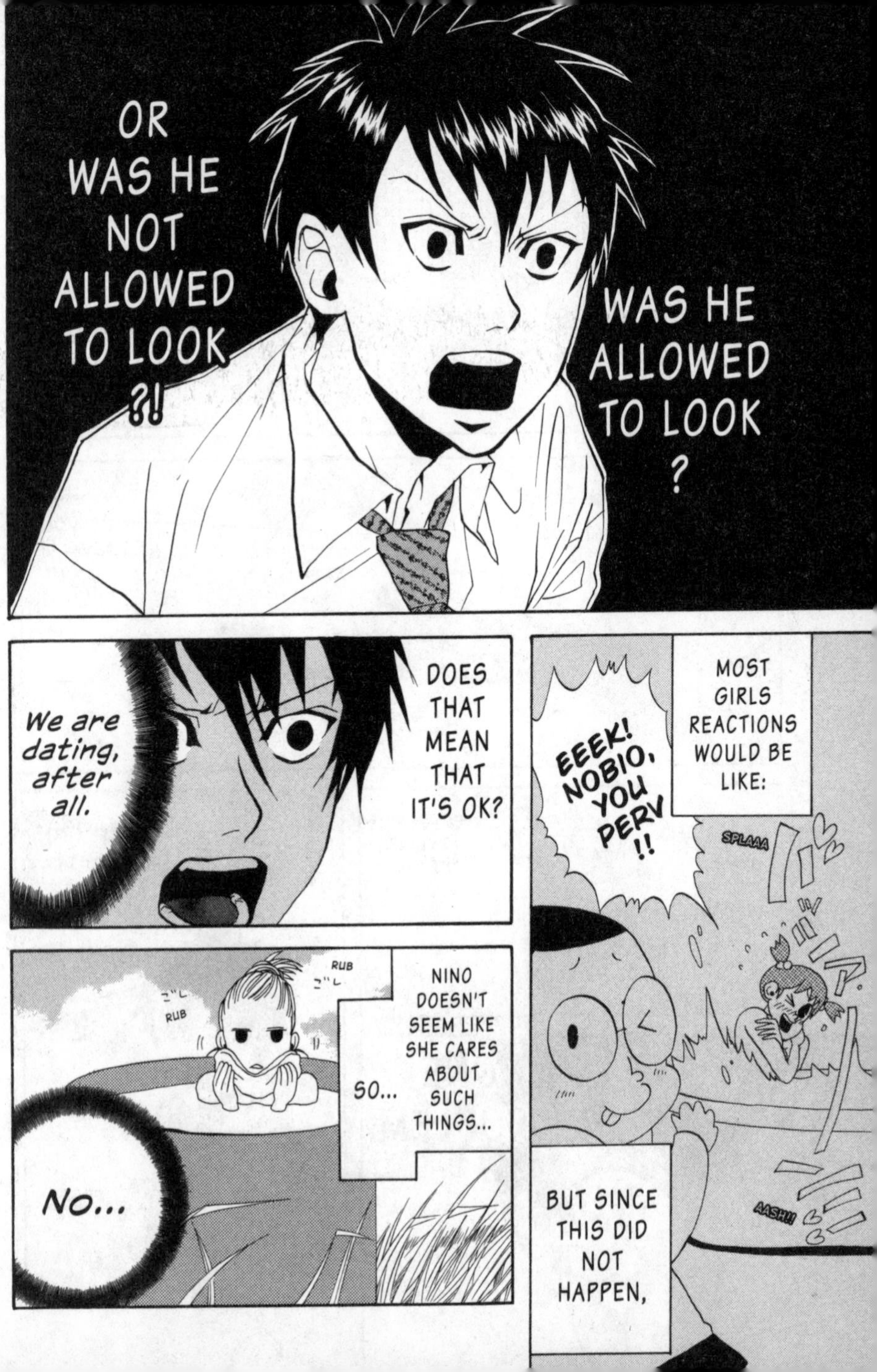
WAS HE ALLOWED TO LOOK?
OR WAS HE NOT ALLOWED TO LOOK?!
MOST GIRLS REACTIONS WOULD BE LIKE:
EEEK! NOBIO, YOU PERV!!
SPLAAA
AASH!!
BUT SINCE THIS DID NOT HAPPEN,
DOES THAT MEAN THAT IT'S OK?
We are dating, after all.
NINO DOESN'T SEEM LIKE SHE CARES ABOUT SUCH THINGS...
RUB
RUB
SO...
NO...

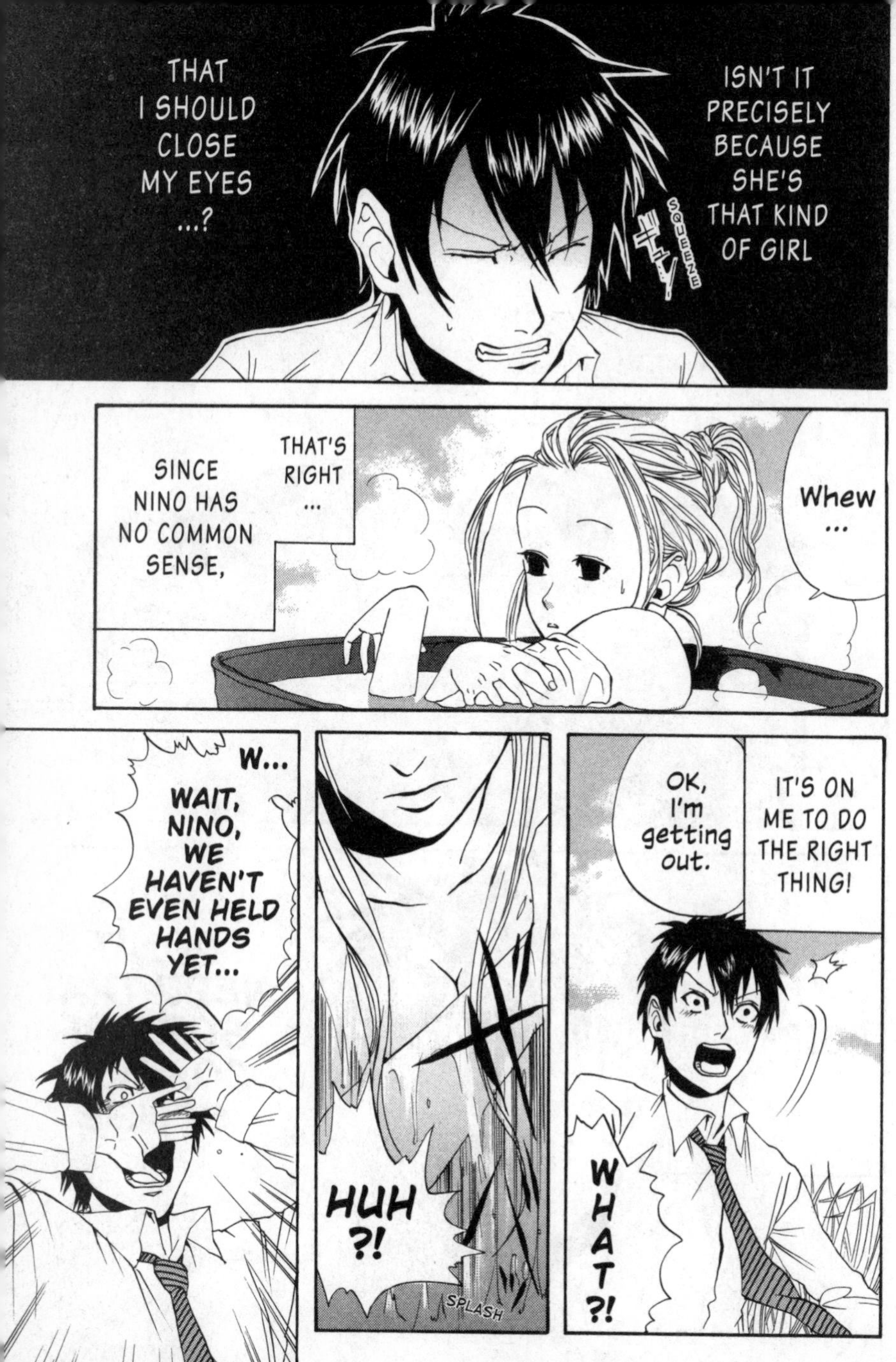
ISN'T IT PRECISELY BECAUSE SHE'S THAT KIND OF GIRL
SQUEEZE
THAT I SHOULD CLOSE MY EYES ...?
Whew ...
THAT'S RIGHT ...
SINCE NINO HAS NO COMMON SENSE,
IT'S ON ME TO DO THE RIGHT THING!
OK, I'm getting out.
WHAT ?!
HUH ?!
SPLASH
W... WAIT, NINO, WE HAVEN'T EVEN HELD HANDS YET...

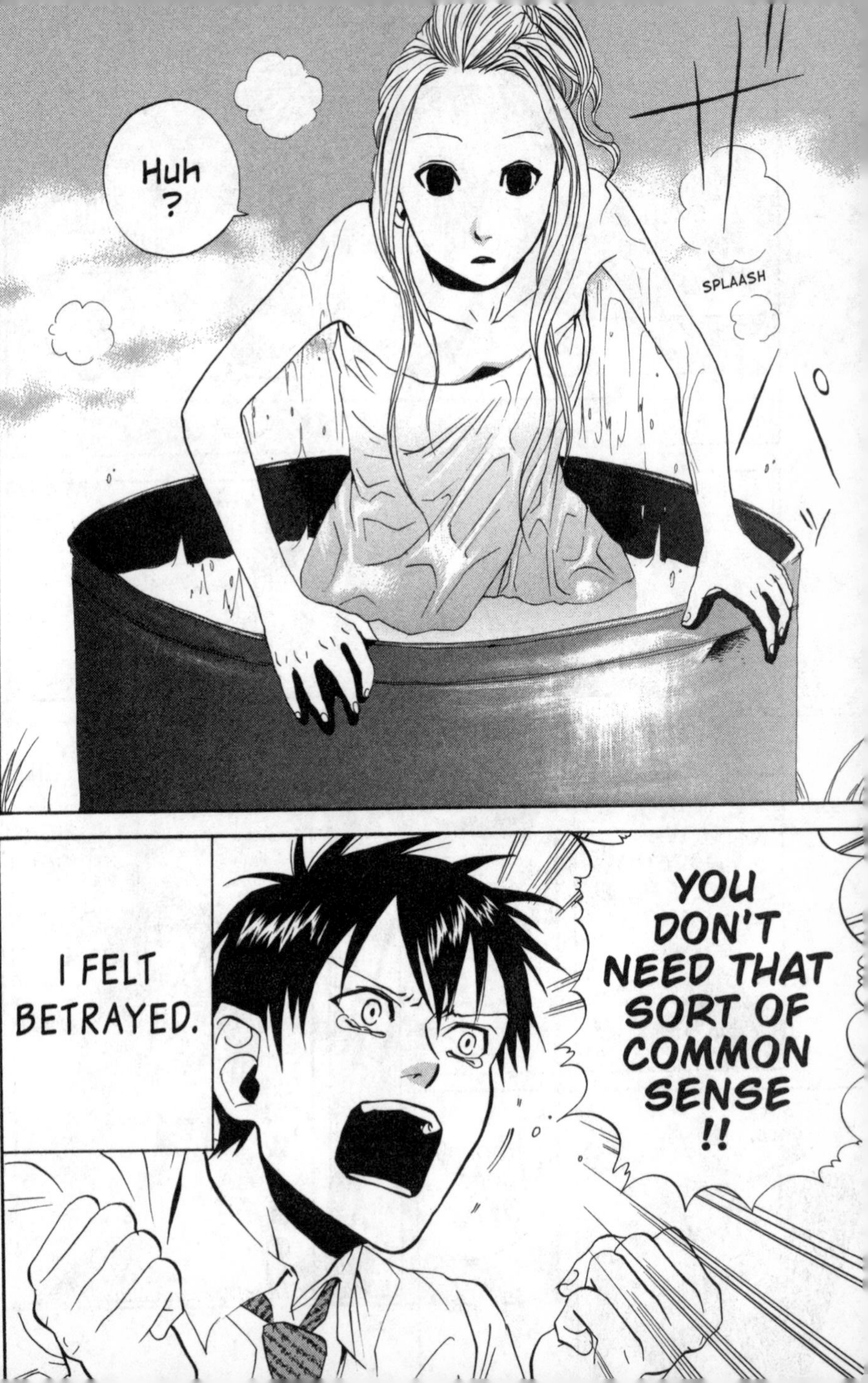
Huh?
SPLAASH
YOU DON'T NEED THAT SORT OF COMMON SENSE!!
I FELT BETRAYED.

☜ Chapter 13: Uni

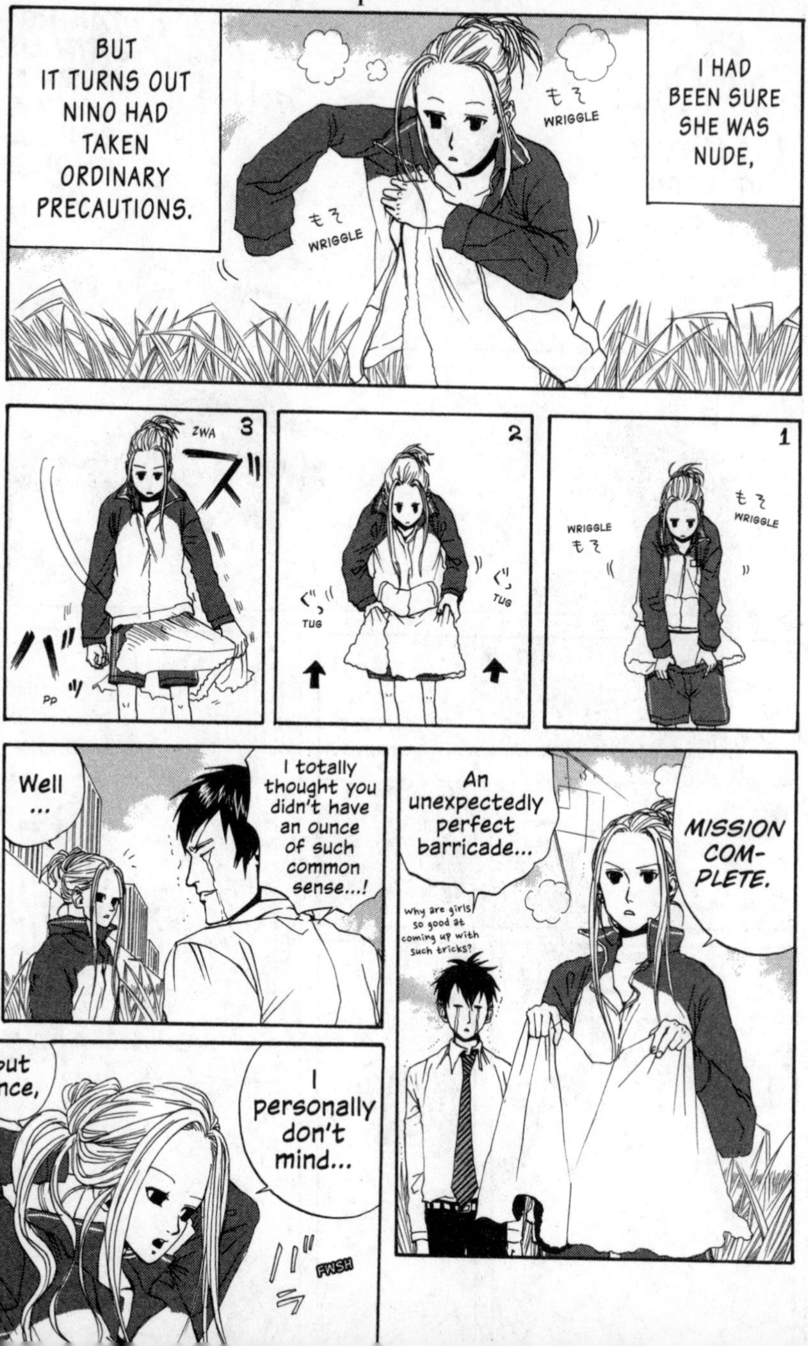

I HAD BEEN SURE SHE WAS NUDE,
もぞ WRIGGLE
もぞ WRIGGLE
BUT IT TURNS OUT NINO HAD TAKEN ORDINARY PRECAUTIONS.
1
もぞ WRIGGLE
WRIGGLE もぞ
2
ぐっ TUG
ぐっ TUG
3
ズ ZWA
バッ PP
MISSION COM-PLETE.
An unexpectedly perfect barricade...
why are girls so good at coming up with such tricks?
I totally thought you didn't have an ounce of such common sense...!
Well ...
I personally don't mind...
but once,
バ FWSH

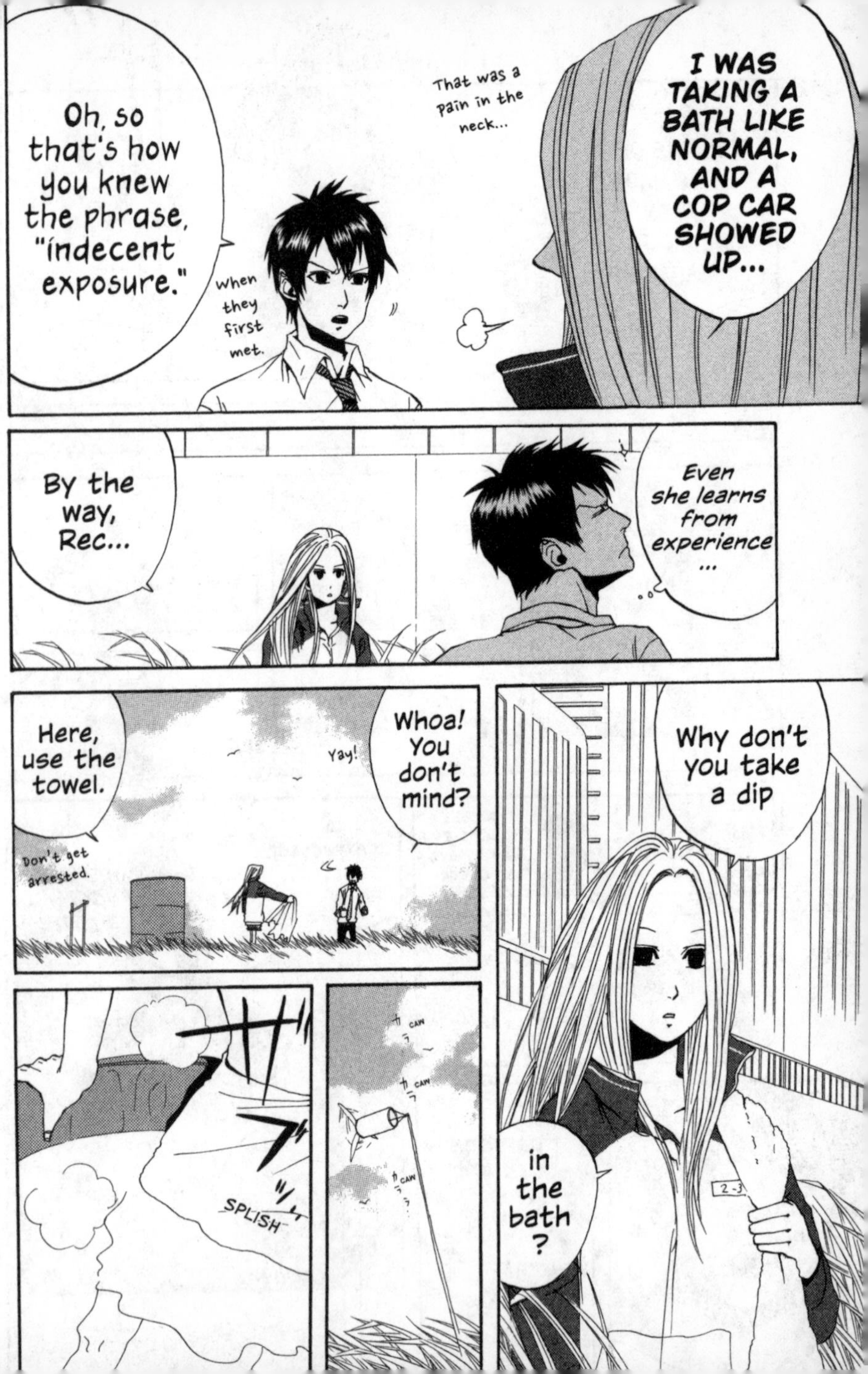
I WAS TAKING A BATH LIKE NORMAL, AND A COP CAR SHOWED UP...
That was a pain in the neck...
Oh, so that's how you knew the phrase, "indecent exposure."
When they first met.
Even she learns from experience ...
By the way, Rec...
Why don't you take a dip
in the bath?
2-3
Whoa! You don't mind?
Yay!
Here, use the towel.
Don't get arrested.
CAW
CAW
CAW
SPLISH

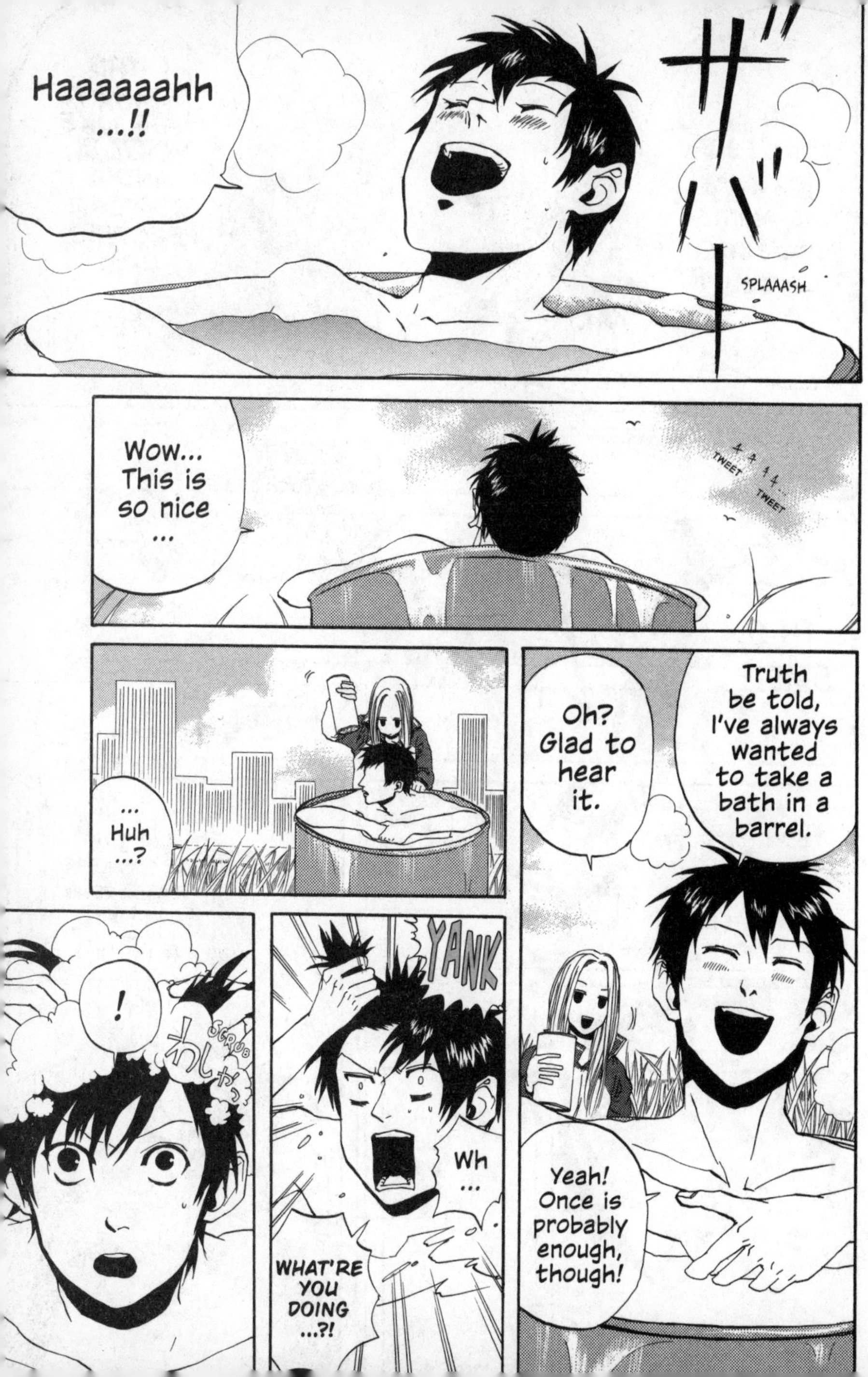

Haaaaaaahh ...!!
ザバー
SPLAAASH
Wow... This is so nice ...
TWEET TWEET
Truth be told, I've always wanted to take a bath in a barrel.
Oh? Glad to hear it.
Yeah! Once is probably enough, though!
... Huh ...?
YANK
Wh ...
WHAT'RE YOU DOING ...?!
!
わしゃっ
SCRUB

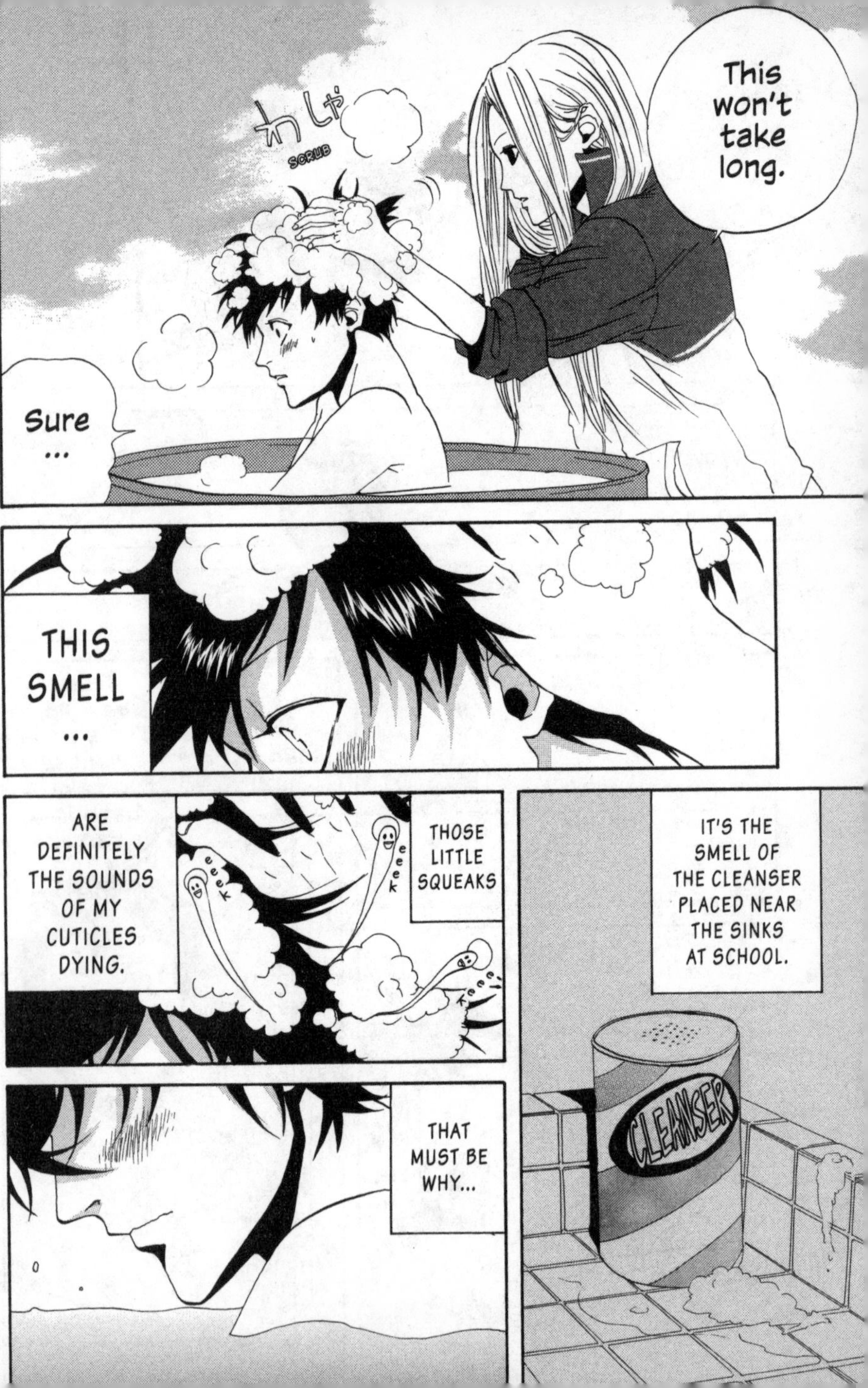
This won't take long.
わしゃ
SCRUB
Sure ...
THIS SMELL ...
IT'S THE SMELL OF THE CLEANSER PLACED NEAR THE SINKS AT SCHOOL.
CLEANSER
THOSE LITTLE SQUEAKS
eeek
eeek
eeek
ARE DEFINITELY THE SOUNDS OF MY CUTICLES DYING.
THAT MUST BE WHY...

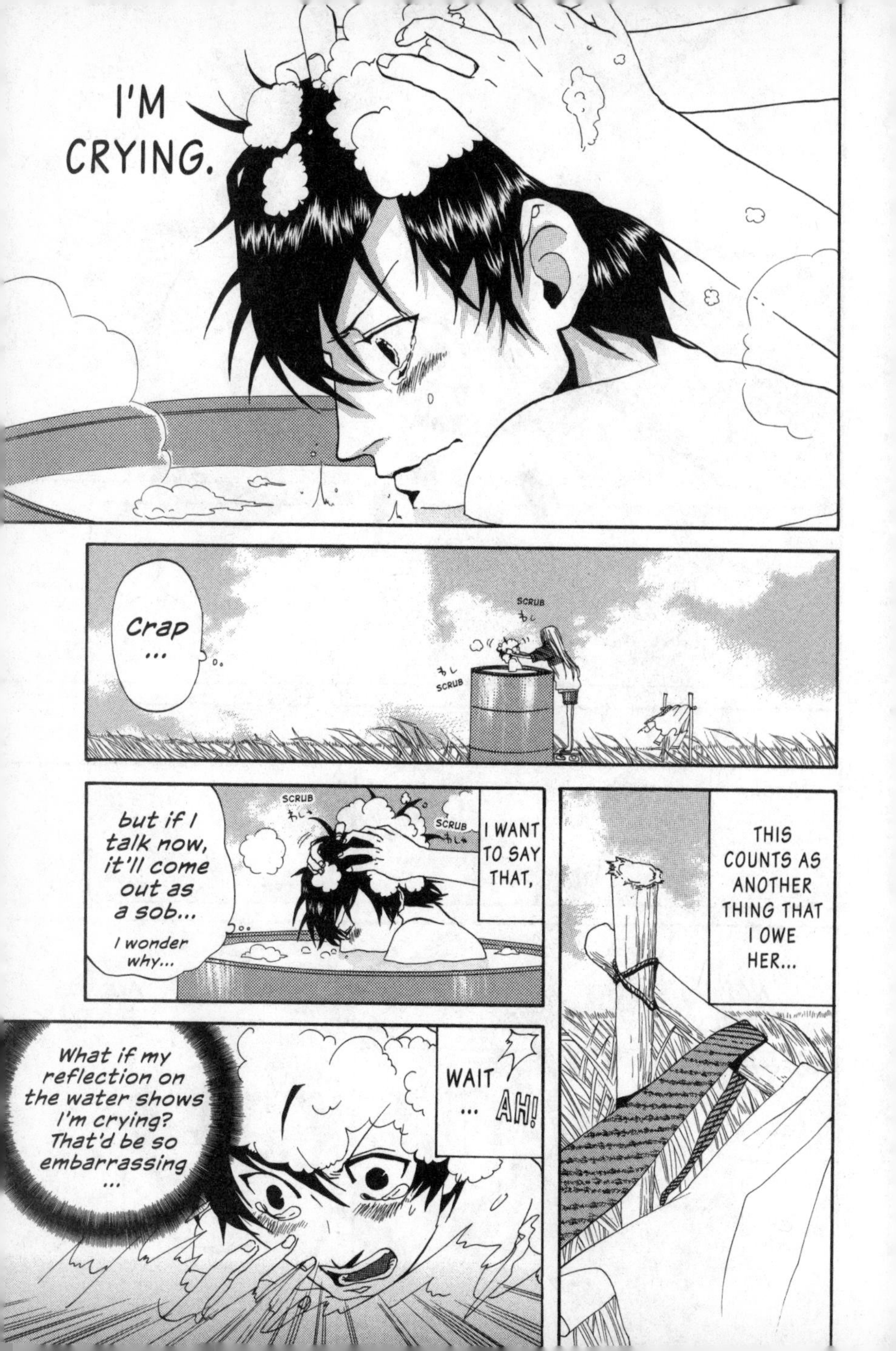
I'M CRYING.
SCRUB
SCRUB
Crap ...
THIS COUNTS AS ANOTHER THING THAT I OWE HER...
I WANT TO SAY THAT,
SCRUB
SCRUB
but if I talk now, it'll come out as a sob...
I wonder why...
AH!
WAIT ...
What if my reflection on the water shows I'm crying? That'd be so embarrassing ...

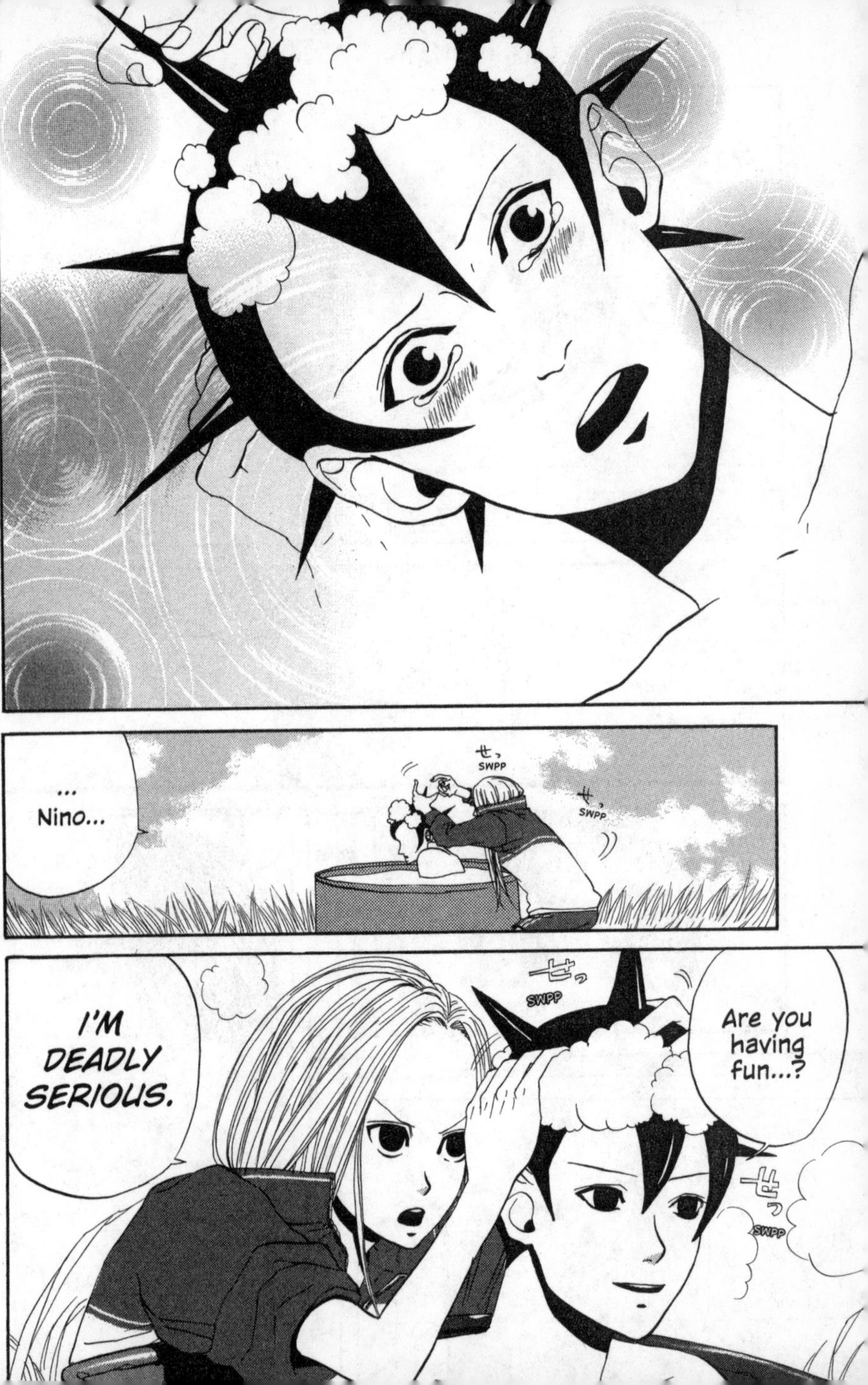
せっ
SWPP
せっ
SWPP
... Nino...
Are you having fun...?
せっ
SWPP
せっ
SWPP
I'M DEADLY SERIOUS.

☜ Chapter 14: Rec's Memories

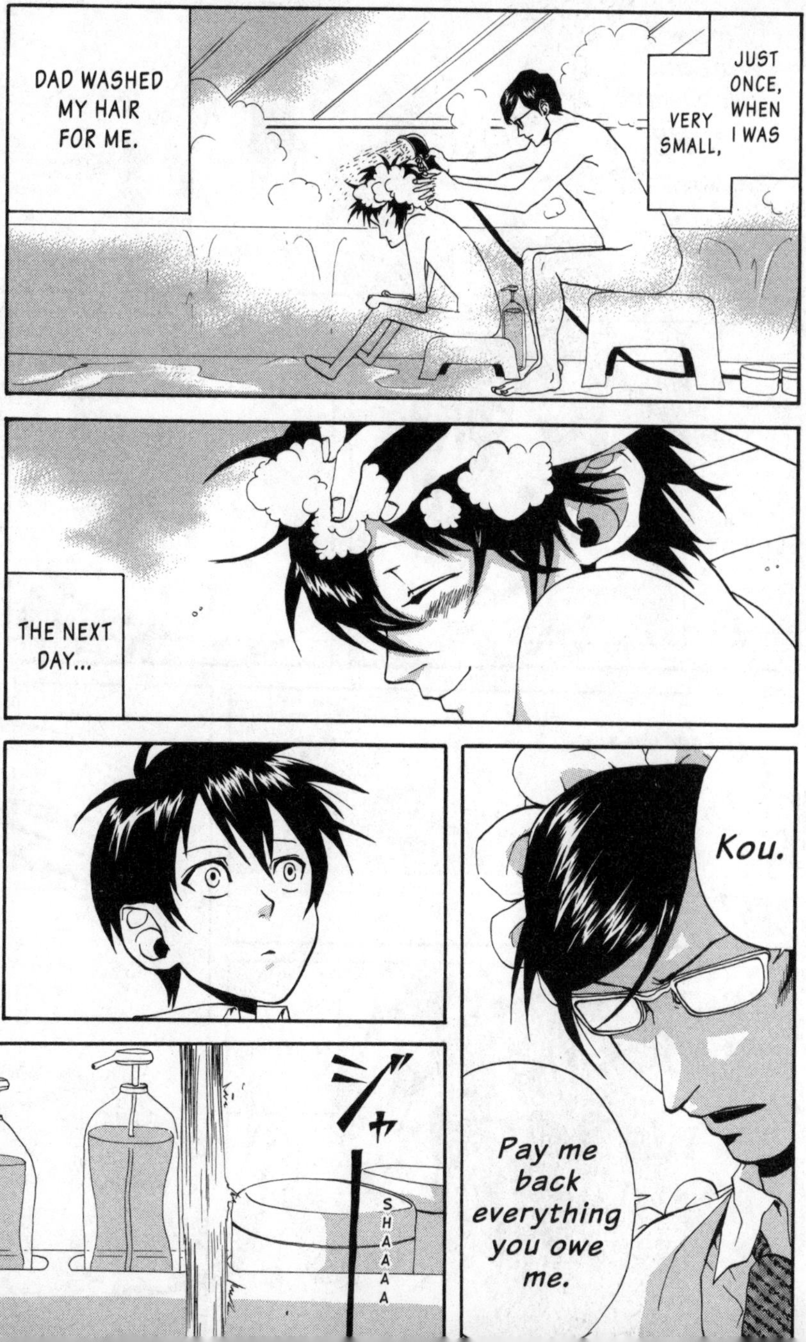

JUST ONCE, WHEN I WAS VERY SMALL,
DAD WASHED MY HAIR FOR ME.
THE NEXT DAY...
Kou.
Pay me back everything you owe me.
ジャ
SHAAAA

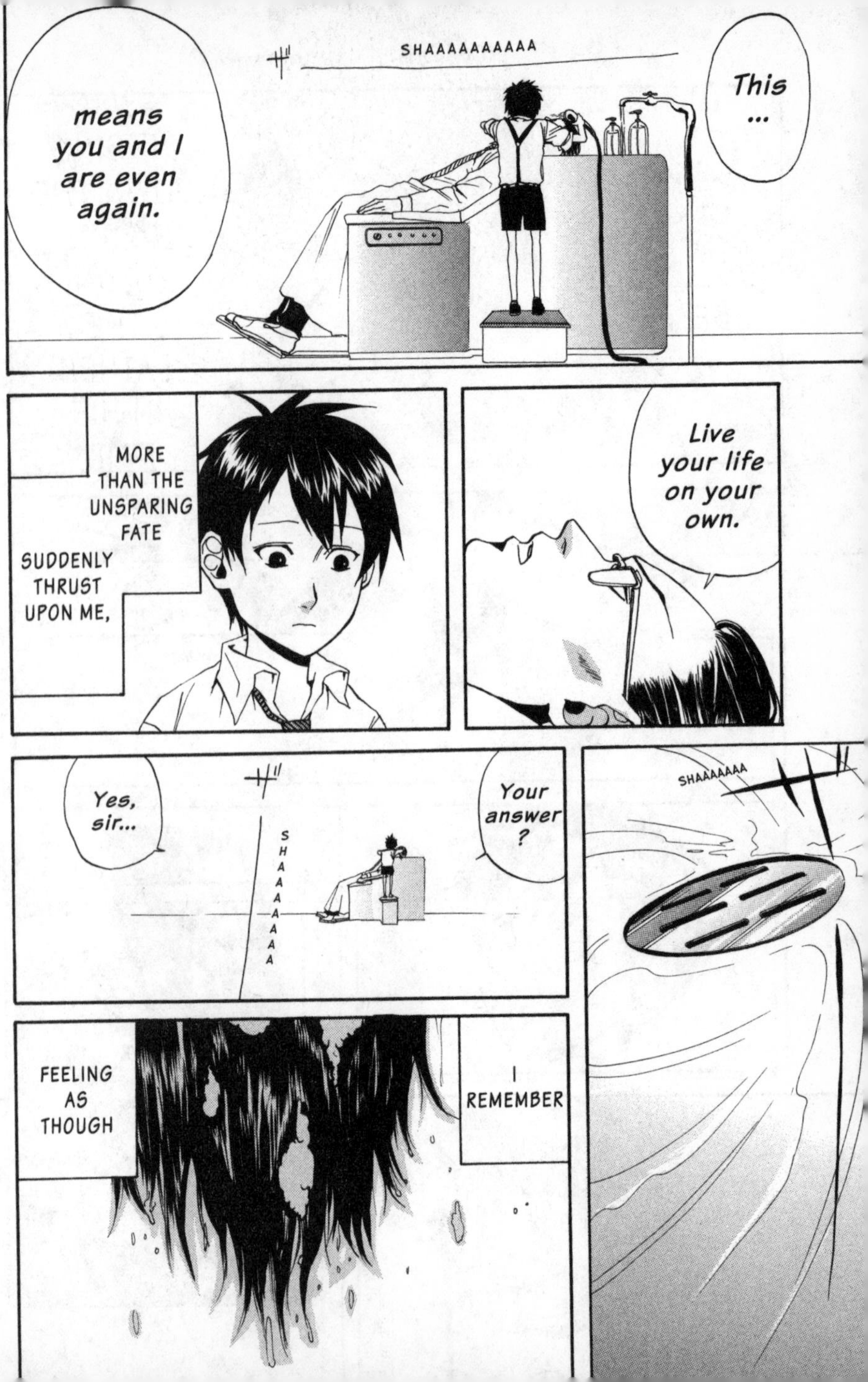
SHAAAAAAAAAA
This ...
means you and I are even again.
Live your life on your own.
MORE THAN THE UNSPARING FATE
SUDDENLY THRUST UPON ME,
SHAAAAAAA
Your answer?
SHAAAAAAAAAAA
Yes, sir...
I REMEMBER
FEELING AS THOUGH

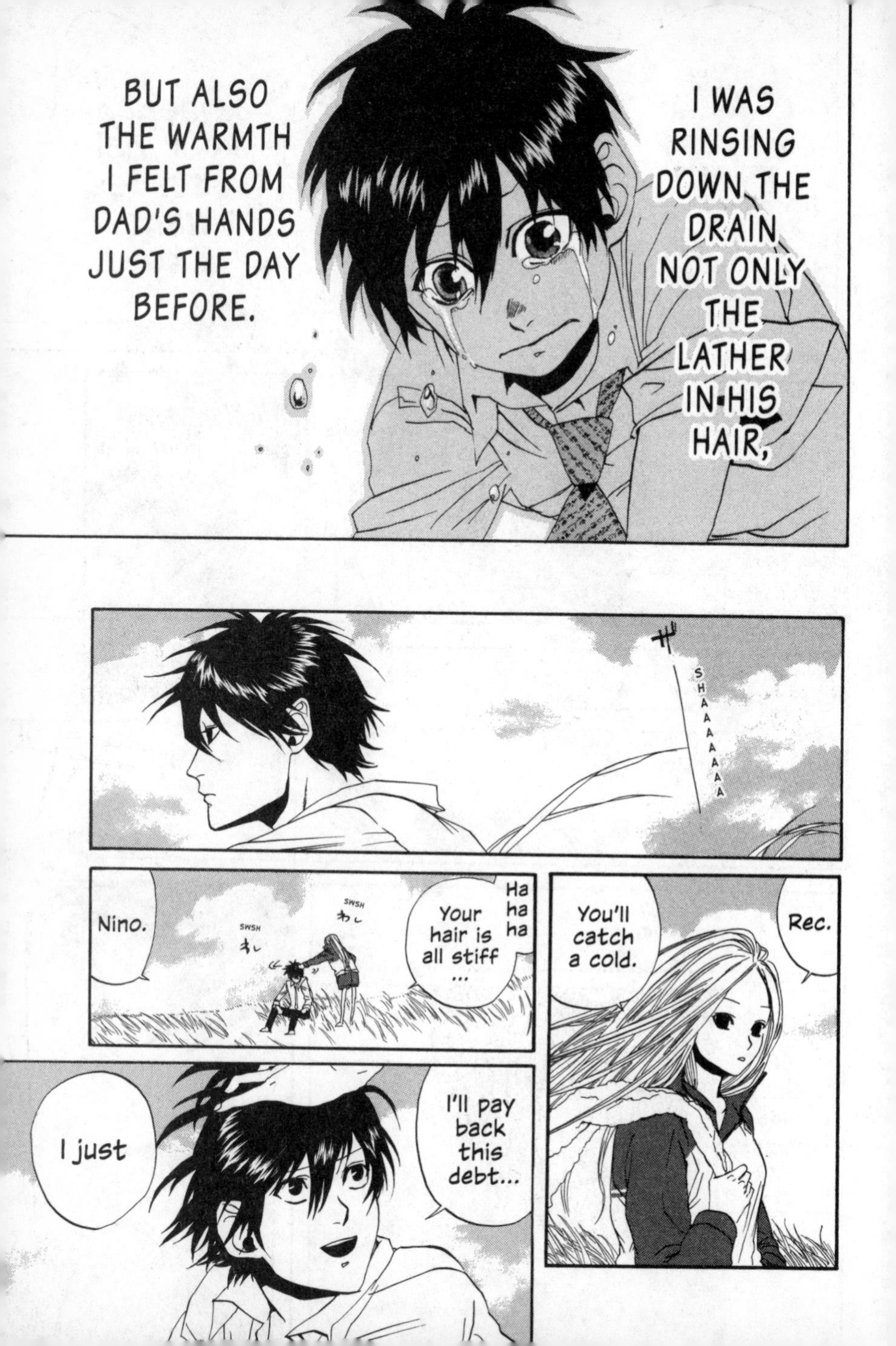
I WAS RINSING DOWN THE DRAIN NOT ONLY THE LATHER IN HIS HAIR,
BUT ALSO THE WARMTH I FELT FROM DAD'S HANDS JUST THE DAY BEFORE.
SHAAAAAAAA
Rec.
You'll catch a cold.
Ha ha ha
Your hair is all stiff ...
SWSH
SWSH
Nino.
I'll pay back this debt...
I just

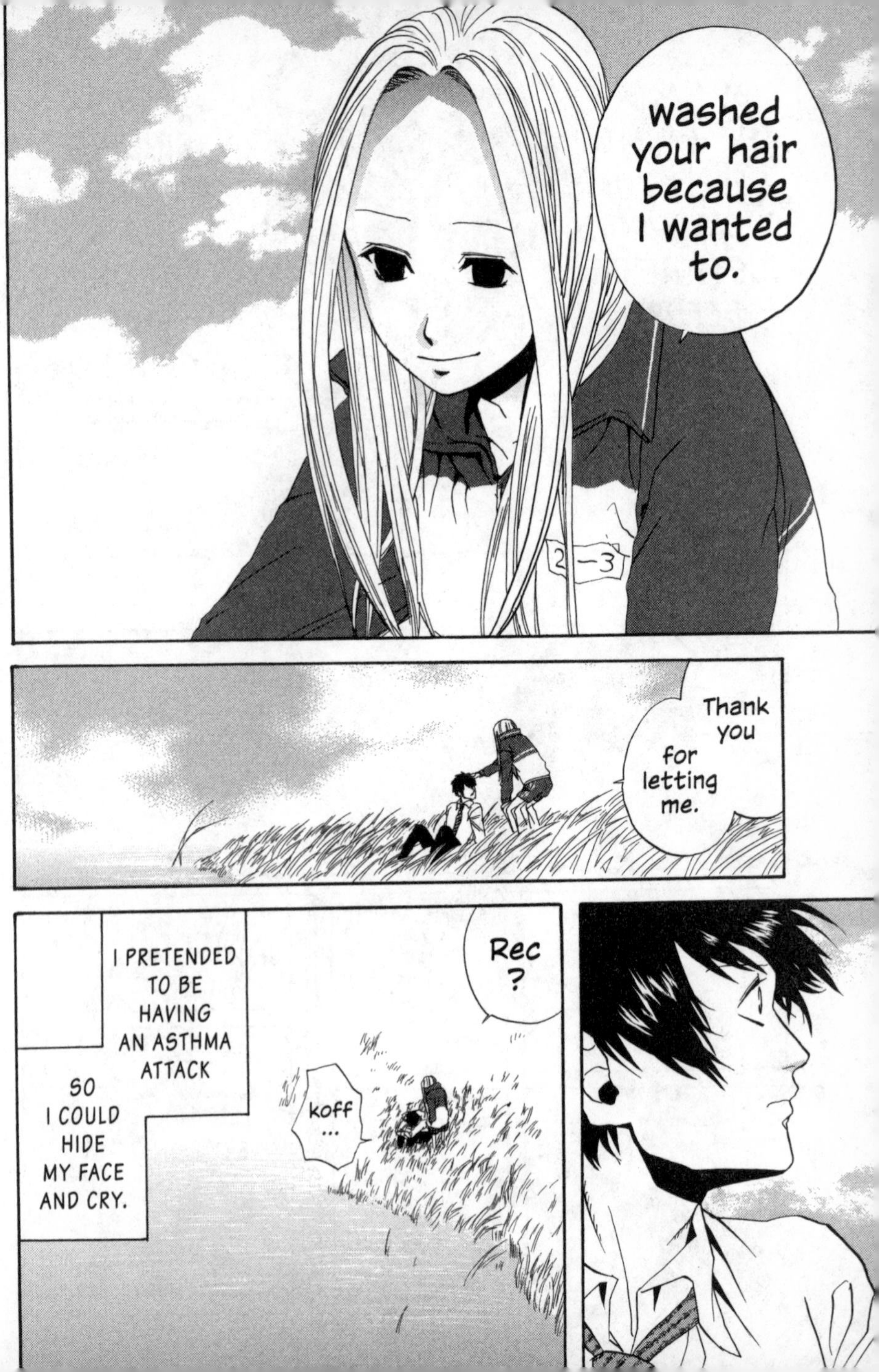
washed your hair because I wanted to.
2-3
Thank you for letting me.
Rec ?
I PRETENDED TO BE HAVING AN ASTHMA ATTACK
SO I COULD HIDE MY FACE AND CRY.
koff ...

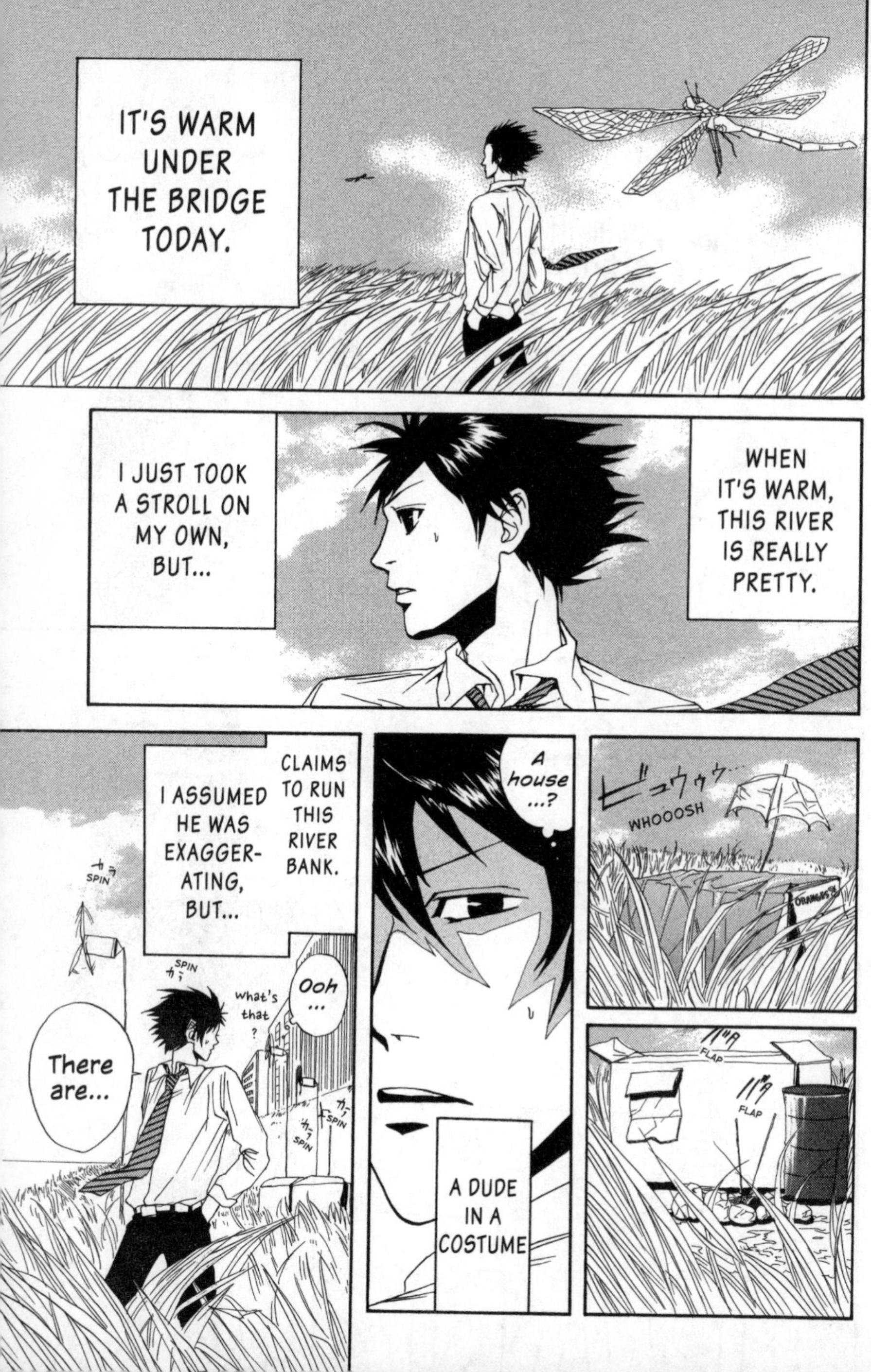

IT'S WARM UNDER THE BRIDGE TODAY.
WHEN IT'S WARM, THIS RIVER IS REALLY PRETTY.
I JUST TOOK A STROLL ON MY OWN, BUT...
WHOOOSH
FLAP
FLAP
A house ...?
A DUDE IN A COSTUME
CLAIMS TO RUN THIS RIVER BANK.
I ASSUMED HE WAS EXAGGER-ATING, BUT...
SPIN
SPIN
Ooh ...
what's that ?
SPIN
SPIN
There are...

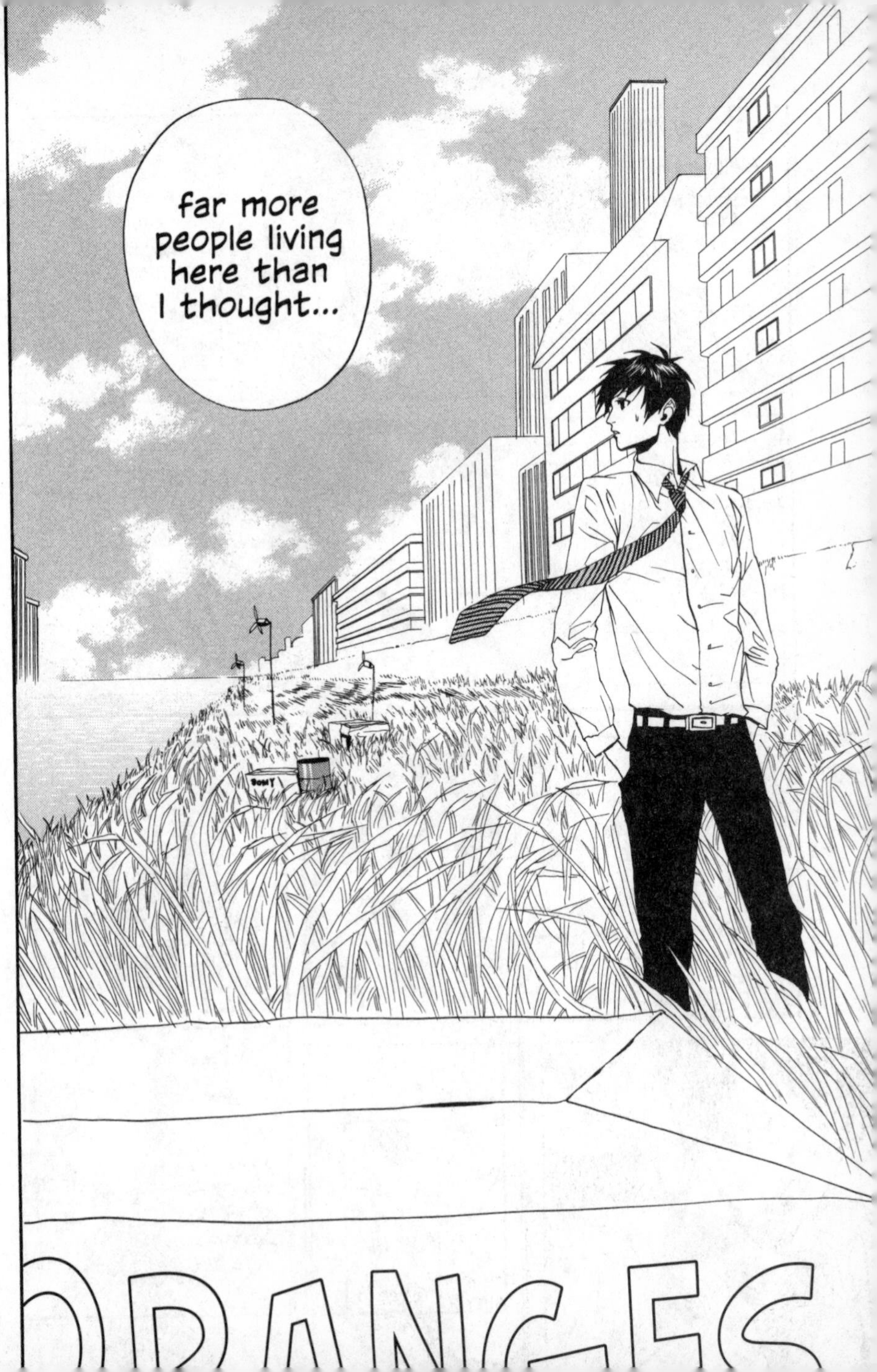
far more people living here than I thought...
ORANGES

☜ Chapter 15: Welcome Party

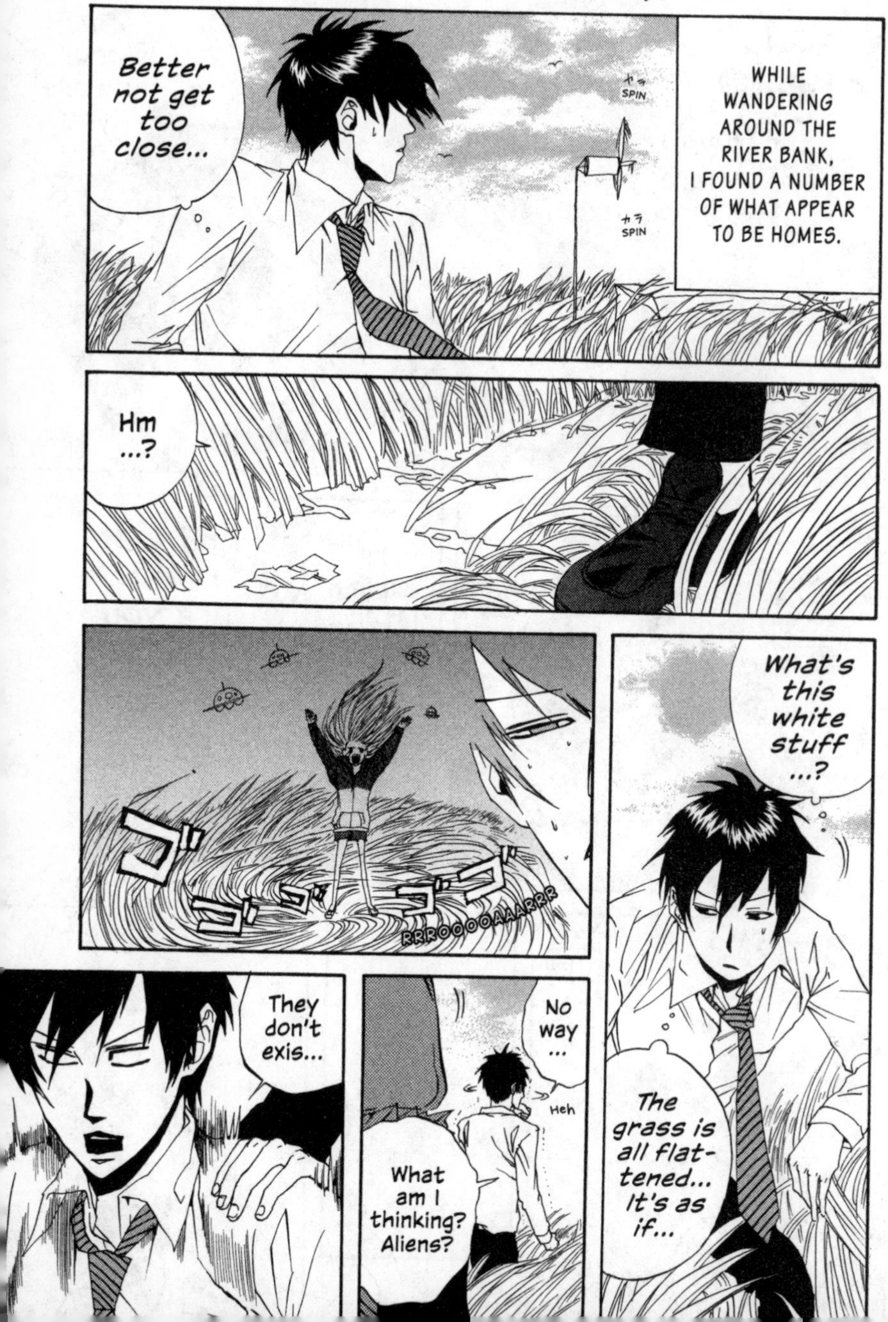
WHILE WANDERING AROUND THE RIVER BANK, I FOUND A NUMBER OF WHAT APPEAR TO BE HOMES.
SPIN
SPIN
Better not get too close...
Hm ...?
What's this white stuff ...?
The grass is all flattened... It's as if...
RRROOOOOAAARRR
No way ...
Heh
What am I thinking? Aliens?
They don't exis...

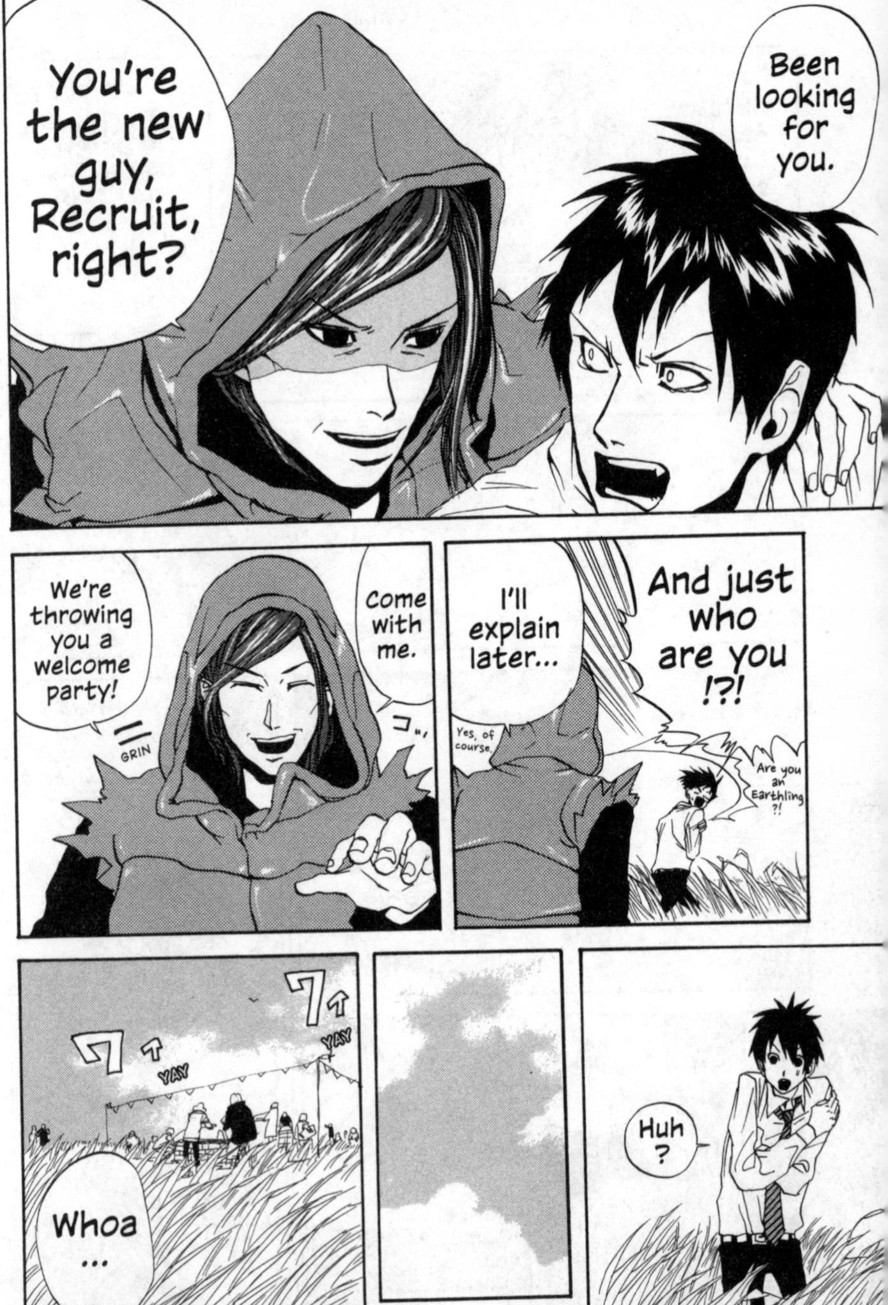
Been looking for you.
You're the new guy, Recruit, right?
And just who are you !?!
Are you an Earthling ?!
I'll explain later...
Yes, of course.
Come with me.
We're throwing you a welcome party!
GRIN
Huh ?
YAY
YAY
Whoa ...

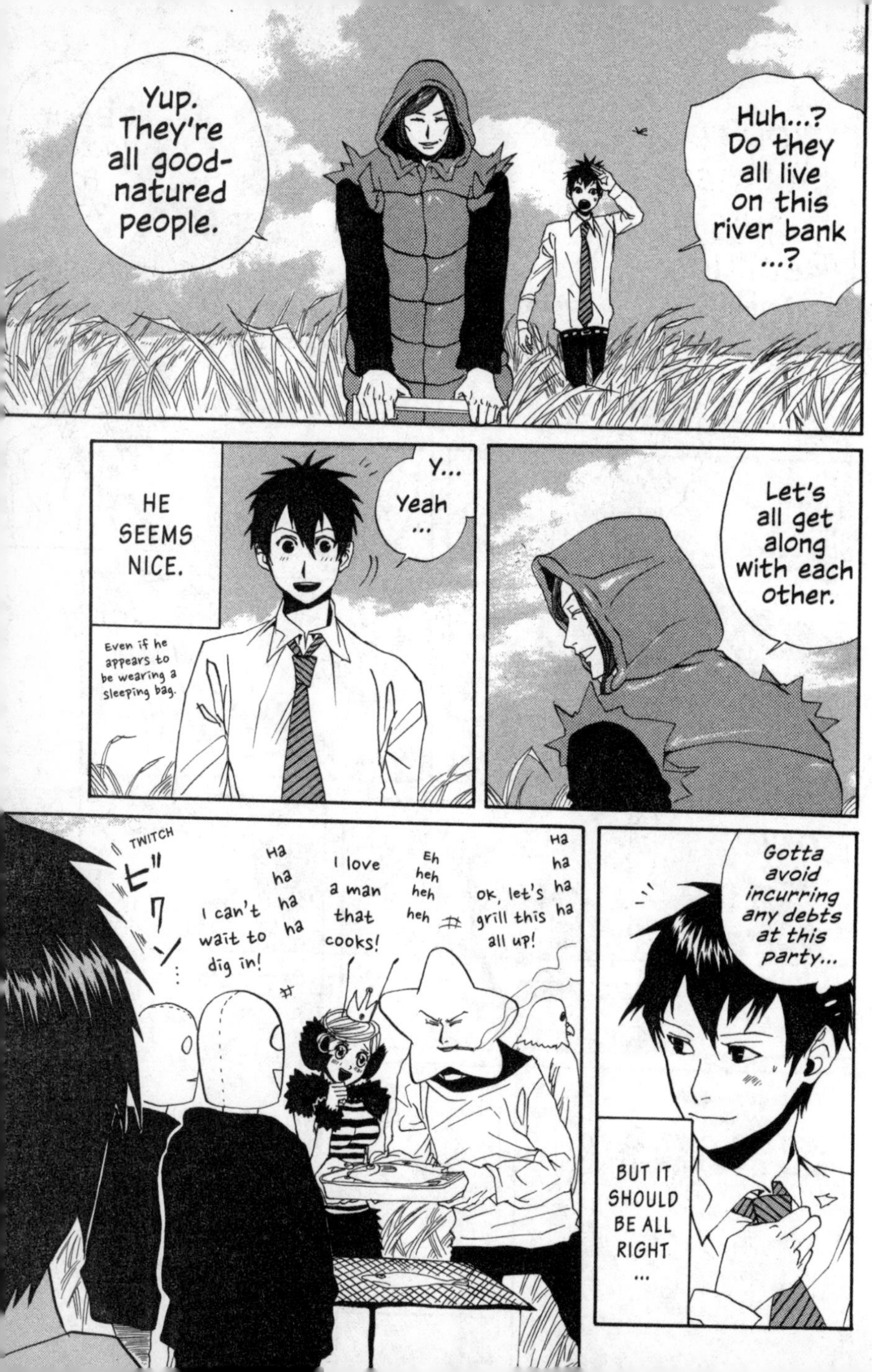
Huh...? Do they all live on this river bank ...?
Yup. They're all good-natured people.
Let's all get along with each other.
Y... Yeah ...
HE SEEMS NICE.
Even if he appears to be wearing a sleeping bag.
Gotta avoid incurring any debts at this party...
BUT IT SHOULD BE ALL RIGHT ...
Ha ha ha ha
OK, let's grill this all up!
Eh heh heh heh
I love a man that cooks!
Ha ha ha ha
I can't wait to dig in!
TWITCH
ビクッ

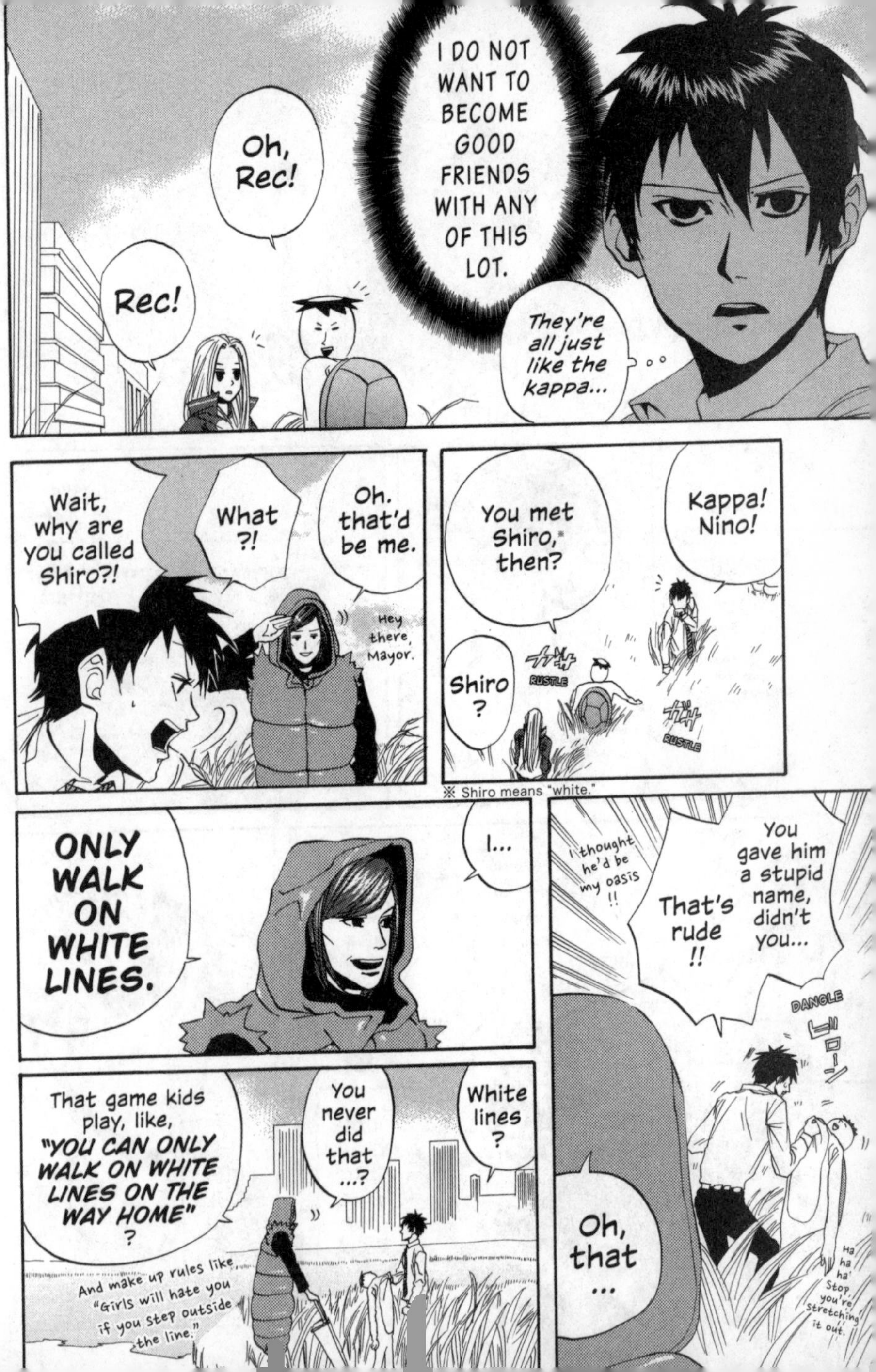
I DO NOT WANT TO BECOME GOOD FRIENDS WITH ANY OF THIS LOT.
They're all just like the kappa...
Oh, Rec!
Rec!
Kappa! Nino!
You met Shiro,* then?
RUSTLE
Shiro?
RUSTLE
Oh. that'd be me.
Hey there, Mayor.
What?!
Wait, why are you called Shiro?!
You gave him a stupid name, didn't you...
That's rude!!
I thought he'd be my oasis!!
DANGLE
Oh, that...
Ha ha ha' Stop, you're stretching it out.
I...
ONLY WALK ON WHITE LINES.
White lines?
You never did that...?
That game kids play, like, "YOU CAN ONLY WALK ON WHITE LINES ON THE WAY HOME"?
And make up rules like "Girls will hate you if you step outside the line."
※ Shiro means "white."

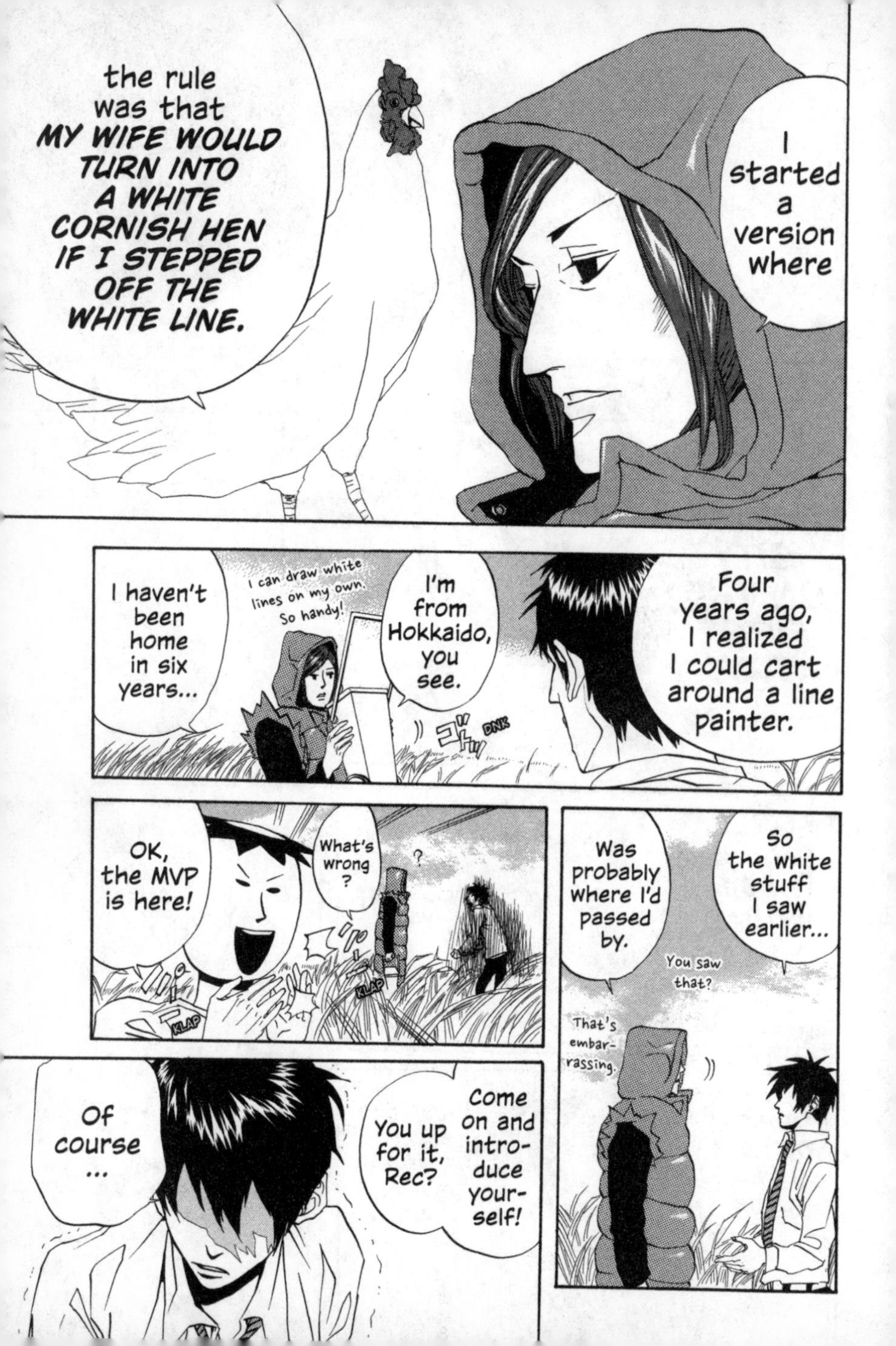
I started a version where
the rule was that MY WIFE WOULD TURN INTO A WHITE CORNISH HEN IF I STEPPED OFF THE WHITE LINE.
Four years ago, I realized I could cart around a line painter.
I'm from Hokkaido, you see.
DNK
I can draw white lines on my own. So handy!
I haven't been home in six years...
So the white stuff I saw earlier...
Was probably where I'd passed by.
You saw that?
That's embar-rassing.
What's wrong?
OK, the MVP is here!
KLAP
KLAP
Come on and intro-duce your-self!
You up for it, Rec?
Of course...

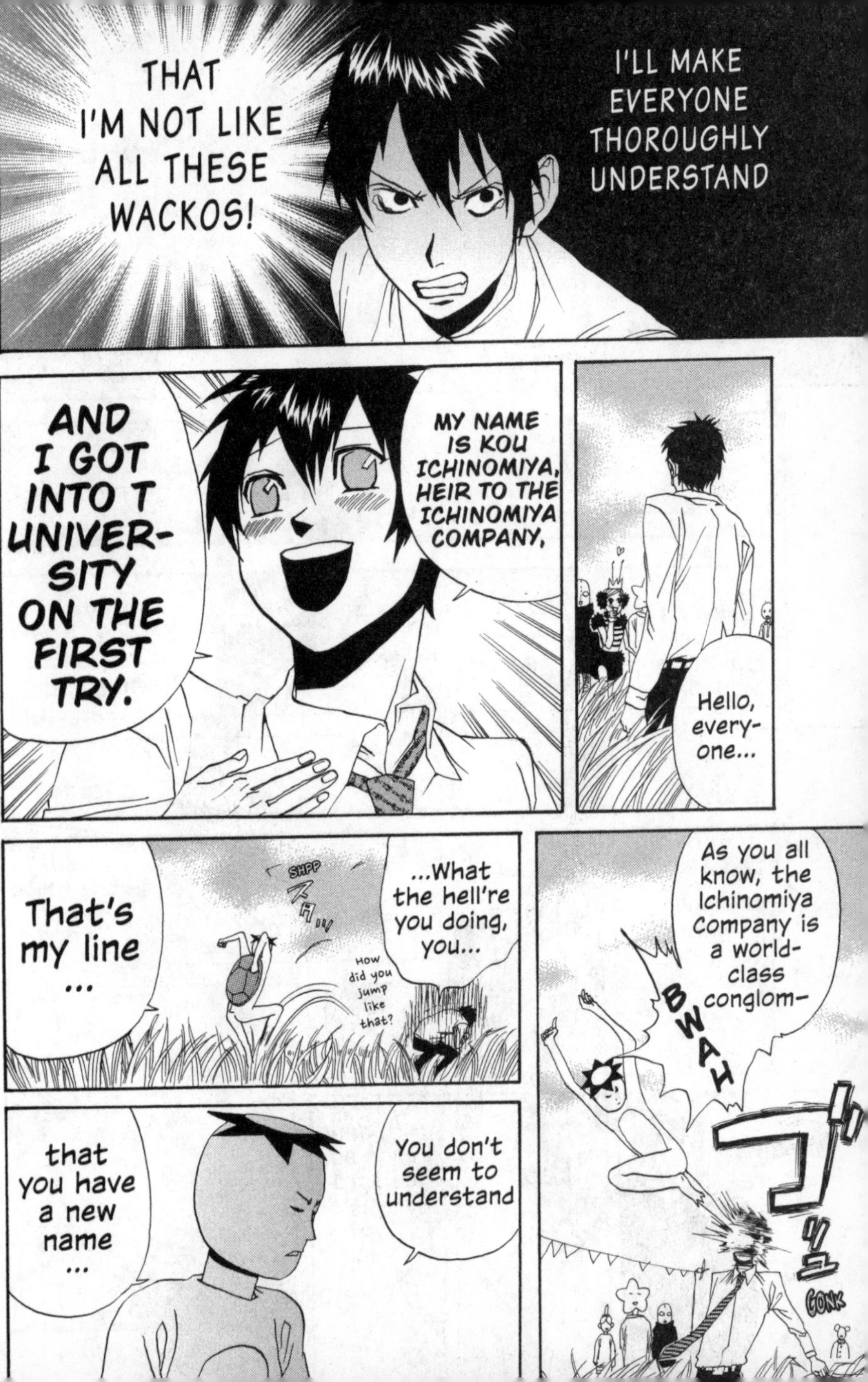
I'LL MAKE EVERYONE THOROUGHLY UNDERSTAND
THAT I'M NOT LIKE ALL THESE WACKOS!
Hello, everyone...
MY NAME IS KOU ICHINOMIYA, HEIR TO THE ICHINOMIYA COMPANY,
AND I GOT INTO T UNIVERSITY ON THE FIRST TRY.
As you all know, the Ichinomiya Company is a world-class conglom-
BWAH
GONK
SHPP
...What the hell're you doing, you...
How did you jump like that?
That's my line ...
You don't seem to understand
that you have a new name ...

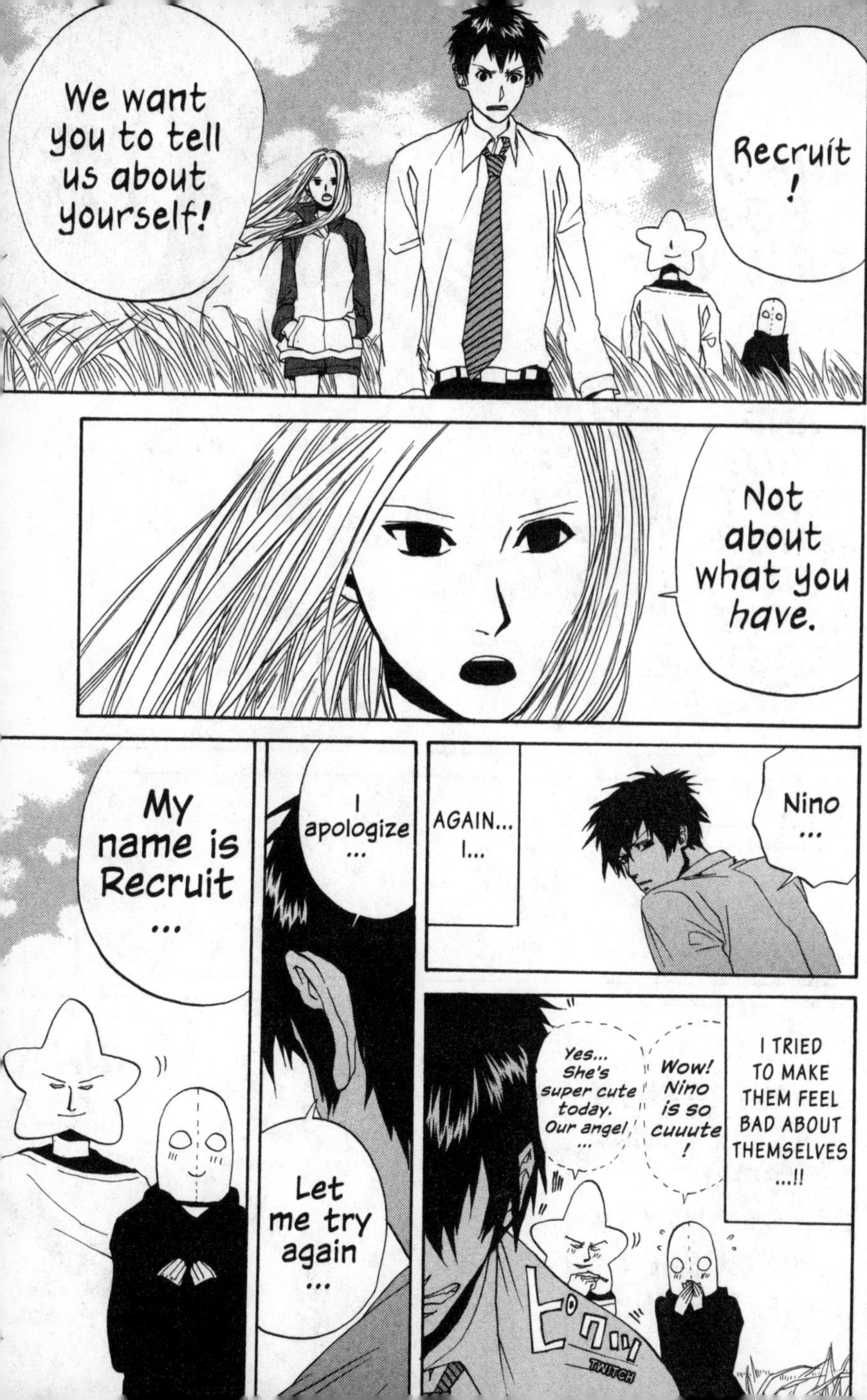

Recruit !
We want you to tell us about yourself!
Not about what you have.
Nino ...
AGAIN... I...
I TRIED TO MAKE THEM FEEL BAD ABOUT THEMSELVES ...!!
Wow! Nino is so cuuute !
Yes... She's super cute today. Our angel ...
ピクッ
TWITCH
I apologize ...
Let me try again ...
My name is Recruit ...

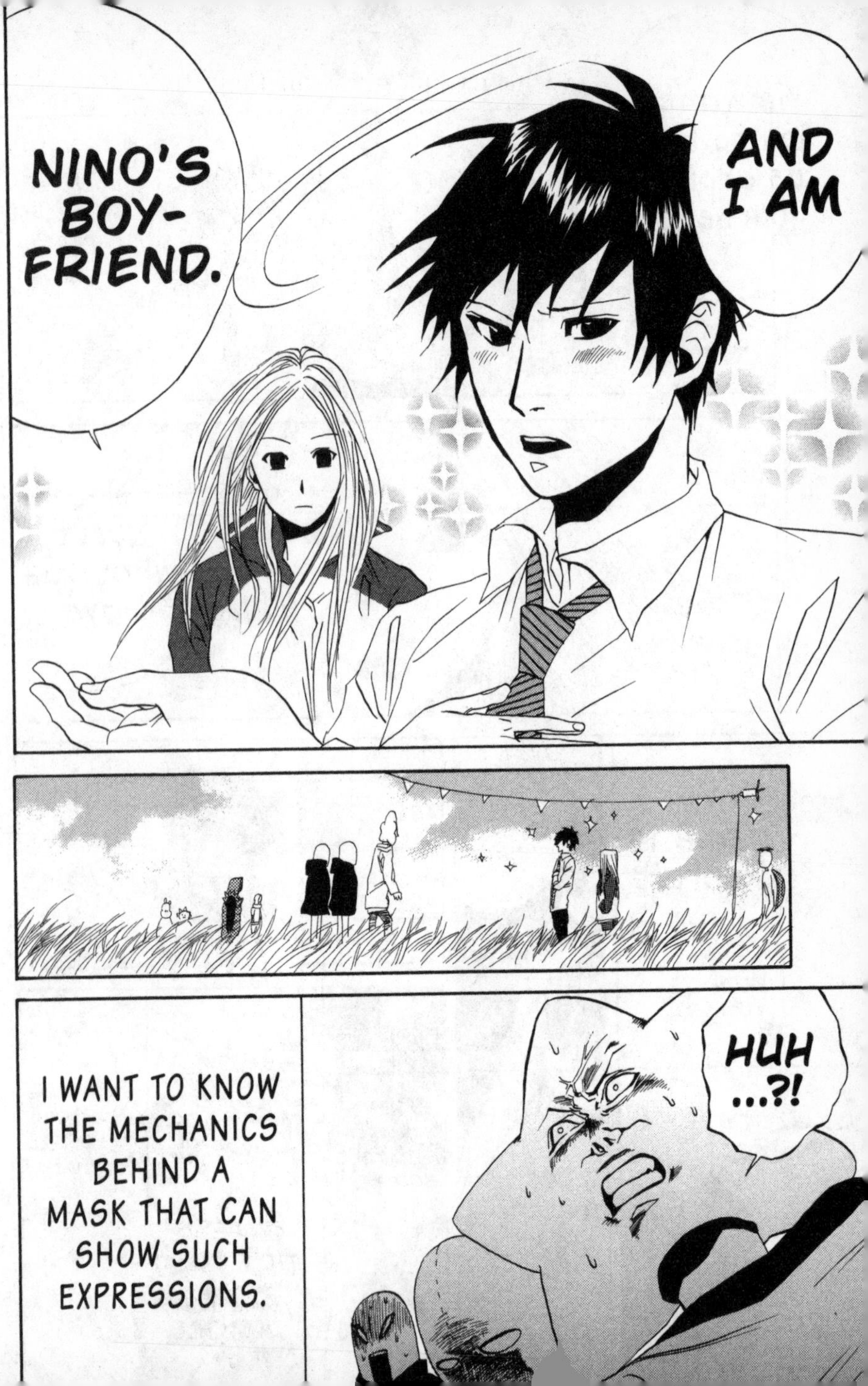
AND I AM
NINO'S BOY-FRIEND.
HUH ...?!
I WANT TO KNOW THE MECHANICS BEHIND A MASK THAT CAN SHOW SUCH EXPRESSIONS.

☜ Chapter 16: Transformation

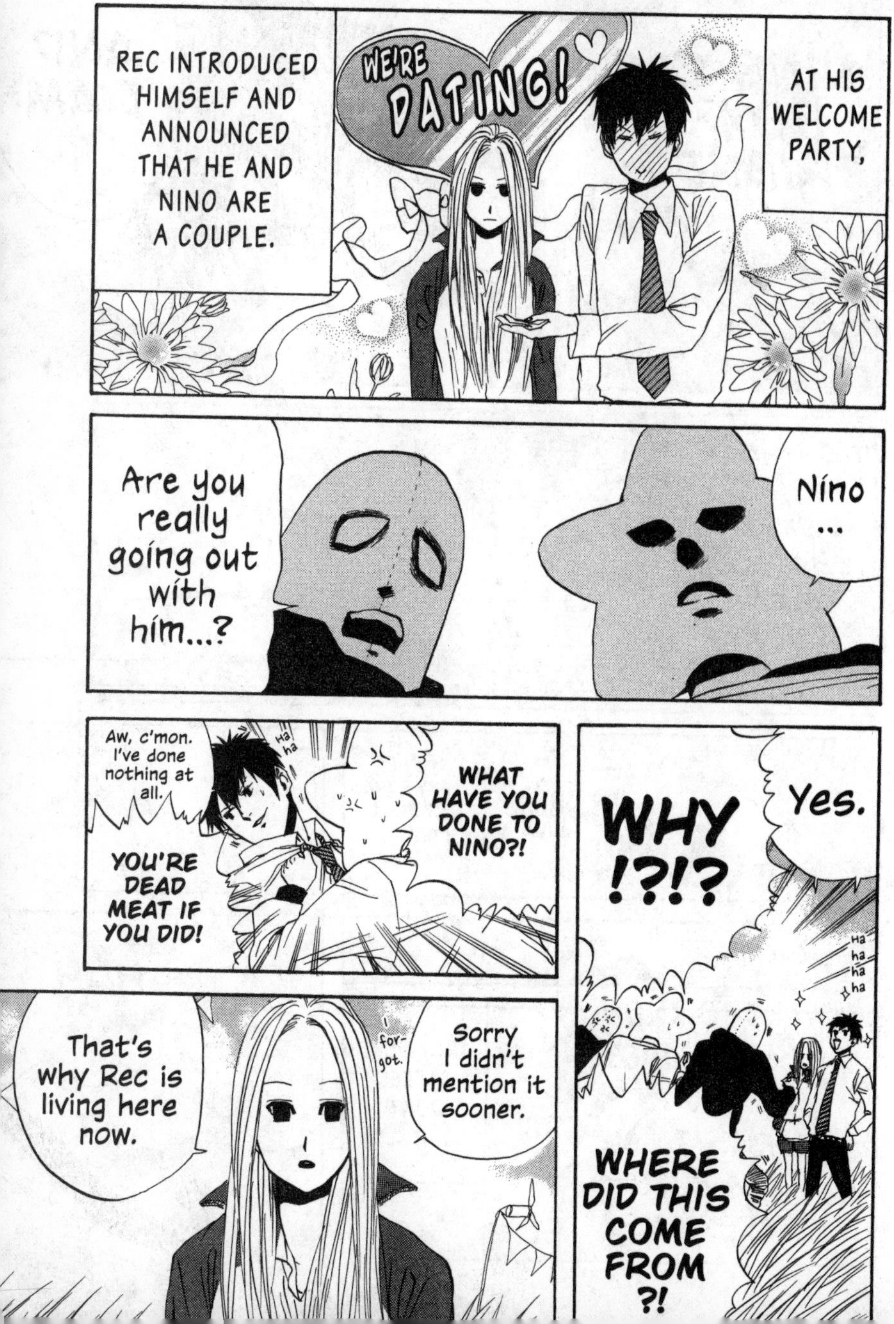
AT HIS WELCOME PARTY,
WE'RE DATING!
REC INTRODUCED HIMSELF AND ANNOUNCED THAT HE AND NINO ARE A COUPLE.
Nino ...
Are you really going out with him...?
Yes.
WHY !?!?
Ha ha ha ha
WHERE DID THIS COME FROM ?!
WHAT HAVE YOU DONE TO NINO?!
YOU'RE DEAD MEAT IF YOU DID!
Aw, c'mon. I've done nothing at all.
Ha ha
Sorry I didn't mention it sooner.
I for-got.
That's why Rec is living here now.

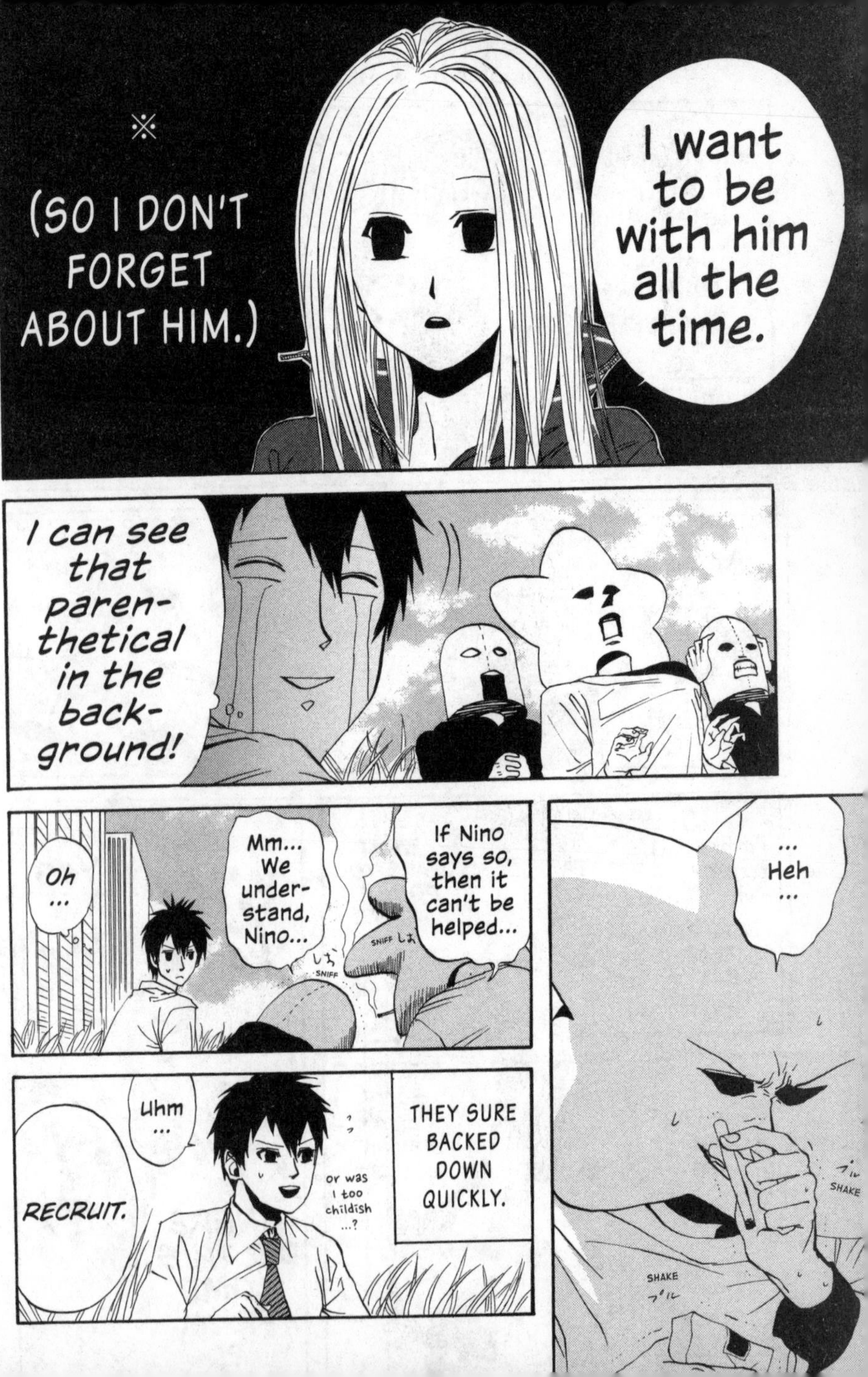
I want to be with him all the time.
※
(SO I DON'T FORGET ABOUT HIM.)
I can see that paren-thetical in the back-ground!
... Heh ...
SHAKE
SHAKE
If Nino says so, then it can't be helped...
SNIFF
Mm... We under-stand, Nino...
SNIFF
Oh ...
THEY SURE BACKED DOWN QUICKLY.
Or was I too childish ...?
Uhm ...
RECRUIT.

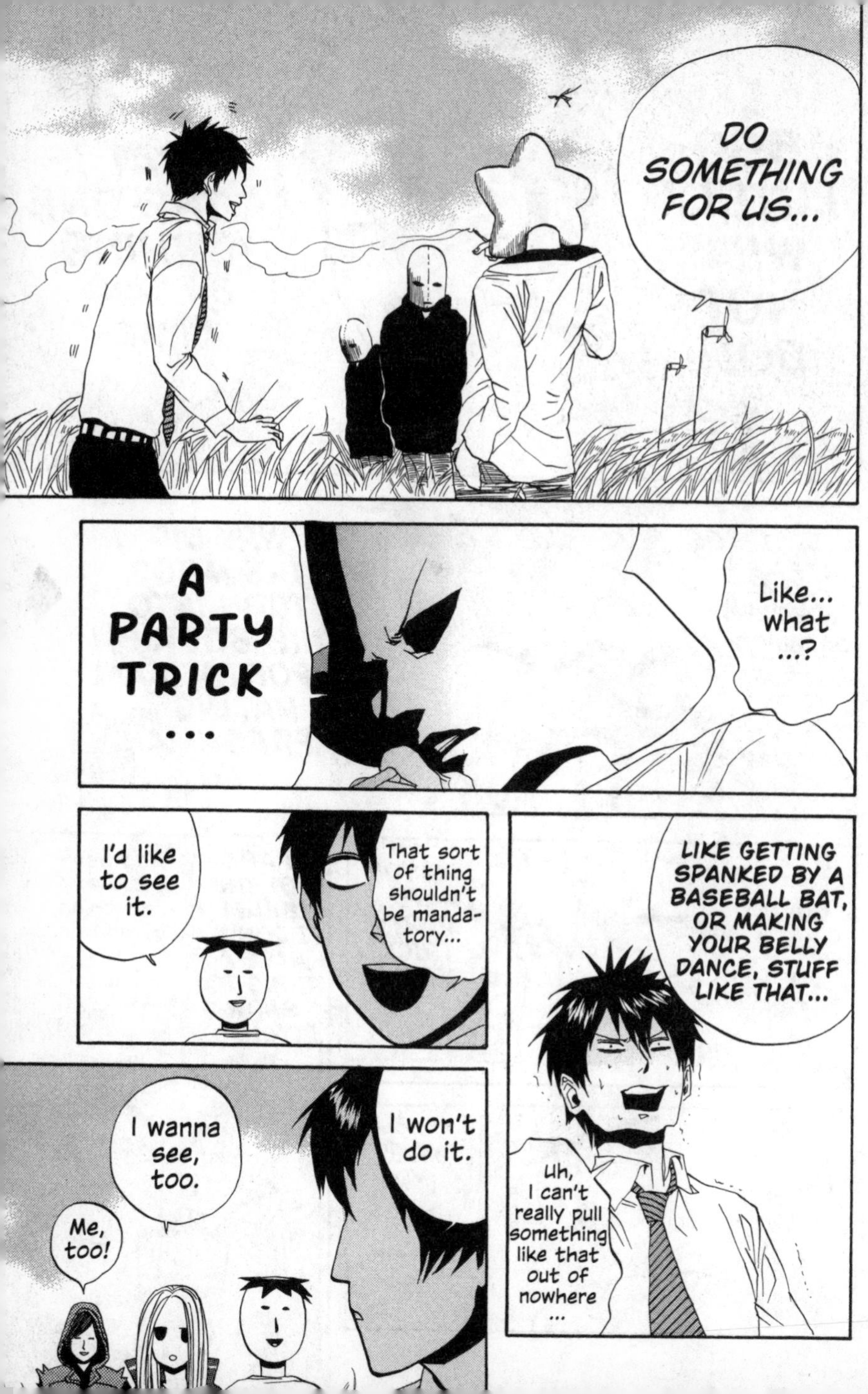
DO SOMETHING FOR US...
Like... what ...?
A PARTY TRICK ...
LIKE GETTING SPANKED BY A BASEBALL BAT, OR MAKING YOUR BELLY DANCE, STUFF LIKE THAT...
Uh, I can't really pull something like that out of nowhere ...
That sort of thing shouldn't be manda-tory...
I'd like to see it.
I won't do it.
I wanna see, too.
Me, too!

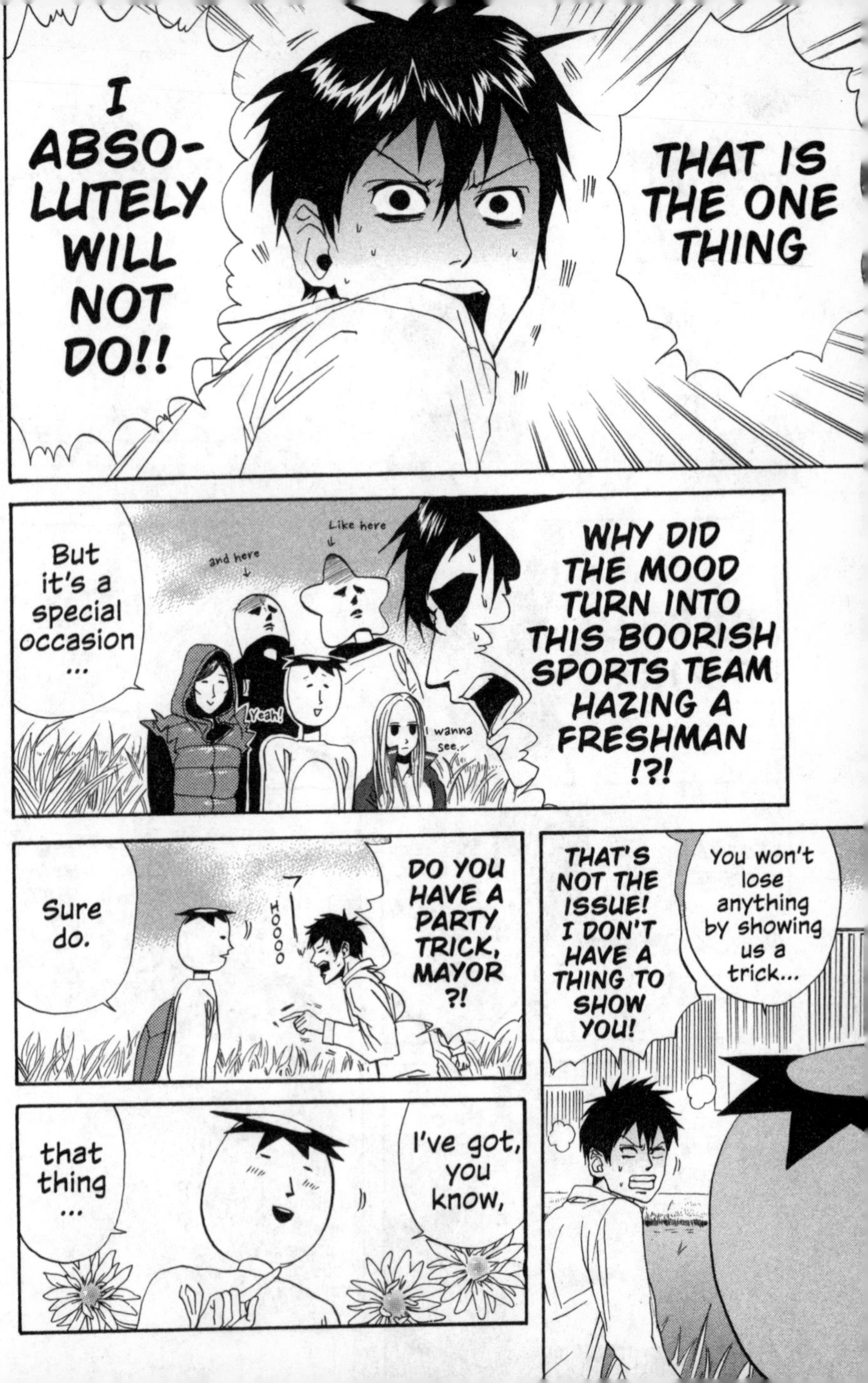
THAT IS THE ONE THING
I ABSO-LUTELY WILL NOT DO!!
WHY DID THE MOOD TURN INTO THIS BOORISH SPORTS TEAM HAZING A FRESHMAN !?!
Like here
and here
I wanna see.
Yeah!
But it's a special occasion ...
You won't lose anything by showing us a trick...
THAT'S NOT THE ISSUE! I DON'T HAVE A THING TO SHOW YOU!
DO YOU HAVE A PARTY TRICK, MAYOR ?!
HOOOO
Sure do.
I've got, you know,
that thing ...

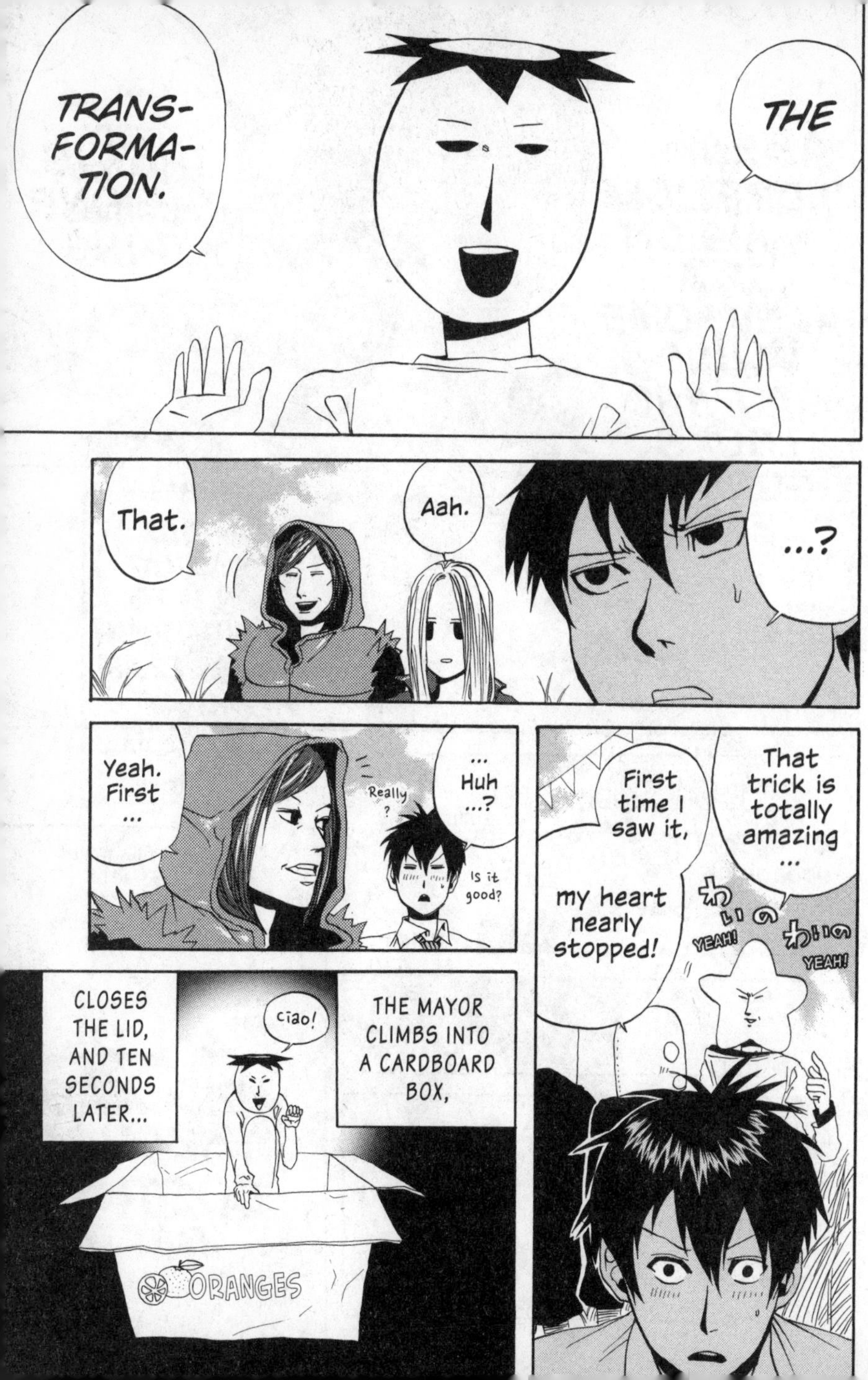

THE
TRANS-FORMA-TION.
...?
Aah.
That.
That trick is totally amazing ...
First time I saw it,
my heart nearly stopped!
わいのわいの
YEAH!
YEAH!
... Huh ...?
Really ?
Is it good?
Yeah. First ...
THE MAYOR CLIMBS INTO A CARDBOARD BOX,
ciao!
CLOSES THE LID, AND TEN SECONDS LATER...
ORANGES

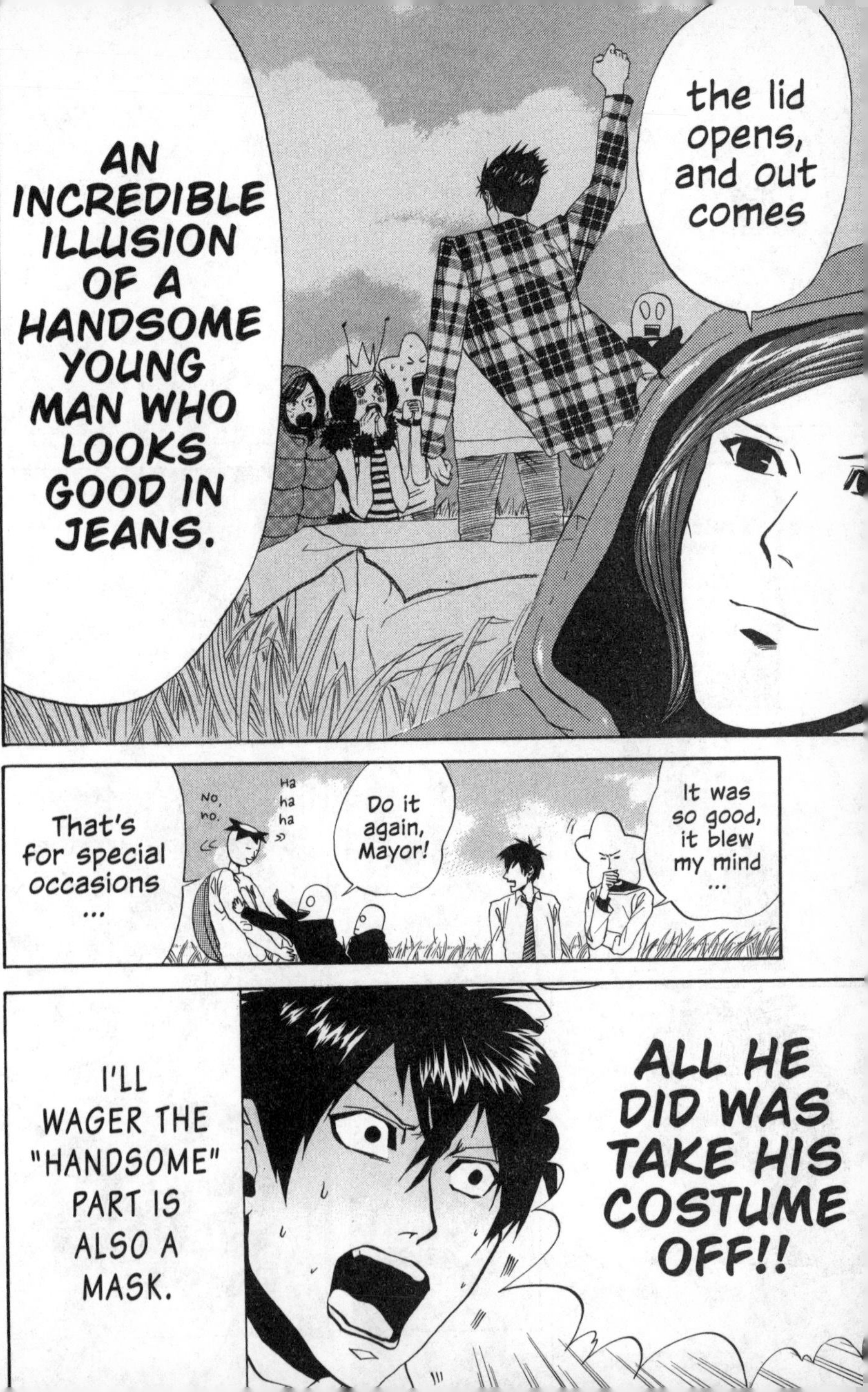
the lid opens, and out comes
AN INCREDIBLE ILLUSION OF A HANDSOME YOUNG MAN WHO LOOKS GOOD IN JEANS.
It was so good, it blew my mind ...
Do it again, Mayor!
Ha ha ha
No, no.
That's for special occasions ...
ALL HE DID WAS TAKE HIS COSTUME OFF!!
I'LL WAGER THE "HANDSOME" PART IS ALSO A MASK.

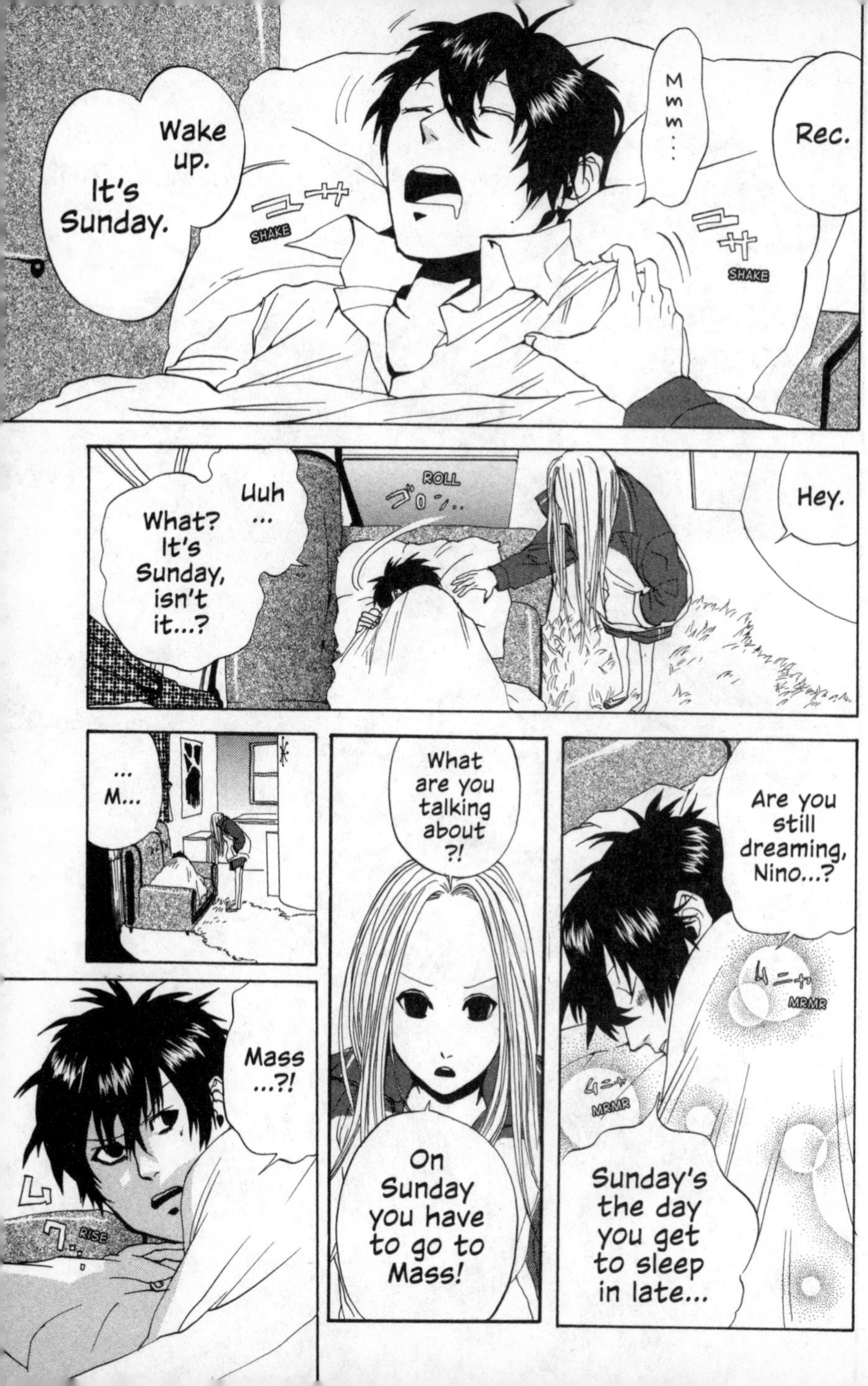
Rec.
Mmm...
SHAKE
SHAKE
Wake up. It's Sunday.
Hey.
ROLL
Uuh... What? It's Sunday, isn't it...?
Are you still dreaming, Nino...?
MRMR
MRMR
Sunday's the day you get to sleep in late...
What are you talking about?!
On Sunday you have to go to Mass!
... M...
Mass...?!
RISE

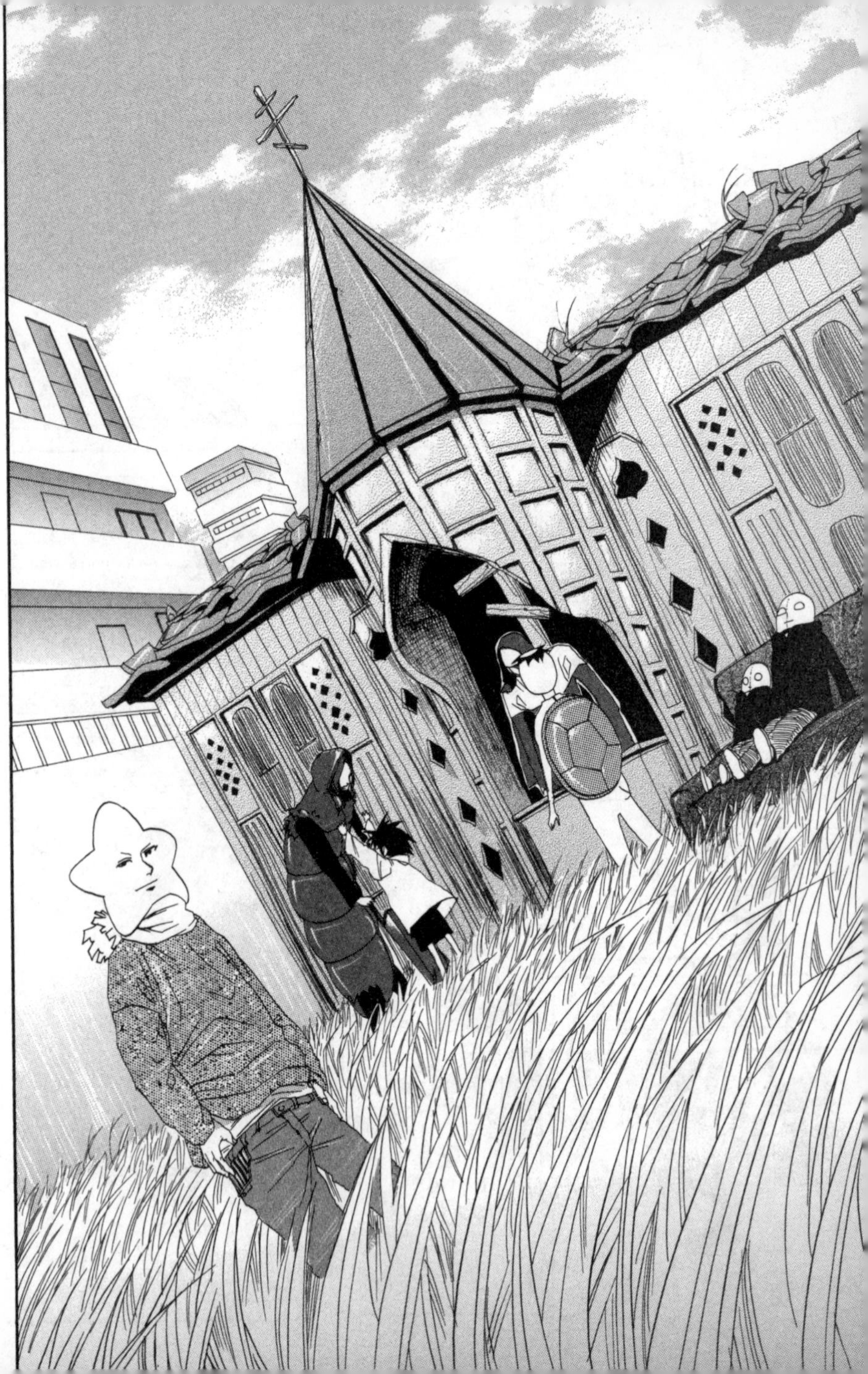

☜ Chapter 17: Battle Sister

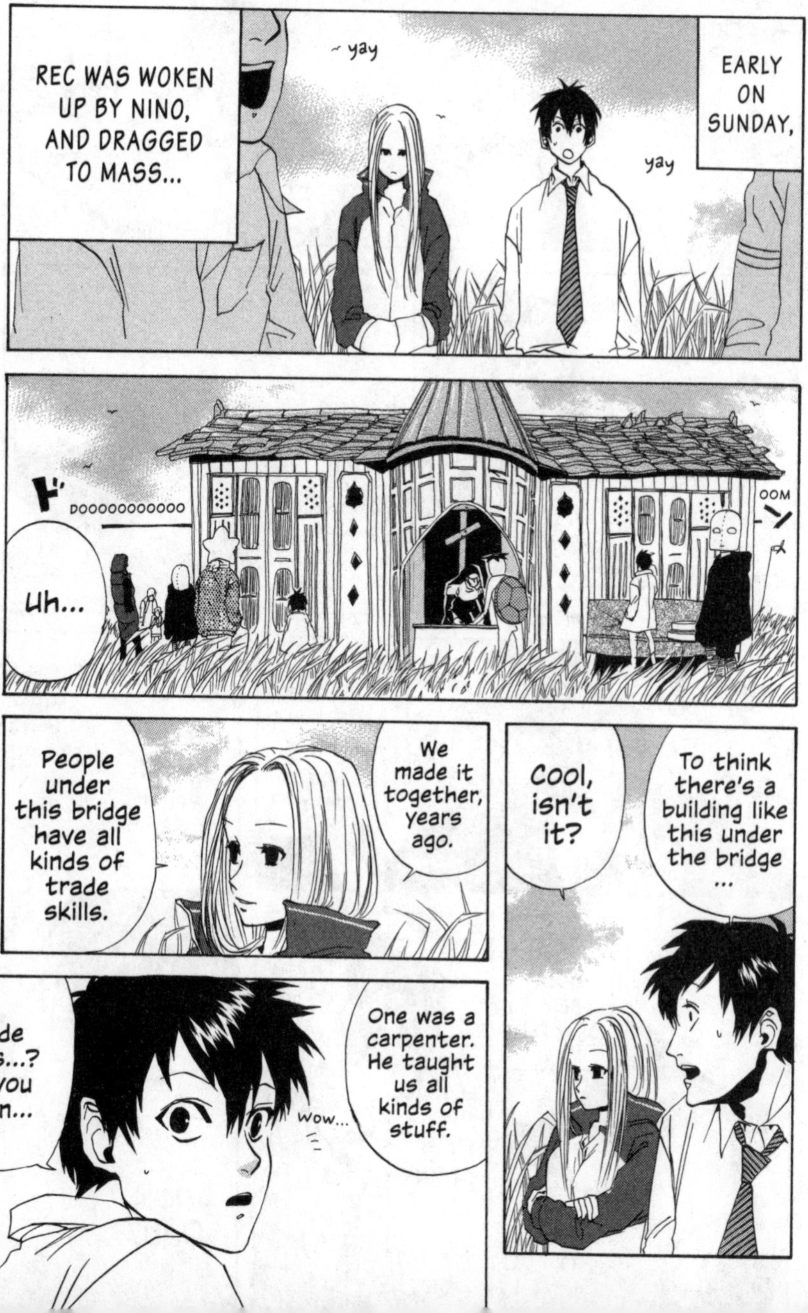
EARLY ON SUNDAY,
yay
~ yay
REC WAS WOKEN UP BY NINO, AND DRAGGED TO MASS...
ド
DOOOOOOOOOOO
OOM
ン
Uh...
To think there's a building like this under the bridge ...
Cool, isn't it?
We made it together, years ago.
People under this bridge have all kinds of trade skills.
One was a carpenter. He taught us all kinds of stuff.
wow...
Trade skills...? So you mean...

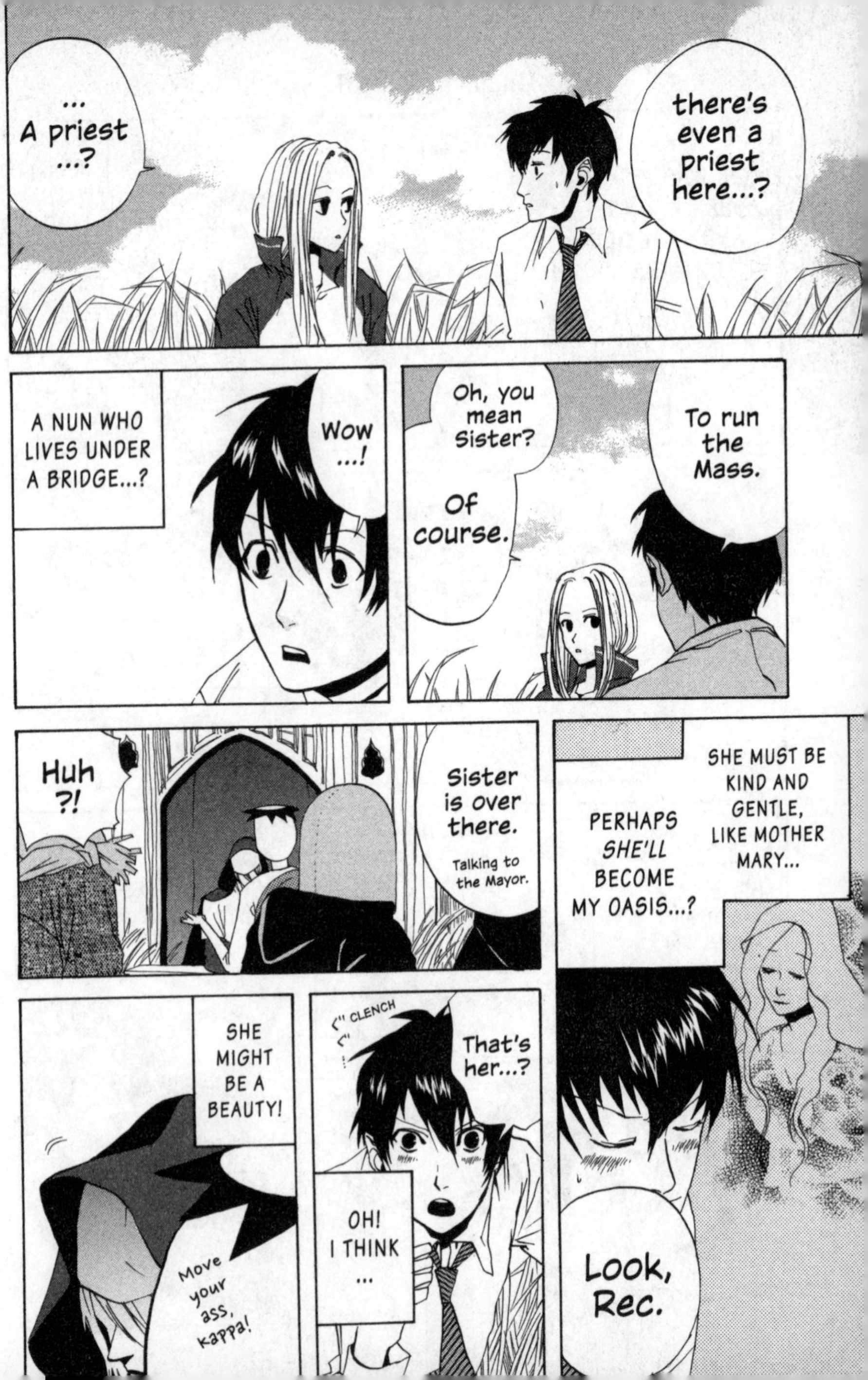
there's even a priest here...?
... A priest ...?
To run the Mass.
Oh, you mean Sister?
Of course.
Wow ...!
A NUN WHO LIVES UNDER A BRIDGE...?
SHE MUST BE KIND AND GENTLE, LIKE MOTHER MARY...
PERHAPS SHE'LL BECOME MY OASIS...?
Sister is over there.
Talking to the Mayor.
Huh ?!
Look, Rec.
CLENCH
That's her...?
OH! I THINK ...
SHE MIGHT BE A BEAUTY!
Move your ass, kappa!

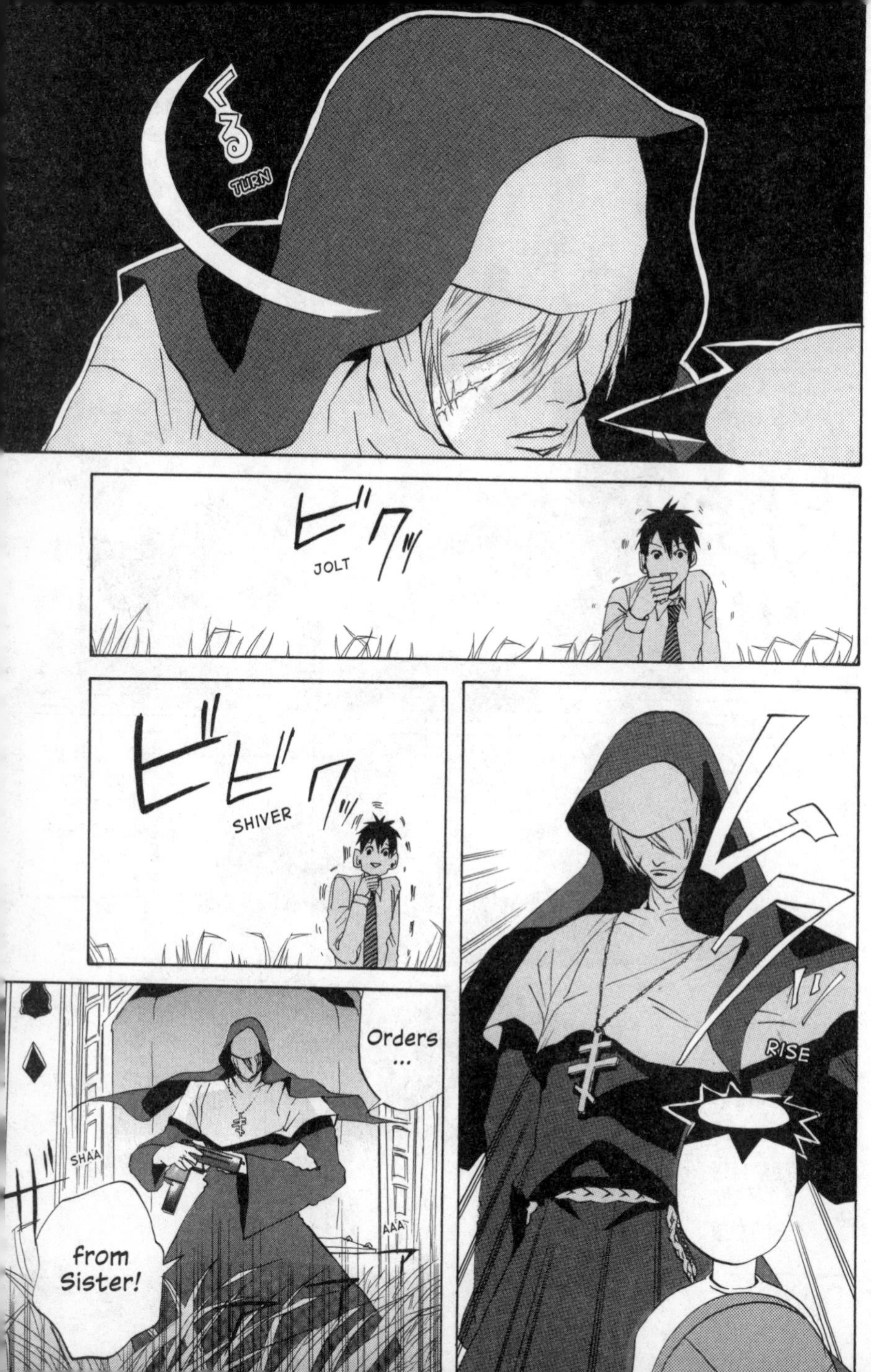

くる
TURN
ビクッ
JOLT
RISE
ビビクッ
SHIVER
Orders...
SHAA
AAA
from Sister!

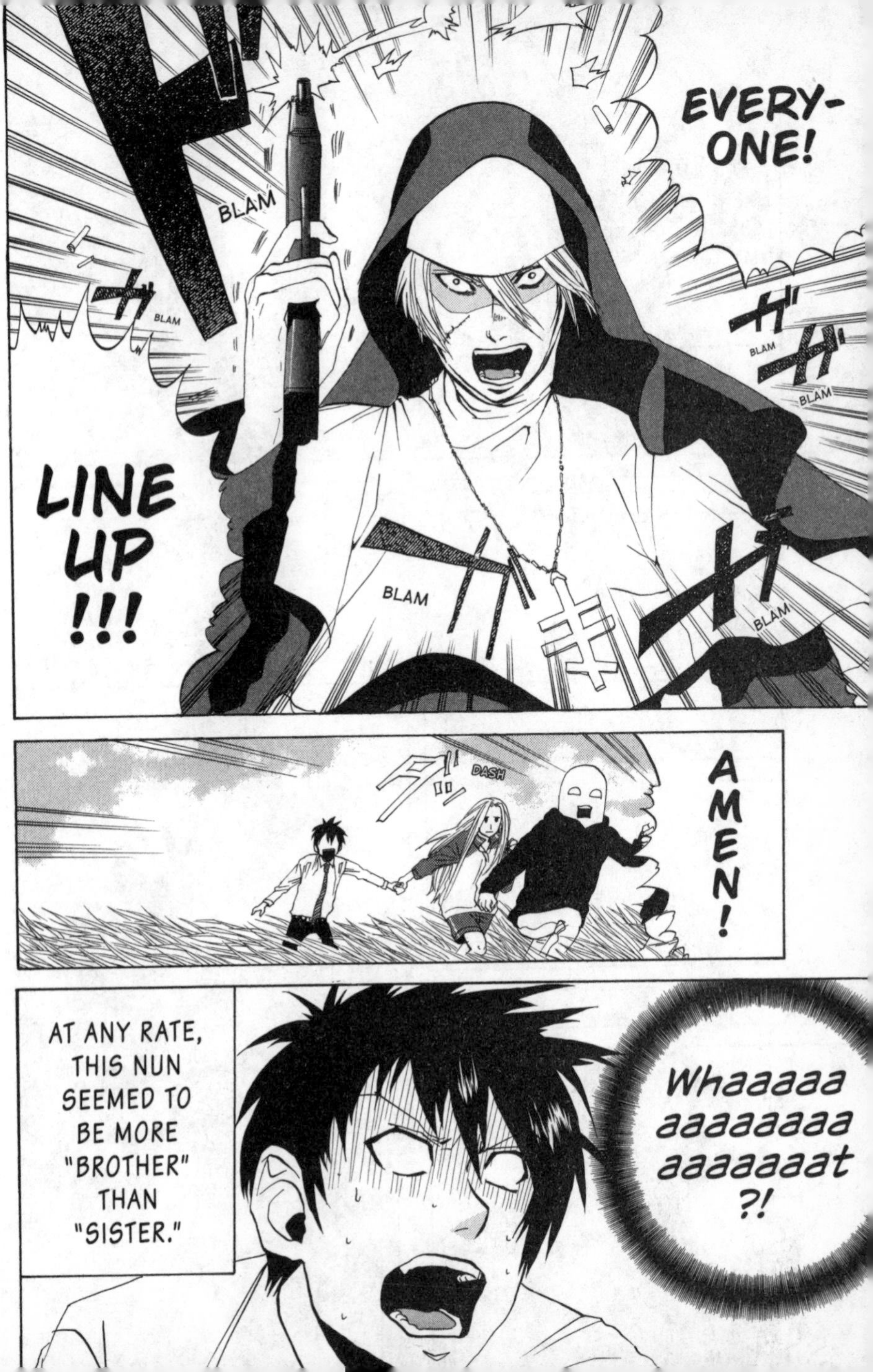
EVERY-ONE!
BLAM
BLAM
BLAM
BLAM
BLAM
BLAM
LINE UP!!!
AMEN!
DASH
Whaaaaaaaaaaaaaaaaaaaaaaat?!
AT ANY RATE, THIS NUN SEEMED TO BE MORE "BROTHER" THAN "SISTER."

Chapter 18: Mass

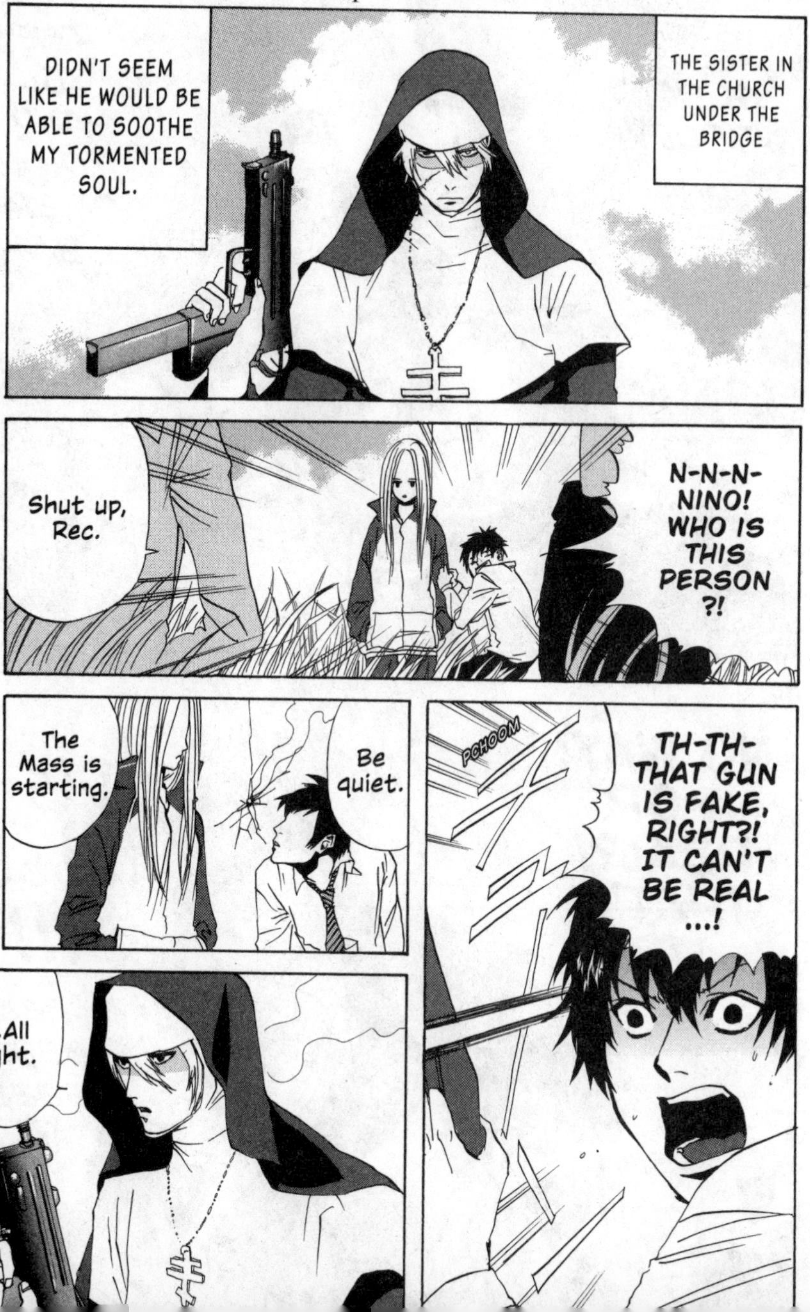

THE SISTER IN THE CHURCH UNDER THE BRIDGE
DIDN'T SEEM LIKE HE WOULD BE ABLE TO SOOTHE MY TORMENTED SOUL.
N-N-N-NINO! WHO IS THIS PERSON?!
Shut up, Rec.
TH-TH-THAT GUN IS FAKE, RIGHT?! IT CAN'T BE REAL ...!
PCHOOM
Be quiet.
The Mass is starting.
...All right.

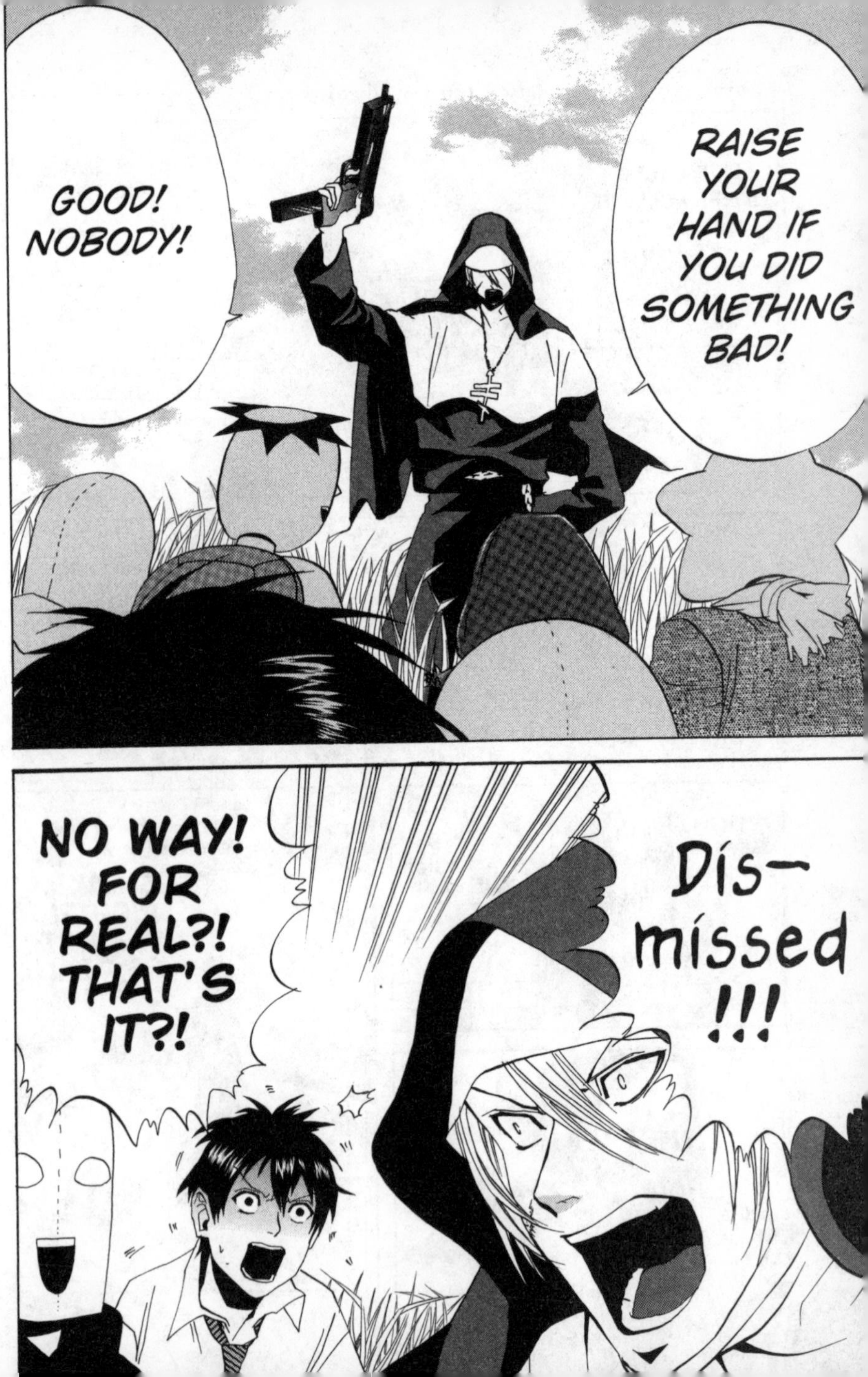
RAISE YOUR HAND IF YOU DID SOMETHING BAD!
GOOD! NOBODY!
Dis-missed!!!
NO WAY! FOR REAL?! THAT'S IT?!

Chapter 19: The Teachings of Jesus

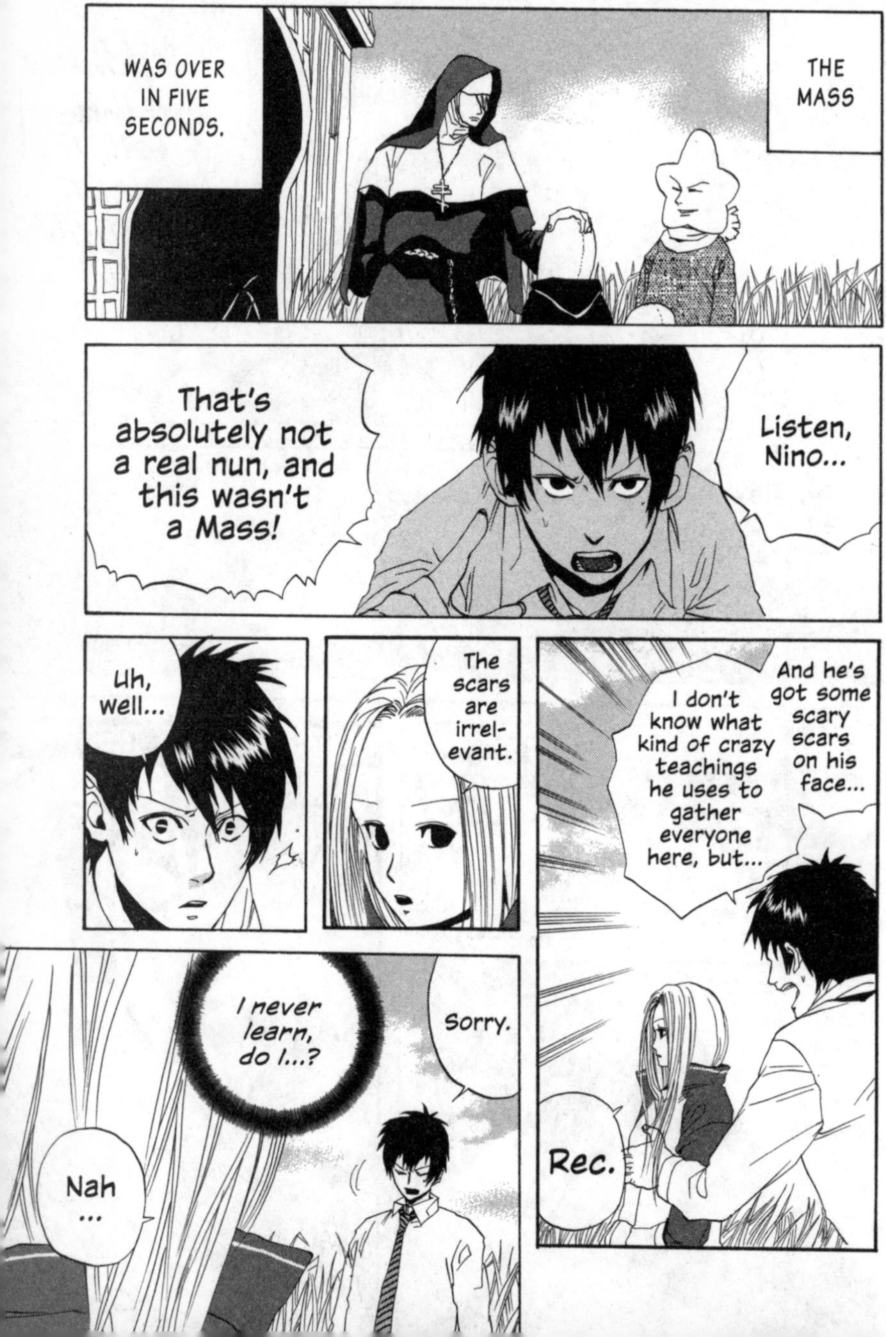
THE MASS
WAS OVER IN FIVE SECONDS.
Listen, Nino...
That's absolutely not a real nun, and this wasn't a Mass!
And he's got some scary scars on his face...
I don't know what kind of crazy teachings he uses to gather everyone here, but...
Rec.
The scars are irrel-evant.
Uh, well...
Sorry.
I never learn, do I...?
Nah ...

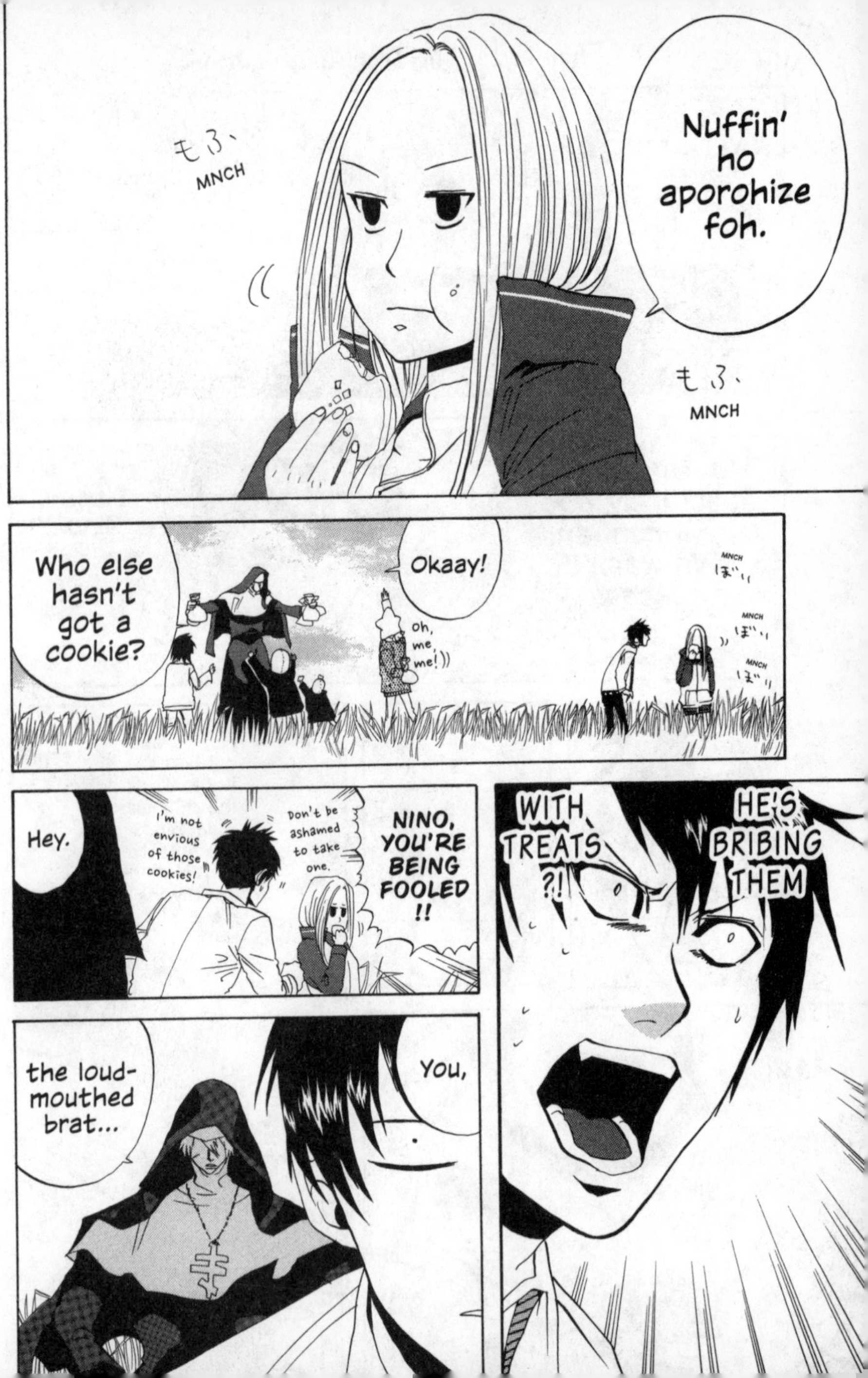
Nuffin' ho aporohize foh.
もふ、
MNCH
もふ、
MNCH
MNCH
MNCH
MNCH
Okaay!
oh, me me!
Who else hasn't got a cookie?
HE'S BRIBING THEM
WITH TREATS?!
NINO, YOU'RE BEING FOOLED!!
Don't be ashamed to take one.
I'm not envious of those cookies!
Hey.
You,
the loud-mouthed brat...

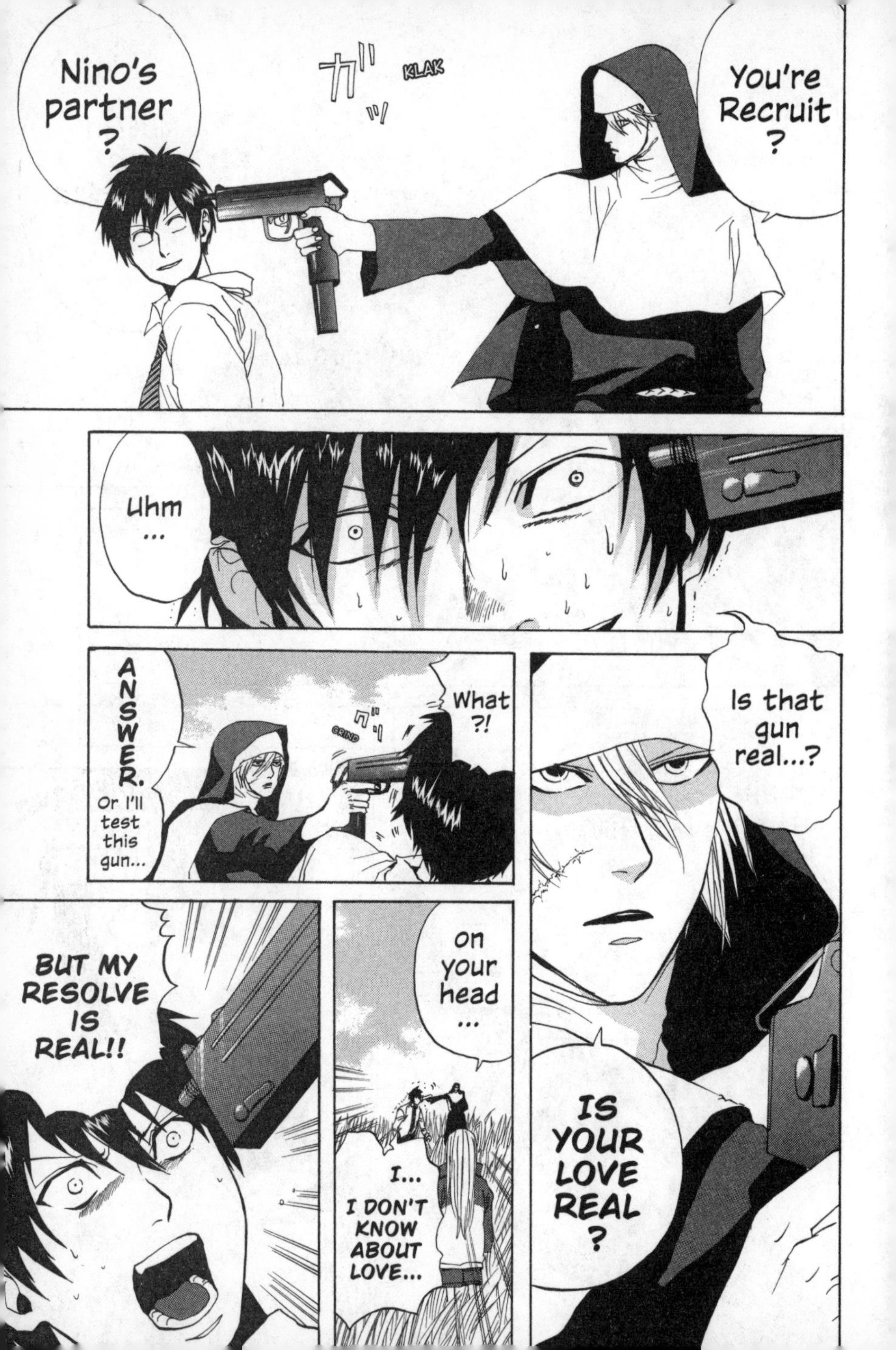
You're Recruit ?
KLAK
Nino's partner ?
Uhm ...
Is that gun real...?
IS YOUR LOVE REAL ?
What ?!
GRIND
ANSWER. Or I'll test this gun...
on your head ...
I... I DON'T KNOW ABOUT LOVE...
BUT MY RESOLVE IS REAL!!

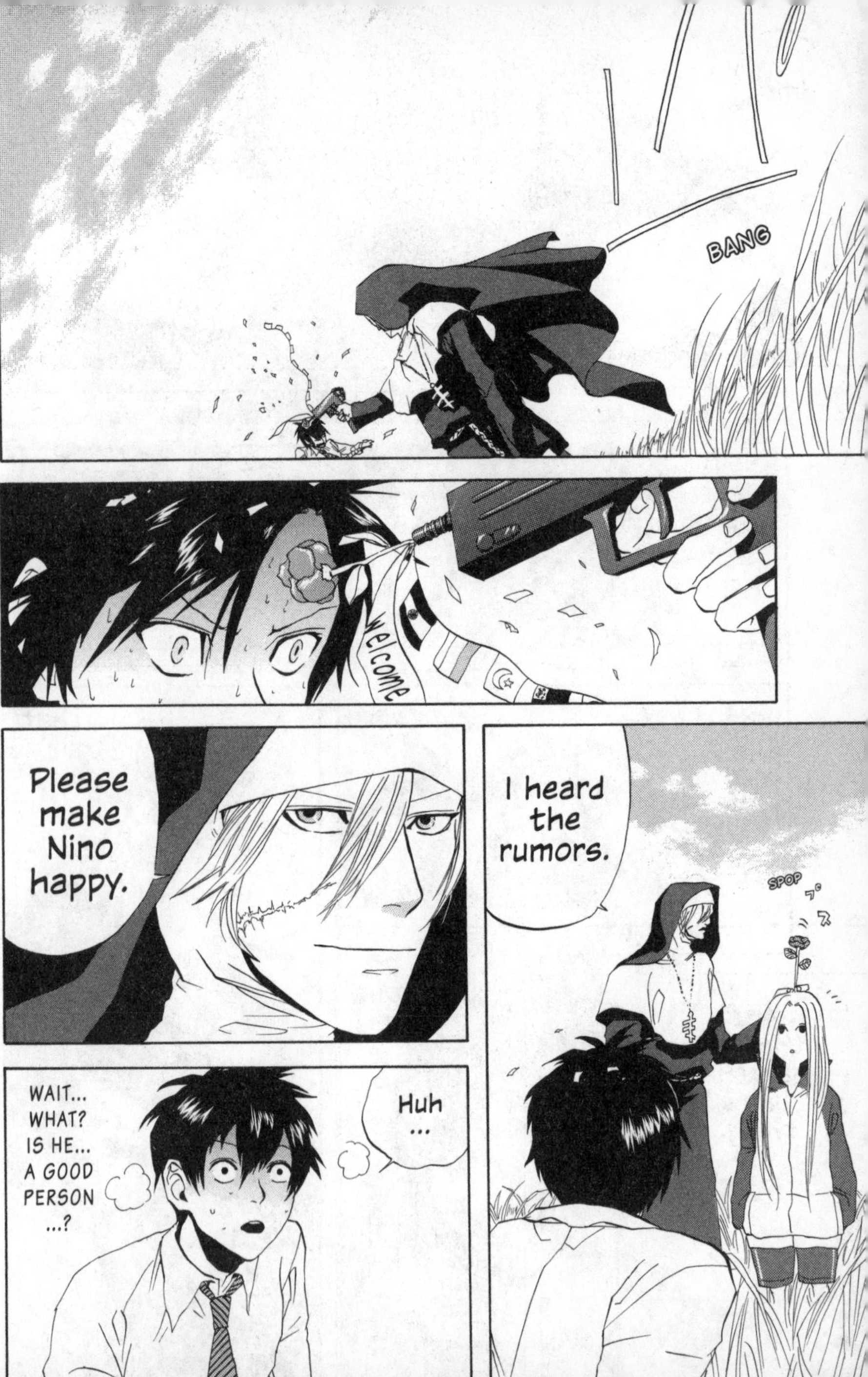
BANG
welcome
I heard the rumors.
SPOP
Please make Nino happy.
Huh ...
WAIT... WHAT? IS HE... A GOOD PERSON ...?

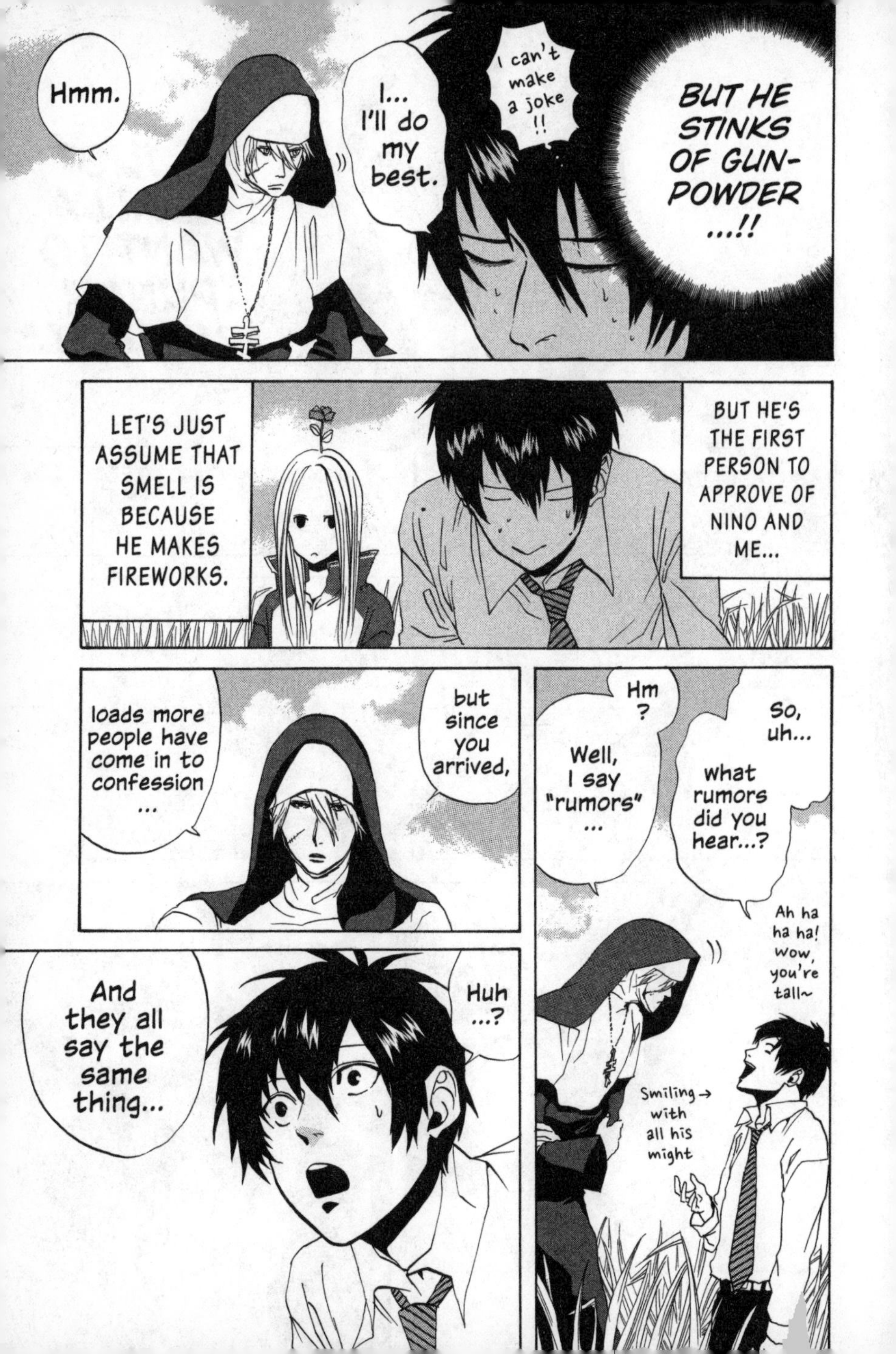
BUT HE STINKS OF GUN-POWDER ...!!
I can't make a joke !!
I... I'll do my best.
Hmm.
BUT HE'S THE FIRST PERSON TO APPROVE OF NINO AND ME...
LET'S JUST ASSUME THAT SMELL IS BECAUSE HE MAKES FIREWORKS.
So, uh... what rumors did you hear...?
Hm ?
Well, I say "rumors" ...
Ah ha ha ha! wow, you're tall~
Smiling → with all his might
but since you arrived,
loads more people have come in to confession ...
Huh ...?
And they all say the same thing...

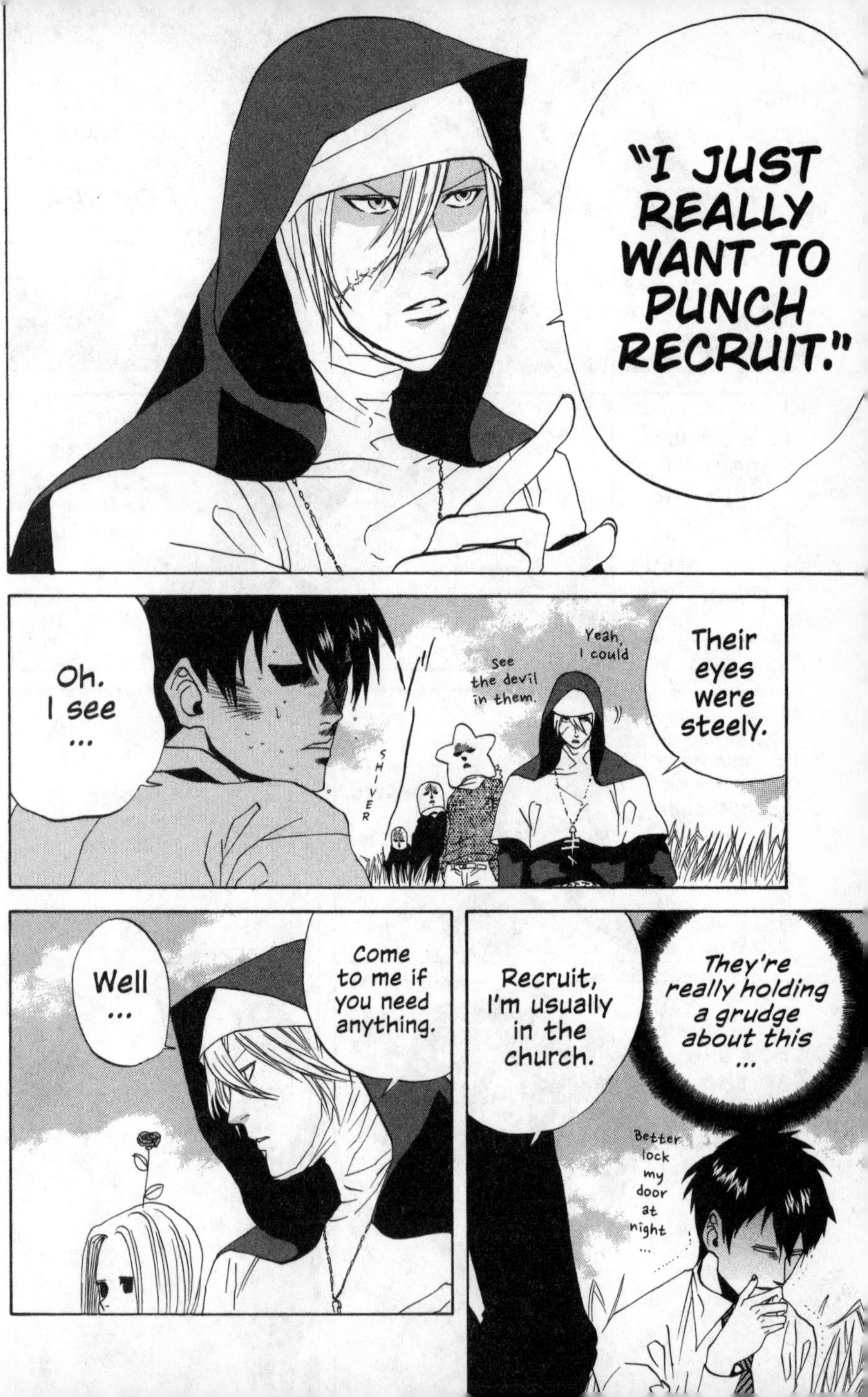
"I JUST REALLY WANT TO PUNCH RECRUIT."
Their eyes were steely.
Yeah, I could see the devil in them.
SHIVER
Oh. I see ...
They're really holding a grudge about this ...
Recruit, I'm usually in the church.
Better lock my door at night ...
Come to me if you need anything.
Well ...

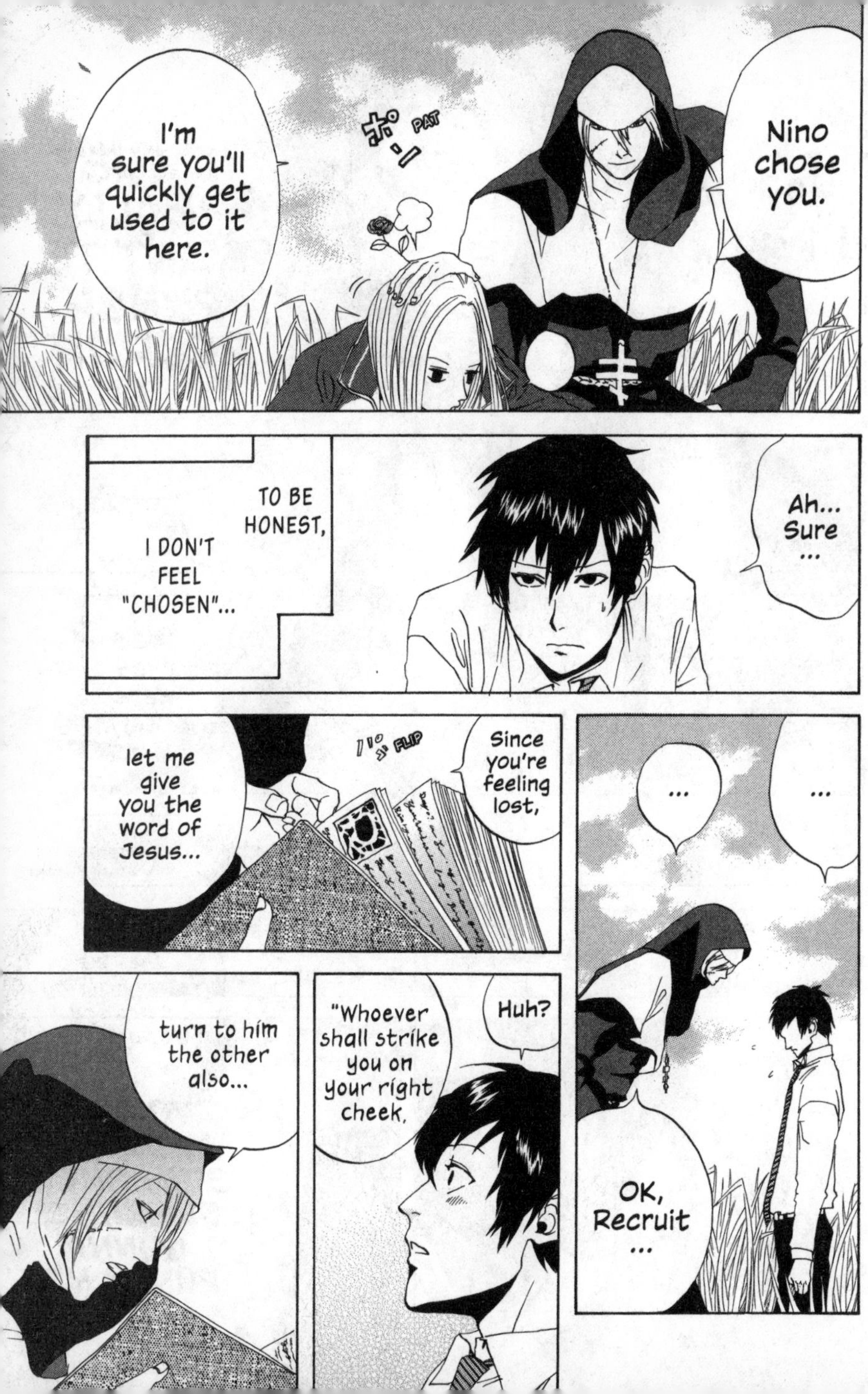
Nino chose you.
PAT
I'm sure you'll quickly get used to it here.
Ah... Sure ...
TO BE HONEST, I DON'T FEEL "CHOSEN"...
...
...
OK, Recruit ...
Since you're feeling lost,
FLIP
let me give you the word of Jesus...
Huh?
"Whoever shall strike you on your right cheek,
turn to him the other also...

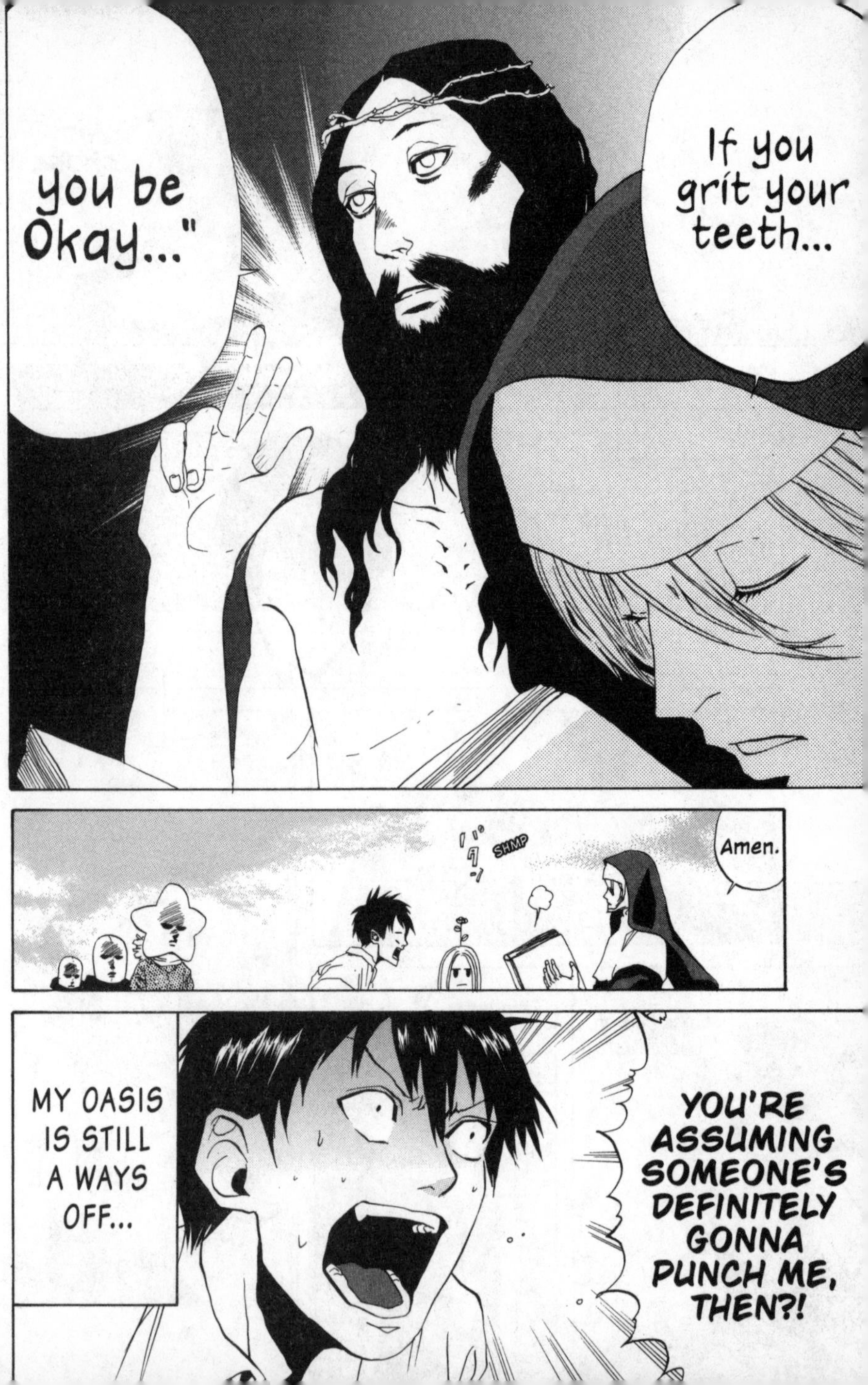
If you grit your teeth...
you be Okay..."
Amen.
SHMP
YOU'RE ASSUMING SOMEONE'S DEFINITELY GONNA PUNCH ME, THEN?!
MY OASIS IS STILL A WAYS OFF...

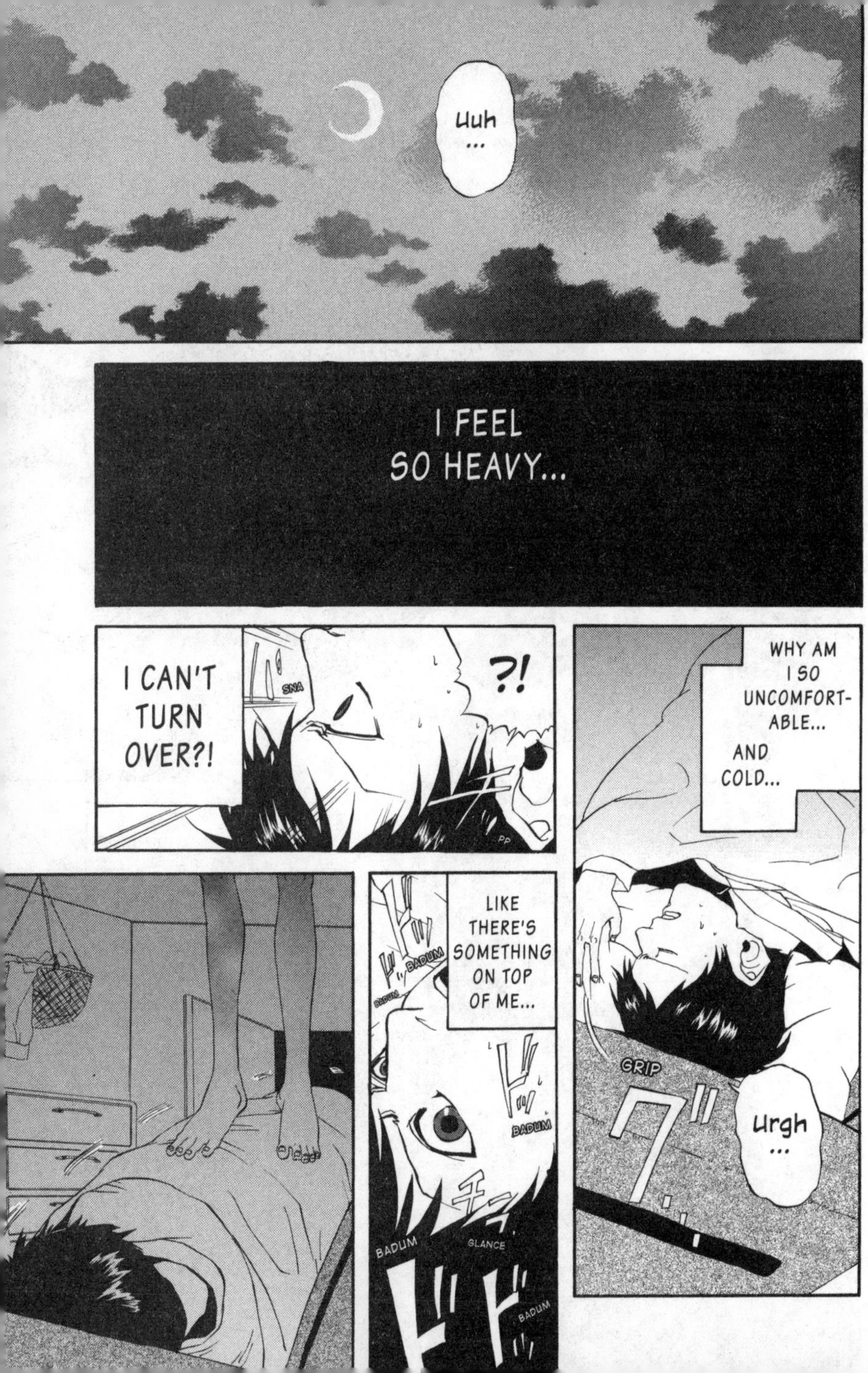

Uuh ...
I FEEL SO HEAVY...
WHY AM I SO UNCOMFORTABLE... AND COLD...
GRIP
Urgh ...
?!
SNA
I CAN'T TURN OVER?!
PP
LIKE THERE'S SOMETHING ON TOP OF ME...
BADUM
BADUM
BADUM
GLANCE
BADUM
BADUM

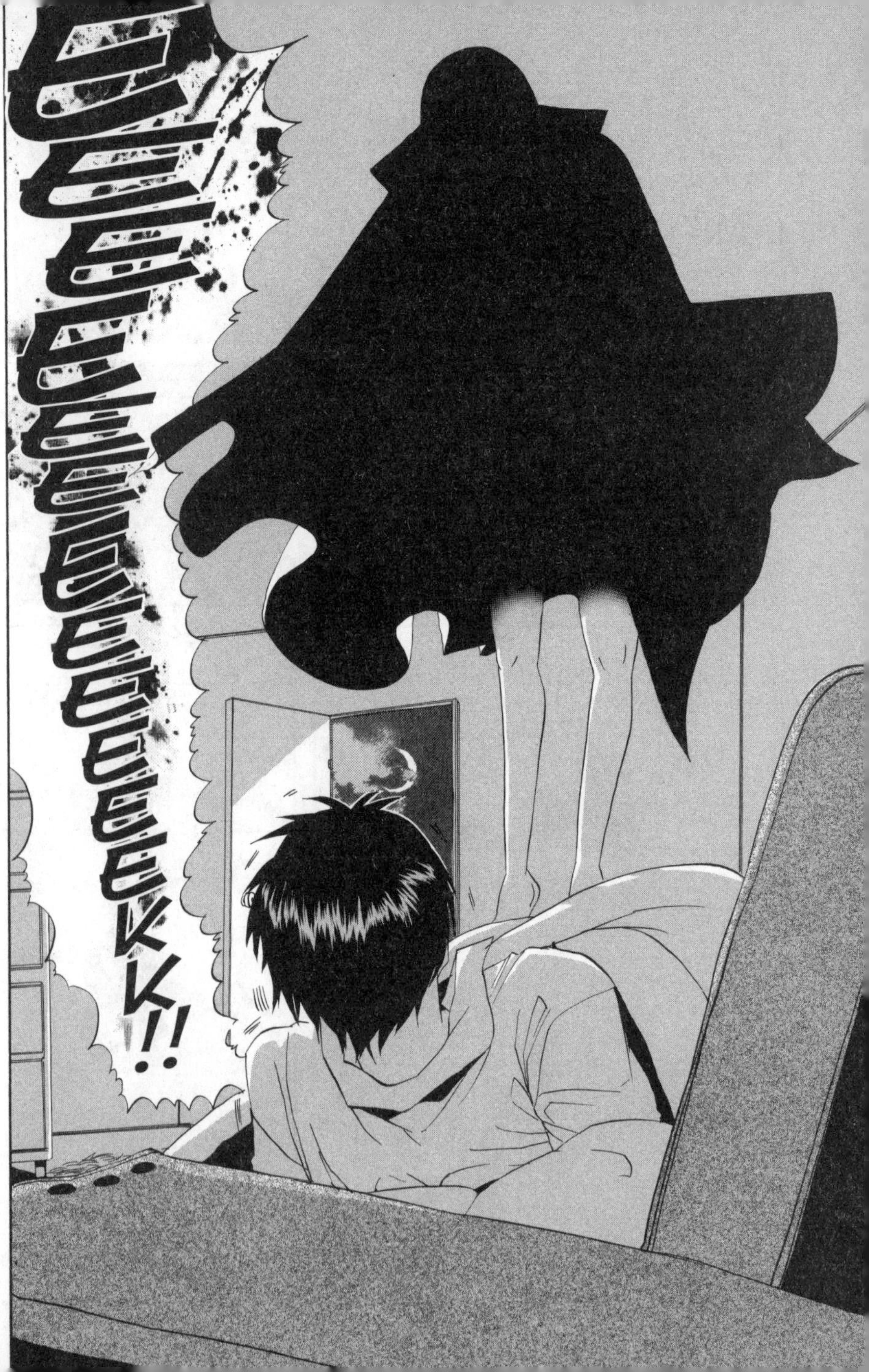
EEEEEEEEEEEEEEEKK!!

☜ Chapter 20: Mid-Winter Mystery

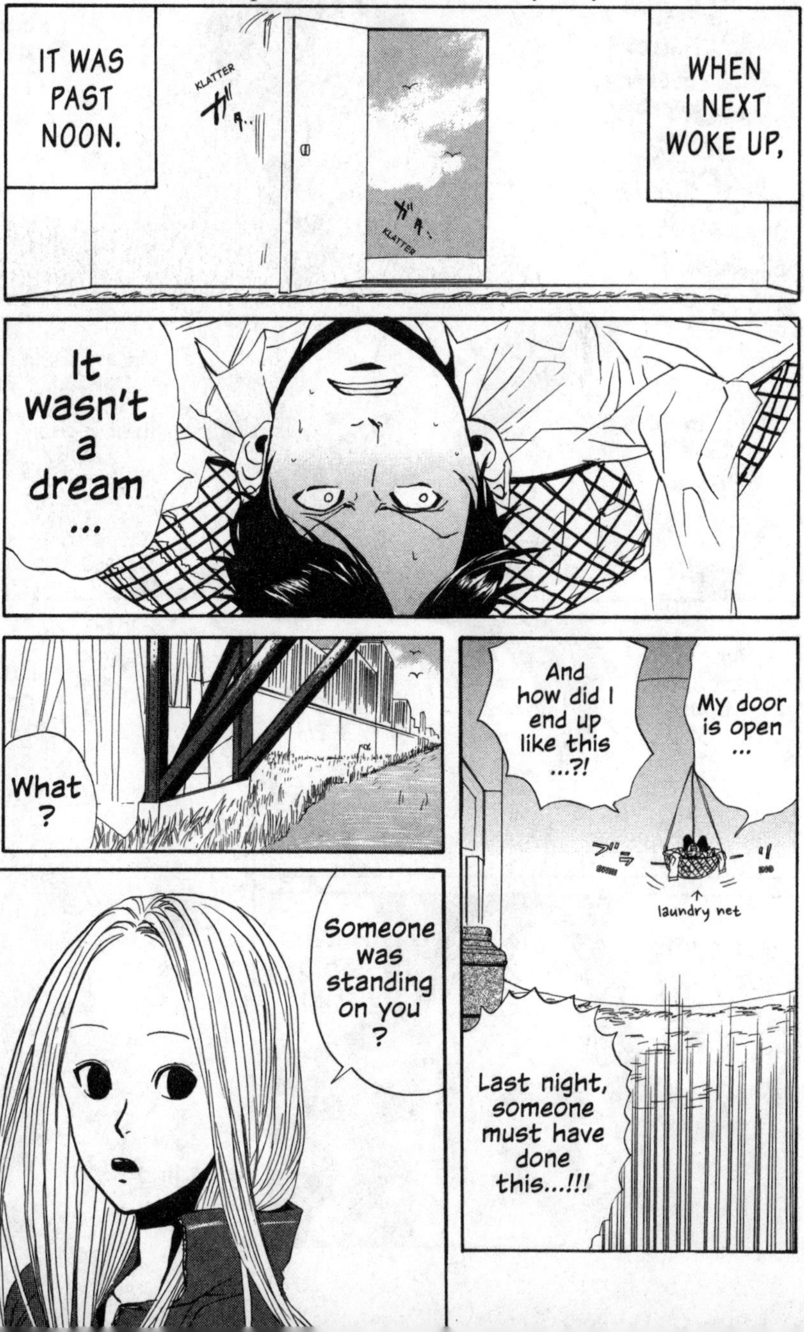
WHEN I NEXT WOKE UP,
IT WAS PAST NOON.
KLATTER
KLATTER
It wasn't a dream...
My door is open...
And how did I end up like this...?!
laundry net
Last night, someone must have done this...!!!
What?
Someone was standing on you?

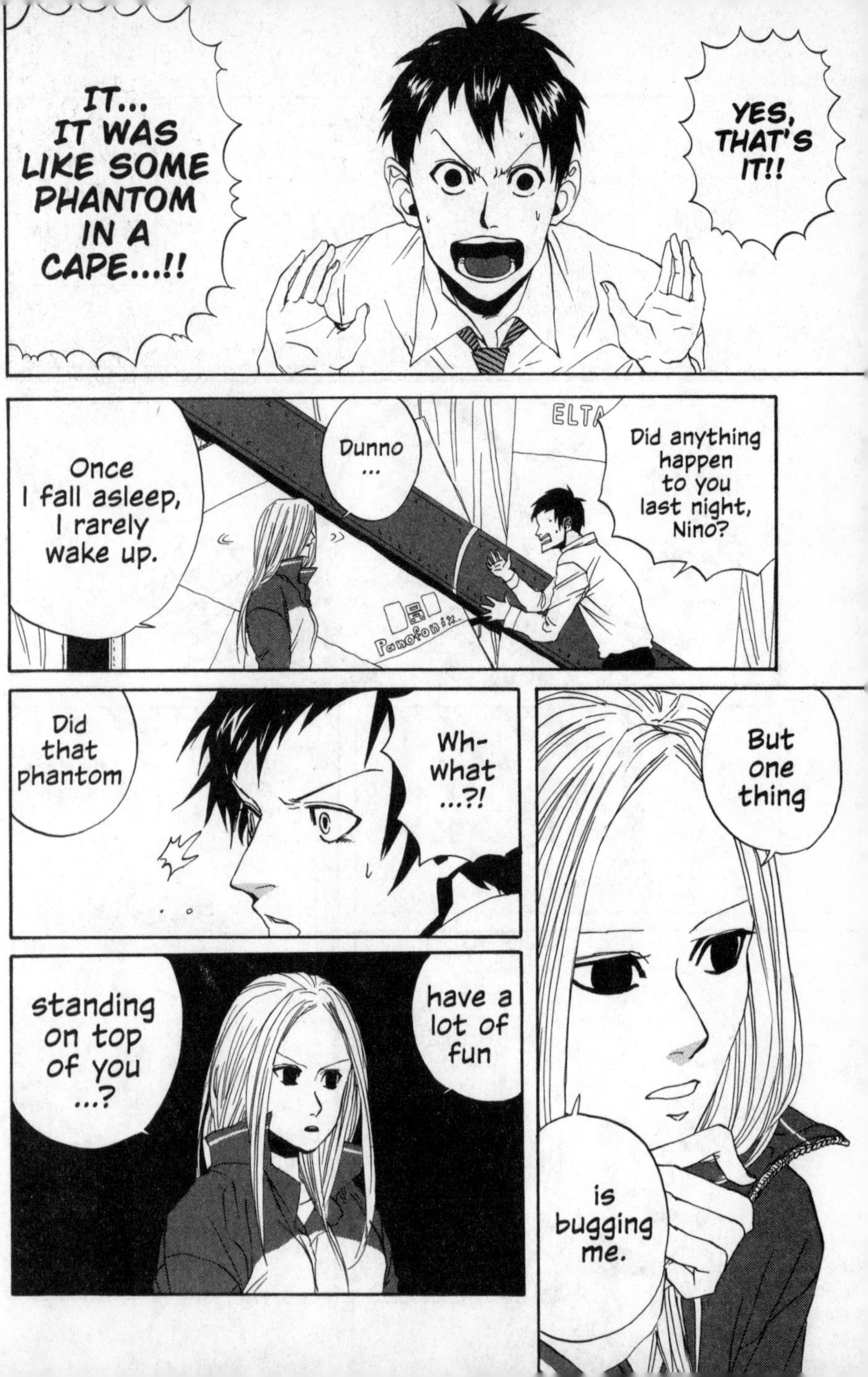
YES, THAT'S IT!!
IT... IT WAS LIKE SOME PHANTOM IN A CAPE...!!
ELTA
Did anything happen to you last night, Nino?
Dunno ...
Once I fall asleep, I rarely wake up.
Panofonix
But one thing
is bugging me.
Wh- what ...?!
Did that phantom
have a lot of fun
standing on top of you ...?

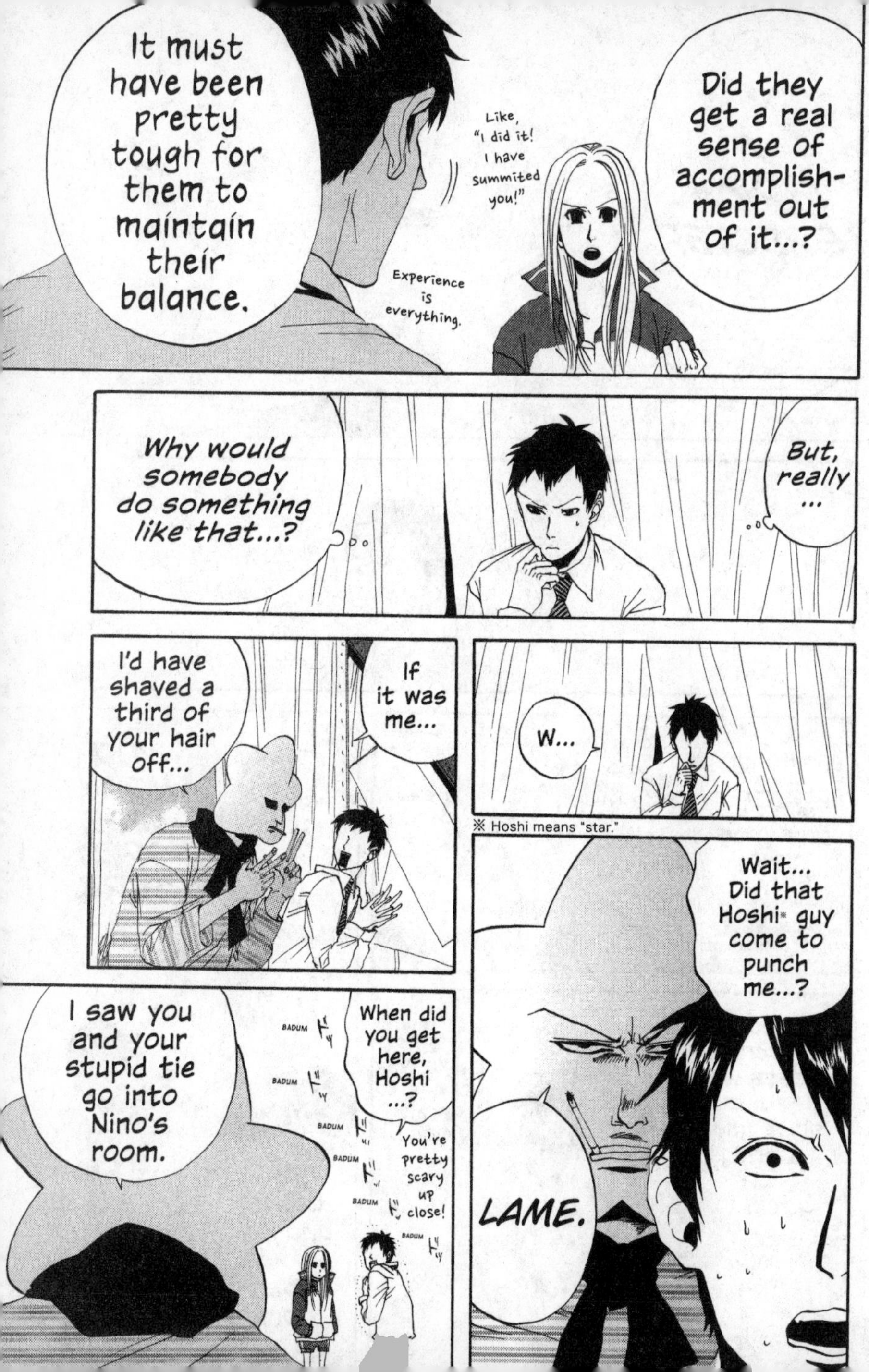
Did they get a real sense of accomplishment out of it...?
Like, "I did it! I have summited you!"
It must have been pretty tough for them to maintain their balance.
Experience is everything.
But, really...
Why would somebody do something like that...?
W...
If it was me...
I'd have shaved a third of your hair off...
Wait... Did that Hoshi※ guy come to punch me...?
LAME.
When did you get here, Hoshi...?
BADUM
BADUM
BADUM
BADUM
BADUM
BADUM
You're pretty scary up close!
I saw you and your stupid tie go into Nino's room.

※ Hoshi means "star."

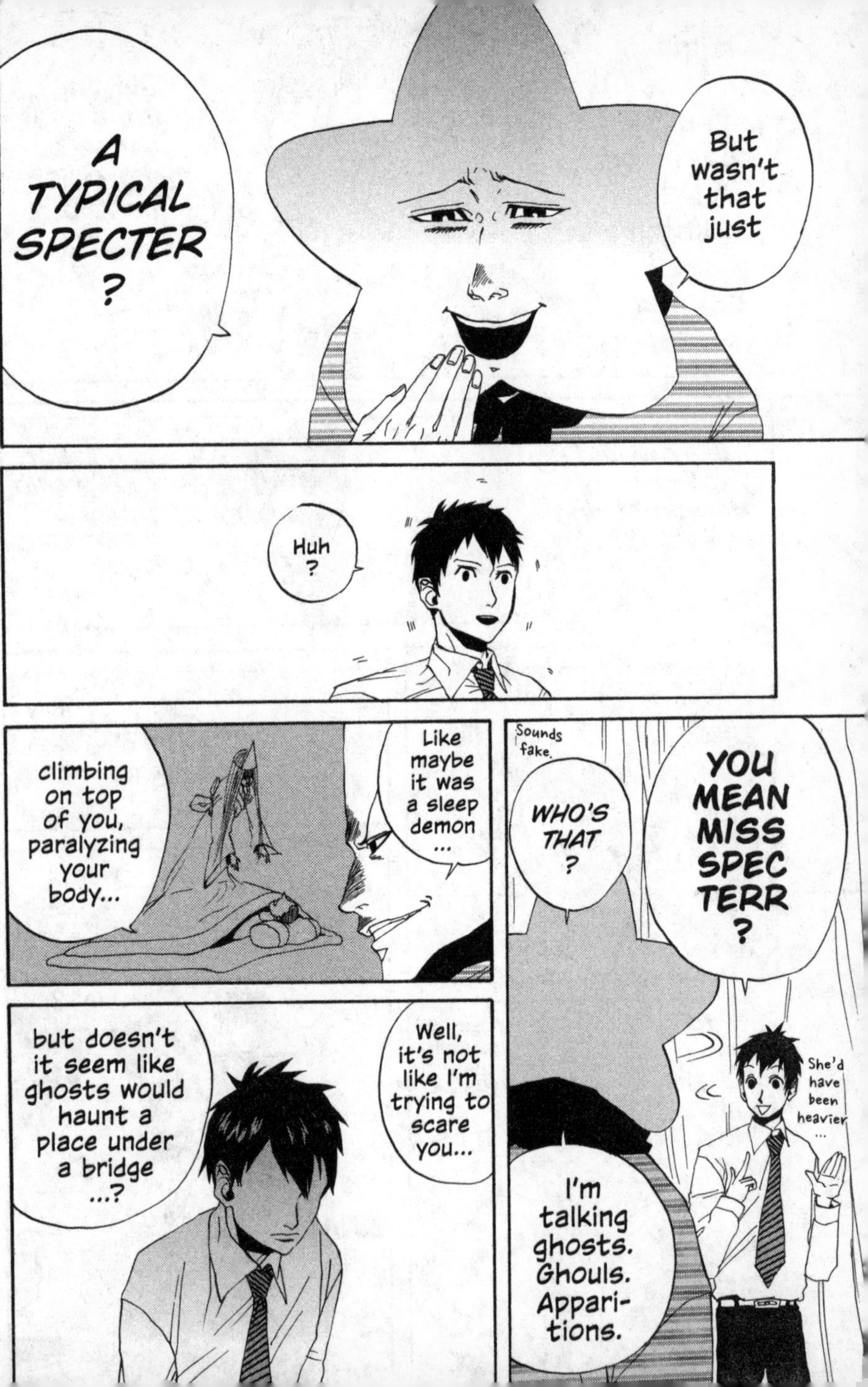

But wasn't that just
A TYPICAL SPECTER ?
Huh ?
YOU MEAN MISS SPEC TERR ?
Sounds fake.
WHO'S THAT ?
She'd have been heavier ...
I'm talking ghosts. Ghouls. Appari- tions.
Like maybe it was a sleep demon ...
climbing on top of you, paralyzing your body...
Well, it's not like I'm trying to scare you...
but doesn't it seem like ghosts would haunt a place under a bridge ...?

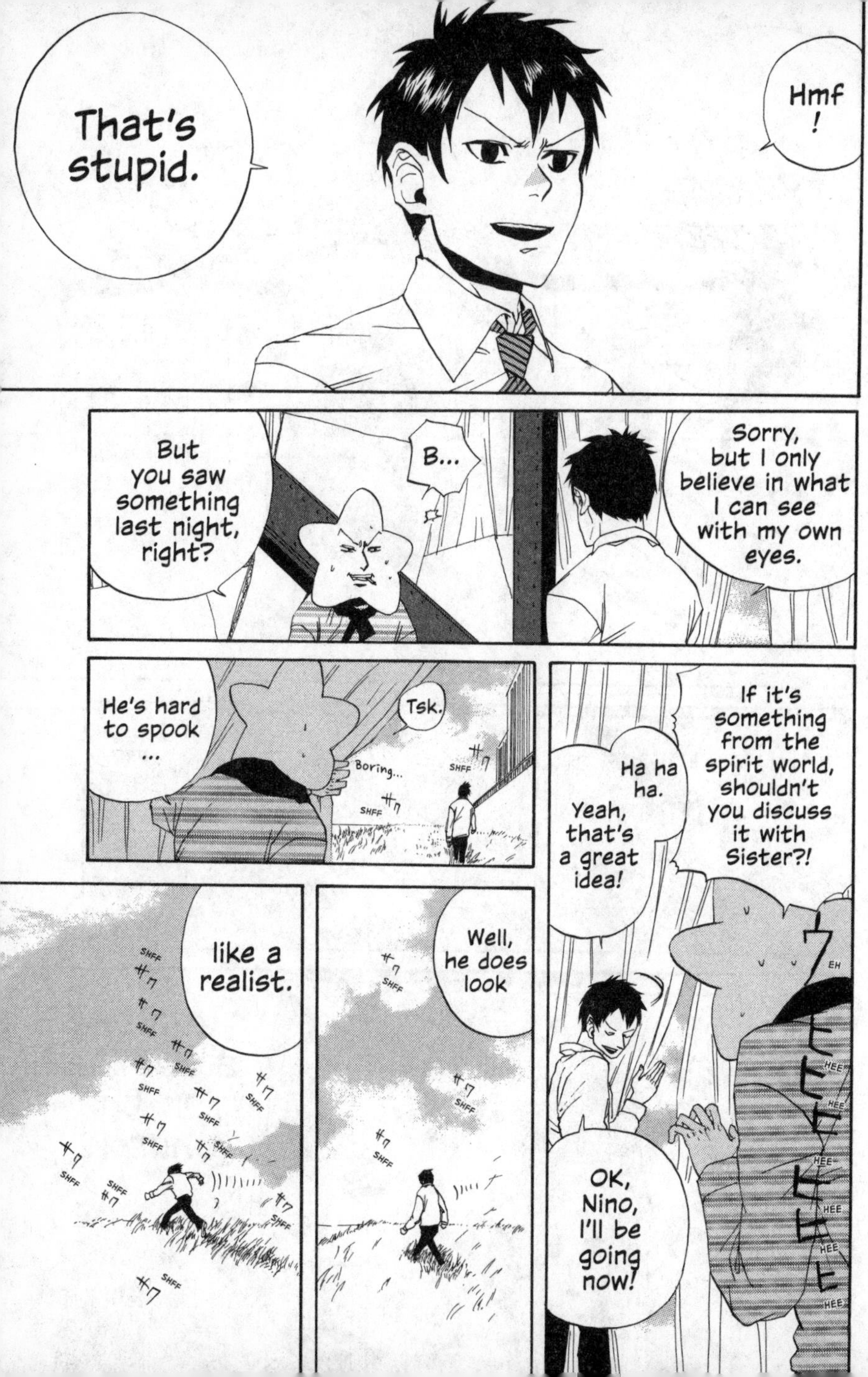
Hmf !
That's stupid.
Sorry, but I only believe in what I can see with my own eyes.
B...
But you saw something last night, right?
If it's something from the spirit world, shouldn't you discuss it with Sister?!
Ha ha ha. Yeah, that's a great idea!
EH
HEE HEE HEE HEE HEE HEE
OK, Nino, I'll be going now!
Tsk.
He's hard to spook ...
Boring...
SHFF
SHFF
Well, he does look
SHFF
SHFF
like a realist.
SHFF

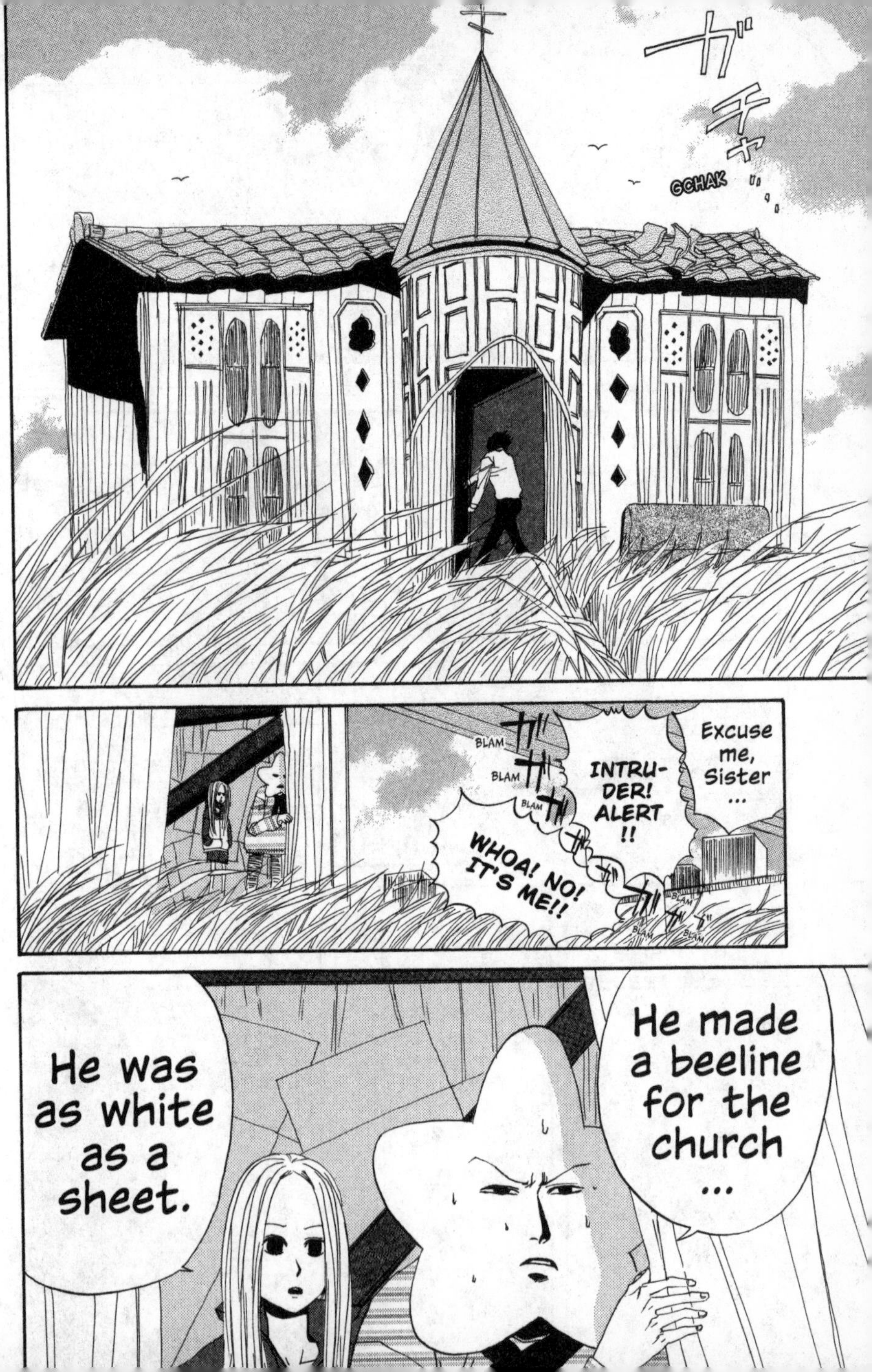
ガチャ
GCHAK
Excuse me, Sister ...
INTRU-DER! ALERT!!
WHOA! NO! IT'S ME!!
BLAM
BLAM
BLAM
BLAM
BLAM
BLAM
He made a beeline for the church ...
He was as white as a sheet.

☜ Chapter 21: Solution

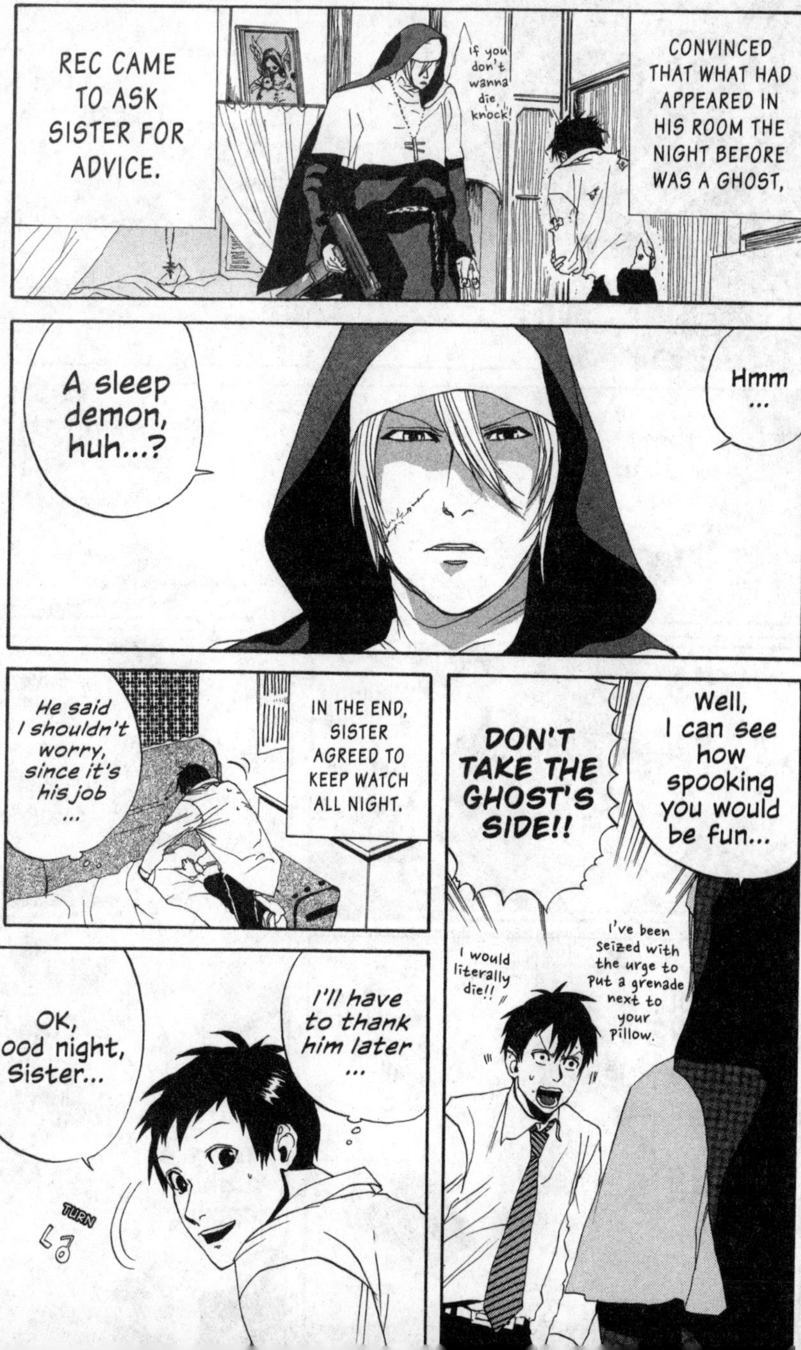

CONVINCED THAT WHAT HAD APPEARED IN HIS ROOM THE NIGHT BEFORE WAS A GHOST,
If you don't wanna die, knock!
REC CAME TO ASK SISTER FOR ADVICE.
Hmm...
A sleep demon, huh...?
Well, I can see how spooking you would be fun...
DON'T TAKE THE GHOST'S SIDE!!
IN THE END, SISTER AGREED TO KEEP WATCH ALL NIGHT.
He said I shouldn't worry, since it's his job...
I've been seized with the urge to put a grenade next to your pillow.
I would literally die!!
I'll have to thank him later...
OK, good night, Sister...
TURN

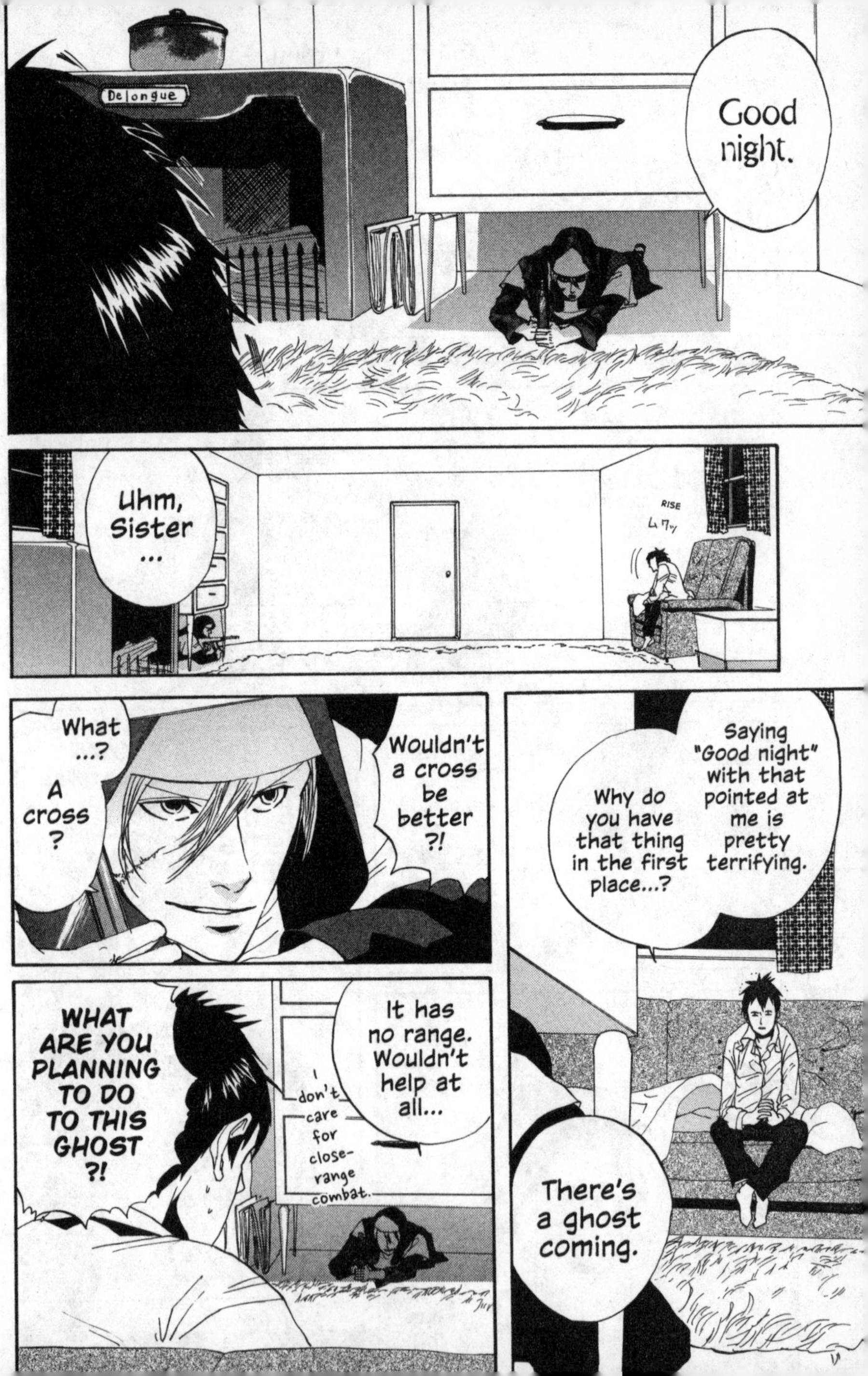

DeLongue
Good night.
RISE
ムワッ
Uhm, Sister ...
Saying "Good night" with that pointed at me is pretty terrifying.
Why do you have that thing in the first place...?
There's a ghost coming.
Wouldn't a cross be better?!
What ...? A cross?
It has no range. Wouldn't help at all...
I don't care for close-range combat.
WHAT ARE YOU PLANNING TO DO TO THIS GHOST?!

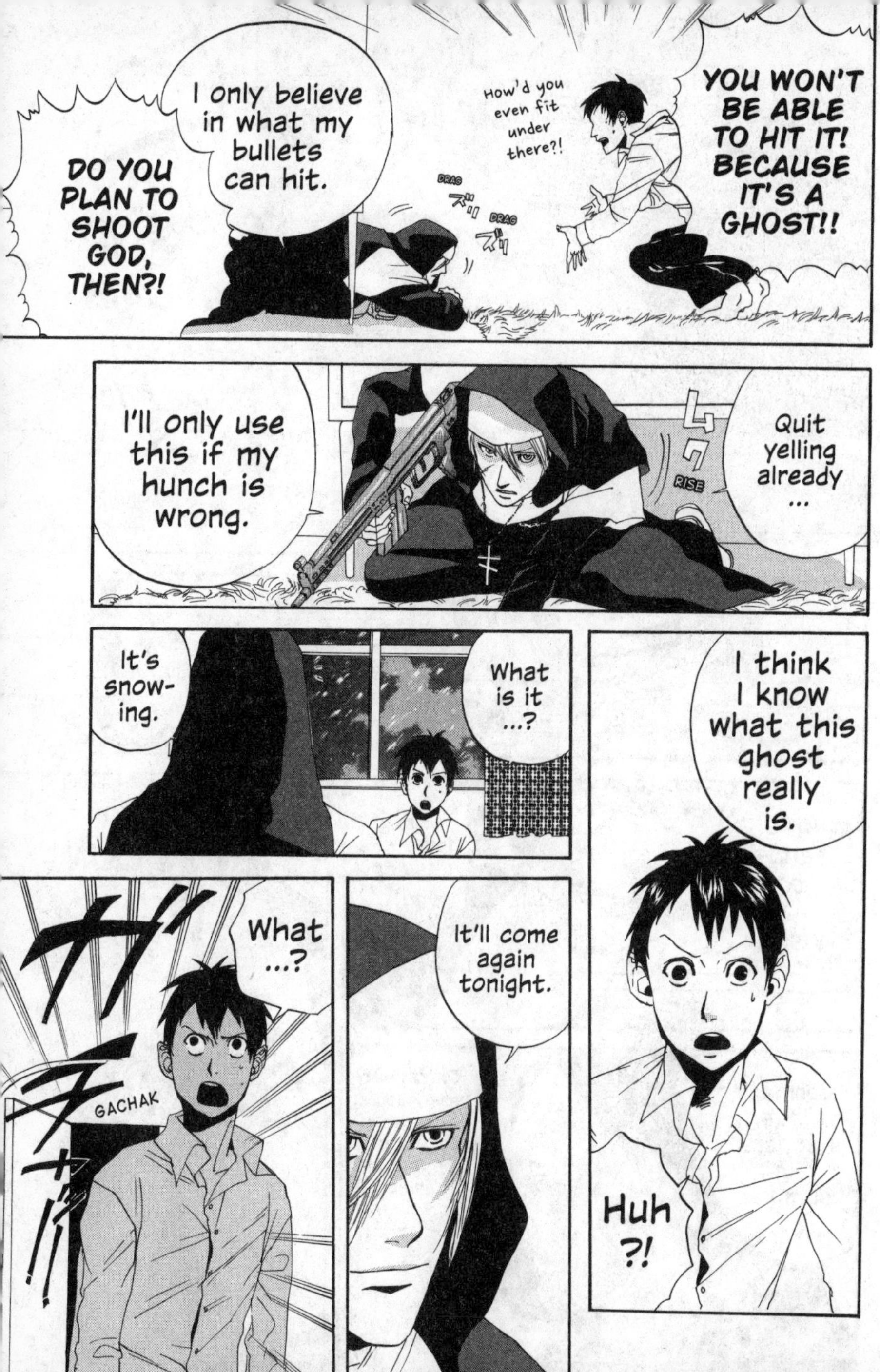
YOU WON'T BE ABLE TO HIT IT! BECAUSE IT'S A GHOST!!
How'd you even fit under there?!
DRAG
DRAG
I only believe in what my bullets can hit.
DO YOU PLAN TO SHOOT GOD, THEN?!
Quit yelling already ...
RISE
I'll only use this if my hunch is wrong.
I think I know what this ghost really is.
Huh ?!
What is it ...?
It's snowing.
It'll come again tonight.
What ...?
GACHAK

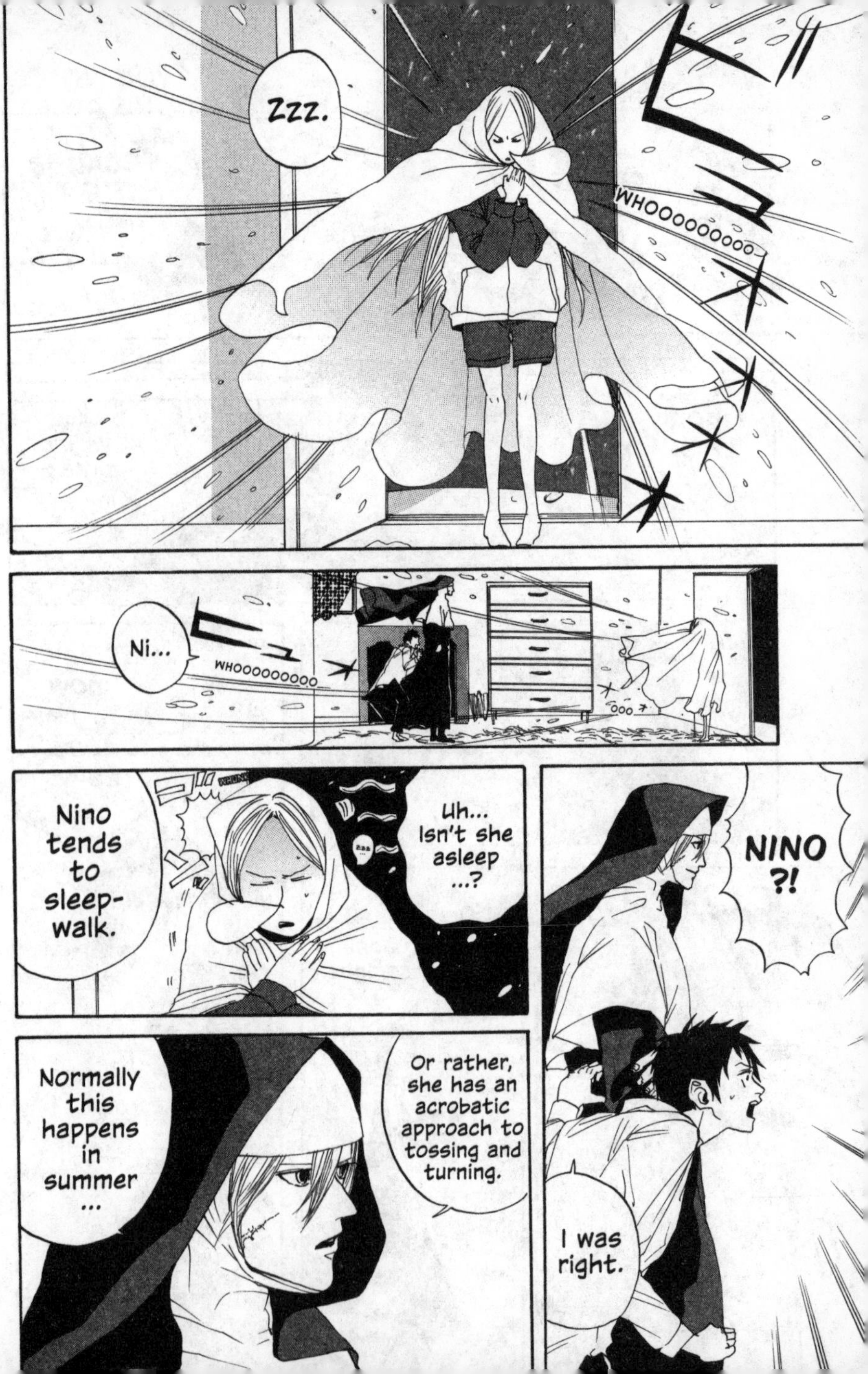
WHOOOOOOOOO
Zzz.
WHOOOOOOOOO
Ni...
NINO ?!
I was right.
Uh... Isn't she asleep ...?
Nino tends to sleep-walk.
Or rather, she has an acrobatic approach to tossing and turning.
Normally this happens in summer ...

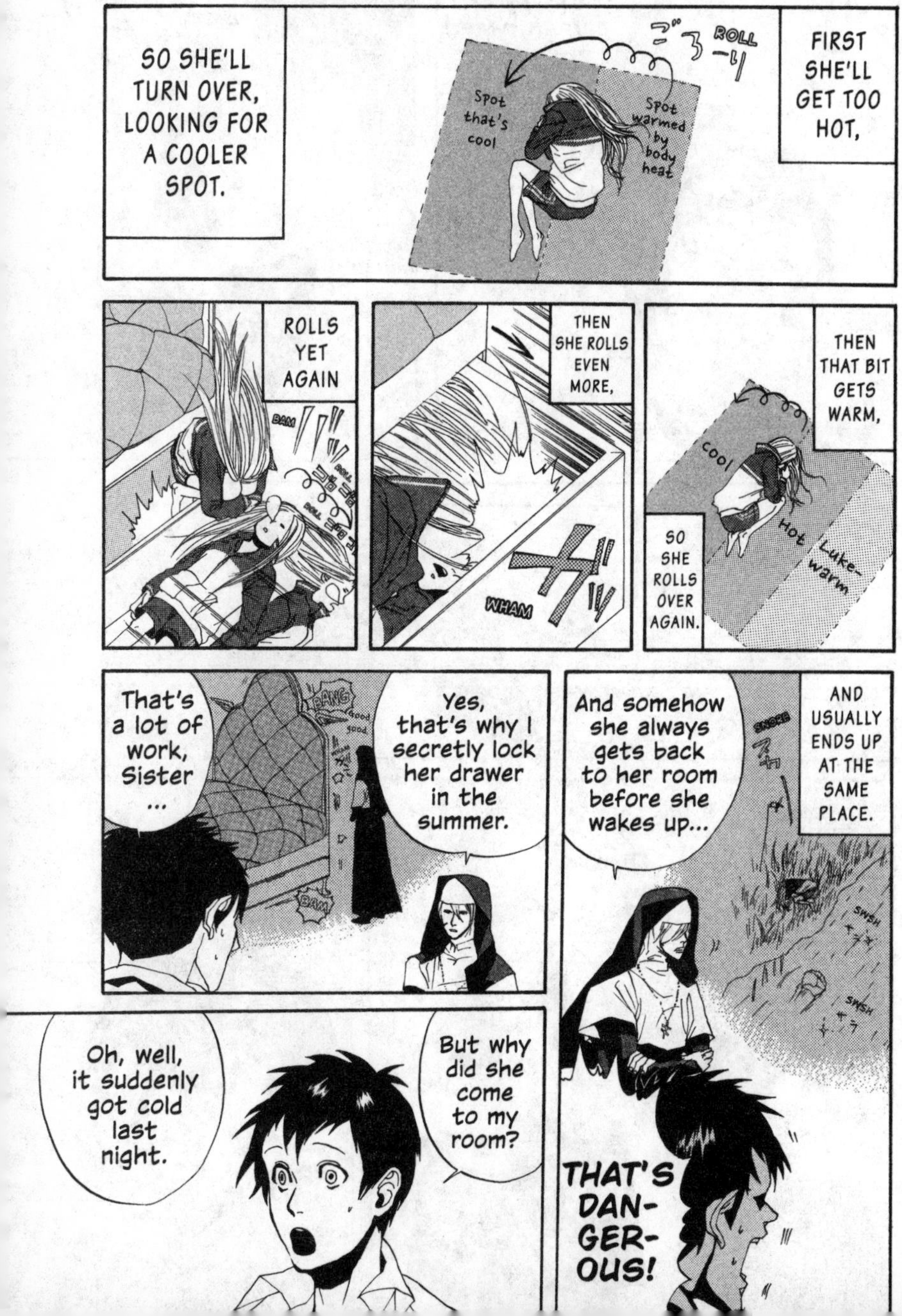
FIRST SHE'LL GET TOO HOT,
ROLL
Spot warmed by body heat
Spot that's cool
SO SHE'LL TURN OVER, LOOKING FOR A COOLER SPOT.
THEN THAT BIT GETS WARM,
Cool
Hot
Luke-warm
SO SHE ROLLS OVER AGAIN.
THEN SHE ROLLS EVEN MORE,
WHAM
ROLLS YET AGAIN
BAM
ROLL
ROLL
AND USUALLY ENDS UP AT THE SAME PLACE.
SNORE
And somehow she always gets back to her room before she wakes up...
SWSH
SWSH
THAT'S DAN-GER-OUS!
Yes, that's why I secretly lock her drawer in the summer.
BANG
good good
BAM
That's a lot of work, Sister ...
But why did she come to my room?
Oh, well, it suddenly got cold last night.

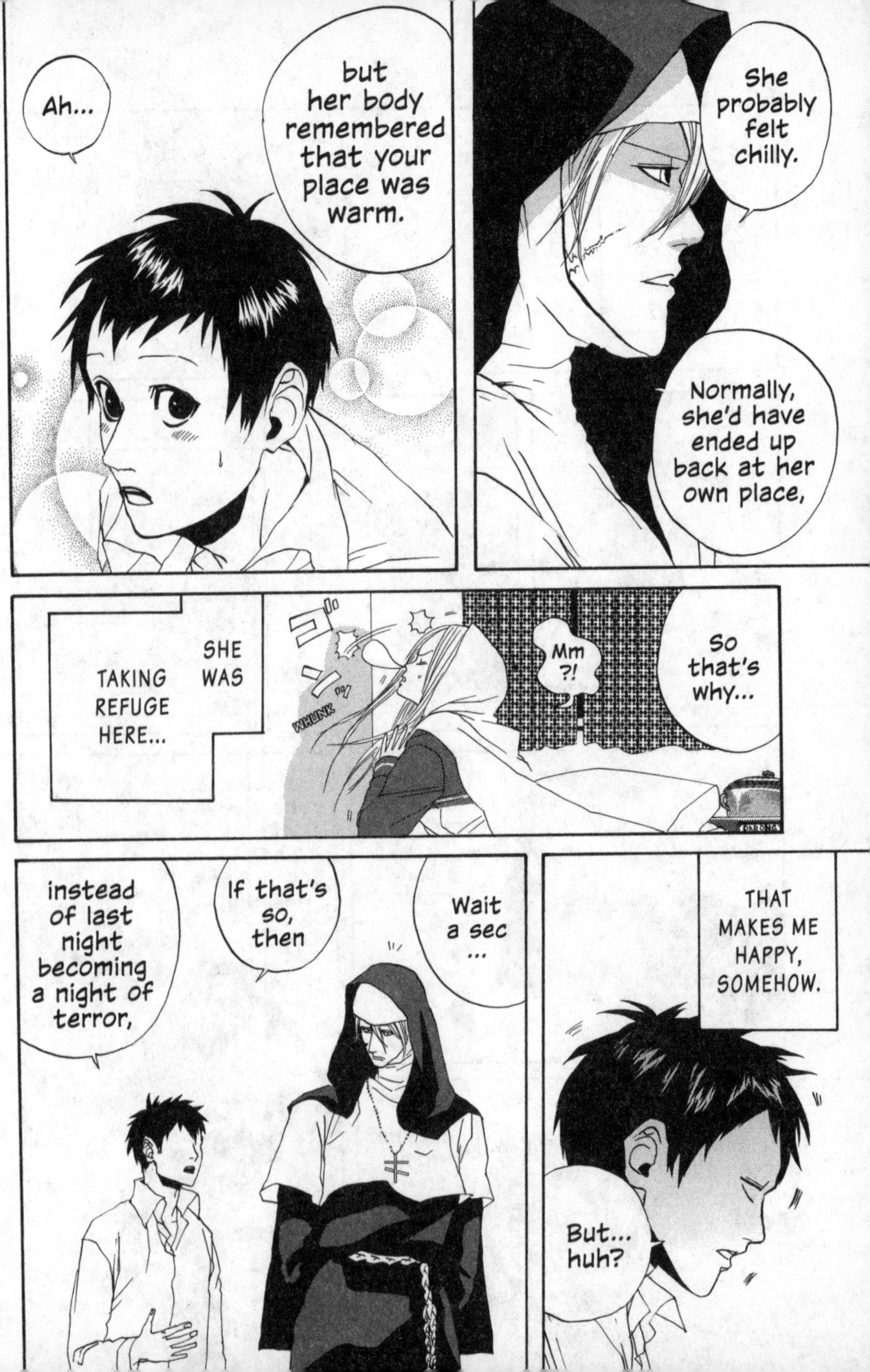
She probably felt chilly.
Normally, she'd have ended up back at her own place,
but her body remembered that your place was warm.
Ah...
So that's why...
Mm ?!
WHUNK
SHE WAS TAKING REFUGE HERE...
THAT MAKES ME HAPPY, SOMEHOW.
But... huh?
Wait a sec ...
If that's so, then
instead of last night becoming a night of terror,

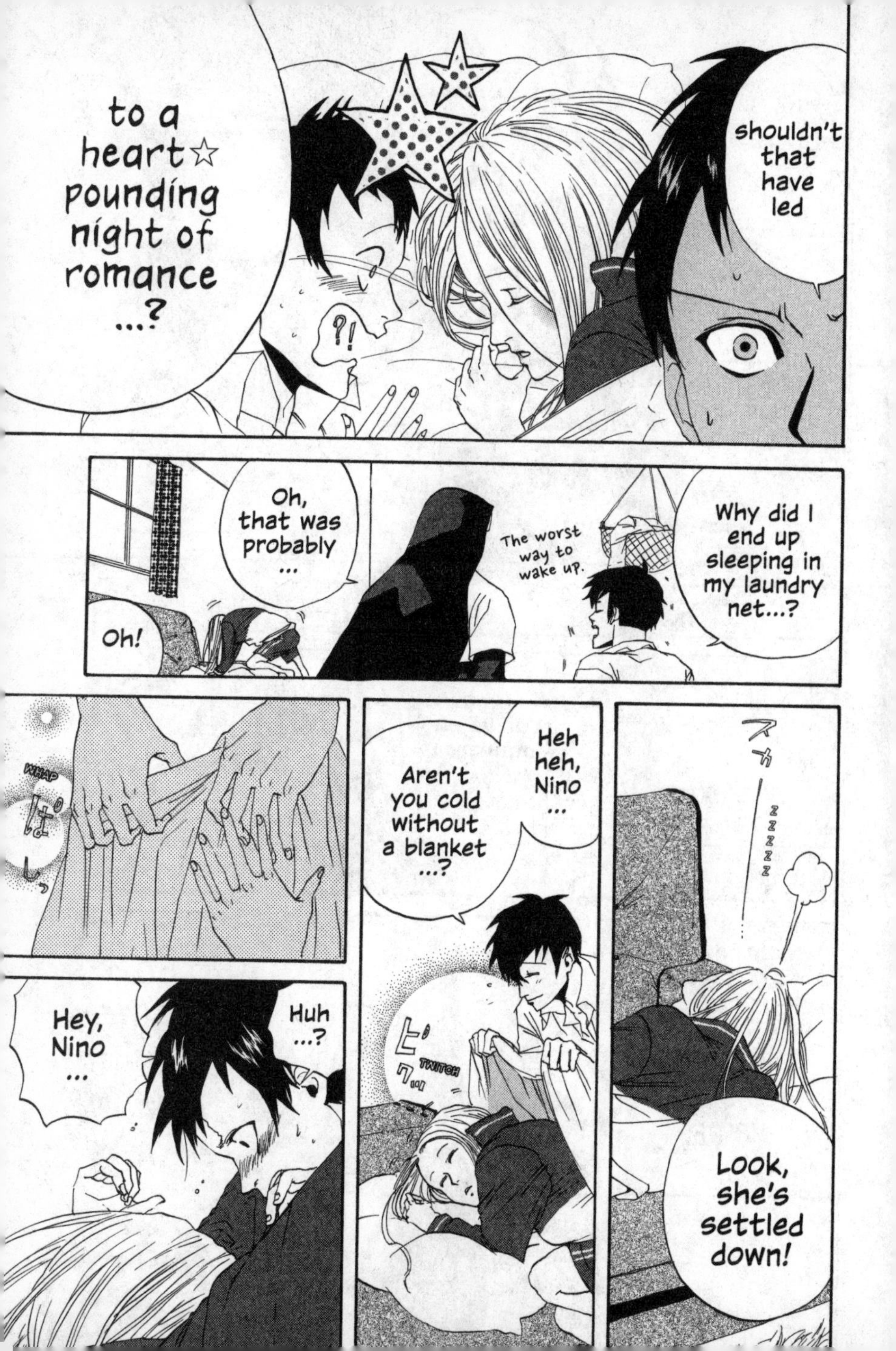
shouldn't that have led
to a heart☆ pounding night of romance ...?
?!
Why did I end up sleeping in my laundry net...?
The worst way to wake up.
Oh, that was probably ...
Oh!
スヤー
ZZZZZ
Look, she's settled down!
Heh heh, Nino ...
Aren't you cold without a blanket ...?
ピクッ
TWITCH
WHAP
ばっ
Huh ...?
Hey, Nino ...

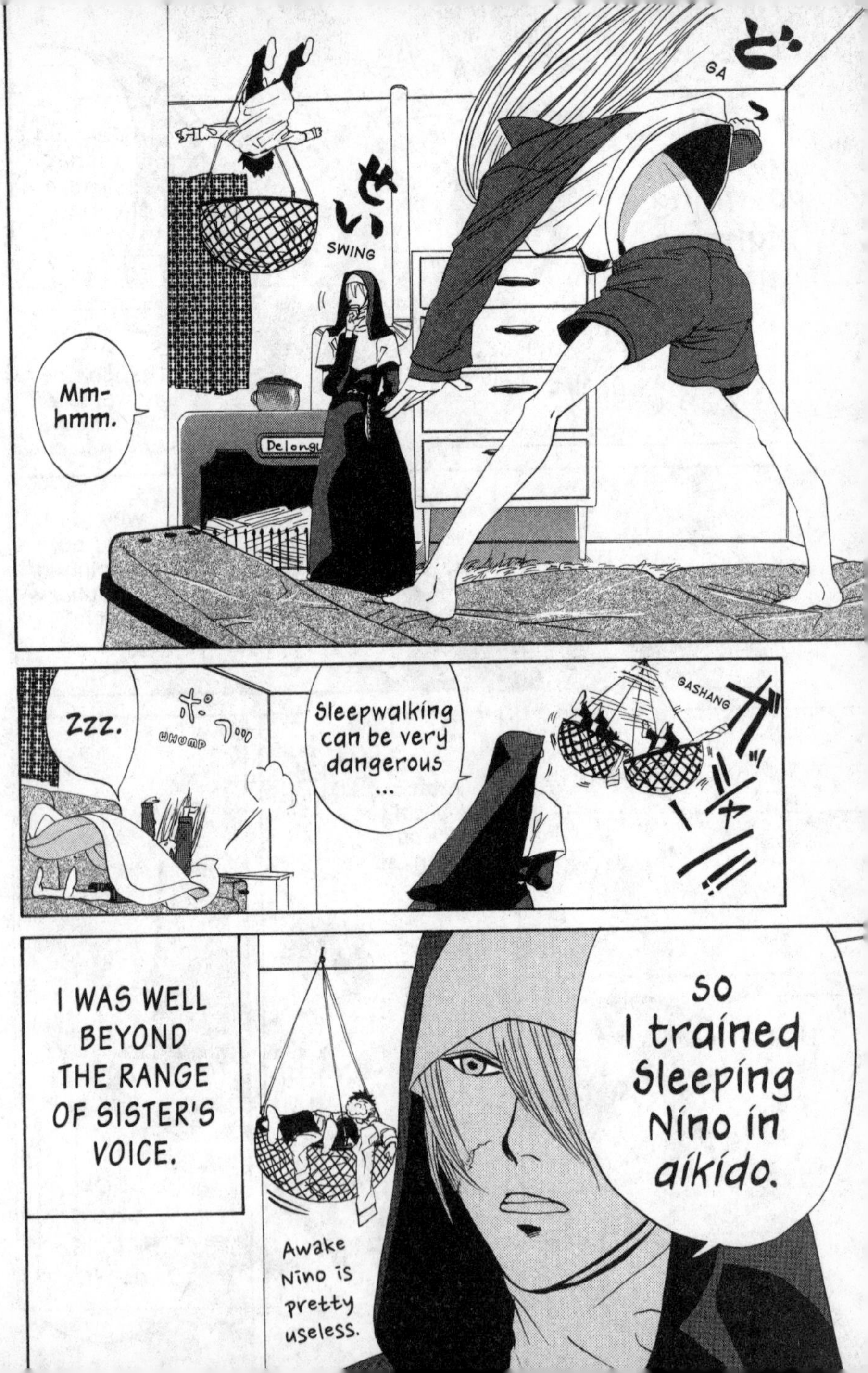
GA
SWING
Mm-hmm.
GASHANG
Sleepwalking can be very dangerous ...
WHOMP
Zzz.
So I trained Sleeping Nino in aikido.
Awake Nino is pretty useless.
I WAS WELL BEYOND THE RANGE OF SISTER'S VOICE.

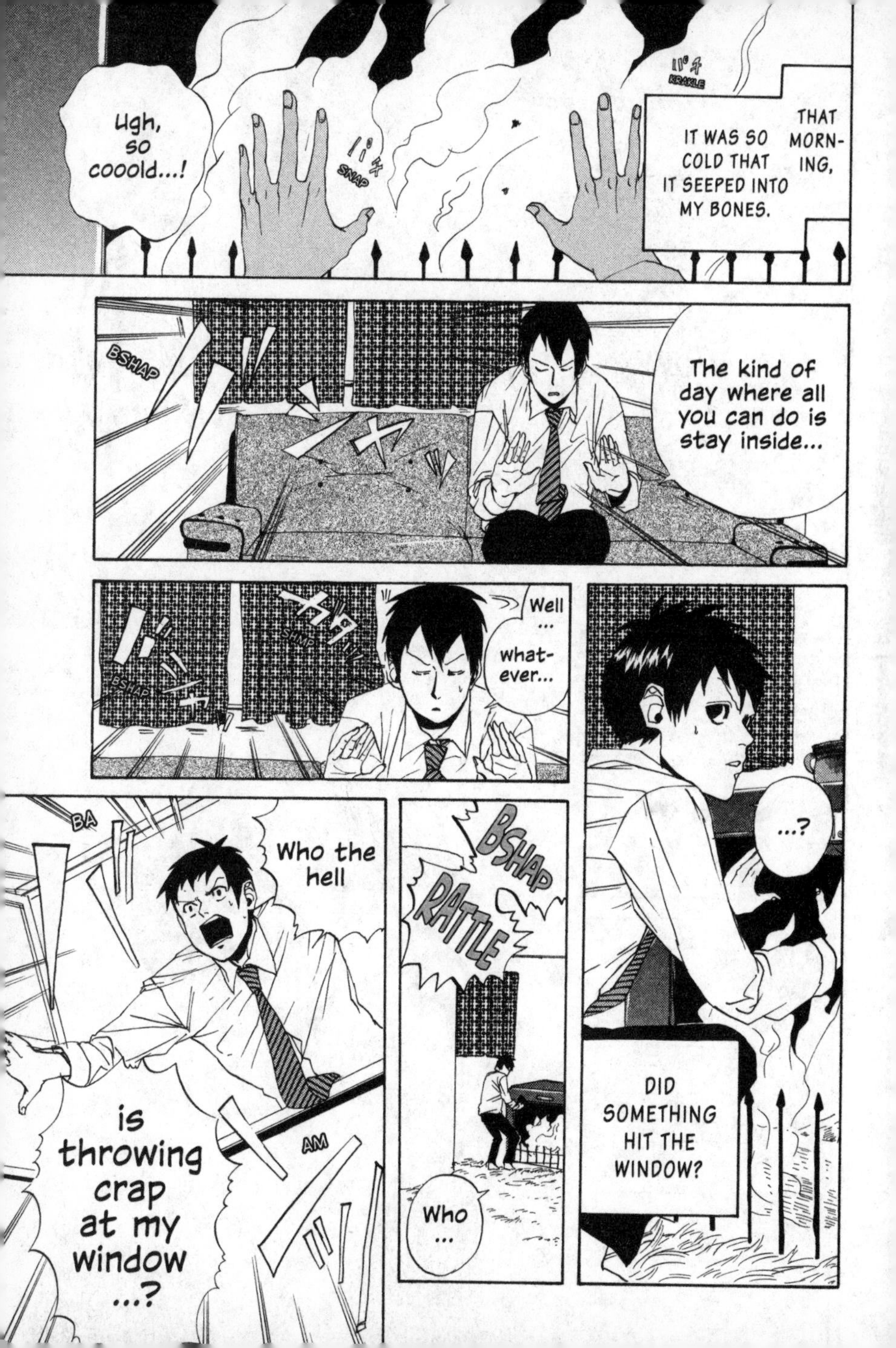
KRAKLE
THAT MORNING, IT WAS SO COLD THAT IT SEEPED INTO MY BONES.
SNAP
Ugh, so cooold...!
The kind of day where all you can do is stay inside...
BSHAP
...?
DID SOMETHING HIT THE WINDOW?
Well ... what-ever...
SHMP
BSHAP
BSHAP
RATTLE
Who ...
BA
Who the hell
AM
is throwing crap at my window ...?

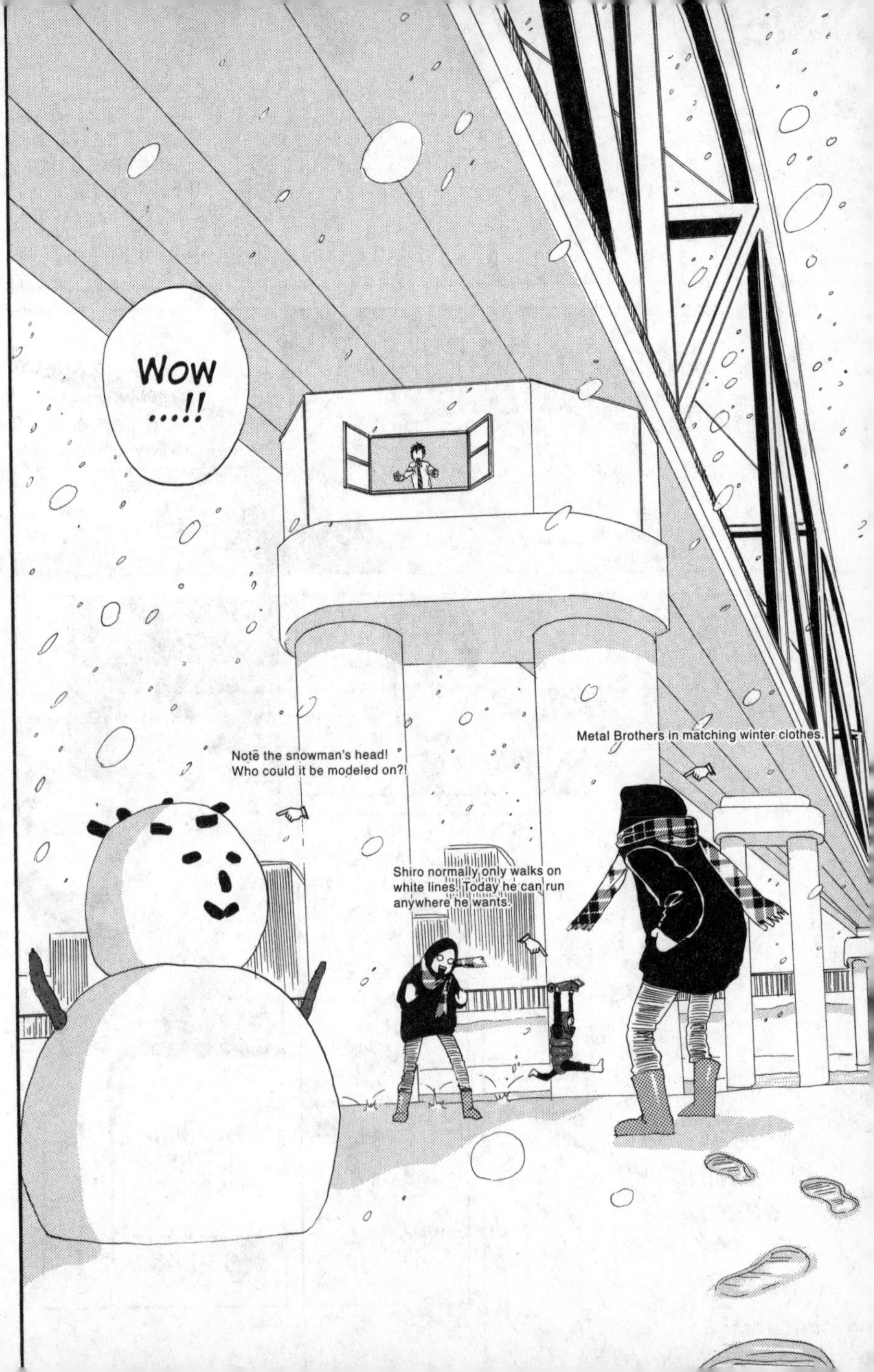
WOW ...!!
Metal Brothers in matching winter clothes.
Note the snowman's head! Who could it be modeled on?!
Shiro normally only walks on white lines. Today he can run anywhere he wants.

Chapter 22: Nino and the Snowy Sky

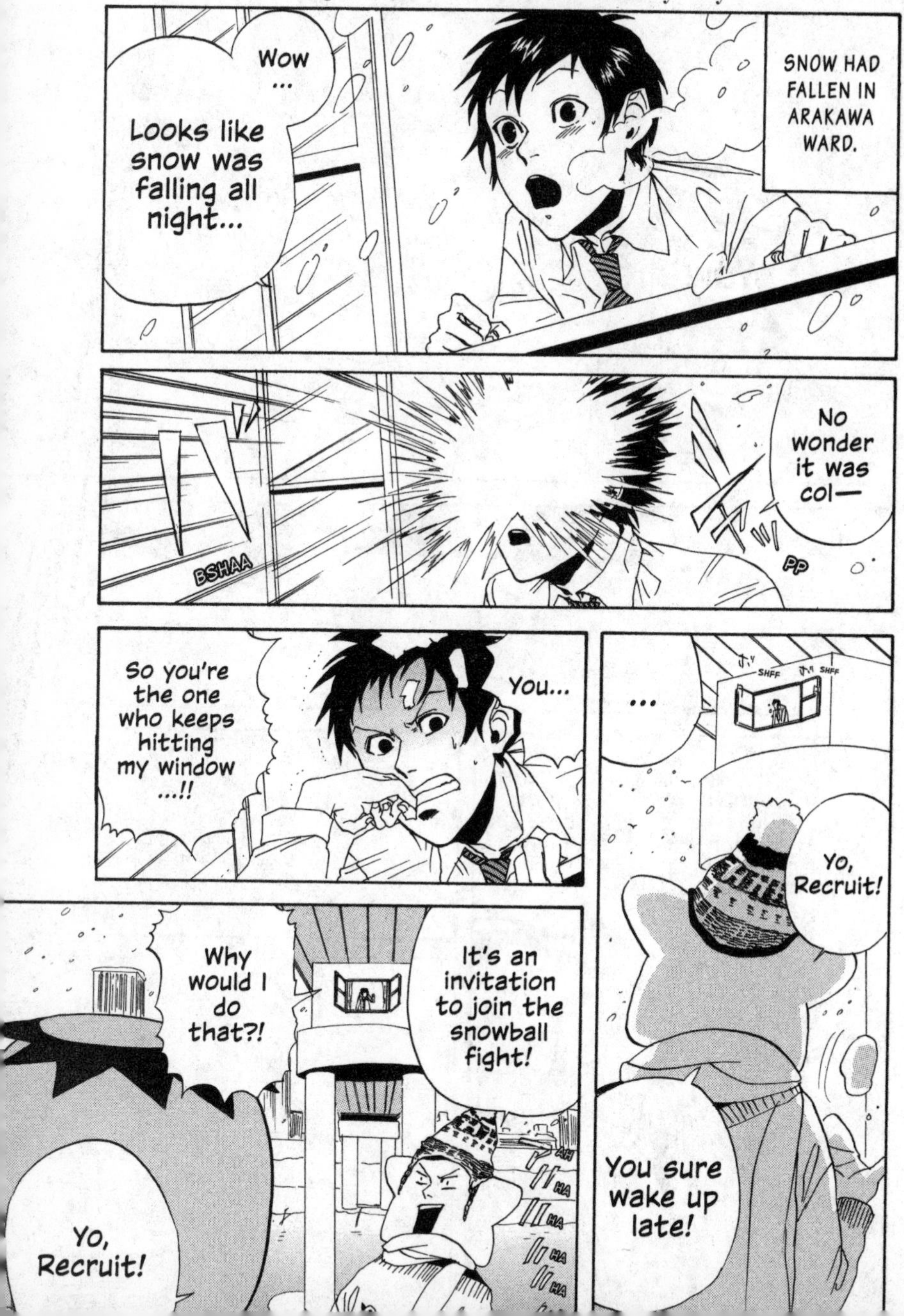
SNOW HAD FALLEN IN ARAKAWA WARD.
Wow ...
Looks like snow was falling all night...
No wonder it was col—
PP
BSHAA
SHFF
SHFF
...
Yo, Recruit!
You sure wake up late!
You...
So you're the one who keeps hitting my window ...!!
It's an invitation to join the snowball fight!
Why would I do that?!
AH
HA
HA
HA
HA
Yo, Recruit!

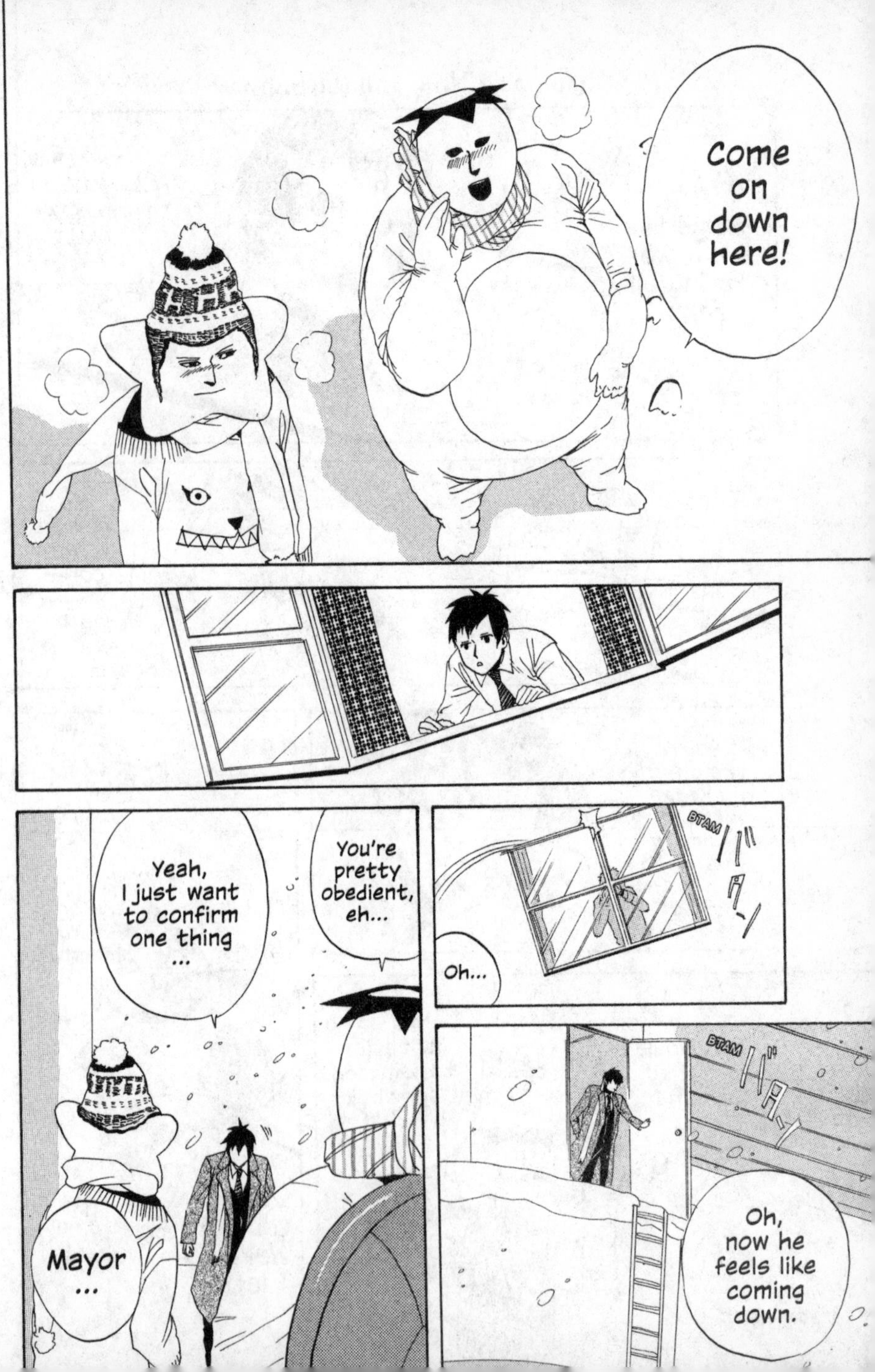
Come on down here!
BTAM
Oh...
BTAM
Oh, now he feels like coming down.
You're pretty obedient, eh...
Yeah, I just want to confirm one thing ...
Mayor ...

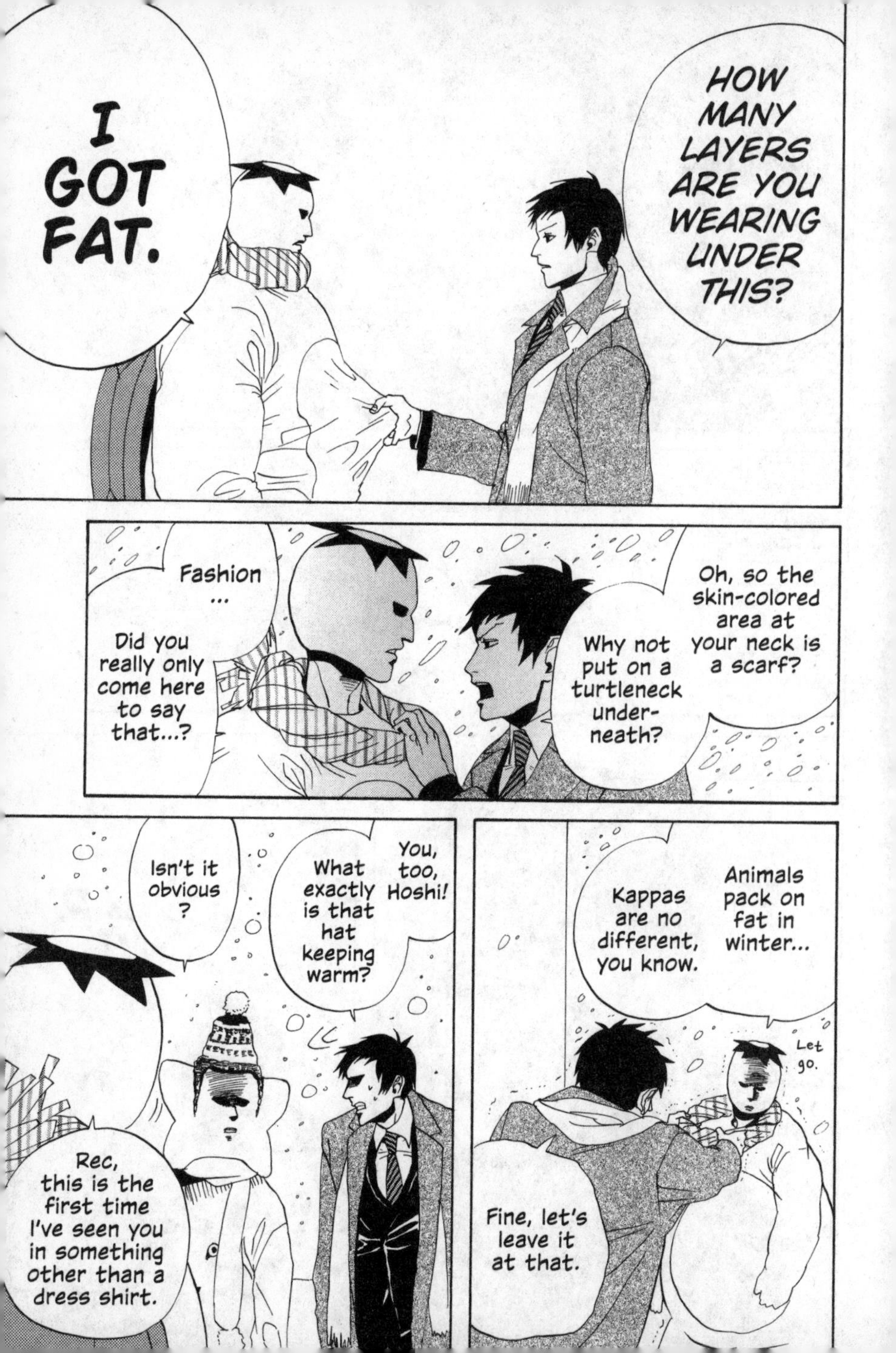
HOW MANY LAYERS ARE YOU WEARING UNDER THIS?
I GOT FAT.
Oh, so the skin-colored area at your neck is a scarf?
Why not put on a turtleneck underneath?
Fashion ...
Did you really only come here to say that...?
Animals pack on fat in winter...
Kappas are no different, you know.
Let go.
Fine, let's leave it at that.
You, too, Hoshi!
What exactly is that hat keeping warm?
Isn't it obvious?
Rec, this is the first time I've seen you in something other than a dress shirt.

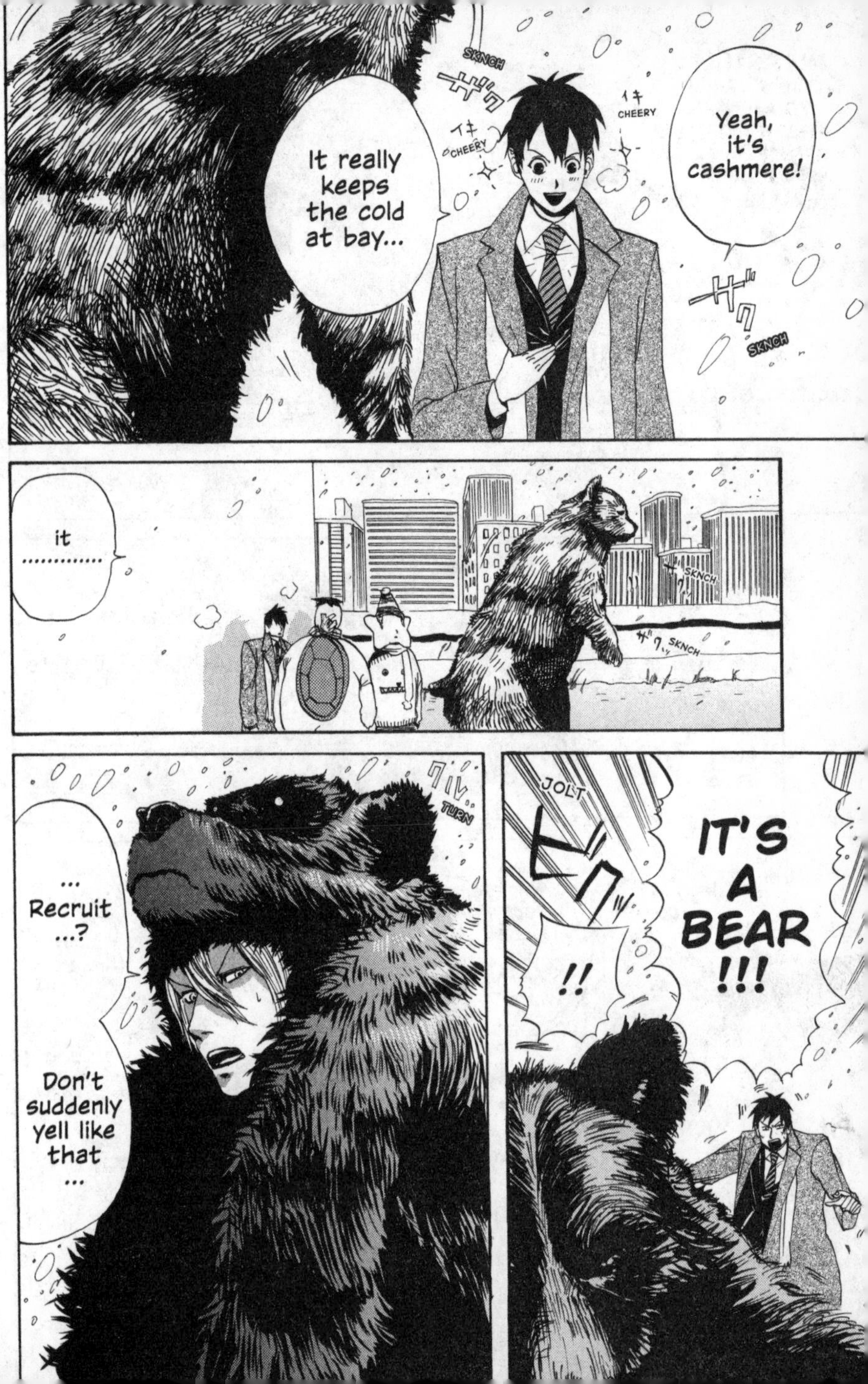

Yeah, it's cashmere!
SKNCH
CHEERY
SKNCH
CHEERY
It really keeps the cold at bay...
SKNCH
SKNCH
it ....
JOLT
IT'S A BEAR !!!
!!
TURN
... Recruit ...?
... Don't suddenly yell like that ...

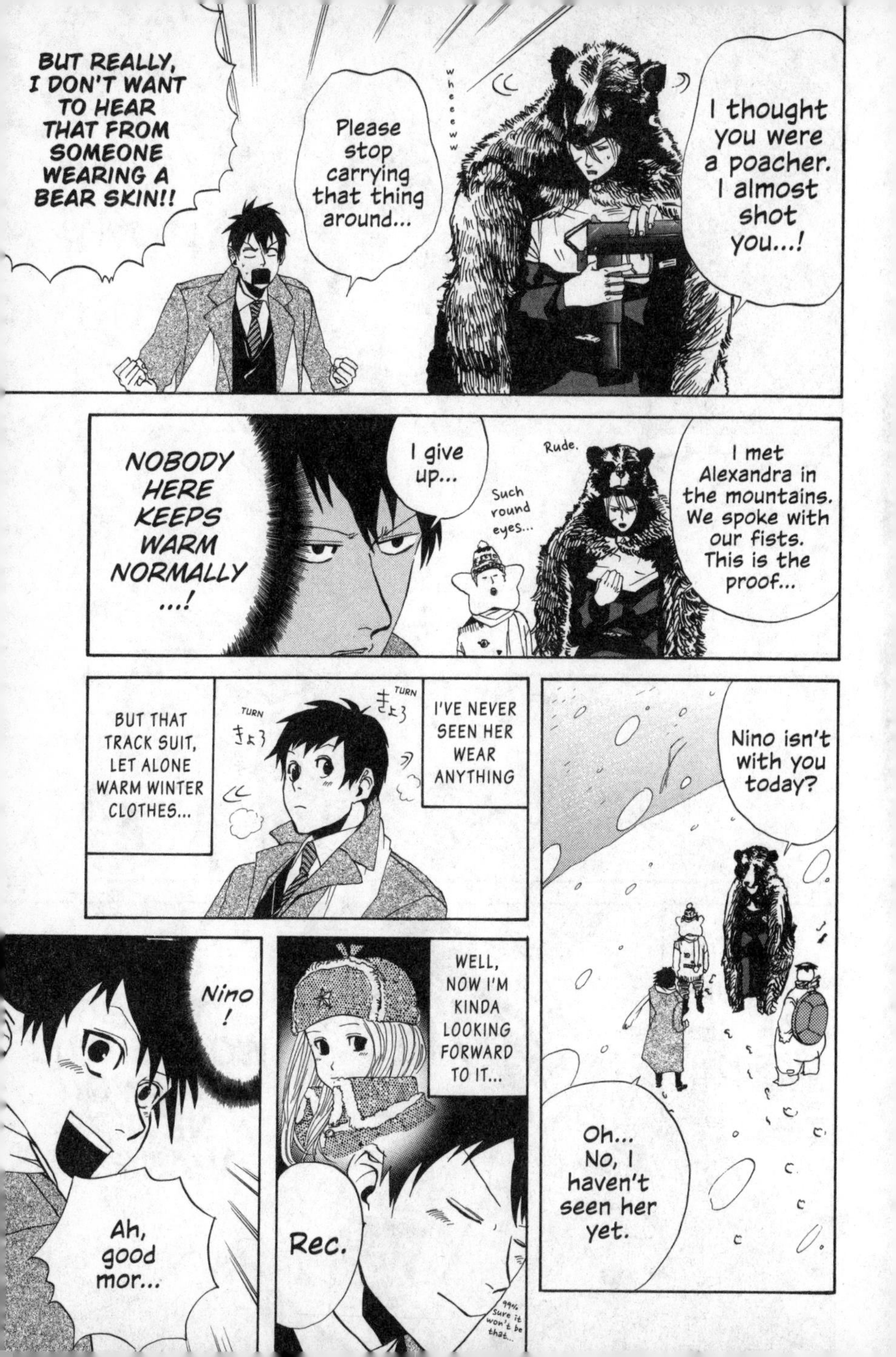
I thought you were a poacher. I almost shot you...!
wheeeww
Please stop carrying that thing around...
BUT REALLY, I DON'T WANT TO HEAR THAT FROM SOMEONE WEARING A BEAR SKIN!!
I met Alexandra in the mountains. We spoke with our fists. This is the proof...
Rude.
Such round eyes...
I give up...
NOBODY HERE KEEPS WARM NORMALLY ...!
Nino isn't with you today?
Oh... No, I haven't seen her yet.
I'VE NEVER SEEN HER WEAR ANYTHING
TURN
きょろ
TURN
きょろ
BUT THAT TRACK SUIT, LET ALONE WARM WINTER CLOTHES...
WELL, NOW I'M KINDA LOOKING FORWARD TO IT...
Rec.
99% Sure it won't be that...
Nino!
Ah, good mor...

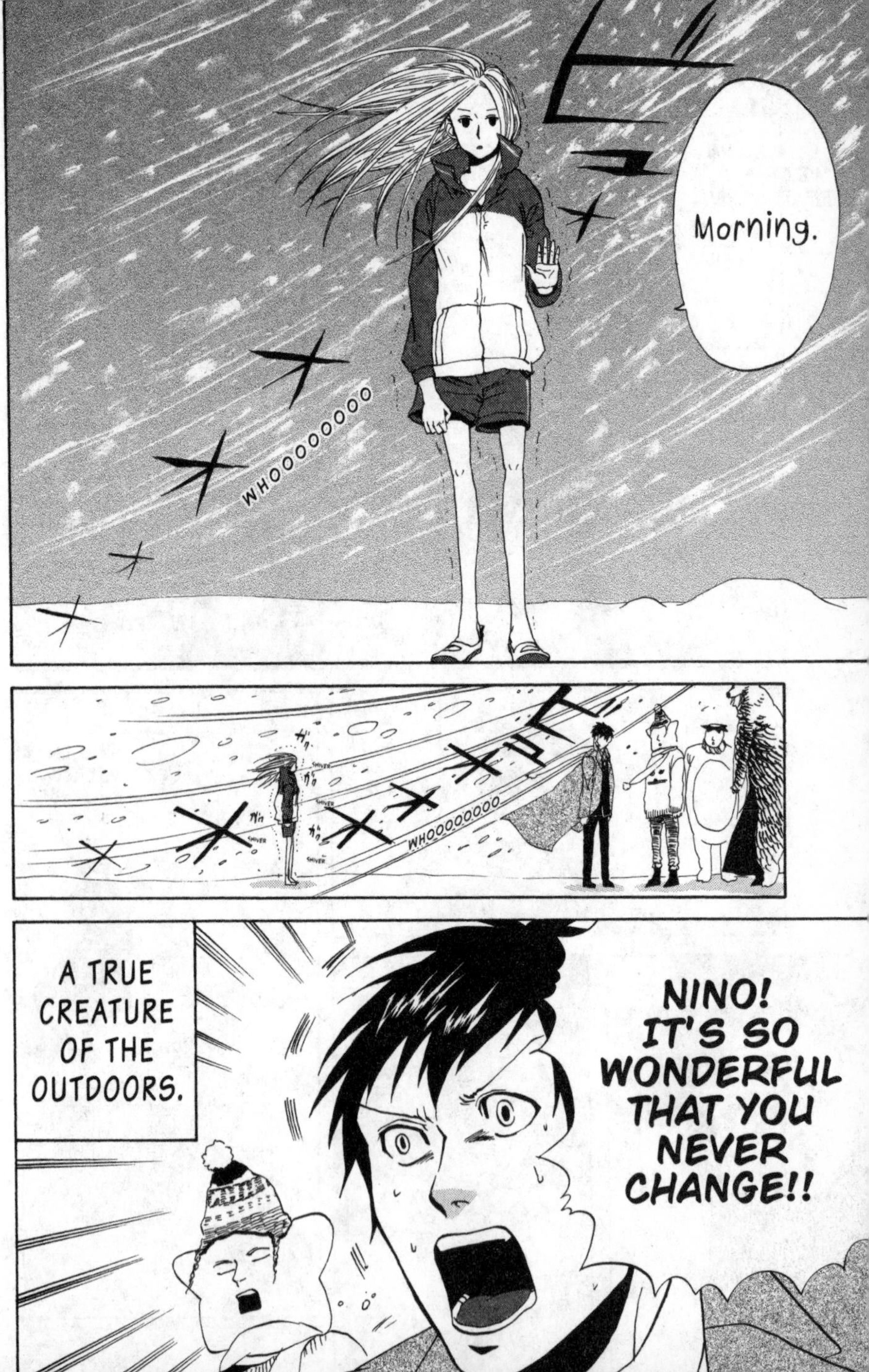
Morning.
WHOOOOOOOOO
WHOOOOOOOOO
SHIVER
SHIVER
SHIVER
SHIVER
NINO! IT'S SO WONDERFUL THAT YOU NEVER CHANGE!!
A TRUE CREATURE OF THE OUTDOORS.

☜Chapter 23: For Love

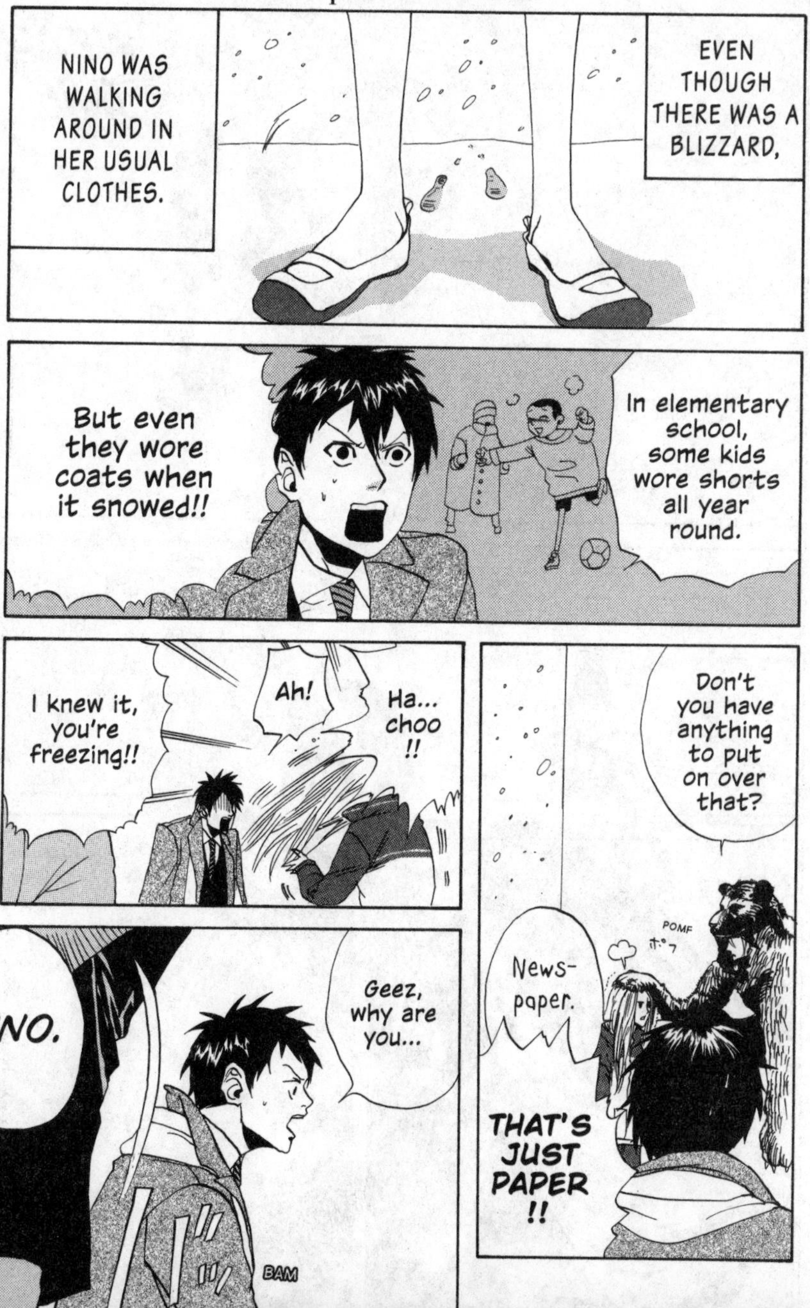
EVEN THOUGH THERE WAS A BLIZZARD,
NINO WAS WALKING AROUND IN HER USUAL CLOTHES.
In elementary school, some kids wore shorts all year round.
But even they wore coats when it snowed!!
Don't you have anything to put on over that?
POMF
ポッ
News-paper.
THAT'S JUST PAPER !!
Ha... choo !!
Ah!
I knew it, you're freezing!!
Geez, why are you...
NINO.
BAM

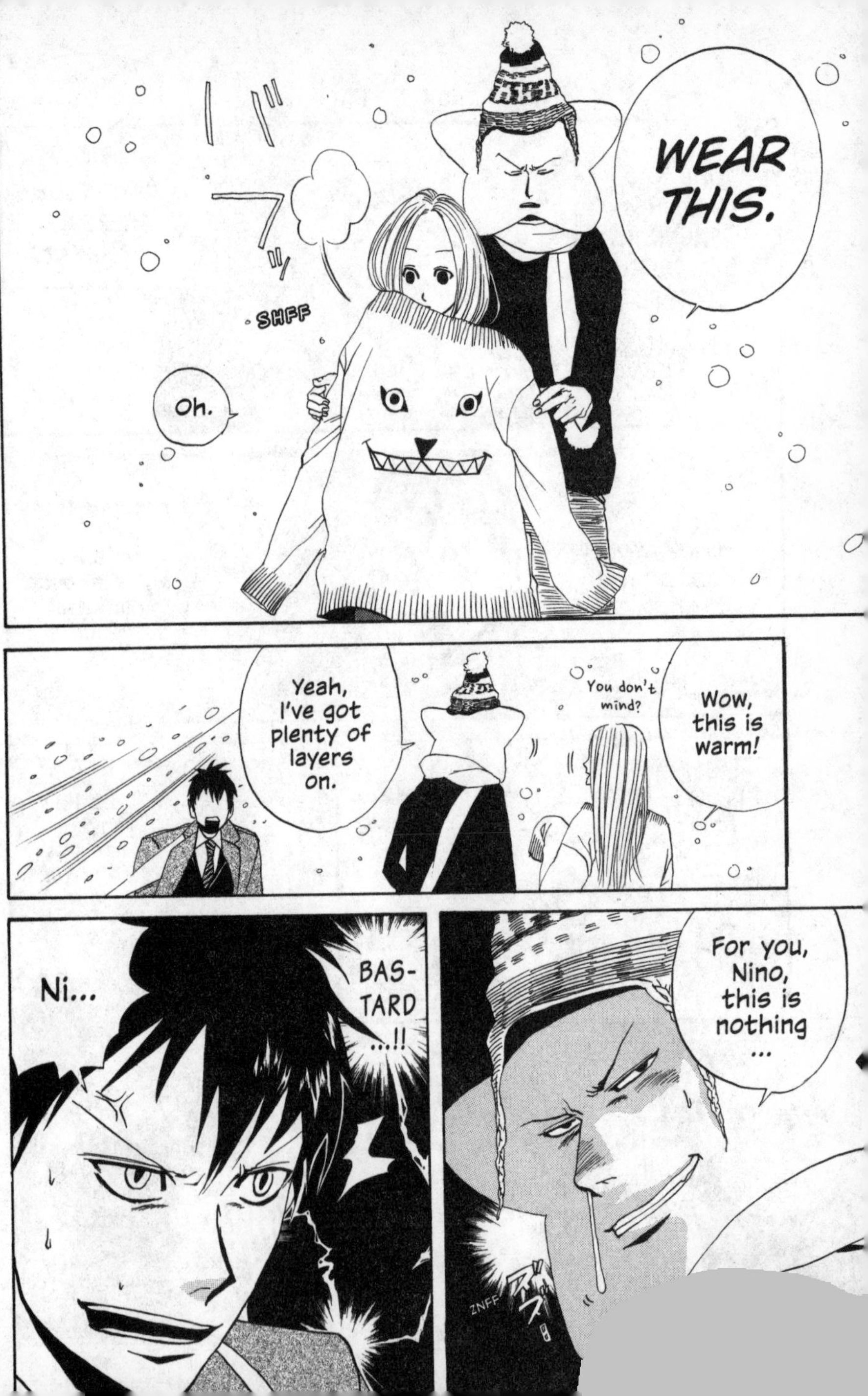
WEAR THIS.
SHFF
Oh.
Wow, this is warm!
You don't mind?
Yeah, I've got plenty of layers on.
For you, Nino, this is nothing ...
ZNFF
BAS-TARD ...!!
Ni...

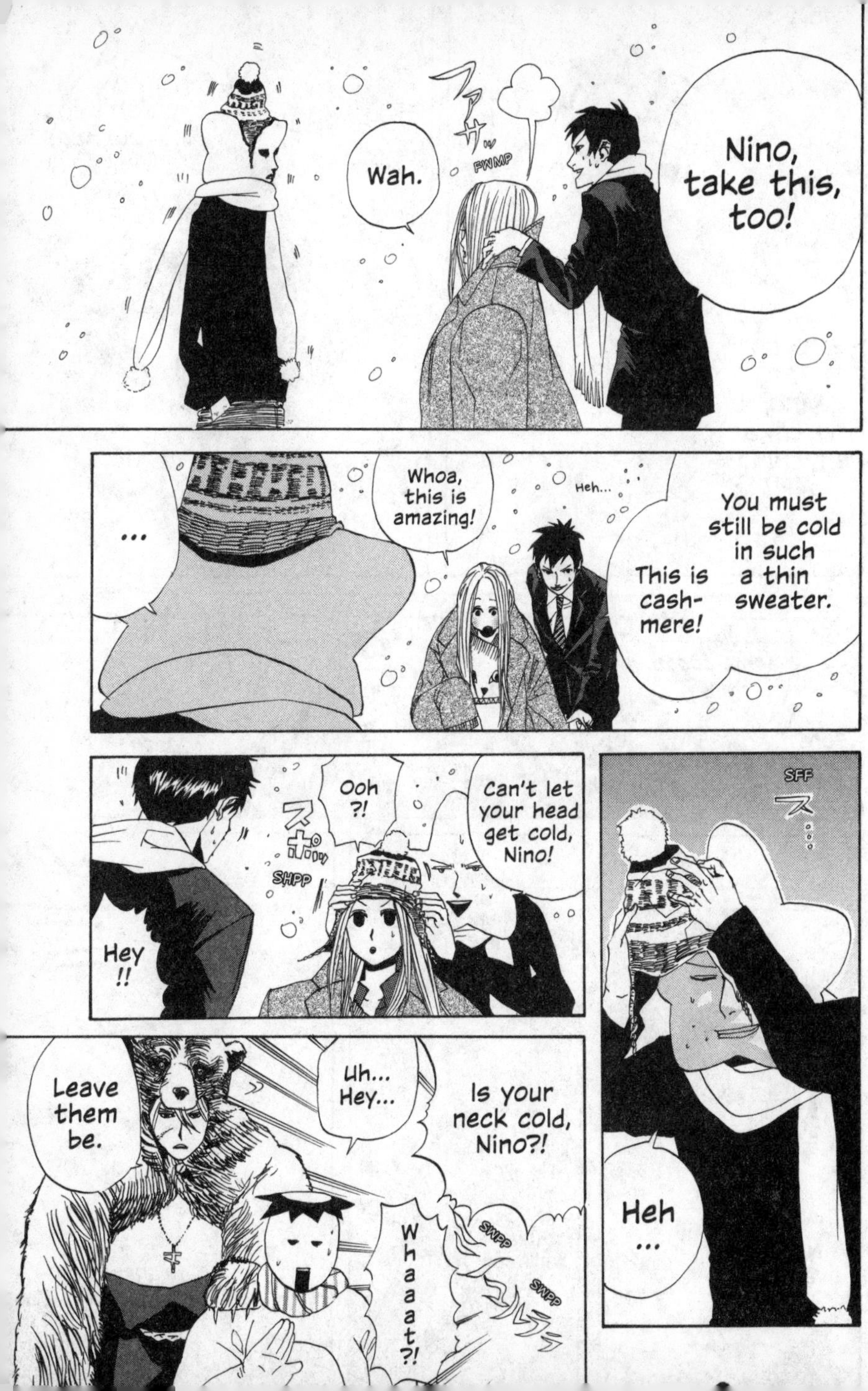
Nino, take this, too!
FWMP
Wah.
You must still be cold in such a thin sweater.
This is cash-mere!
Heh...
Whoa, this is amazing!
...
SFF
Heh ...
Can't let your head get cold, Nino!
Ooh ?!
SHPP
Hey !!
Is your neck cold, Nino?!
Uh... Hey...
Leave them be.
SWPP
SWPP
Whaaaat?!

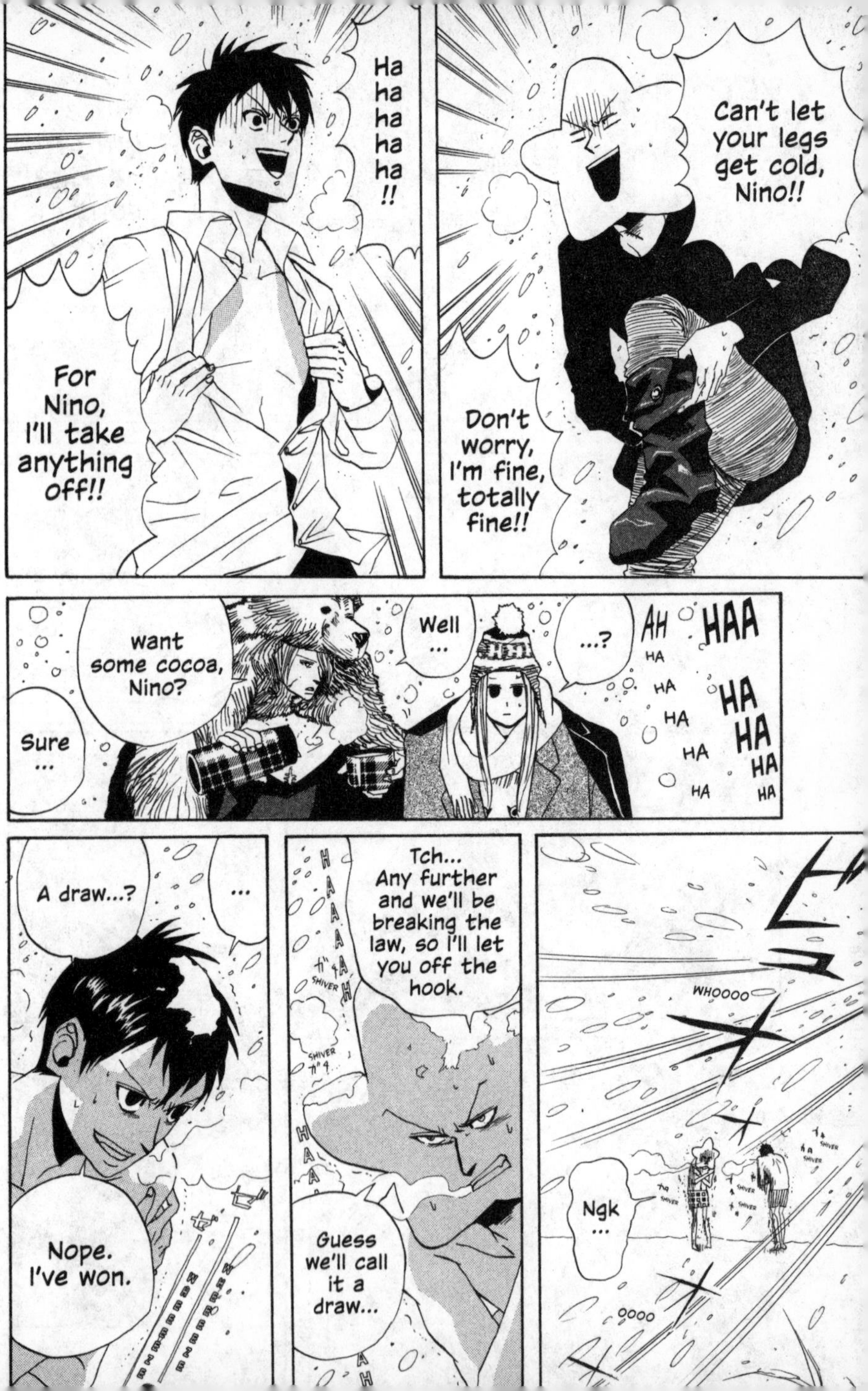
Can't let your legs get cold, Nino!!
Don't worry, I'm fine, totally fine!!
Ha ha ha ha ha!!
For Nino, I'll take anything off!!
AH HAA HA HA HA HA HA HA HA HA HA
...?
Well ...
want some cocoa, Nino?
Sure ...
WHOOOO
SHIVER
SHIVER
SHIVER
SHIVER
SHIVER
Ngk ...
OOOO
Tch... Any further and we'll be breaking the law, so I'll let you off the hook.
HAAAAAH
SHIVER
SHIVER
Guess we'll call it a draw...
A draw...?
...
Nope. I've won.

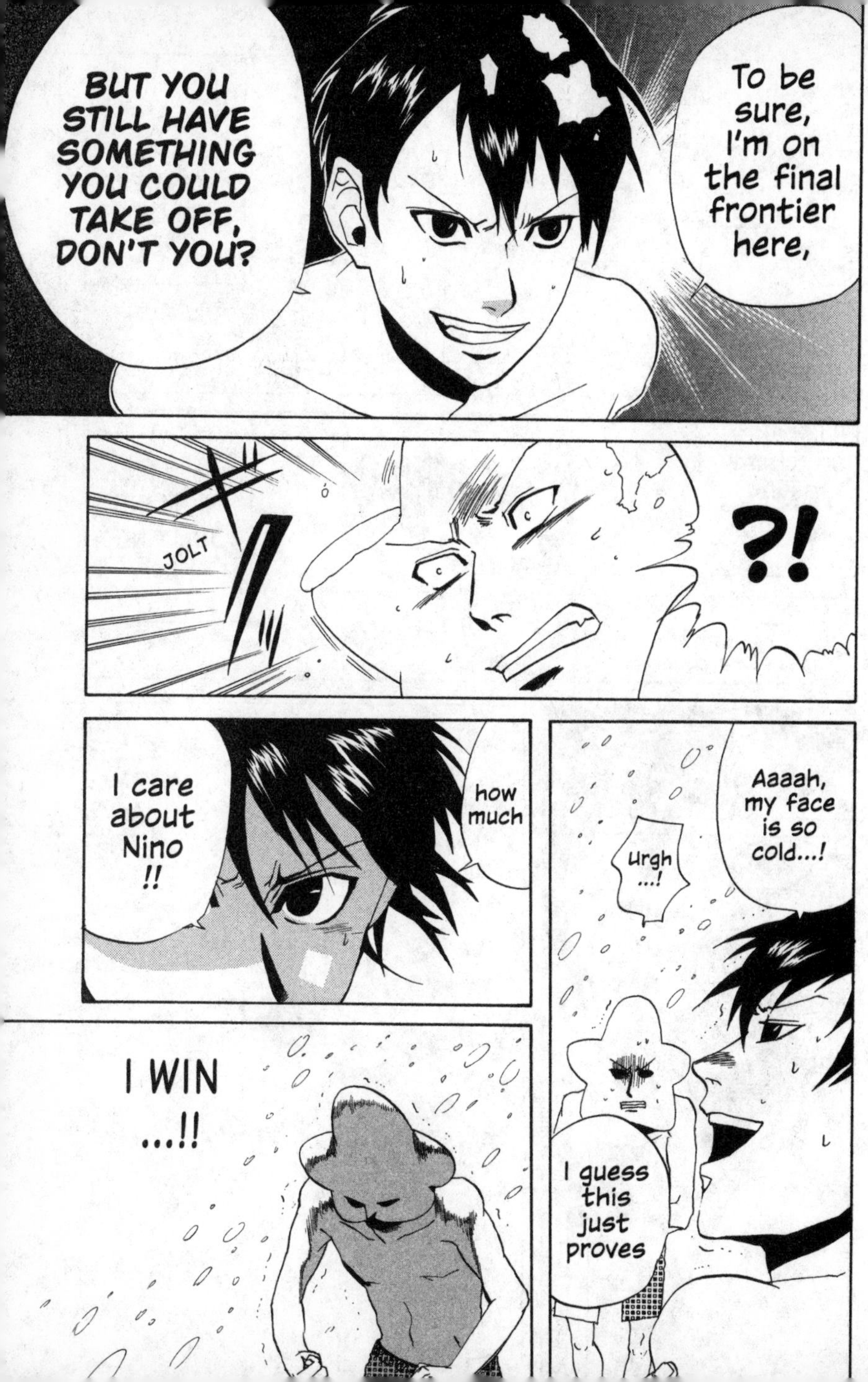
To be sure, I'm on the final frontier here,
BUT YOU STILL HAVE SOMETHING YOU COULD TAKE OFF, DON'T YOU?
?!
JOLT
Aaaah, my face is so cold...!
Urgh ...!
I guess this just proves
how much
I care about Nino !!
I WIN ...!!

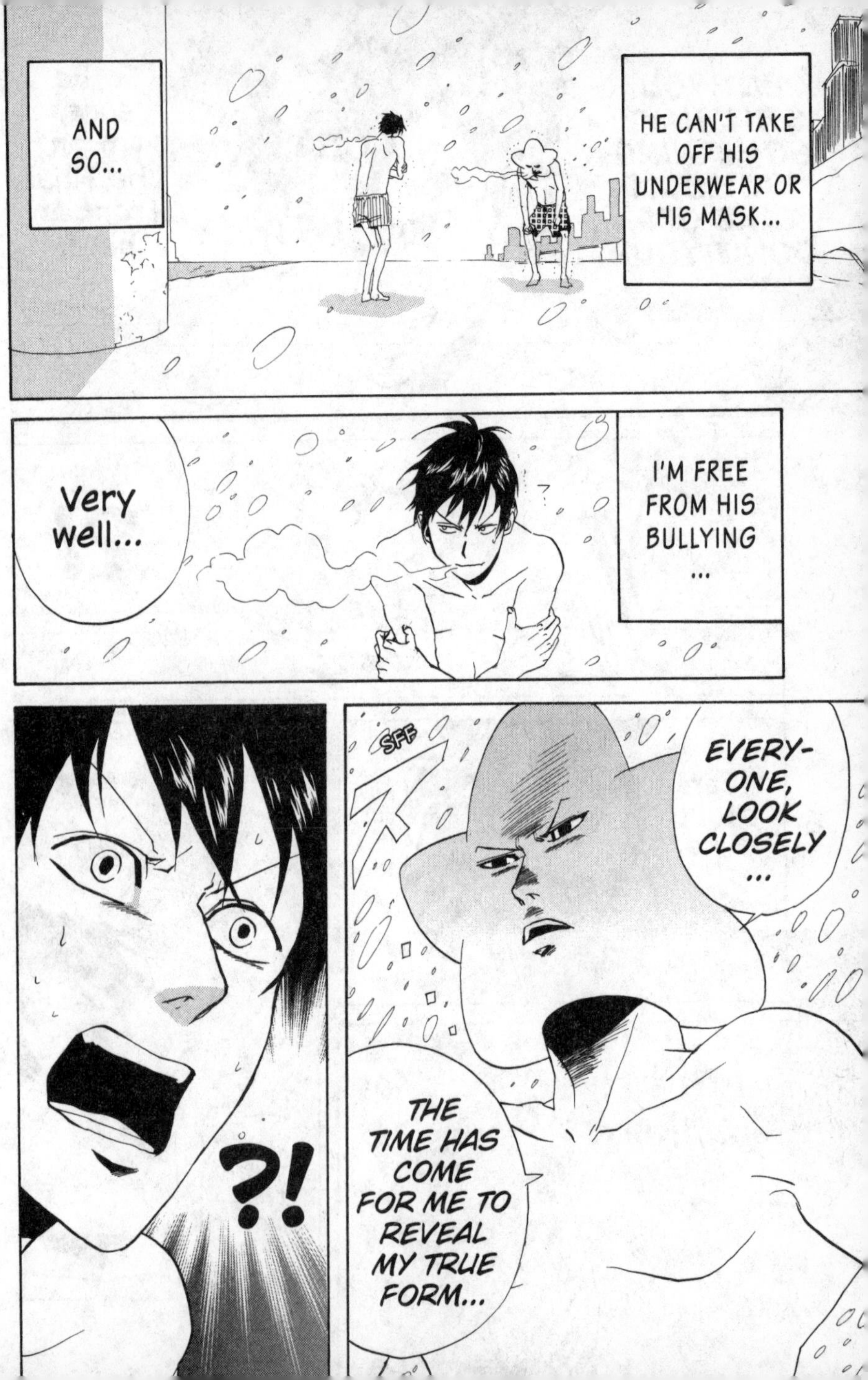
HE CAN'T TAKE OFF HIS UNDERWEAR OR HIS MASK...
AND SO...
I'M FREE FROM HIS BULLYING ...
Very well...
SFF
EVERY-ONE, LOOK CLOSELY ...
THE TIME HAS COME FOR ME TO REVEAL MY TRUE FORM...
?!

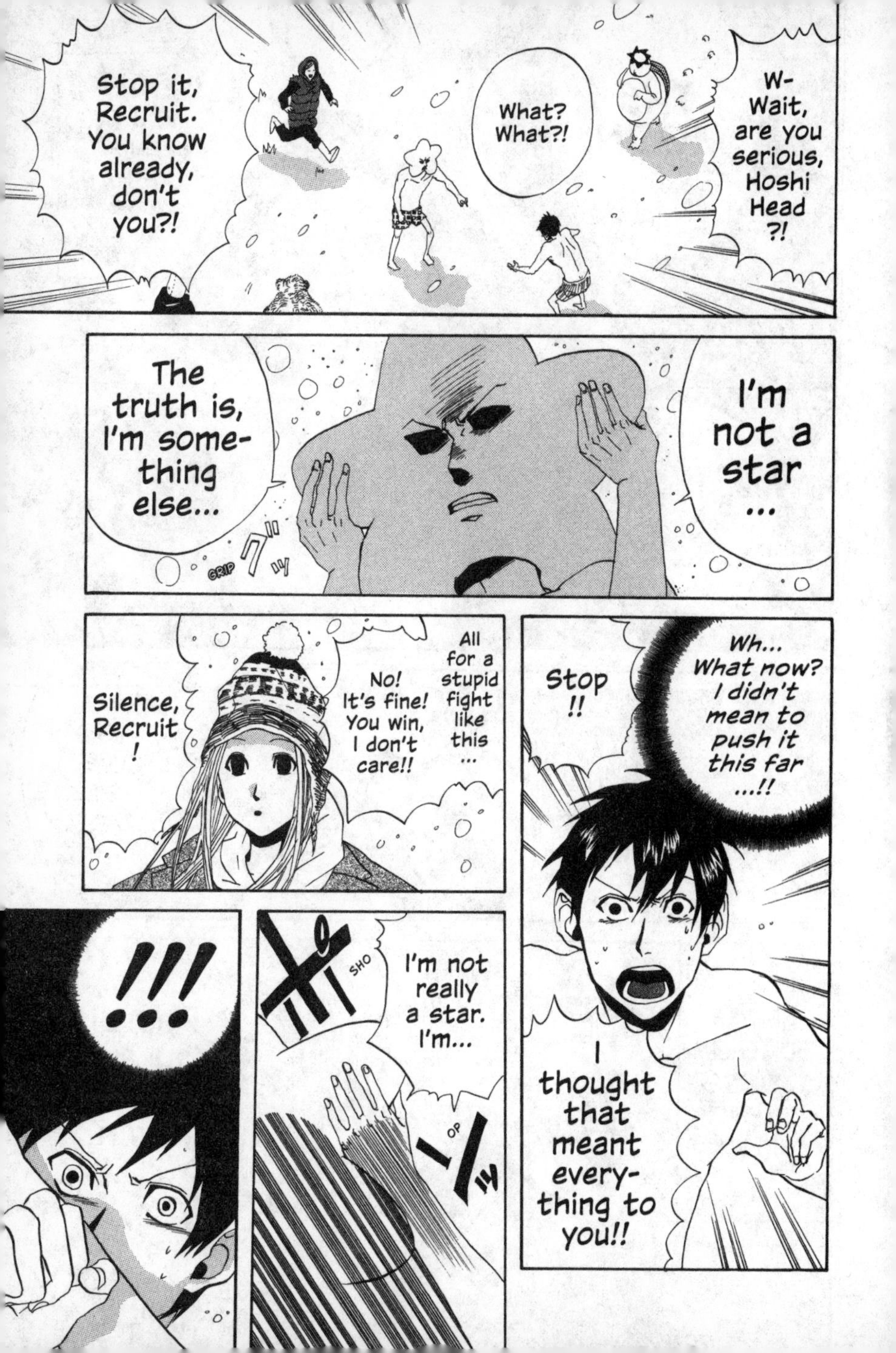
W- Wait, are you serious, Hoshi Head ?!
What? What?!
Stop it, Recruit. You know already, don't you?!
I'm not a star ...
The truth is, I'm some-thing else...
GRIP
Wh... What now? I didn't mean to push it this far ...!!
Stop !!
I thought that meant every-thing to you!!
All for a stupid fight like this ...
No! It's fine! You win, I don't care!!
Silence, Recruit !
SHO
I'm not really a star. I'm...
OP
!!!

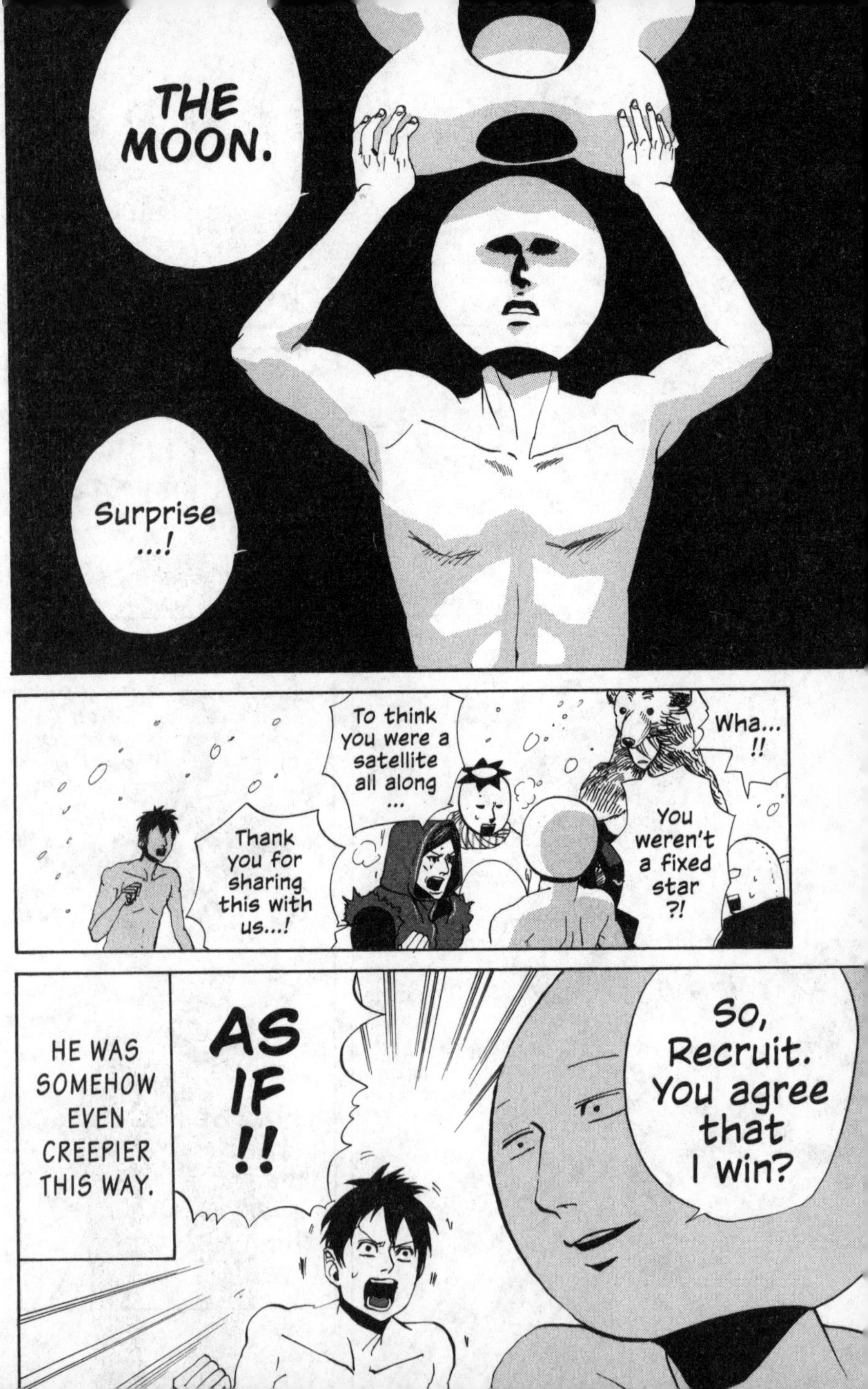
THE MOON.
Surprise ...!
Wha... !!
You weren't a fixed star ?!
To think you were a satellite all along ...
Thank you for sharing this with us...!
So, Recruit. You agree that I win?
AS IF !!
HE WAS SOMEHOW EVEN CREEPIER THIS WAY.

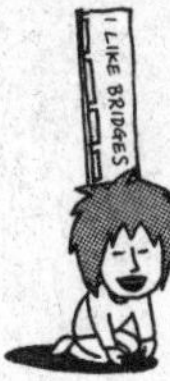
I LIKE BRIDGES

AFTERWORD

Thank you for buying Arakawa Under the the Bridge volume 1. Personally, I have a lot of fun drawing this manga, and I really love it. If I have entertained you thus far, dear reader, then I am thrilled. I hope we will meet again next volume!

June 9, 2005 -- Hikaru Nakamura

Information

Truth is these ↓ characters were created for the comedic manga "Nakamura Studio" volumes 1-3. It's a collection of short gag stories, so if you're interested, please read it!

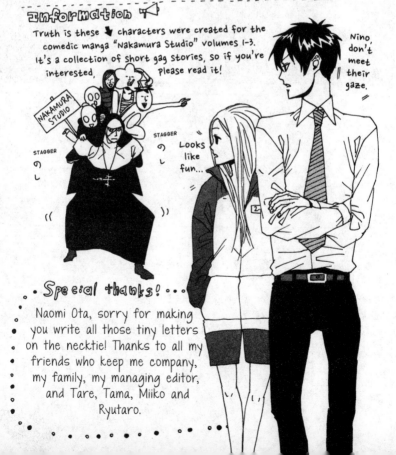

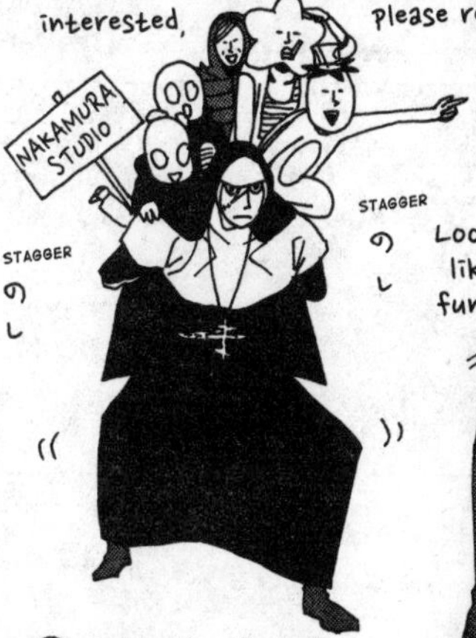
NAKAMURA STUDIO
STAGGER
STAGGER

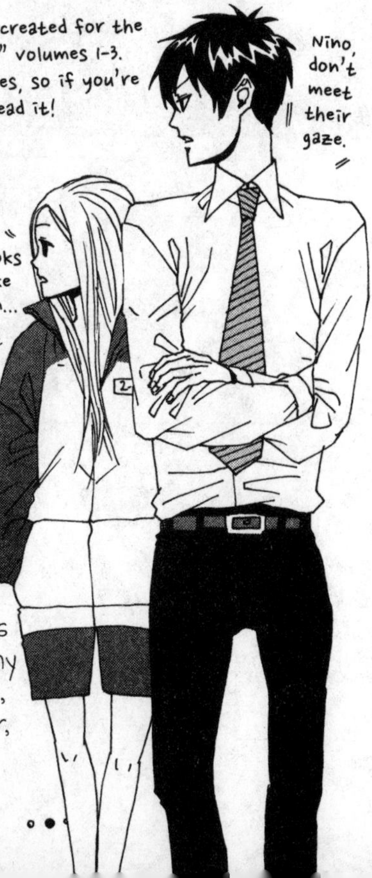
Nino, don't meet their gaze.
Looks like fun...

Special thanks!

Naomi Ota, sorry for making you write all those tiny letters on the necktie! Thanks to all my friends who keep me company, my family, my managing editor, and Tare, Tama, Miiko and Ryutaro.

Ichinomiya Heirloom Necktie

Hand-woven.
I feel sorry for
the artisan who
made it.

Sister's cookies

Hand-made, and actually pretty tasty.

Probably because he can apply a lot of pressure when kneading the dough.

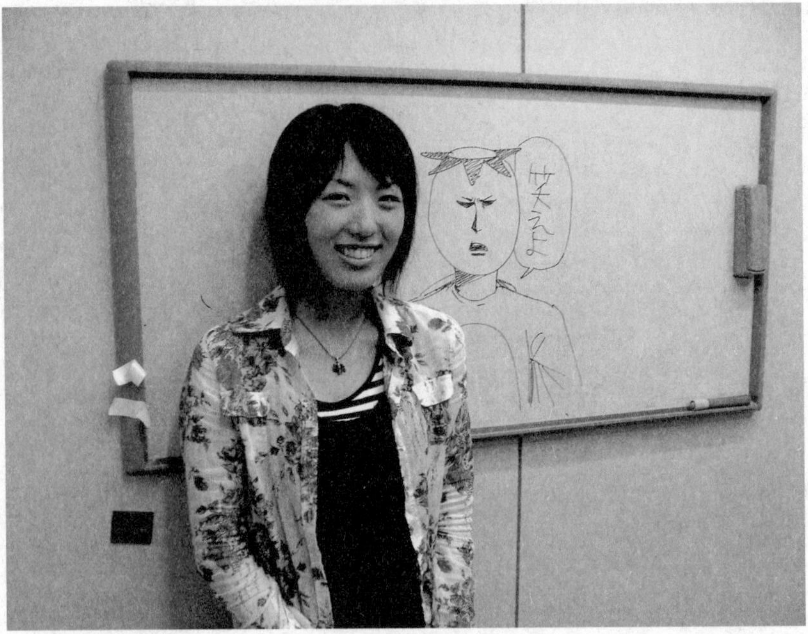
笑えよ

When I was small, we often stopped at the river bank on the way home. Sunlight would reflect off the water, so it was light even under the bridge. I loved that place, and living under there was one of my dreams as a child. In a sense, that dream has come true with this manga. Thank you, *Arakawa Under the Bridge*. Yet I give my most heart-felt thanks to you, dear reader, for picking up this book.

—Hikaru Nakamura

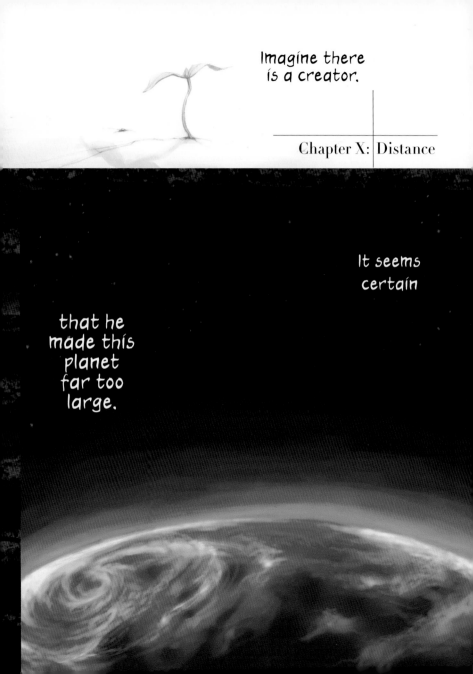

Imagine there is a creator.

Chapter X: Distance

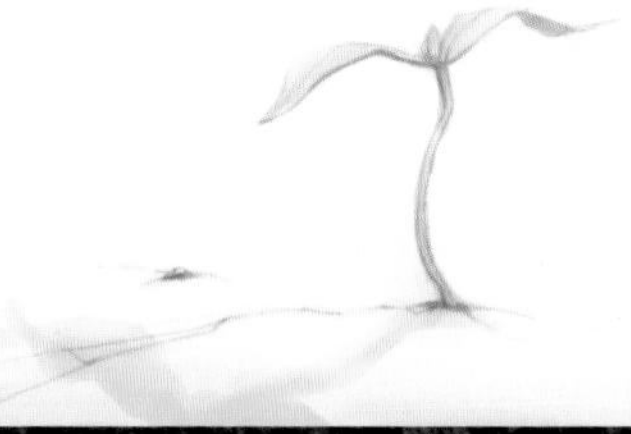

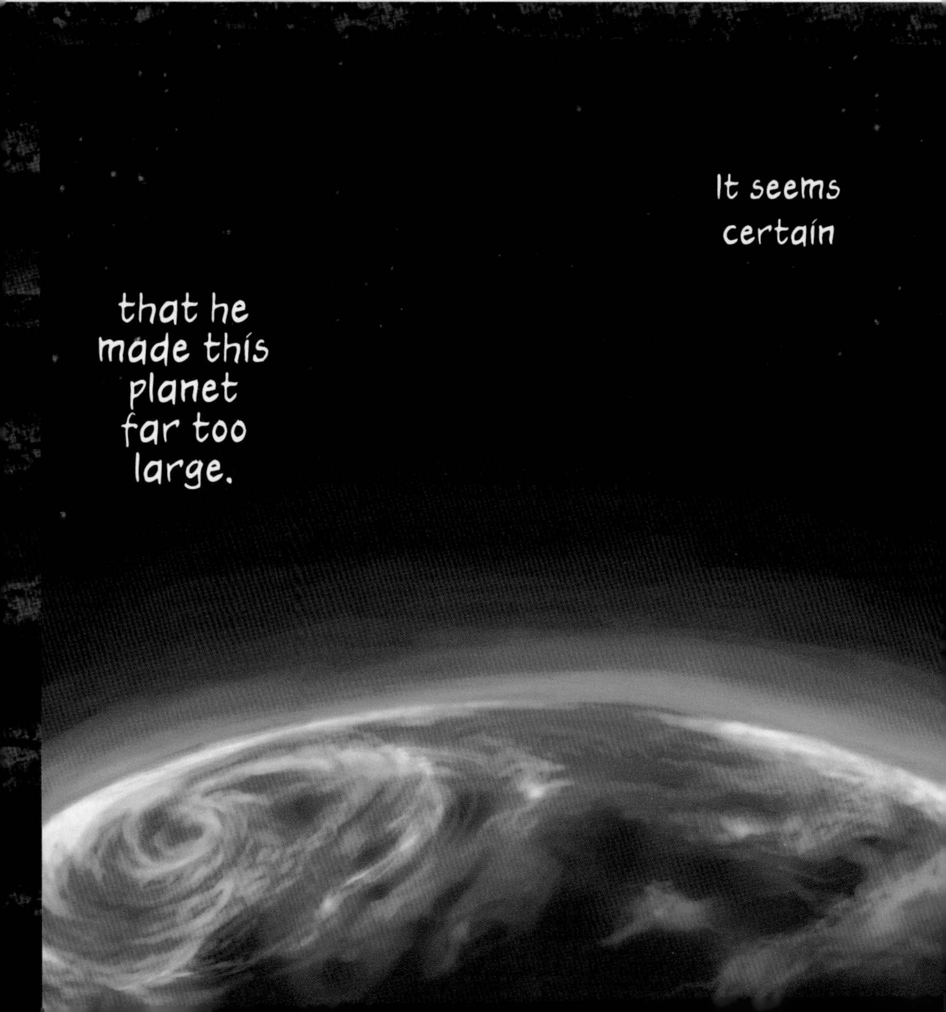
It seems certain
that he made this planet far too large.

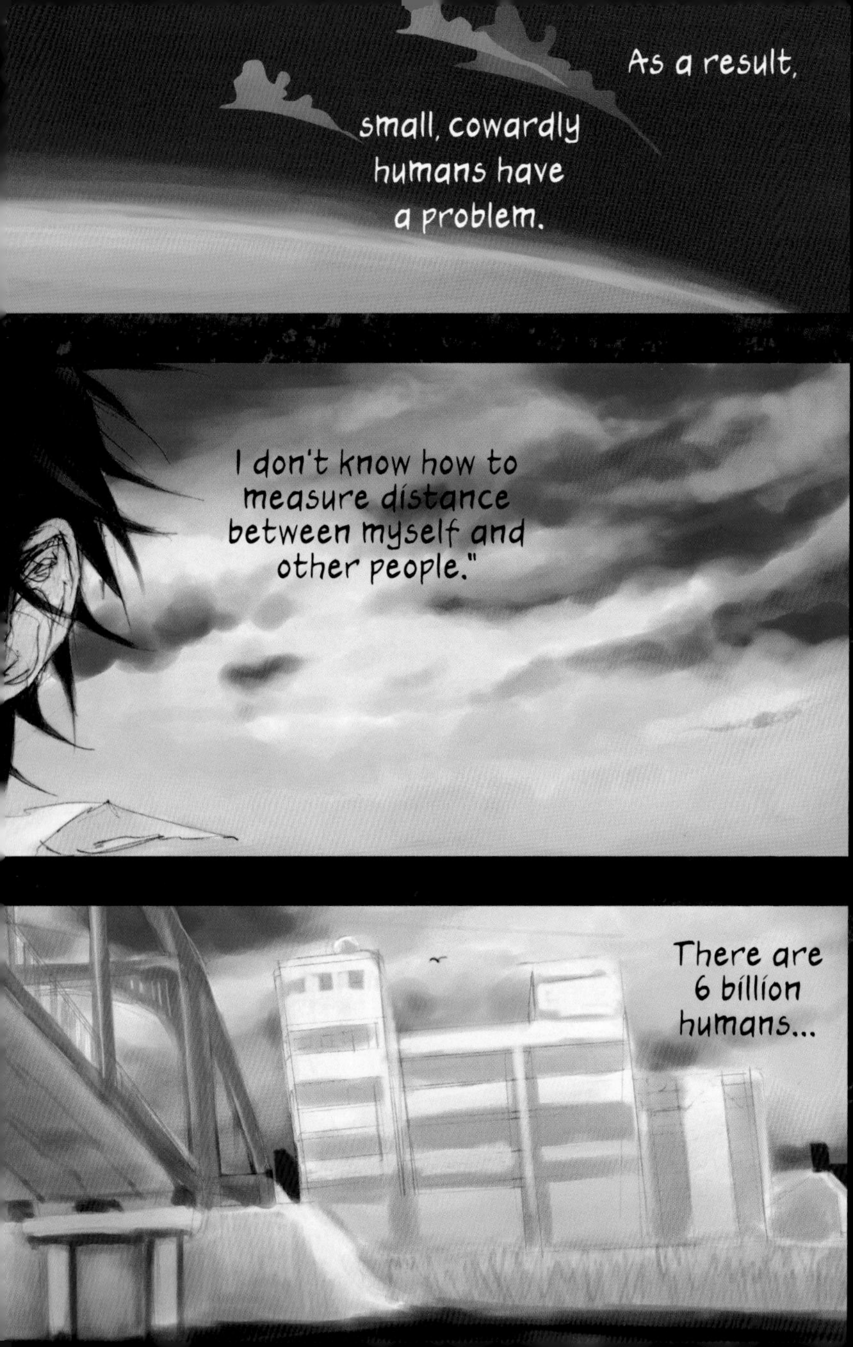
As a result,
small, cowardly humans have a problem.
I don't know how to measure distance between myself and other people."
There are 6 billion humans...

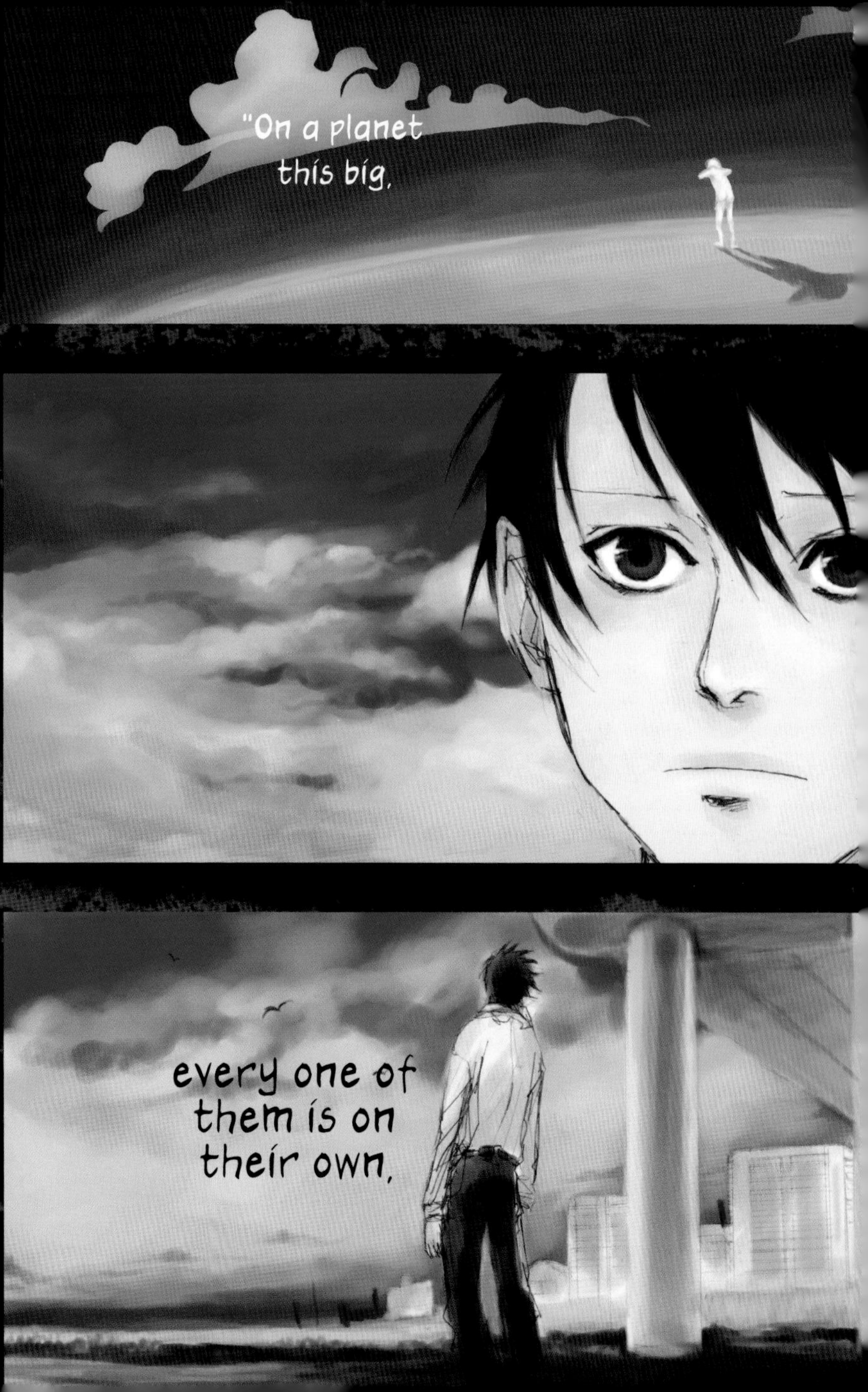
"On a planet this big,
every one of them is on their own,

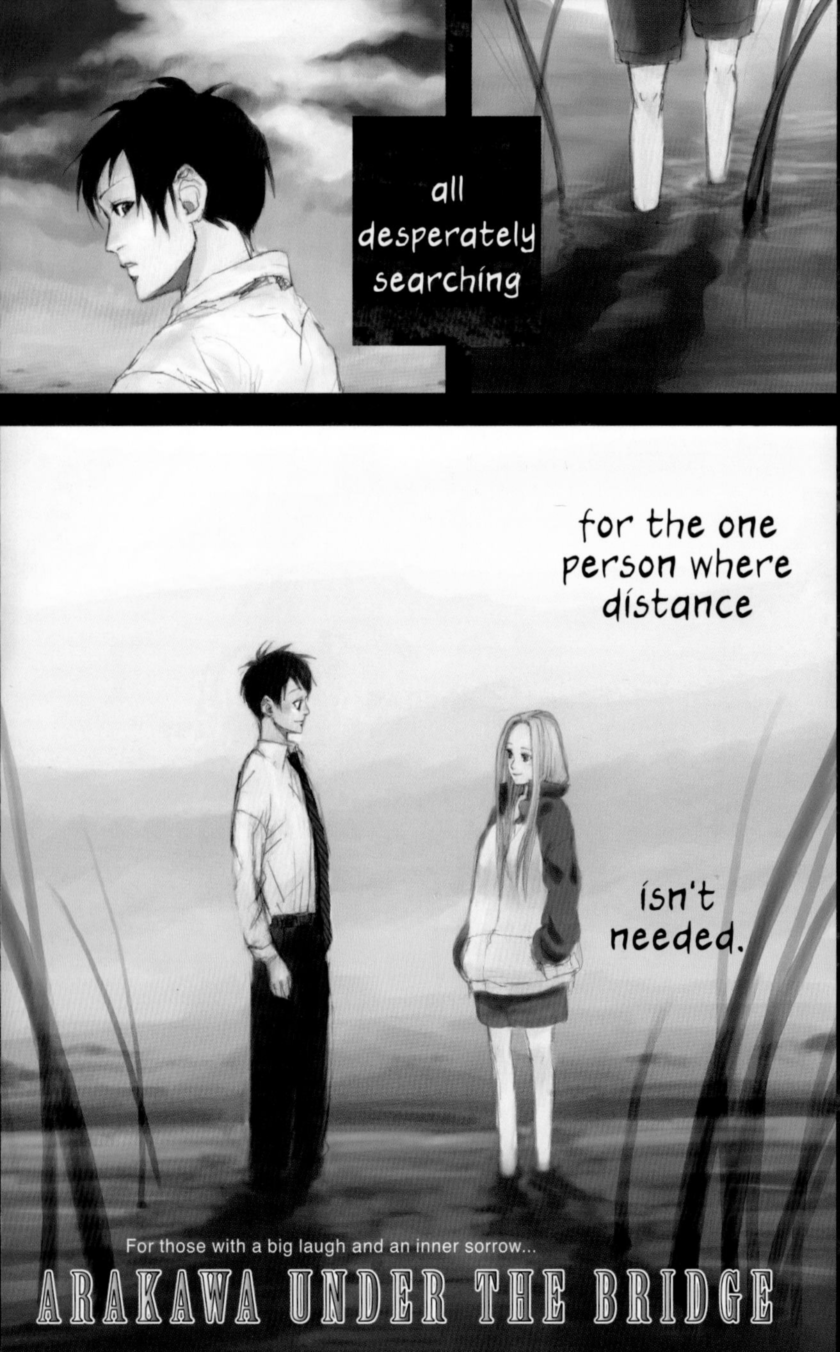
all desperately searching
for the one person where distance
isn't needed.
For those with a big laugh and an inner sorrow...
ARAKAWA UNDER THE BRIDGE

ARAKAWA UNDER THE BRIDGE

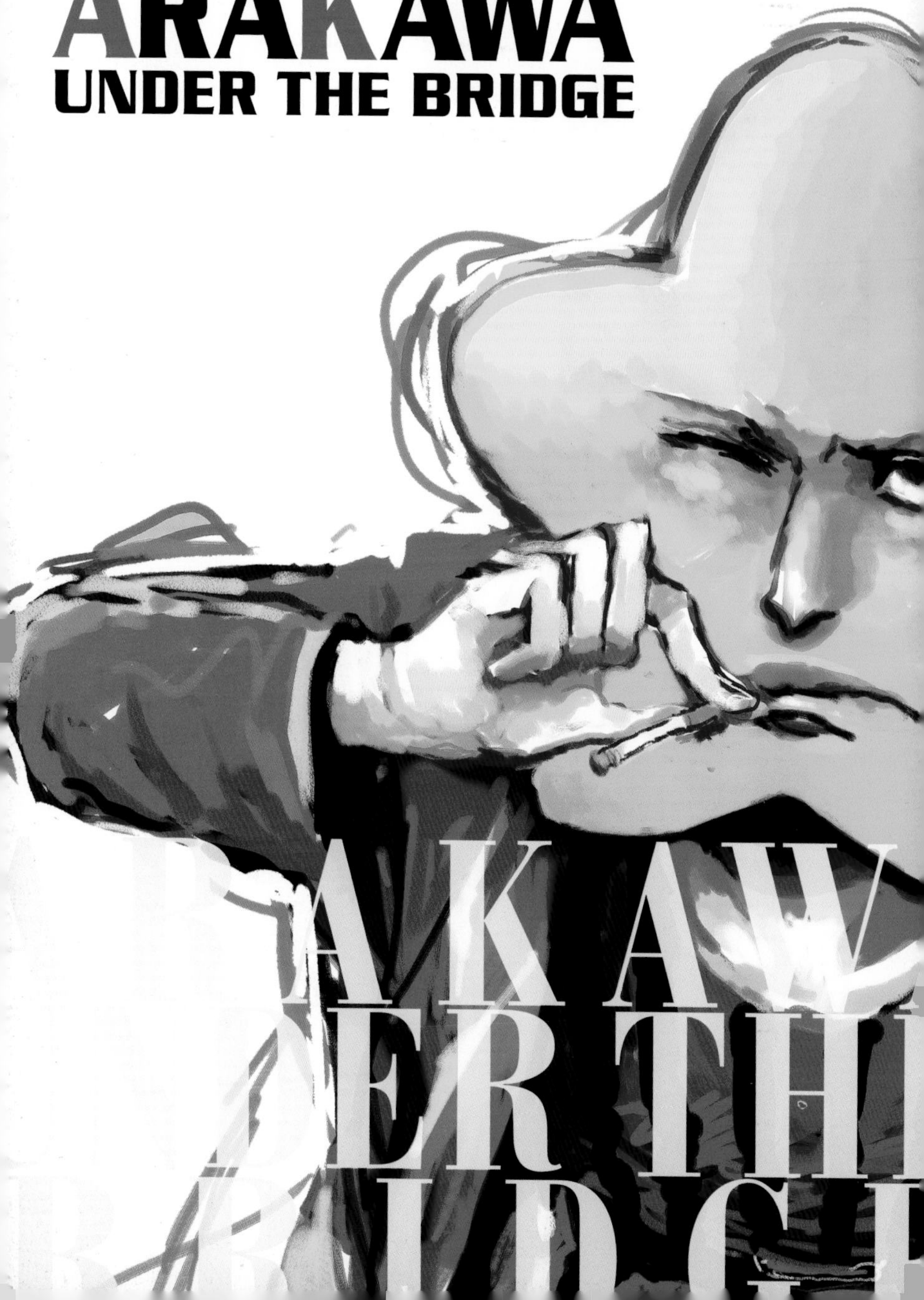

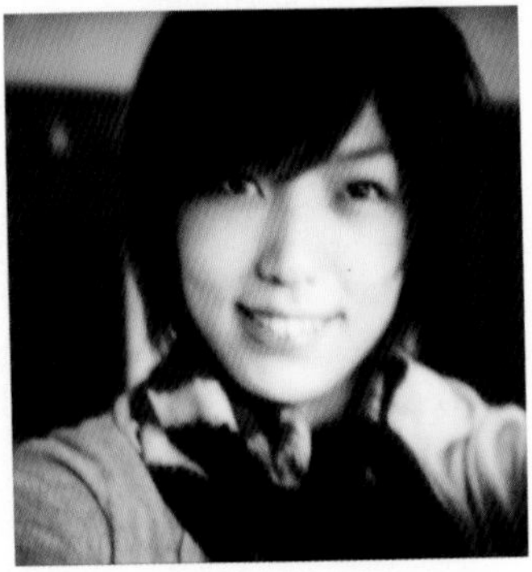

This volume came out successfully. I'm so happy! Thank you. I've started to want to live near a river, so I'm slowly putting together a plan to move. I'd like to live in a place where I can walk down to the river bed.

—Hikaru Nakamura

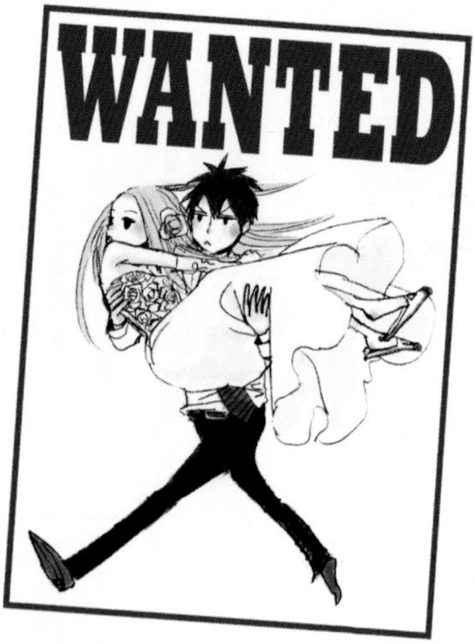
WANTED

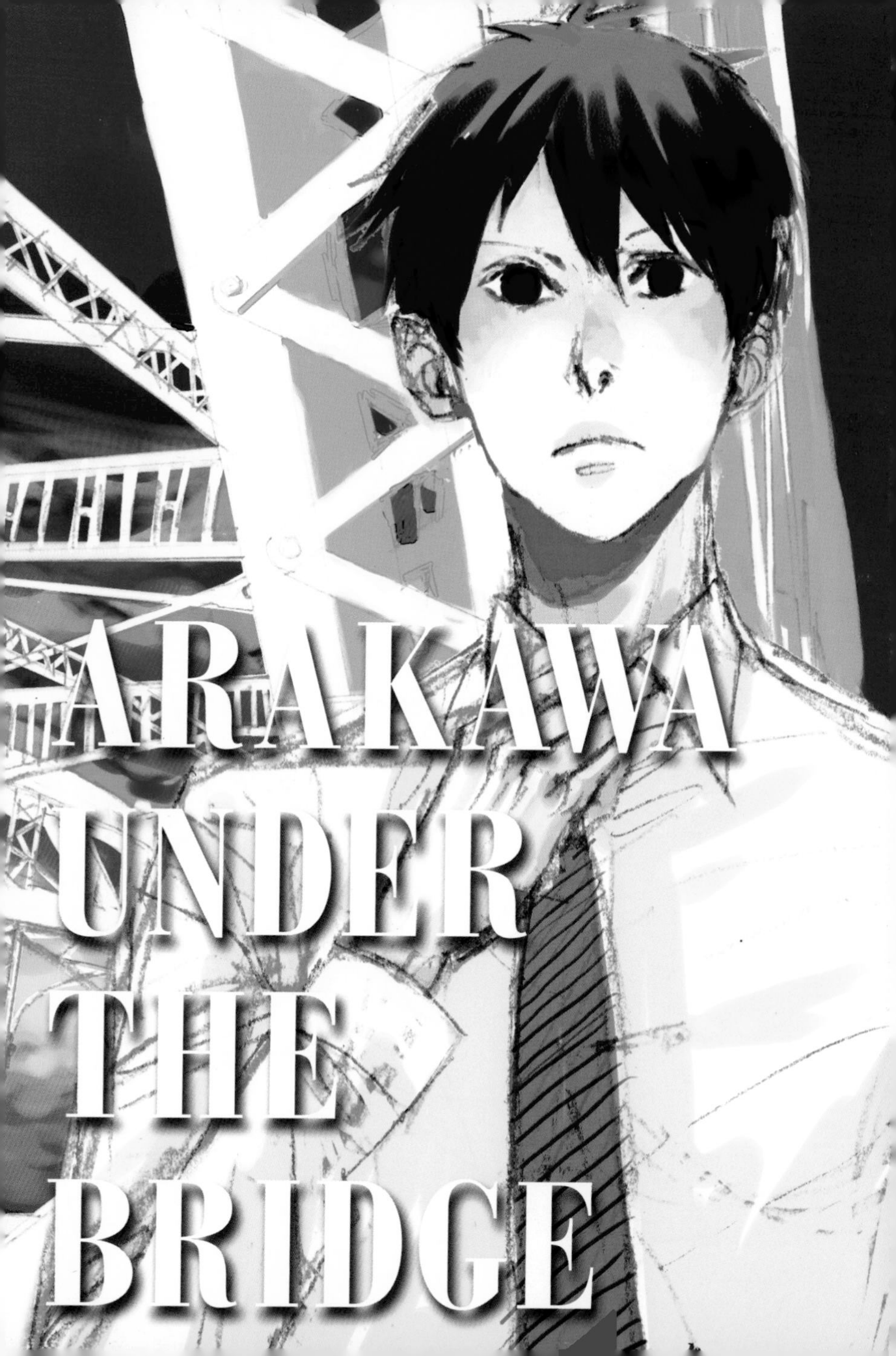
ARAKAWA
UNDER
THE
BRIDGE

C O N T E N T S

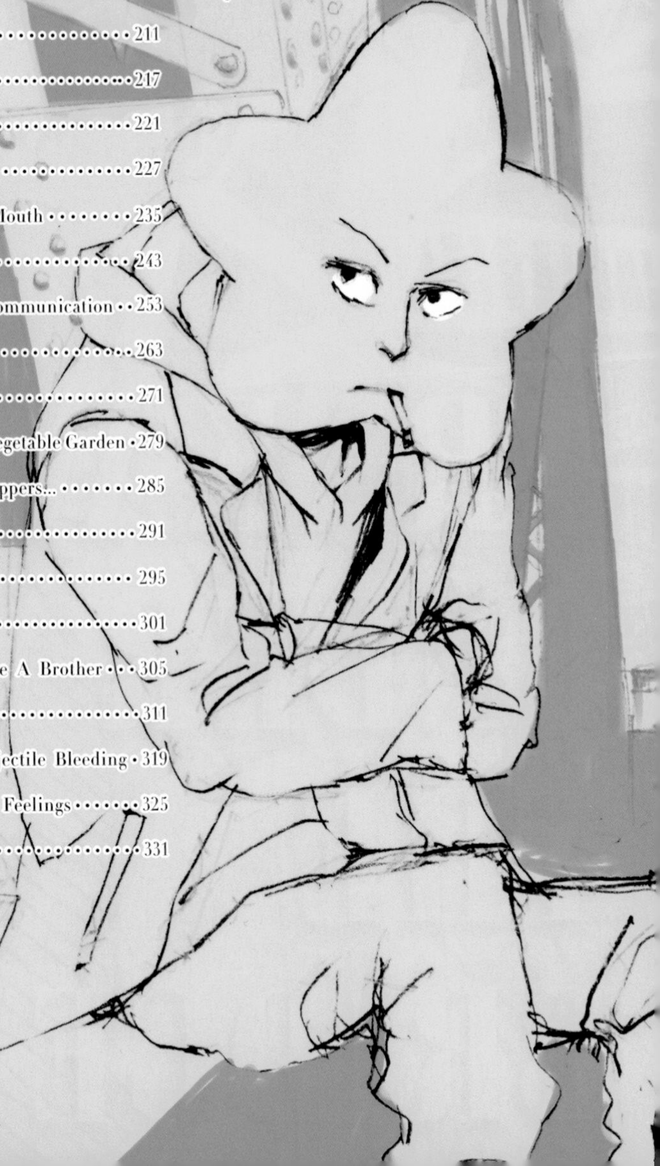

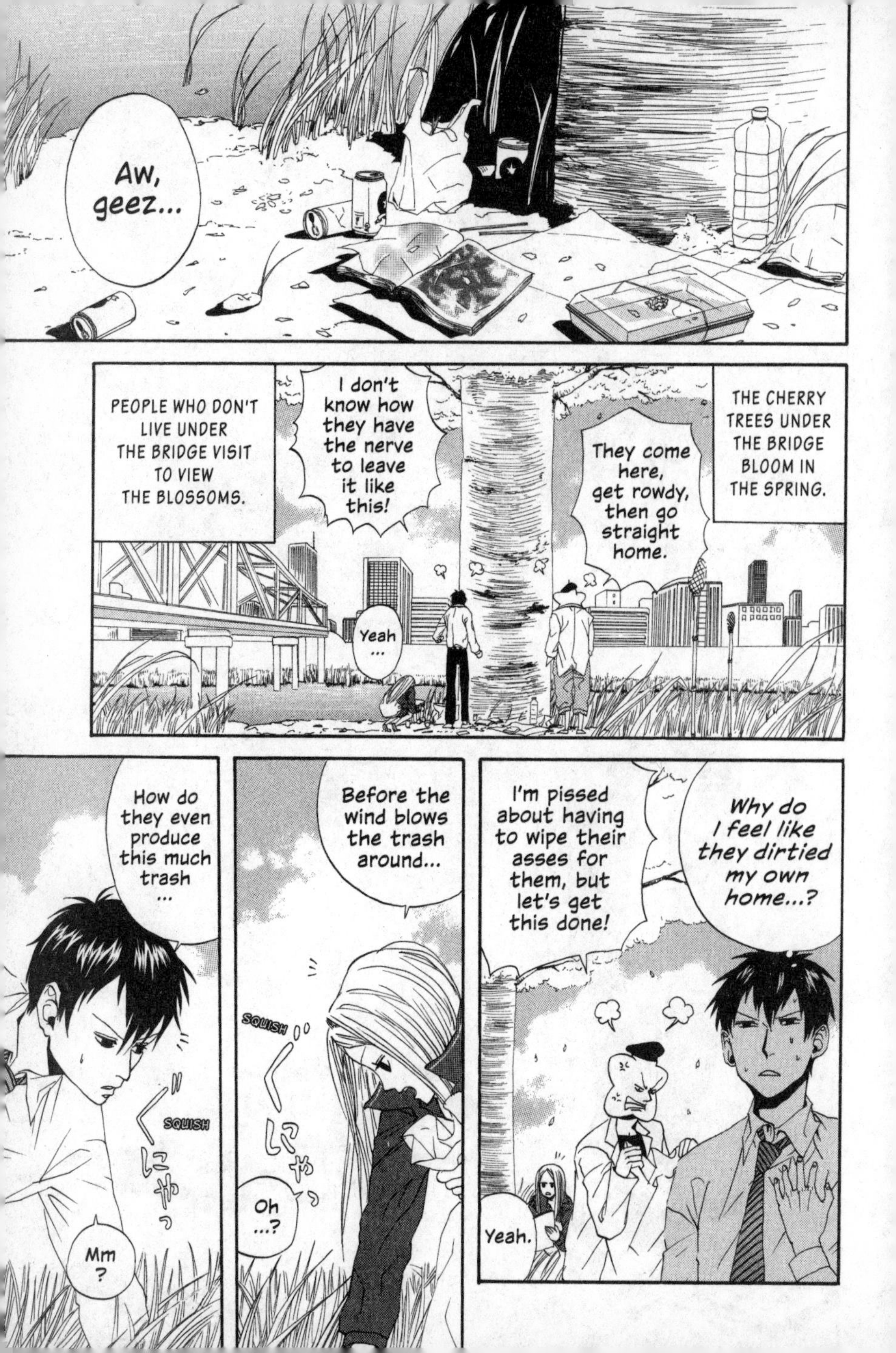
Aw, geez...
THE CHERRY TREES UNDER THE BRIDGE BLOOM IN THE SPRING.
They come here, get rowdy, then go straight home.
I don't know how they have the nerve to leave it like this!
PEOPLE WHO DON'T LIVE UNDER THE BRIDGE VISIT TO VIEW THE BLOSSOMS.
Yeah ...
Why do I feel like they dirtied my own home...?
I'm pissed about having to wipe their asses for them, but let's get this done!
Yeah.
Before the wind blows the trash around...
SQUISH
Oh ...?
How do they even produce this much trash ...
SQUISH
Mm ?

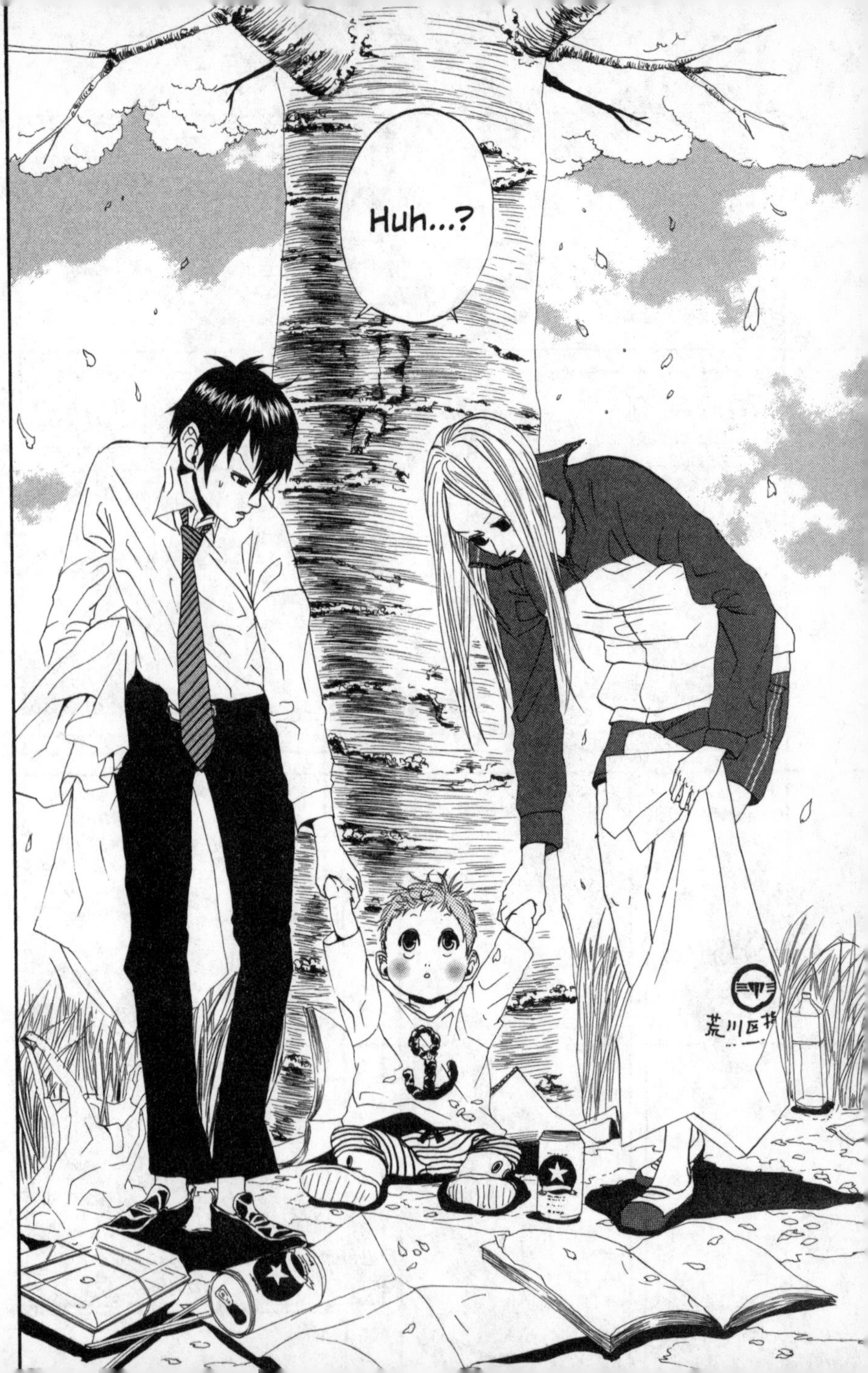
Huh...?
荒川区

☜ Chapter 24: The Baby and Nino

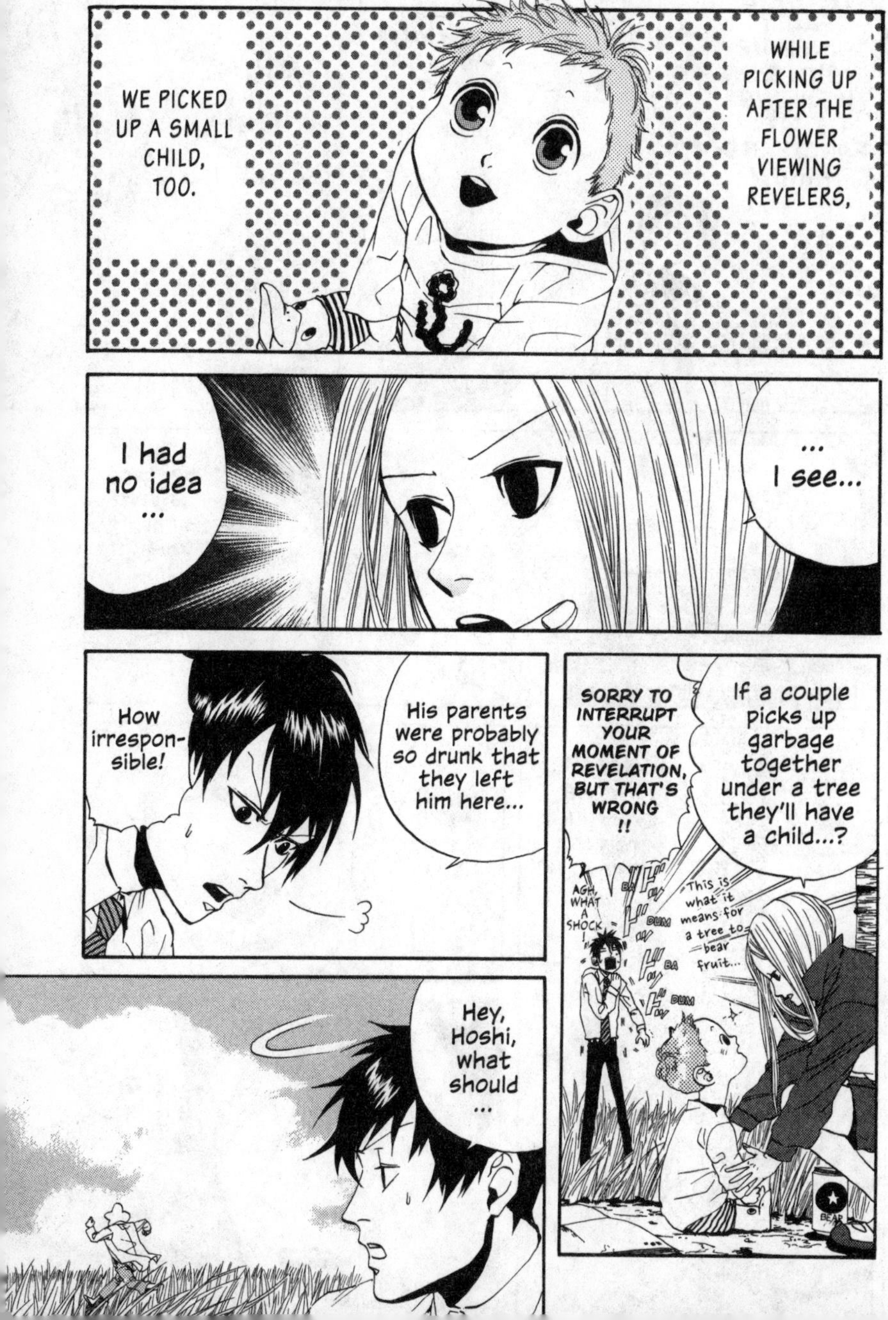
WHILE PICKING UP AFTER THE FLOWER VIEWING REVELERS,
WE PICKED UP A SMALL CHILD, TOO.
... I see...
I had no idea ...
If a couple picks up garbage together under a tree they'll have a child...?
SORRY TO INTERRUPT YOUR MOMENT OF REVELATION, BUT THAT'S WRONG !!
This is what it means for a tree to bear fruit...
AGH, WHAT A SHOCK !
BA DUM BA DUM
BEAR
His parents were probably so drunk that they left him here...
How irrespon-sible!
Hey, Hoshi, what should ...

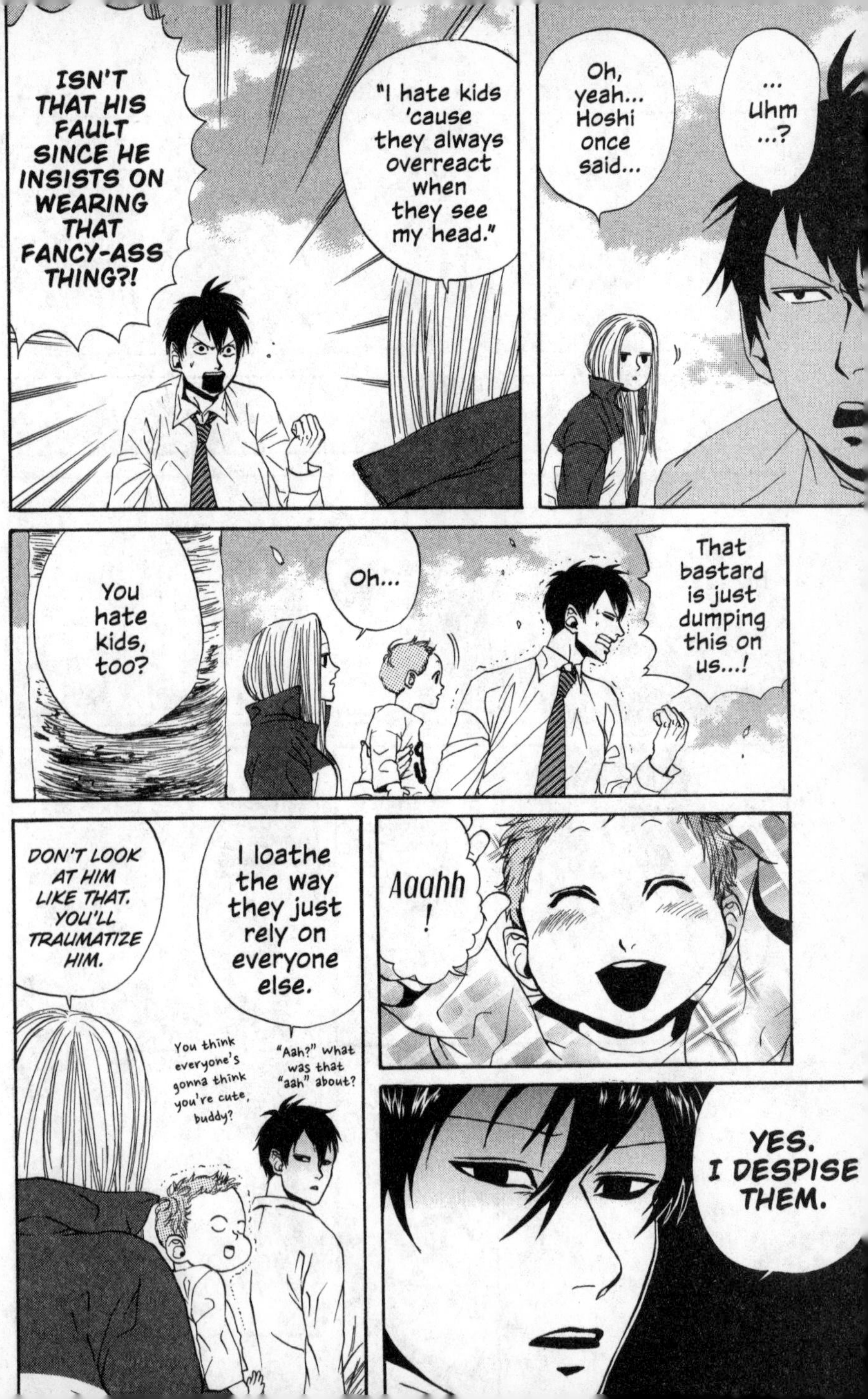
... Uhm ...?
Oh, yeah... Hoshi once said...
"I hate kids 'cause they always overreact when they see my head."
ISN'T THAT HIS FAULT SINCE HE INSISTS ON WEARING THAT FANCY-ASS THING?!
That bastard is just dumping this on us...!
Oh...
You hate kids, too?
Aaahh!
YES. I DESPISE THEM.
I loathe the way they just rely on everyone else.
DON'T LOOK AT HIM LIKE THAT. YOU'LL TRAUMATIZE HIM.
"Aah?" what was that "aah" about?
You think everyone's gonna think you're cute, buddy?

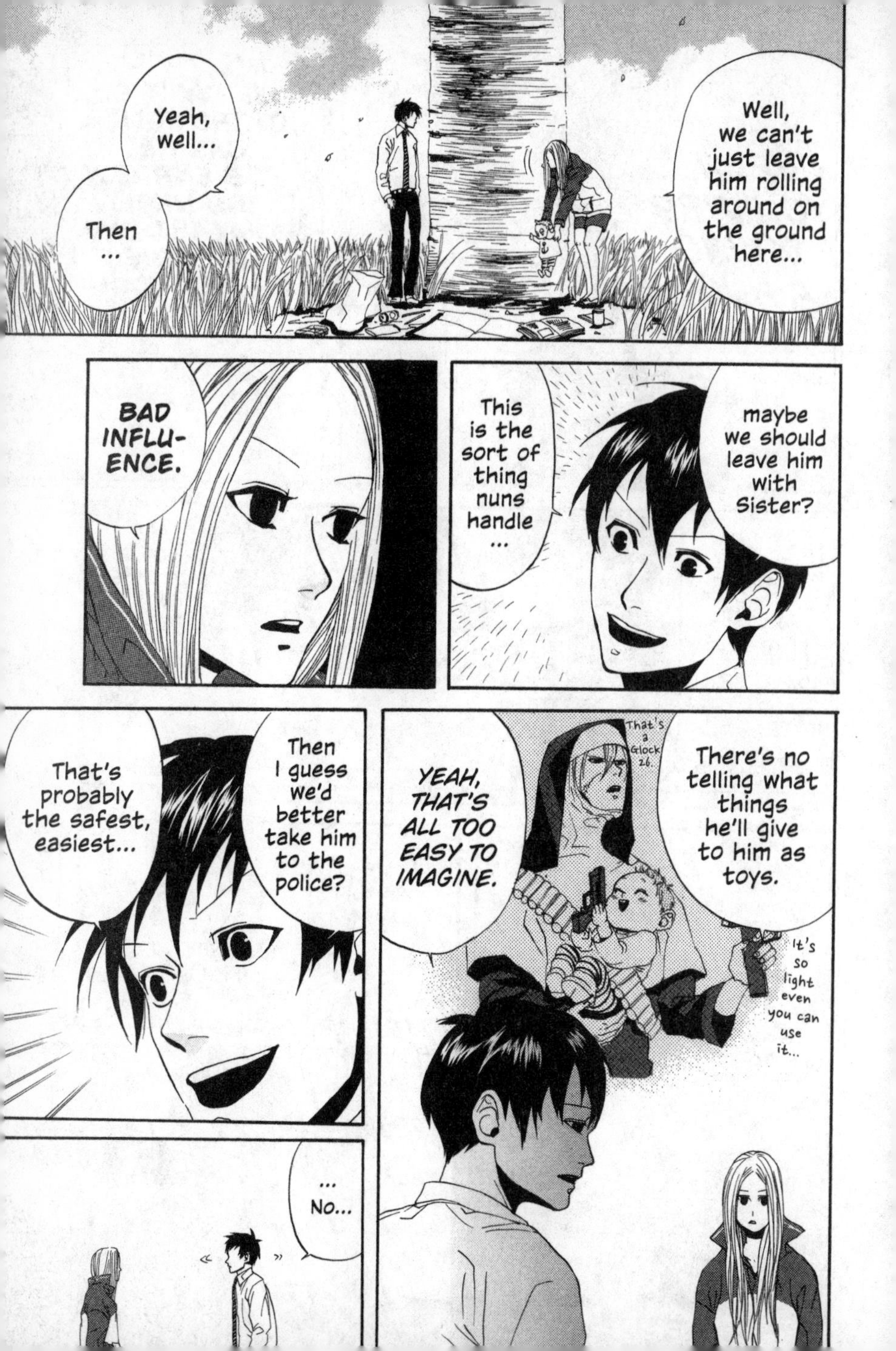

Well, we can't just leave him rolling around on the ground here...
Yeah, well...
Then ...
maybe we should leave him with Sister?
This is the sort of thing nuns handle ...
BAD INFLUENCE.
There's no telling what things he'll give to him as toys.
That's a Glock 26.
YEAH, THAT'S ALL TOO EASY TO IMAGINE.
It's so light even you can use it...
Then I guess we'd better take him to the police?
That's probably the safest, easiest...
... No...

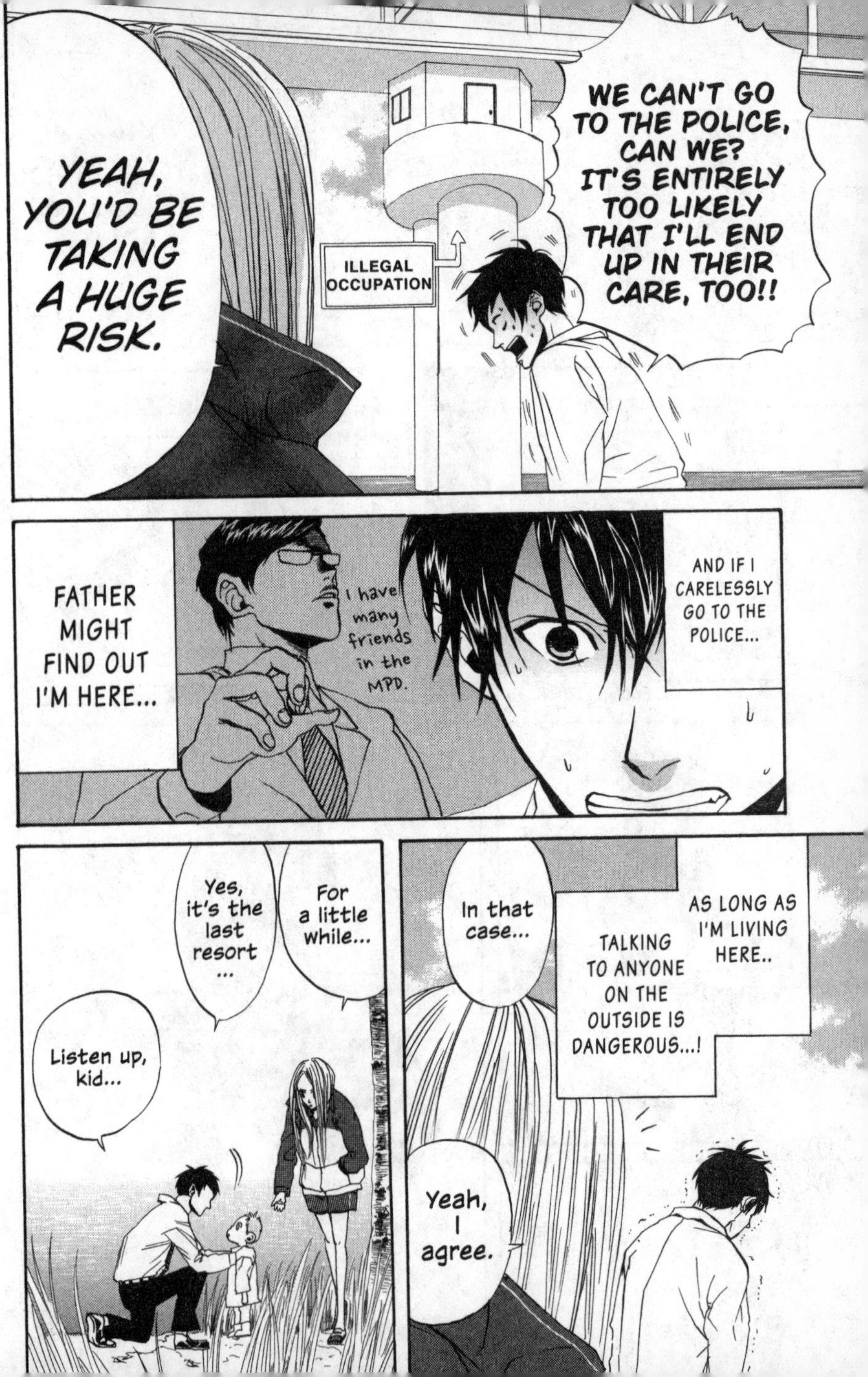
WE CAN'T GO TO THE POLICE, CAN WE? IT'S ENTIRELY TOO LIKELY THAT I'LL END UP IN THEIR CARE, TOO!!
ILLEGAL OCCUPATION
YEAH, YOU'D BE TAKING A HUGE RISK.
AND IF I CARELESSLY GO TO THE POLICE...
I have many friends in the MPD.
FATHER MIGHT FIND OUT I'M HERE...
AS LONG AS I'M LIVING HERE..
TALKING TO ANYONE ON THE OUTSIDE IS DANGEROUS...!
In that case...
Yeah, I agree.
For a little while...
Yes, it's the last resort ...
Listen up, kid...

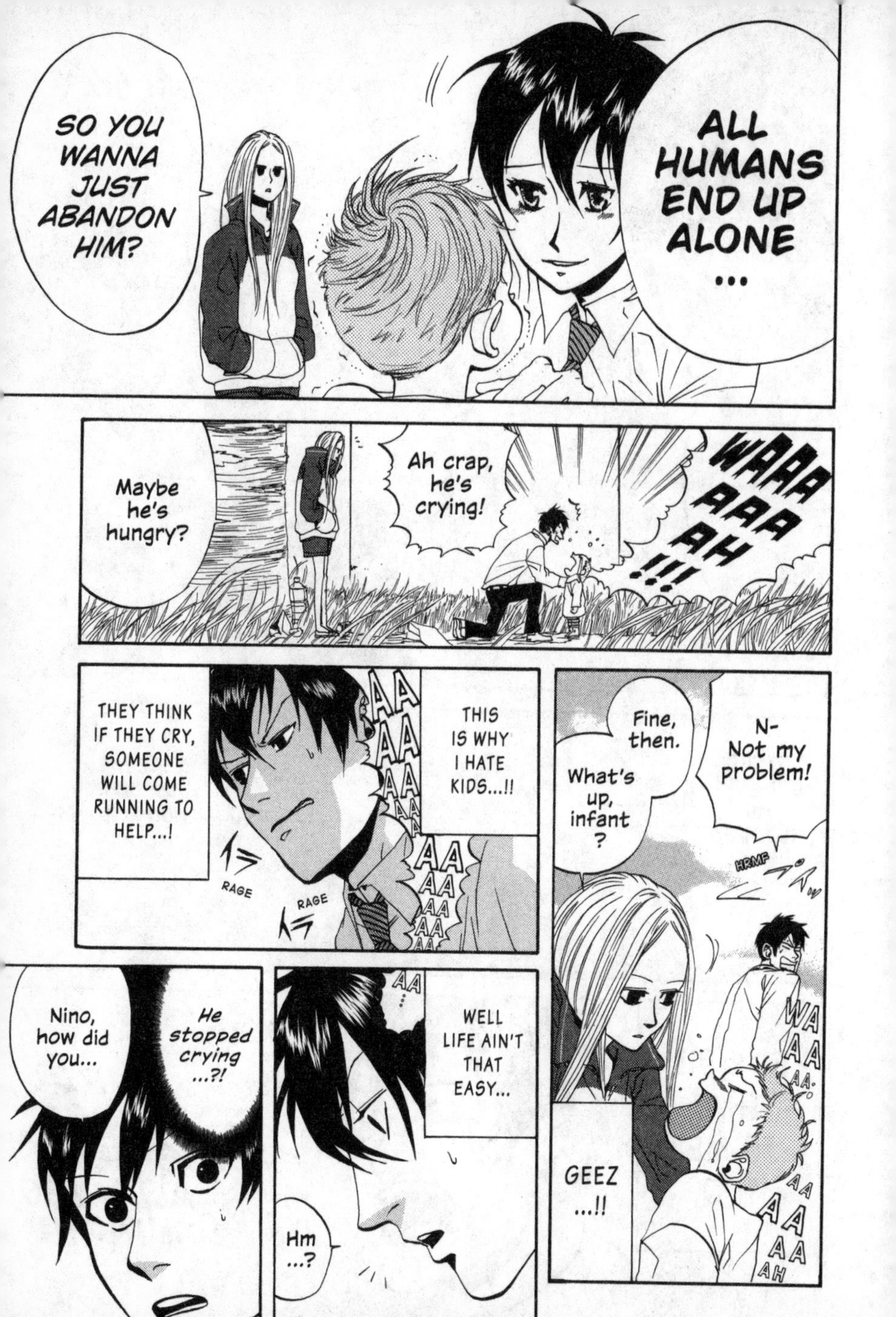
ALL HUMANS END UP ALONE ...
SO YOU WANNA JUST ABANDON HIM?
WAAAAAAAH!!!
Ah crap, he's crying!
Maybe he's hungry?
N- Not my problem!
Fine, then.
What's up, infant?
HRMF
WAAAA...
GEEZ ...!!
AA AAAAA AH
THIS IS WHY I HATE KIDS...!!
AAAAAAA
THEY THINK IF THEY CRY, SOMEONE WILL COME RUNNING TO HELP...!
RAGE
RAGE
AA...
WELL LIFE AIN'T THAT EASY...
Hm ...?
He stopped crying ...?!
Nino, how did you...

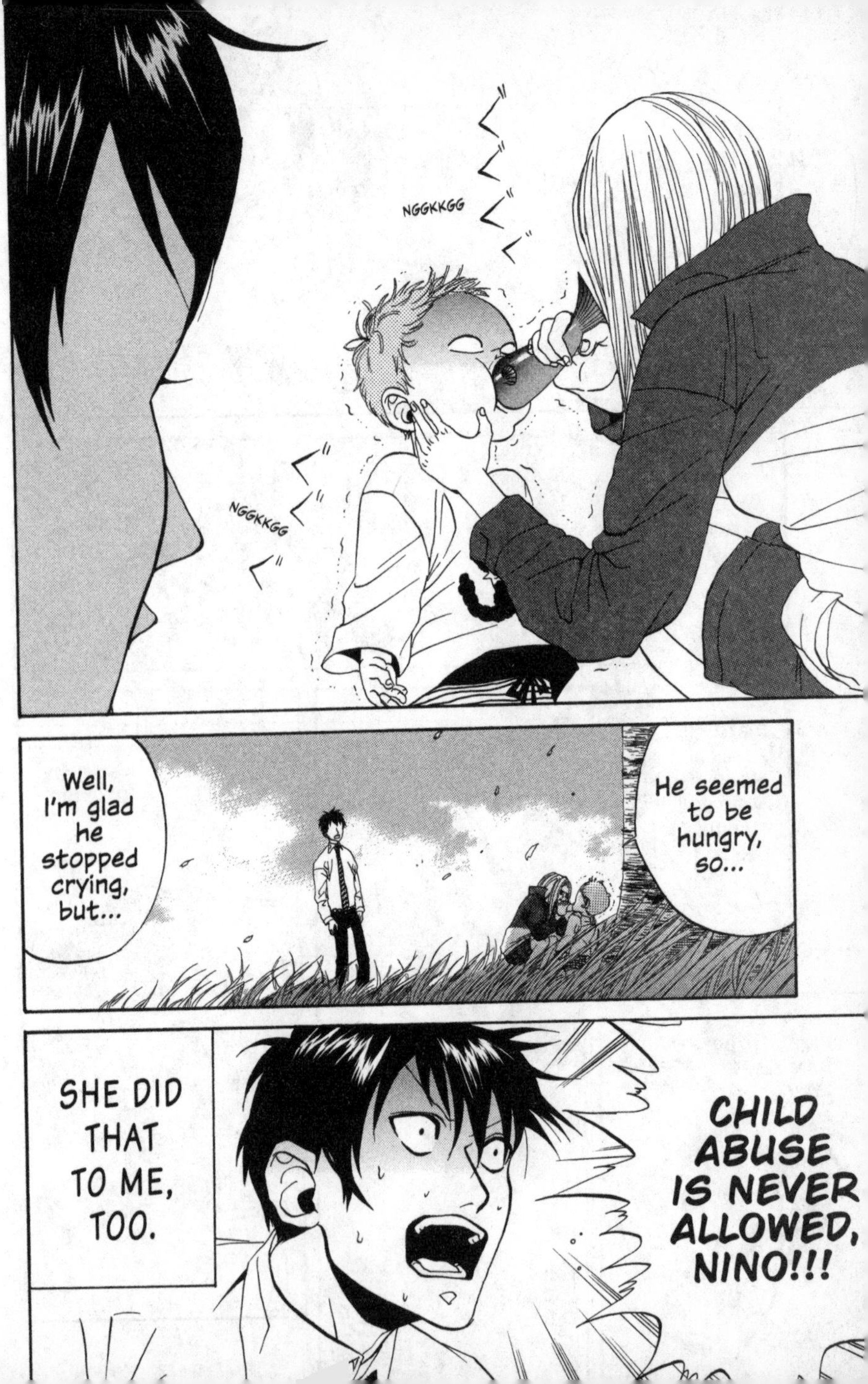
NGGKKGG
NGGKKGG
He seemed to be hungry, so...
Well, I'm glad he stopped crying, but...
CHILD ABUSE IS NEVER ALLOWED, NINO!!!
SHE DID THAT TO ME, TOO.

Chapter 25: Partner

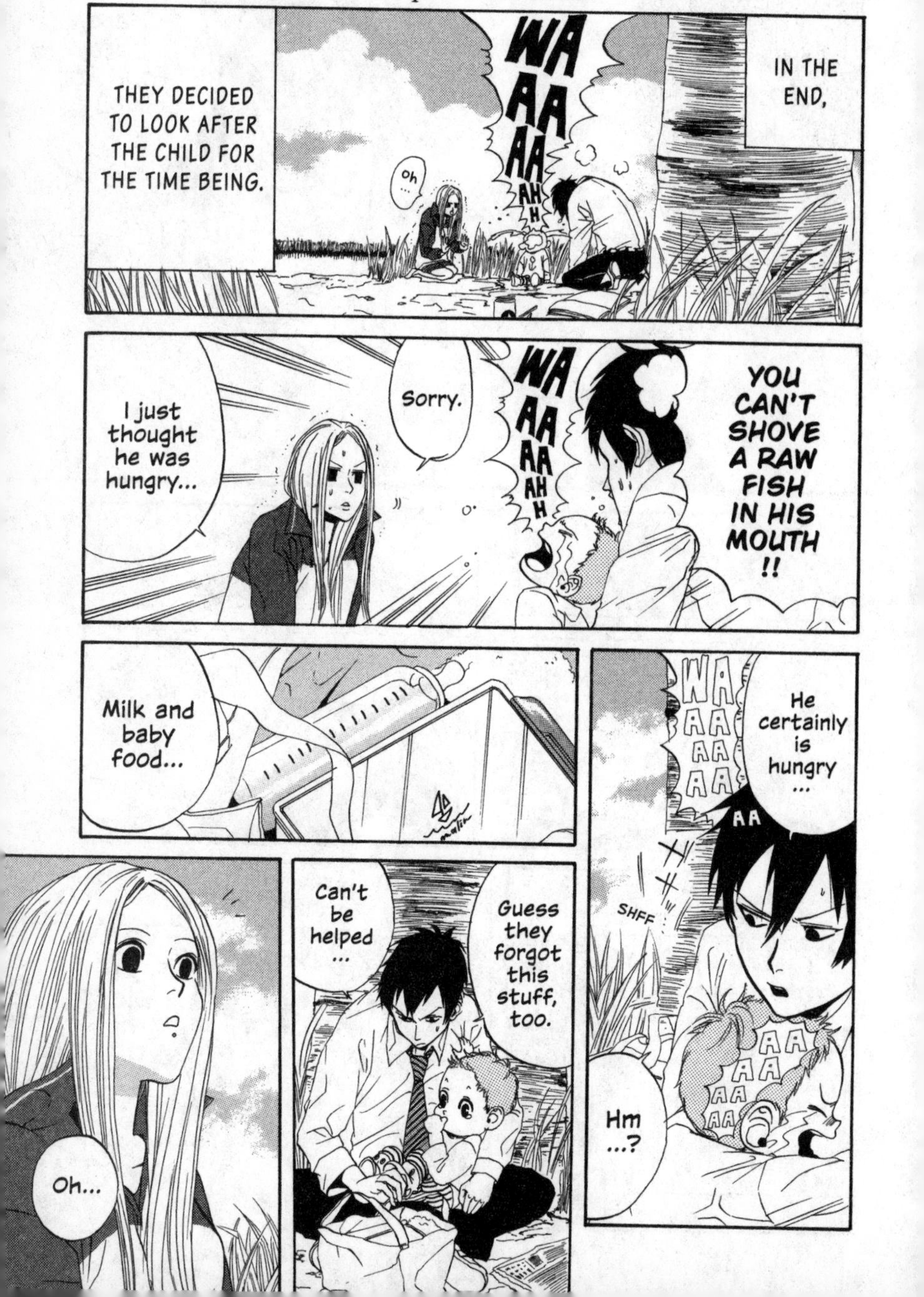
IN THE END,
WAAAAAAHH
Oh ...
THEY DECIDED TO LOOK AFTER THE CHILD FOR THE TIME BEING.
YOU CAN'T SHOVE A RAW FISH IN HIS MOUTH !!
WAAAAAAHH
Sorry.
I just thought he was hungry...
He certainly is hungry ...
WAAAAAAAAA
SHFF
Hm ...?
Milk and baby food...
Guess they forgot this stuff, too.
Can't be helped ...
Oh...

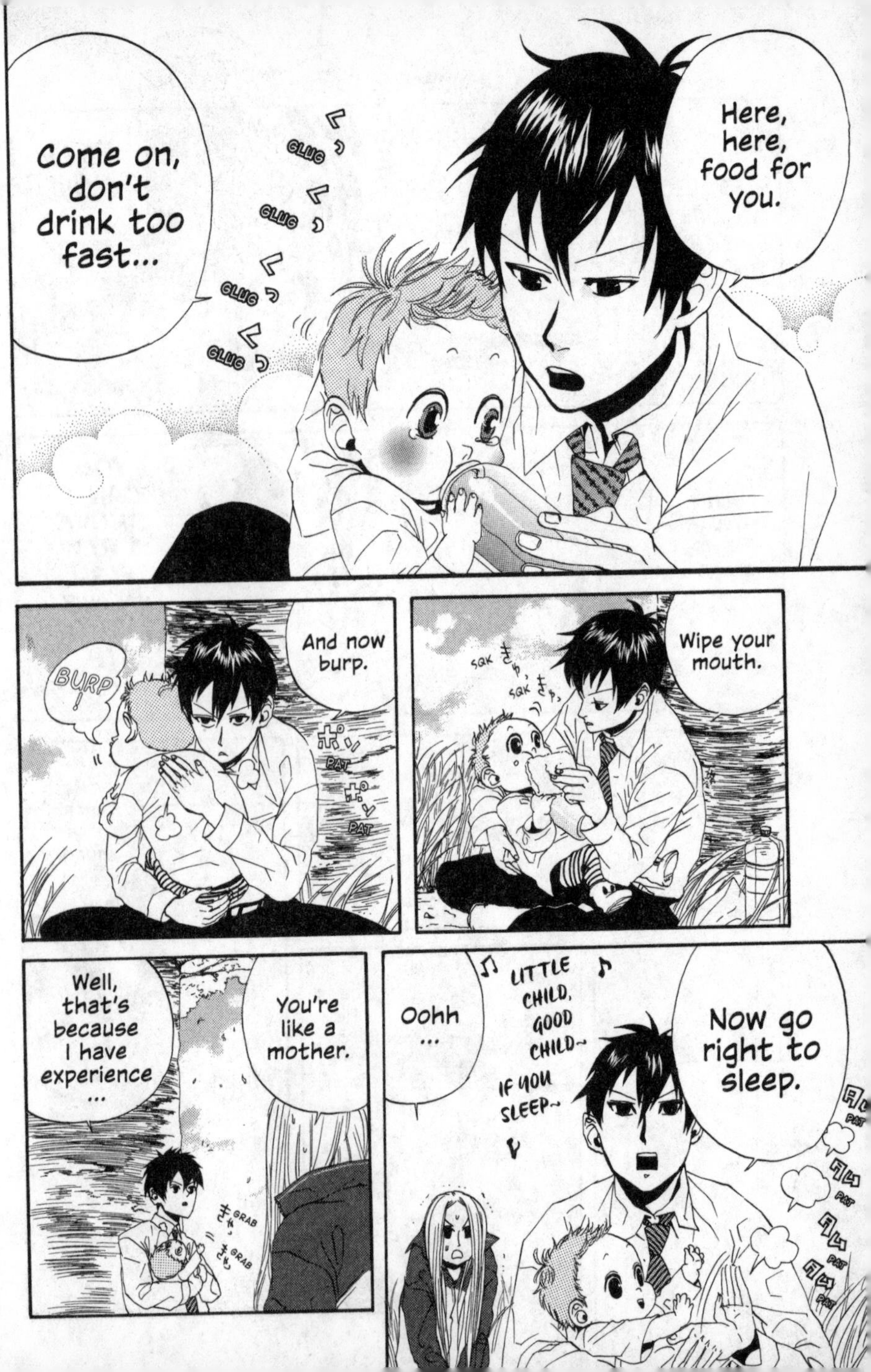
Here, here, food for you.
GLUG GLUG GLUG GLUG
Come on, don't drink too fast...
Wipe your mouth.
SQK SQK
And now burp.
BURP!
PAT PAT
Now go right to sleep.
LITTLE CHILD, GOOD CHILD~ IF YOU SLEEP~
Oohh...
PAT PAT PAT PAT
You're like a mother.
Well, that's because I have experience...
GRAB GRAB

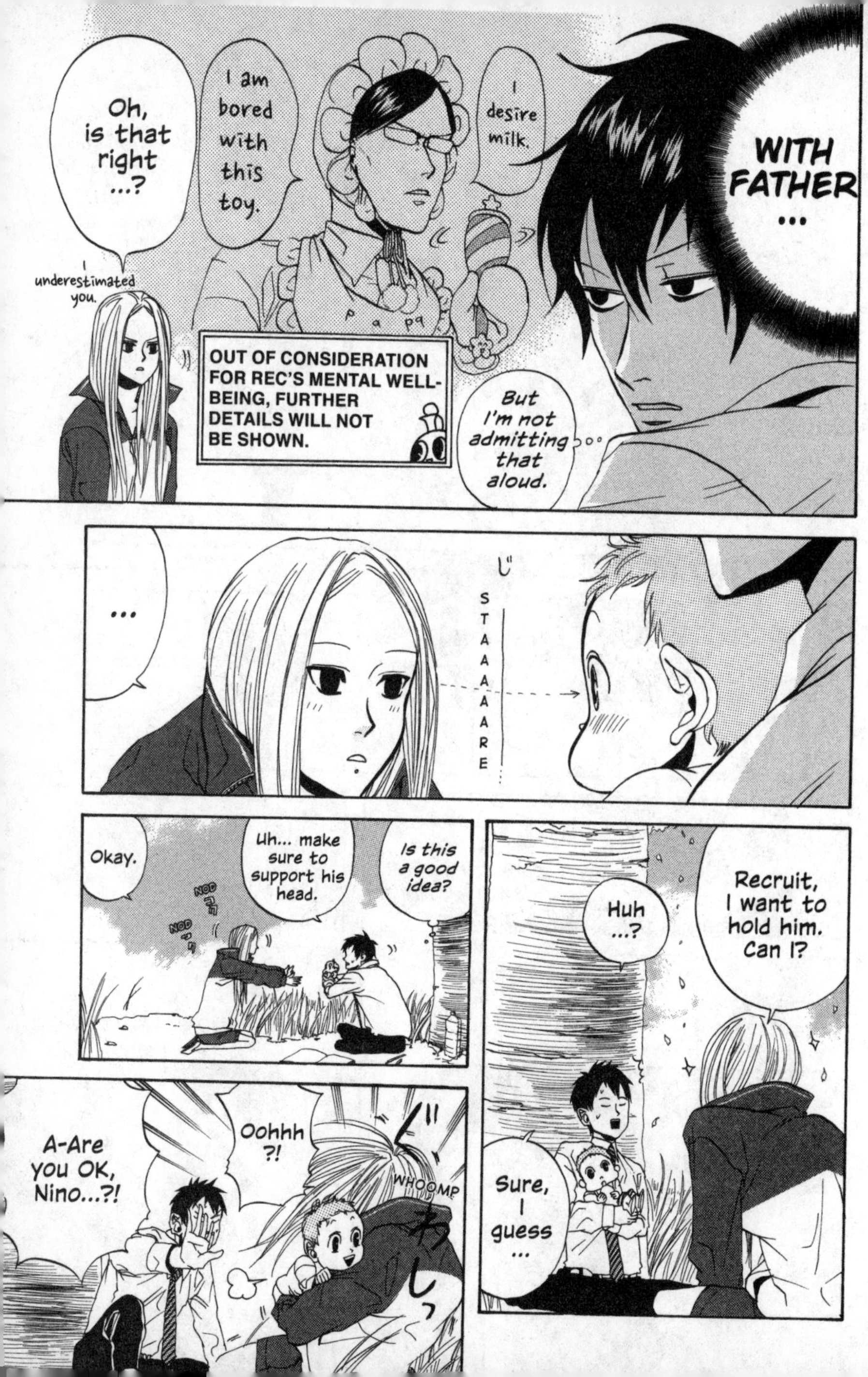
WITH FATHER ...
I desire milk.
I am bored with this toy.
But I'm not admitting that aloud.
OUT OF CONSIDERATION FOR REC'S MENTAL WELL-BEING, FURTHER DETAILS WILL NOT BE SHOWN.
Oh, is that right ...?
I underestimated you.
STAAAAAARE
...
Recruit, I want to hold him. Can I?
Huh ...?
Sure, I guess ...
Is this a good idea?
Uh... make sure to support his head.
Okay.
NOD
NOD
WHOOMP
Oohhh ?!
A-Are you OK, Nino...?!

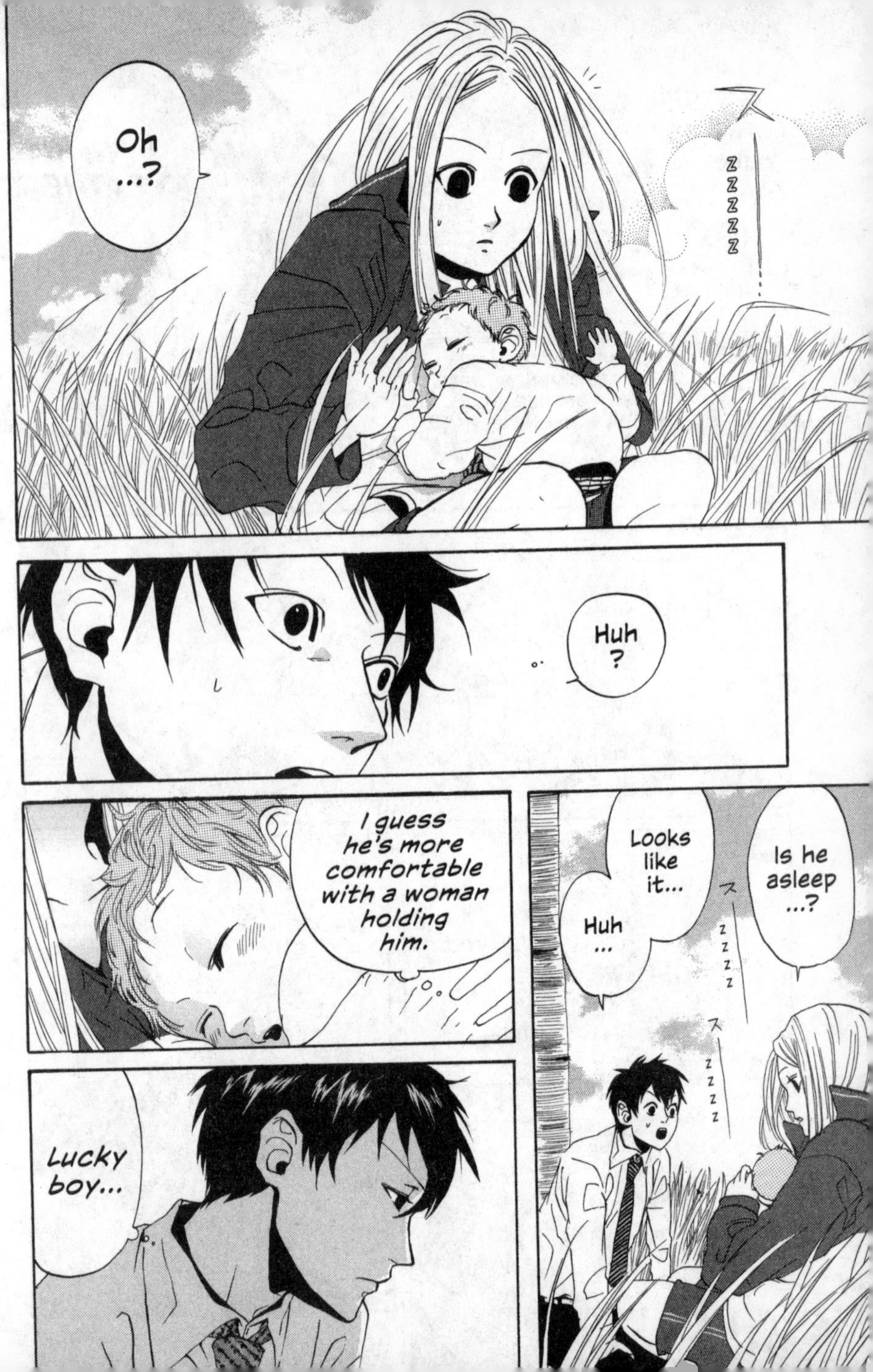
Oh ...?
ス
ZZZZZ
Huh ?
Is he asleep ...?
Looks like it...
Huh ...
ス
ZZZZ
ス
ZZZZ
I guess he's more comfortable with a woman holding him.
Lucky boy...

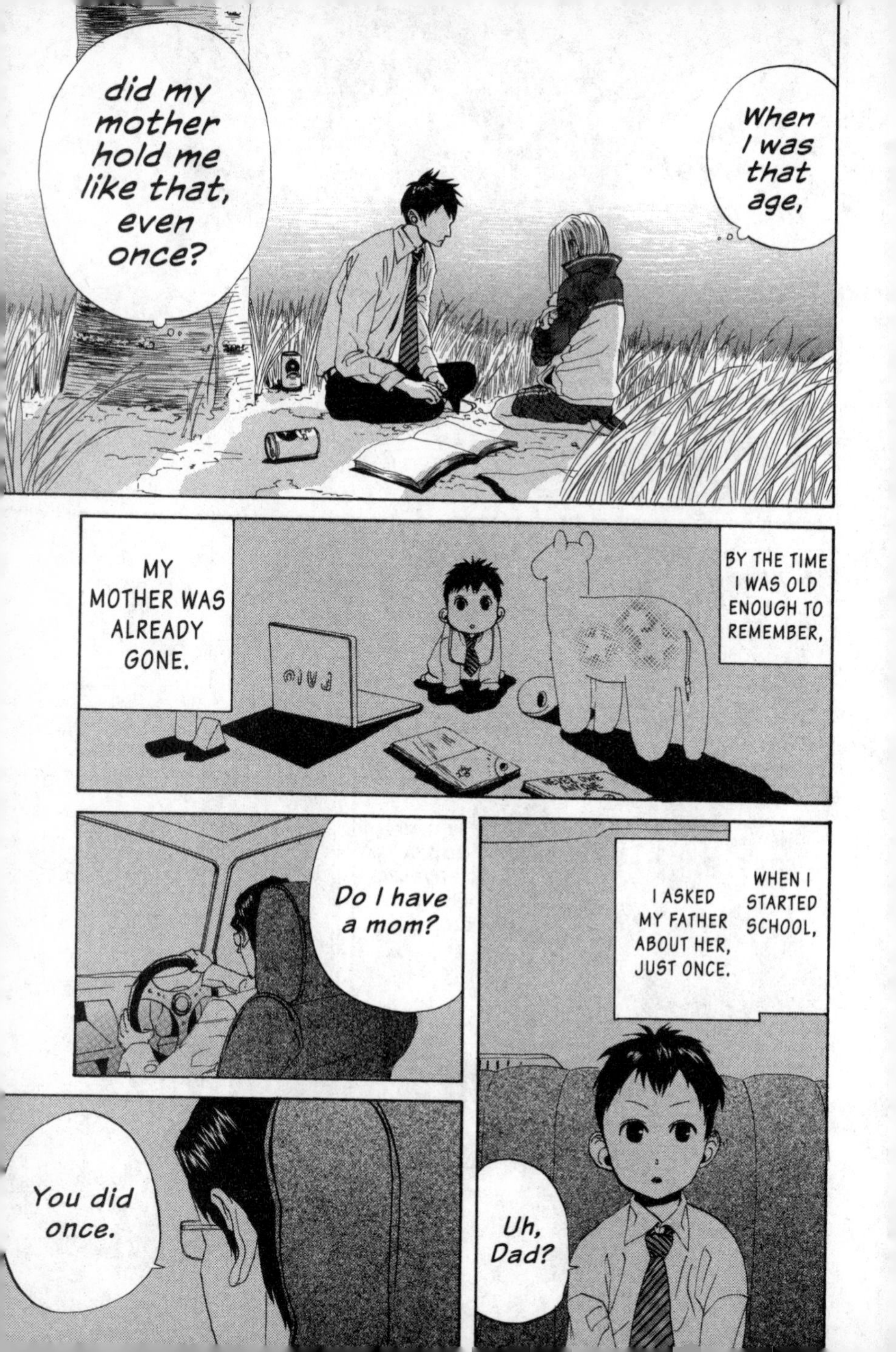
When I was that age,
did my mother hold me like that, even once?
BY THE TIME I WAS OLD ENOUGH TO REMEMBER,
MY MOTHER WAS ALREADY GONE.
WHEN I STARTED SCHOOL,
I ASKED MY FATHER ABOUT HER, JUST ONCE.
Uh, Dad?
Do I have a mom?
You did once.

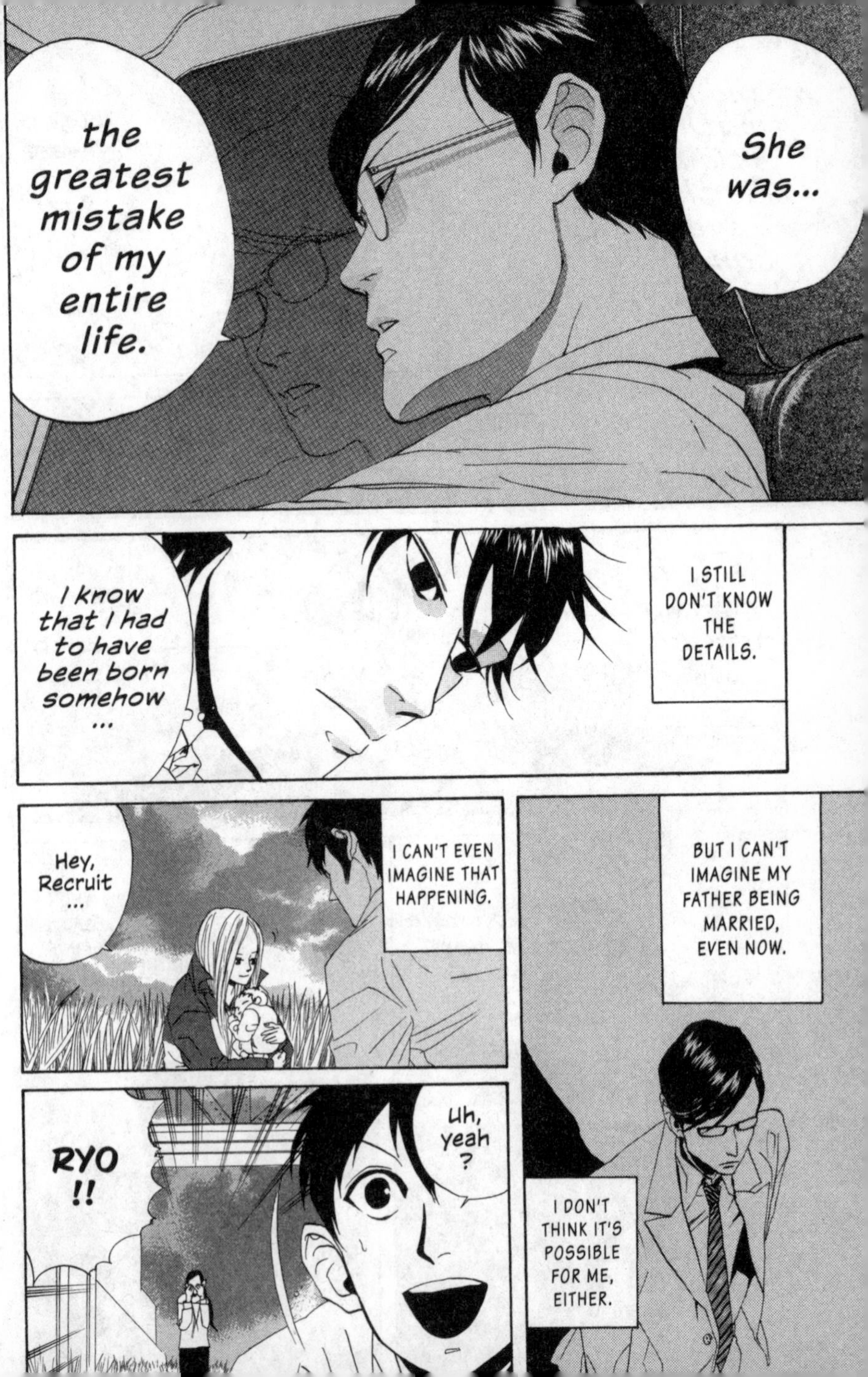
She was...
the greatest mistake of my entire life.
I STILL DON'T KNOW THE DETAILS.
I know that I had to have been born somehow...
BUT I CAN'T IMAGINE MY FATHER BEING MARRIED, EVEN NOW.
I DON'T THINK IT'S POSSIBLE FOR ME, EITHER.
I CAN'T EVEN IMAGINE THAT HAPPENING.
Hey, Recruit...
Uh, yeah?
RYO!!

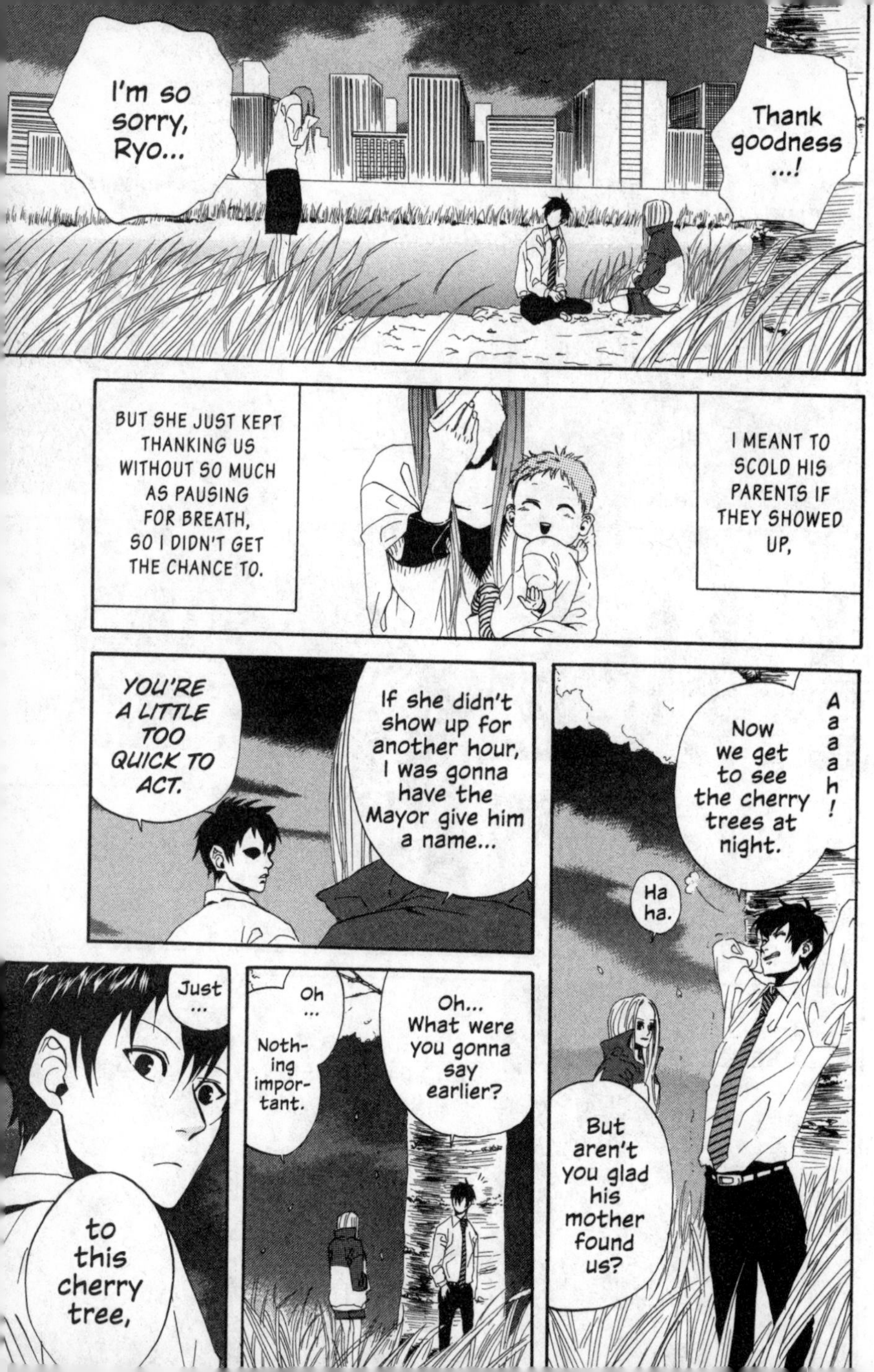
Thank goodness ...!
I'm so sorry, Ryo...
I MEANT TO SCOLD HIS PARENTS IF THEY SHOWED UP,
BUT SHE JUST KEPT THANKING US WITHOUT SO MUCH AS PAUSING FOR BREATH, SO I DIDN'T GET THE CHANCE TO.
Aaaah!
Now we get to see the cherry trees at night.
Ha ha.
But aren't you glad his mother found us?
If she didn't show up for another hour, I was gonna have the Mayor give him a name...
YOU'RE A LITTLE TOO QUICK TO ACT.
Oh... What were you gonna say earlier?
Oh ...
Nothing important.
Just ...
to this cherry tree,

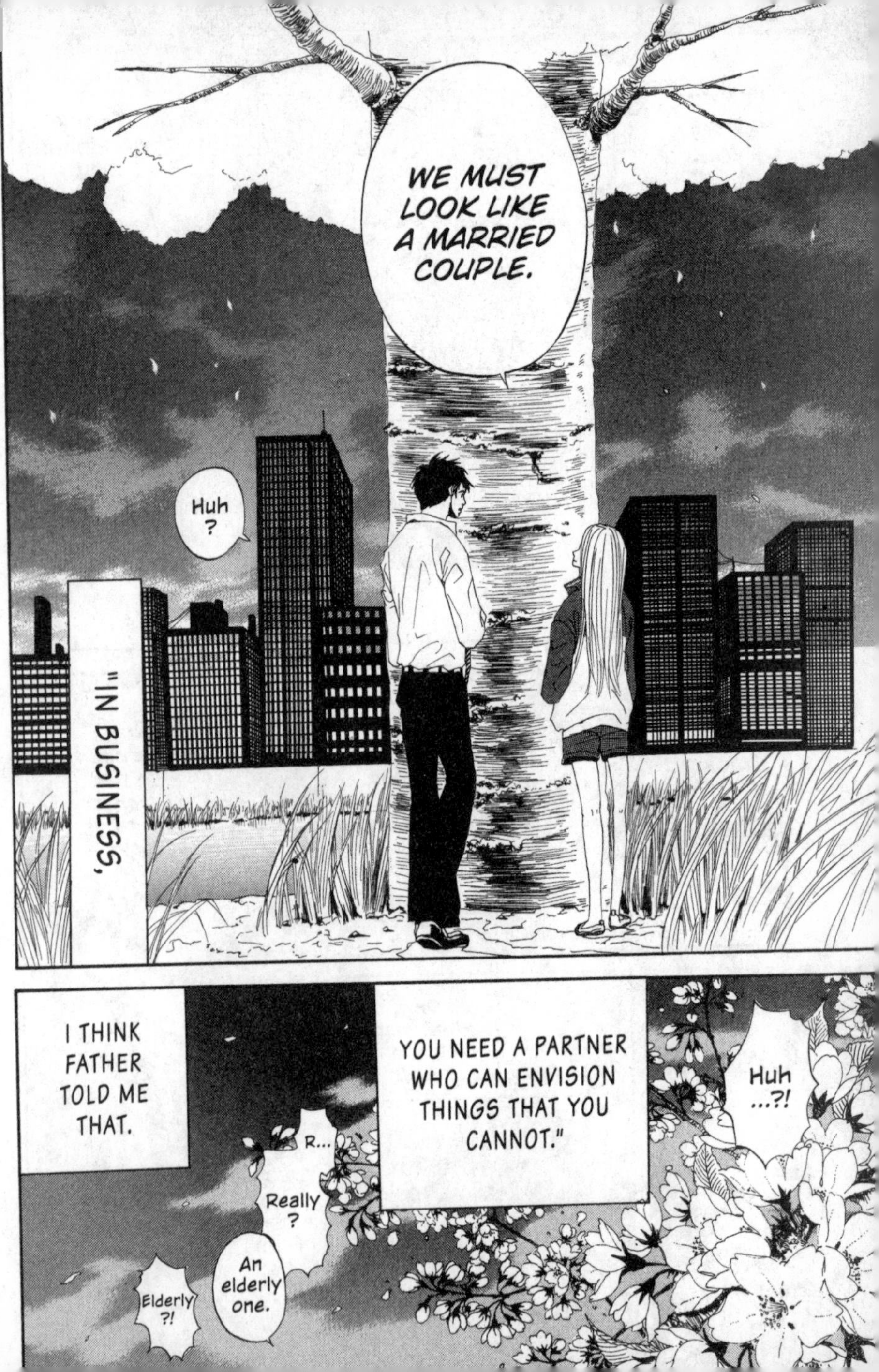
WE MUST LOOK LIKE A MARRIED COUPLE.
Huh?
"IN BUSINESS,
Huh ...?!
YOU NEED A PARTNER WHO CAN ENVISION THINGS THAT YOU CANNOT."
I THINK FATHER TOLD ME THAT.
R...
Really?
An elderly one.
Elderly?!

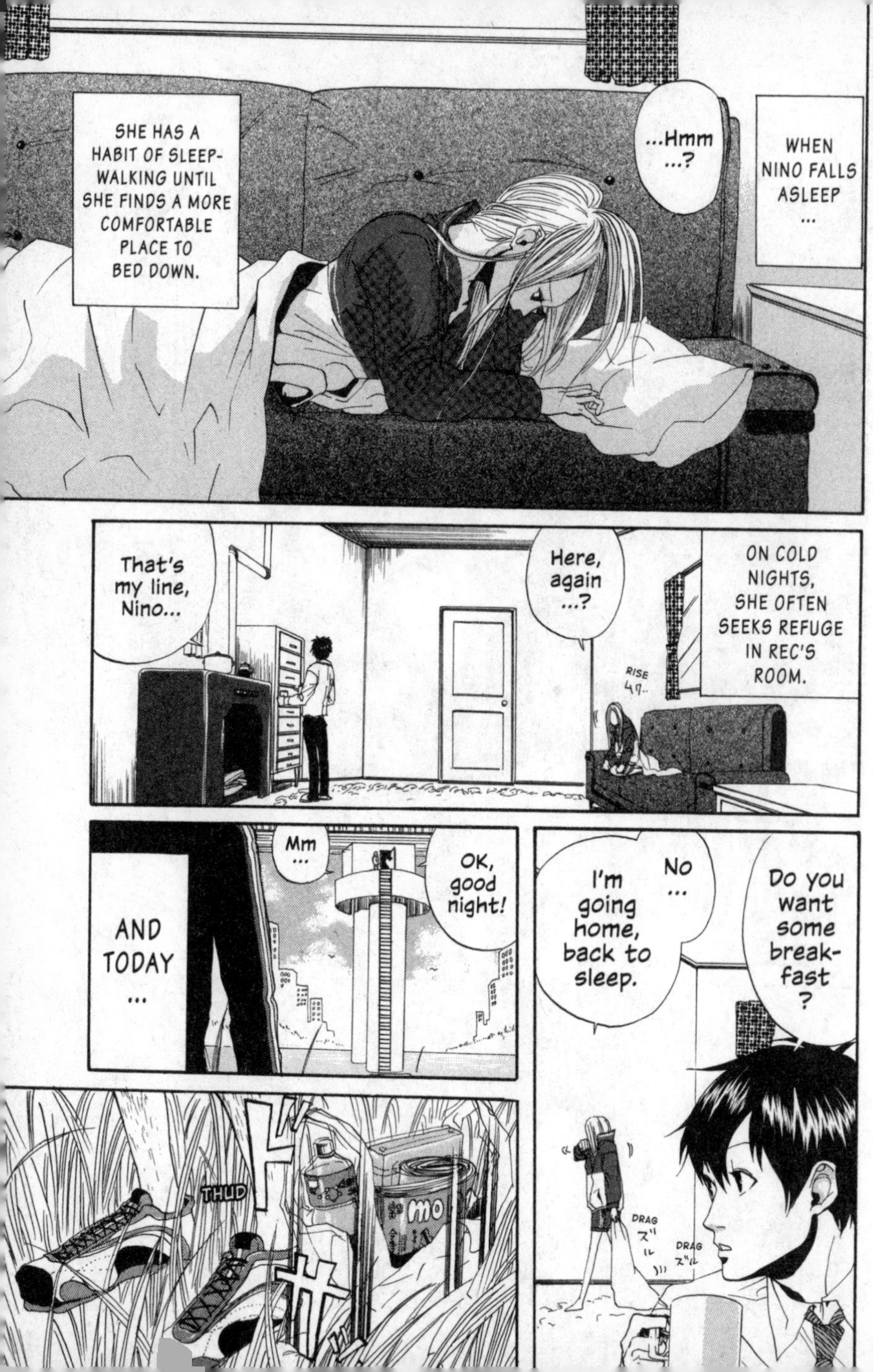
WHEN NINO FALLS ASLEEP ...
...Hmm ...?
SHE HAS A HABIT OF SLEEP-WALKING UNTIL SHE FINDS A MORE COMFORTABLE PLACE TO BED DOWN.
ON COLD NIGHTS, SHE OFTEN SEEKS REFUGE IN REC'S ROOM.
RISE
Here, again ...?
That's my line, Nino...
Do you want some break-fast?
No ...
I'm going home, back to sleep.
DRAG
DRAG
OK, good night!
Mm ...
AND TODAY ...
THUD

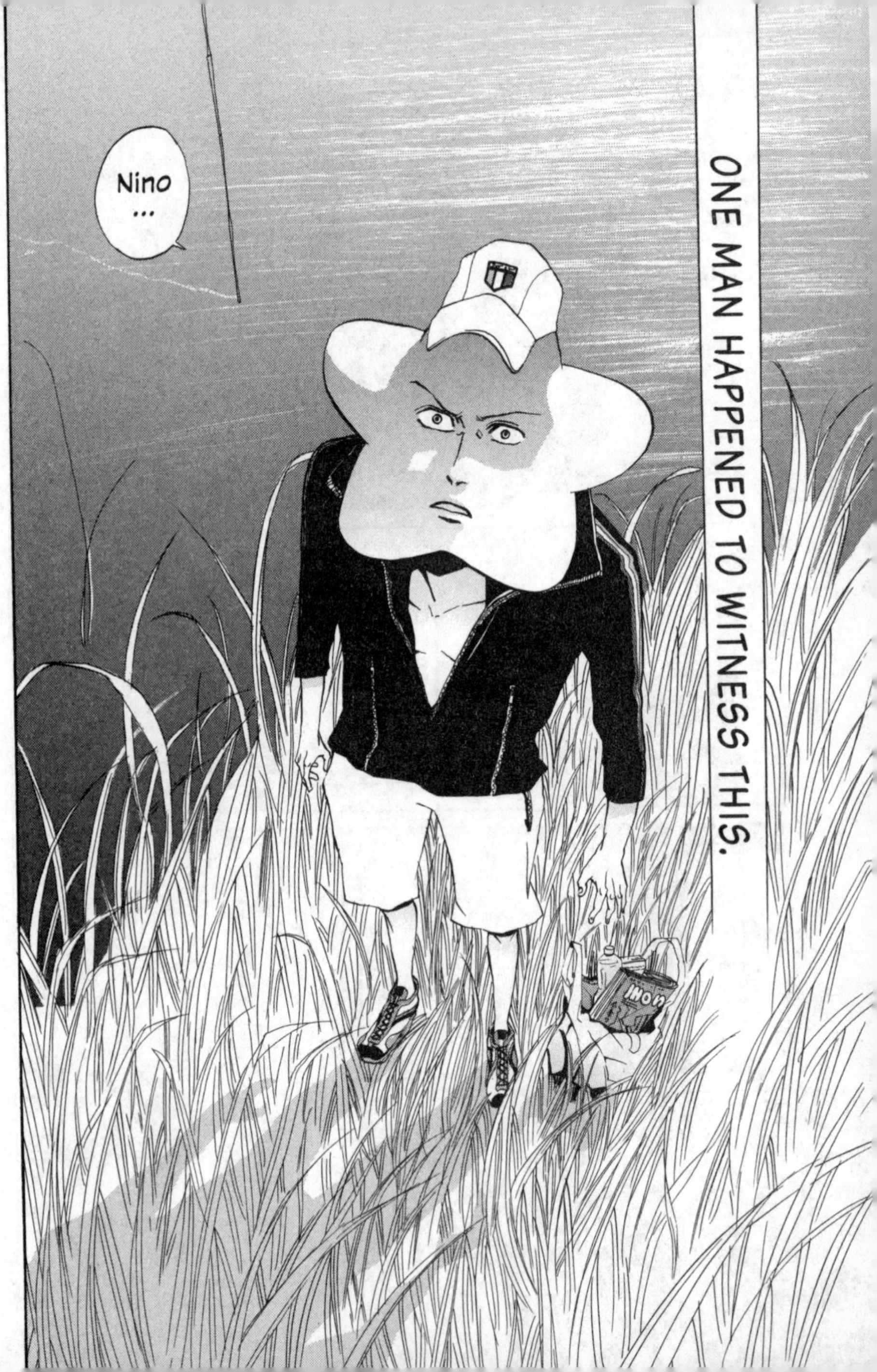
ONE MAN HAPPENED TO WITNESS THIS.
Nino ...

Chapter 26: Sister's Confessional Booth

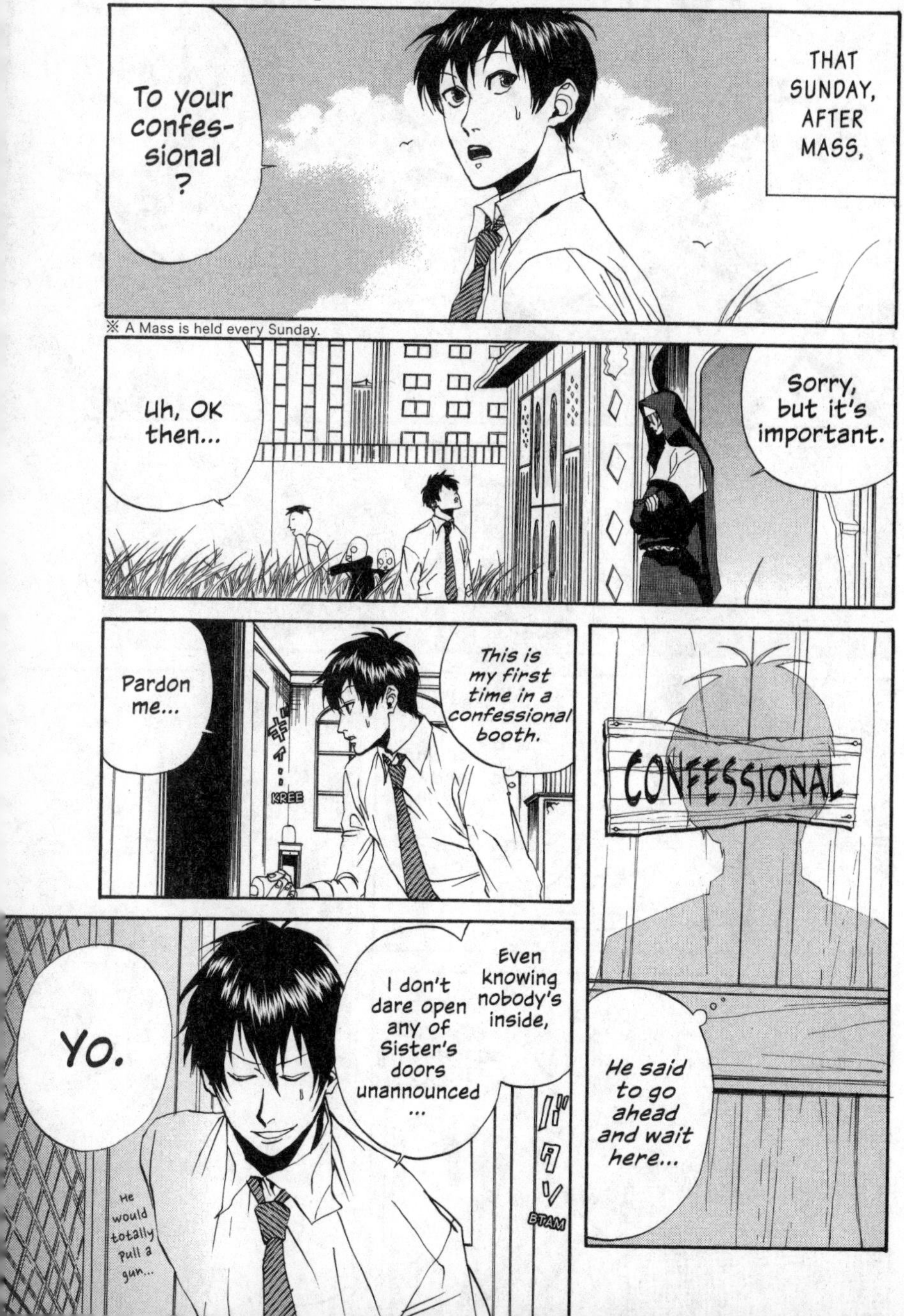
THAT SUNDAY, AFTER MASS,
To your confes-sional?
Sorry, but it's important.
Uh, OK then...
CONFESSIONAL
He said to go ahead and wait here...
This is my first time in a confessional booth.
KREE
Pardon me...
BTAM
Even knowing nobody's inside,
I don't dare open any of Sister's doors unannounced ...
YO.
He would totally pull a gun...

※ A Mass is held every Sunday.

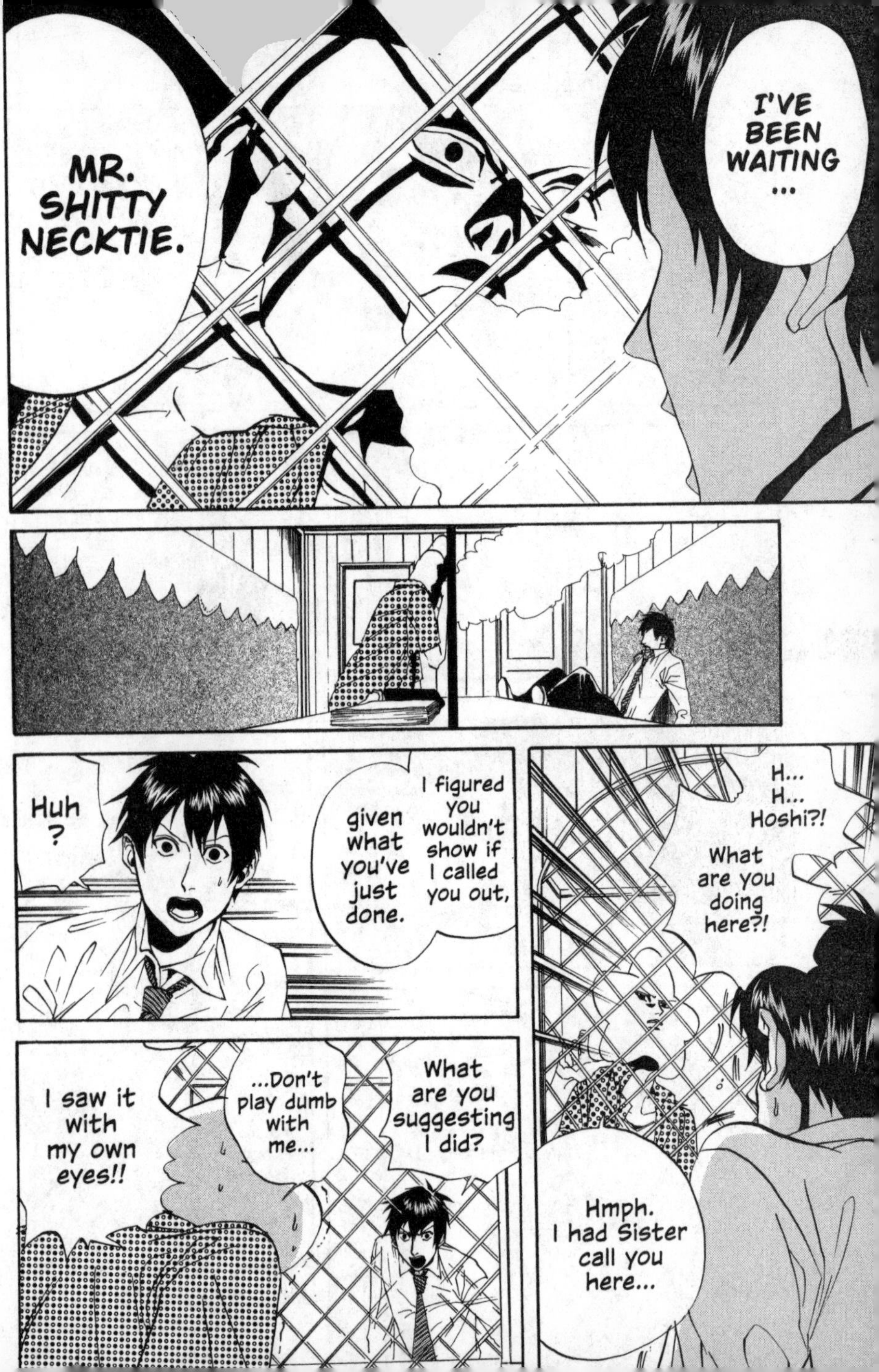
I'VE BEEN WAITING ...
MR. SHITTY NECKTIE.
H... H... Hoshi?!
What are you doing here?!
Hmph. I had Sister call you here...
I figured you wouldn't show if I called you out,
given what you've just done.
Huh?
What are you suggesting I did?
...Don't play dumb with me...
I saw it with my own eyes!!

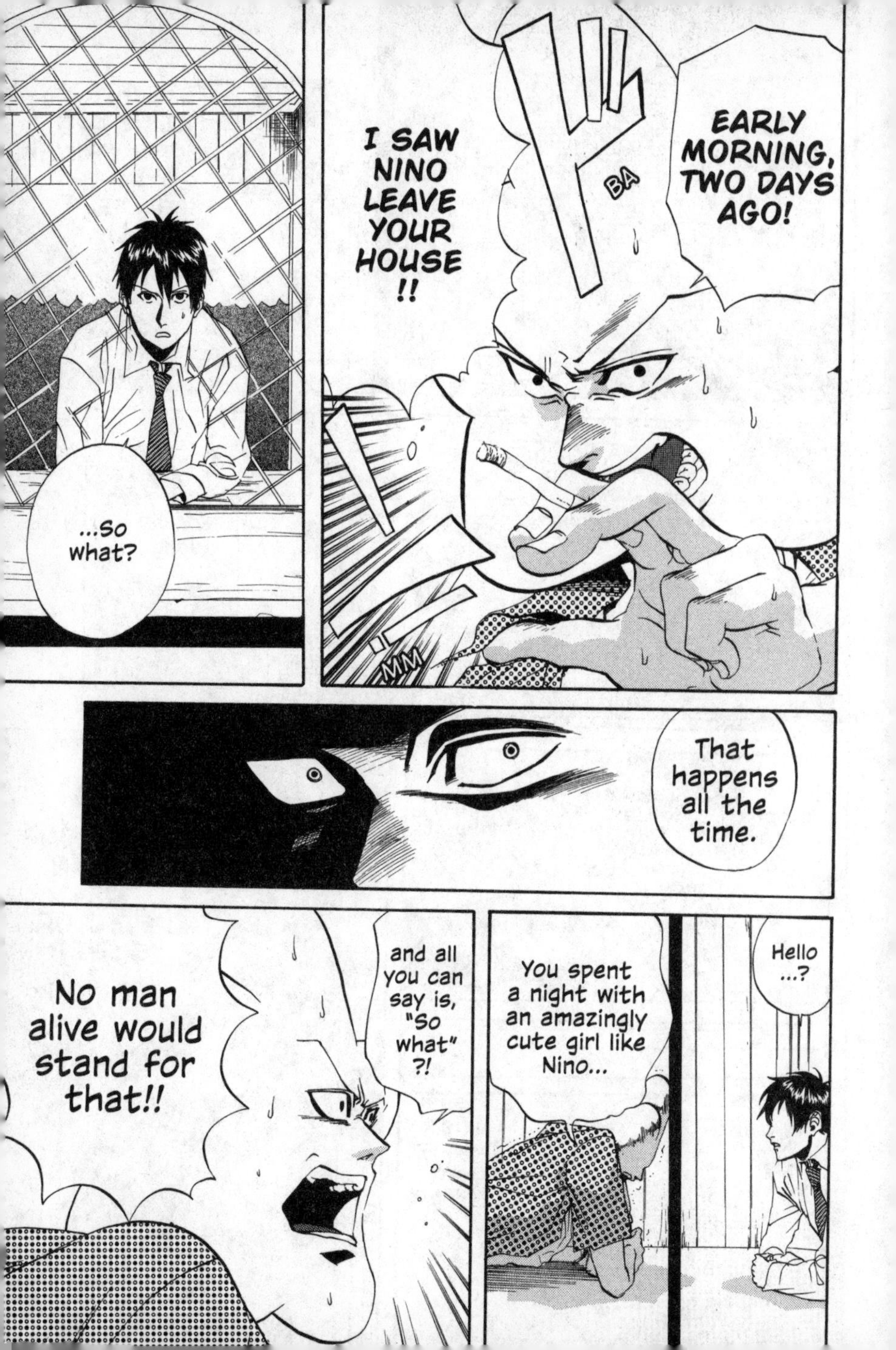
EARLY MORNING, TWO DAYS AGO!
BA
I SAW NINO LEAVE YOUR HOUSE !!
MM
...So what?
That happens all the time.
Hello ...?
You spent a night with an amazingly cute girl like Nino...
and all you can say is, "So what" ?!
No man alive would stand for that!!

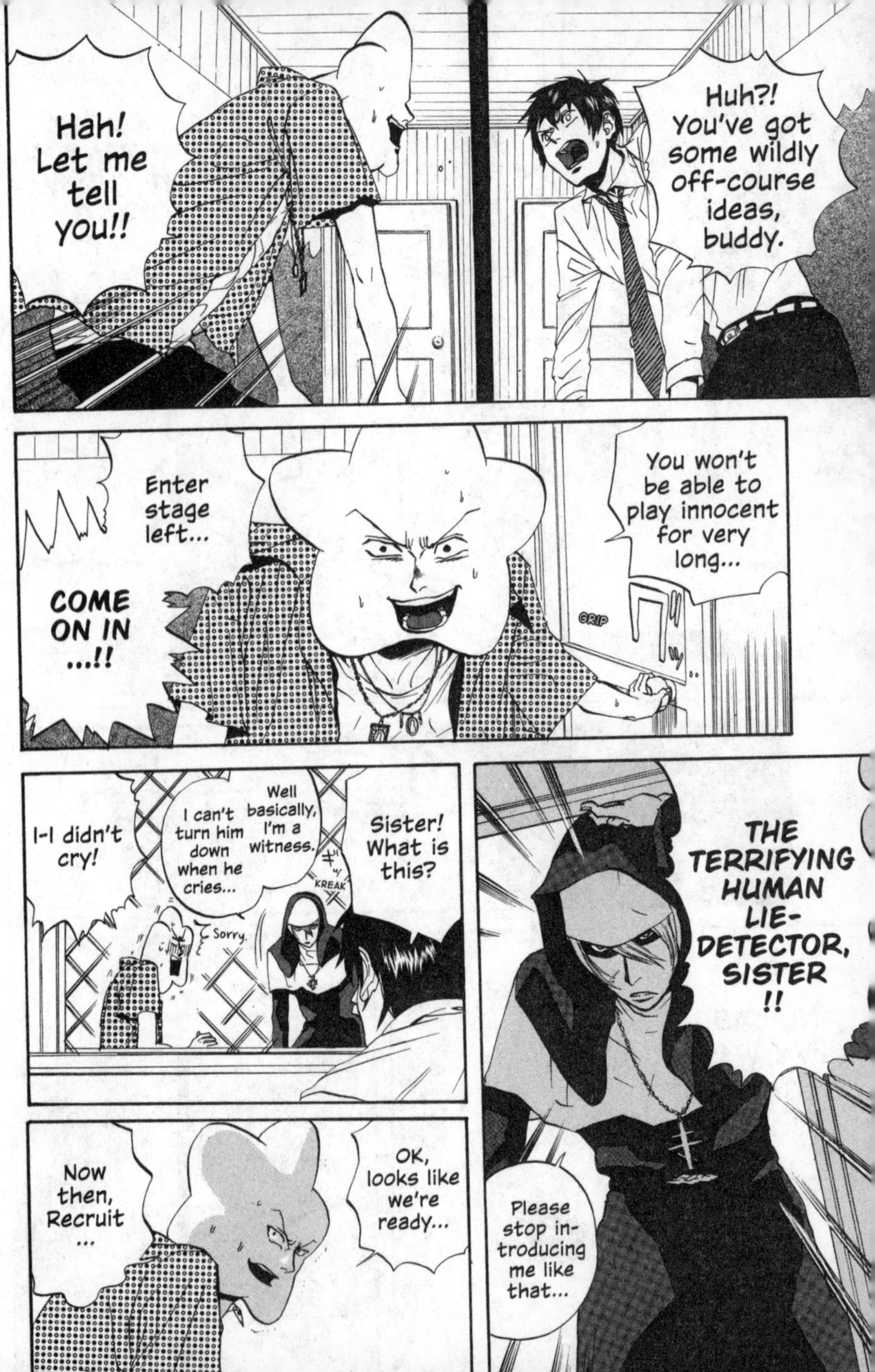
Huh?! You've got some wildly off-course ideas, buddy.
Hah! Let me tell you!!
You won't be able to play innocent for very long...
GRIP
Enter stage left...
COME ON IN ...!!
THE TERRIFYING HUMAN LIE-DETECTOR, SISTER !!
Please stop in-troducing me like that...
Sister! What is this?
KREAK
Well basically, I'm a witness.
I can't turn him down when he cries...
Sorry.
I-I didn't cry!
OK, looks like we're ready...
Now then, Recruit ...

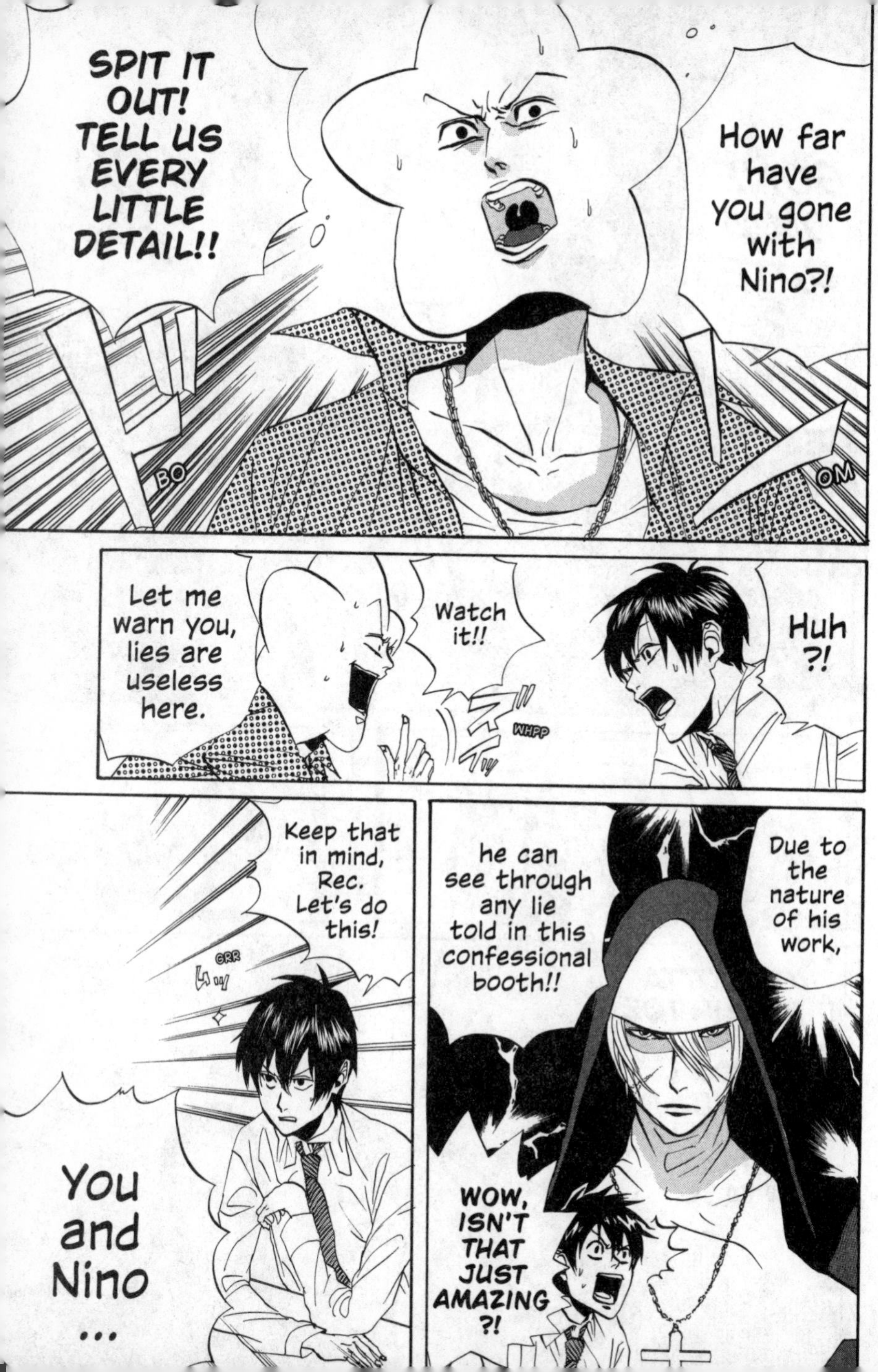
How far have you gone with Nino?!
SPIT IT OUT! TELL US EVERY LITTLE DETAIL!!
BO
OM
Huh ?!
Watch it!!
WHPP
Let me warn you, lies are useless here.
Due to the nature of his work,
he can see through any lie told in this confessional booth!!
WOW, ISN'T THAT JUST AMAZING ?!
Keep that in mind, Rec. Let's do this!
GRR
You and Nino ...

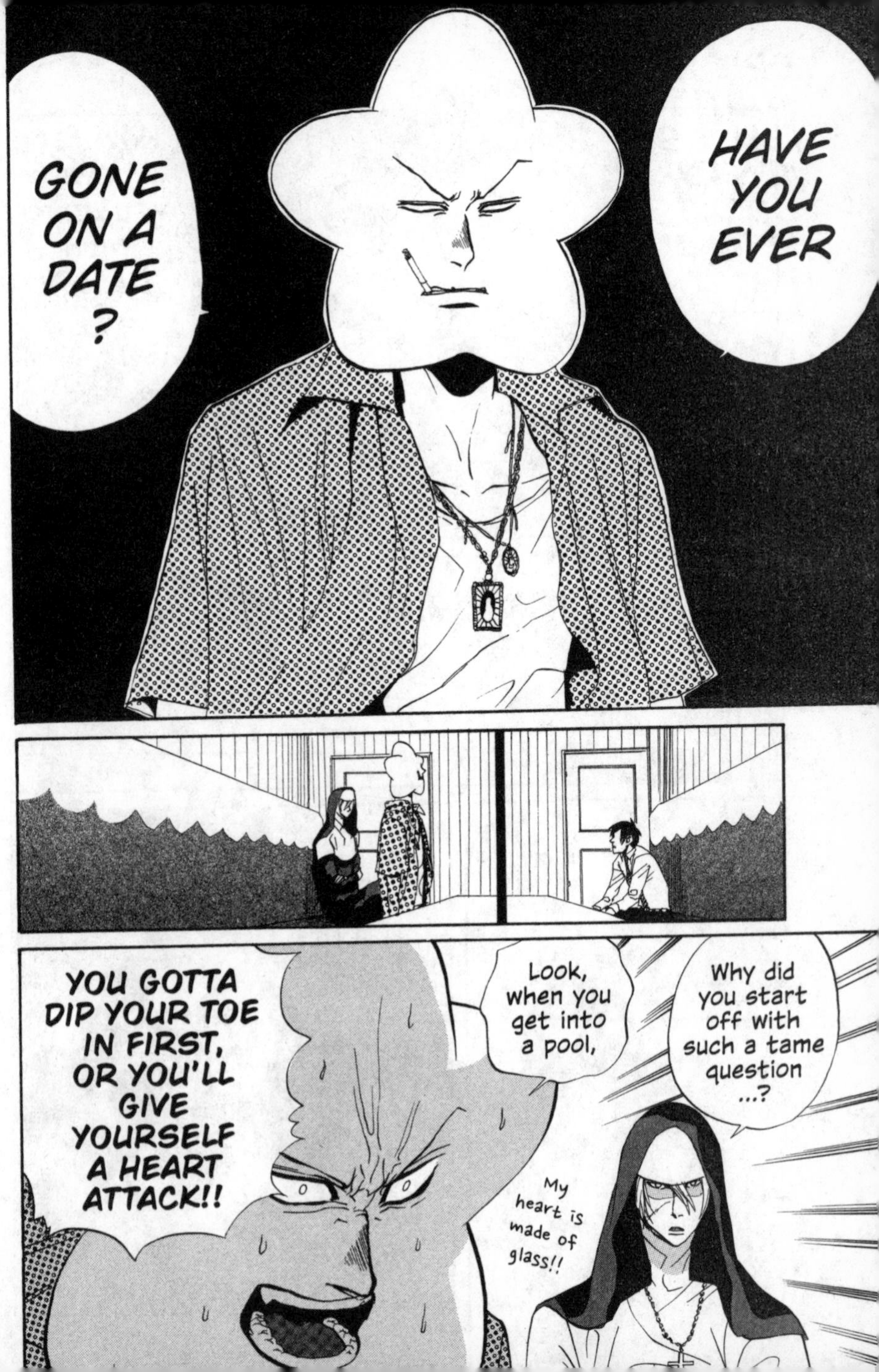
HAVE YOU EVER
GONE ON A DATE?
Why did you start off with such a tame question...?
Look, when you get into a pool,
YOU GOTTA DIP YOUR TOE IN FIRST, OR YOU'LL GIVE YOURSELF A HEART ATTACK!!
My heart is made of glass!!

Chapter 27: Bromance

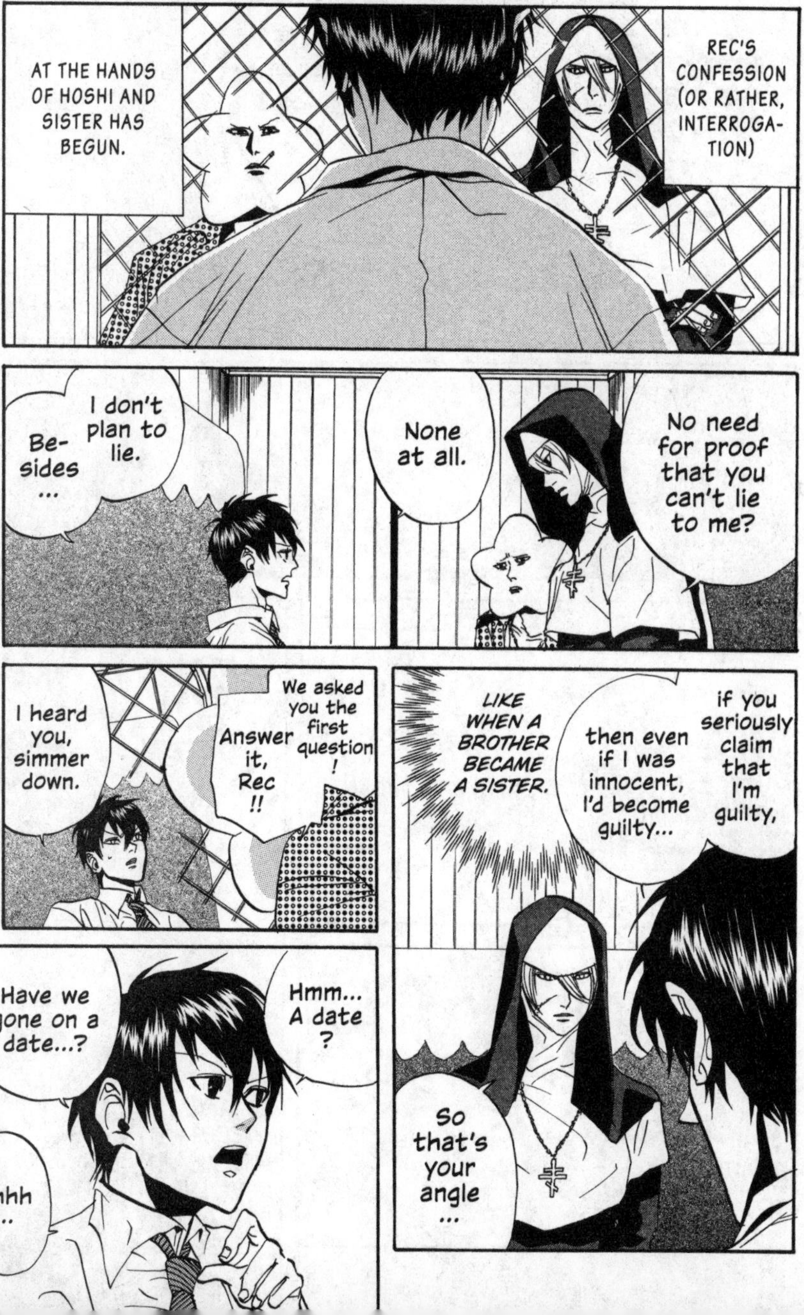
REC'S CONFESSION (OR RATHER, INTERROGATION)
AT THE HANDS OF HOSHI AND SISTER HAS BEGUN.
No need for proof that you can't lie to me?
None at all.
Besides... I don't plan to lie.
if you seriously claim that I'm guilty,
then even if I was innocent, I'd become guilty...
LIKE WHEN A BROTHER BECAME A SISTER.
We asked you the first question!
Answer it, Rec!!
I heard you, simmer down.
So that's your angle...
Hmm... A date?
Have we gone on a date...?
Uhhh...

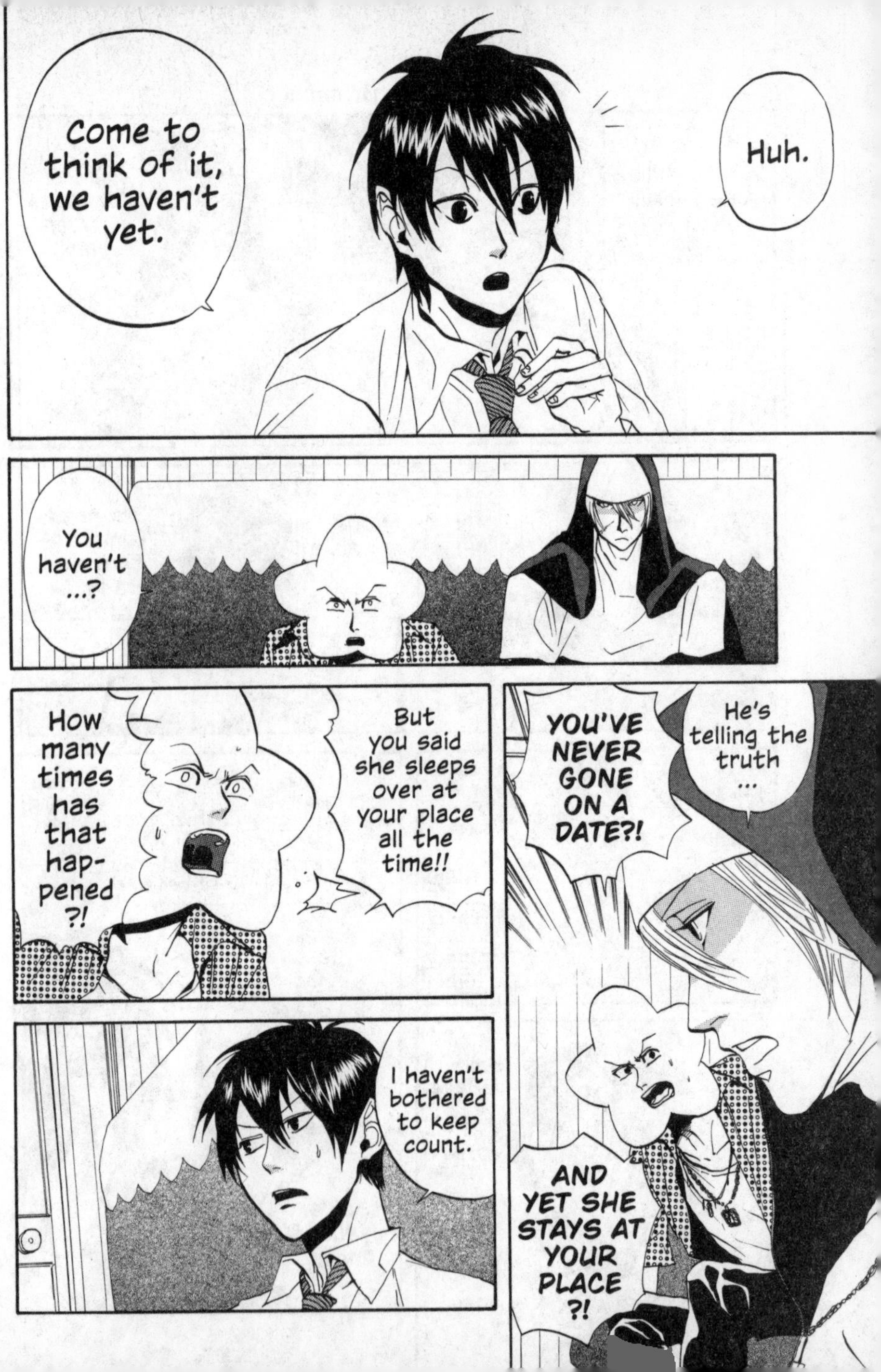
Huh.
Come to think of it, we haven't yet.
You haven't ...?
He's telling the truth ...
YOU'VE NEVER GONE ON A DATE?!
AND YET SHE STAYS AT YOUR PLACE ?!
But you said she sleeps over at your place all the time!!
How many times has that hap-pened ?!
I haven't bothered to keep count.

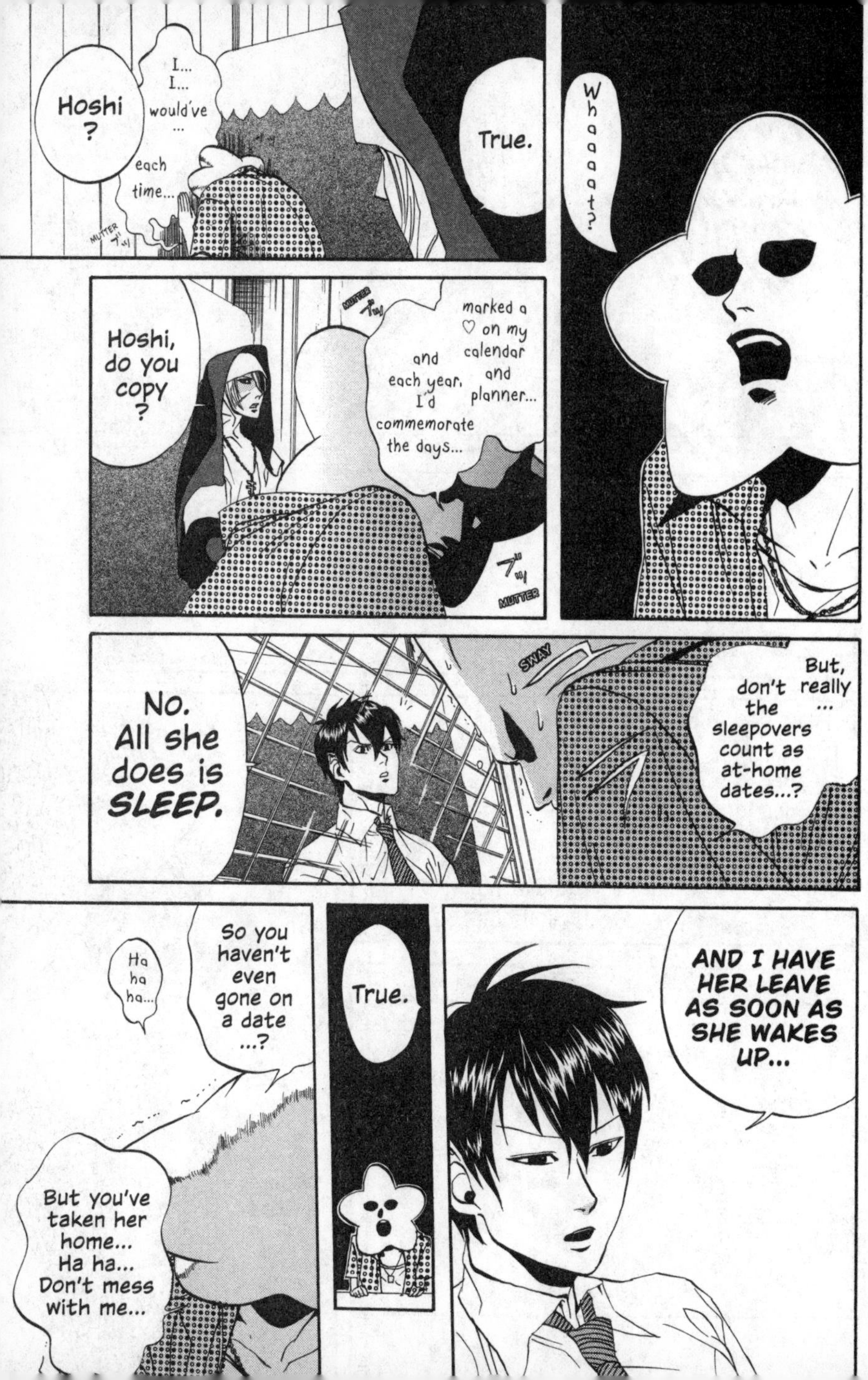

Whaaaat?
True.
Hoshi?
I... I... would've... each time...
MUTTER
Hoshi, do you copy?
MUTTER
marked a ♡ on my calendar and planner...
and each year, I'd commemorate the days...
MUTTER
But, really... don't the sleepovers count as at-home dates...?
SWAY
No. All she does is SLEEP.
AND I HAVE HER LEAVE AS SOON AS SHE WAKES UP...
True.
So you haven't even gone on a date...?
Ha ha ha...
But you've taken her home... Ha ha... Don't mess with me...

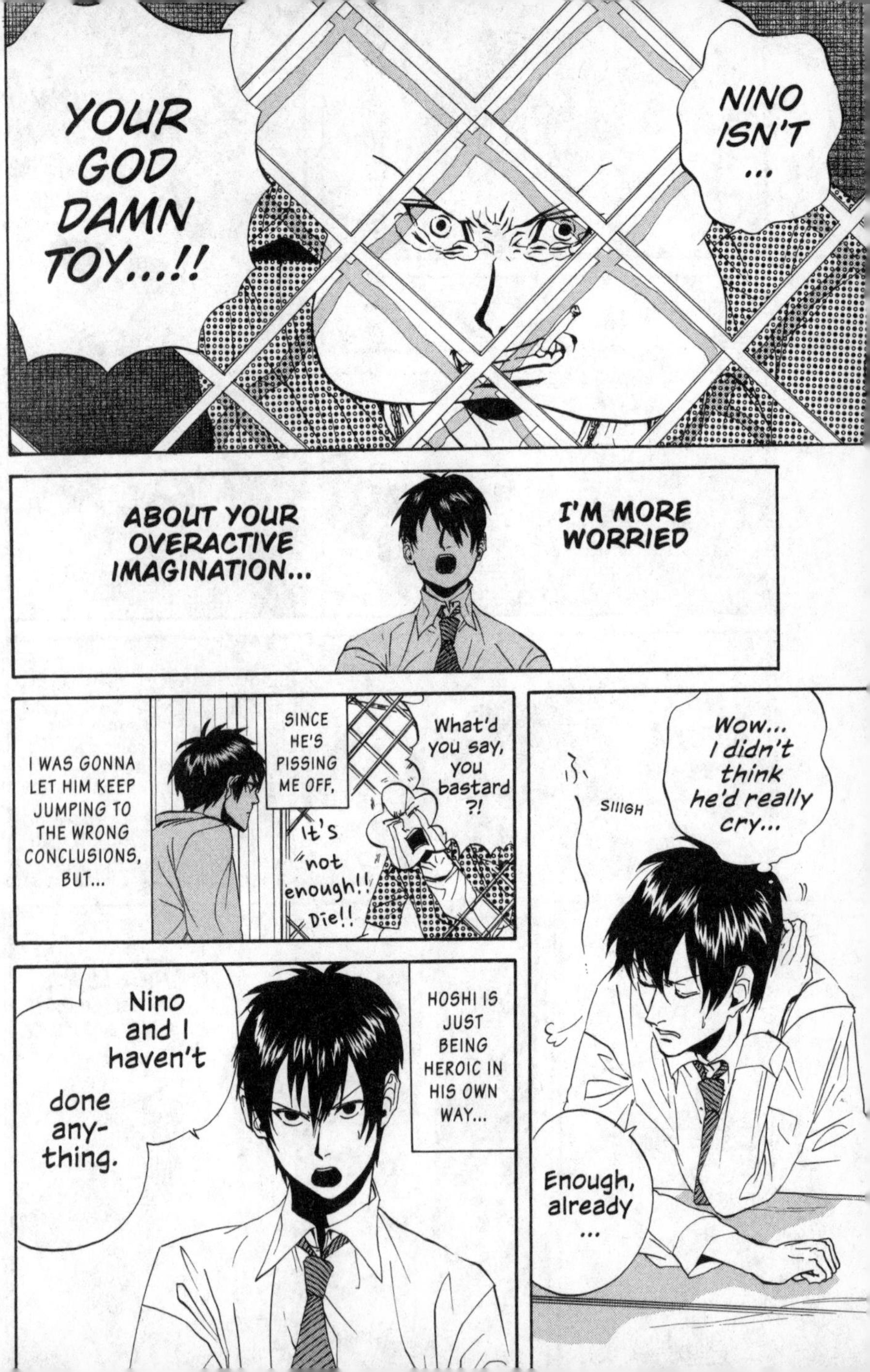
NINO ISN'T ...
YOUR GOD DAMN TOY...!!
I'M MORE WORRIED
ABOUT YOUR OVERACTIVE IMAGINATION...
Wow... I didn't think he'd really cry...
SIIGH
Enough, already ...
What'd you say, you bastard ?!
SINCE HE'S PISSING ME OFF,
It's not enough!! Die!!
I WAS GONNA LET HIM KEEP JUMPING TO THE WRONG CONCLUSIONS, BUT...
HOSHI IS JUST BEING HEROIC IN HIS OWN WAY...
Nino and I haven't done any-thing.

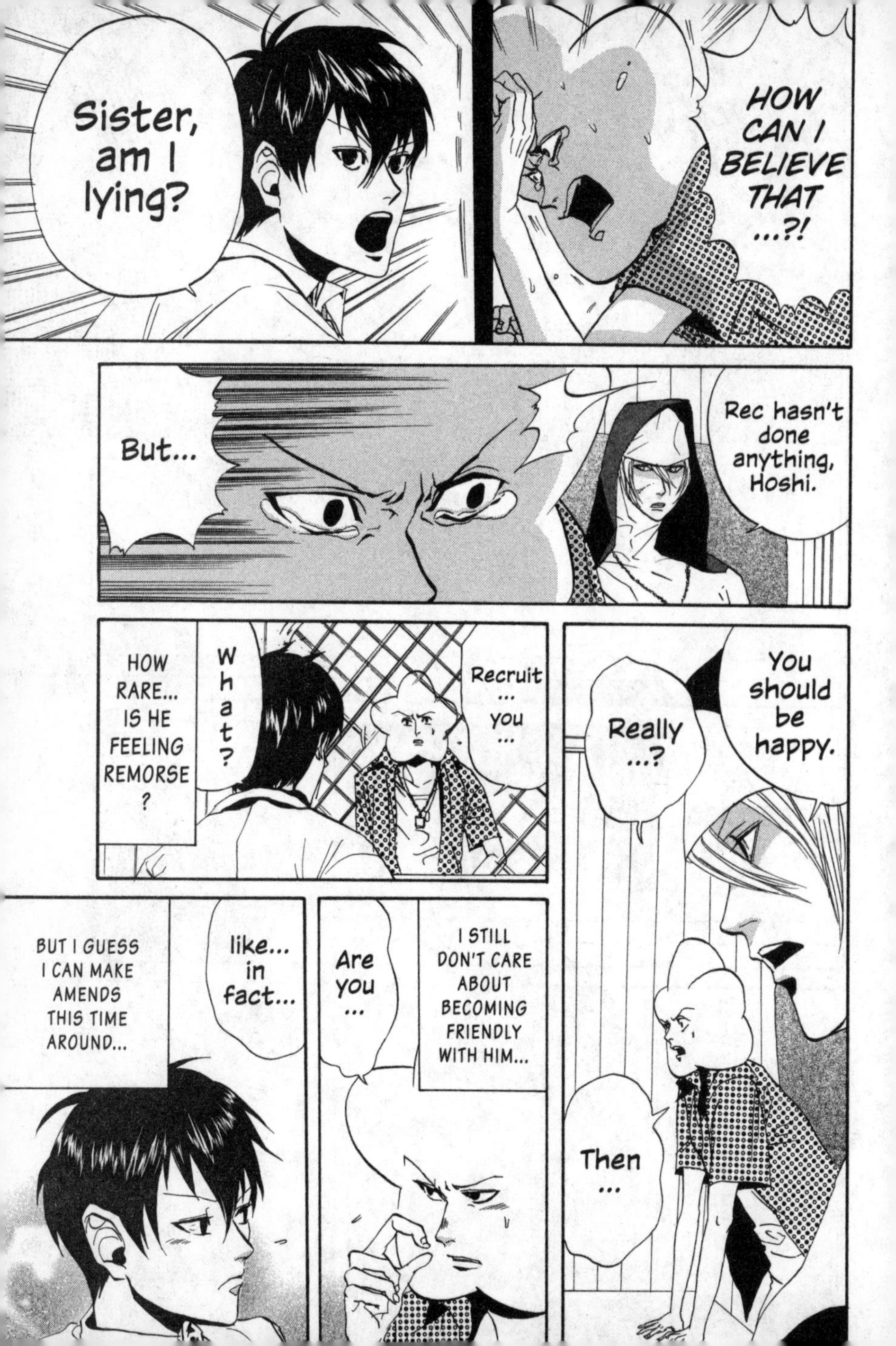
HOW CAN I BELIEVE THAT ...?!
Sister, am I lying?
Rec hasn't done anything, Hoshi.
But...
You should be happy.
Really ...?
Then ...
Recruit ... you ...
What?
HOW RARE... IS HE FEELING REMORSE?
I STILL DON'T CARE ABOUT BECOMING FRIENDLY WITH HIM...
Are you ...
like... in fact...
BUT I GUESS I CAN MAKE AMENDS THIS TIME AROUND...

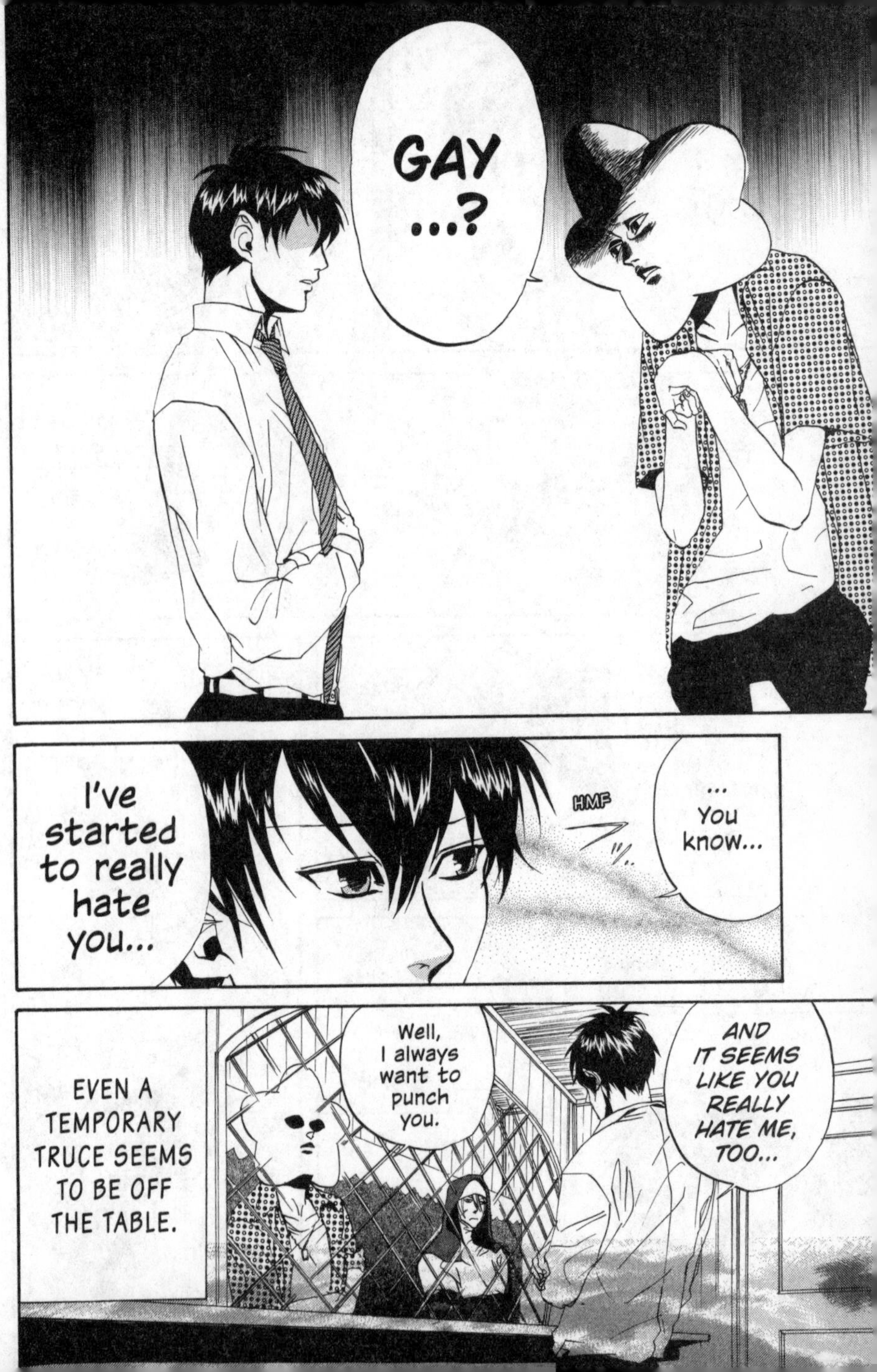
GAY ...?
... You know...
HMF
I've started to really hate you...
AND IT SEEMS LIKE YOU REALLY HATE ME, TOO...
Well, I always want to punch you.
EVEN A TEMPORARY TRUCE SEEMS TO BE OFF THE TABLE.

Chapter 28: Rec's Resolve

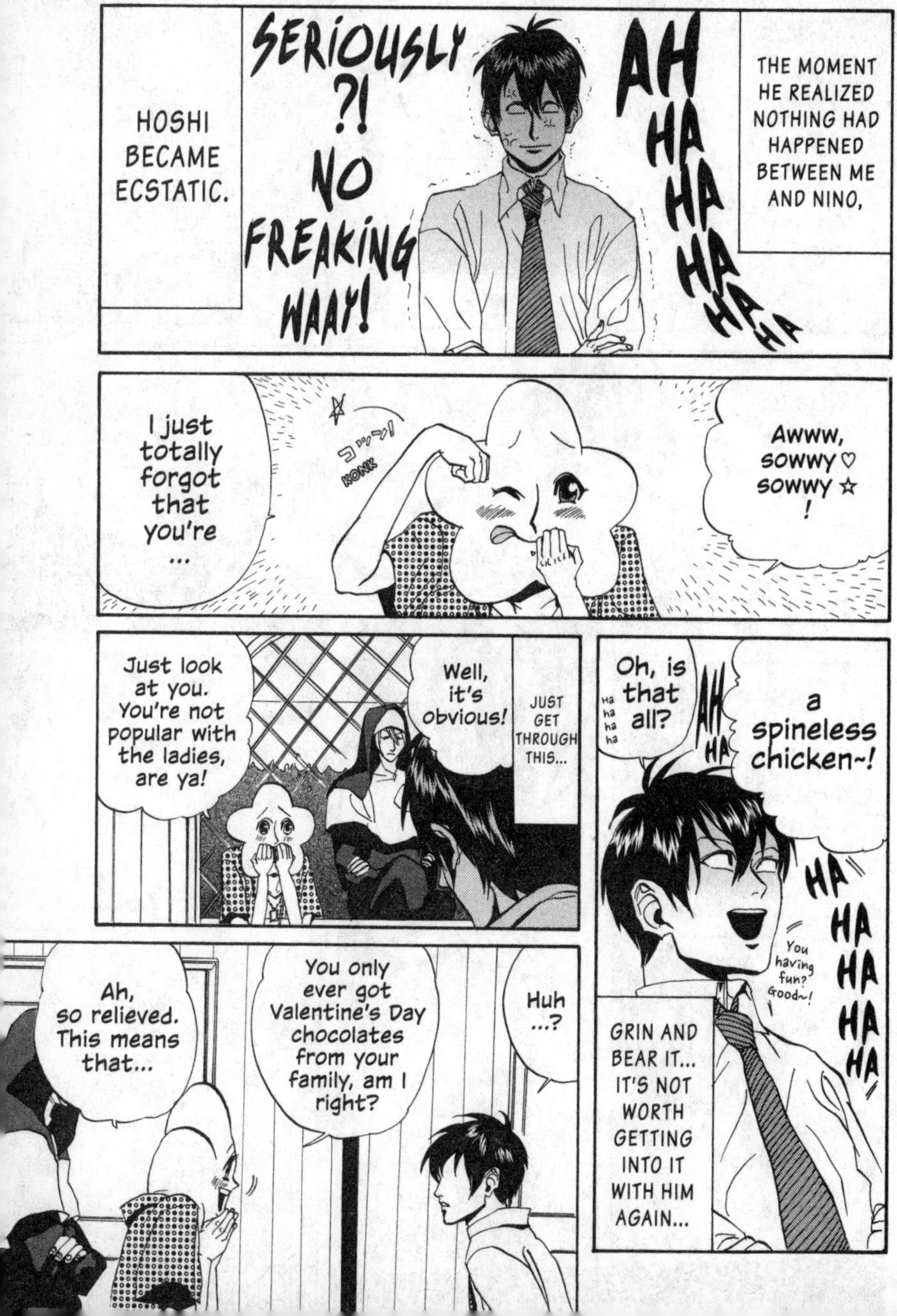
THE MOMENT HE REALIZED NOTHING HAD HAPPENED BETWEEN ME AND NINO,
AH HA HA HA HA HA HA
SERIOUSLY?! NO FREAKING WAAY!
HOSHI BECAME ECSTATIC.
Awww, sowwy♡ sowwy☆!
KONK
I just totally forgot that you're ...
a spineless chicken~!
AH HA
Oh, is that all?
Ha ha ha ha
HA HA HA HA HA
You having fun? Good~!
GRIN AND BEAR IT... IT'S NOT WORTH GETTING INTO IT WITH HIM AGAIN...
Well, it's obvious!
JUST GET THROUGH THIS...
Just look at you. You're not popular with the ladies, are ya!
Huh ...?
You only ever got Valentine's Day chocolates from your family, am I right?
Ah, so relieved. This means that...

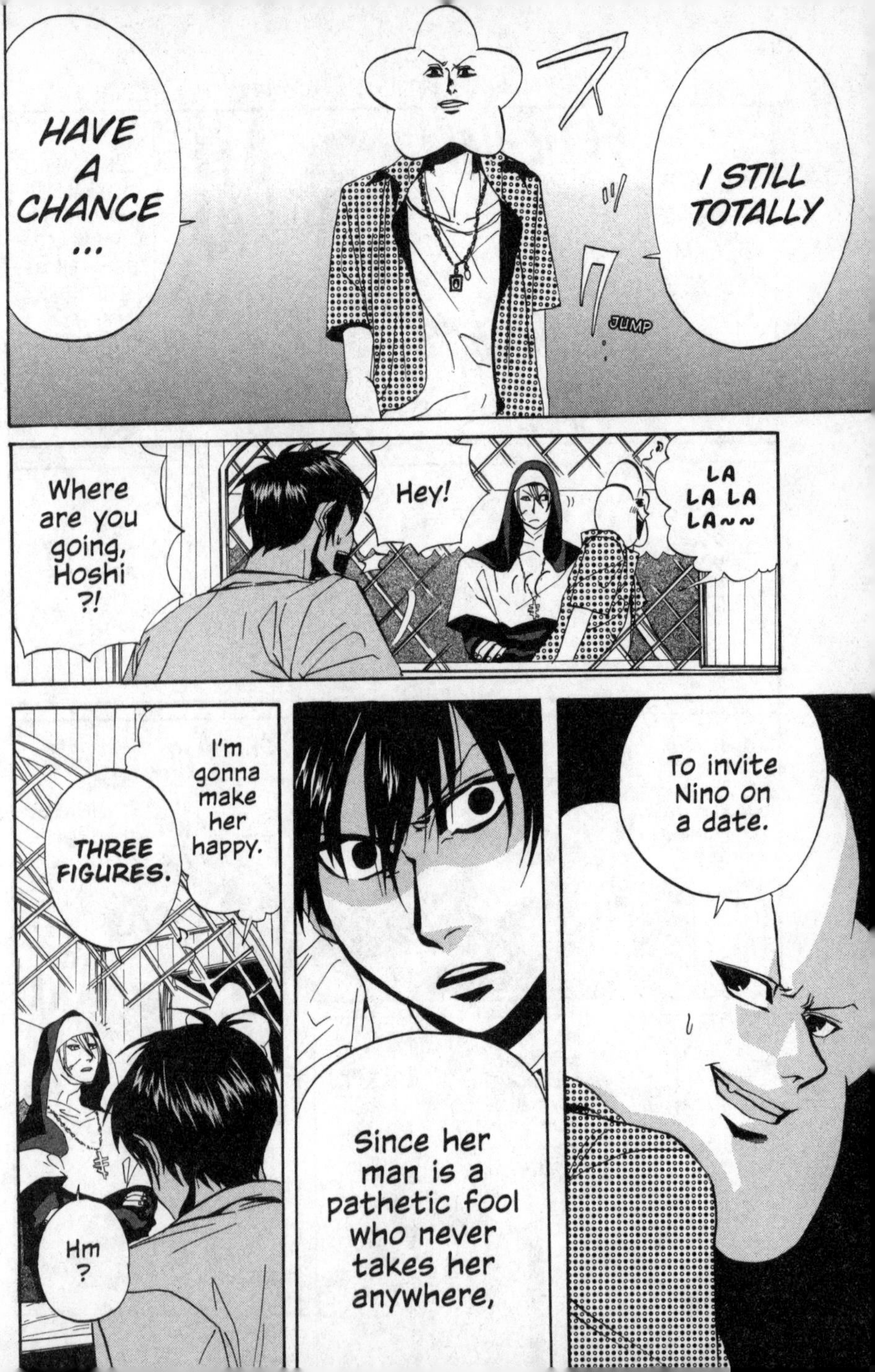
I STILL TOTALLY
JUMP
HAVE A CHANCE ...
LA LA LA LA~~
Hey!
Where are you going, Hoshi ?!
To invite Nino on a date.
Since her man is a pathetic fool who never takes her anywhere,
I'm gonna make her happy.
THREE FIGURES.
Hm ?

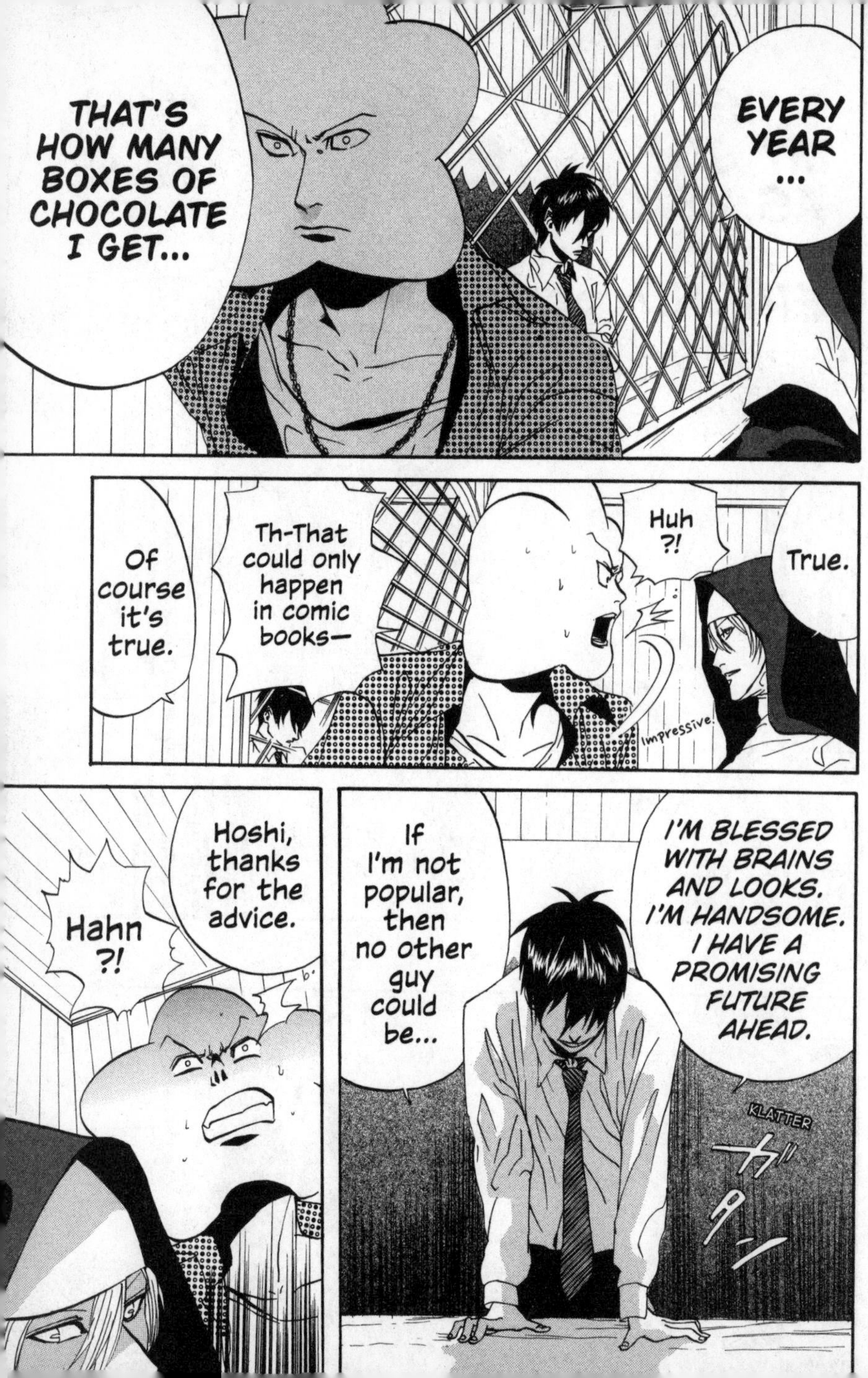
EVERY YEAR ...
THAT'S HOW MANY BOXES OF CHOCOLATE I GET...
True.
Huh ?!
Impressive!
Th-That could only happen in comic books—
Of course it's true.
I'M BLESSED WITH BRAINS AND LOOKS. I'M HANDSOME. I HAVE A PROMISING FUTURE AHEAD.
KLATTER
If I'm not popular, then no other guy could be...
Hoshi, thanks for the advice.
Hahn ?!

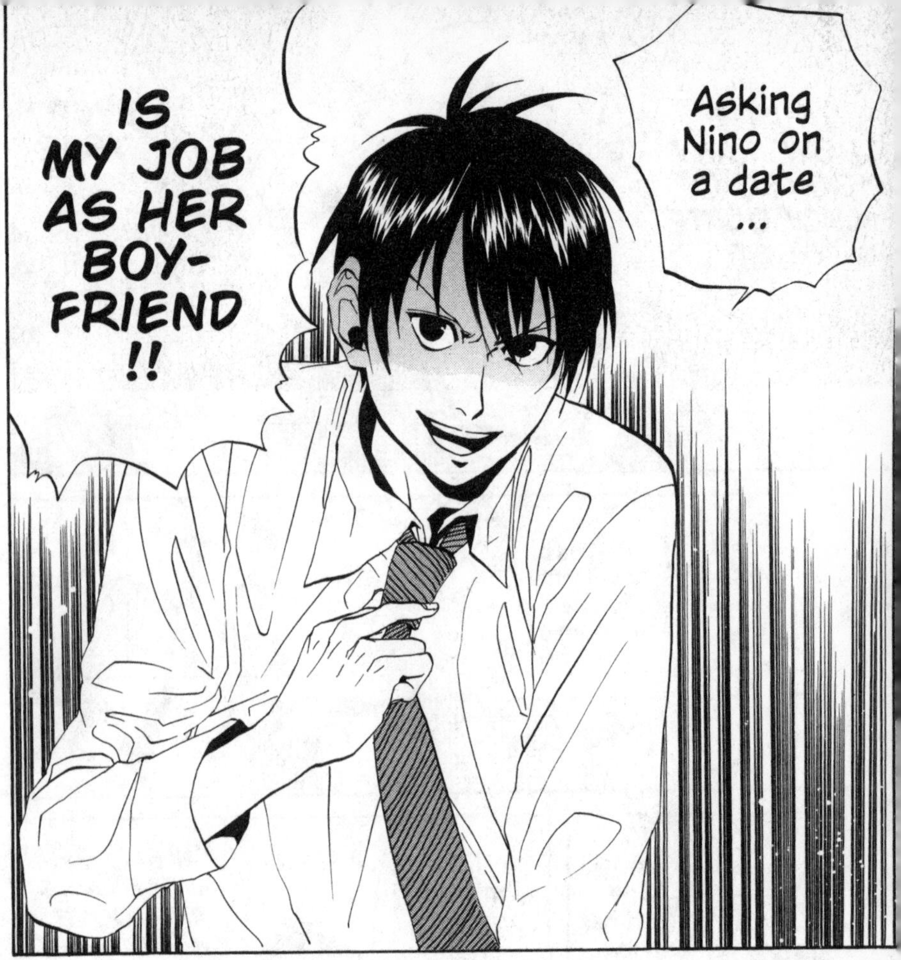
Asking Nino on a date ...
IS MY JOB AS HER BOY-FRIEND !!

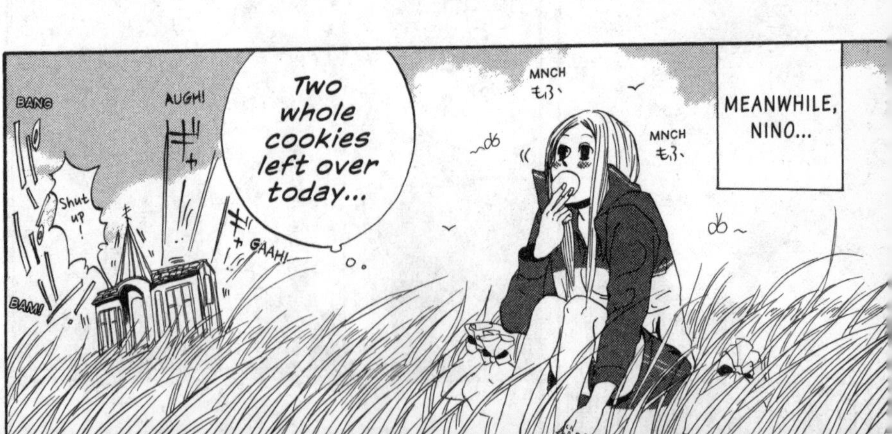
MEANWHILE, NINO...
MNCH
MNCH
Two whole cookies left over today...
AUGH!
GAAH!
BANG
Shut up!
BAM!

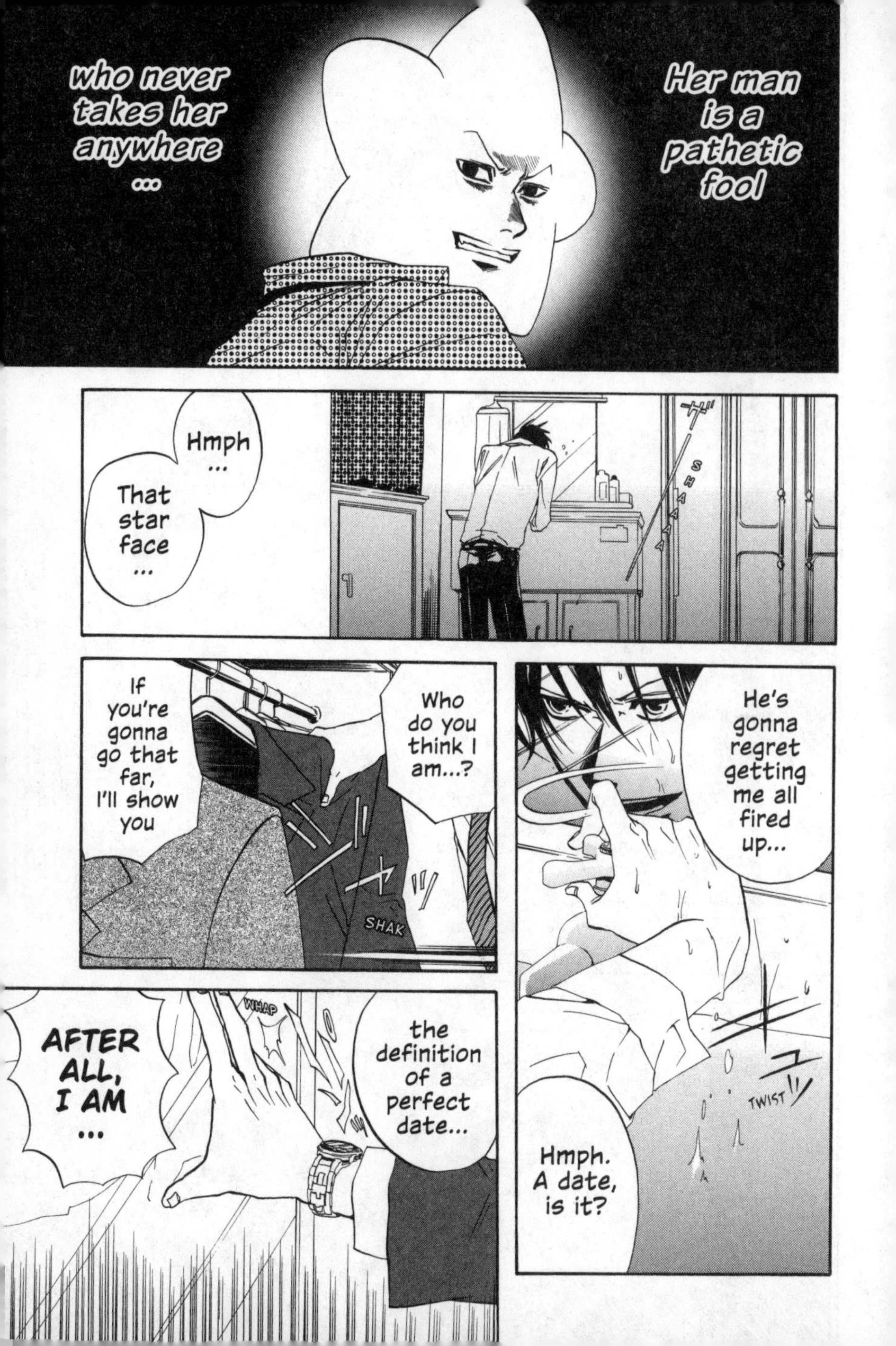
Her man is a pathetic fool
who never takes her anywhere ...
SHAAAA
Hmph ...
That star face ...
He's gonna regret getting me all fired up...
TWIST
Hmph. A date, is it?
Who do you think I am...?
If you're gonna go that far, I'll show you
SHAK
WHAP
the definition of a perfect date...
AFTER ALL, I AM ...

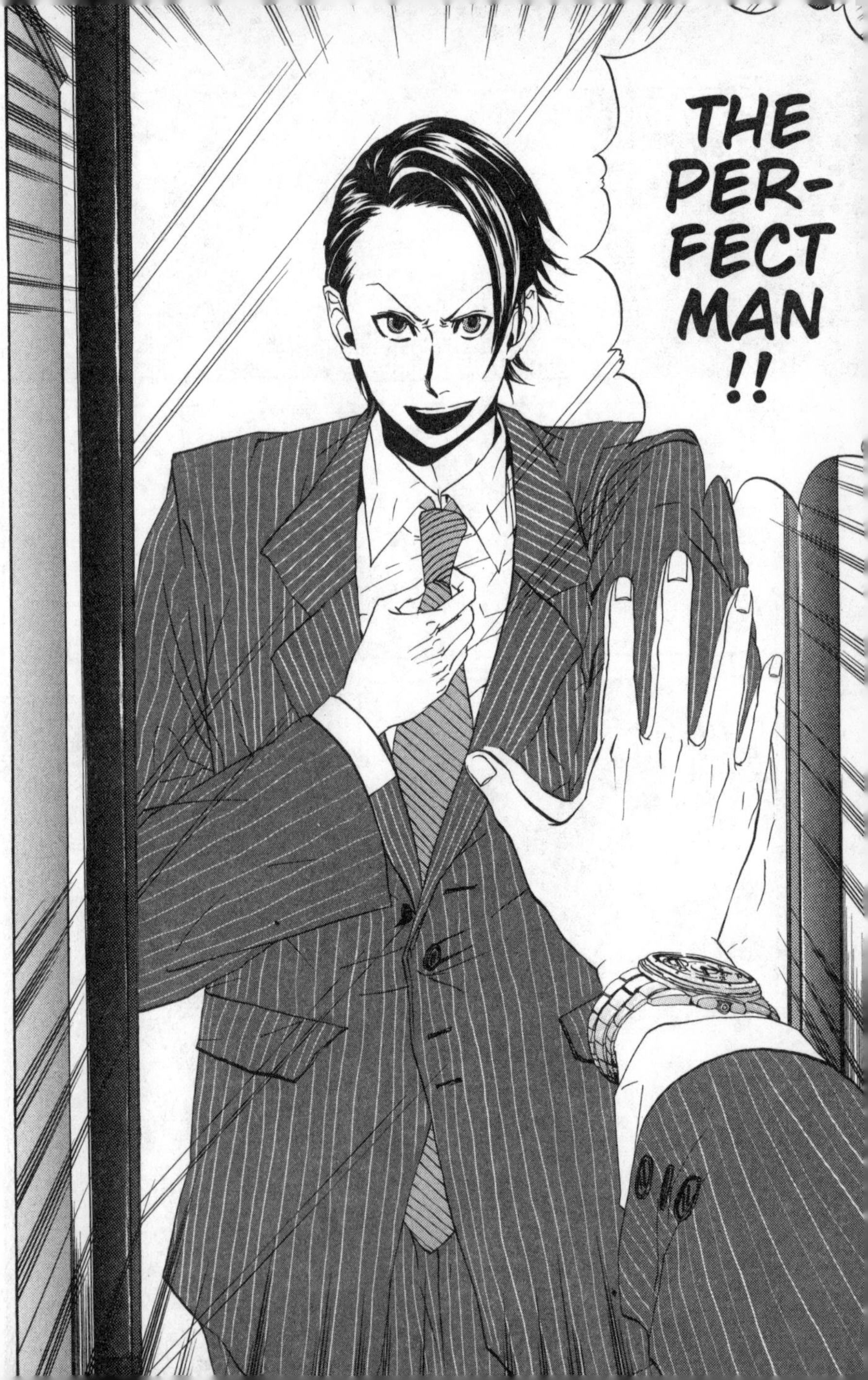
THE PER-FECT MAN !!

☜ Chapter 29: Invitation

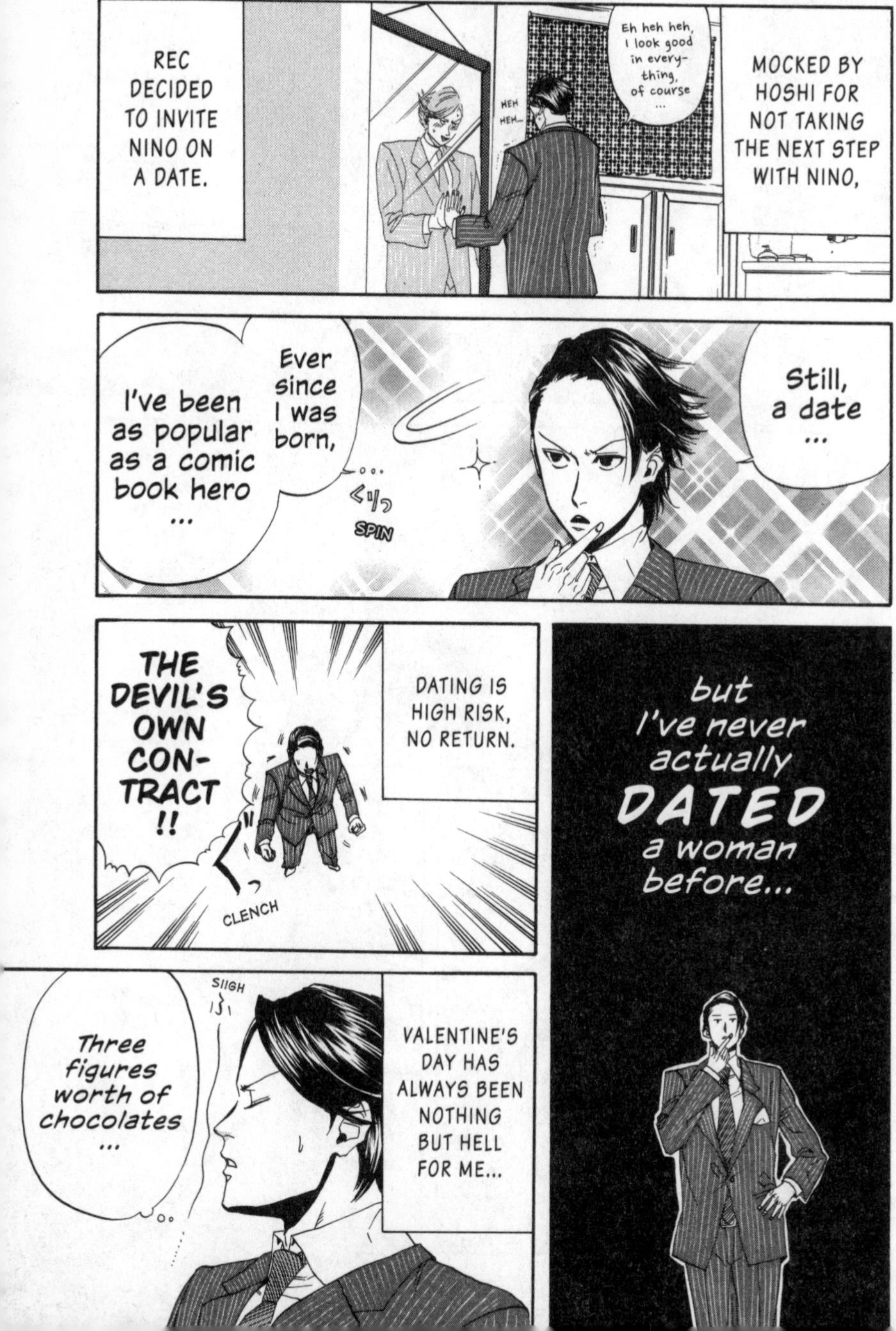
MOCKED BY HOSHI FOR NOT TAKING THE NEXT STEP WITH NINO,
Eh heh heh, I look good in every-thing, of course ...
HEH HEH...
REC DECIDED TO INVITE NINO ON A DATE.
Still, a date ...
SPIN
Ever since I was born,
I've been as popular as a comic book hero ...
but I've never actually DATED a woman before...
DATING IS HIGH RISK, NO RETURN.
THE DEVIL'S OWN CON-TRACT !!
CLENCH
VALENTINE'S DAY HAS ALWAYS BEEN NOTHING BUT HELL FOR ME...
SIIGH
Three figures worth of chocolates ...

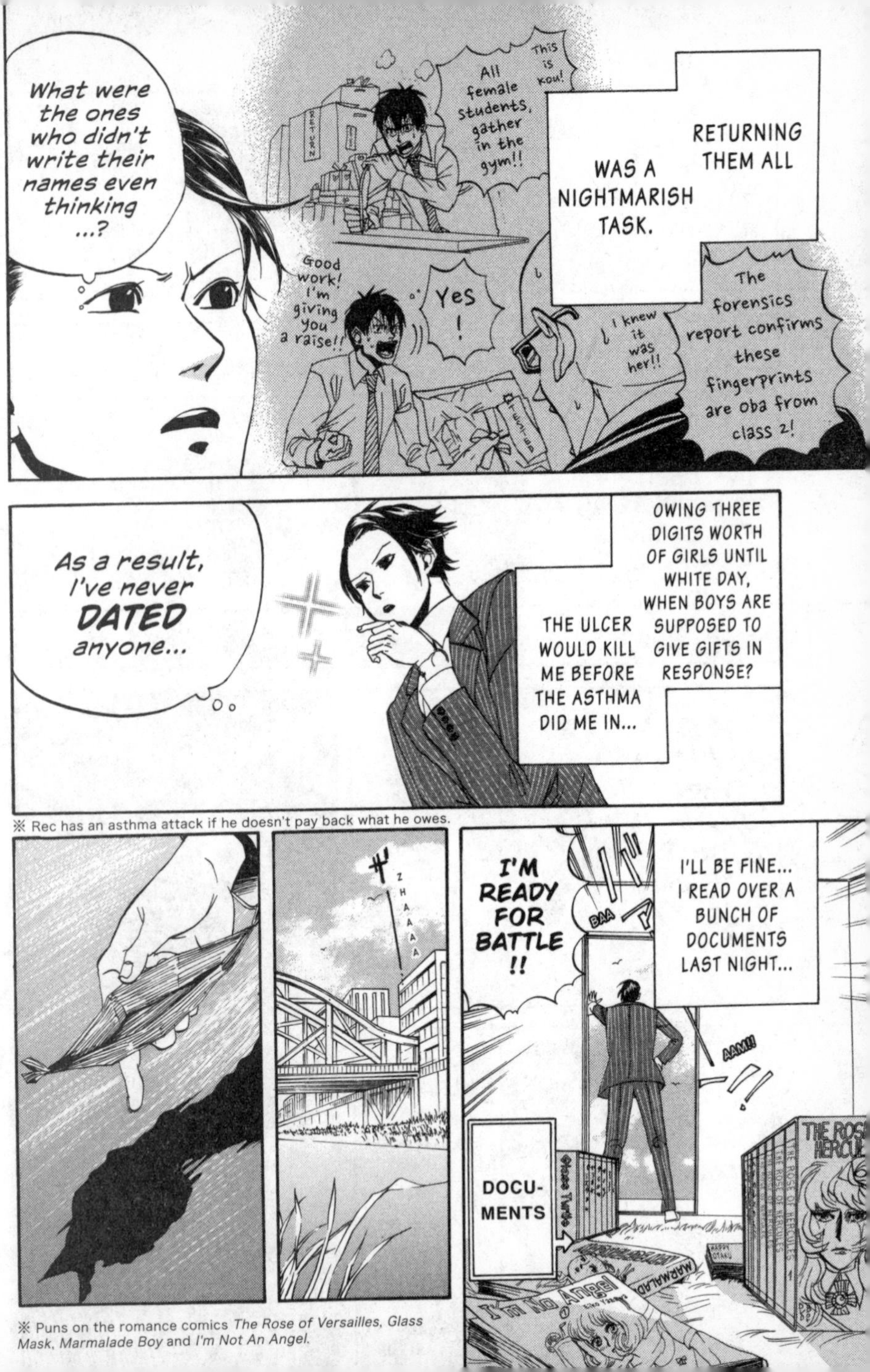
RETURNING THEM ALL
WAS A NIGHTMARISH TASK.
This is kou!
All female students, gather in the gym!!
The forensics report confirms these fingerprints are oba from class 2!
I knew it was her!!
Yes!
Good work! I'm giving you a raise!!
What were the ones who didn't write their names even thinking ...?
OWING THREE DIGITS WORTH OF GIRLS UNTIL WHITE DAY, WHEN BOYS ARE SUPPOSED TO GIVE GIFTS IN RESPONSE?
THE ULCER WOULD KILL ME BEFORE THE ASTHMA DID ME IN...
As a result, I've never **DATED** anyone...
I'LL BE FINE... I READ OVER A BUNCH OF DOCUMENTS LAST NIGHT...
BAA
AAM!!
I'M READY FOR BATTLE !!
DOCU-MENTS
HAPPY OTAKU
I'm No Angel
ZHAAAAA

※ Rec has an asthma attack if he doesn't pay back what he owes.

※ Puns on the romance comics *The Rose of Versailles, Glass Mask, Marmalade Boy* and *I'm Not An Angel*.

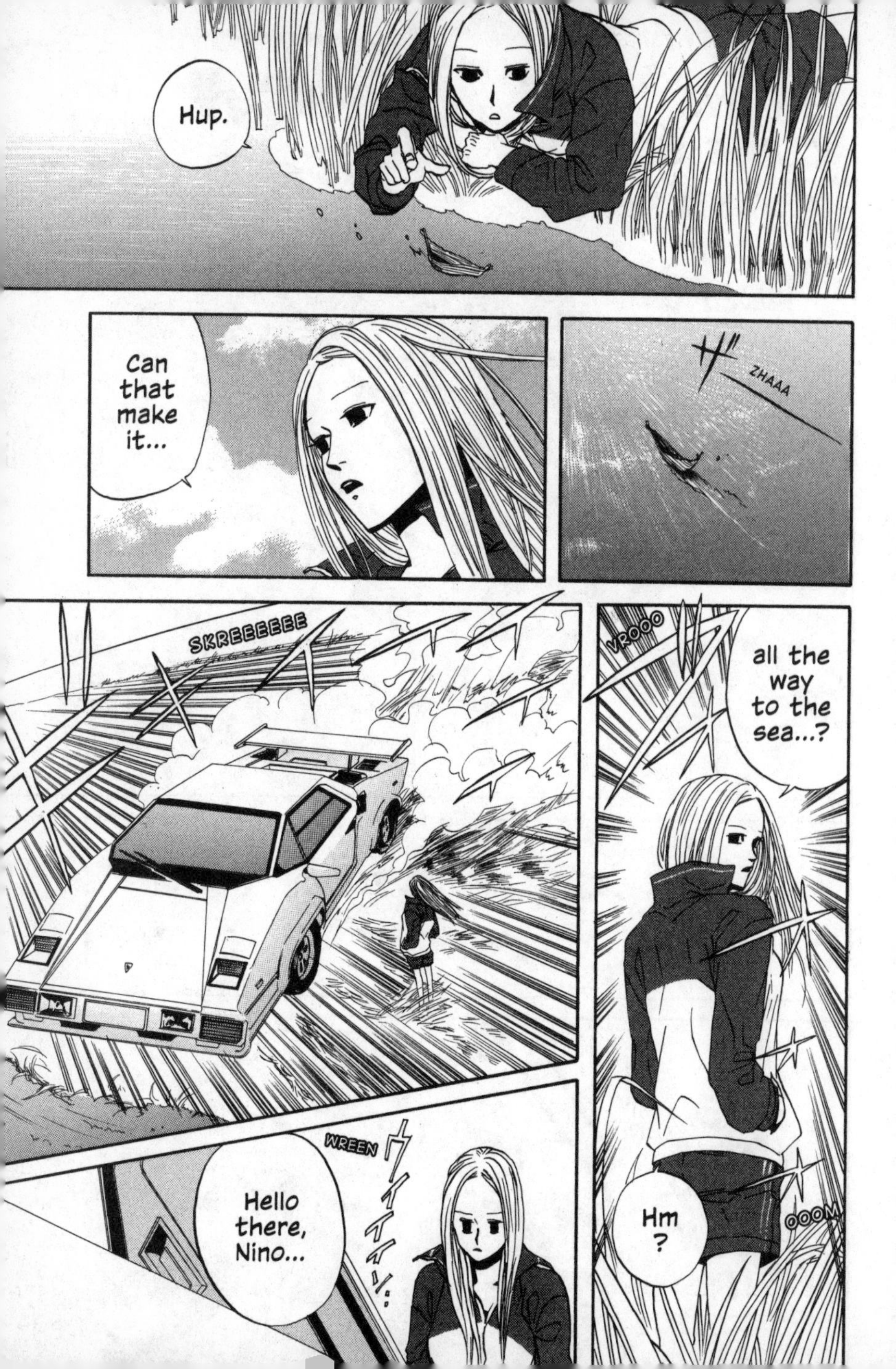
Hup.
ZHAAA
Can that make it...
VROOO
all the way to the sea...?
OOOM
Hm ?
SKREEEEEEE
WREEN
Hello there, Nino...

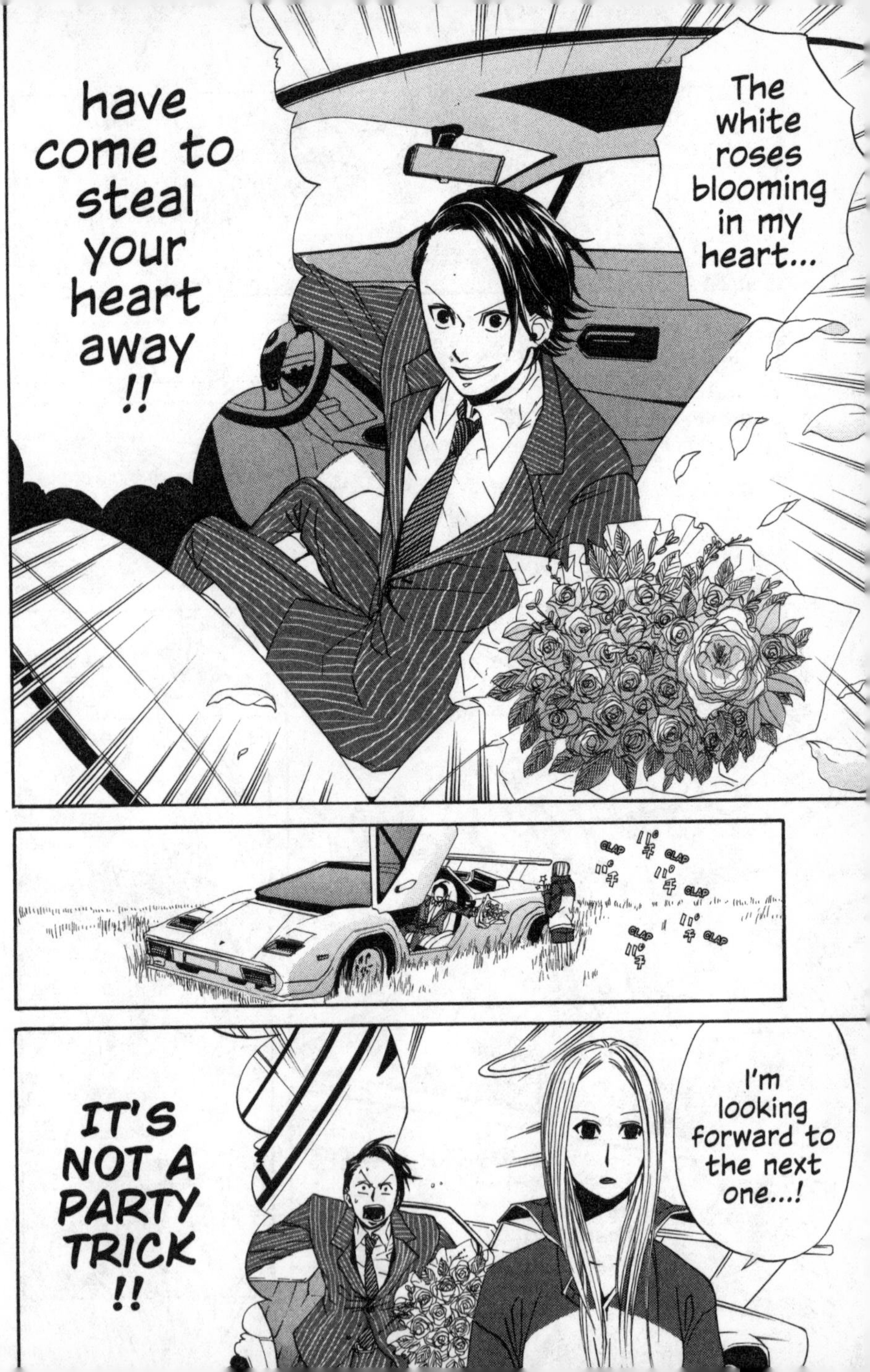
The white roses blooming in my heart...
have come to steal your heart away!!
CLAP
CLAP
CLAP
CLAP
CLAP
I'm looking forward to the next one...!
IT'S NOT A PARTY TRICK!!

☜ Chapter 30: Plan

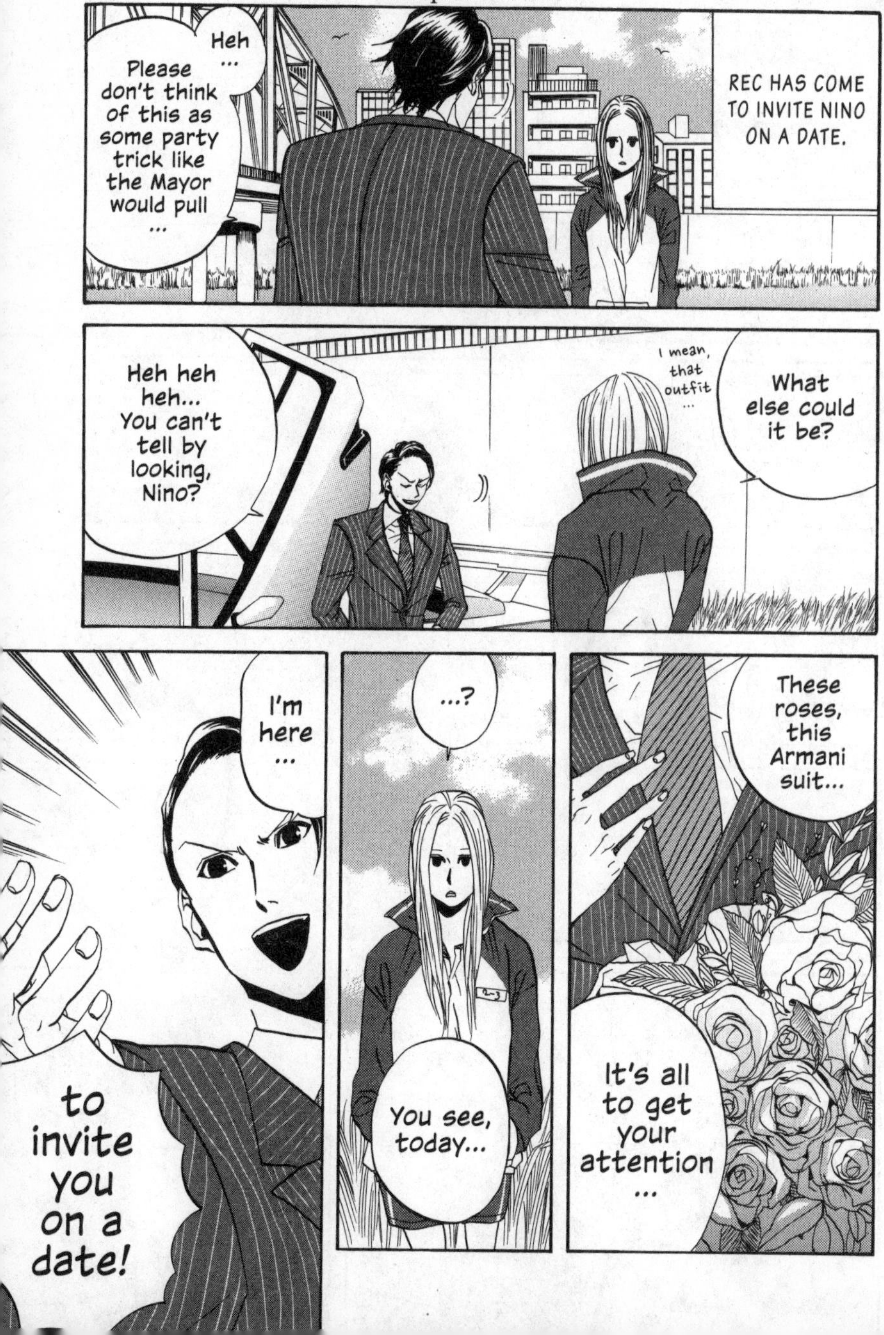
REC HAS COME TO INVITE NINO ON A DATE.
Heh ...
Please don't think of this as some party trick like the Mayor would pull ...
What else could it be?
I mean, that outfit ...
Heh heh heh... You can't tell by looking, Nino?
These roses, this Armani suit...
It's all to get your attention ...
...?
You see, today...
I'm here ...
to invite you on a date!

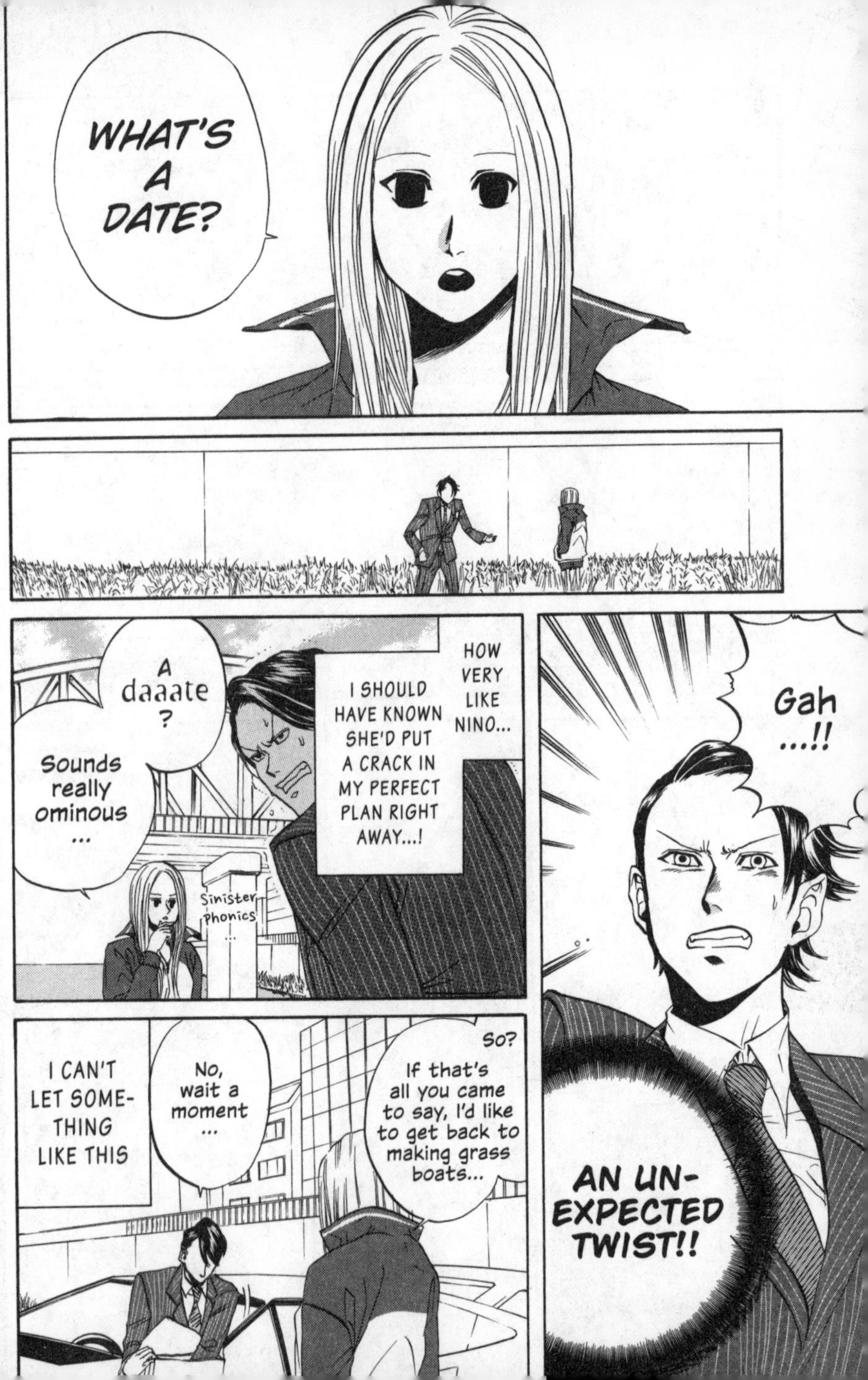
WHAT'S A DATE?
Gah ...!!
AN UN-EXPECTED TWIST!!
HOW VERY LIKE NINO...
I SHOULD HAVE KNOWN SHE'D PUT A CRACK IN MY PERFECT PLAN RIGHT AWAY...!
A daaate?
Sounds really ominous ...
Sinister Phonics ...
So?
If that's all you came to say, I'd like to get back to making grass boats...
No, wait a moment ...
I CAN'T LET SOME-THING LIKE THIS

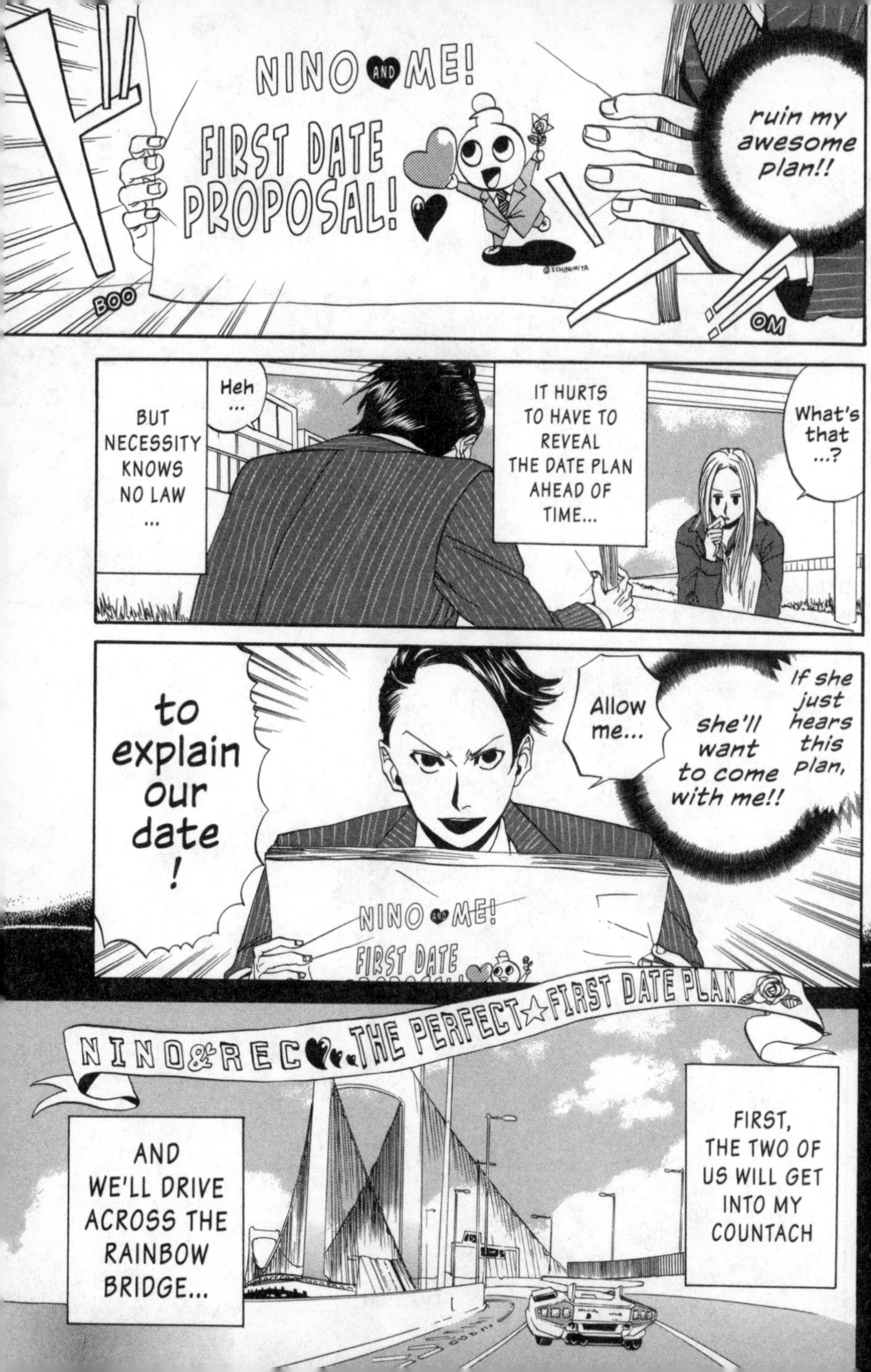
ruin my awesome plan!!
NINO AND ME!
FIRST DATE PROPOSAL!
©ICHINOMIYA
BOO
OM
What's that ...?
IT HURTS TO HAVE TO REVEAL THE DATE PLAN AHEAD OF TIME...
Heh ...
BUT NECESSITY KNOWS NO LAW ...
If she just hears this plan,
she'll want to come with me!!
Allow me...
to explain our date !
NINO AND ME!
FIRST DATE
NINO & REC THE PERFECT☆FIRST DATE PLAN
FIRST, THE TWO OF US WILL GET INTO MY COUNTACH
AND WE'LL DRIVE ACROSS THE RAINBOW BRIDGE...

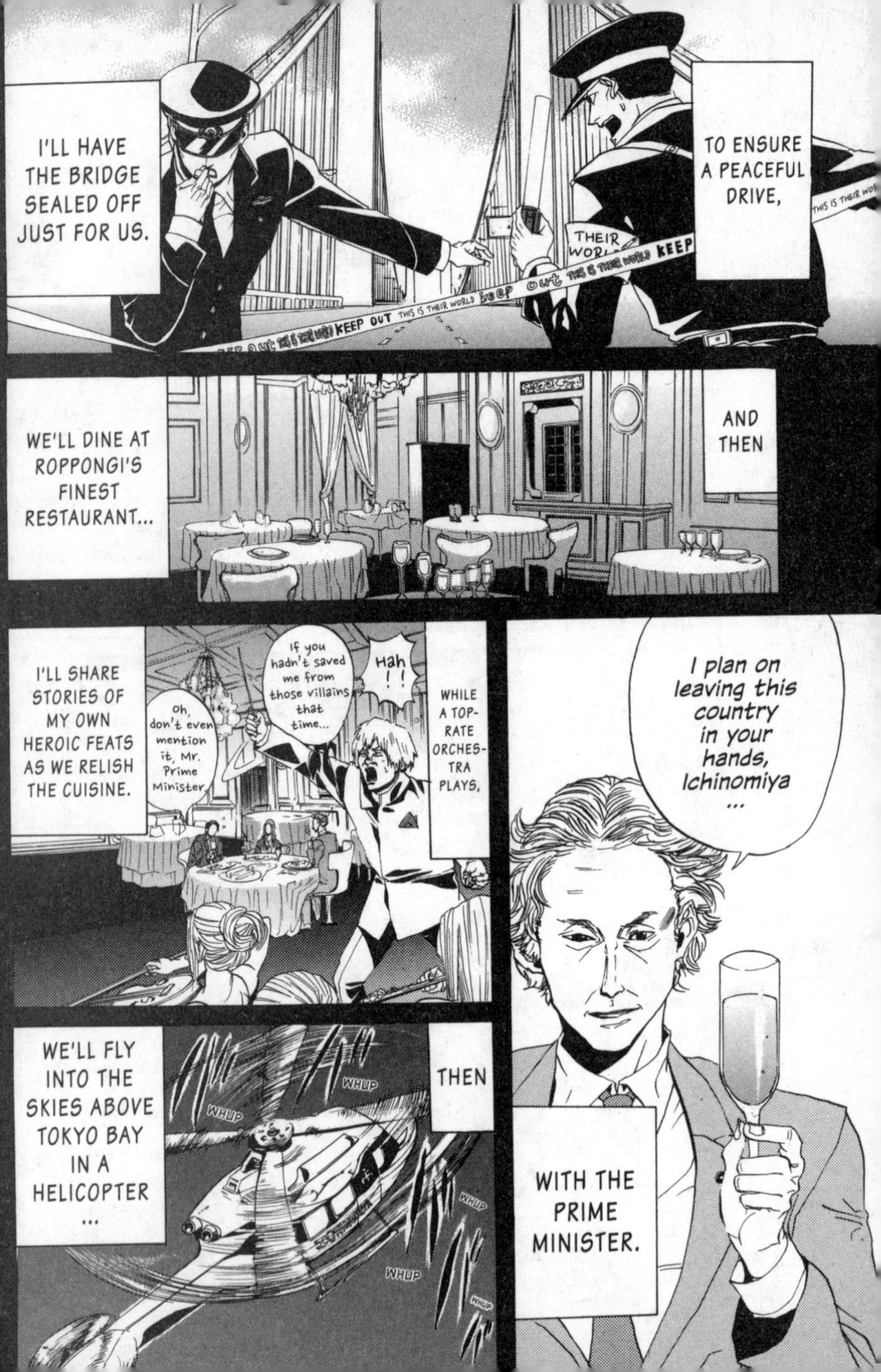
TO ENSURE A PEACEFUL DRIVE,
THIS IS THEIR WORLD
THEIR WORLD KEEP
I'LL HAVE THE BRIDGE SEALED OFF JUST FOR US.
KEEP OUT THIS IS THEIR WORLD
AND THEN
WE'LL DINE AT ROPPONGI'S FINEST RESTAURANT...
I plan on leaving this country in your hands, Ichinomiya ...
WITH THE PRIME MINISTER.
WHILE A TOP-RATE ORCHESTRA PLAYS,
Hah!!
If you hadn't saved me from those villains that time...
Oh, don't even mention it, Mr. Prime Minister.
I'LL SHARE STORIES OF MY OWN HEROIC FEATS AS WE RELISH THE CUISINE.
THEN
WHUP
WHUP
WHUP
WHUP
WHUP
WE'LL FLY INTO THE SKIES ABOVE TOKYO BAY IN A HELICOPTER ...

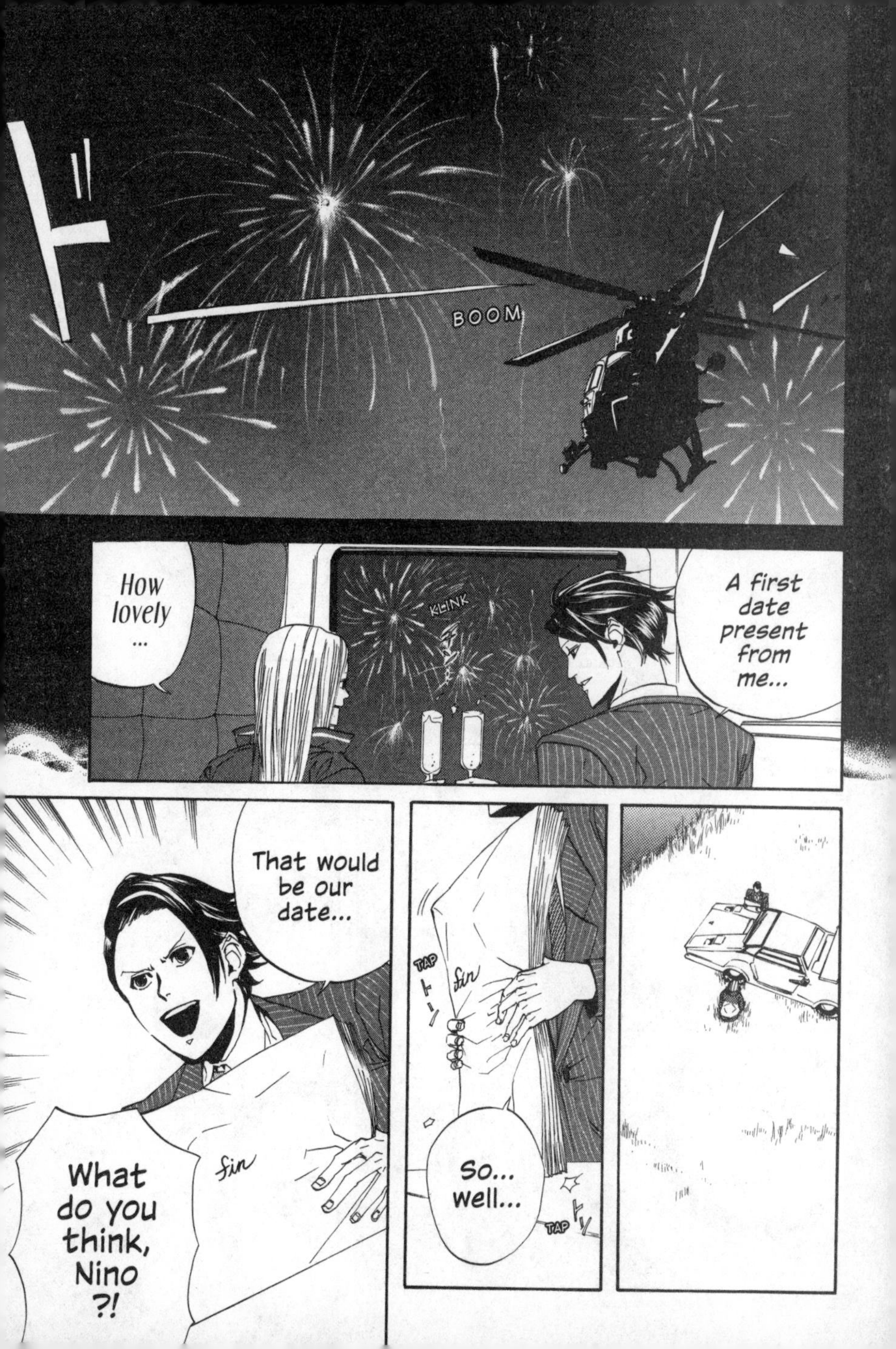
ド
BOOM
A first date present from me...
KLINK
How lovely ...
fin
TAP
So... well...
TAP
That would be our date...
fin
What do you think, Nino ?!

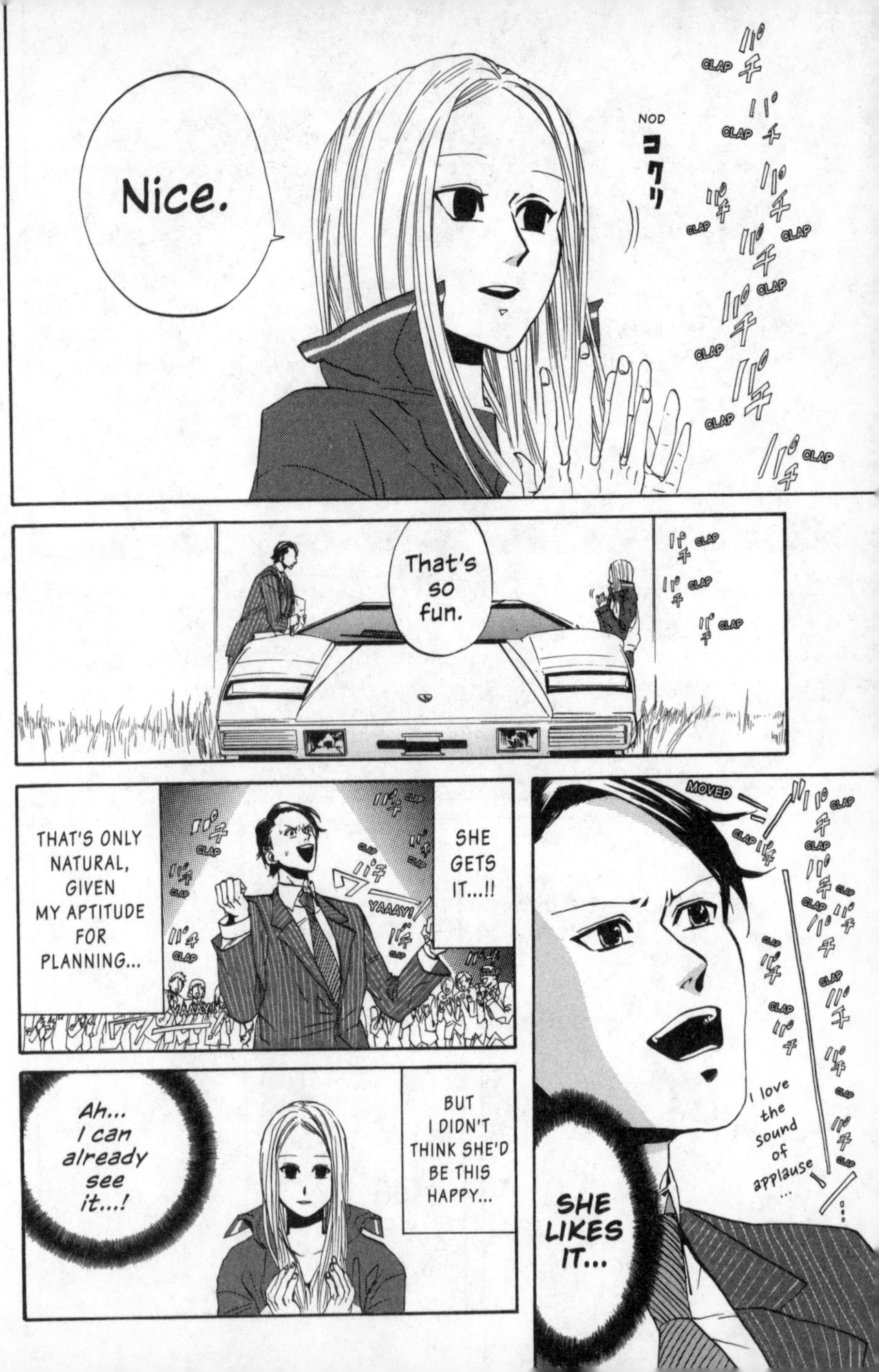
CLAP
NOD
コクリ
Nice.
CLAP
That's so fun.
MOVED
CLAP
I love the sound of applause...
SHE LIKES IT...
SHE GETS IT...!!
YAAAY!
CLAP
THAT'S ONLY NATURAL, GIVEN MY APTITUDE FOR PLANNING...
BUT I DIDN'T THINK SHE'D BE THIS HAPPY...
Ah... I can already see it...!

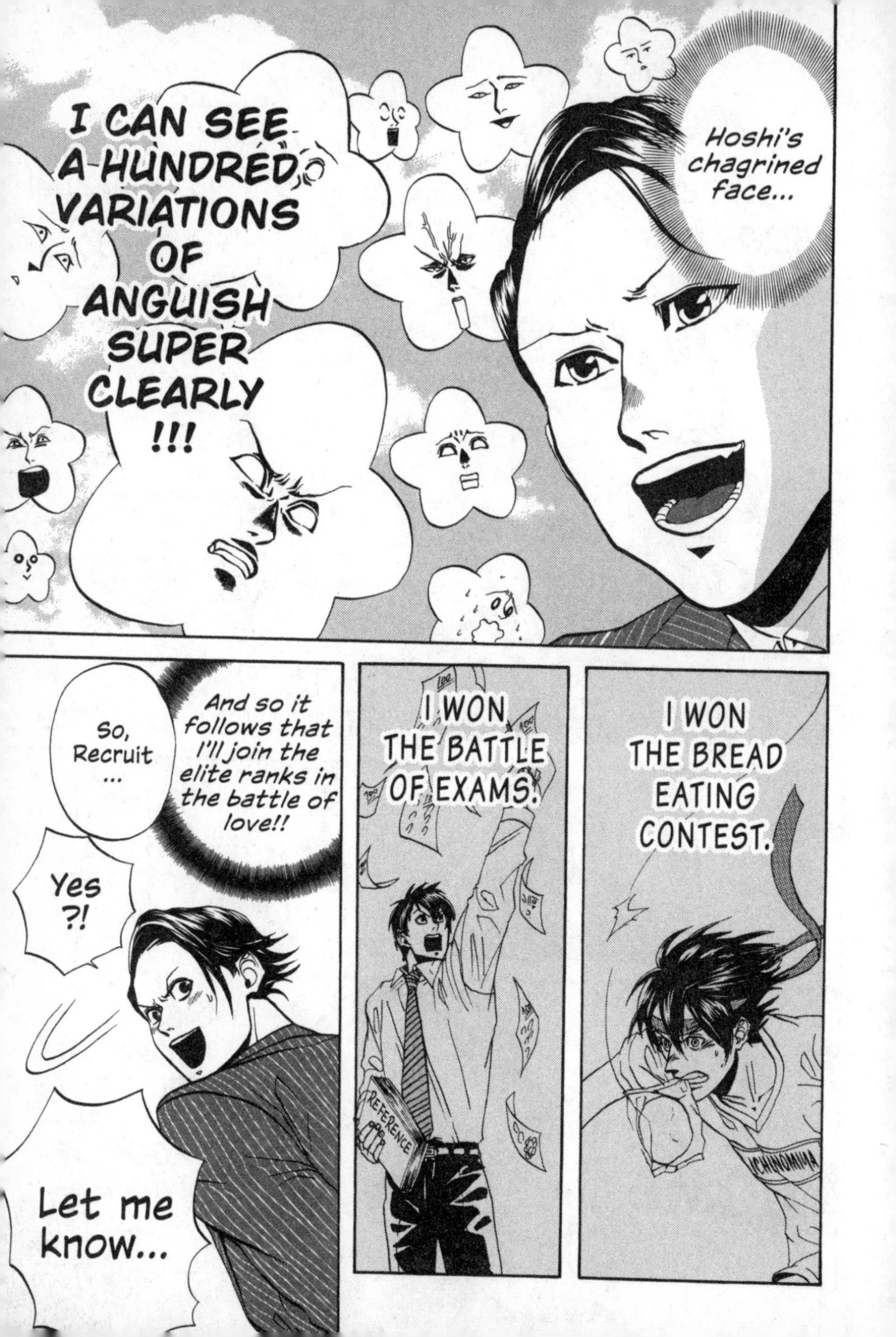
Hoshi's chagrined face...
I CAN SEE A HUNDRED VARIATIONS OF ANGUISH SUPER CLEARLY !!!
I WON THE BREAD EATING CONTEST.
ICHINOMIYA
I WON THE BATTLE OF EXAMS.
REFERENCE
And so it follows that I'll join the elite ranks in the battle of love!!
So, Recruit ...
Yes ?!
Let me know...

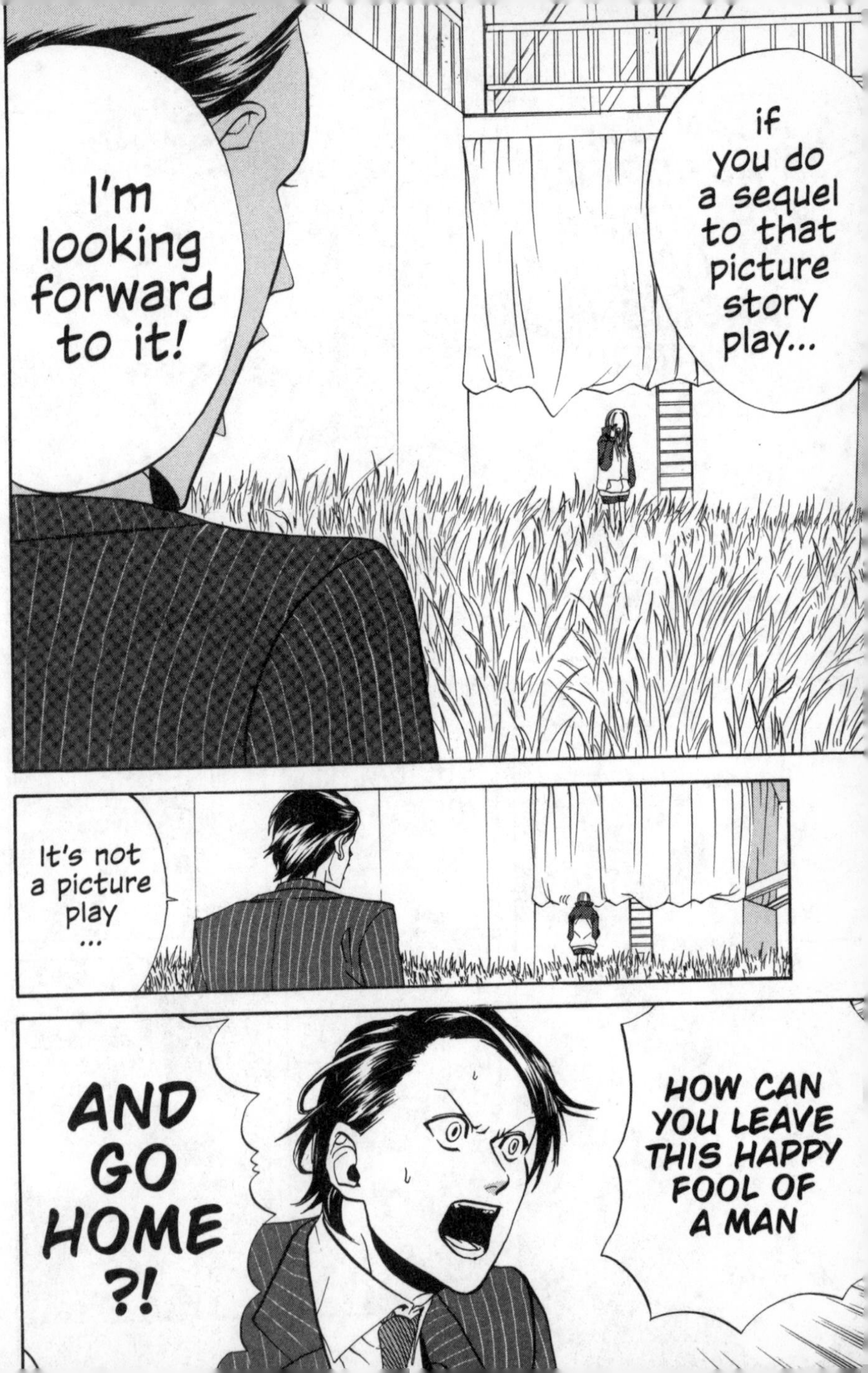

if you do a sequel to that picture story play...
I'm looking forward to it!
It's not a picture play ...
HOW CAN YOU LEAVE THIS HAPPY FOOL OF A MAN
AND GO HOME ?!

☜ Chapter 31: To the River Mouth

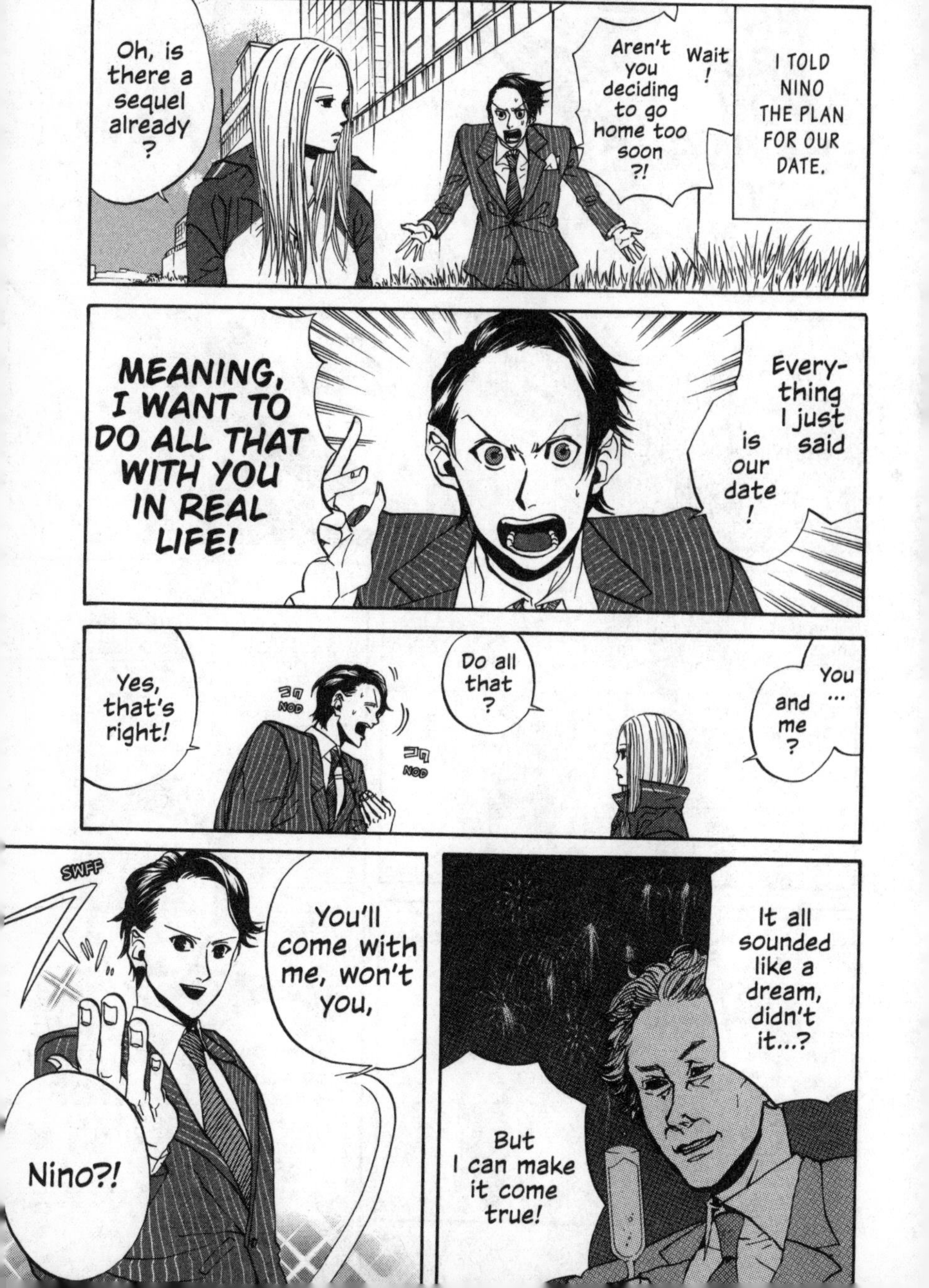
I TOLD NINO THE PLAN FOR OUR DATE.
Wait!
Aren't you deciding to go home too soon?!
Oh, is there a sequel already?
Everything I just said is our date!
MEANING, I WANT TO DO ALL THAT WITH YOU IN REAL LIFE!
You... and me?
Do all that?
Yes, that's right!
NOD
NOD
It all sounded like a dream, didn't it...?
But I can make it come true!
SWFF
You'll come with me, won't you,
Nino?!

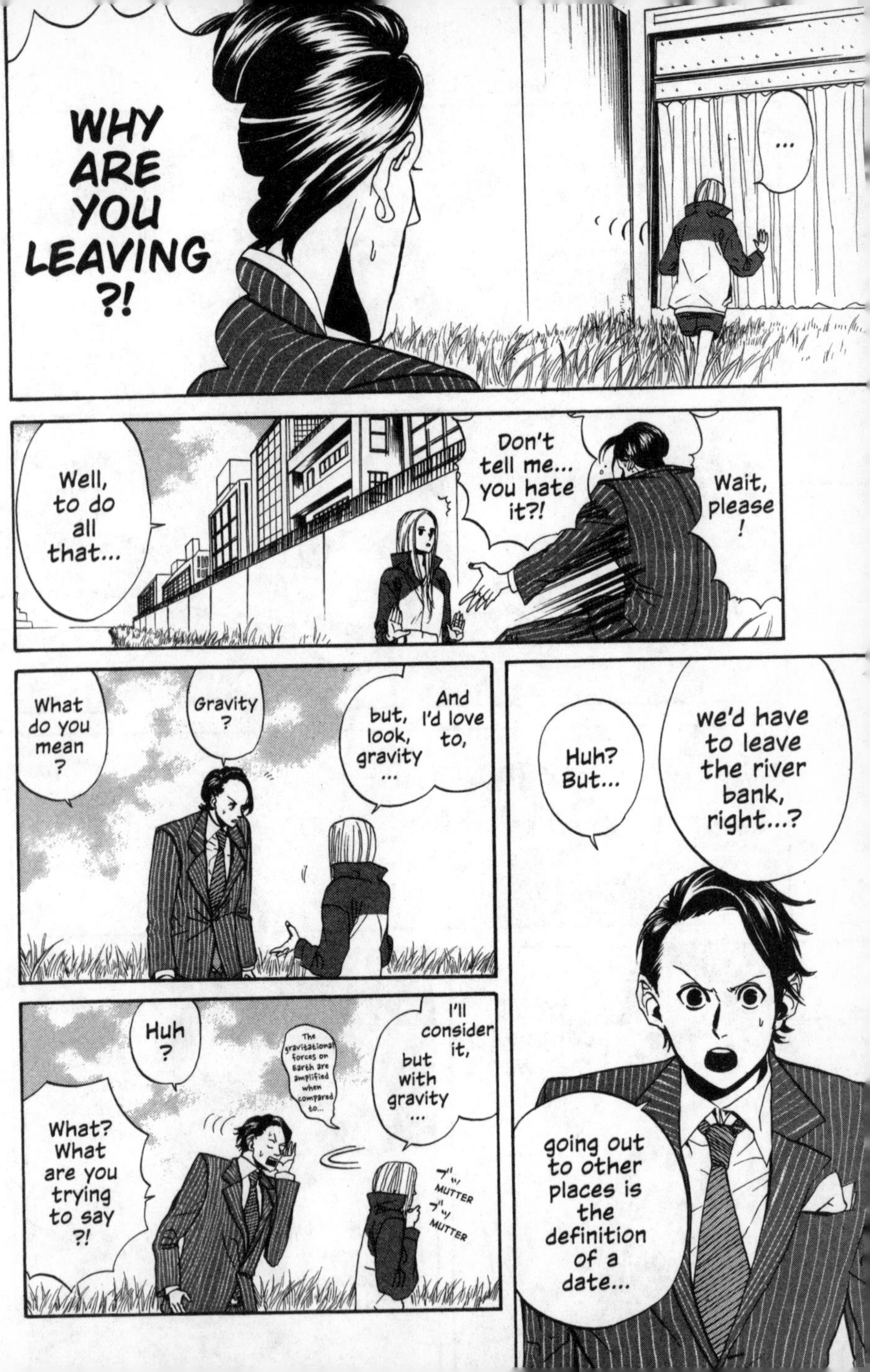

...
WHY ARE YOU LEAVING ?!
Wait, please !
Don't tell me... you hate it?!
Well, to do all that...
we'd have to leave the river bank, right...?
Huh? But...
going out to other places is the definition of a date...
And I'd love to,
but, look, gravity ...
Gravity ?
What do you mean ?
I'll consider it,
but with gravity ...
The gravitational forces on Earth are amplified when compared to...
Huh ?
What? What are you trying to say ?!
ブツ MUTTER
ブツ MUTTER

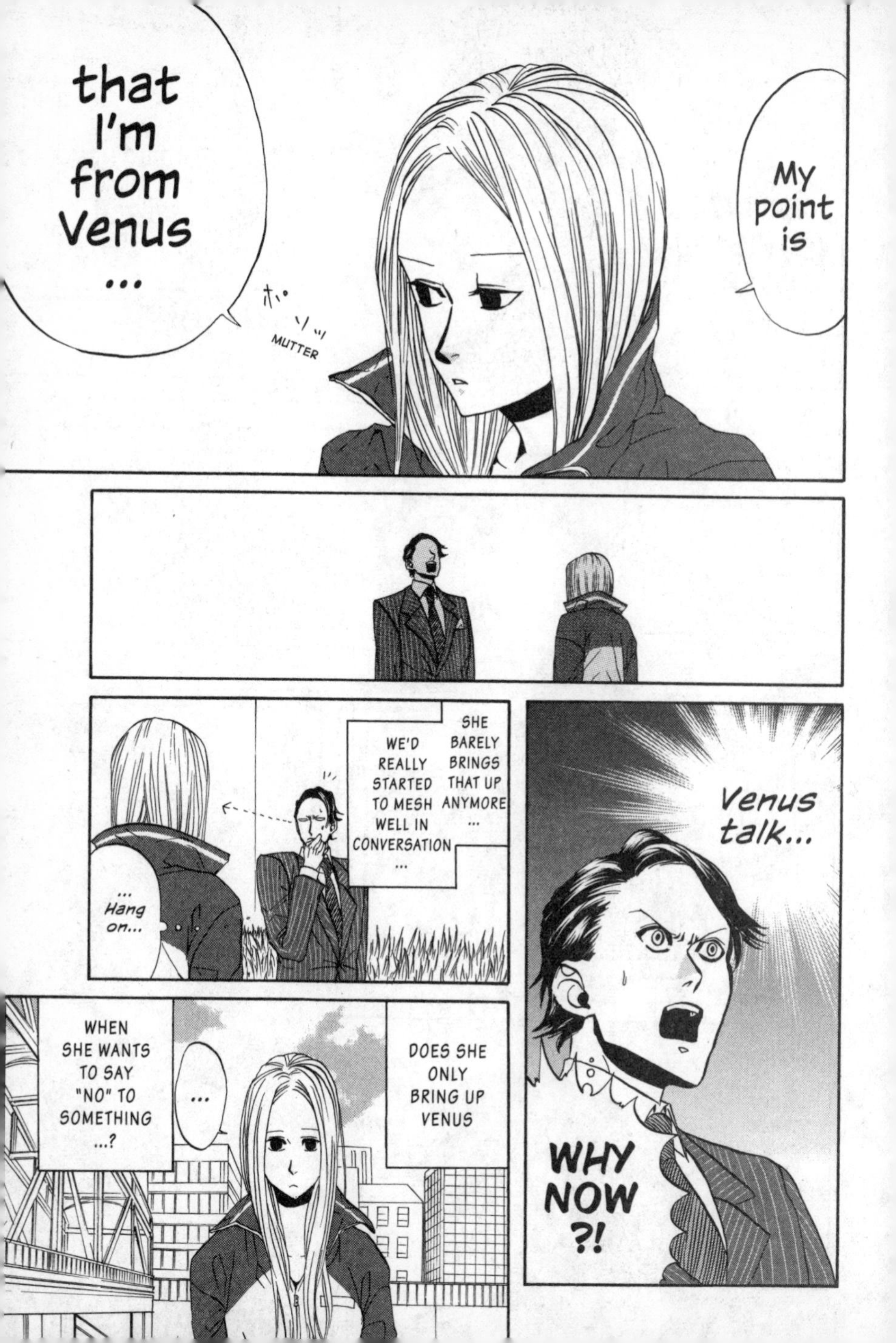
My point is
that I'm from Venus ...
ボソッ
MUTTER
Venus talk...
WHY NOW ?!
SHE BARELY BRINGS THAT UP ANYMORE ...
WE'D REALLY STARTED TO MESH WELL IN CONVERSATION ...
... Hang on...
DOES SHE ONLY BRING UP VENUS
WHEN SHE WANTS TO SAY "NO" TO SOMETHING ...?
...

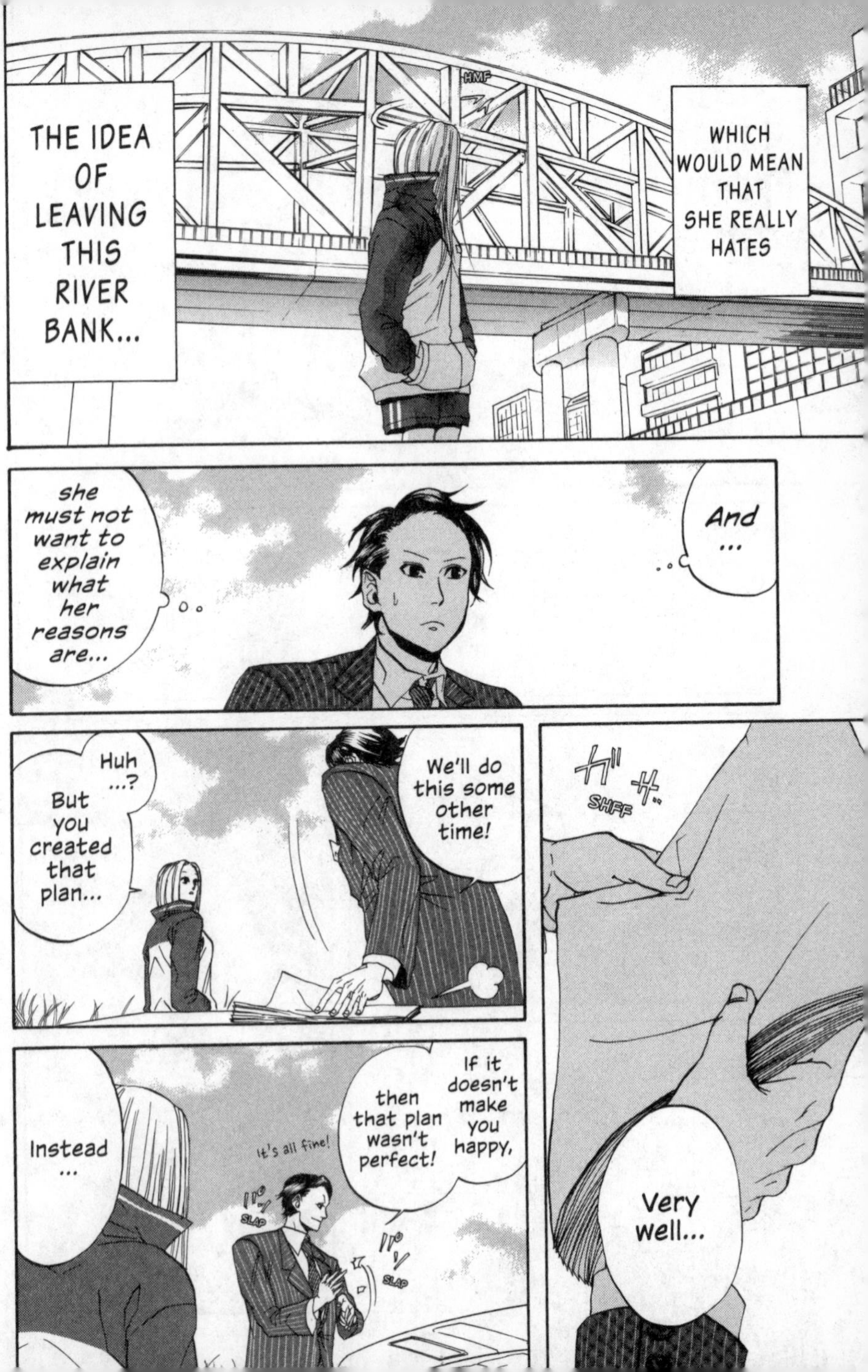
WHICH WOULD MEAN THAT SHE REALLY HATES
HMF
THE IDEA OF LEAVING THIS RIVER BANK...
And...
she must not want to explain what her reasons are...
SHFF
Very well...
We'll do this some other time!
Huh...? But you created that plan...
If it doesn't make you happy,
then that plan wasn't perfect!
It's all fine!
SLAP
SLAP
Instead...

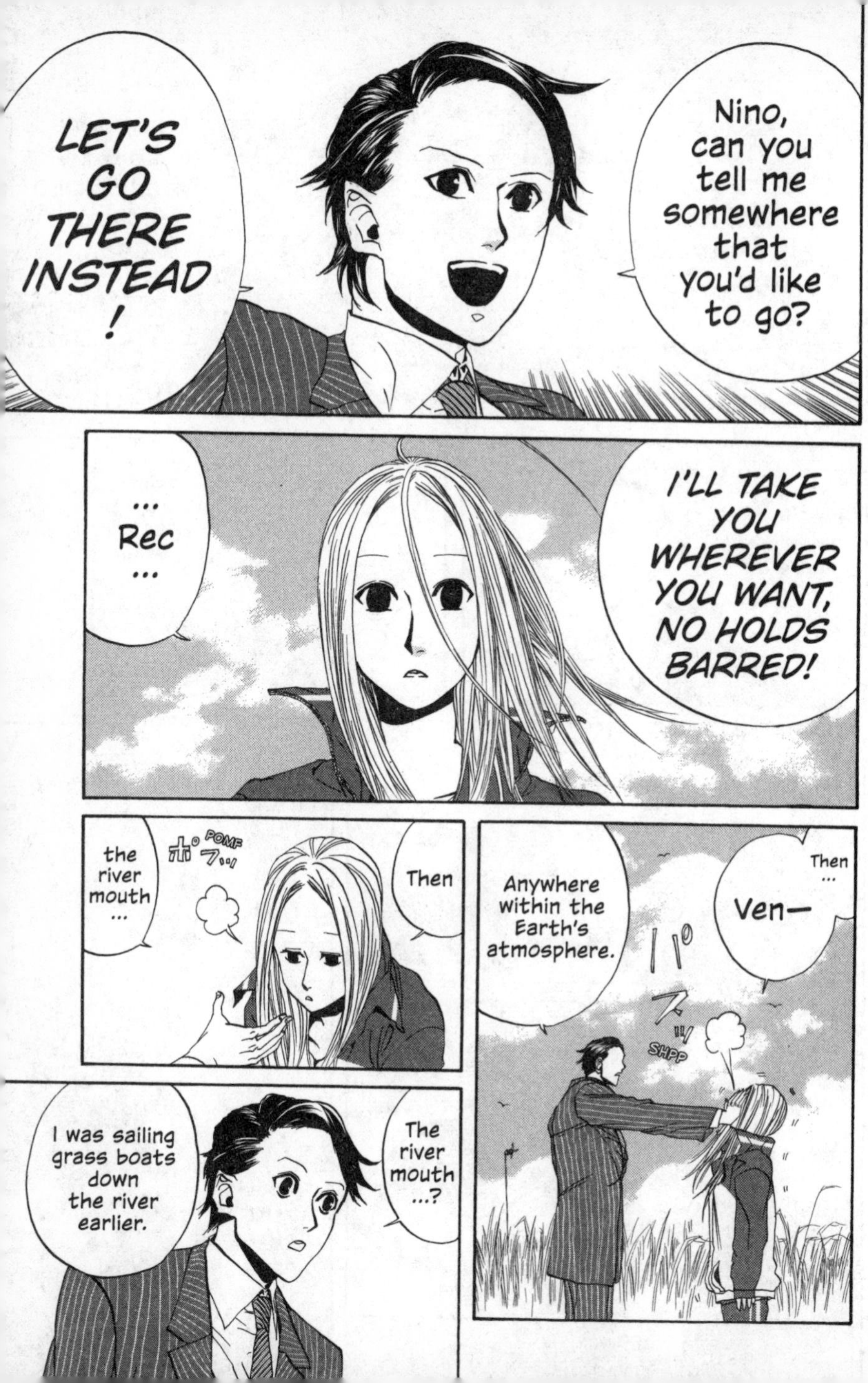
Nino, can you tell me somewhere that you'd like to go?
LET'S GO THERE INSTEAD!
I'LL TAKE YOU WHEREVER YOU WANT, NO HOLDS BARRED!
... Rec ...
Then ...
Ven—
Anywhere within the Earth's atmosphere.
SHPP
Then
the river mouth ...
POMF
The river mouth ...?
I was sailing grass boats down the river earlier.

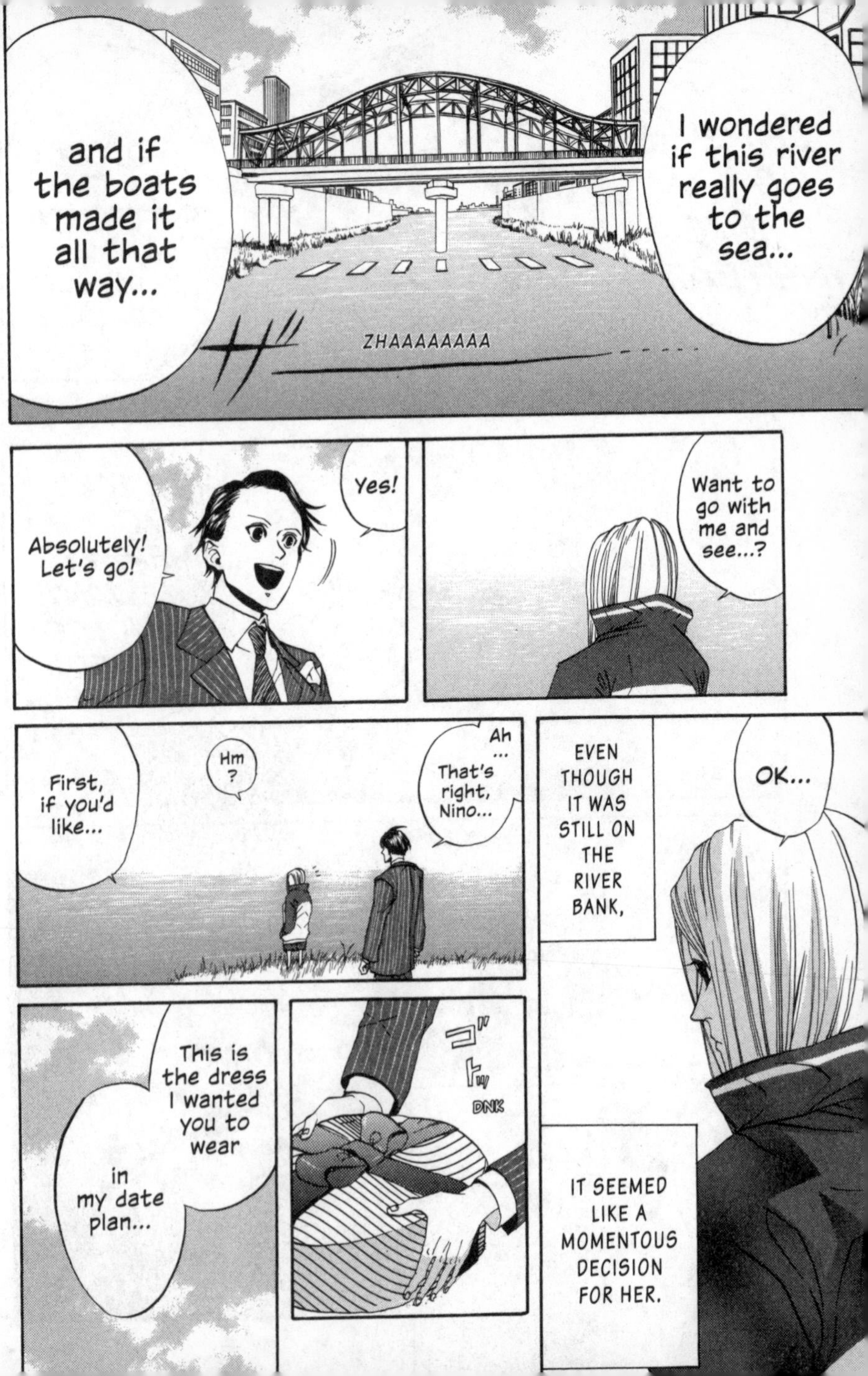

I wondered if this river really goes to the sea...
and if the boats made it all that way...
ZHAAAAAAAA
Want to go with me and see...?
Yes!
Absolutely! Let's go!
OK...
EVEN THOUGH IT WAS STILL ON THE RIVER BANK,
IT SEEMED LIKE A MOMENTOUS DECISION FOR HER.
Ah... That's right, Nino...
Hm?
First, if you'd like...
DNK
This is the dress I wanted you to wear
in my date plan...

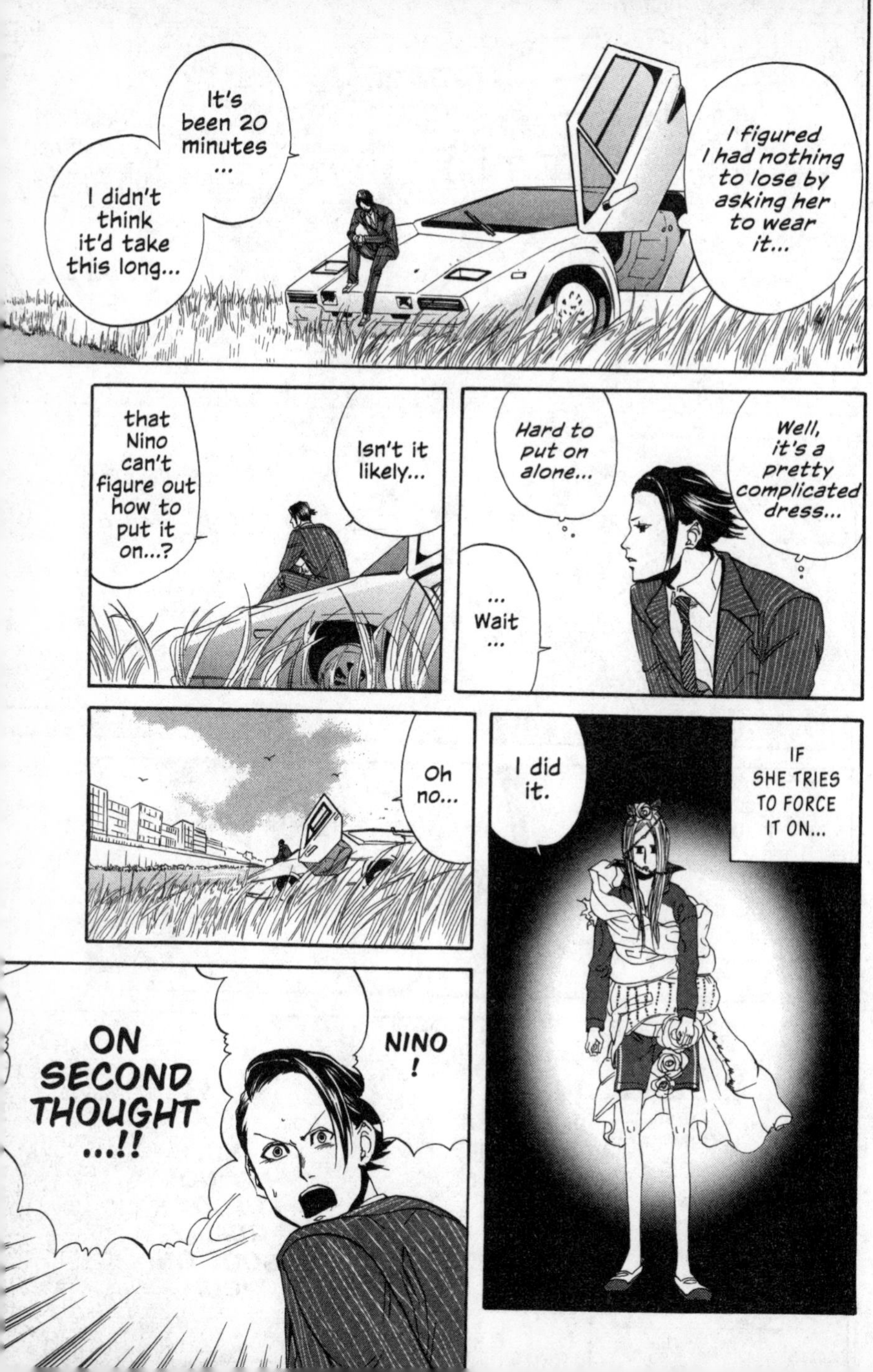
I figured I had nothing to lose by asking her to wear it...
It's been 20 minutes ...
I didn't think it'd take this long...
Well, it's a pretty complicated dress...
Hard to put on alone...
... Wait ...
Isn't it likely...
that Nino can't figure out how to put it on...?
IF SHE TRIES TO FORCE IT ON...
I did it.
Oh no...
NINO!
ON SECOND THOUGHT ...!!

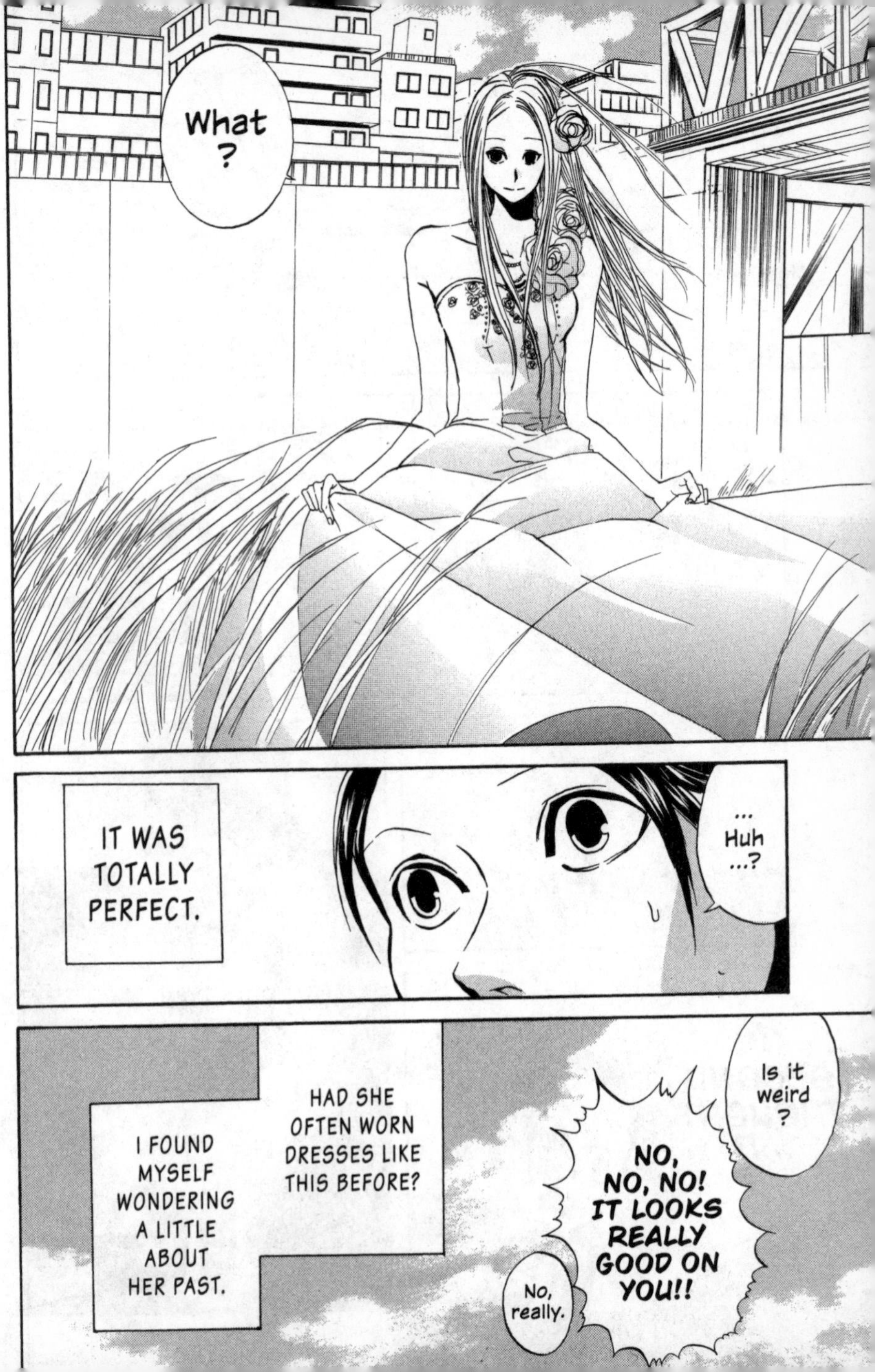
What?
... Huh ...?
IT WAS TOTALLY PERFECT.
Is it weird?
NO, NO, NO! IT LOOKS REALLY GOOD ON YOU!!
No, really.
HAD SHE OFTEN WORN DRESSES LIKE THIS BEFORE?
I FOUND MYSELF WONDERING A LITTLE ABOUT HER PAST.

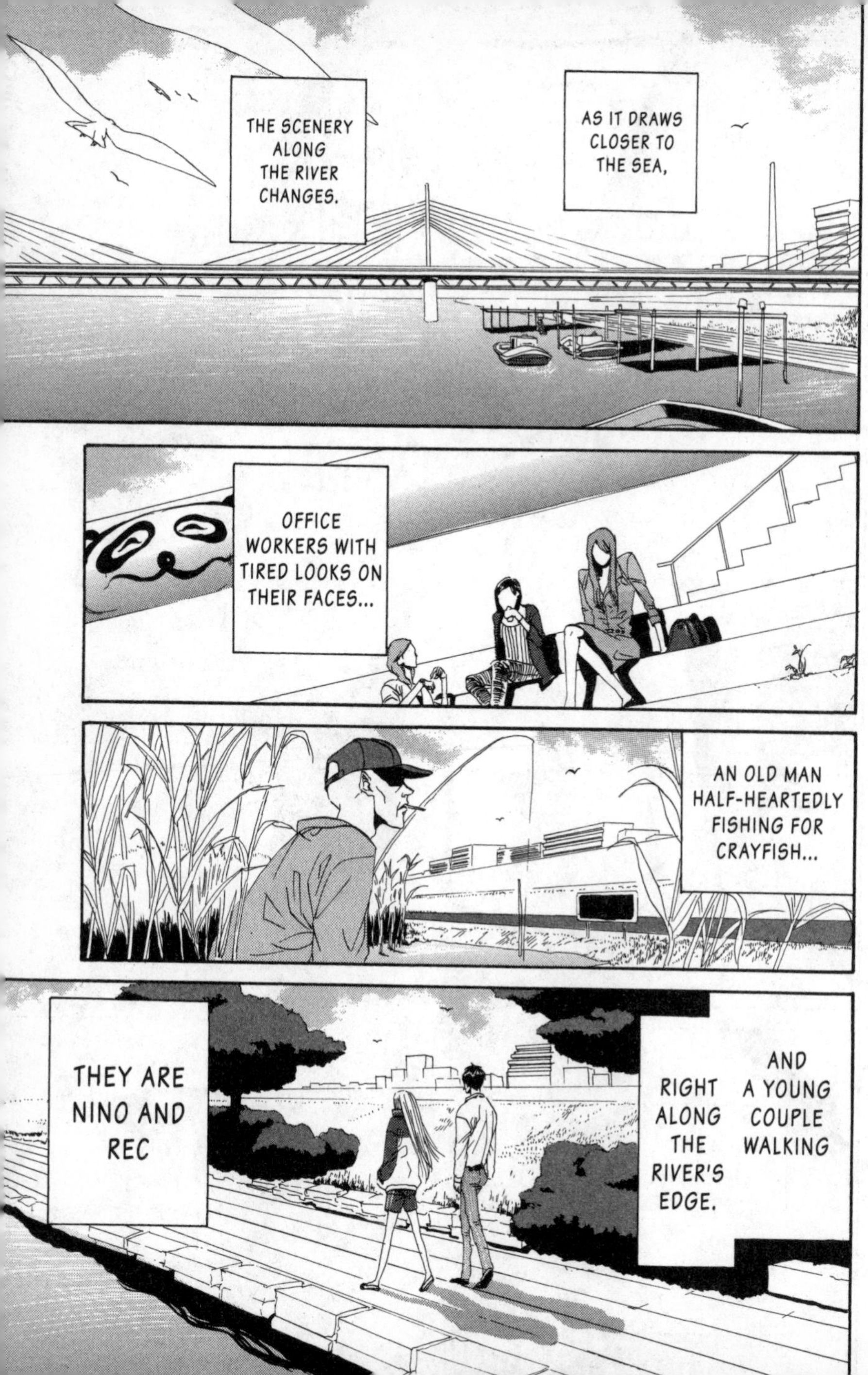
AS IT DRAWS CLOSER TO THE SEA,
THE SCENERY ALONG THE RIVER CHANGES.
OFFICE WORKERS WITH TIRED LOOKS ON THEIR FACES...
AN OLD MAN HALF-HEARTEDLY FISHING FOR CRAYFISH...
AND A YOUNG COUPLE WALKING
RIGHT ALONG THE RIVER'S EDGE.
THEY ARE NINO AND REC

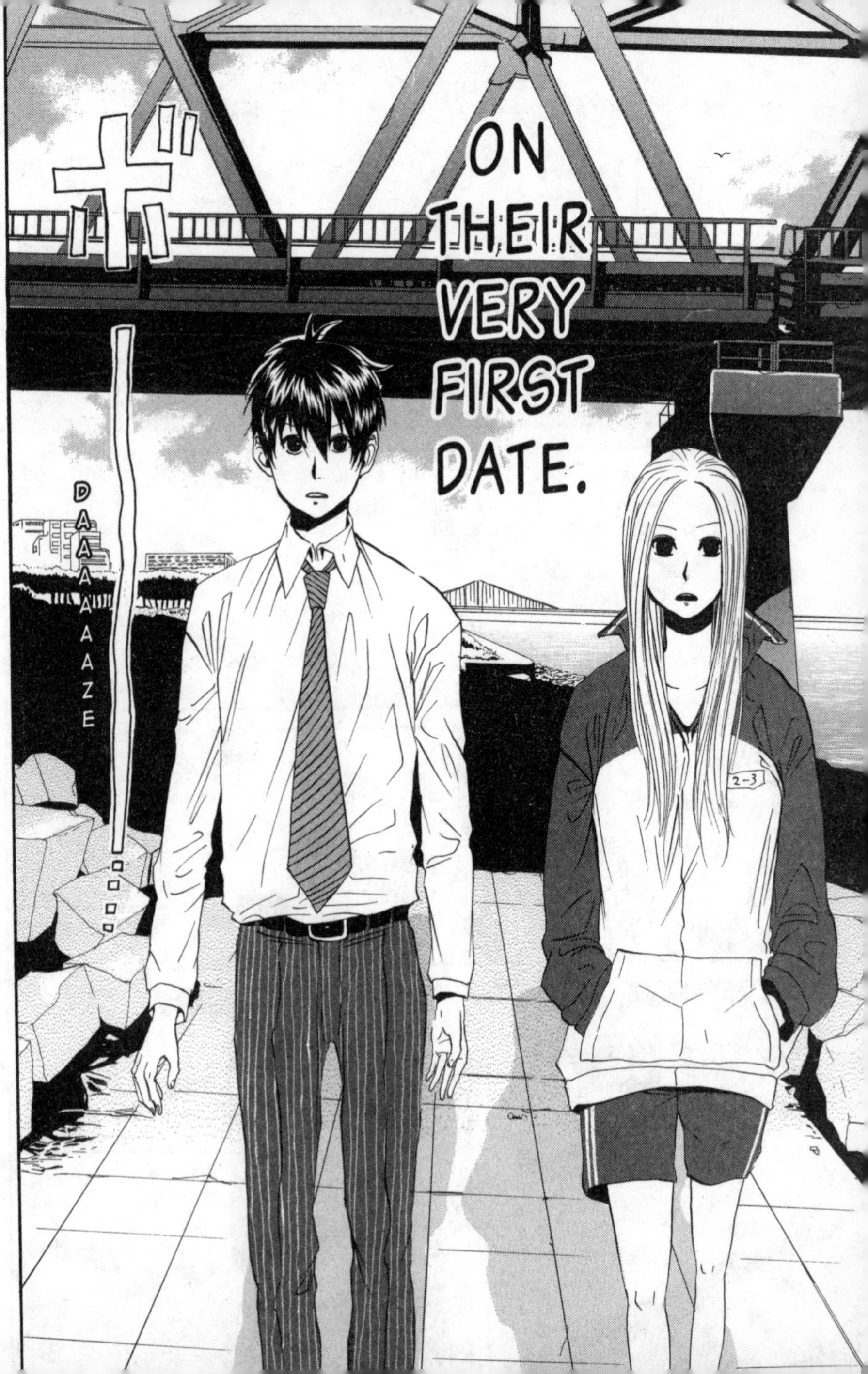
ON THEIR VERY FIRST DATE.
DAAAAAAZE
2-3

Chapter 32: First Date

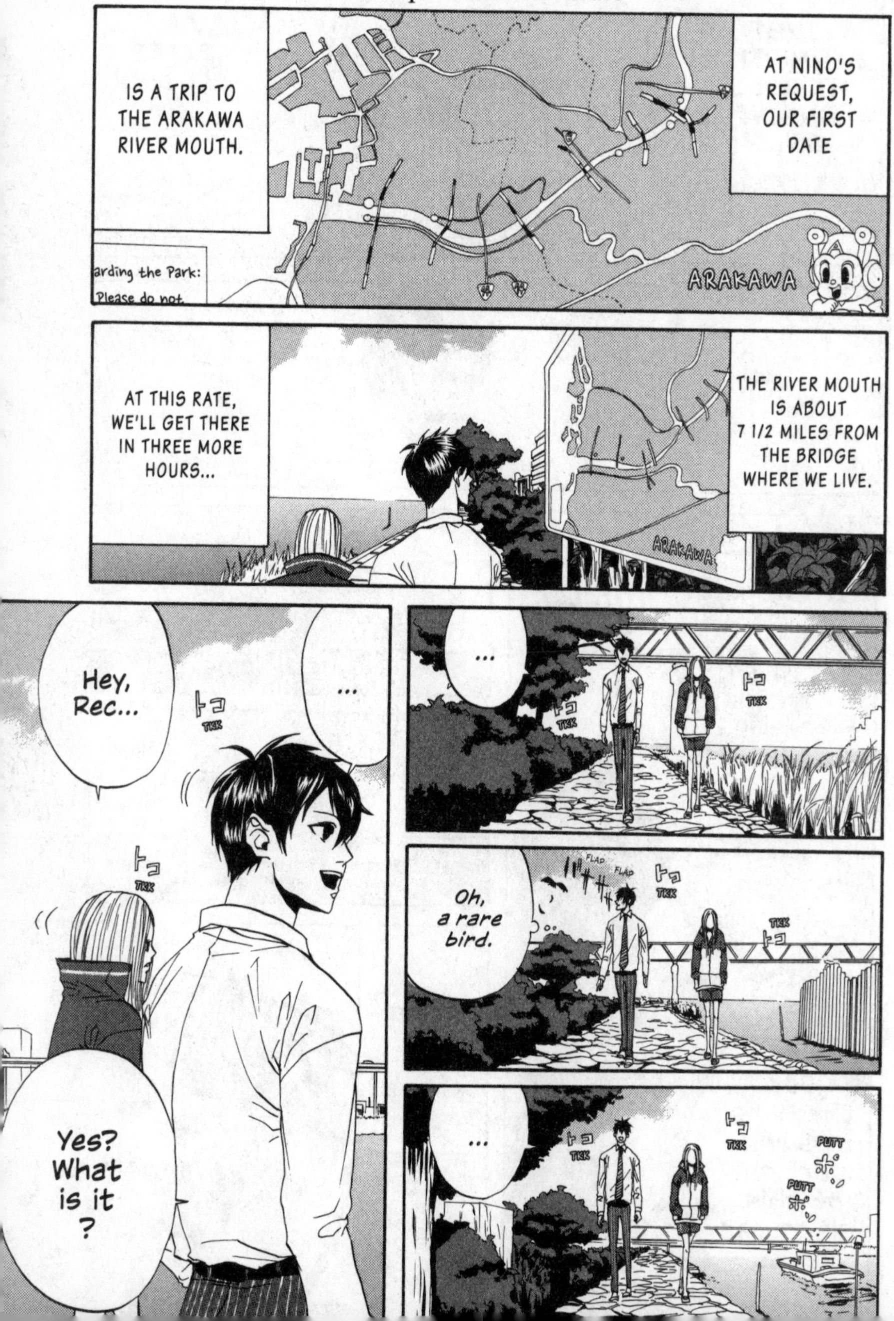
AT NINO'S REQUEST, OUR FIRST DATE
IS A TRIP TO THE ARAKAWA RIVER MOUTH.
ARAKAWA
arding the Park:
Please do not
THE RIVER MOUTH IS ABOUT 7 1/2 MILES FROM THE BRIDGE WHERE WE LIVE.
AT THIS RATE, WE'LL GET THERE IN THREE MORE HOURS...
ARAKAWA
...
TKK
TKK
FLAP
FLAP
TKK
Oh, a rare bird.
TKK
...
TKK
TKK
PUTT
PUTT
...
Hey, Rec...
TKK
TKK
Yes? What is it ?

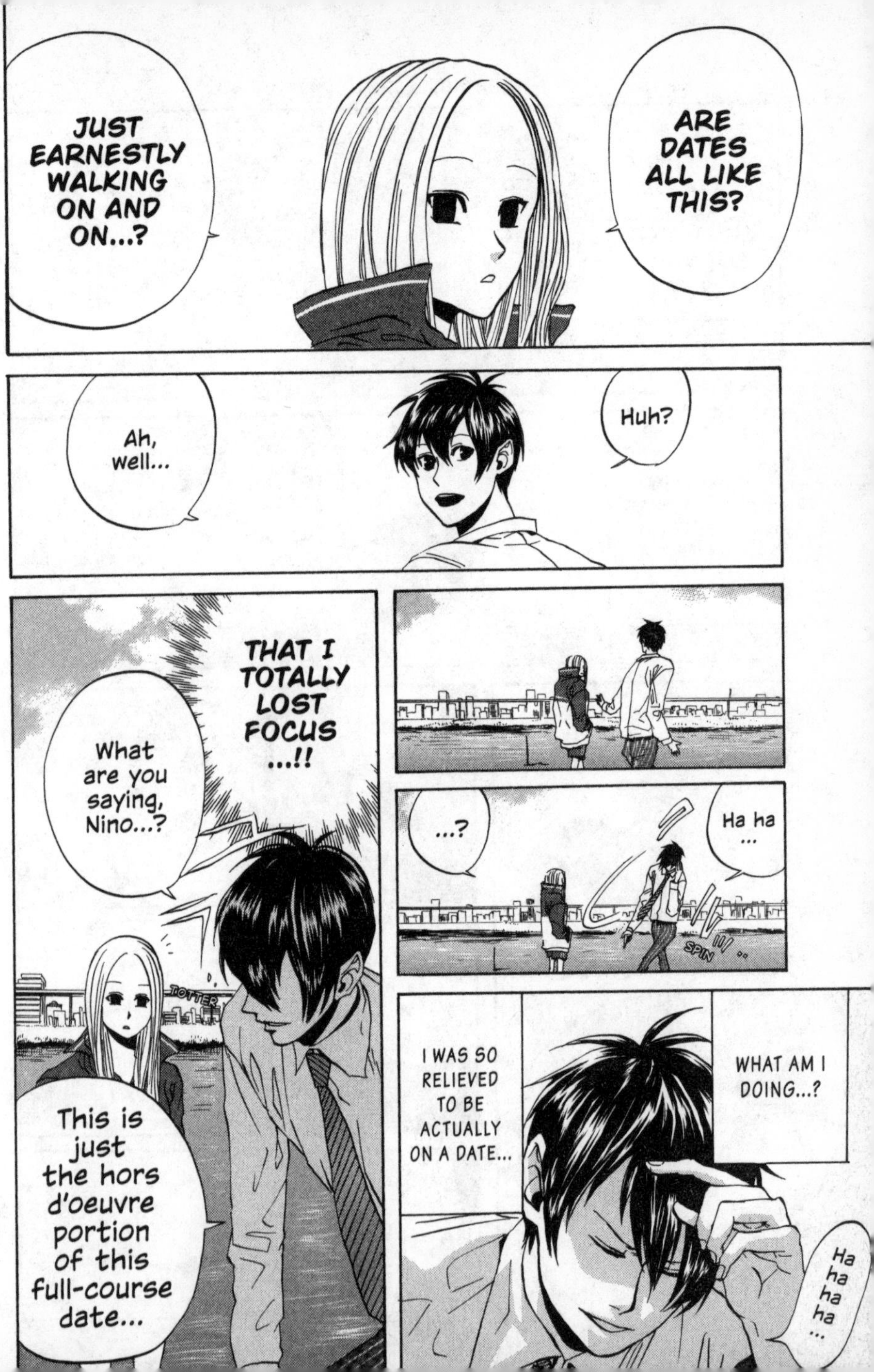
ARE DATES ALL LIKE THIS?
JUST EARNESTLY WALKING ON AND ON...?
Huh?
Ah, well...
Ha ha ...
...?
SPIN
WHAT AM I DOING...?
I WAS SO RELIEVED TO BE ACTUALLY ON A DATE...
Ha ha ha ha ...
THAT I TOTALLY LOST FOCUS ...!!
What are you saying, Nino...?
TOTTER
This is just the hors d'oeuvre portion of this full-course date...

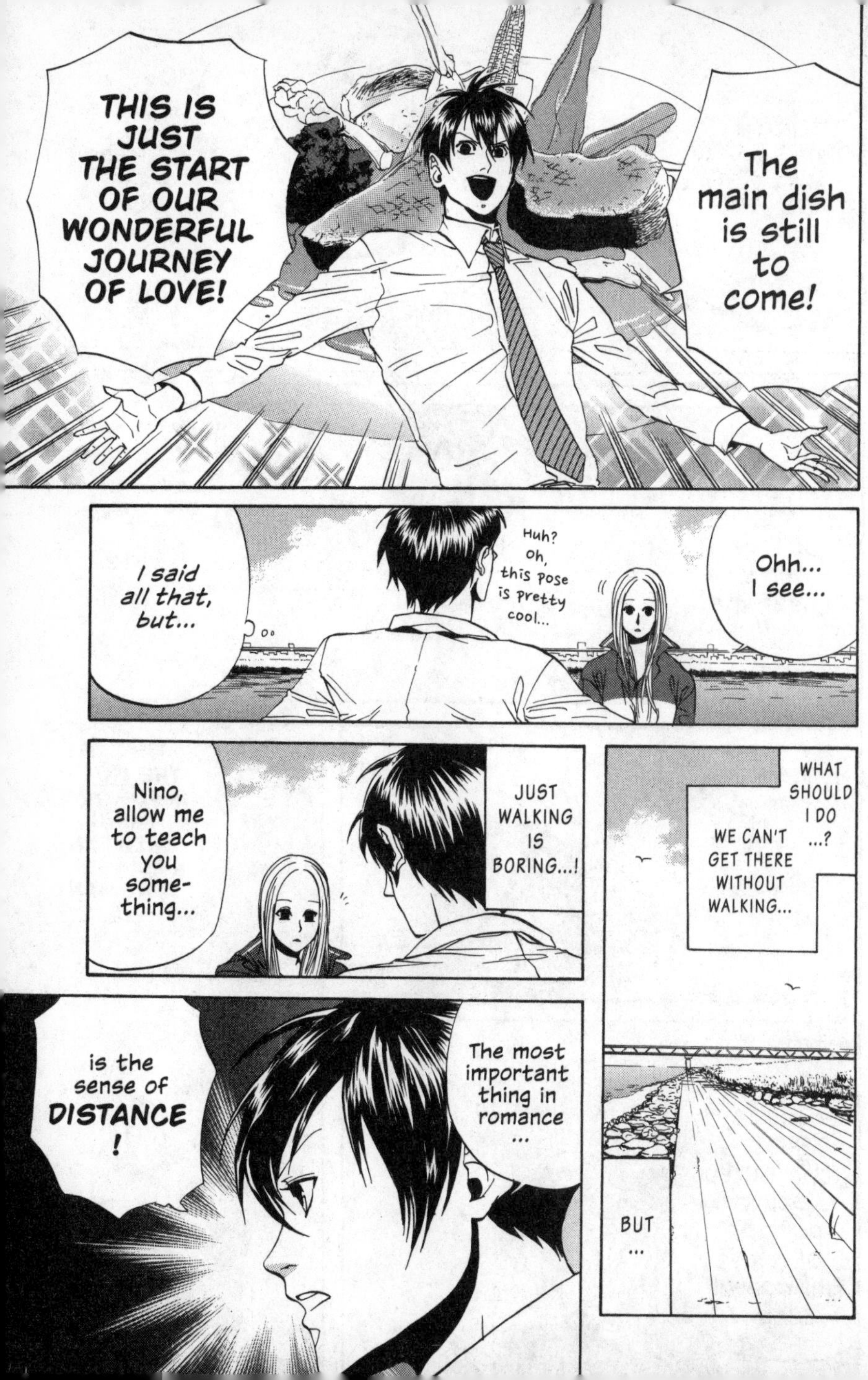

The main dish is still to come!
THIS IS JUST THE START OF OUR WONDERFUL JOURNEY OF LOVE!
Ohh... I see...
Huh? Oh, this pose is pretty cool...
I said all that, but...
WHAT SHOULD I DO ...?
WE CAN'T GET THERE WITHOUT WALKING...
BUT ...
JUST WALKING IS BORING...!
Nino, allow me to teach you some-thing...
The most important thing in romance ...
is the sense of DISTANCE !

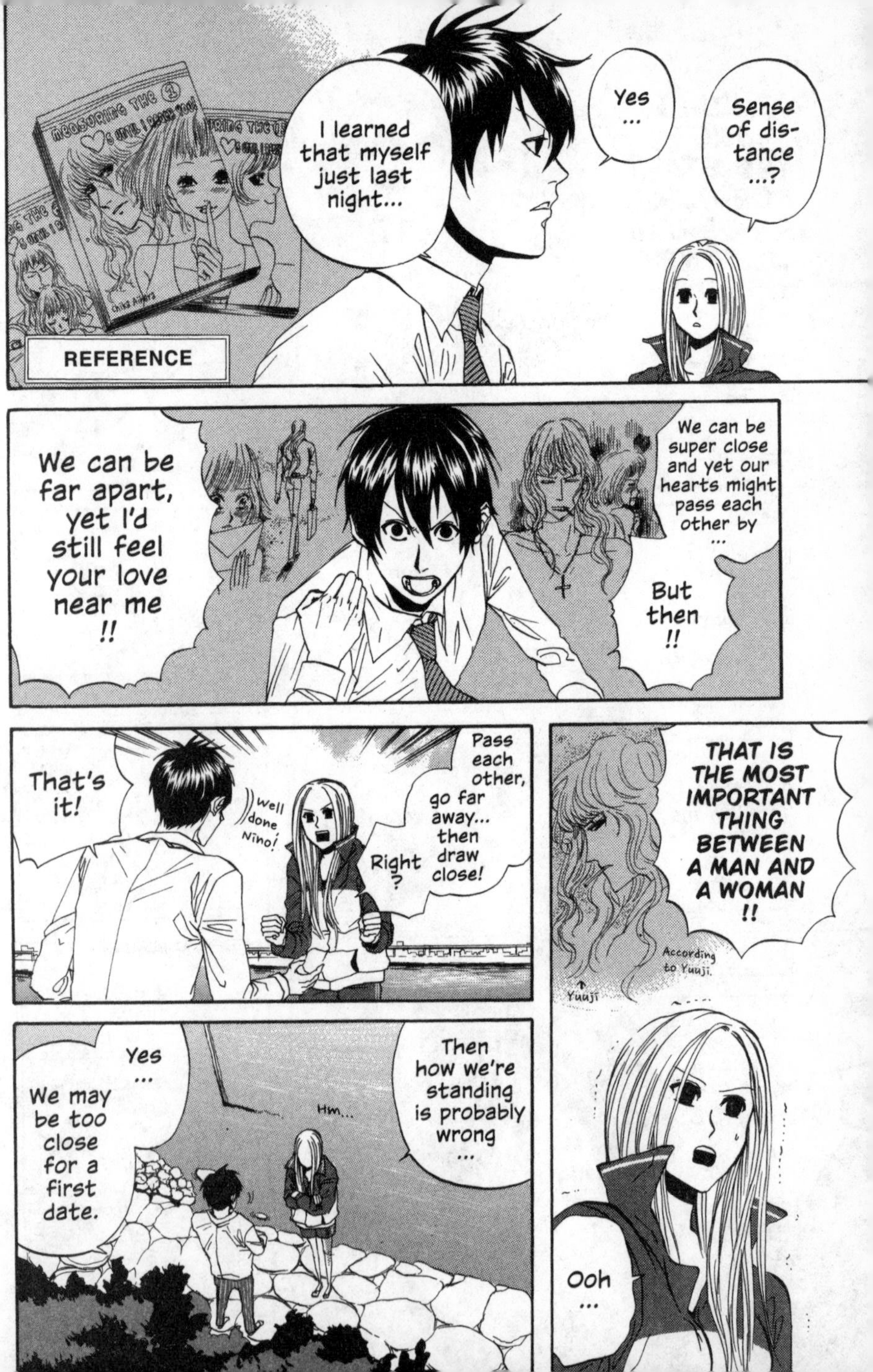
Sense of dis-tance ...?
Yes ...
I learned that myself just last night...
REFERENCE
We can be super close and yet our hearts might pass each other by ...
But then !!
We can be far apart, yet I'd still feel your love near me !!
THAT IS THE MOST IMPORTANT THING BETWEEN A MAN AND A WOMAN !!
According to Yuuji.
↑ Yuuji
Pass each other, go far away... then draw close!
Right ?
Well done Nino!
That's it!
Ooh ...
Then how we're standing is probably wrong ...
Hm...
Yes ...
We may be too close for a first date.

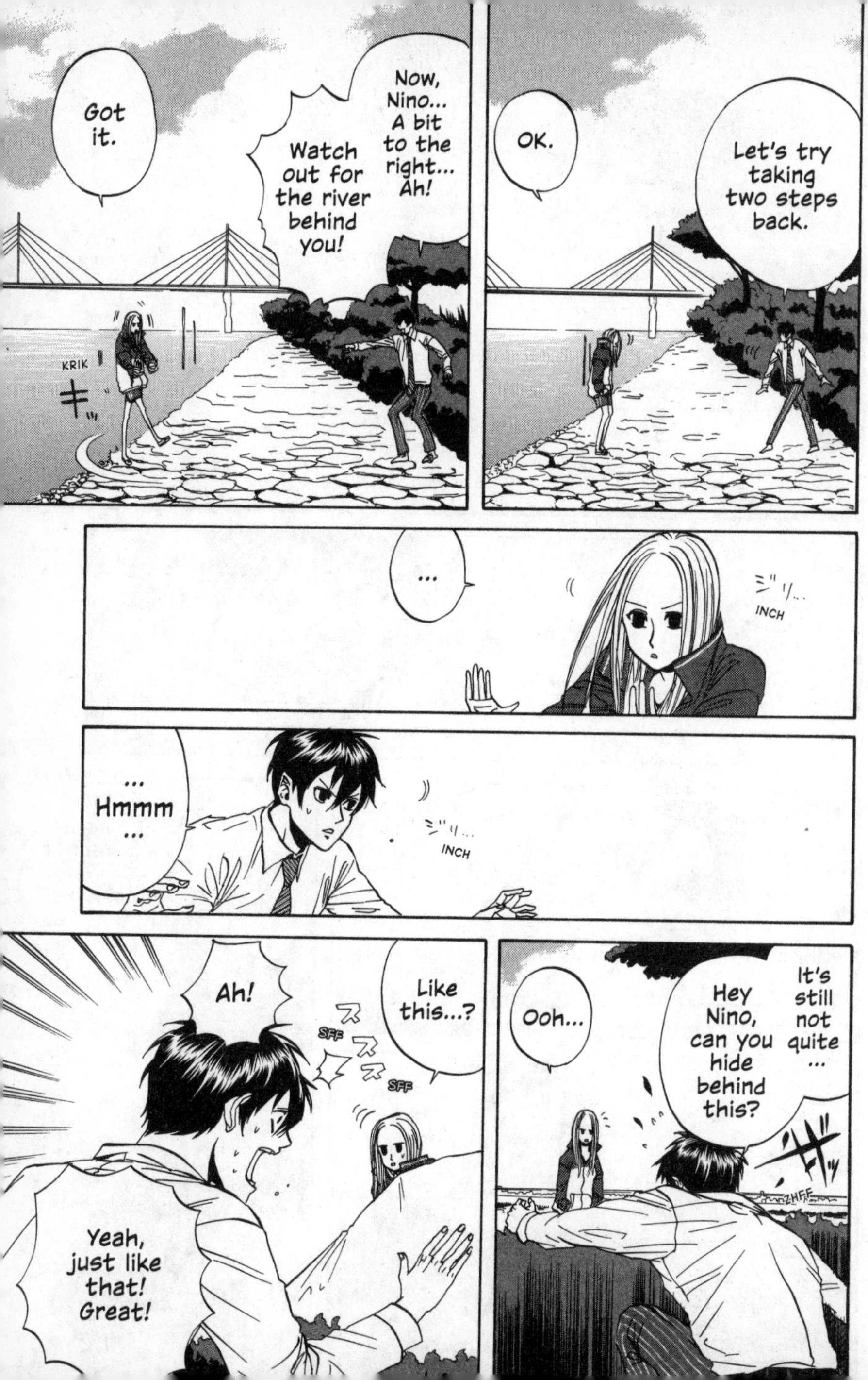
Let's try taking two steps back.
OK.
Now, Nino... A bit to the right... Ah!
Watch out for the river behind you!
Got it.
KRIK
...
INCH
... Hmmm ...
INCH
It's still not quite ...
Hey Nino, can you hide behind this?
Ooh...
ZHFF
Like this...?
SFF
SFF
Ah!
Yeah, just like that! Great!

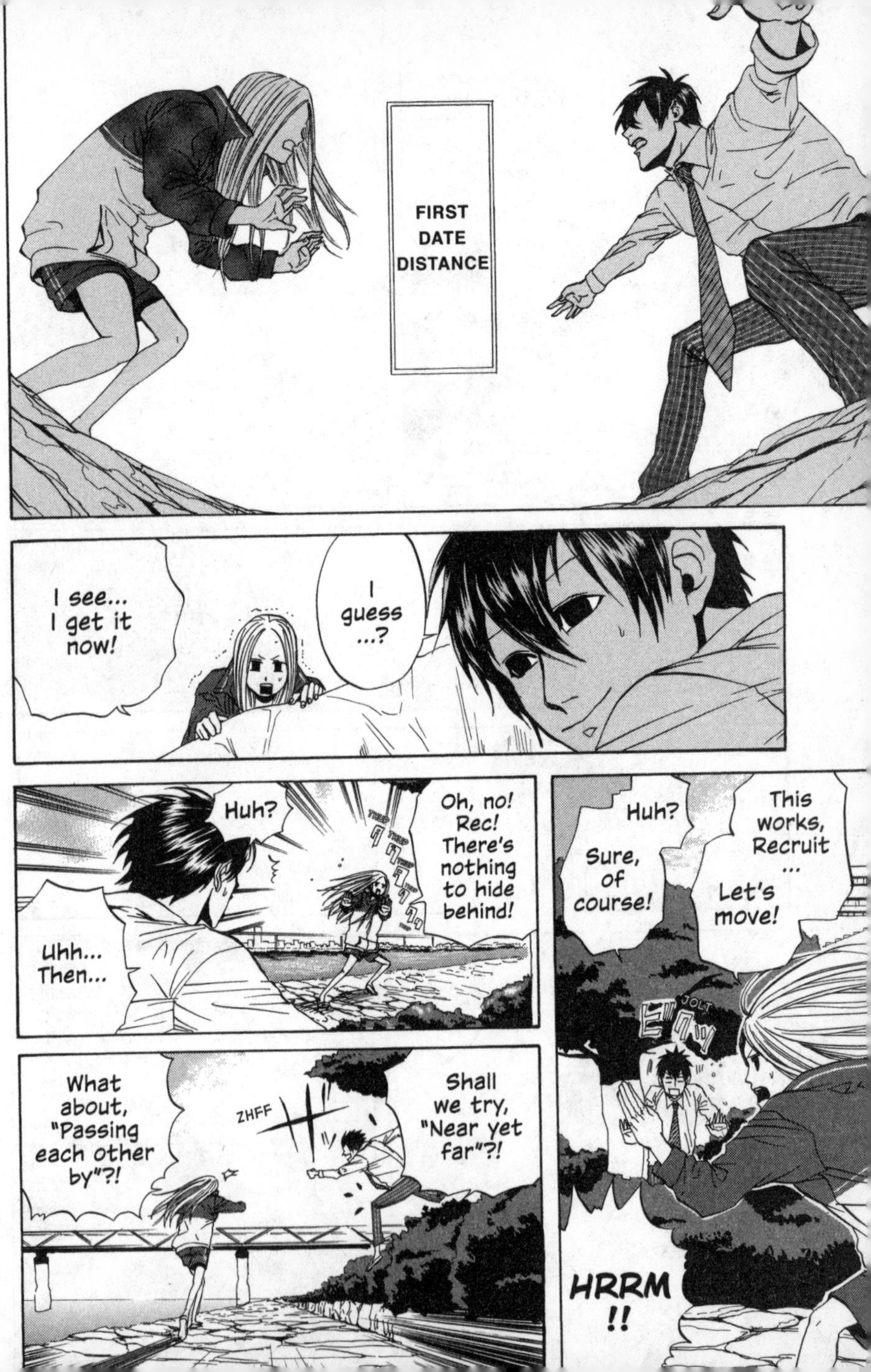

FIRST DATE DISTANCE
I guess ...?
I see... I get it now!
This works, Recruit ...
Let's move!
Huh?
Sure, of course!
JOLI
HRRM !!
Oh, no! Rec! There's nothing to hide behind!
THUP
Huh?
Uhh... Then...
Shall we try, "Near yet far"?!
ZHFF
What about, "Passing each other by"?!

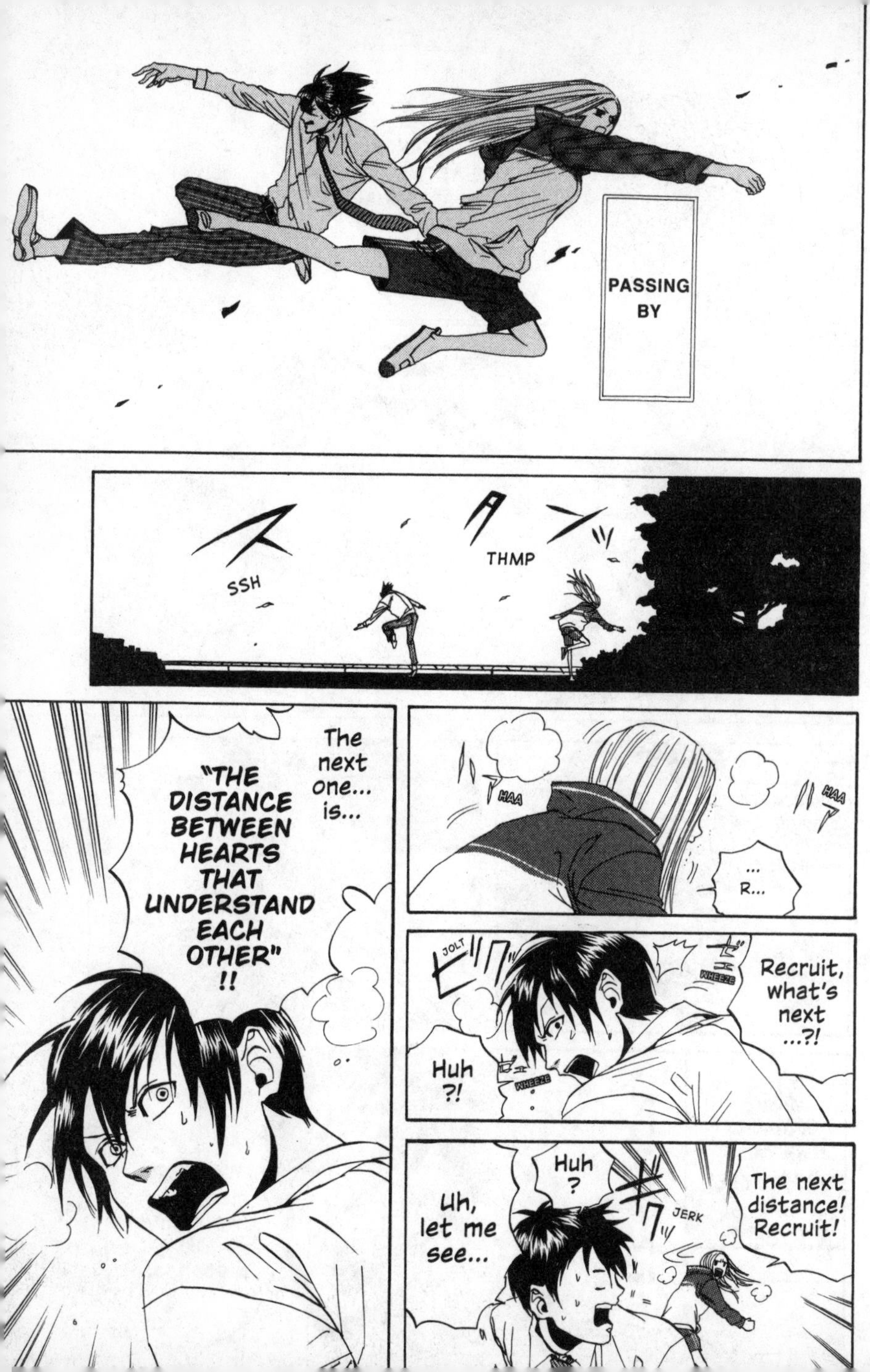
PASSING BY
THMP
SSH
HAA
HAA
... R...
Recruit, what's next ...?!
WHEEZE
JOLT
Huh ?!
WHEEZE
The next distance! Recruit!
JERK
Huh ?
Uh, let me see...
The next one... is...
"THE DISTANCE BETWEEN HEARTS THAT UNDERSTAND EACH OTHER" !!

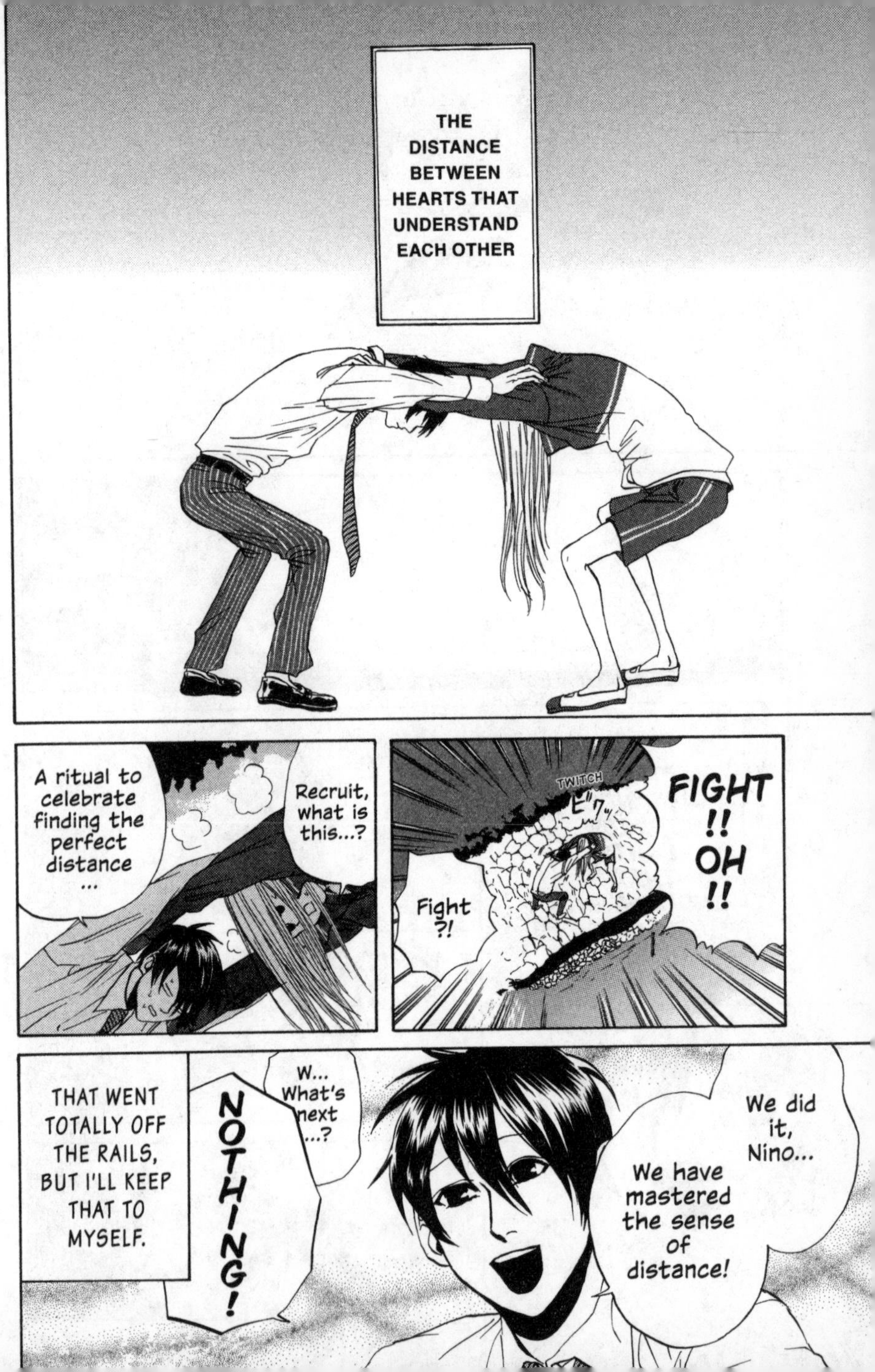
THE DISTANCE BETWEEN HEARTS THAT UNDERSTAND EACH OTHER
FIGHT!! OH!!
TWITCH
Fight?!
Recruit, what is this...?
A ritual to celebrate finding the perfect distance...
We did it, Nino...
We have mastered the sense of distance!
W... What's next...?
NOTHING!
THAT WENT TOTALLY OFF THE RAILS, BUT I'LL KEEP THAT TO MYSELF.

Chapter 33: Inter-Gender Communication

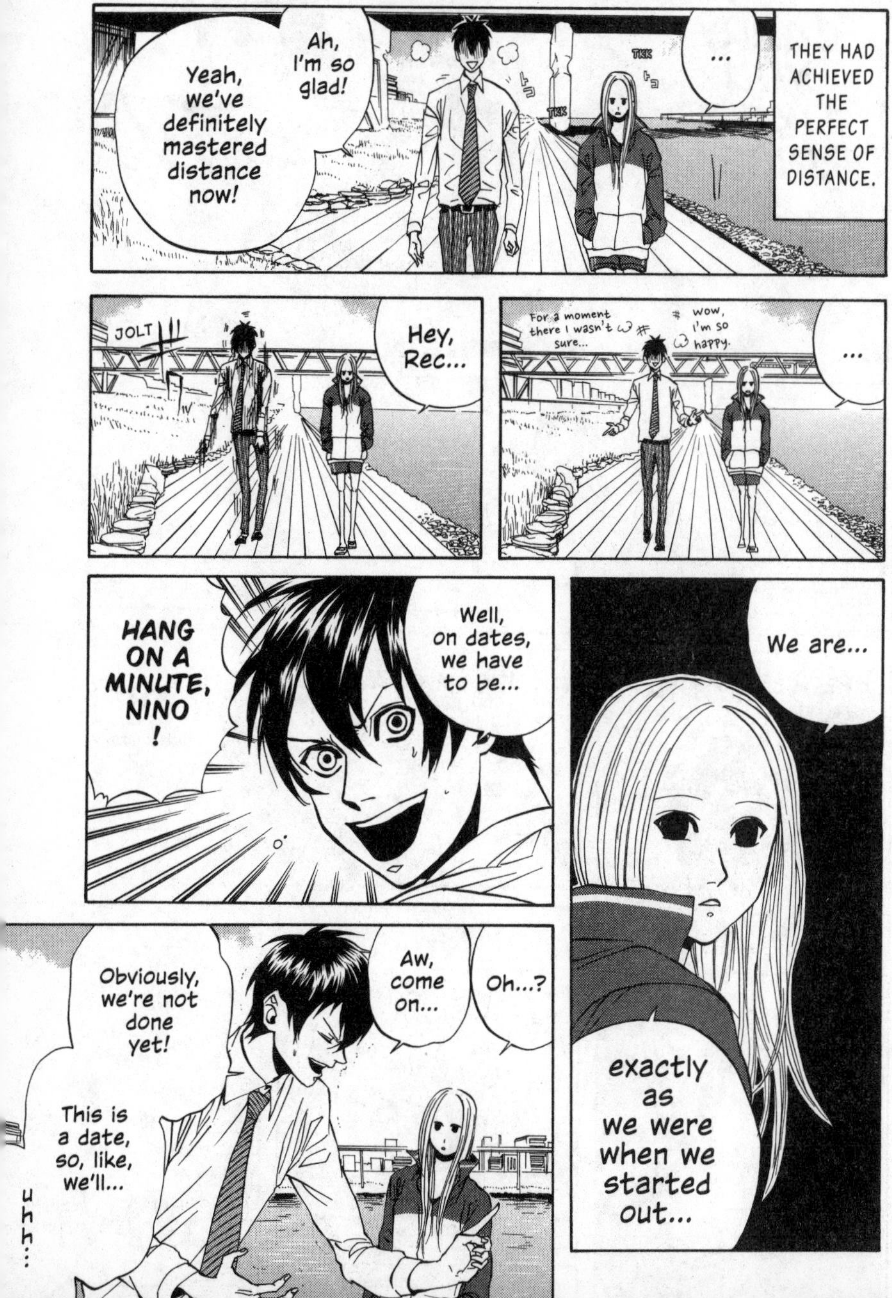
THEY HAD ACHIEVED THE PERFECT SENSE OF DISTANCE.
...
TKK
TKK
Ah, I'm so glad!
Yeah, we've definitely mastered distance now!
...
Wow, I'm so happy.
For a moment there I wasn't sure...
Hey, Rec...
JOLT
We are...
exactly as we were when we started out...
Well, on dates, we have to be...
HANG ON A MINUTE, NINO!
Oh...?
Aw, come on...
Obviously, we're not done yet!
This is a date, so, like, we'll...
uhh...

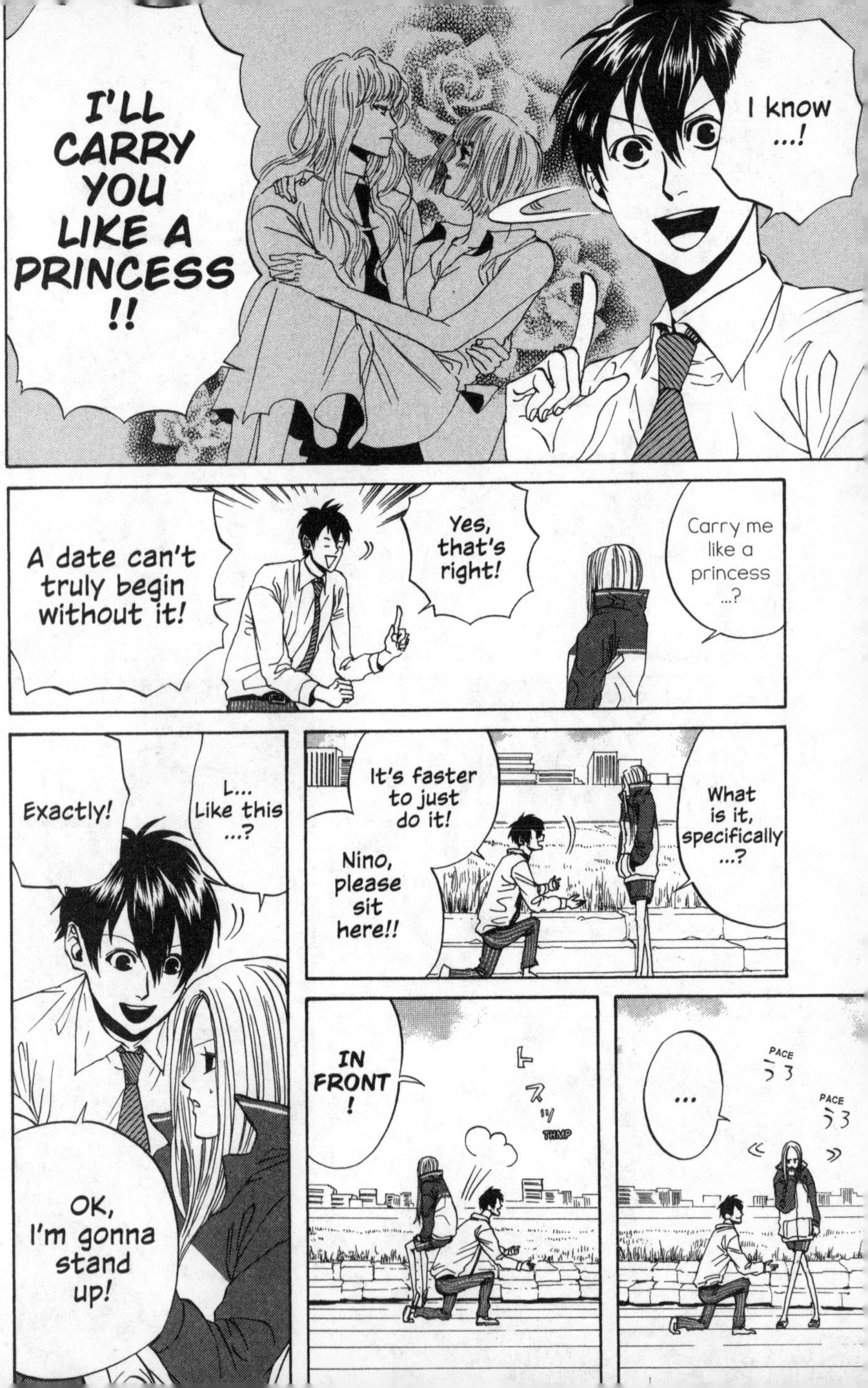
I know ...!
I'LL CARRY YOU LIKE A PRINCESS !!
Carry me like a princess ...?
Yes, that's right!
A date can't truly begin without it!
What is it, specifically ...?
It's faster to just do it!
Nino, please sit here!!
...
PACE
PACE
IN FRONT !
THMP
L... Like this ...?
Exactly!
OK, I'm gonna stand up!

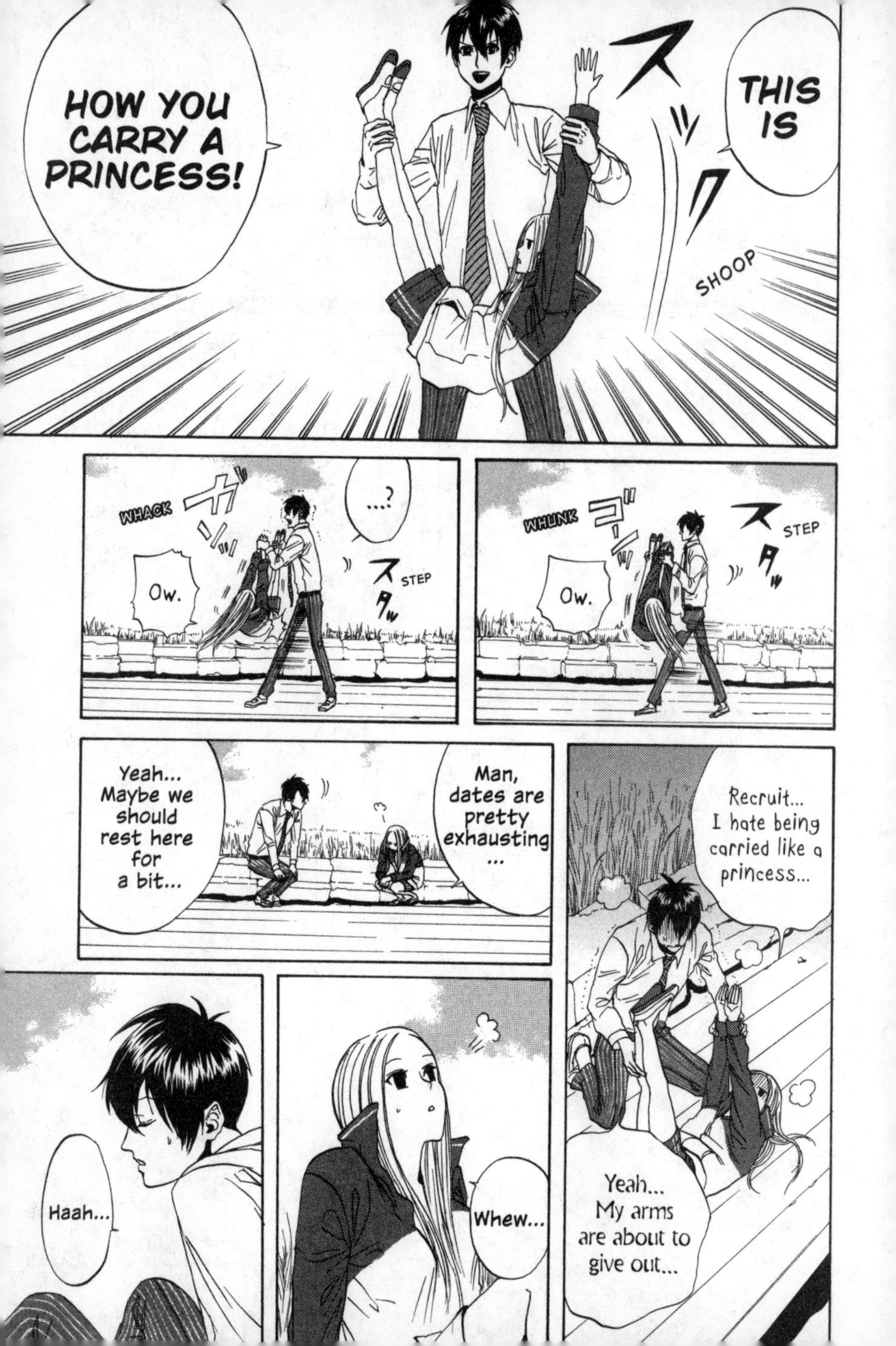
THIS IS
SHOOP
HOW YOU CARRY A PRINCESS!
WHUNK
STEP
Ow.
...?
WHACK
STEP
Ow.
Recruit... I hate being carried like a princess...
Yeah... My arms are about to give out...
Man, dates are pretty exhausting...
Yeah... Maybe we should rest here for a bit...
Whew...
Haah...

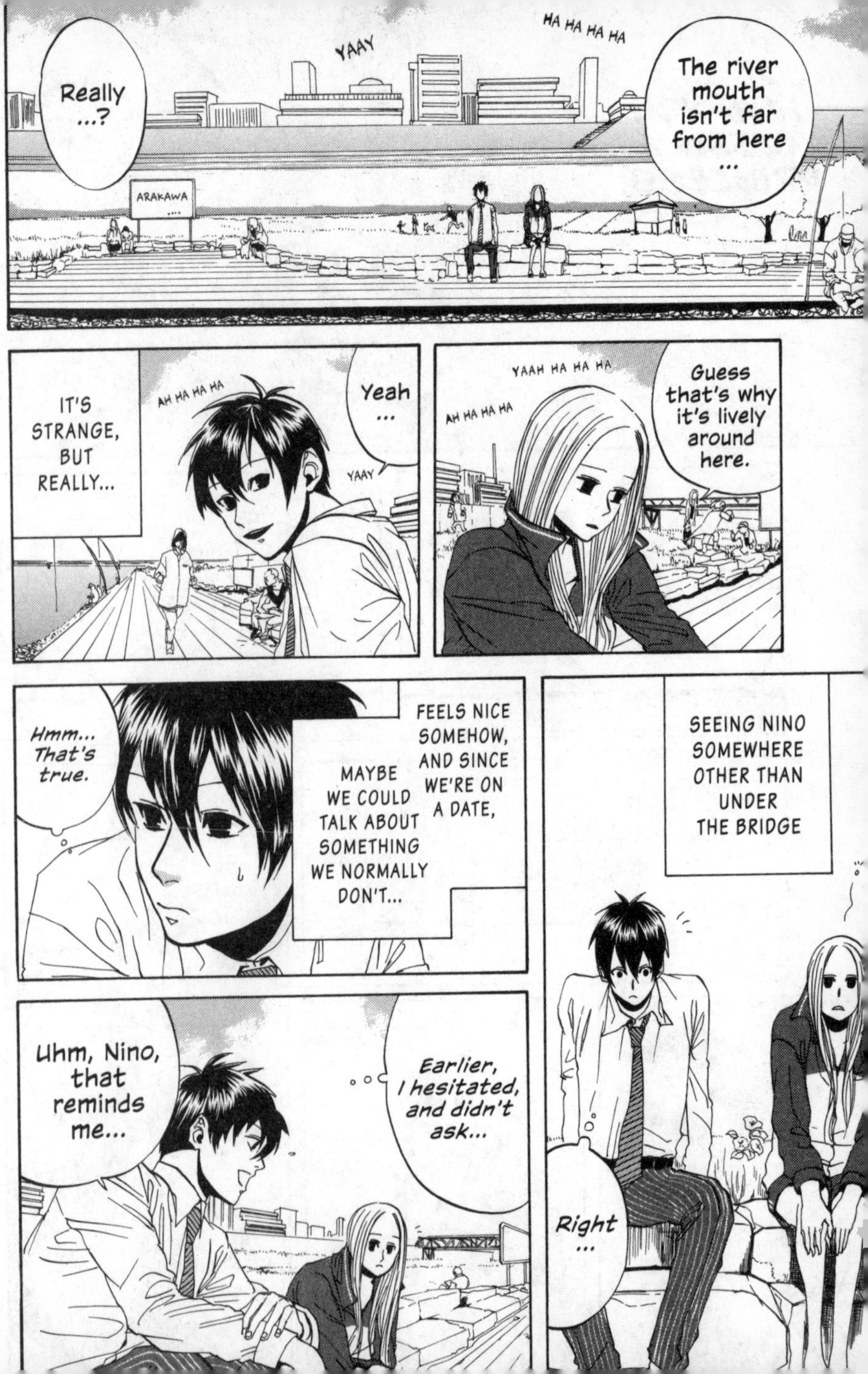
HA HA HA HA
YAAY
The river mouth isn't far from here ...
Really ...?
ARAKAWA ...
YAAH HA HA HA
AH HA HA HA
Guess that's why it's lively around here.
Yeah ...
AH HA HA HA
YAAY
IT'S STRANGE, BUT REALLY...
SEEING NINO SOMEWHERE OTHER THAN UNDER THE BRIDGE
Right ...
FEELS NICE SOMEHOW, AND SINCE WE'RE ON A DATE,
MAYBE WE COULD TALK ABOUT SOMETHING WE NORMALLY DON'T...
Hmm... That's true.
Earlier, I hesitated, and didn't ask...
Uhm, Nino, that reminds me...

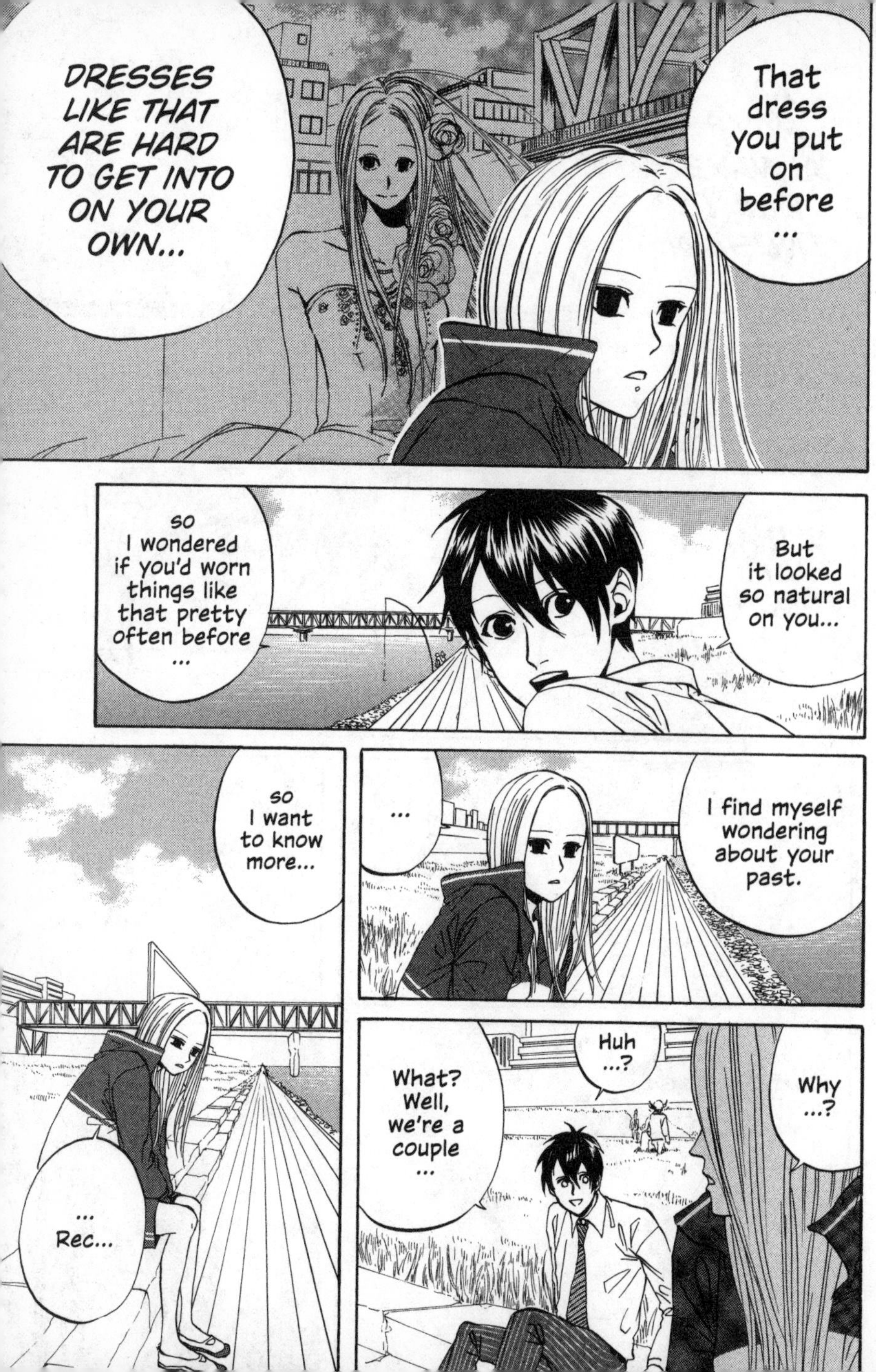
That dress you put on before ...
DRESSES LIKE THAT ARE HARD TO GET INTO ON YOUR OWN...
But it looked so natural on you...
so I wondered if you'd worn things like that pretty often before ...
I find myself wondering about your past.
...
Why ...?
Huh ...?
What? Well, we're a couple ...
so I want to know more...
... Rec...

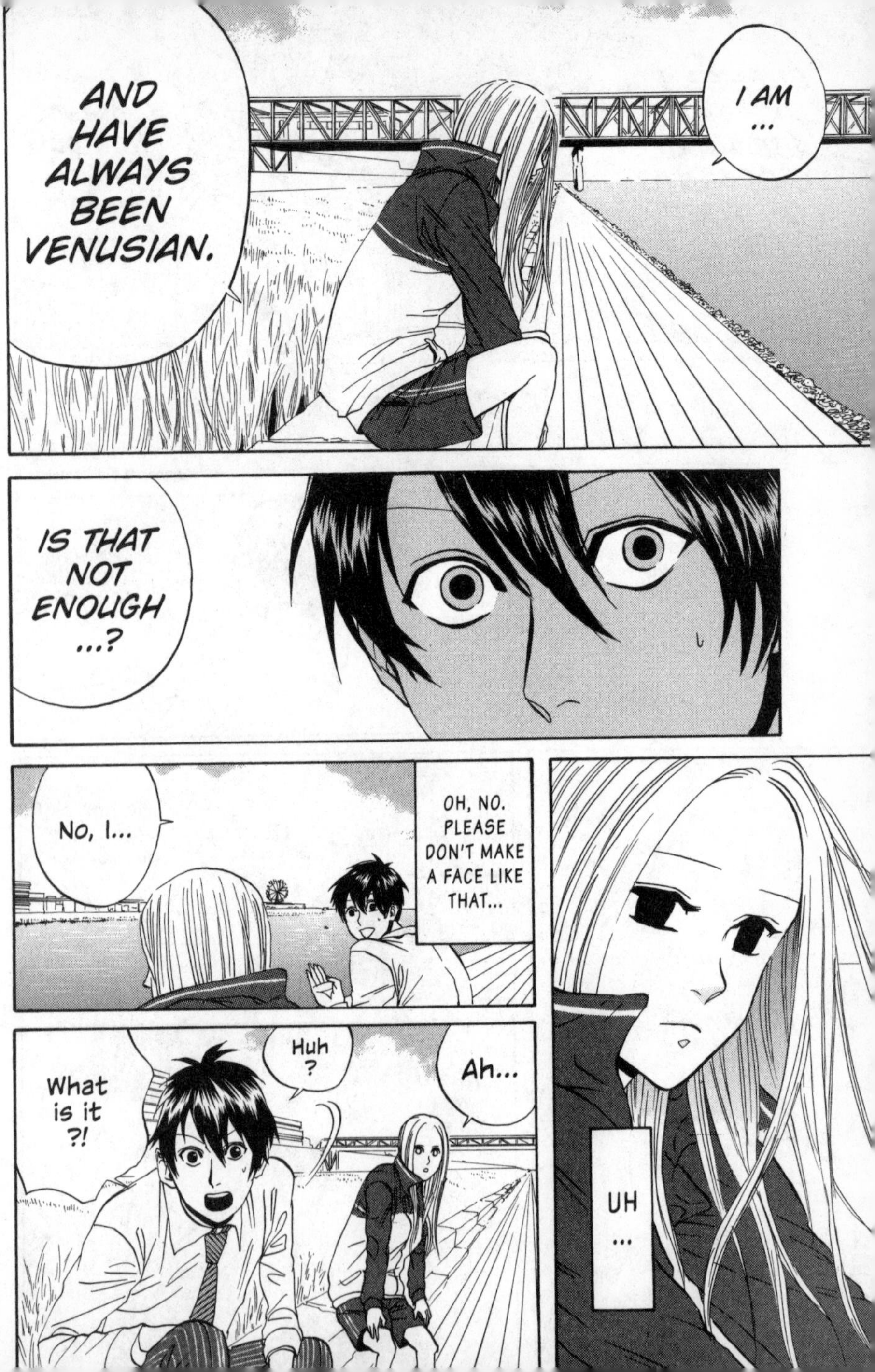
I AM ...
AND HAVE ALWAYS BEEN VENUSIAN.
IS THAT NOT ENOUGH ...?
UH ...
OH, NO. PLEASE DON'T MAKE A FACE LIKE THAT...
No, I...
Ah...
Huh ?
What is it ?!

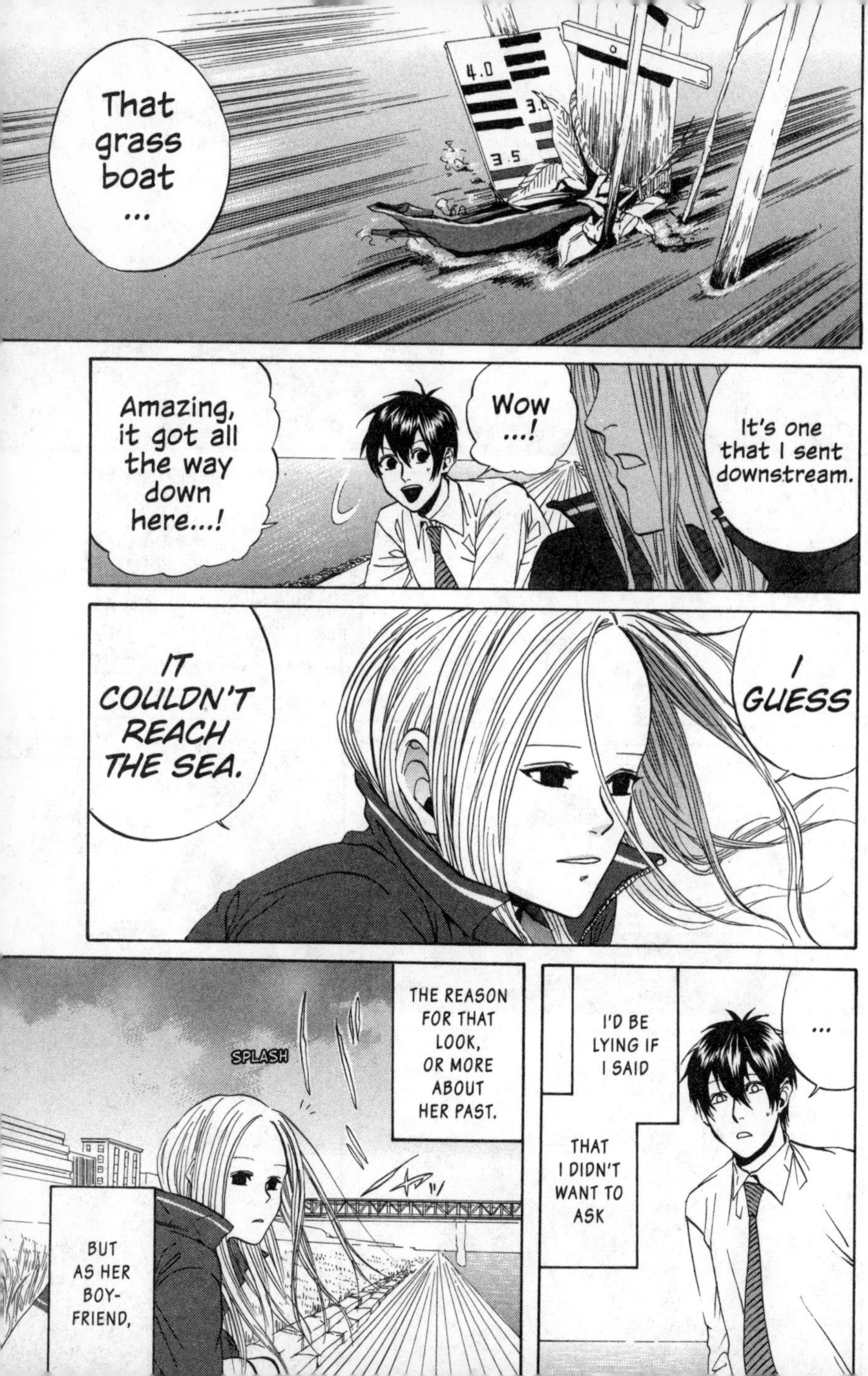
That grass boat ...
4.0
3.5
It's one that I sent downstream.
Wow ...!
Amazing, it got all the way down here...!
I GUESS
IT COULDN'T REACH THE SEA.
...
I'D BE LYING IF I SAID
THAT I DIDN'T WANT TO ASK
THE REASON FOR THAT LOOK, OR MORE ABOUT HER PAST.
SPLASH
BUT AS HER BOY-FRIEND,

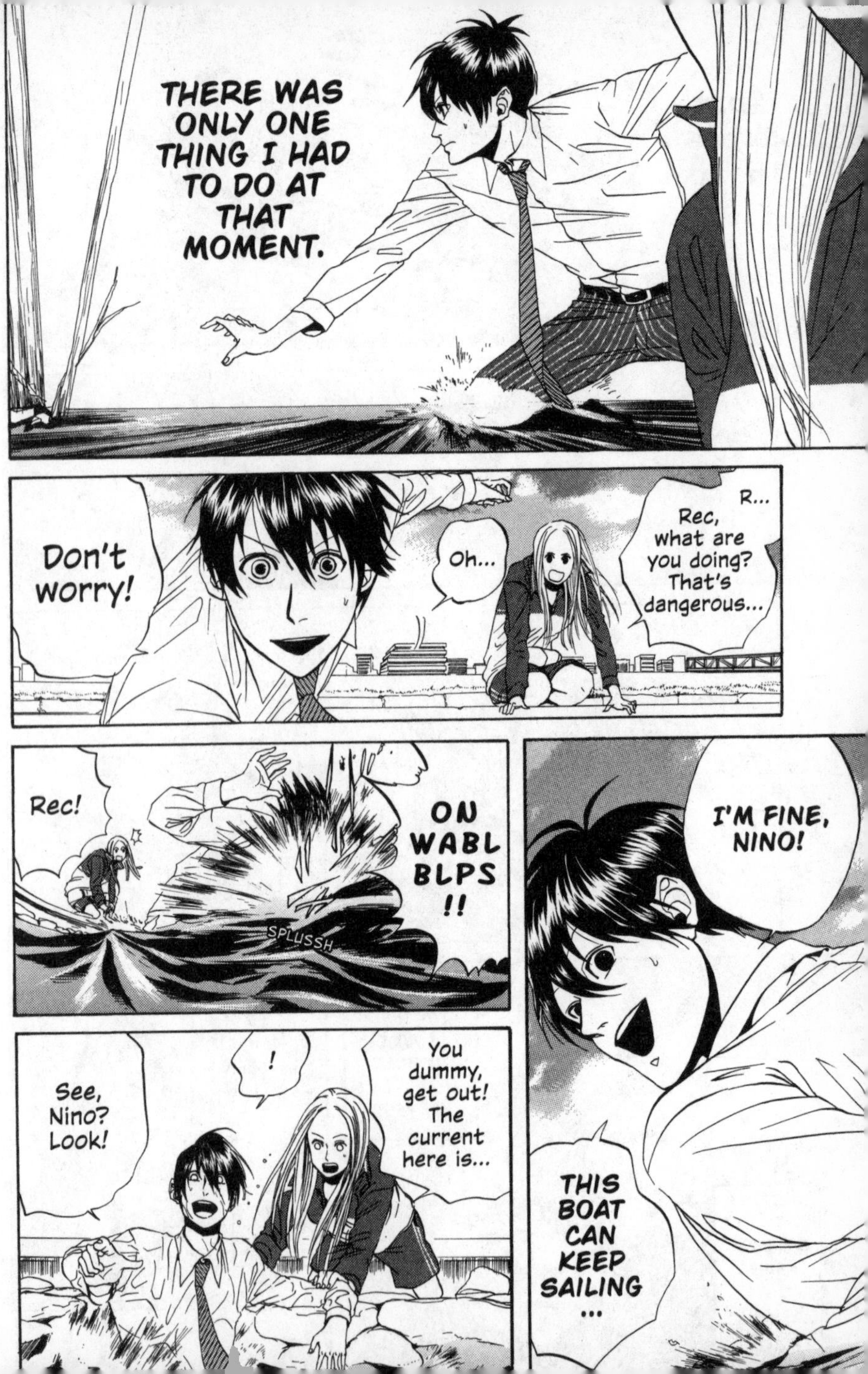
THERE WAS ONLY ONE THING I HAD TO DO AT THAT MOMENT.
R... Rec, what are you doing? That's dangerous...
Oh...
Don't worry!
I'M FINE, NINO!
THIS BOAT CAN KEEP SAILING ...
ON WABL BLPS !!
Rec!
SPLUSSH
You dummy, get out! The current here is...
!
See, Nino? Look!

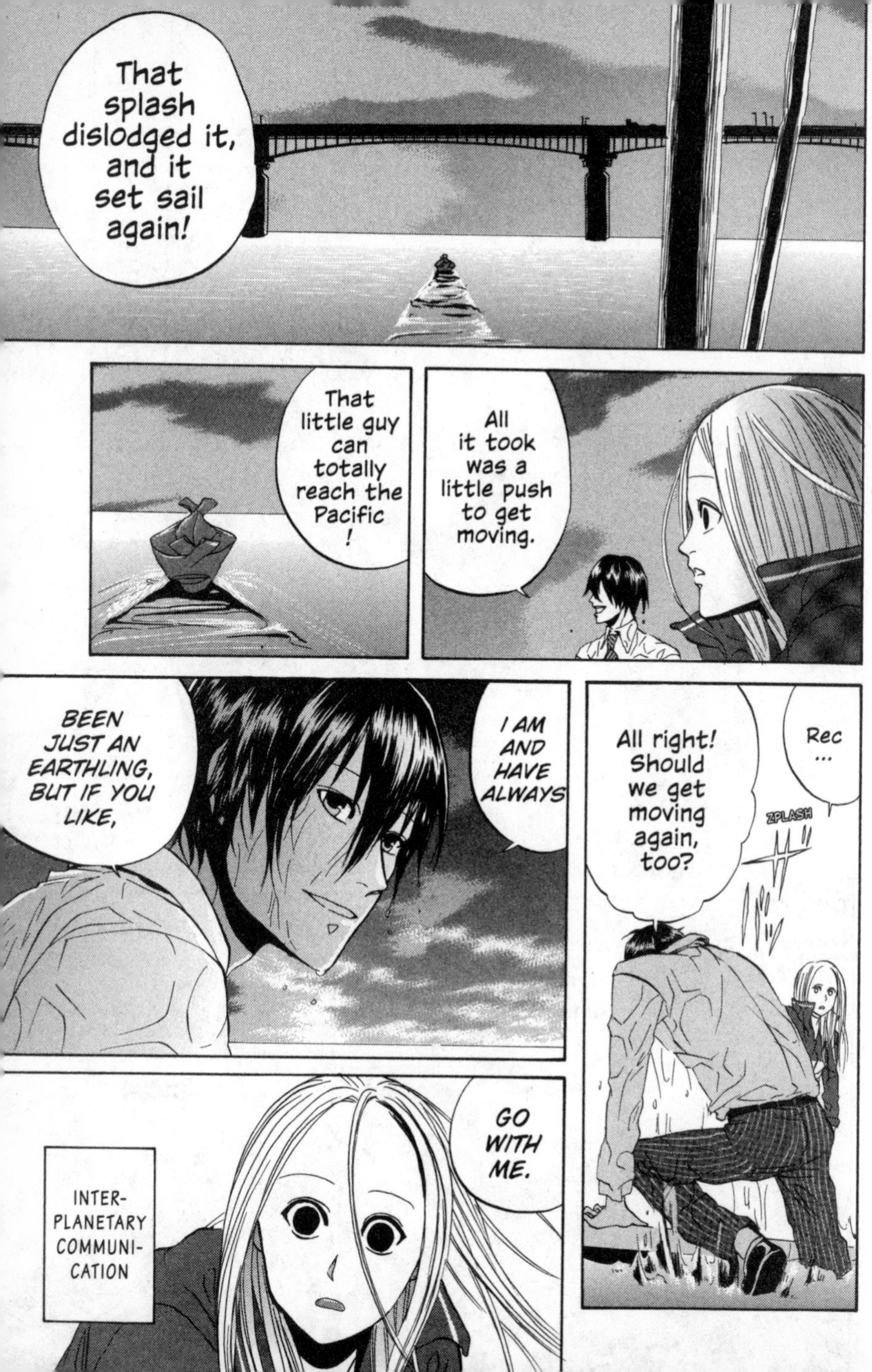
That splash dislodged it, and it set sail again!
All it took was a little push to get moving.
That little guy can totally reach the Pacific!
Rec ...
All right! Should we get moving again, too?
ZPLASH
I AM AND HAVE ALWAYS
BEEN JUST AN EARTHLING, BUT IF YOU LIKE,
GO WITH ME.
INTER-PLANETARY COMMUNICATION

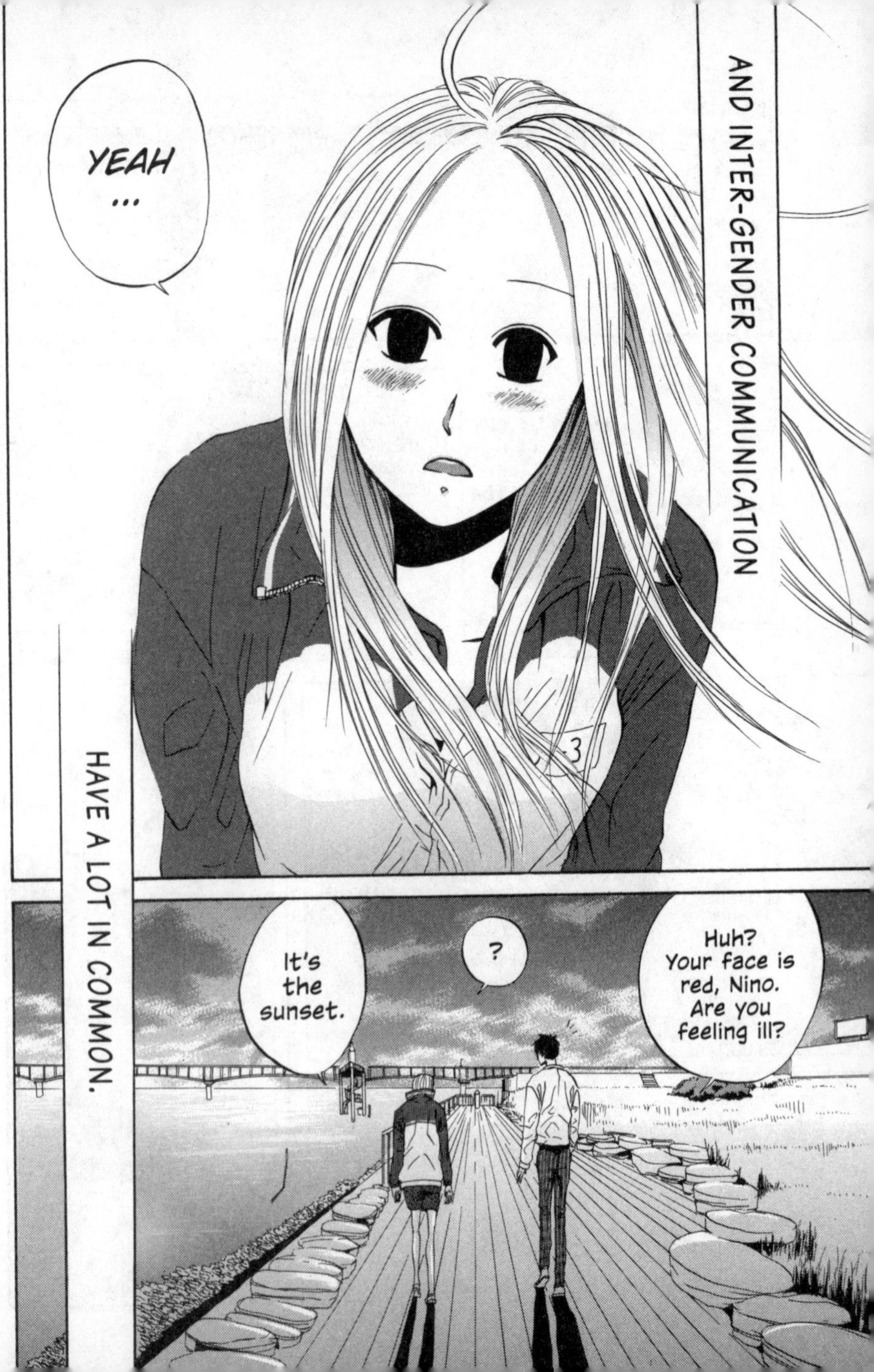
AND INTER-GENDER COMMUNICATION
YEAH ...
HAVE A LOT IN COMMON.
Huh? Your face is red, Nino. Are you feeling ill?
?
It's the sunset.

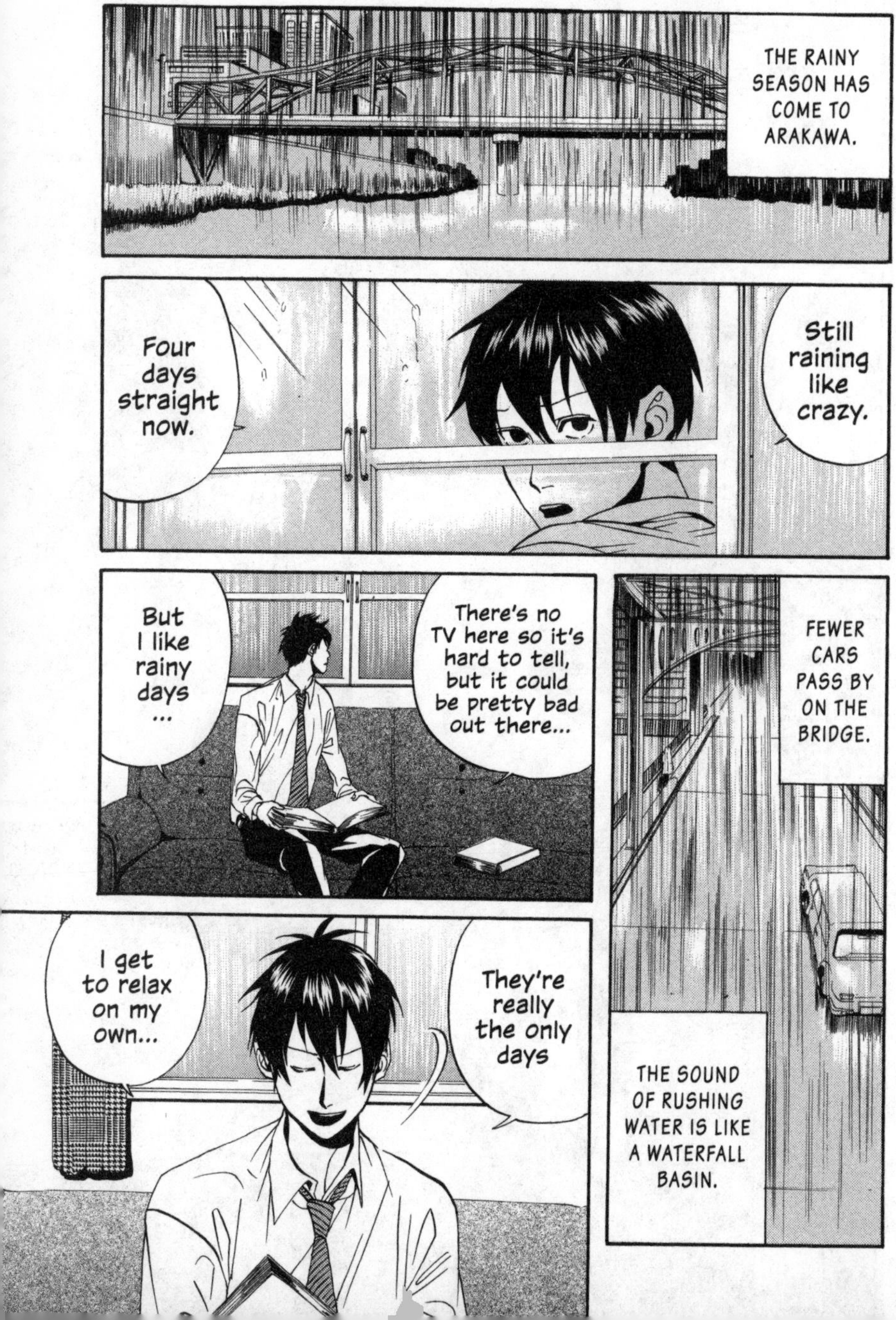
THE RAINY SEASON HAS COME TO ARAKAWA.
Still raining like crazy.
Four days straight now.
FEWER CARS PASS BY ON THE BRIDGE.
THE SOUND OF RUSHING WATER IS LIKE A WATERFALL BASIN.
There's no TV here so it's hard to tell, but it could be pretty bad out there...
But I like rainy days ...
They're really the only days
I get to relax on my own...

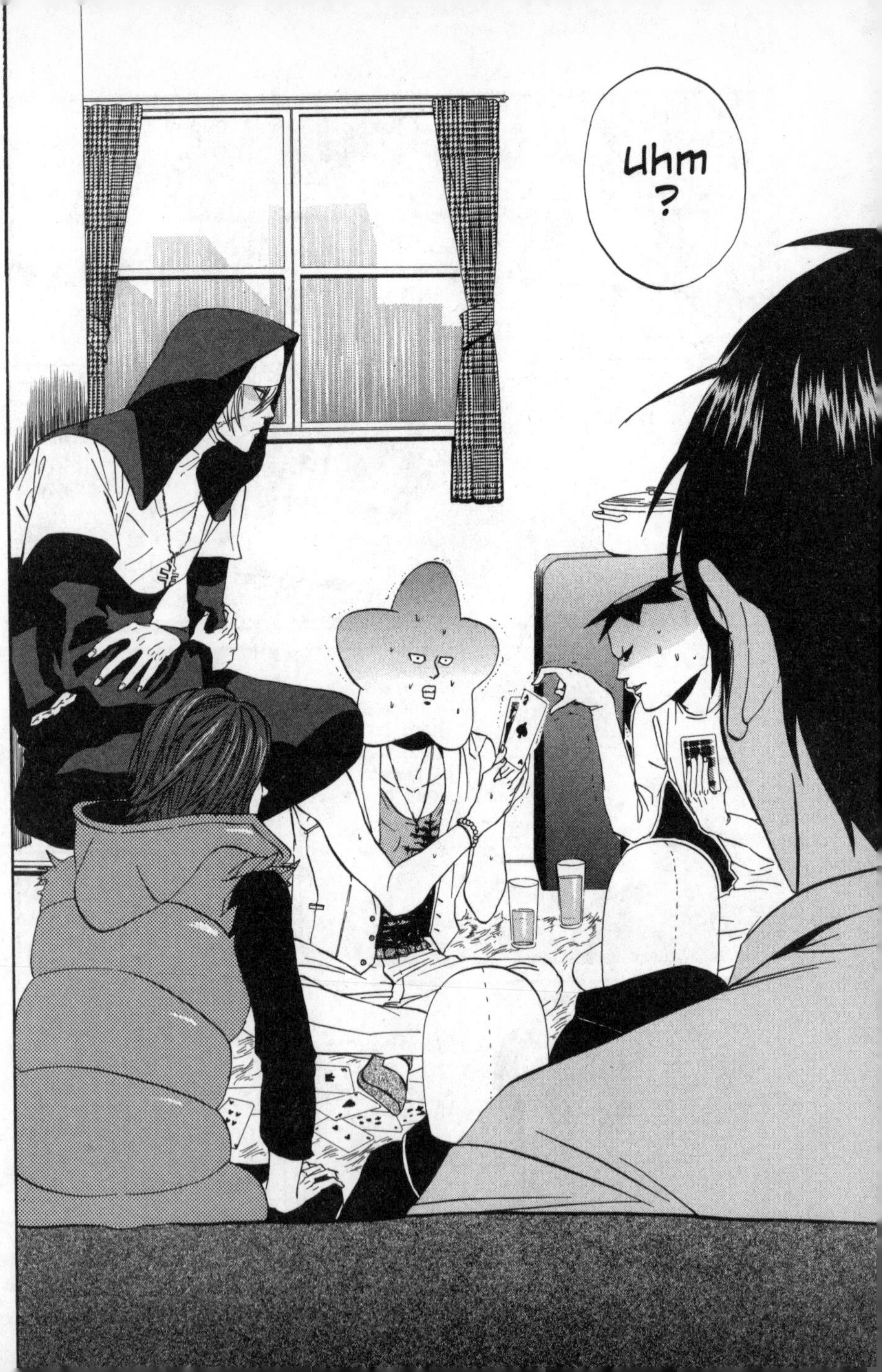
Uhm
?

Chapter 34: Rainy Season

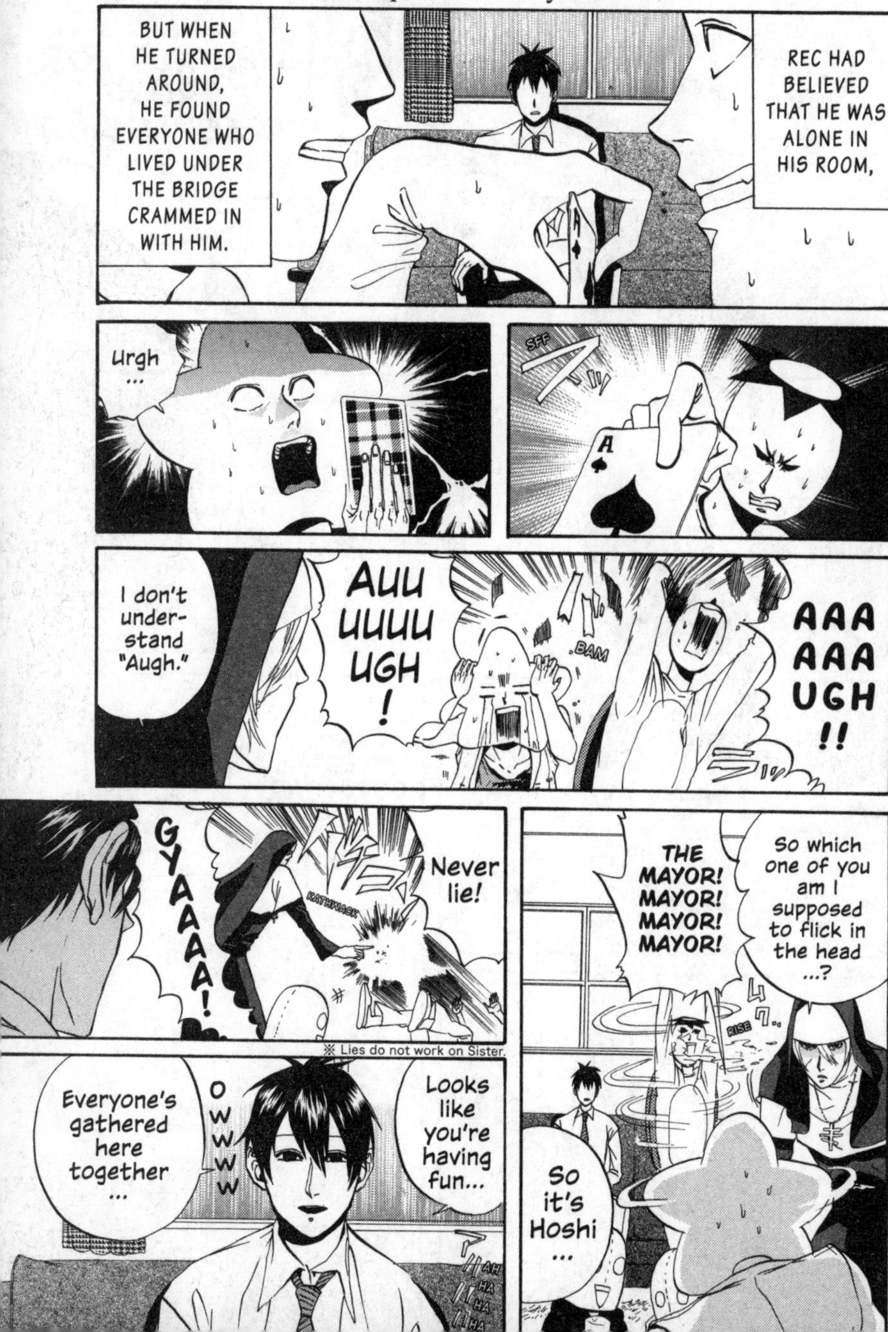
REC HAD BELIEVED THAT HE WAS ALONE IN HIS ROOM,
BUT WHEN HE TURNED AROUND, HE FOUND EVERYONE WHO LIVED UNDER THE BRIDGE CRAMMED IN WITH HIM.
SFF
Urgh ...
AAAAAAUGH!!
BAM
AUUUUUUUGH!
I don't under-stand "Augh."
So which one of you am I supposed to flick in the head ...?
THE MAYOR! MAYOR! MAYOR! MAYOR!
RISE
So it's Hoshi ...
Never lie!
KATHWACK
GYAAAAA!
※ Lies do not work on Sister.
Looks like you're having fun...
OWWWWW
Everyone's gathered here together ...
AH HA HA HA

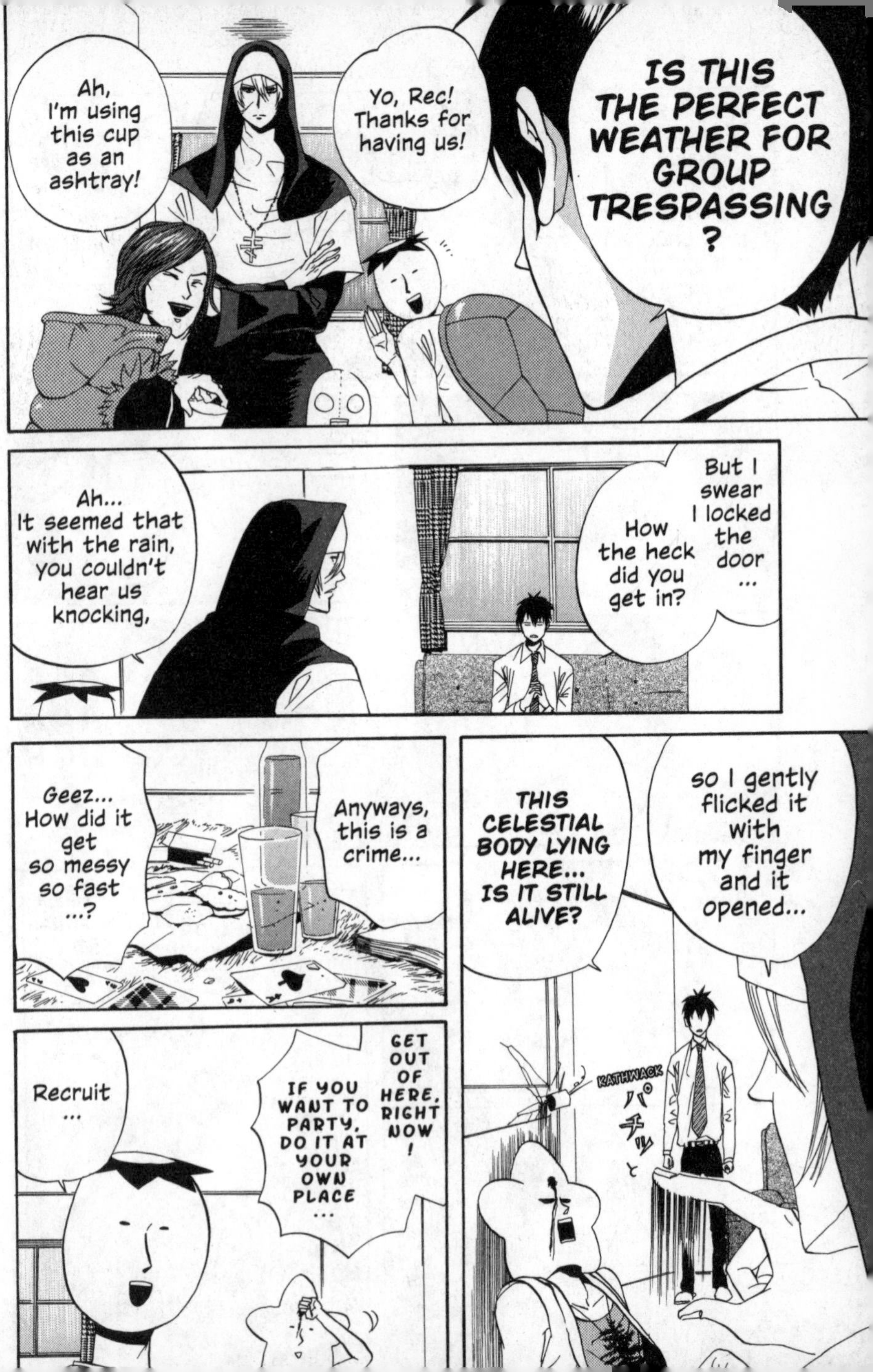
IS THIS THE PERFECT WEATHER FOR GROUP TRESPASSING?
Yo, Rec! Thanks for having us!
Ah, I'm using this cup as an ashtray!
But I swear I locked the door...
How the heck did you get in?
Ah... It seemed that with the rain, you couldn't hear us knocking,
so I gently flicked it with my finger and it opened...
THIS CELESTIAL BODY LYING HERE... IS IT STILL ALIVE?
KATHWACK
Anyways, this is a crime...
Geez... How did it get so messy so fast...?
GET OUT OF HERE, RIGHT NOW!
IF YOU WANT TO PARTY, DO IT AT YOUR OWN PLACE...
Recruit...

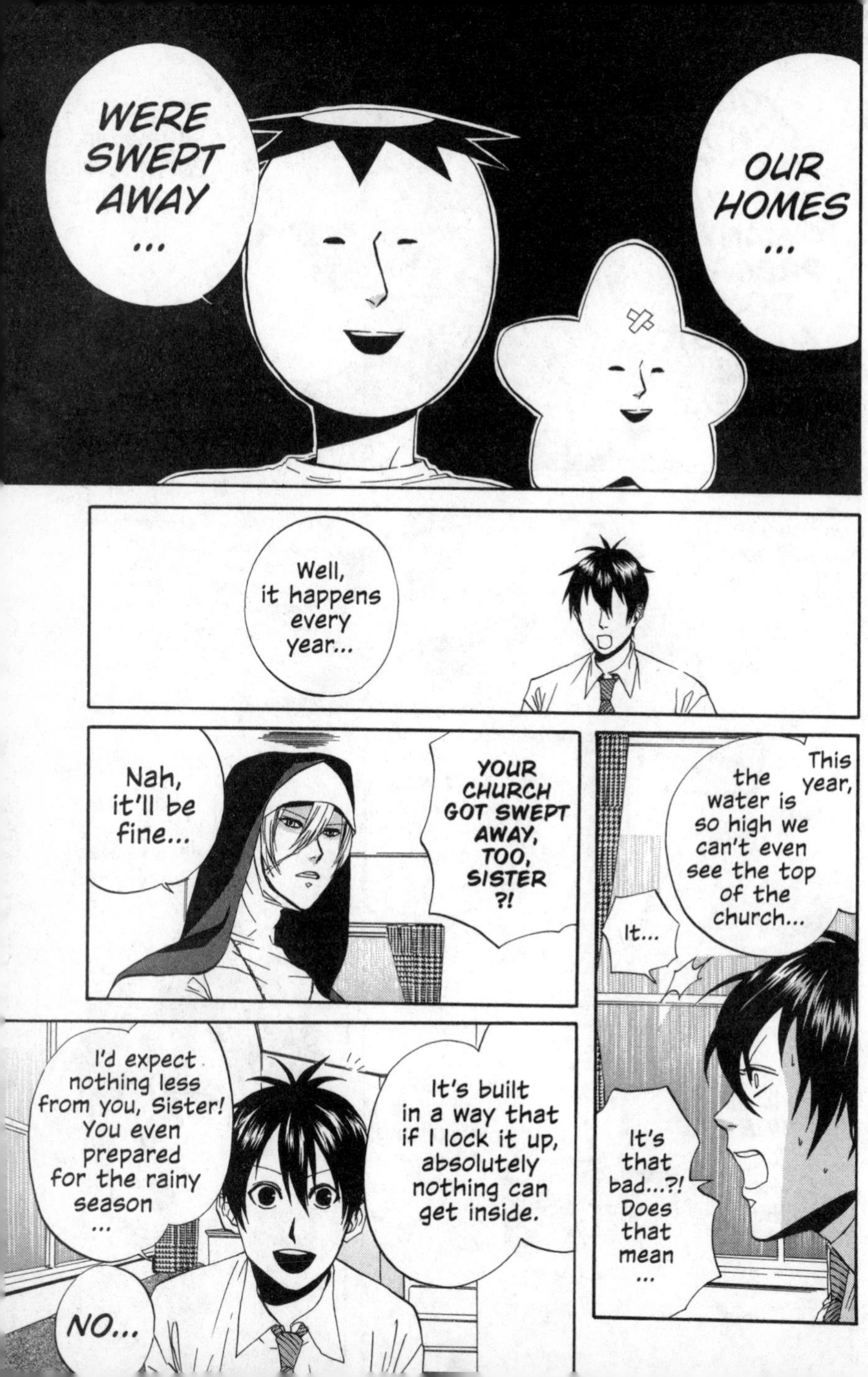
OUR HOMES ...
WERE SWEPT AWAY ...
Well, it happens every year...
This year, the water is so high we can't even see the top of the church...
It...
It's that bad...?! Does that mean ...
YOUR CHURCH GOT SWEPT AWAY, TOO, SISTER ?!
Nah, it'll be fine...
It's built in a way that if I lock it up, absolutely nothing can get inside.
I'd expect nothing less from you, Sister! You even prepared for the rainy season ...
NO...

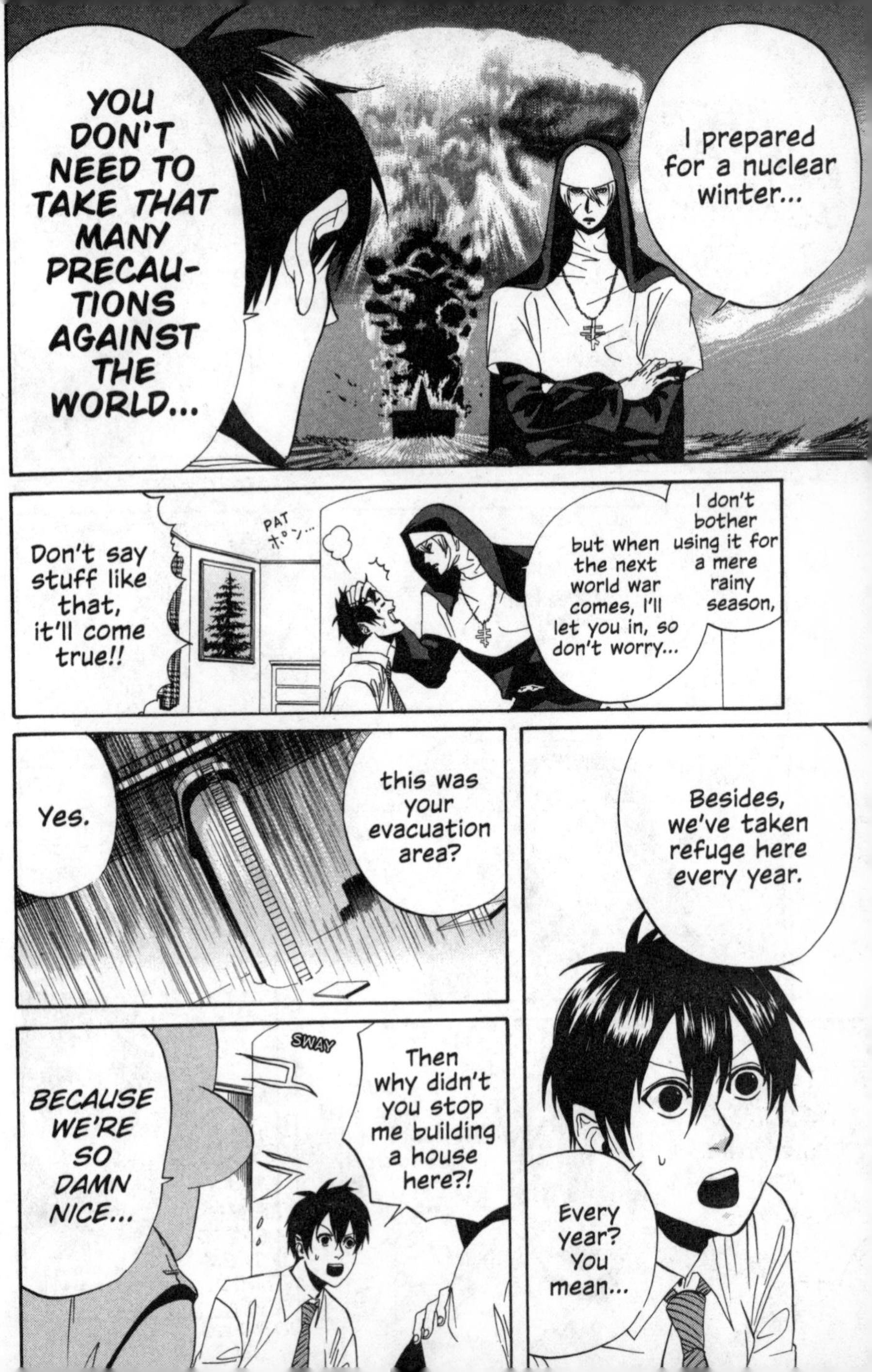

I prepared for a nuclear winter...
YOU DON'T NEED TO TAKE THAT MANY PRECAUTIONS AGAINST THE WORLD...
I don't bother using it for a mere rainy season,
but when the next world war comes, I'll let you in, so don't worry...
PAT ポン…
Don't say stuff like that, it'll come true!!
Besides, we've taken refuge here every year.
Every year? You mean...
this was your evacuation area?
Yes.
SWAY
Then why didn't you stop me building a house here?!
BECAUSE WE'RE SO DAMN NICE...

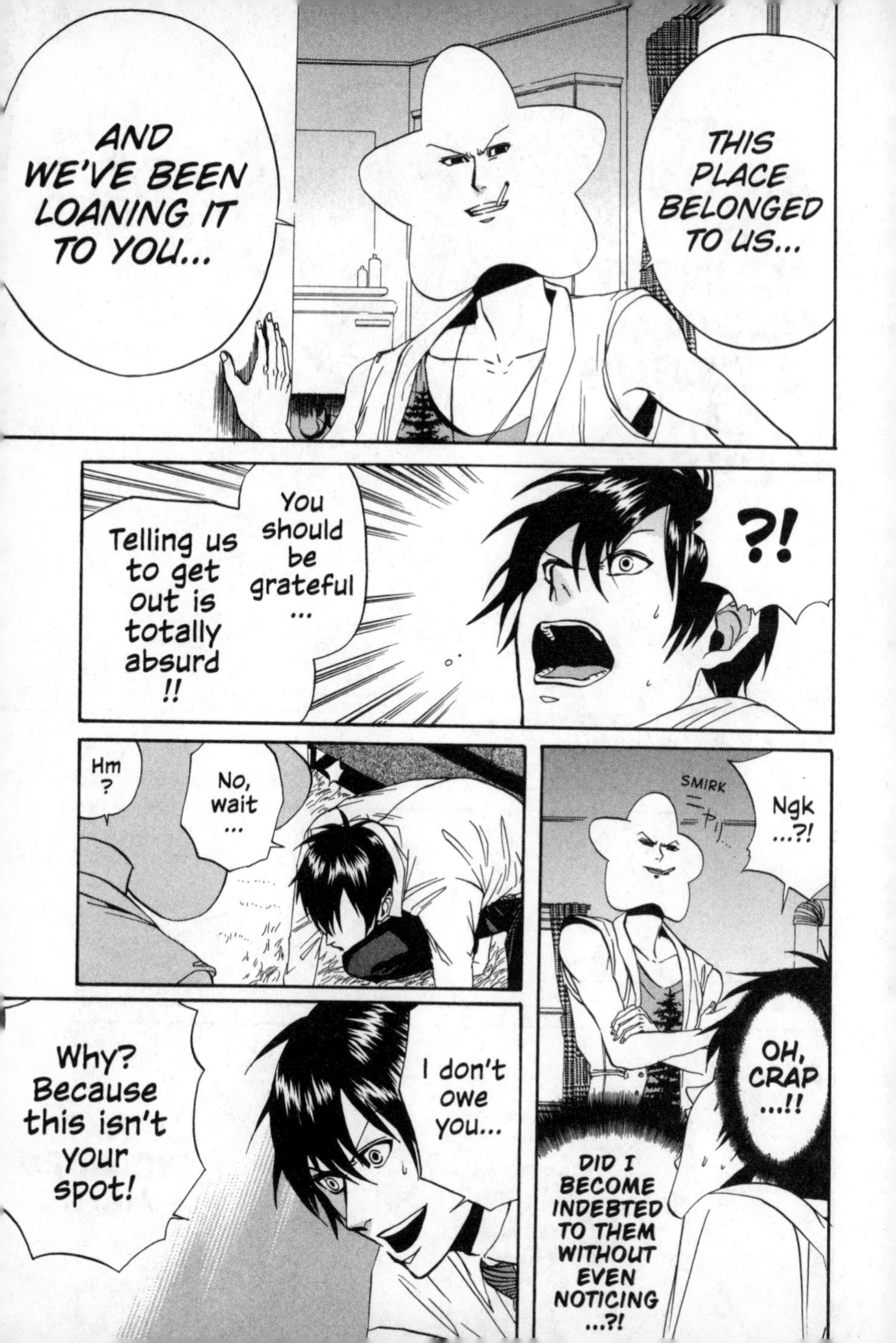
THIS PLACE BELONGED TO US...
AND WE'VE BEEN LOANING IT TO YOU...
?!
You should be grateful ...
Telling us to get out is totally absurd !!
Ngk ...?!
SMIRK
OH, CRAP ...!!
DID I BECOME INDEBTED TO THEM WITHOUT EVEN NOTICING ...?!
No, wait ...
Hm ?
I don't owe you...
Why? Because this isn't your spot!

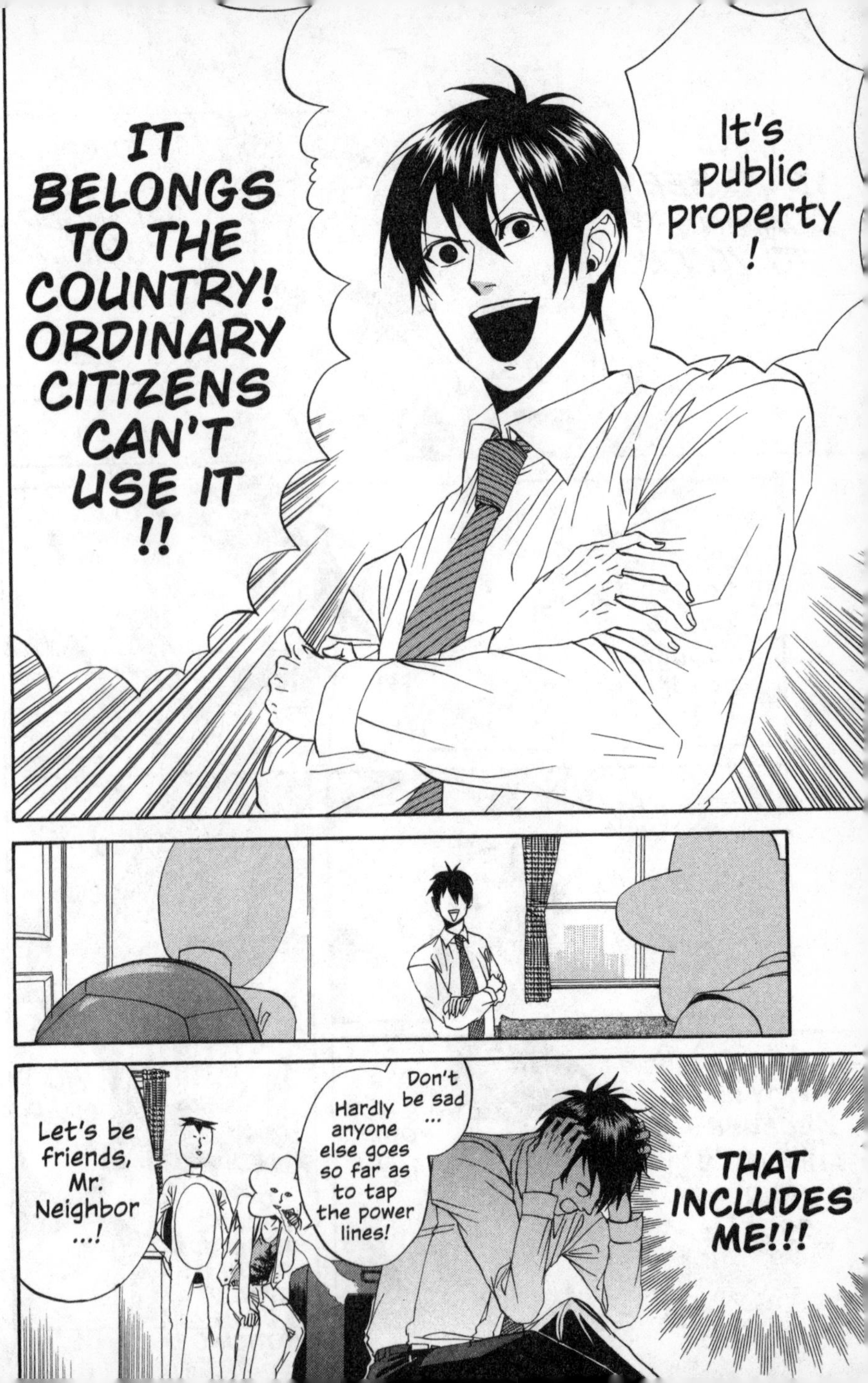
It's public property!
IT BELONGS TO THE COUNTRY! ORDINARY CITIZENS CAN'T USE IT!!
THAT INCLUDES ME!!!
Don't be sad ...
Hardly anyone else goes so far as to tap the power lines!
Let's be friends, Mr. Neighbor ...!

☜ Chapter 35: King

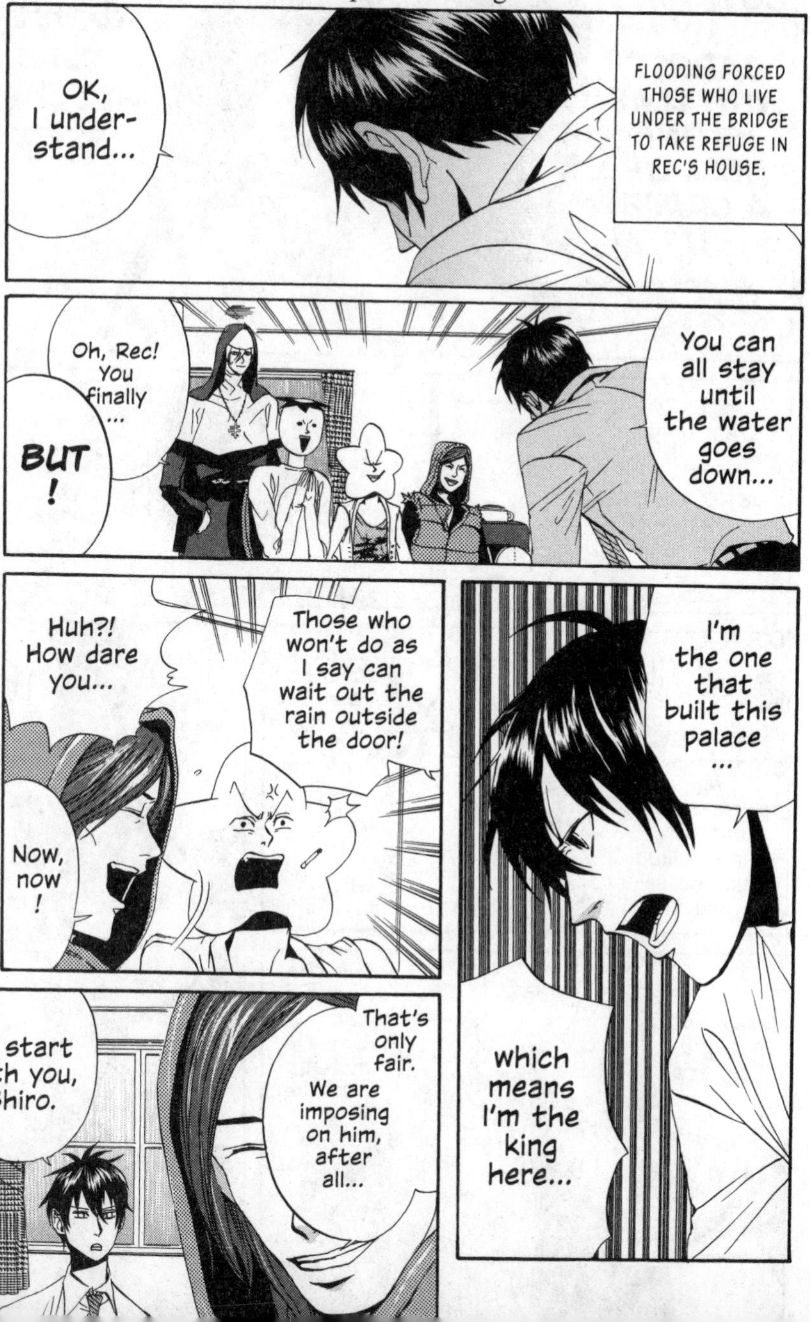

FLOODING FORCED THOSE WHO LIVE UNDER THE BRIDGE TO TAKE REFUGE IN REC'S HOUSE.
OK, I under-stand...
You can all stay until the water goes down...
Oh, Rec! You finally...
BUT!
I'm the one that built this palace...
which means I'm the king here...
Those who won't do as I say can wait out the rain outside the door!
Huh?! How dare you...
Now, now!
That's only fair. We are imposing on him, after all...
I'll start with you, Shiro.

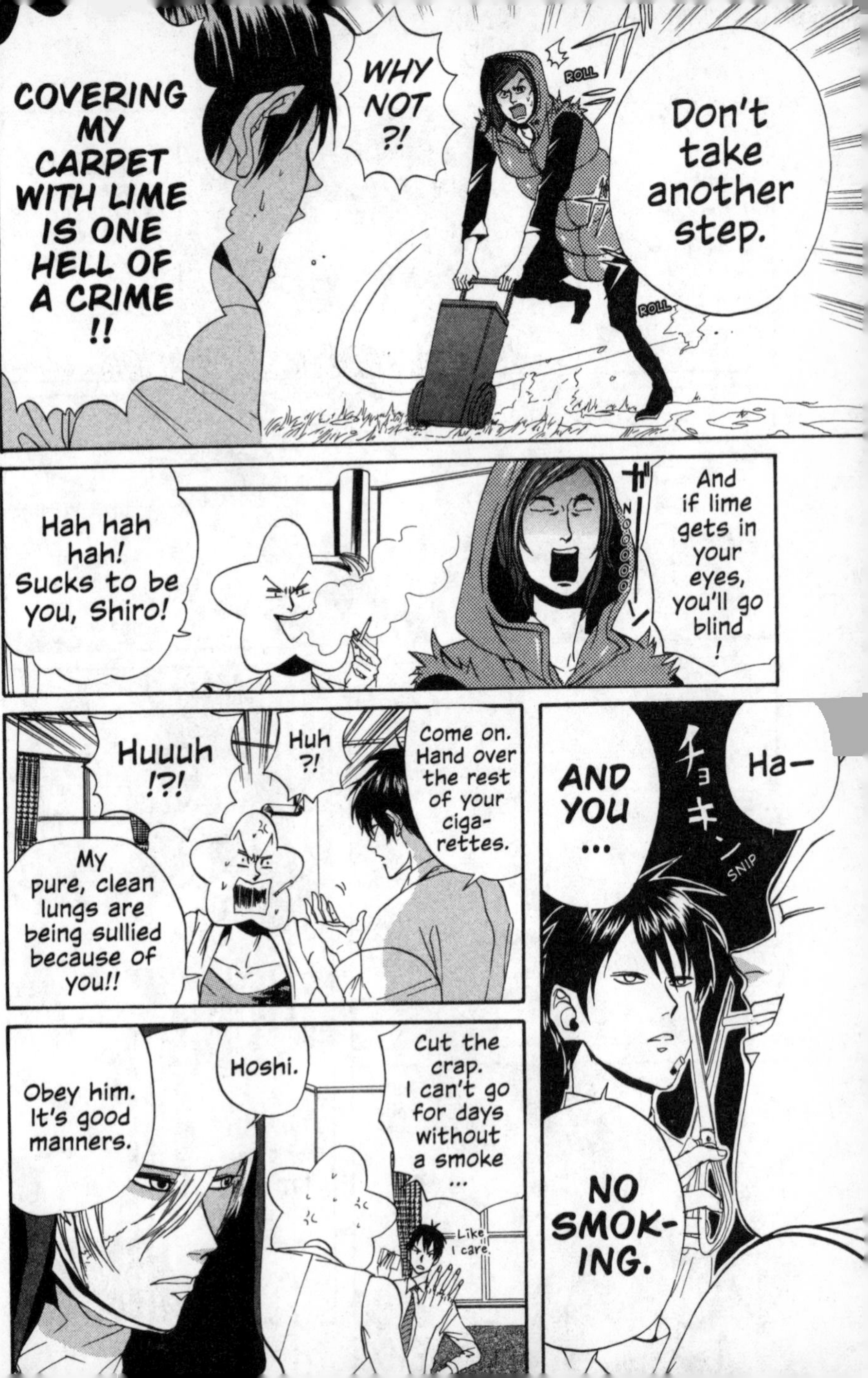

Don't take another step.
ROLL
ROLL
WHY NOT ?!
COVERING MY CARPET WITH LIME IS ONE HELL OF A CRIME !!
And if lime gets in your eyes, you'll go blind !
Hah hah hah! Sucks to be you, Shiro!
Ha—
AND YOU ...
SNIP
NO SMOK-ING.
Come on. Hand over the rest of your ciga-rettes.
Huh ?!
Huuuh !?!
My pure, clean lungs are being sullied because of you!!
Cut the crap. I can't go for days without a smoke ...
Hoshi.
Obey him. It's good manners.
Like I care.

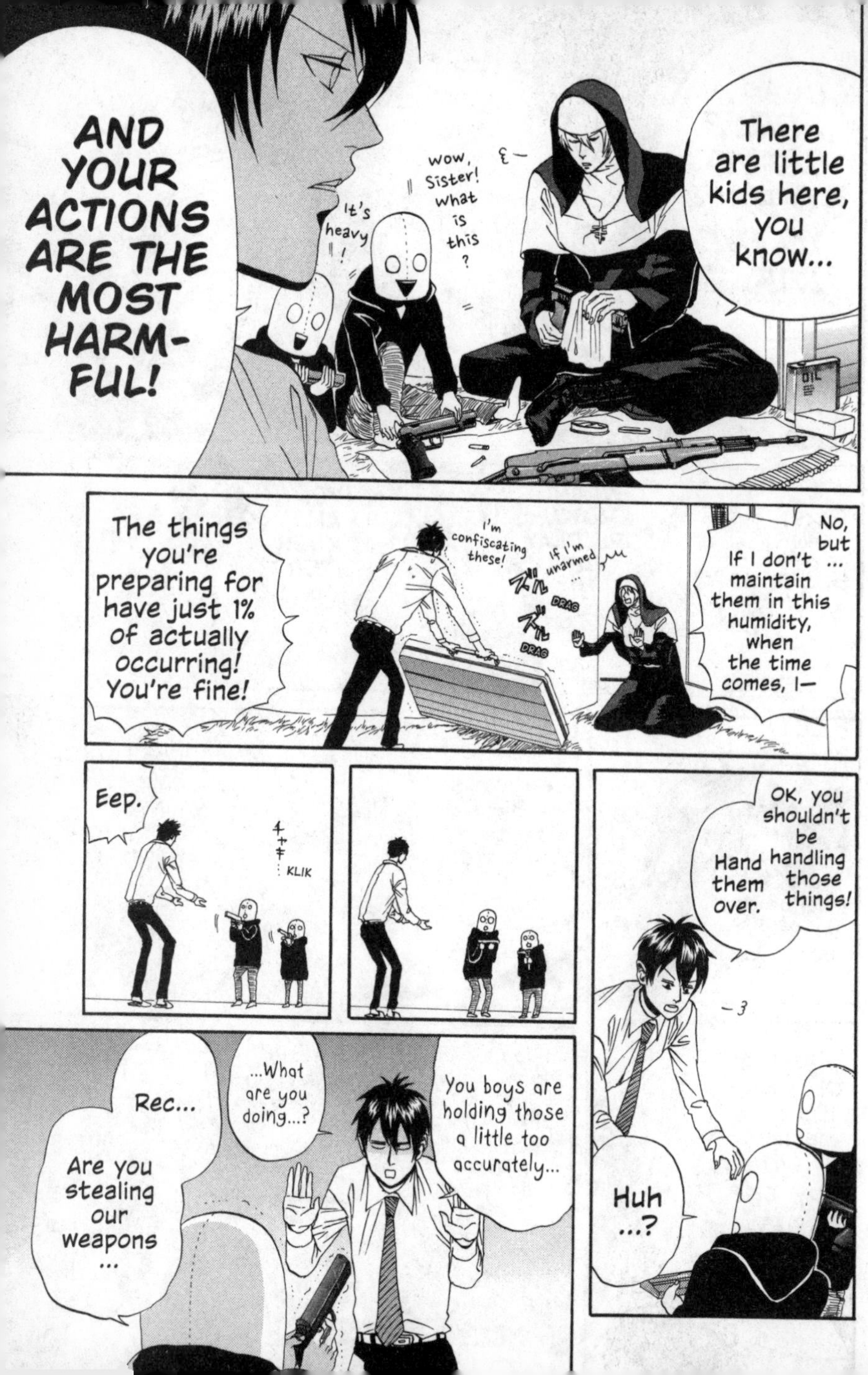
There are little kids here, you know...
wow, Sister! what is this?
It's heavy!
AND YOUR ACTIONS ARE THE MOST HARM-FUL!
No, but ... If I don't maintain them in this humidity, when the time comes, I—
If I'm unarmed ...
I'm confiscating these!
DRAG
DRAG
The things you're preparing for have just 1% of actually occurring! You're fine!
OK, you shouldn't be handling those things!
Hand them over.
Huh ...?
Eep.
KLIK
You boys are holding those a little too accurately...
...What are you doing...?
Rec...
Are you stealing our weapons ...

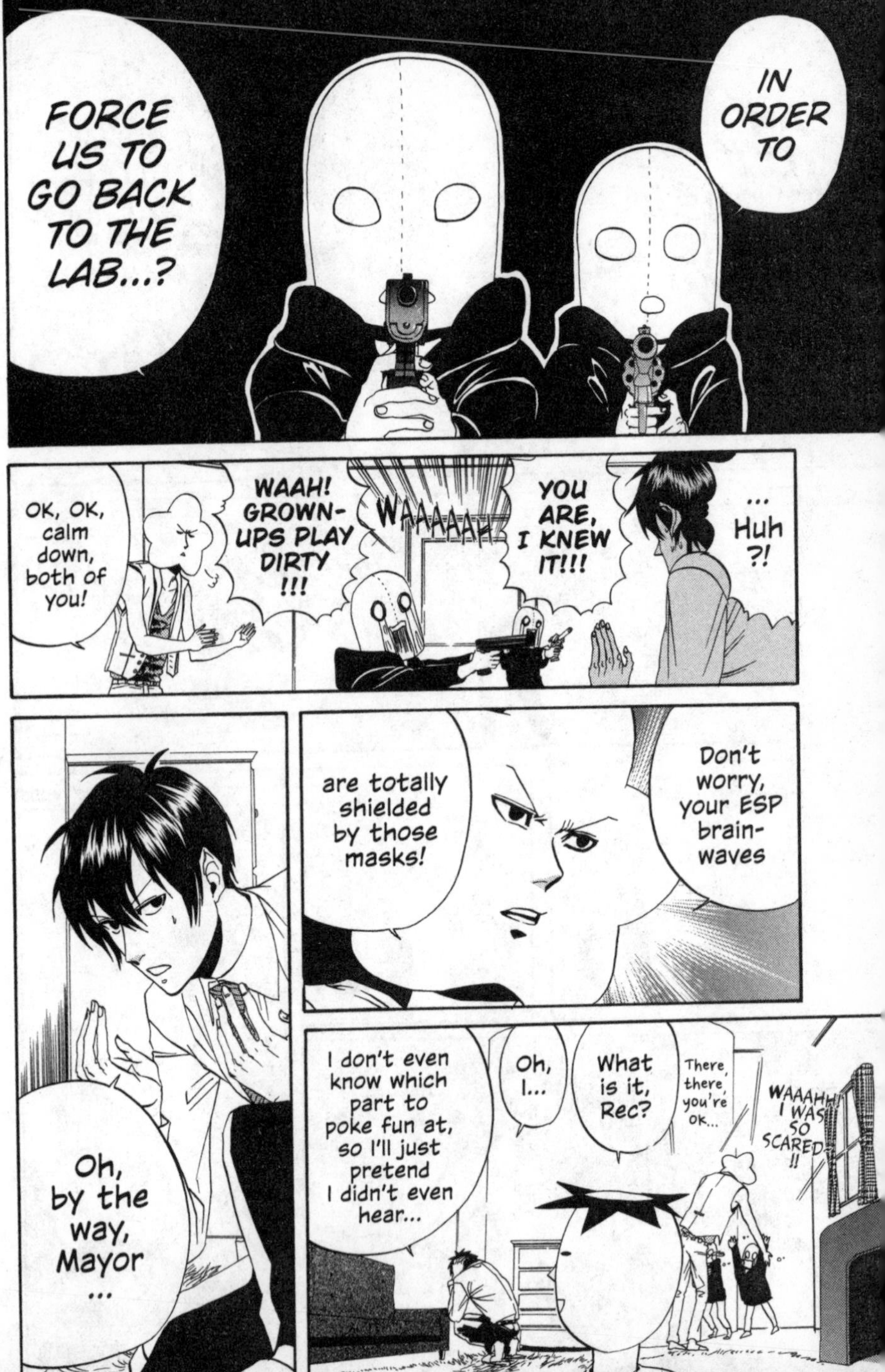

IN ORDER TO
FORCE US TO GO BACK TO THE LAB...?
... Huh?!
YOU ARE, I KNEW IT!!!
WAAAAAH
WAAH! GROWN-UPS PLAY DIRTY !!!
OK, OK, calm down, both of you!
Don't worry, your ESP brain-waves
are totally shielded by those masks!
WAAAHH! I WAS SO SCARED !!
There, there, you're ok...
What is it, Rec?
Oh, I...
I don't even know which part to poke fun at, so I'll just pretend I didn't even hear...
Oh, by the way, Mayor ...

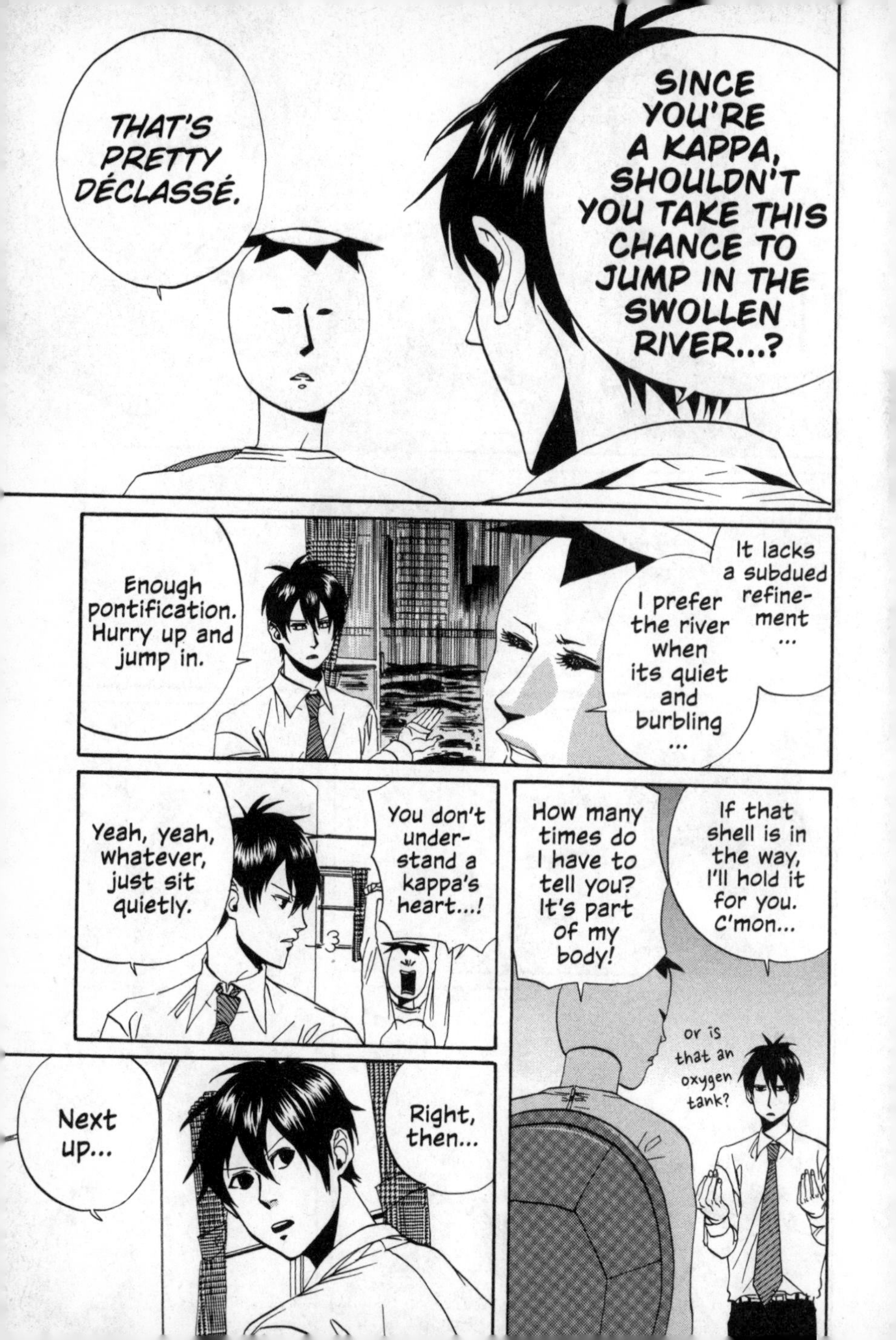

SINCE YOU'RE A KAPPA, SHOULDN'T YOU TAKE THIS CHANCE TO JUMP IN THE SWOLLEN RIVER...?
THAT'S PRETTY DÉCLASSÉ.
It lacks a subdued refinement ...
I prefer the river when its quiet and burbling ...
Enough pontification. Hurry up and jump in.
If that shell is in the way, I'll hold it for you. C'mon...
How many times do I have to tell you? It's part of my body!
or is that an oxygen tank?
You don't understand a kappa's heart...!
Yeah, yeah, whatever, just sit quietly.
Right, then...
Next up...

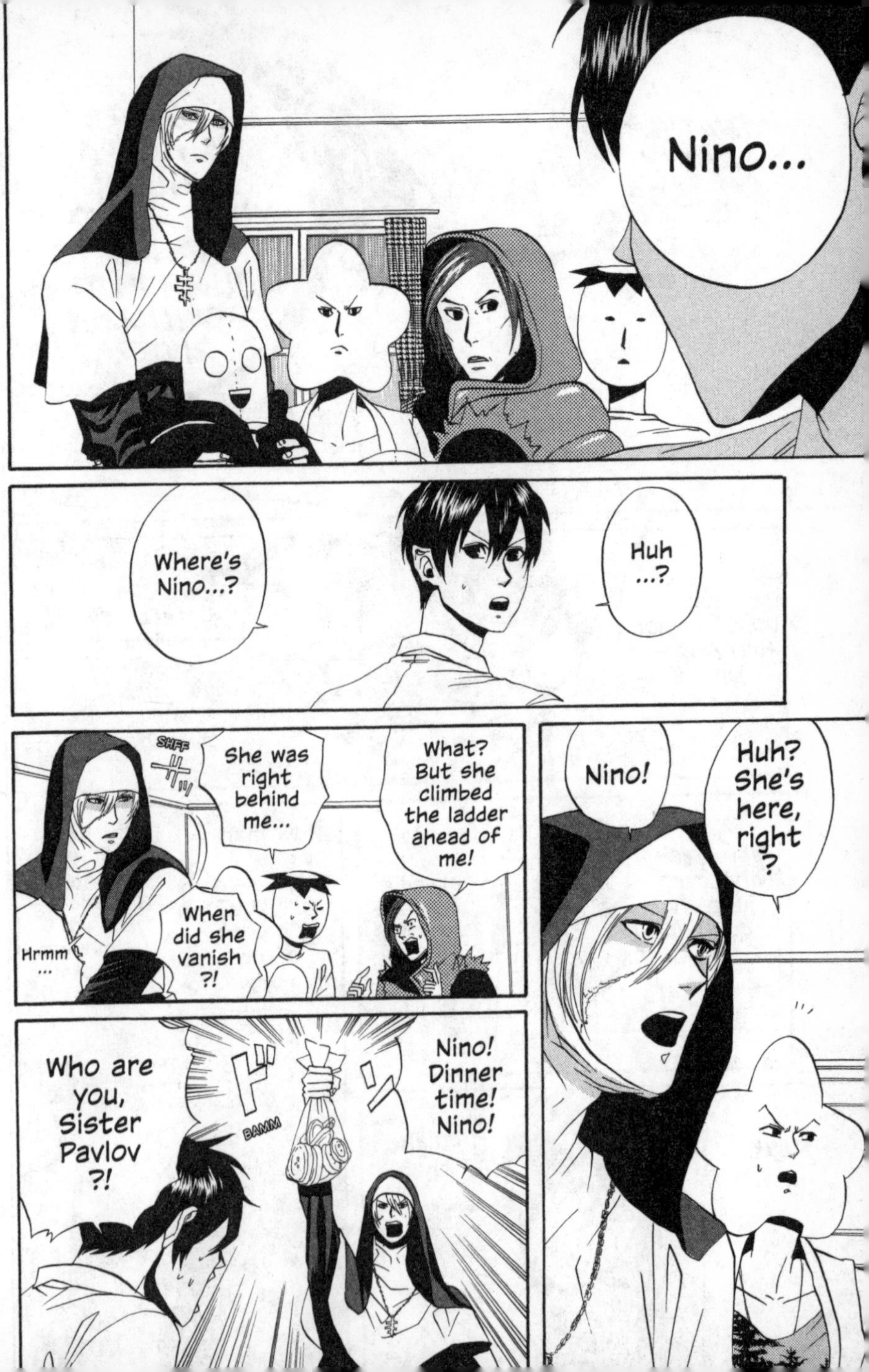
Nino...
Huh ...?
Where's Nino...?
Huh? She's here, right?
Nino!
What? But she climbed the ladder ahead of me!
She was right behind me...
SHFF
When did she vanish?!
Hrmm...
Nino! Dinner time! Nino!
BAMM
Who are you, Sister Pavlov?!

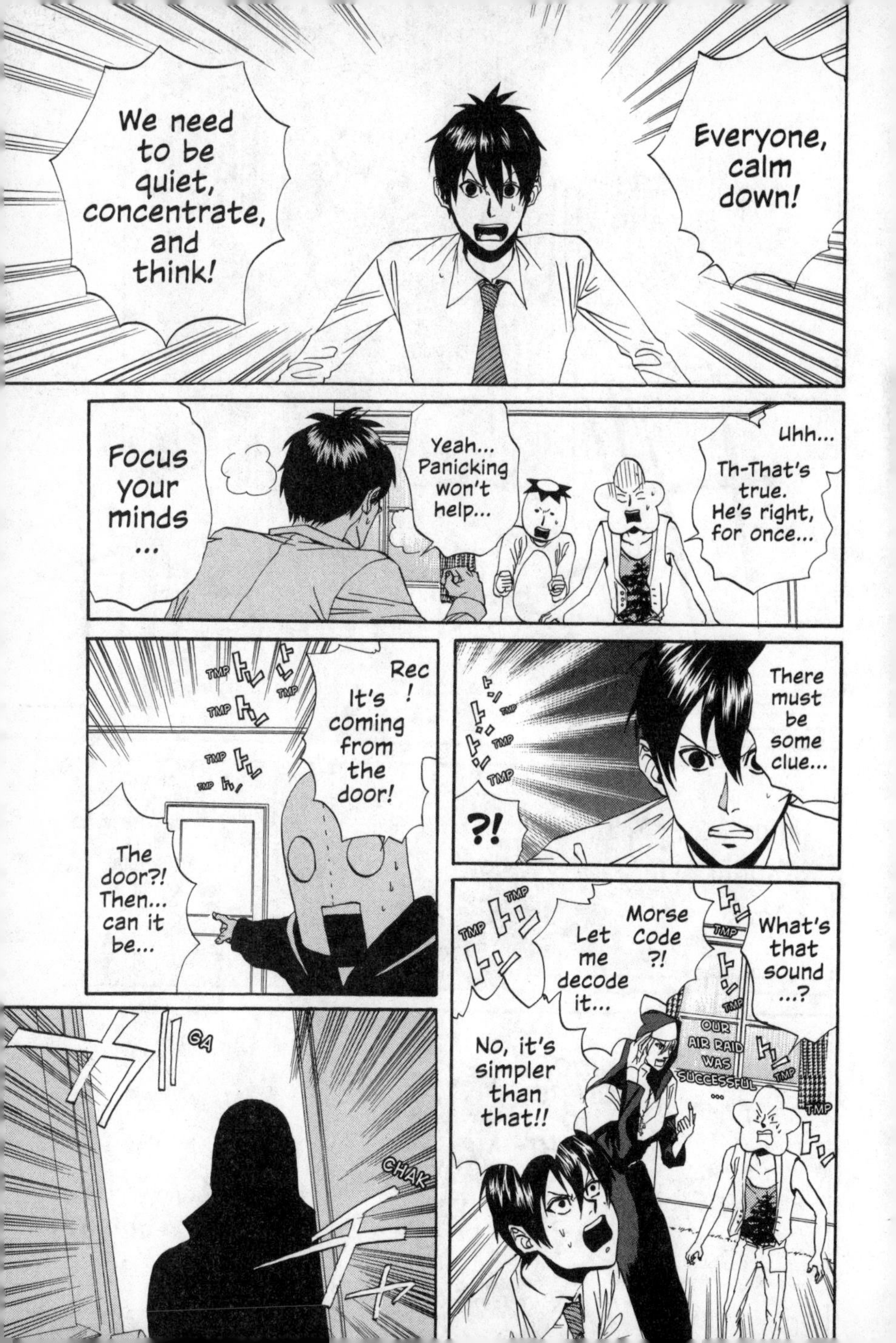
Everyone, calm down!
We need to be quiet, concentrate, and think!
Uhh... Th-That's true. He's right, for once...
Yeah... Panicking won't help...
Focus your minds ...
TMP
TMP
TMP
?!
There must be some clue...
TMP
TMP
TMP
TMP
Rec! It's coming from the door!
The door?! Then... can it be...
TMP
TMP
What's that sound ...?
Morse Code ?!
Let me decode it...
OUR AIR RAID WAS SUCCESSFUL ...
TMP
TMP
No, it's simpler than that!!
GA
CHAK

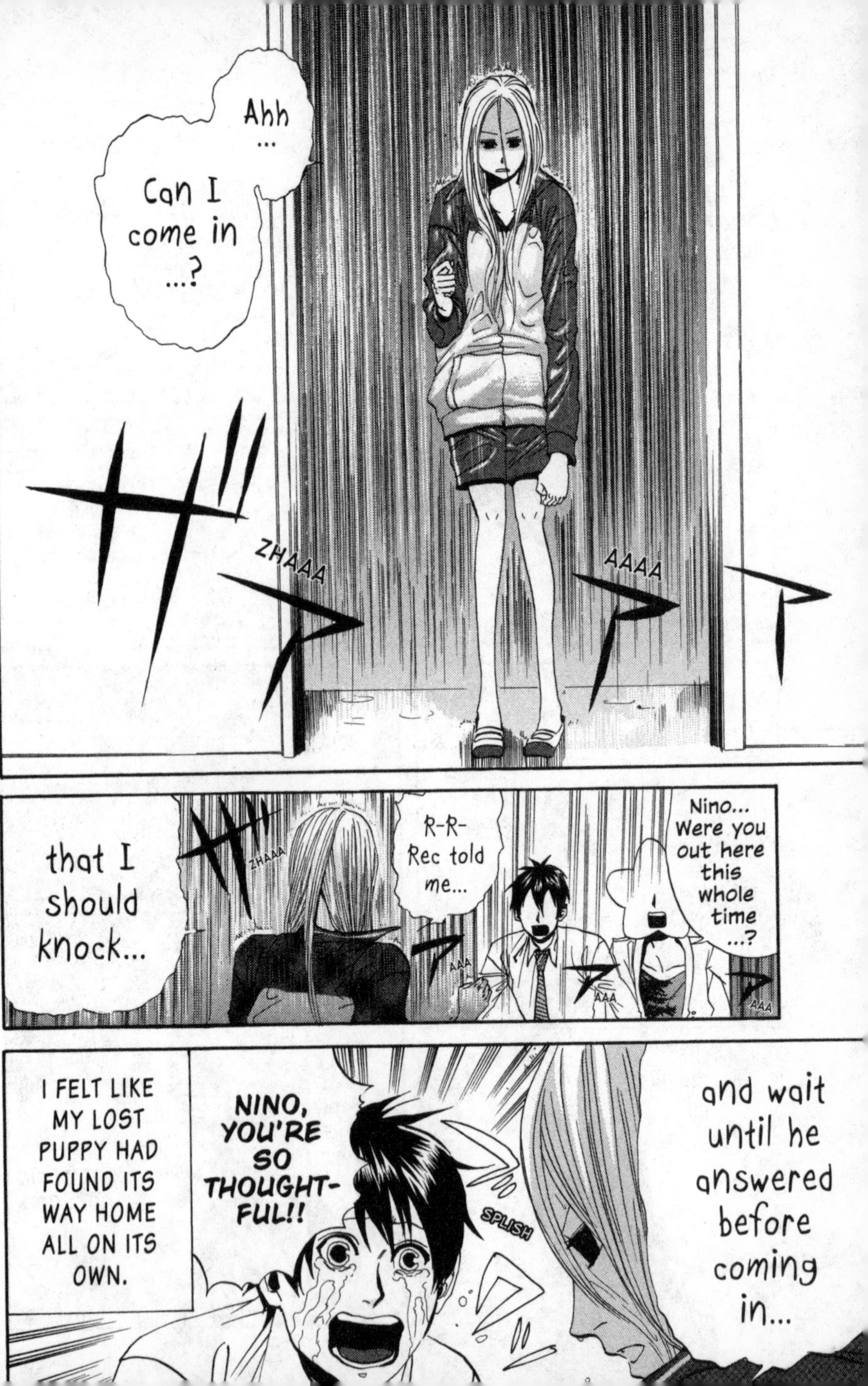
Ahh ... Can I come in ...?
ZHAAA
AAAA
Nino... Were you out here this whole time ...?
R-R-Rec told me...
that I should knock...
ZHAAA
AAA
AAA
AAA
and wait until he answered before coming in...
SPLISH
NINO, YOU'RE SO THOUGHTFUL!!
I FELT LIKE MY LOST PUPPY HAD FOUND ITS WAY HOME ALL ON ITS OWN.

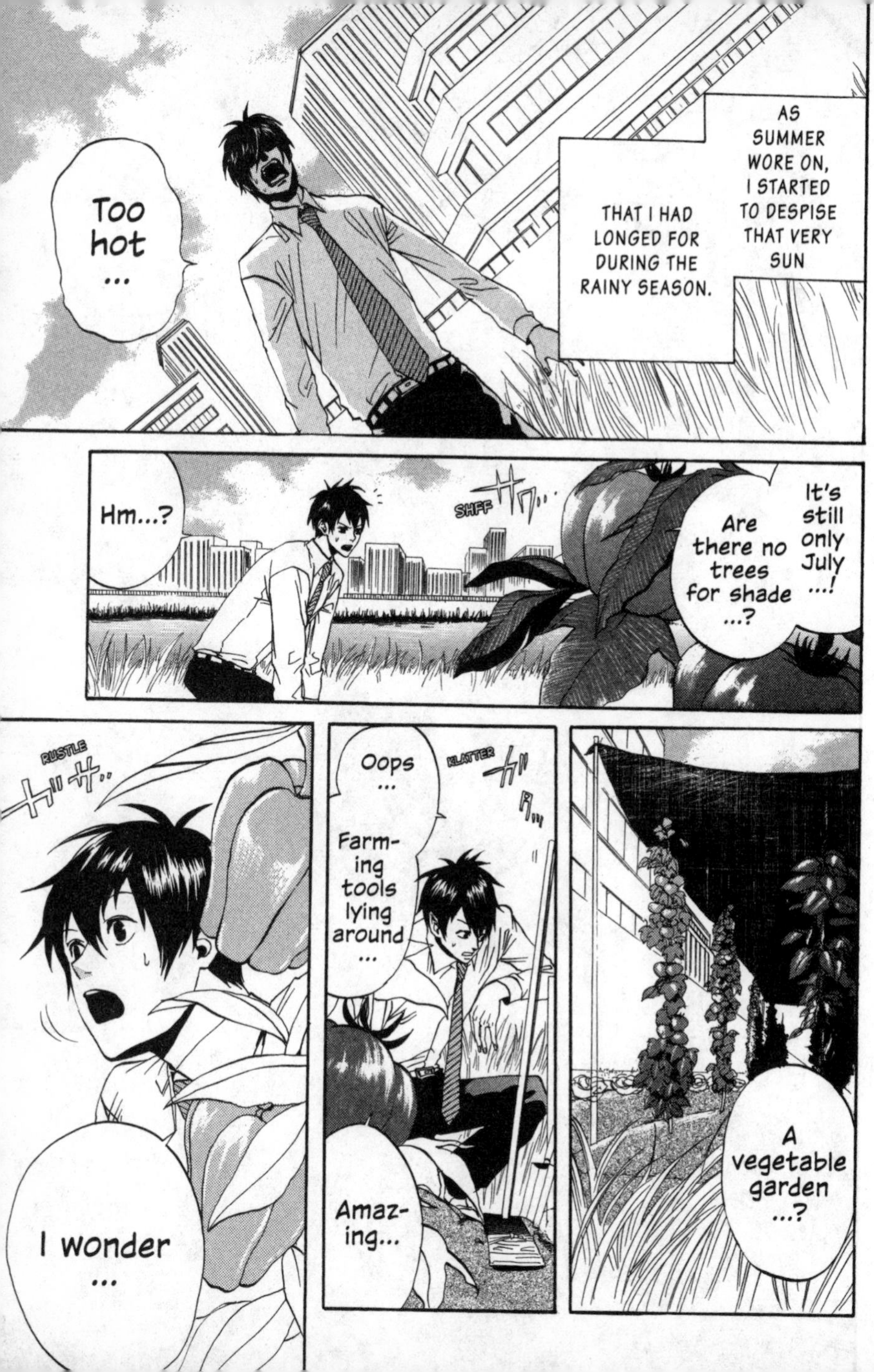
AS SUMMER WORE ON, I STARTED TO DESPISE THAT VERY SUN
THAT I HAD LONGED FOR DURING THE RAINY SEASON.
Too hot ...
It's still only July ...!
Are there no trees for shade ...?
SHFF
Hm...?
A vegetable garden ...?
KLATTER
Oops ...
Farming tools lying around ...
Amazing...
RUSTLE
I wonder ...

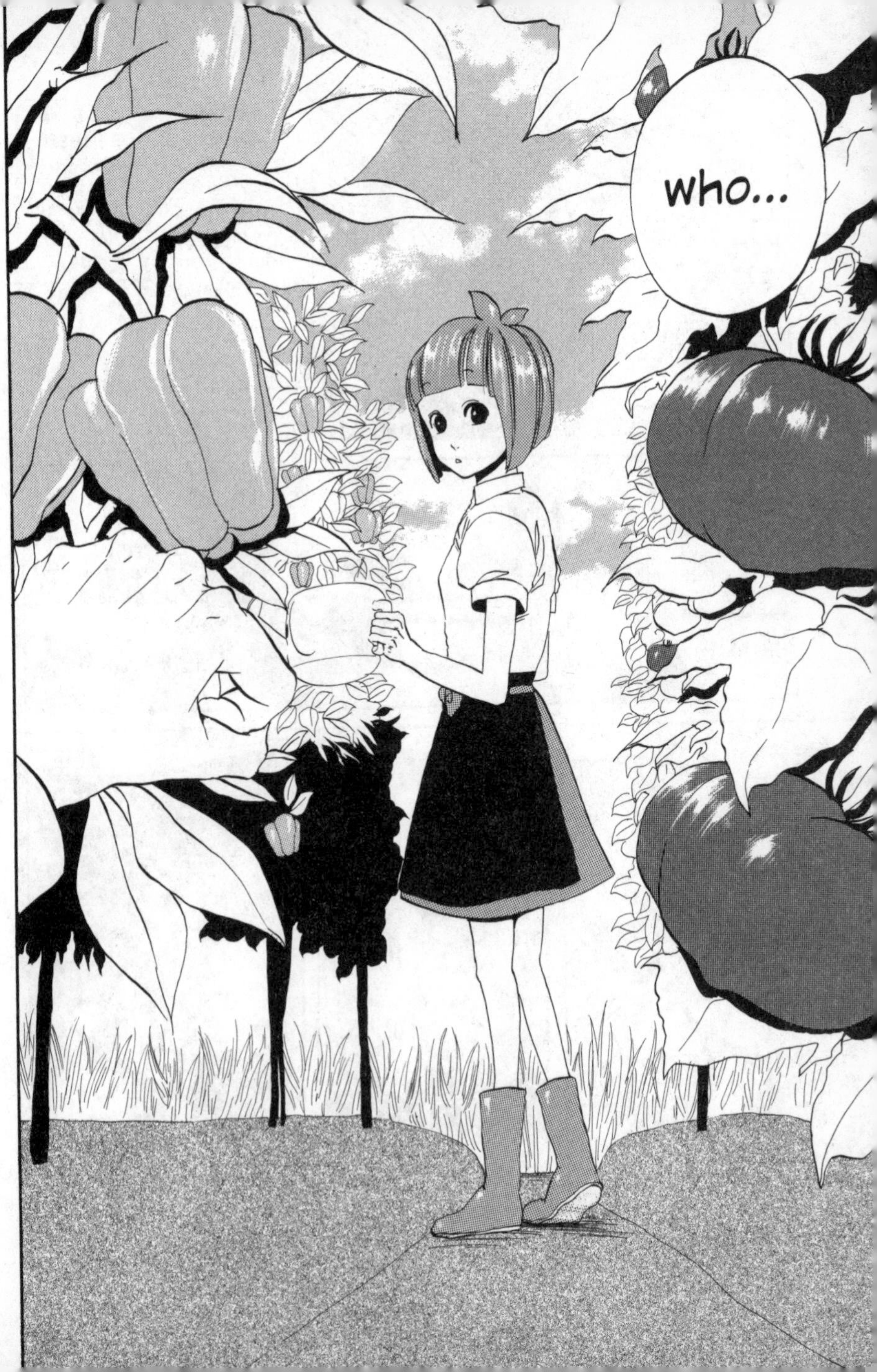
who...

☜ Chapter 36: Greetings in a Vegetable Garden

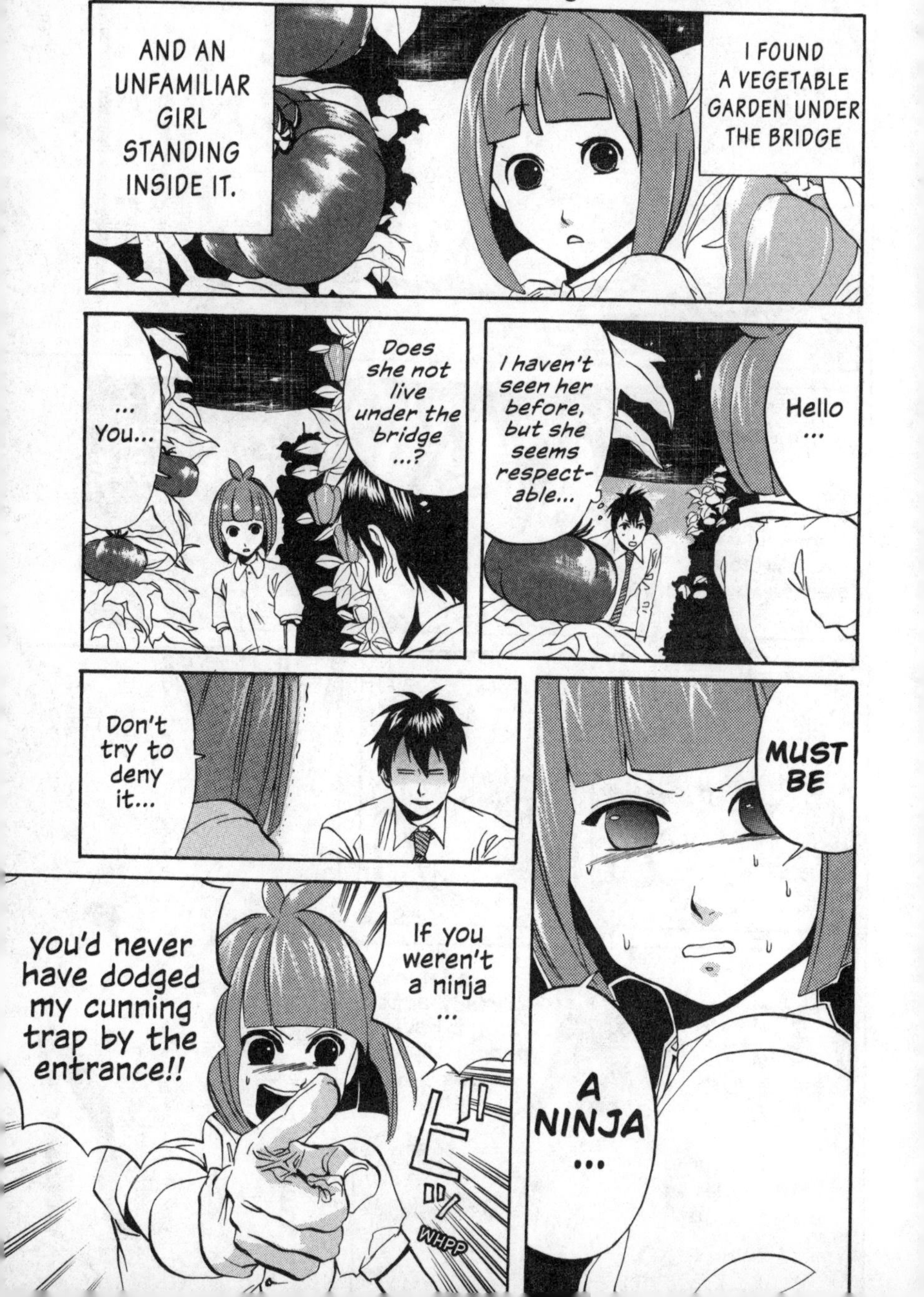
I FOUND A VEGETABLE GARDEN UNDER THE BRIDGE
AND AN UNFAMILIAR GIRL STANDING INSIDE IT.
Hello ...
I haven't seen her before, but she seems respect-able...
Does she not live under the bridge ...?
... You...
MUST BE
A NINJA ...
Don't try to deny it...
If you weren't a ninja ...
you'd never have dodged my cunning trap by the entrance!!
WHPP

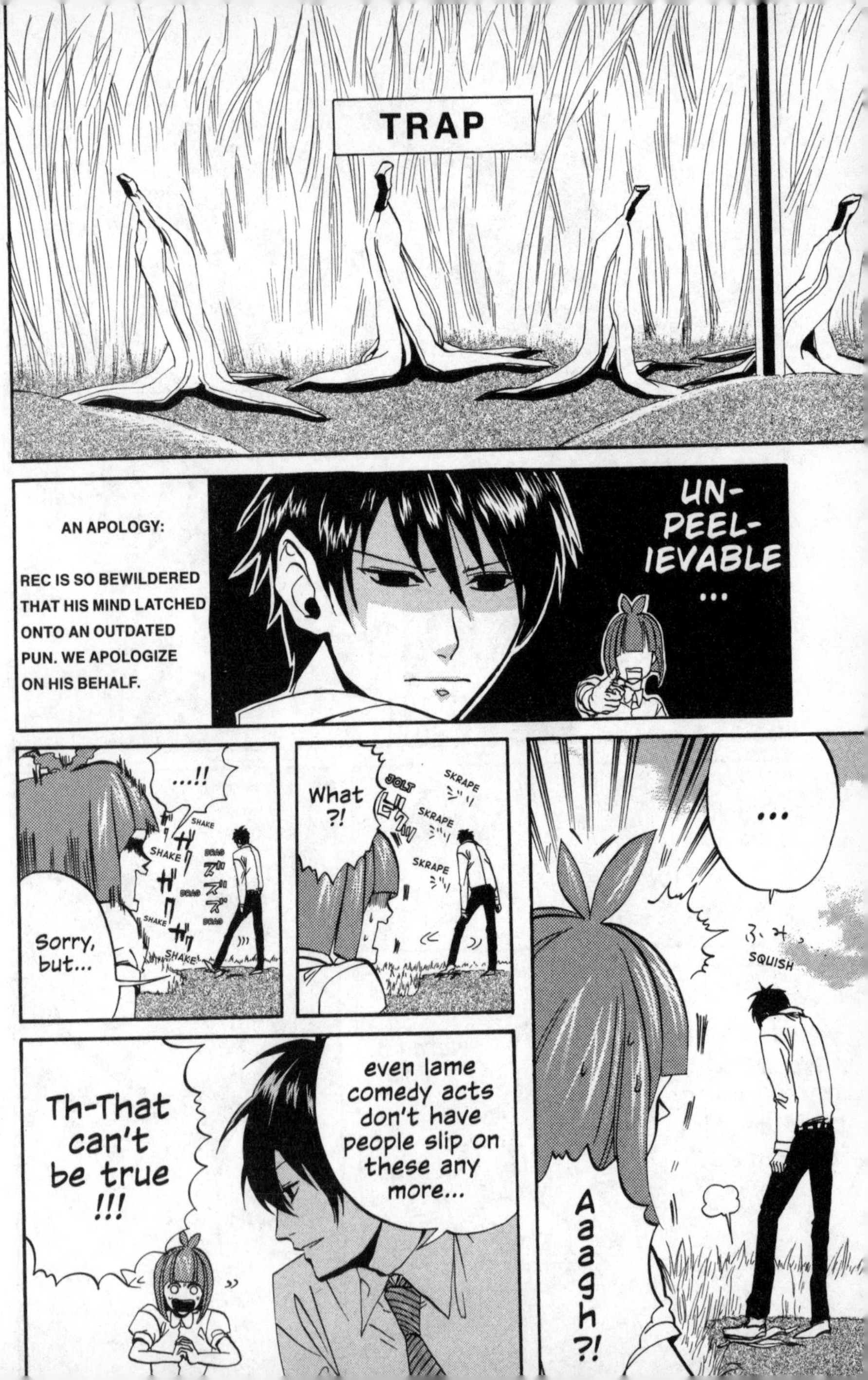

TRAP
UN-PEEL-IEVABLE ...
AN APOLOGY:
REC IS SO BEWILDERED THAT HIS MIND LATCHED ONTO AN OUTDATED PUN. WE APOLOGIZE ON HIS BEHALF.
...
ふみっ
SQUISH
Aaagh?!
What ?!
JOLT
SKRAPE
SKRAPE
SKRAPE
...!!
SHAKE
SHAKE
DRAG
DRAG
DRAG
SHAKE
SHAKE
Sorry, but...
even lame comedy acts don't have people slip on these any more...
Th-That can't be true !!!

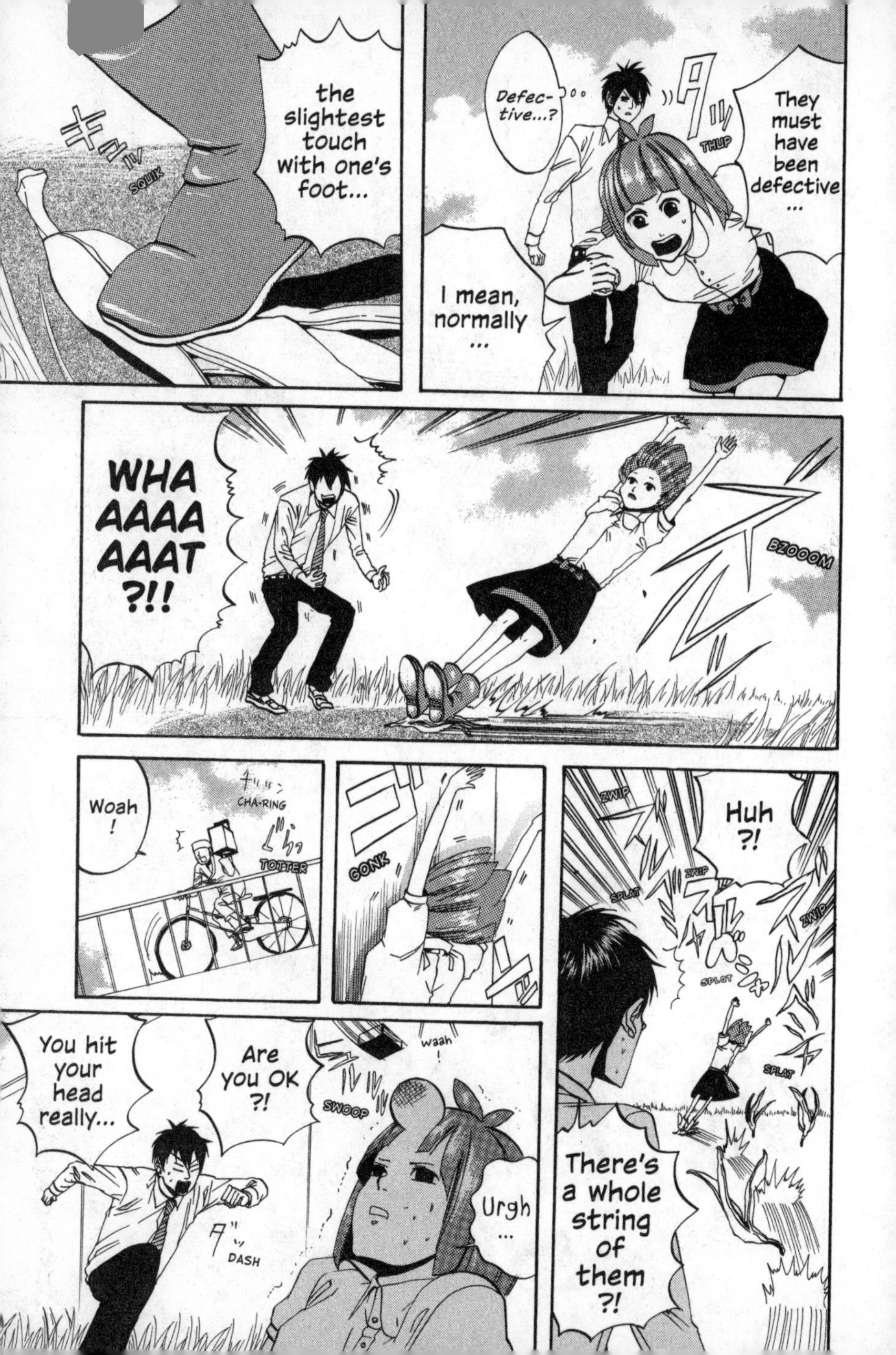
They must have been defective...
Defective...?
THUP
I mean, normally...
the slightest touch with one's foot...
SQUIK
BZOOOM
WHAAAAAAAT?!!
Huh?!
ZWIP
ZWIP
ZWIP
SPLAT
SPLOT
SPLAT
There's a whole string of them?!
GONK
Woah!
CHA-RING
TOTTER
waah!
SWOOP
Urgh...
Are you OK?!
You hit your head really...
DASH

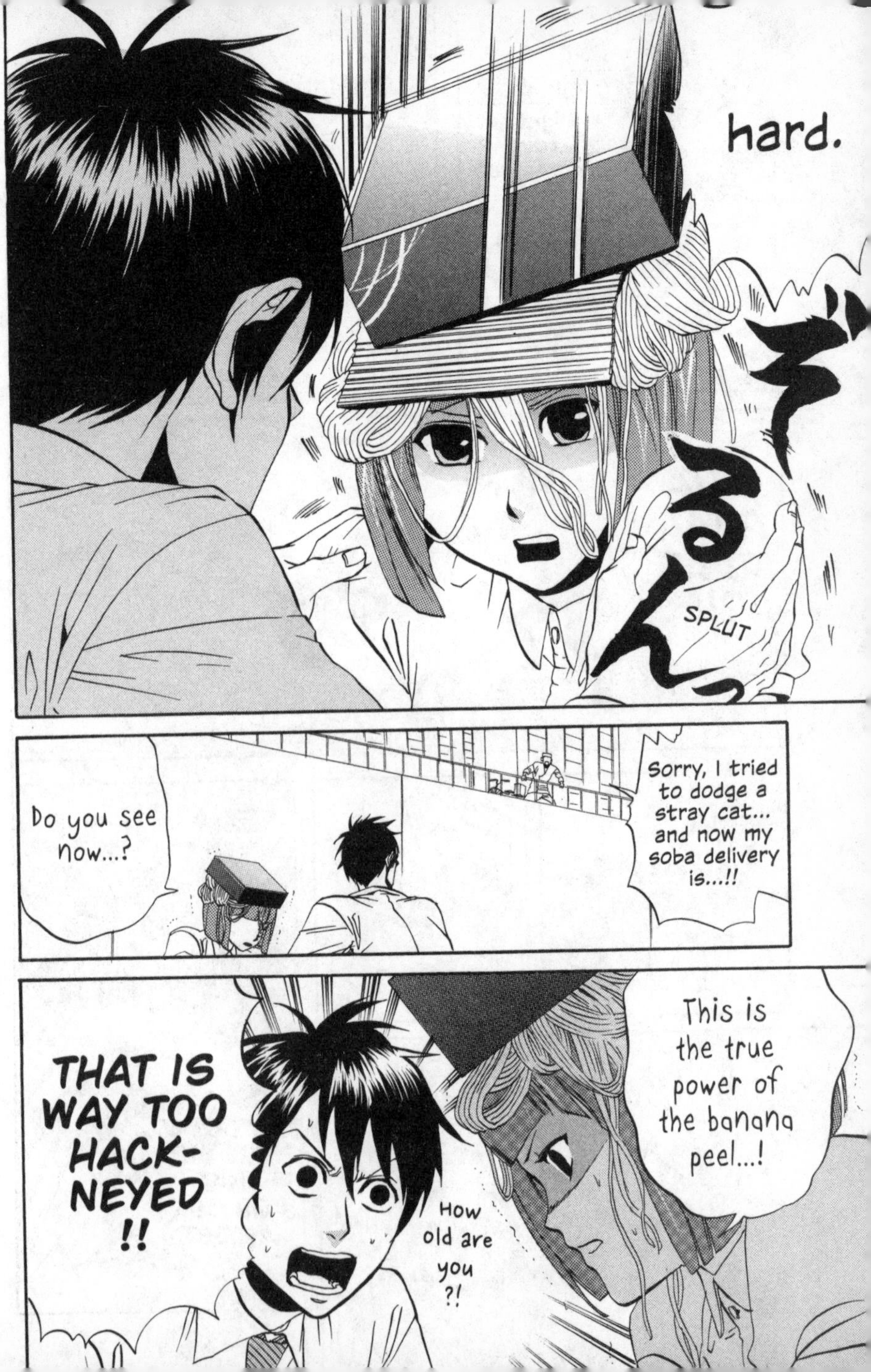
hard.
ずるんっ
SPLUT
Sorry, I tried to dodge a stray cat... and now my soba delivery is...!!
Do you see now...?
This is the true power of the banana peel...!
How old are you ?!
THAT IS WAY TOO HACK-NEYED !!

Chapter 37: Maybe Bell Peppers...

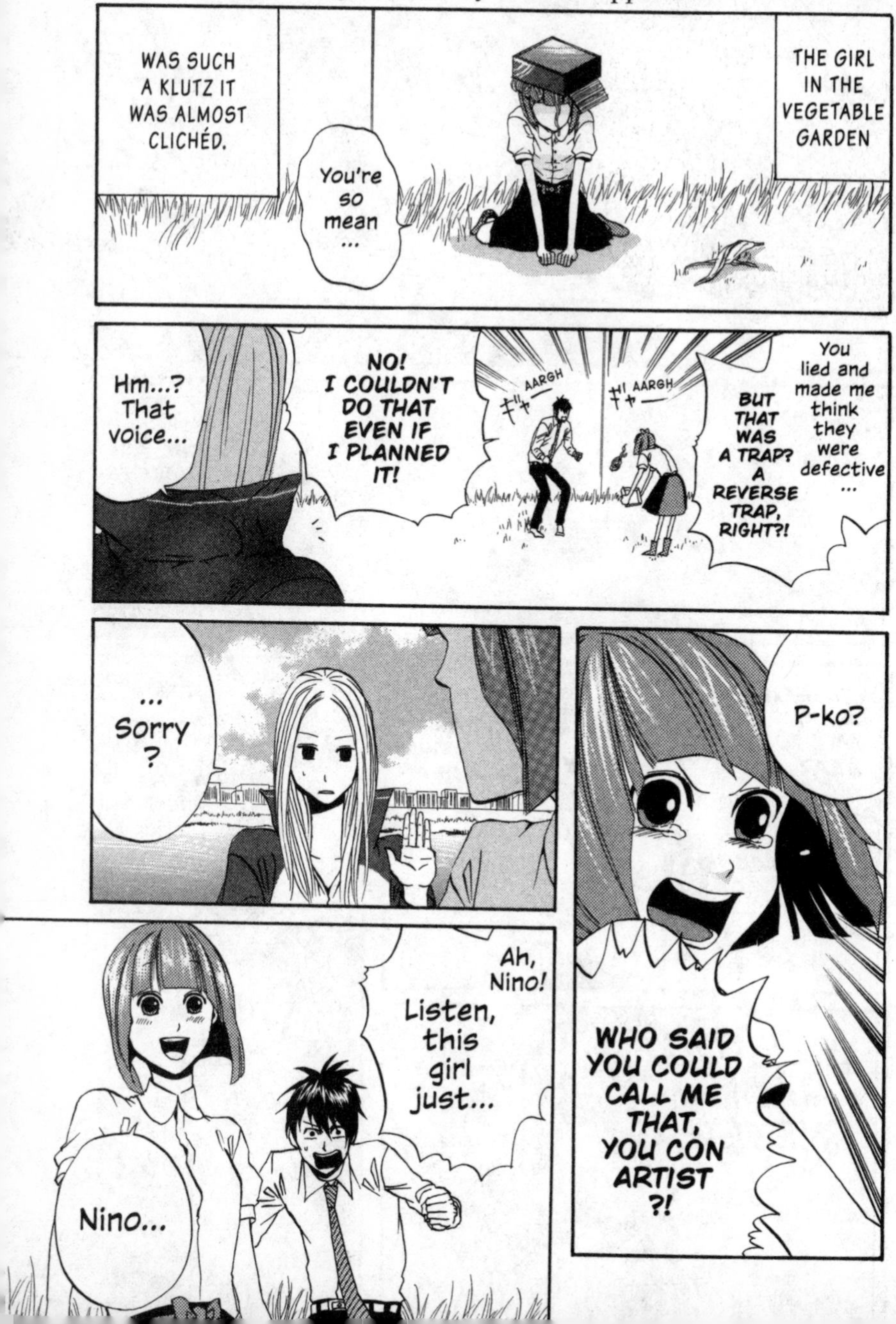
THE GIRL IN THE VEGETABLE GARDEN
WAS SUCH A KLUTZ IT WAS ALMOST CLICHÉD.
You're so mean ...
You lied and made me think they were defective ...
BUT THAT WAS A TRAP? A REVERSE TRAP, RIGHT?!
AARGH
AARGH
NO! I COULDN'T DO THAT EVEN IF I PLANNED IT!
Hm...? That voice...
P-ko?
WHO SAID YOU COULD CALL ME THAT, YOU CON ARTIST ?!
... Sorry ?
Ah, Nino!
Listen, this girl just...
Nino...

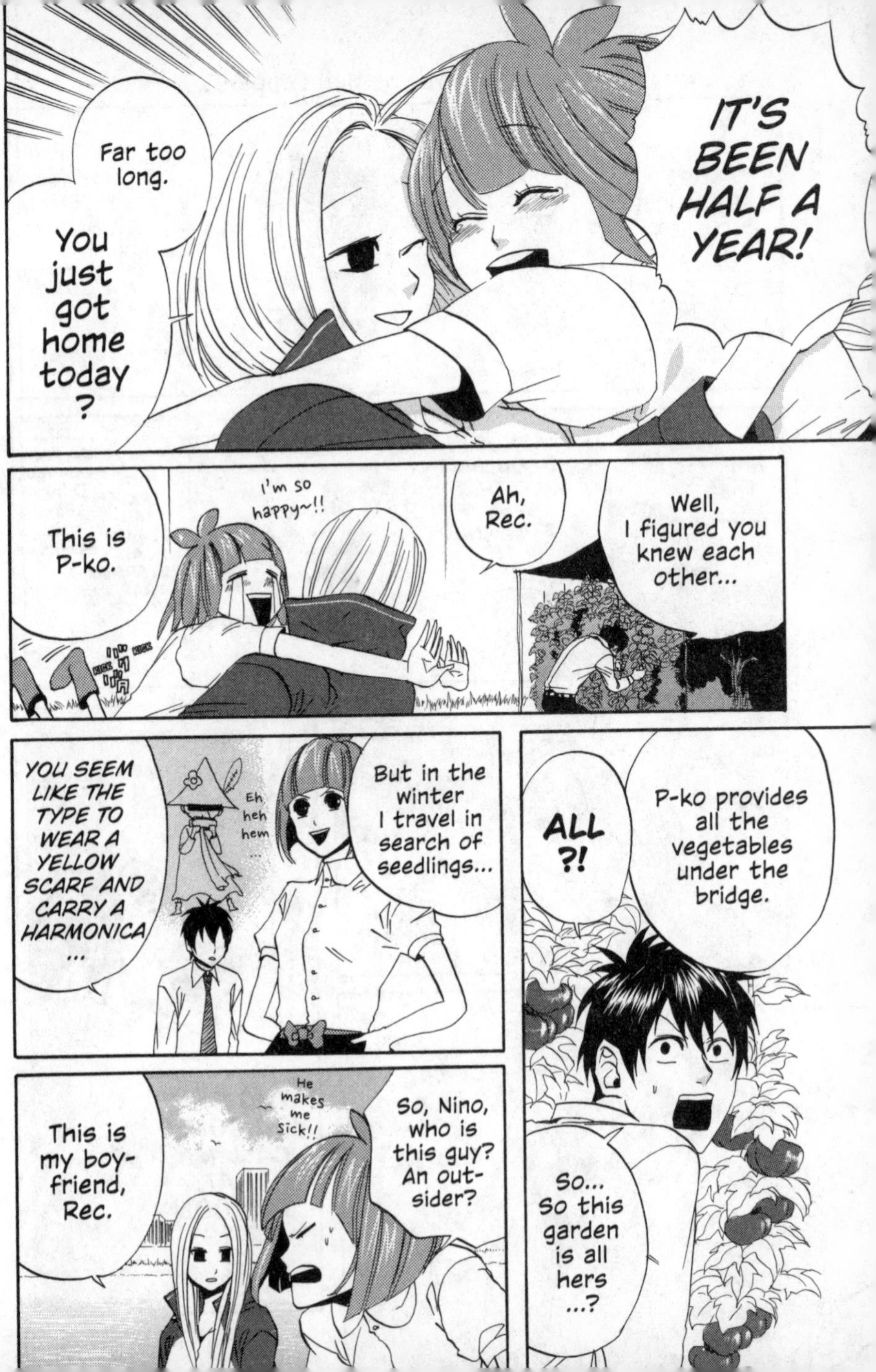
IT'S BEEN HALF A YEAR!
Far too long.
You just got home today?
Well, I figured you knew each other...
Ah, Rec.
I'm so happy~!!
This is P-ko.
P-ko provides all the vegetables under the bridge.
ALL?!
So... So this garden is all hers...?
But in the winter I travel in search of seedlings...
Eh heh hem...
YOU SEEM LIKE THE TYPE TO WEAR A YELLOW SCARF AND CARRY A HARMONICA...
So, Nino, who is this guy? An outsider?
He makes me sick!!
This is my boy-friend, Rec.

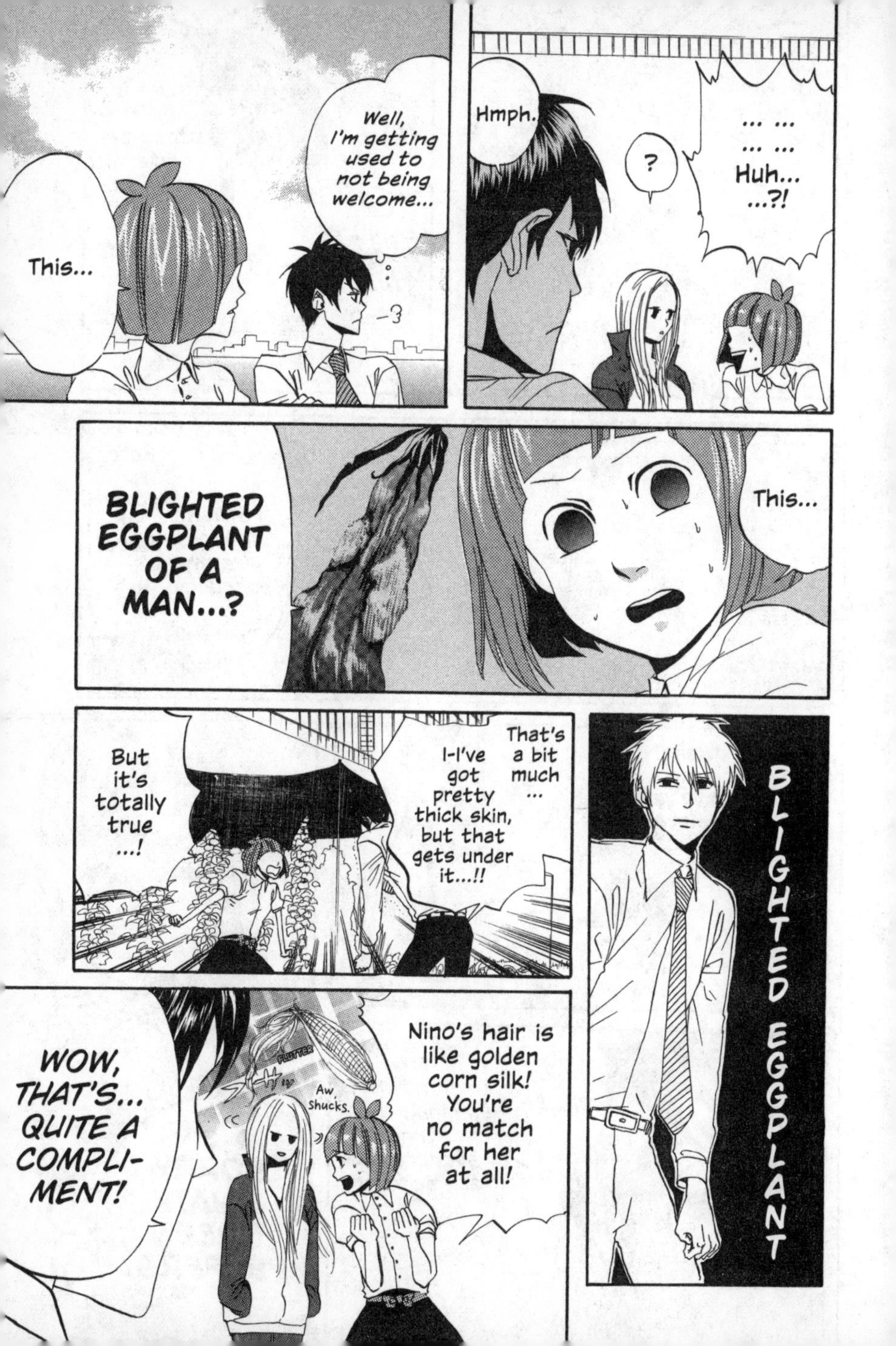
... ... Huh... ...?!
?
Hmph.
Well, I'm getting used to not being welcome...
This...
This...
BLIGHTED EGGPLANT OF A MAN...?
BLIGHTED EGGPLANT
That's a bit much ...
I-I've got pretty thick skin, but that gets under it...!!
But it's totally true ...!
Nino's hair is like golden corn silk! You're no match for her at all!
Aw, Shucks.
FLUTTER
WOW, THAT'S... QUITE A COMPLIMENT!

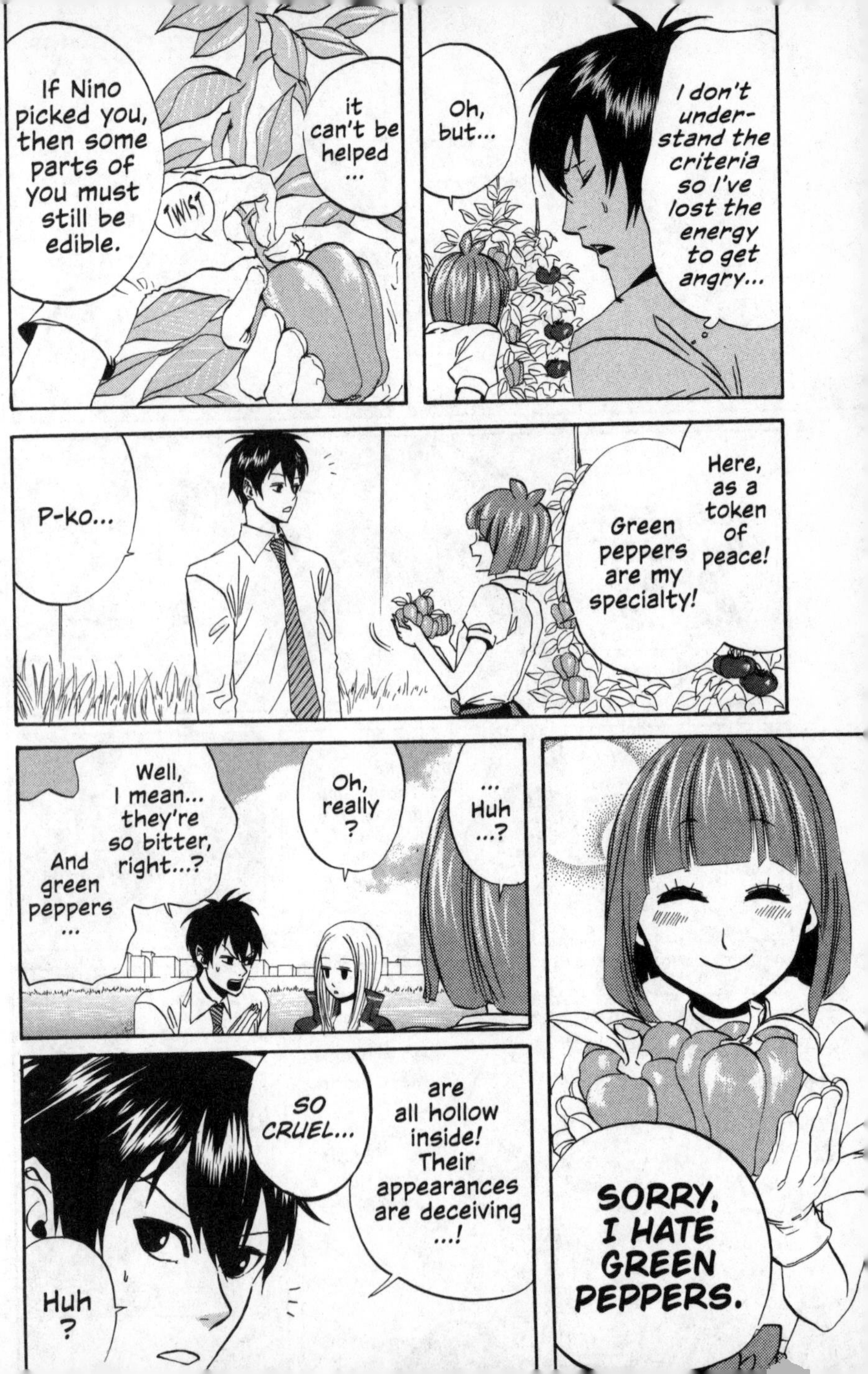
I don't under-stand the criteria so I've lost the energy to get angry...
Oh, but...
it can't be helped ...
TWIST
If Nino picked you, then some parts of you must still be edible.
Here, as a token of peace!
Green peppers are my specialty!
P-ko...
SORRY, I HATE GREEN PEPPERS.
... Huh ...?
Oh, really ?
Well, I mean... they're so bitter, right...?
And green peppers ...
are all hollow inside! Their appearances are deceiving ...!
SO CRUEL...
Huh ?

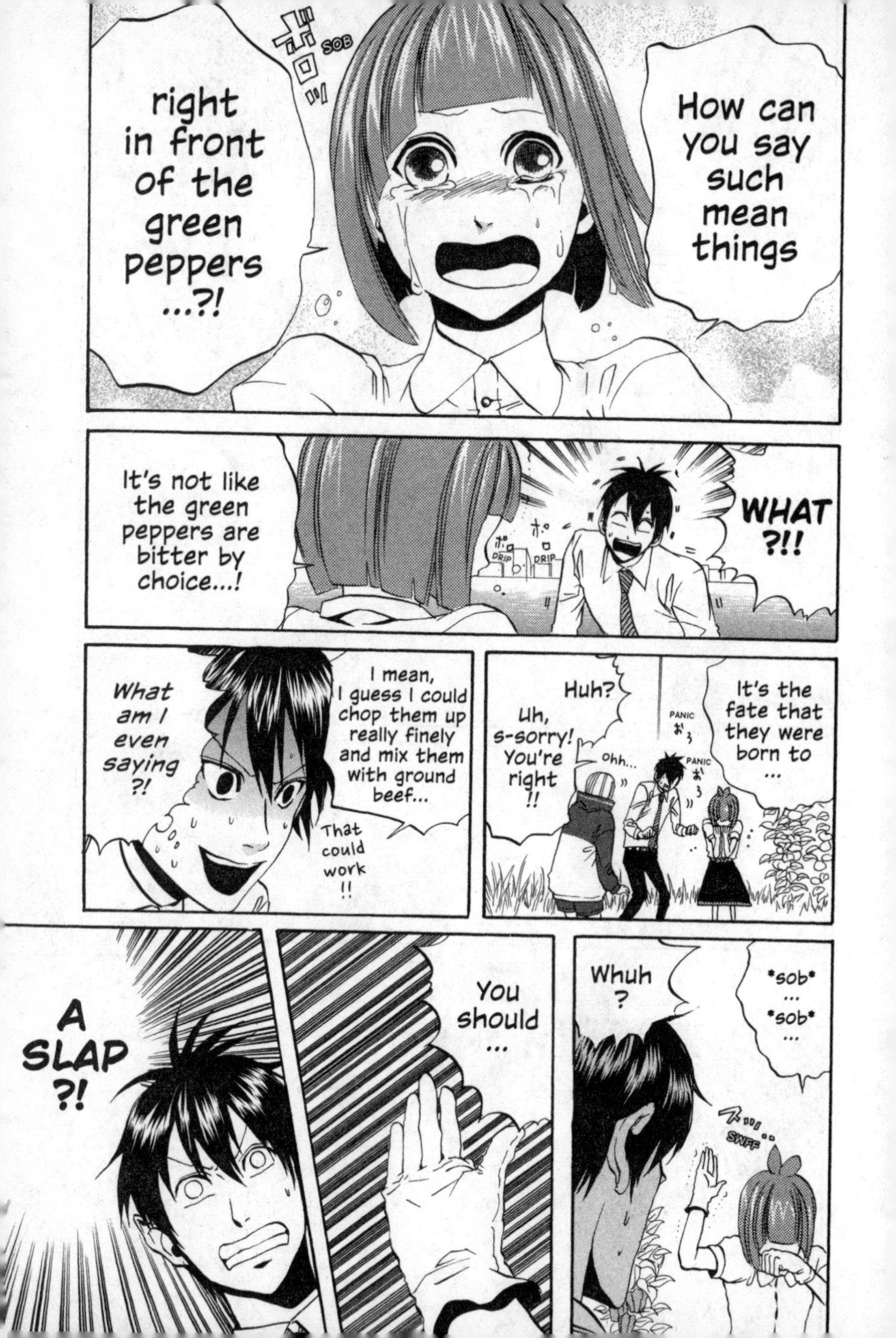
How can you say such mean things
SOB
right in front of the green peppers ...?!
WHAT ?!!
DRIP
DRIP
It's not like the green peppers are bitter by choice...!
It's the fate that they were born to ...
Huh?
PANIC
PANIC
Uh, s-sorry! You're right !!
Ohh...
I mean, I guess I could chop them up really finely and mix them with ground beef...
What am I even saying ?!
That could work !!
sob ... *sob* ...
Whuh ?
SWFF
You should ...
A SLAP ?!

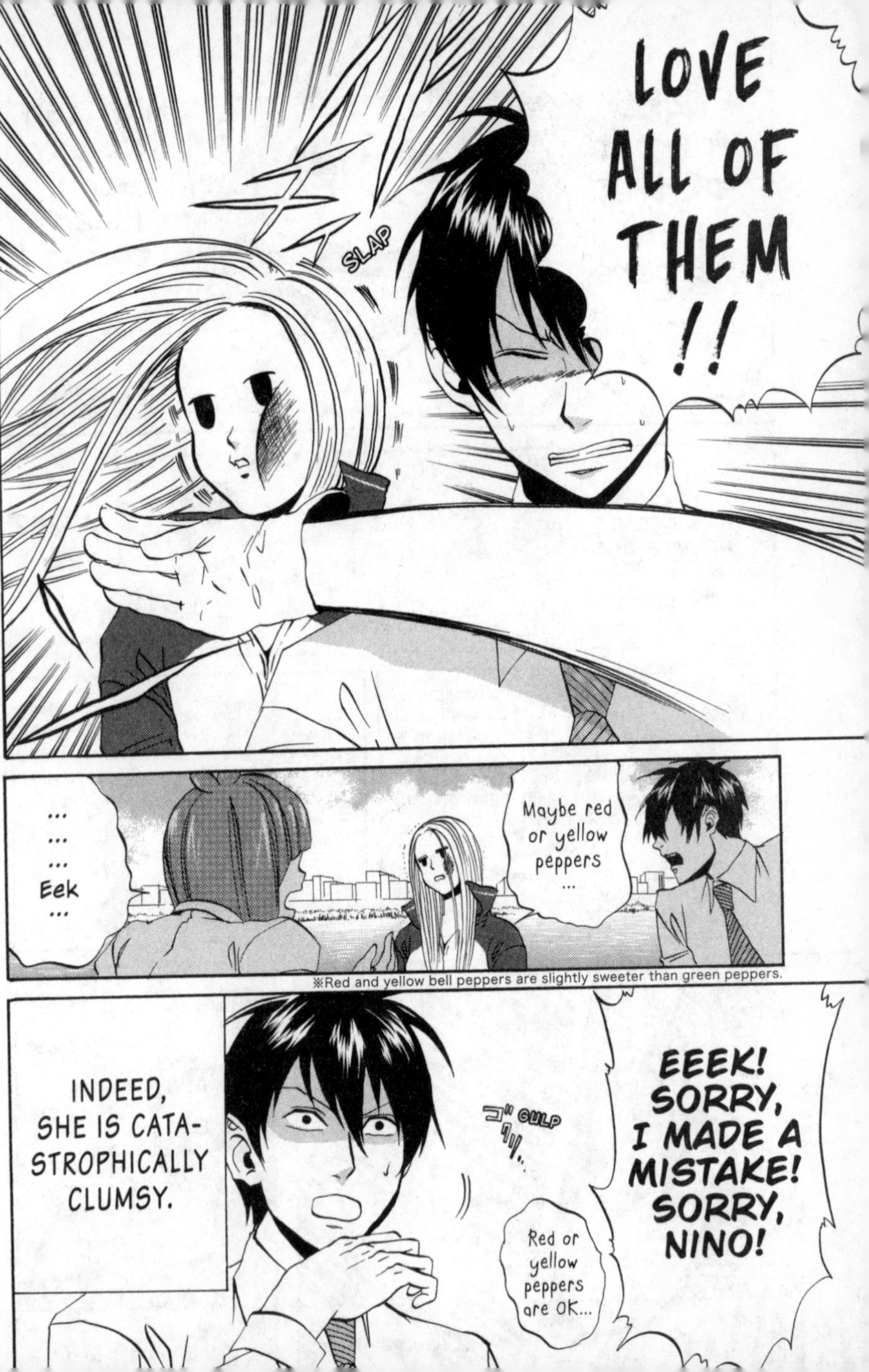
LOVE ALL OF THEM!!
SLAP
Maybe red or yellow peppers ...
... ... Eek ...
EEEK! SORRY, I MADE A MISTAKE! SORRY, NINO!
Red or yellow peppers are OK...
GULP
INDEED, SHE IS CATA-STROPHICALLY CLUMSY.
※Red and yellow bell peppers are slightly sweeter than green peppers.

Chapter 38: For You

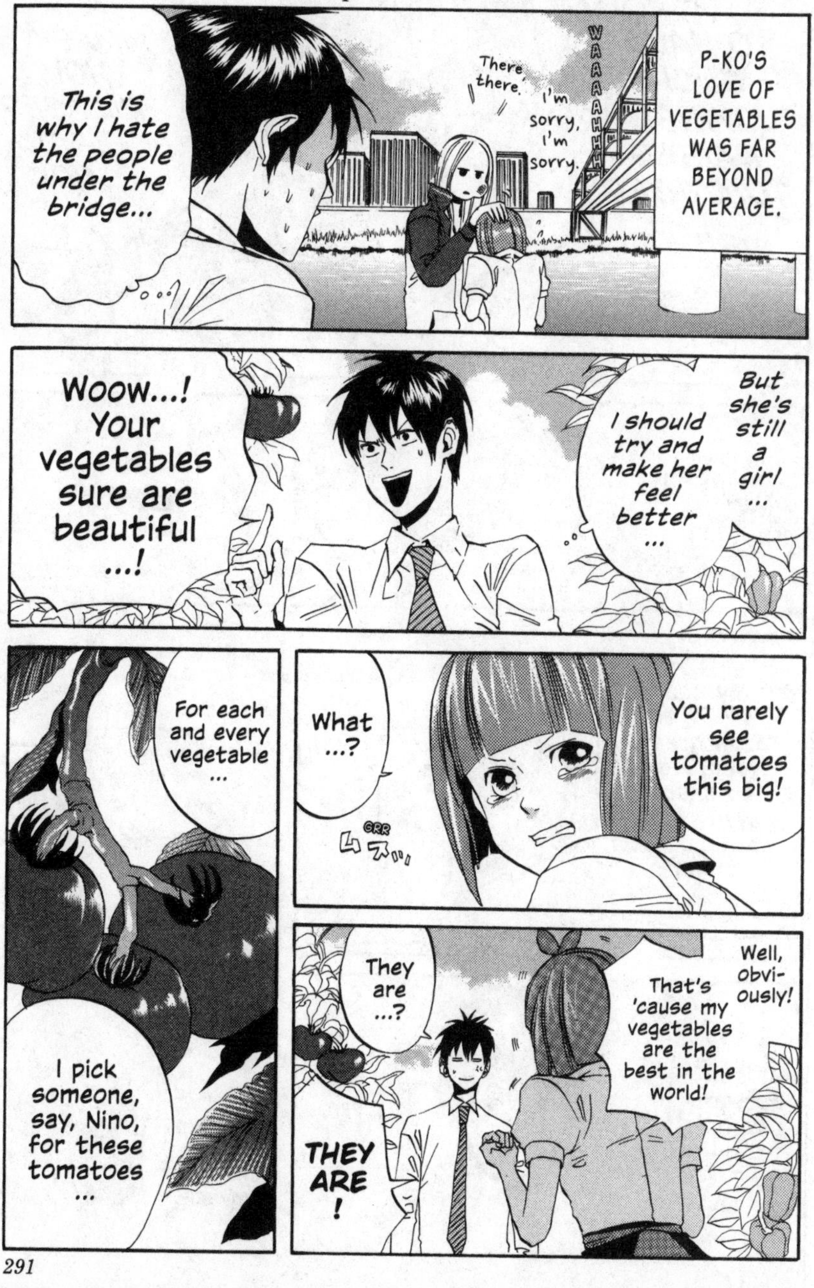
P-KO'S LOVE OF VEGETABLES WAS FAR BEYOND AVERAGE.
WAAAAAHHH
There there.
I'm sorry, I'm sorry.
This is why I hate the people under the bridge...
But she's still a girl...
I should try and make her feel better...
Woow...! Your vegetables sure are beautiful...!
You rarely see tomatoes this big!
What...?
GRR
Well, obvi-ously!
That's 'cause my vegetables are the best in the world!
They are...?
THEY ARE!
For each and every vegetable...
I pick someone, say, Nino, for these tomatoes...

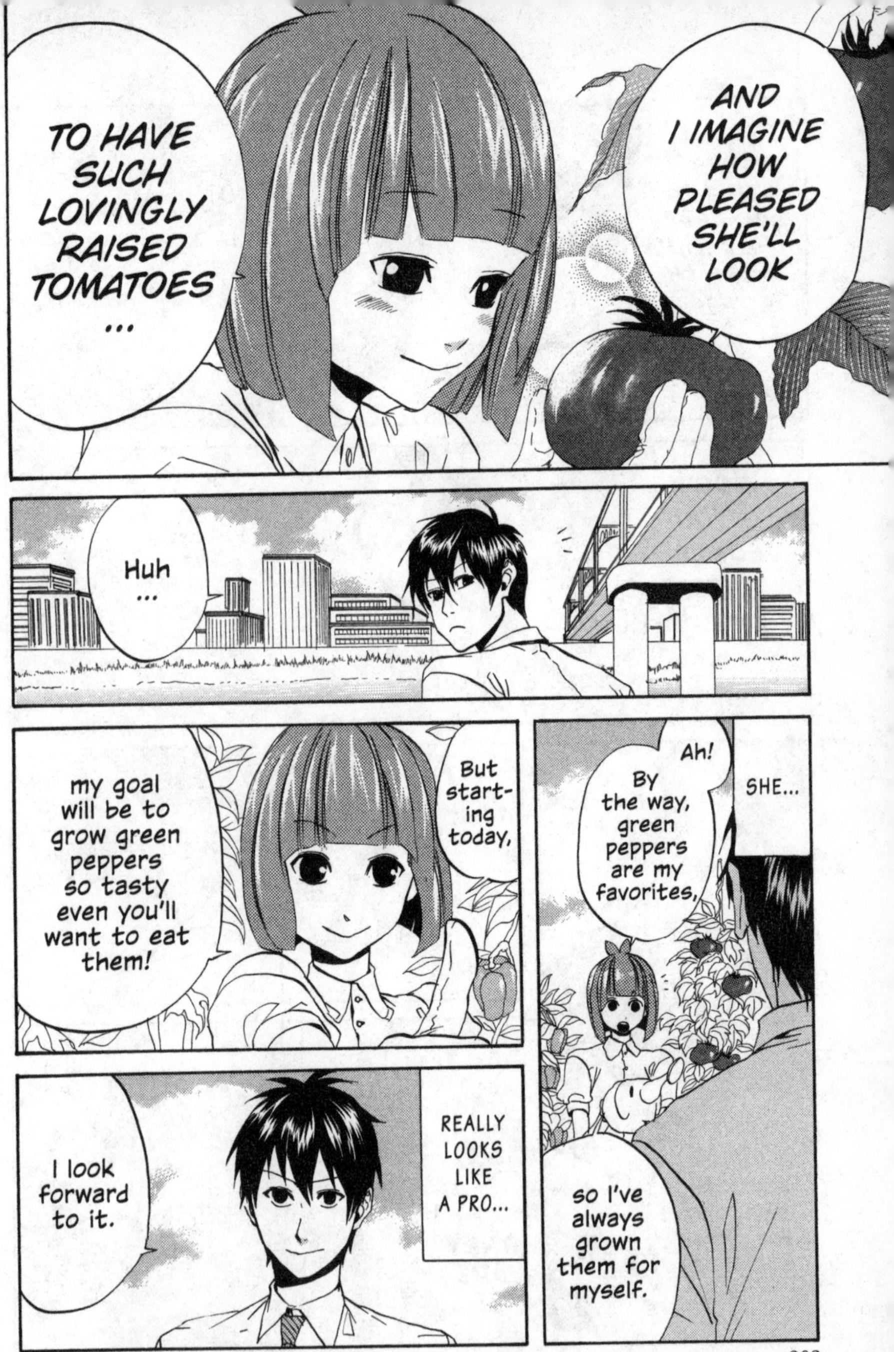
TO HAVE SUCH LOVINGLY RAISED TOMATOES ...
AND I IMAGINE HOW PLEASED SHE'LL LOOK
Huh ...
SHE...
Ah! By the way, green peppers are my favorites,
so I've always grown them for myself.
But start-ing today,
my goal will be to grow green peppers so tasty even you'll want to eat them!
REALLY LOOKS LIKE A PRO...
I look forward to it.

She picks which vegetables to grow in this garden according to what the people who live under the bridge like...

Oh, I see...

Hm...?

That explains why there's a little bit of so many varieties...

ZHAAAA

STAAAARE...!!

Huh...?

BUT IT SEEMS LIKE THERE ARE QUITE A NUMBER OF CUCUMBERS...

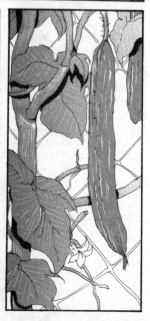

...?

What's she staring at...

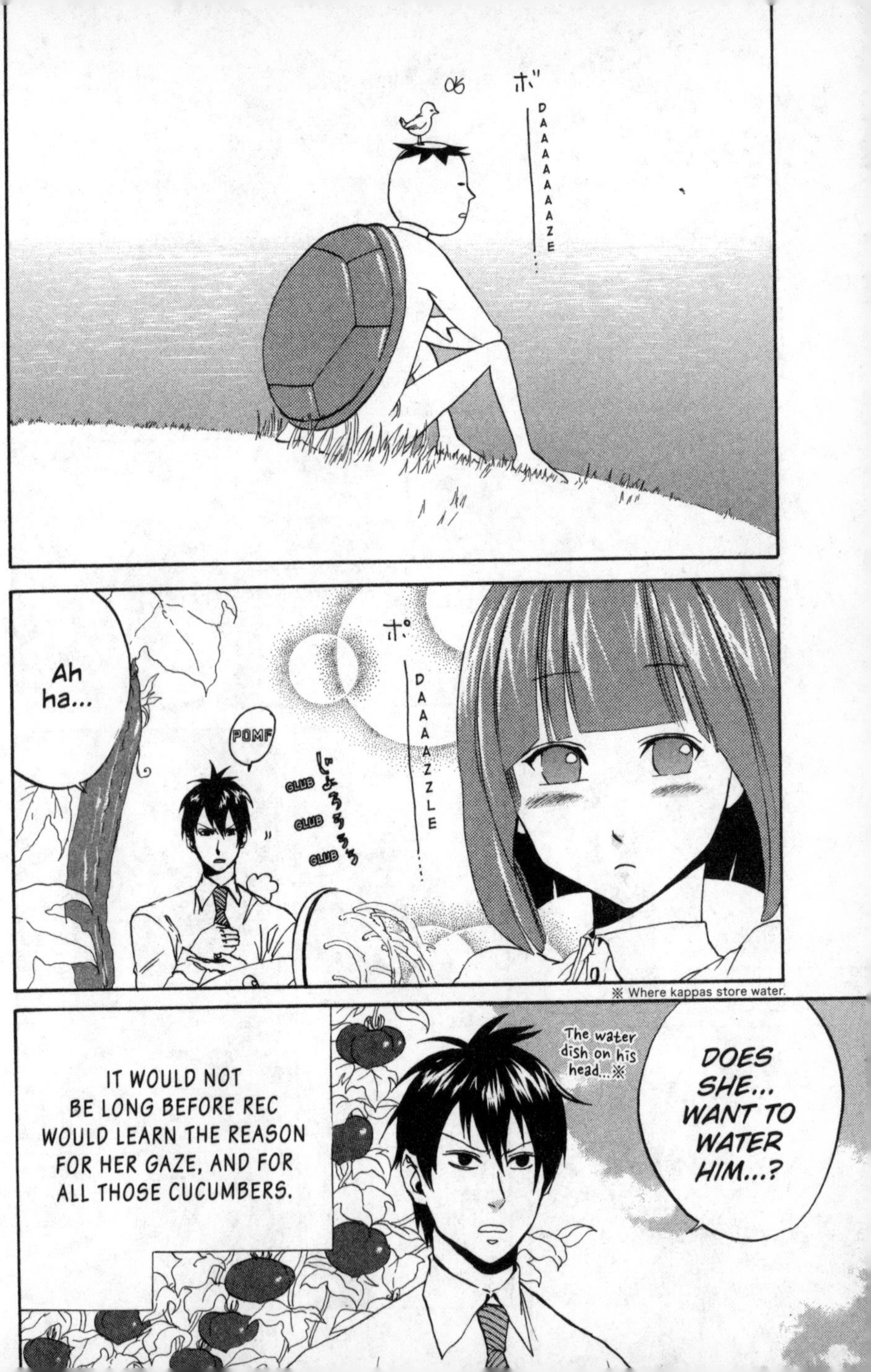

ボ
DAAAAAAAAZE...
ポ
DAAAAZZLE...
じょろろろ
CLUB CLUB CLUB
POMF
Ah ha...
DOES SHE... WANT TO WATER HIM...?
The water dish on his head...※
IT WOULD NOT BE LONG BEFORE REC WOULD LEARN THE REASON FOR HER GAZE, AND FOR ALL THOSE CUCUMBERS.

※ Where kappas store water.

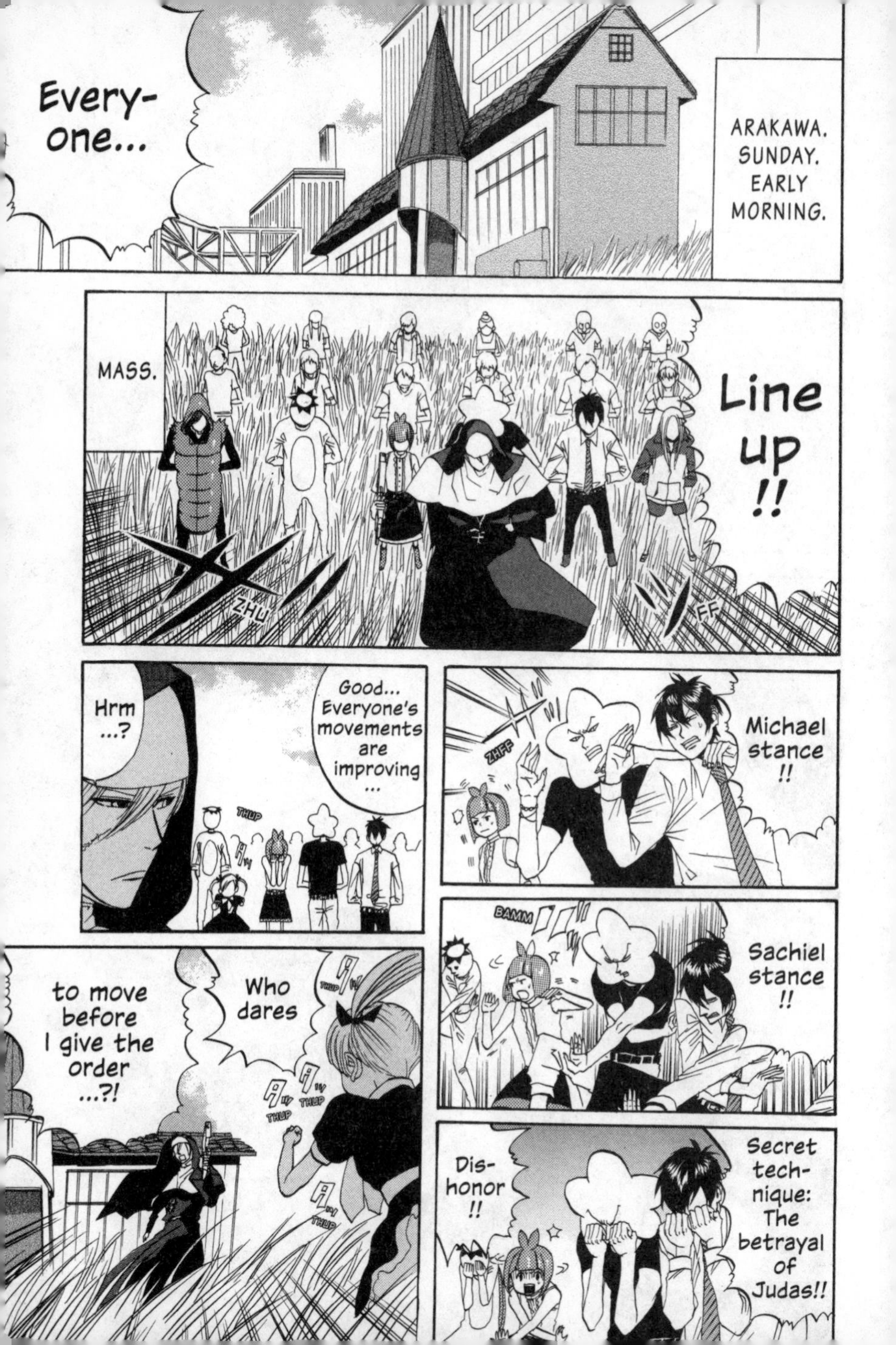
ARAKAWA. SUNDAY. EARLY MORNING.
Every-one...
Line up!!
MASS.
FF
ZHU
Michael stance!!
ZHFF
Good... Everyone's movements are improving...
Hrm...?
THUP
Sachiel stance!!
BAMM
Secret tech-nique: The betrayal of Judas!!
Dis-honor!!
Who dares
to move before I give the order...?!
THUP
THUP
THUP
THUP

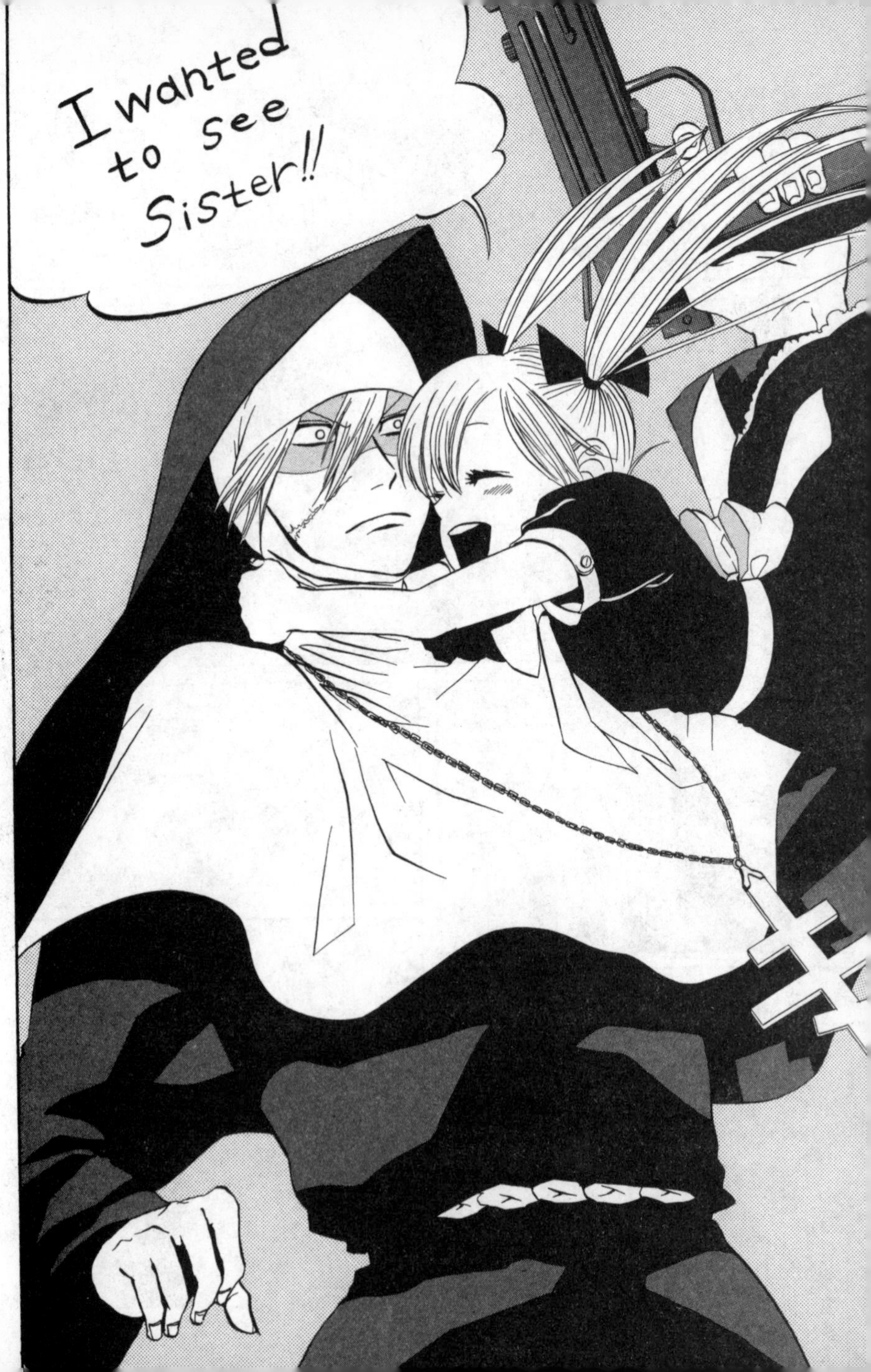
I wanted to see Sister!!

Chapter 39: Stella

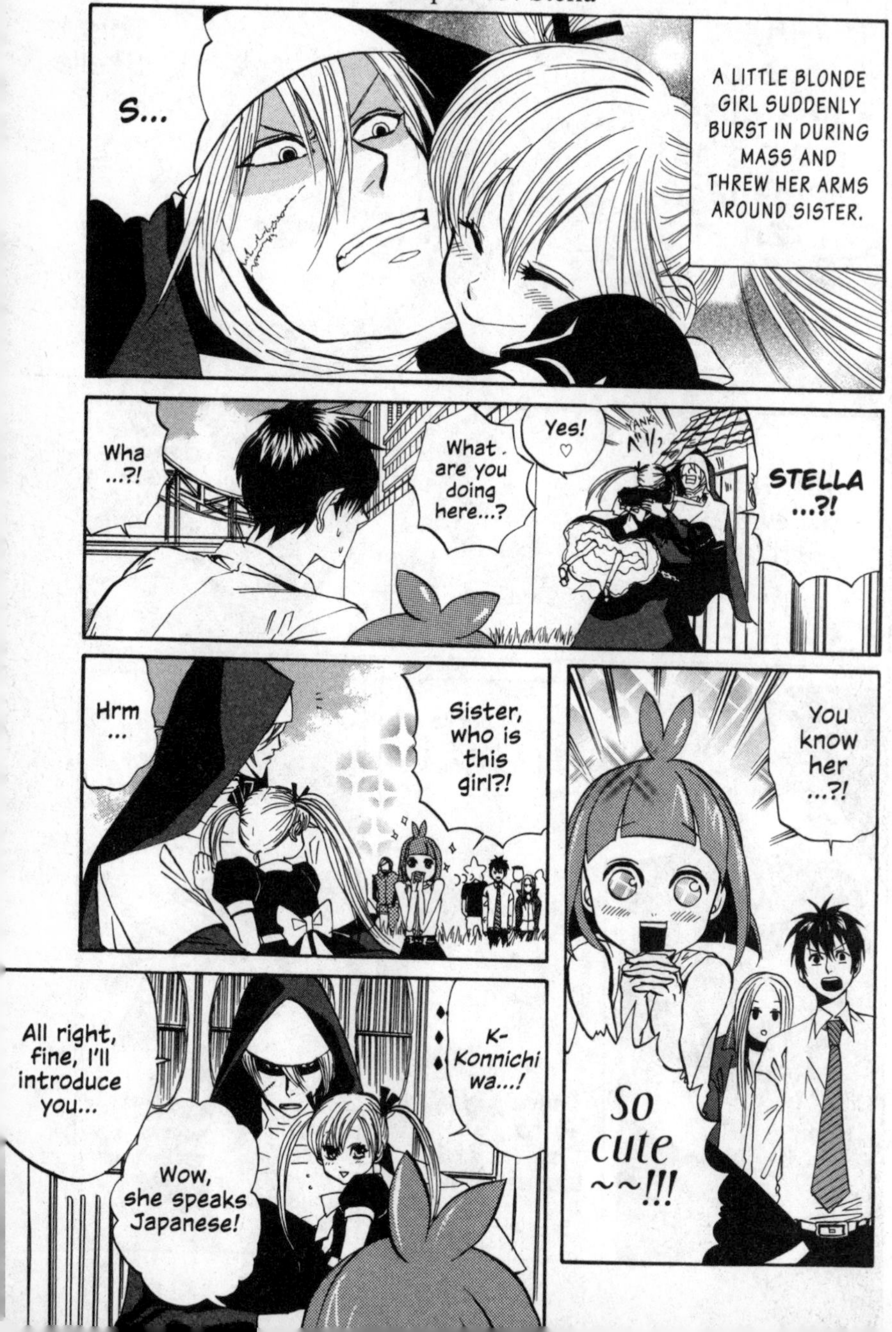
A LITTLE BLONDE GIRL SUDDENLY BURST IN DURING MASS AND THREW HER ARMS AROUND SISTER.
S...
STELLA ...?!
YANK
Yes! ♡
What are you doing here...?
Wha ...?!
You know her ...?!
So cute ~~!!!
Sister, who is this girl?!
Hrm ...
K-Konnichi wa...!
All right, fine, I'll introduce you...
Wow, she speaks Japanese!

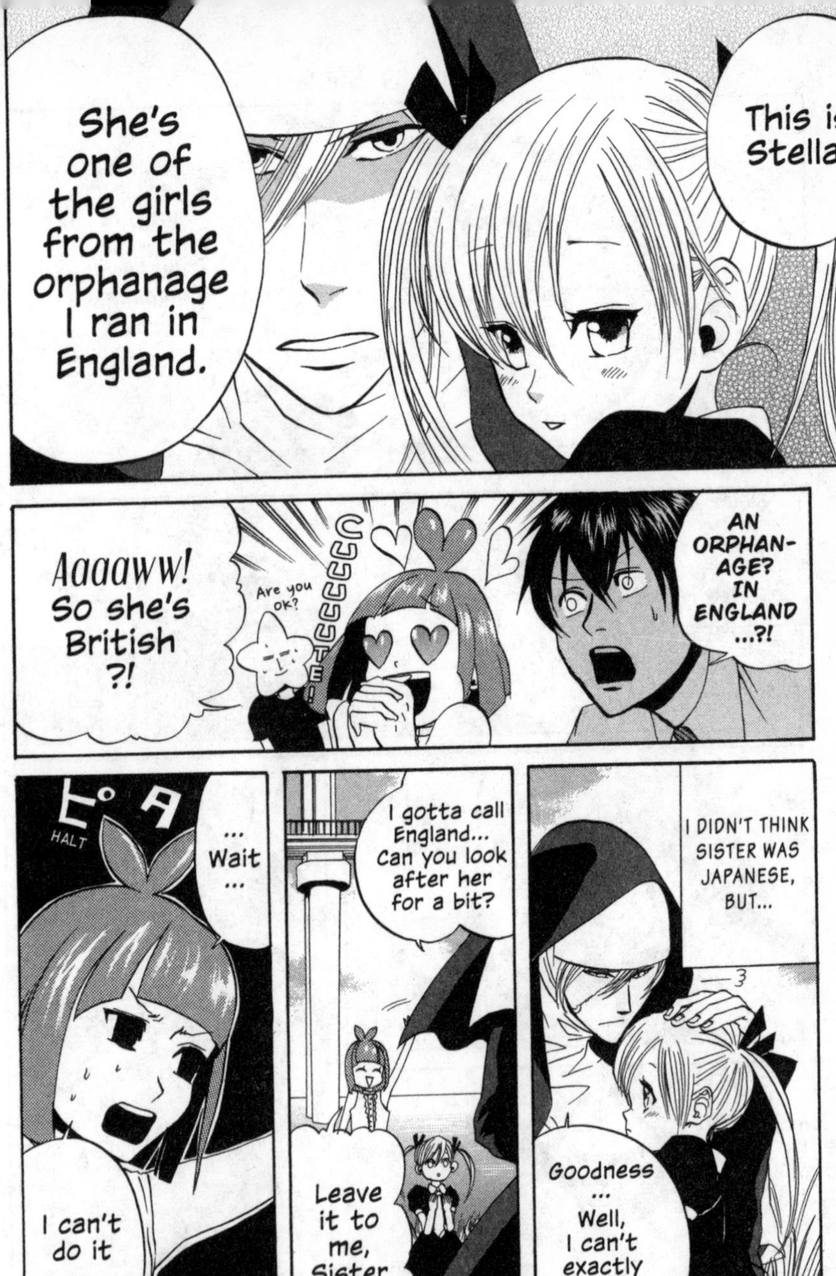
This is Stella.
She's one of the girls from the orphanage I ran in England.
AN ORPHAN-AGE? IN ENGLAND ...?!
CUUUUUUTE!
Are you ok?
Aaaaww! So she's British ?!
I DIDN'T THINK SISTER WAS JAPANESE, BUT...
Goodness ... Well, I can't exactly send you away...
I gotta call England... Can you look after her for a bit?
Leave it to me, Sister !
ピタ
HALT
... Wait ...
I can't do it ...

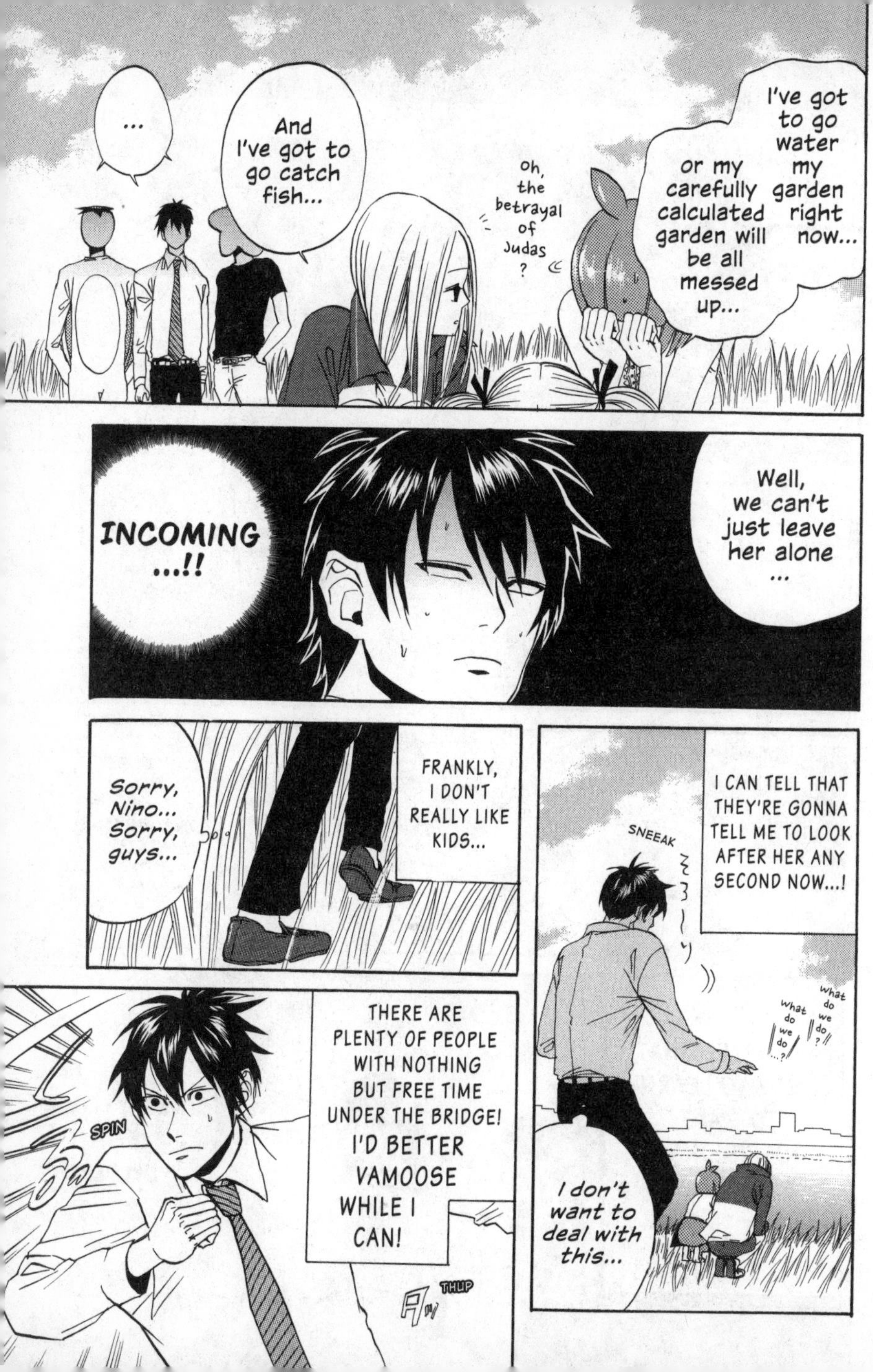
I've got to go water my garden right now... or my carefully calculated garden will be all messed up...
Oh, the betrayal of Judas?
And I've got to go catch fish...
...
Well, we can't just leave her alone...
INCOMING...!!
I CAN TELL THAT THEY'RE GONNA TELL ME TO LOOK AFTER HER ANY SECOND NOW...!
SNEEAK
what do we do?
what do we do...?
I don't want to deal with this...
FRANKLY, I DON'T REALLY LIKE KIDS...
Sorry, Nino... Sorry, guys...
THERE ARE PLENTY OF PEOPLE WITH NOTHING BUT FREE TIME UNDER THE BRIDGE! I'D BETTER VAMOOSE WHILE I CAN!
SPIN
THUP

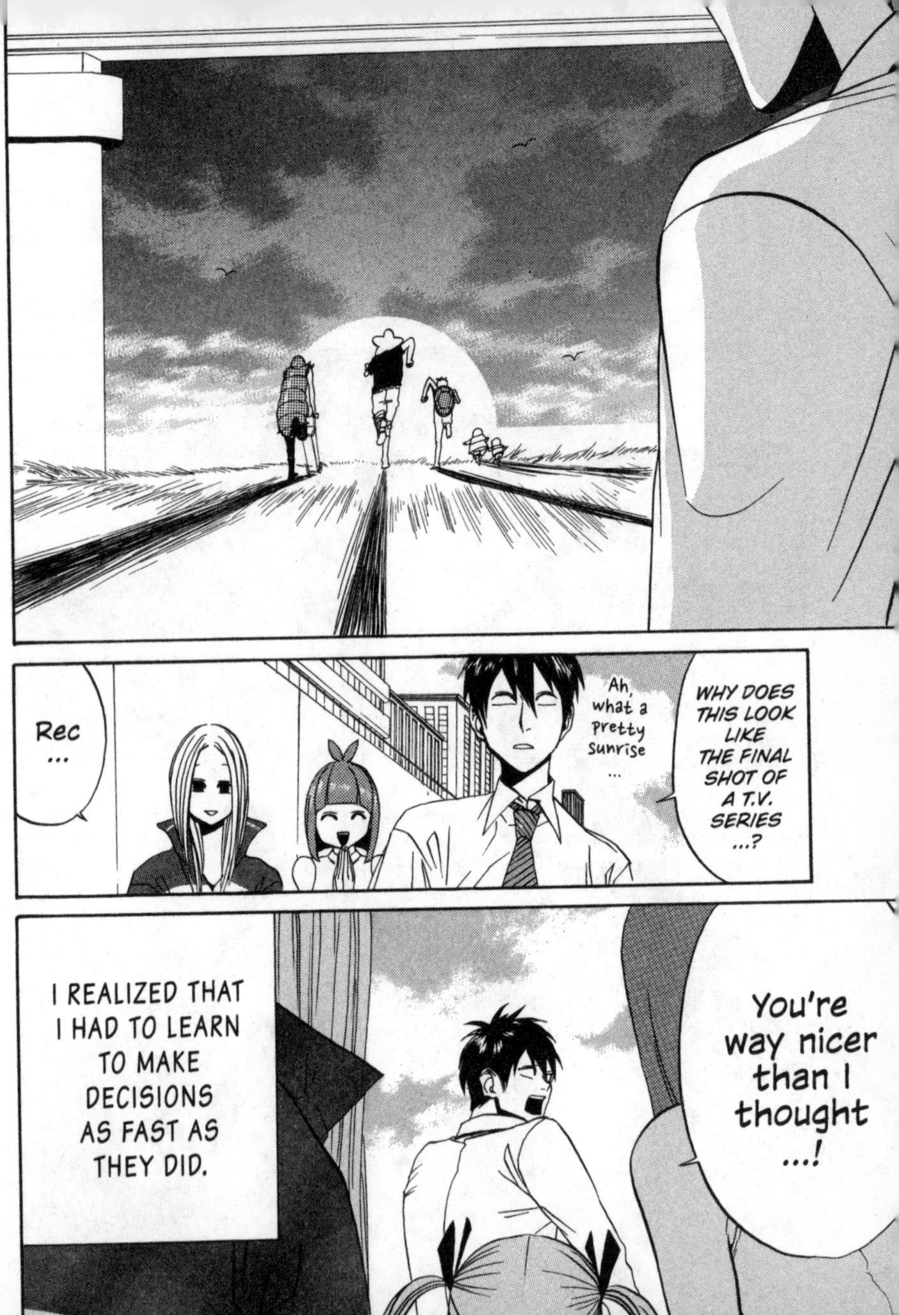
WHY DOES THIS LOOK LIKE THE FINAL SHOT OF A T.V. SERIES ...?
Ah, what a pretty sunrise ...
Rec ...
You're way nicer than I thought ...!
I REALIZED THAT I HAD TO LEARN TO MAKE DECISIONS AS FAST AS THEY DID.

Chapter 40: Let's Play!

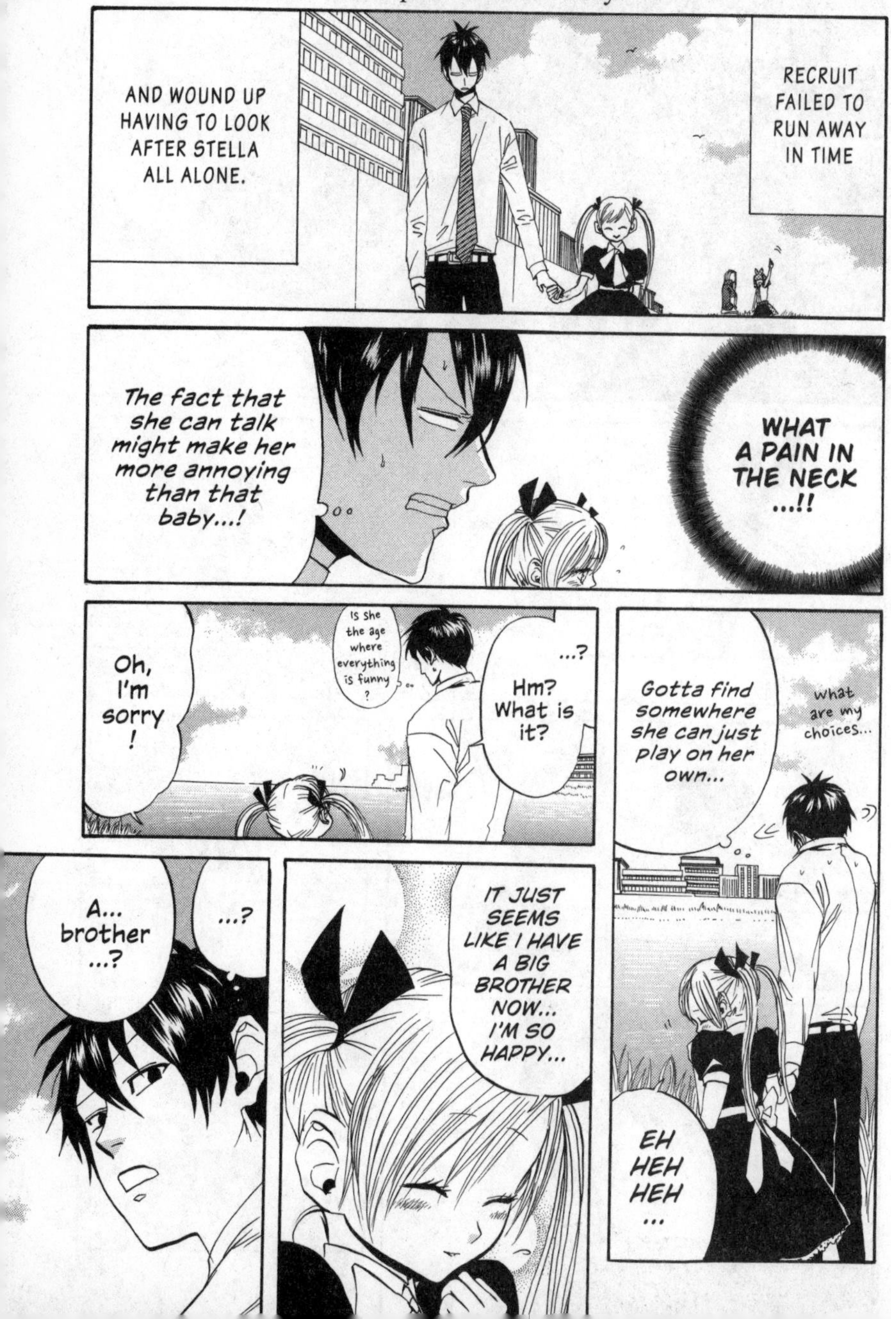
RECRUIT FAILED TO RUN AWAY IN TIME
AND WOUND UP HAVING TO LOOK AFTER STELLA ALL ALONE.
WHAT A PAIN IN THE NECK ...!!
The fact that she can talk might make her more annoying than that baby...!
what are my choices...
Gotta find somewhere she can just play on her own...
EH HEH HEH ...
...? Hm? What is it?
Is she the age where everything is funny?
Oh, I'm sorry!
IT JUST SEEMS LIKE I HAVE A BIG BROTHER NOW... I'M SO HAPPY...
...?
A... brother ...?

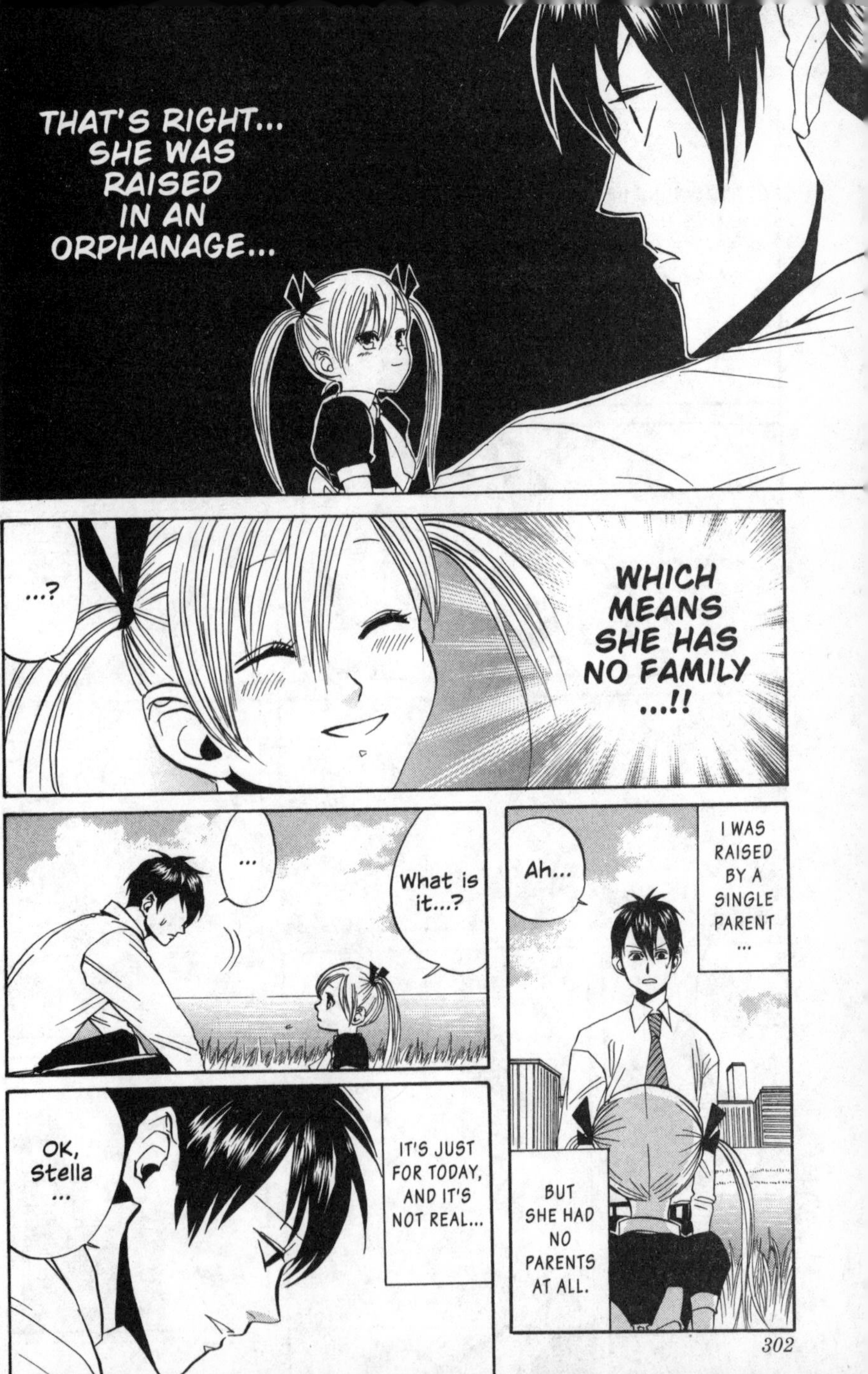
THAT'S RIGHT... SHE WAS RAISED IN AN ORPHANAGE...
WHICH MEANS SHE HAS NO FAMILY ...!!
...?
I WAS RAISED BY A SINGLE PARENT ...
Ah...
BUT SHE HAD NO PARENTS AT ALL.
What is it...?
...
IT'S JUST FOR TODAY, AND IT'S NOT REAL...
OK, Stella ...

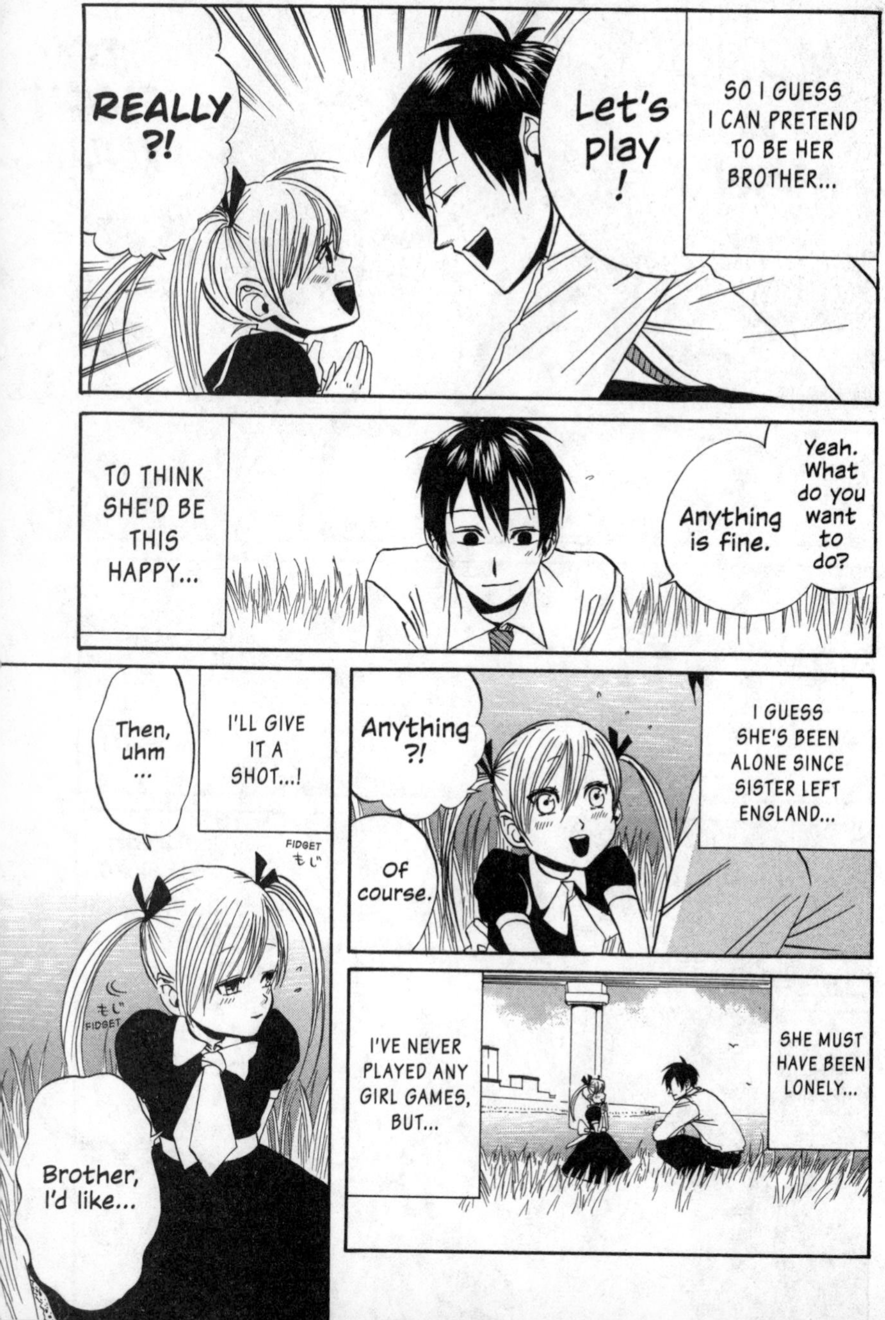
SO I GUESS I CAN PRETEND TO BE HER BROTHER...
Let's play!
REALLY?!
Yeah. What do you want to do?
Anything is fine.
TO THINK SHE'D BE THIS HAPPY...
I GUESS SHE'S BEEN ALONE SINCE SISTER LEFT ENGLAND...
Anything?!
Of course.
SHE MUST HAVE BEEN LONELY...
I'VE NEVER PLAYED ANY GIRL GAMES, BUT...
I'LL GIVE IT A SHOT...!
Then, uhm ...
FIDGET もじ
もじ FIDGET
Brother, I'd like...

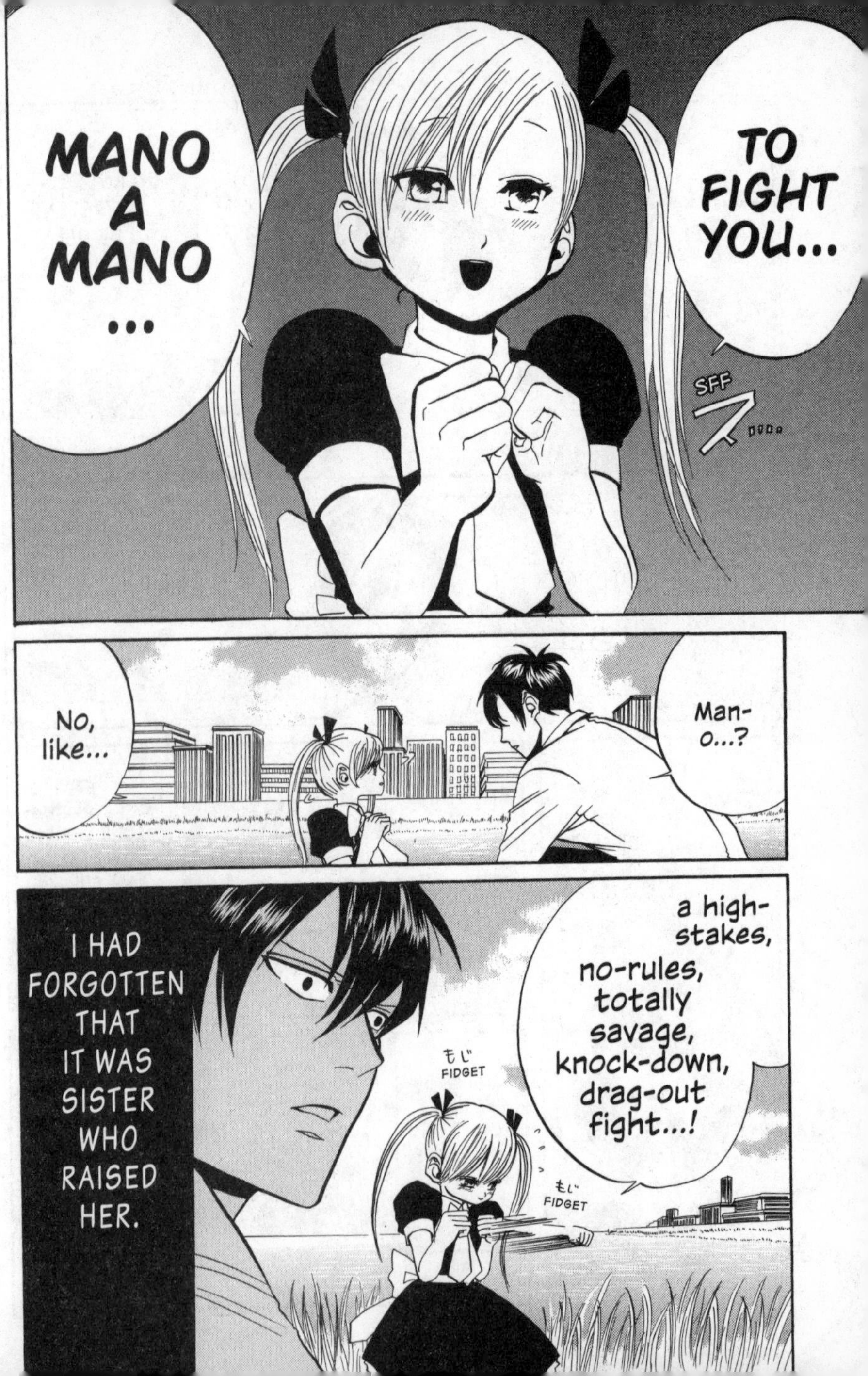
TO FIGHT YOU...
MANO A MANO ...
SFF
Man-o...?
No, like...
a high-stakes, no-rules, totally savage, knock-down, drag-out fight...!
もじ FIDGET
もじ FIDGET
I HAD FORGOTTEN THAT IT WAS SISTER WHO RAISED HER.

Chapter 41: Qualified to be A Brother

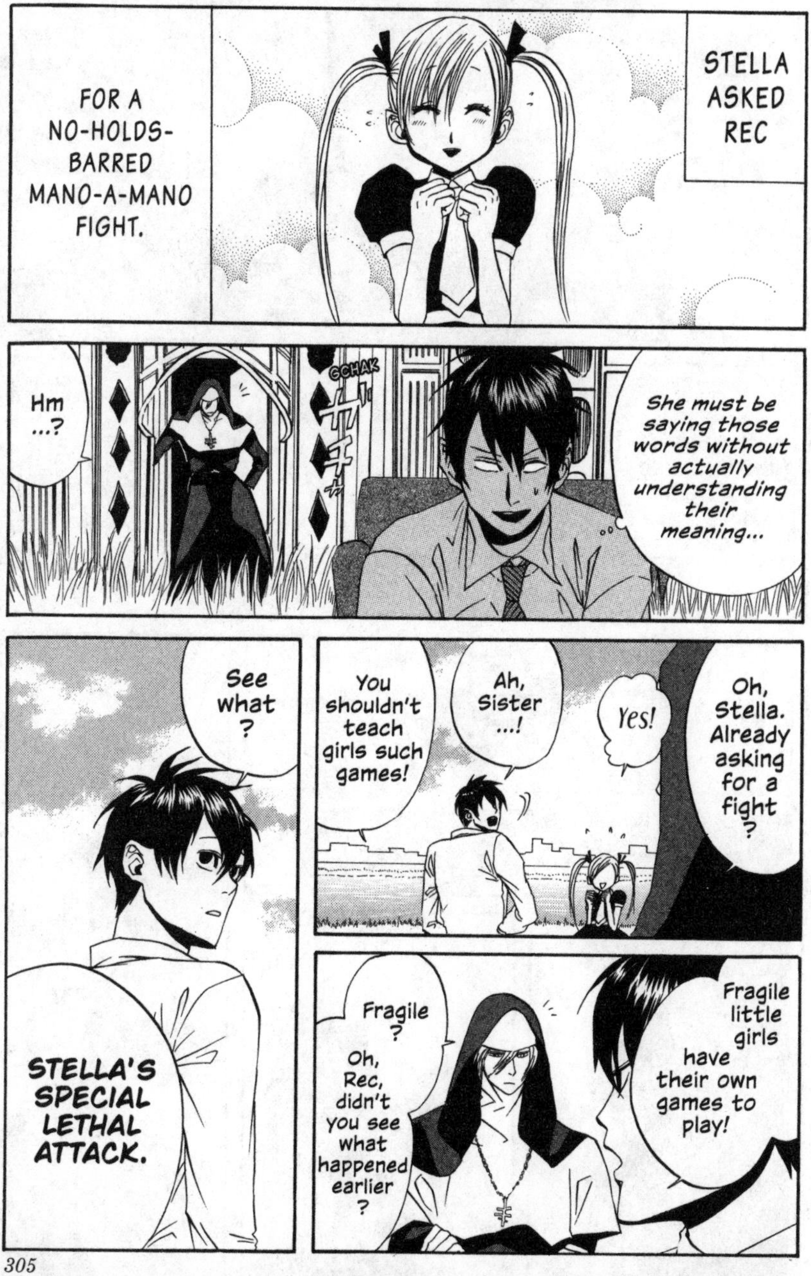
STELLA ASKED REC
FOR A NO-HOLDS-BARRED MANO-A-MANO FIGHT.
She must be saying those words without actually understanding their meaning...
GCHAK
Hm ...?
Oh, Stella. Already asking for a fight?
Yes!
Ah, Sister ...!
You shouldn't teach girls such games!
Fragile little girls have their own games to play!
Fragile?
Oh, Rec, didn't you see what happened earlier?
See what?
STELLA'S SPECIAL LETHAL ATTACK.

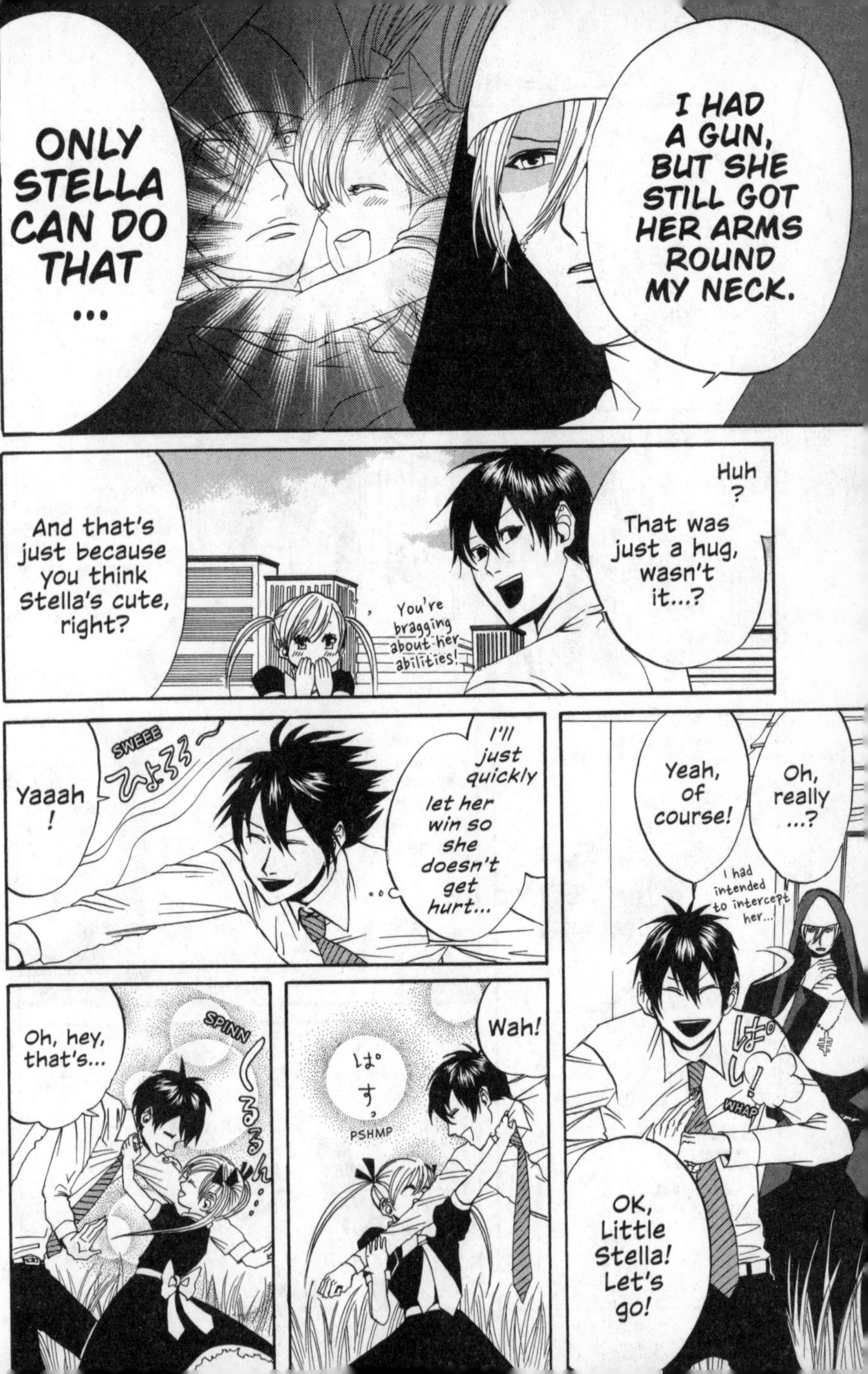
I HAD A GUN, BUT SHE STILL GOT HER ARMS ROUND MY NECK.
ONLY STELLA CAN DO THAT ...
Huh?
That was just a hug, wasn't it...?
You're bragging about her abilities!
And that's just because you think Stella's cute, right?
Oh, really ...?
Yeah, of course!
I had intended to intercept her...
ぱしッ
WHAP
OK, Little Stella! Let's go!
I'll just quickly let her win so she doesn't get hurt...
SWEEE
ひょろろ~
Yaaah!
Wah!
ぱす。
PSHMP
Oh, hey, that's...
SPINN
くるるん

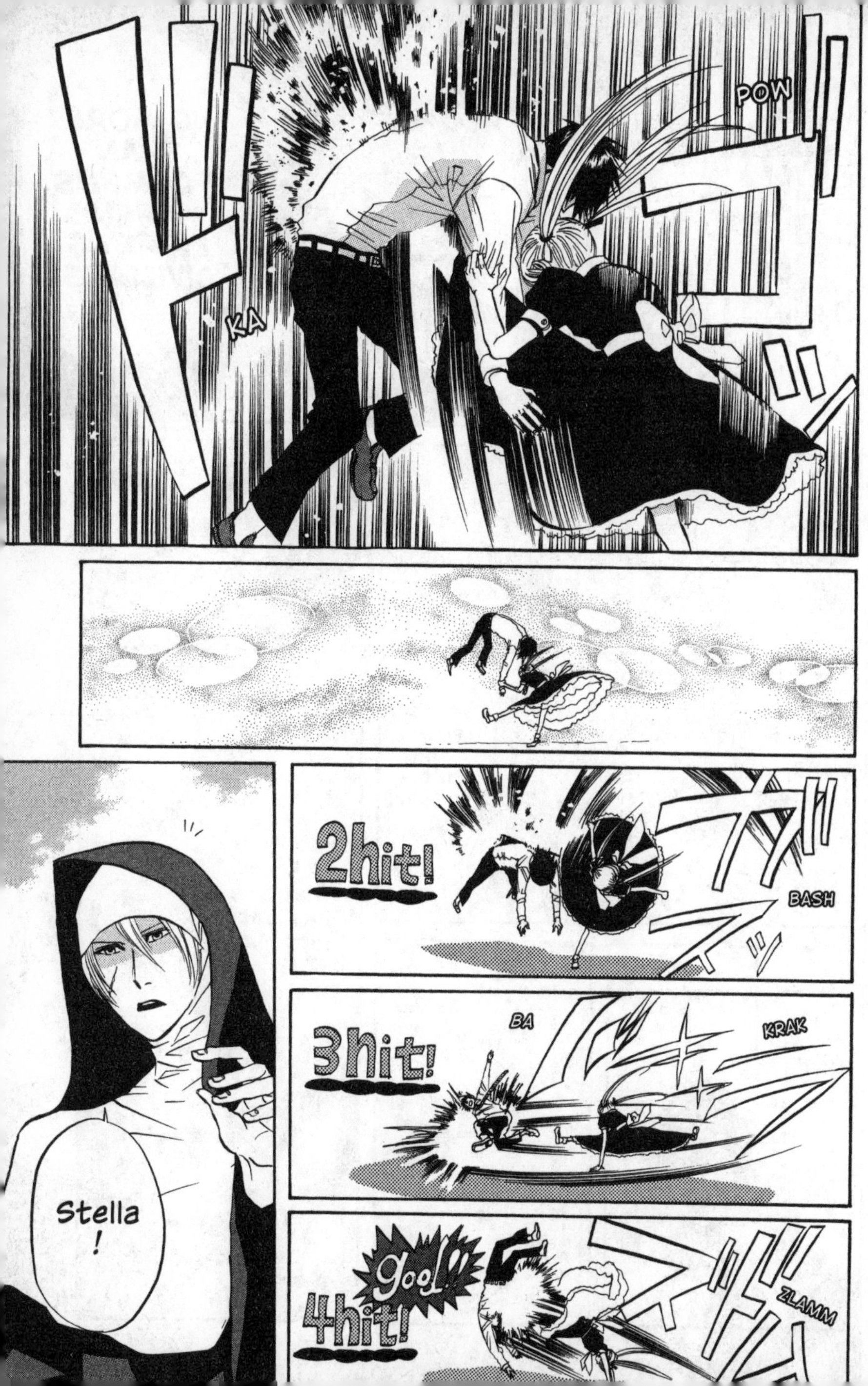
POW
KA
BASH
2hit!
KRAK
BA
3hit!
ZLAMM
gool!!
4hit!
Stella
!

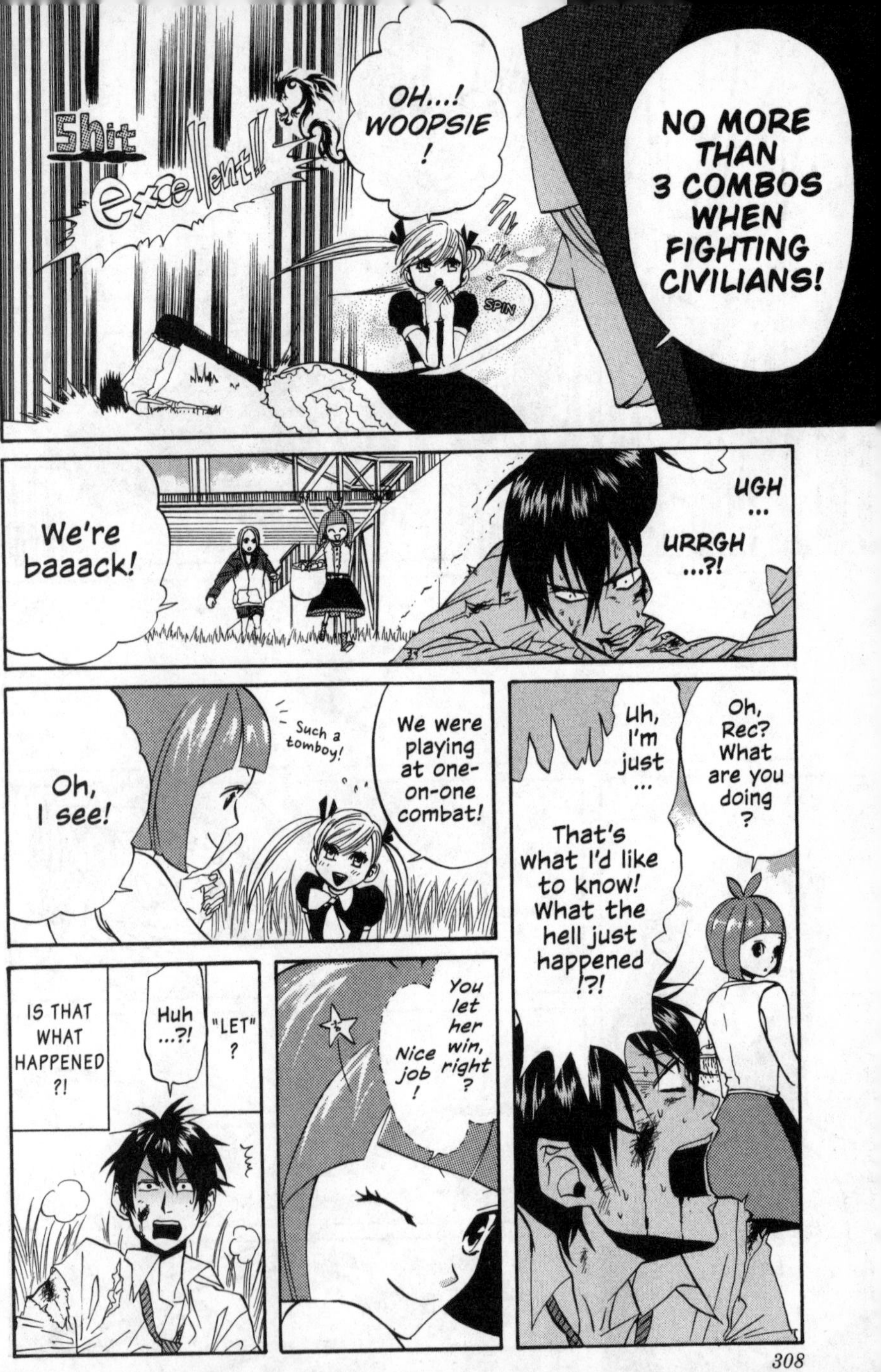
NO MORE THAN 3 COMBOS WHEN FIGHTING CIVILIANS!
OH...! WOOPSIE!
SPIN
Shit excellent!!
UGH ... URRGH ...?!
We're baaack!
Oh, Rec? What are you doing?
Uh, I'm just ...
That's what I'd like to know! What the hell just happened!?!
We were playing at one-on-one combat!
Such a tomboy!
Oh, I see!
You let her win, right?
Nice job!
"LET"?
Huh ...?!
IS THAT WHAT HAPPENED?!

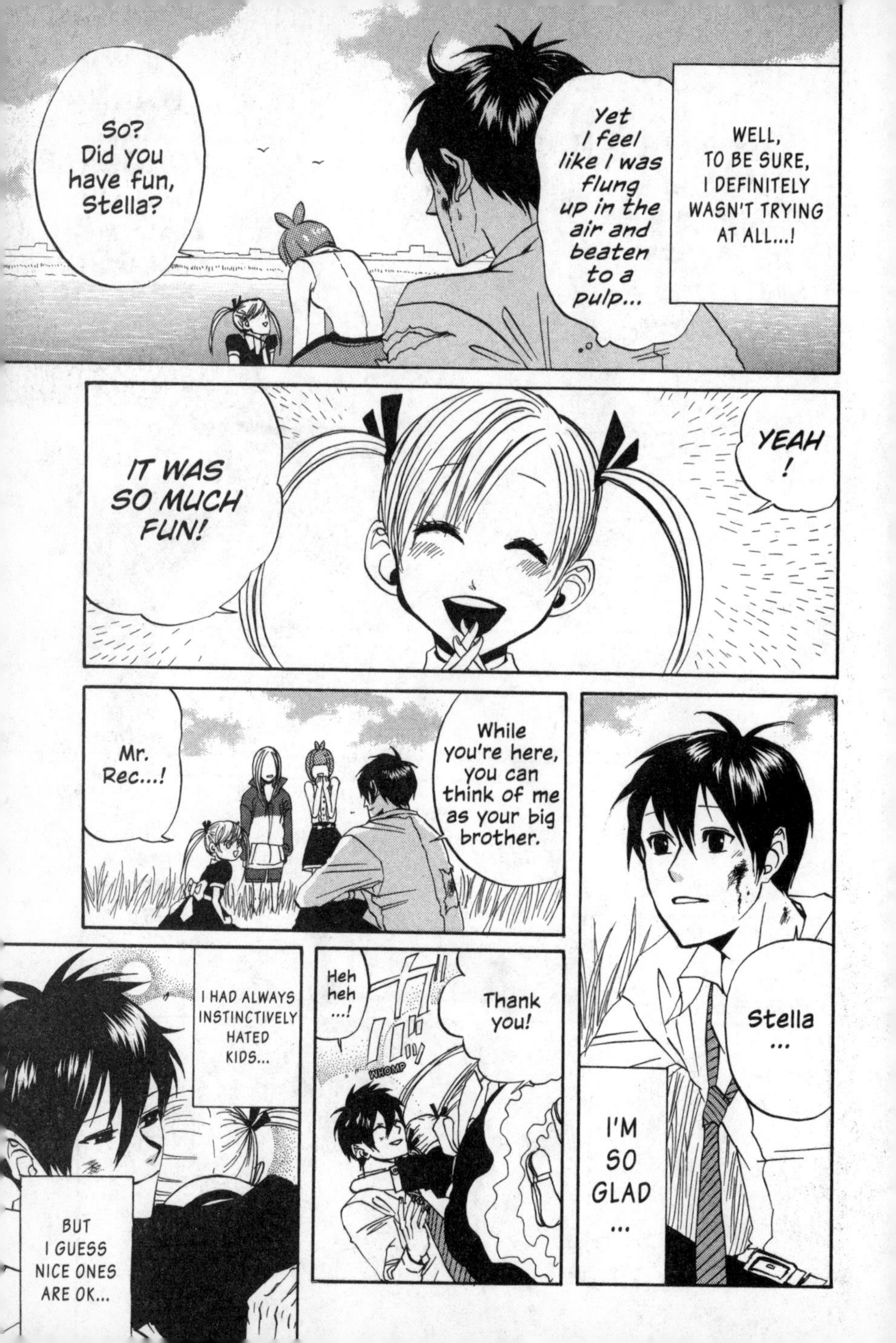
WELL, TO BE SURE, I DEFINITELY WASN'T TRYING AT ALL...!
Yet I feel like I was flung up in the air and beaten to a pulp...
So? Did you have fun, Stella?
YEAH!
IT WAS SO MUCH FUN!
Stella ...
I'M SO GLAD ...
While you're here, you can think of me as your big brother.
Mr. Rec...!
Thank you!
WHOMP
Heh heh ...!
I HAD ALWAYS INSTINCTIVELY HATED KIDS...
BUT I GUESS NICE ONES ARE OK...

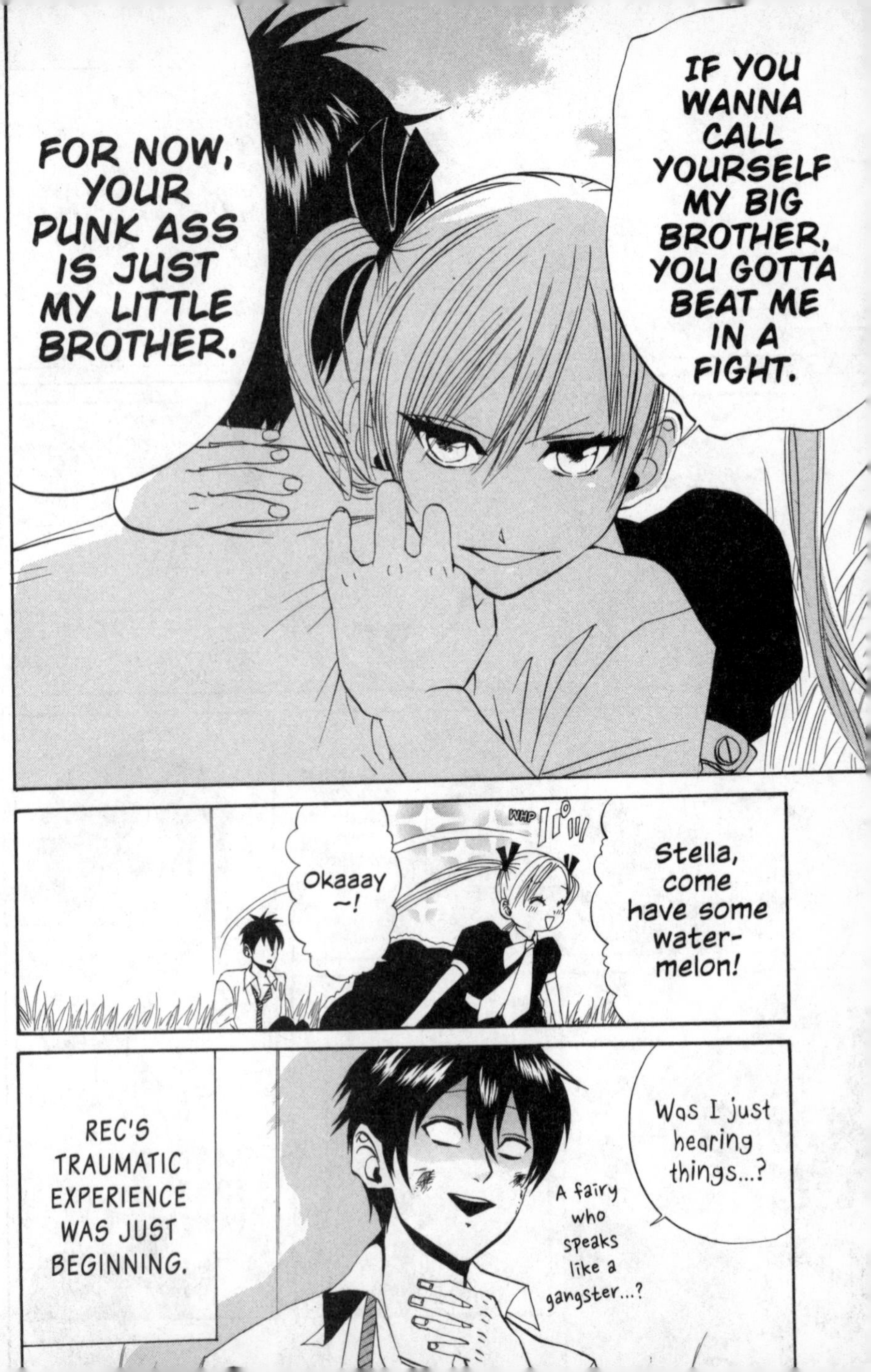
IF YOU WANNA CALL YOURSELF MY BIG BROTHER, YOU GOTTA BEAT ME IN A FIGHT.
FOR NOW, YOUR PUNK ASS IS JUST MY LITTLE BROTHER.
Stella, come have some water-melon!
WHP
Okaaay ~!
Was I just hearing things...?
A fairy who speaks like a gangster...?
REC'S TRAUMATIC EXPERIENCE WAS JUST BEGINNING.

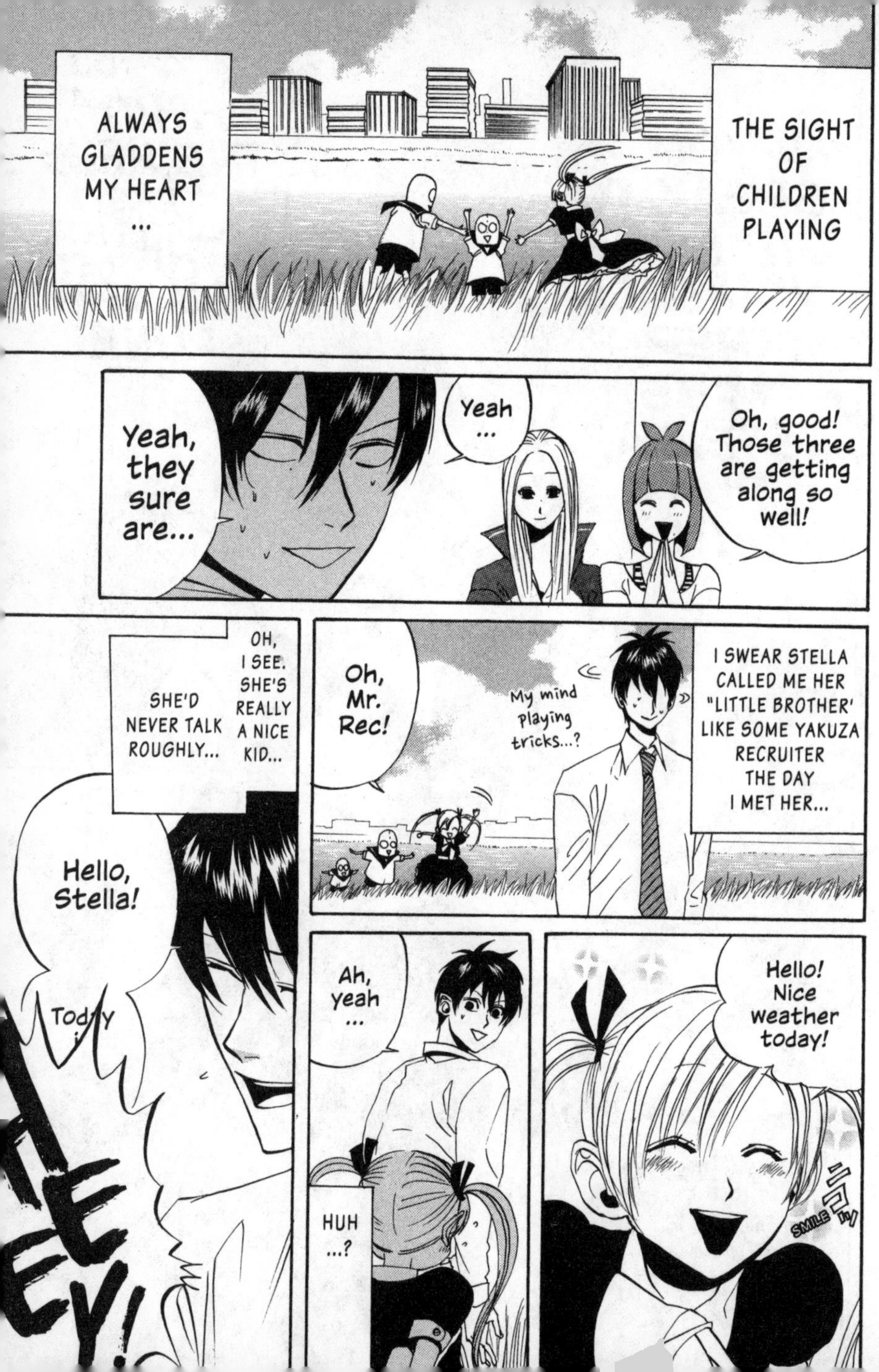
THE SIGHT OF CHILDREN PLAYING
ALWAYS GLADDENS MY HEART ...
Oh, good! Those three are getting along so well!
Yeah ...
Yeah, they sure are...
I SWEAR STELLA CALLED ME HER "LITTLE BROTHER' LIKE SOME YAKUZA RECRUITER THE DAY I MET HER...
My mind playing tricks...?
Oh, Mr. Rec!
Hello! Nice weather today!
SMILE
Ah, yeah ...
HUH ...?
OH, I SEE. SHE'S REALLY A NICE KID...
SHE'D NEVER TALK ROUGHLY...
Hello, Stella!
HEEEY!

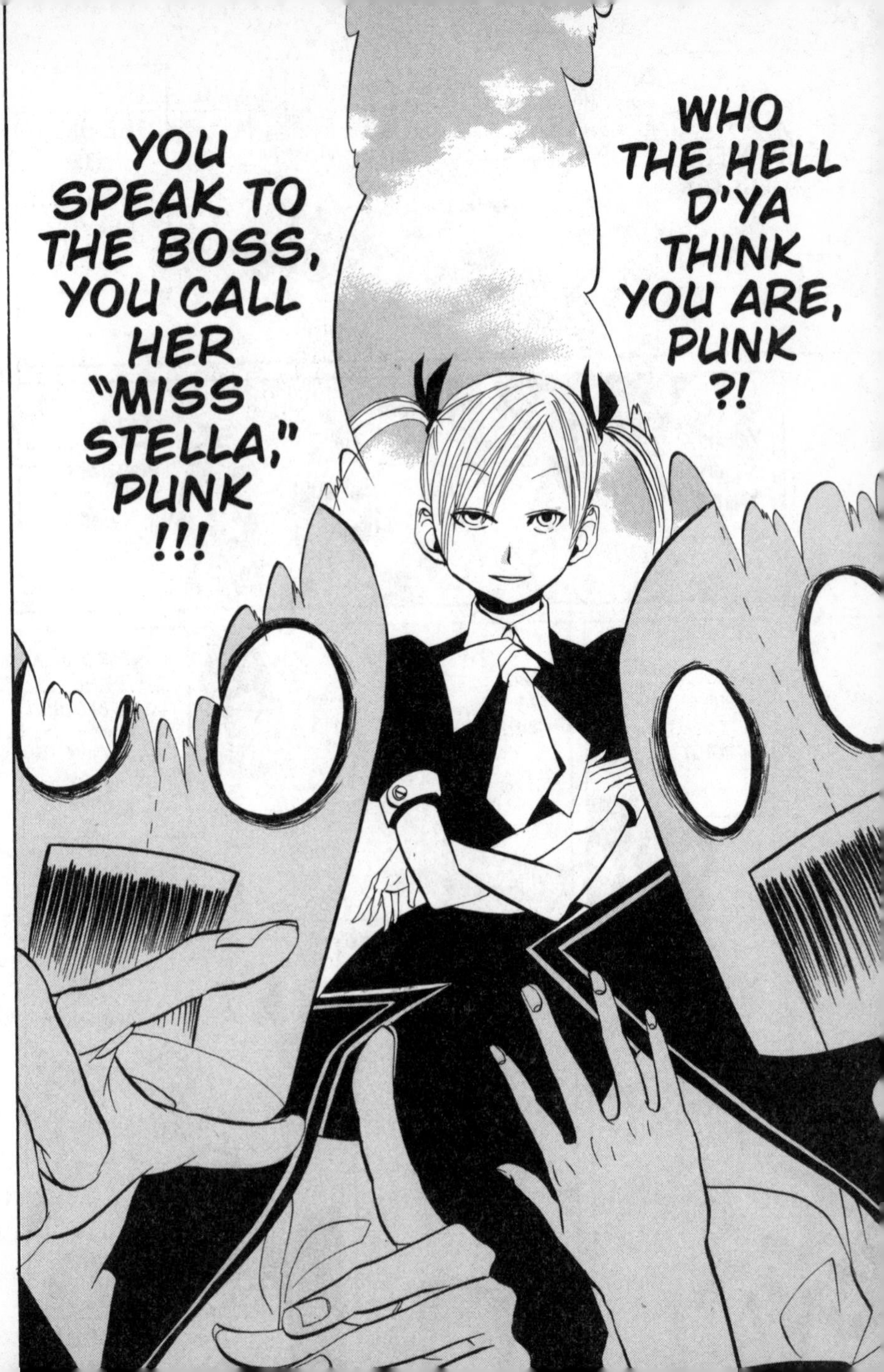
WHO THE HELL D'YA THINK YOU ARE, PUNK ?!
YOU SPEAK TO THE BOSS, YOU CALL HER "MISS STELLA," PUNK !!!

☜ Chapter 42: Maria

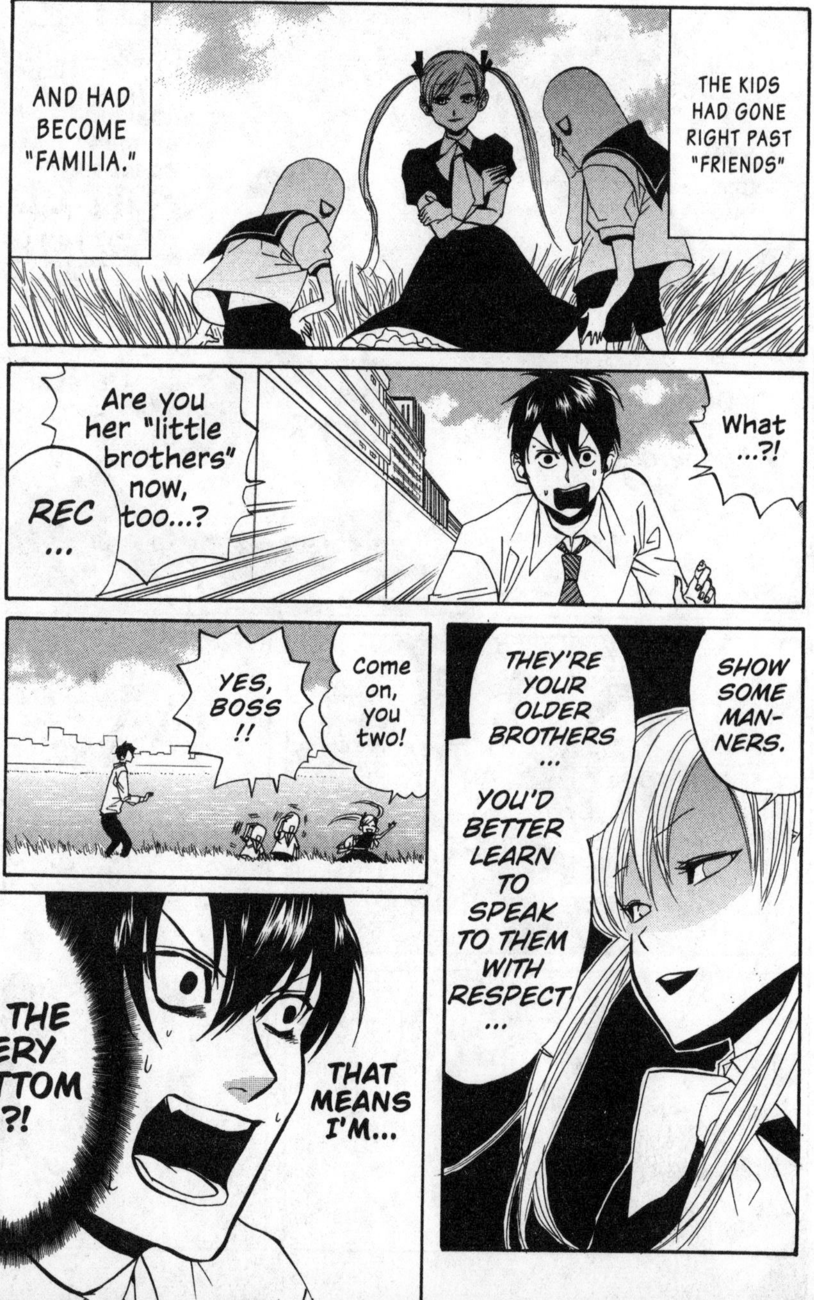
THE KIDS HAD GONE RIGHT PAST "FRIENDS"
AND HAD BECOME "FAMILIA."
What ...?!
Are you her "little brothers" now, too...?
REC ...
SHOW SOME MAN-NERS.
THEY'RE YOUR OLDER BROTHERS ...
YOU'D BETTER LEARN TO SPEAK TO THEM WITH RESPECT ...
Come on, you two!
YES, BOSS !!
THAT MEANS I'M...
AT THE VERY BOTTOM !?!

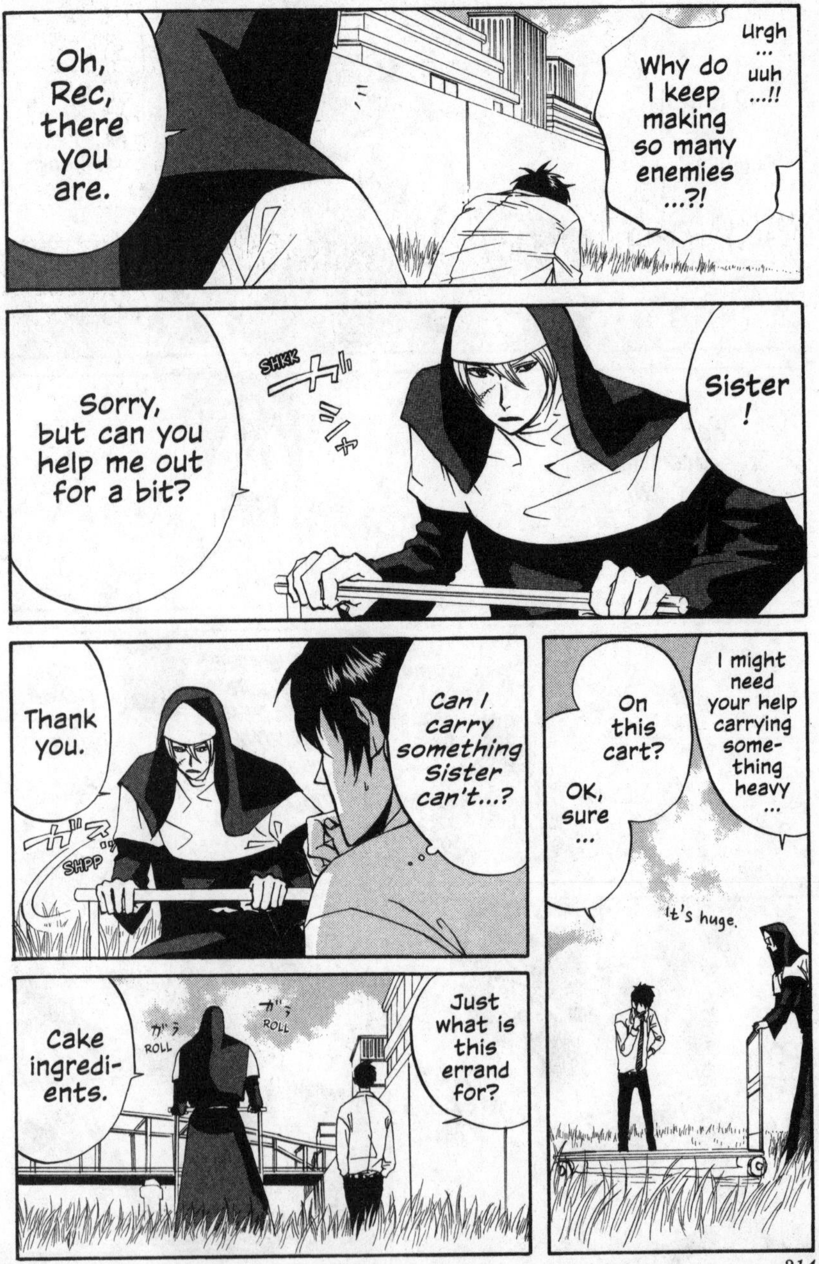
Urgh ... uuh ...!!
Why do I keep making so many enemies ...?!
Oh, Rec, there you are.
Sister!
SHKK
Sorry, but can you help me out for a bit?
I might need your help carrying some-thing heavy ...
On this cart?
OK, sure ...
It's huge.
Can I carry something Sister can't...?
SHPP
Thank you.
Just what is this errand for?
ROLL
ROLL
Cake ingredi-ents.

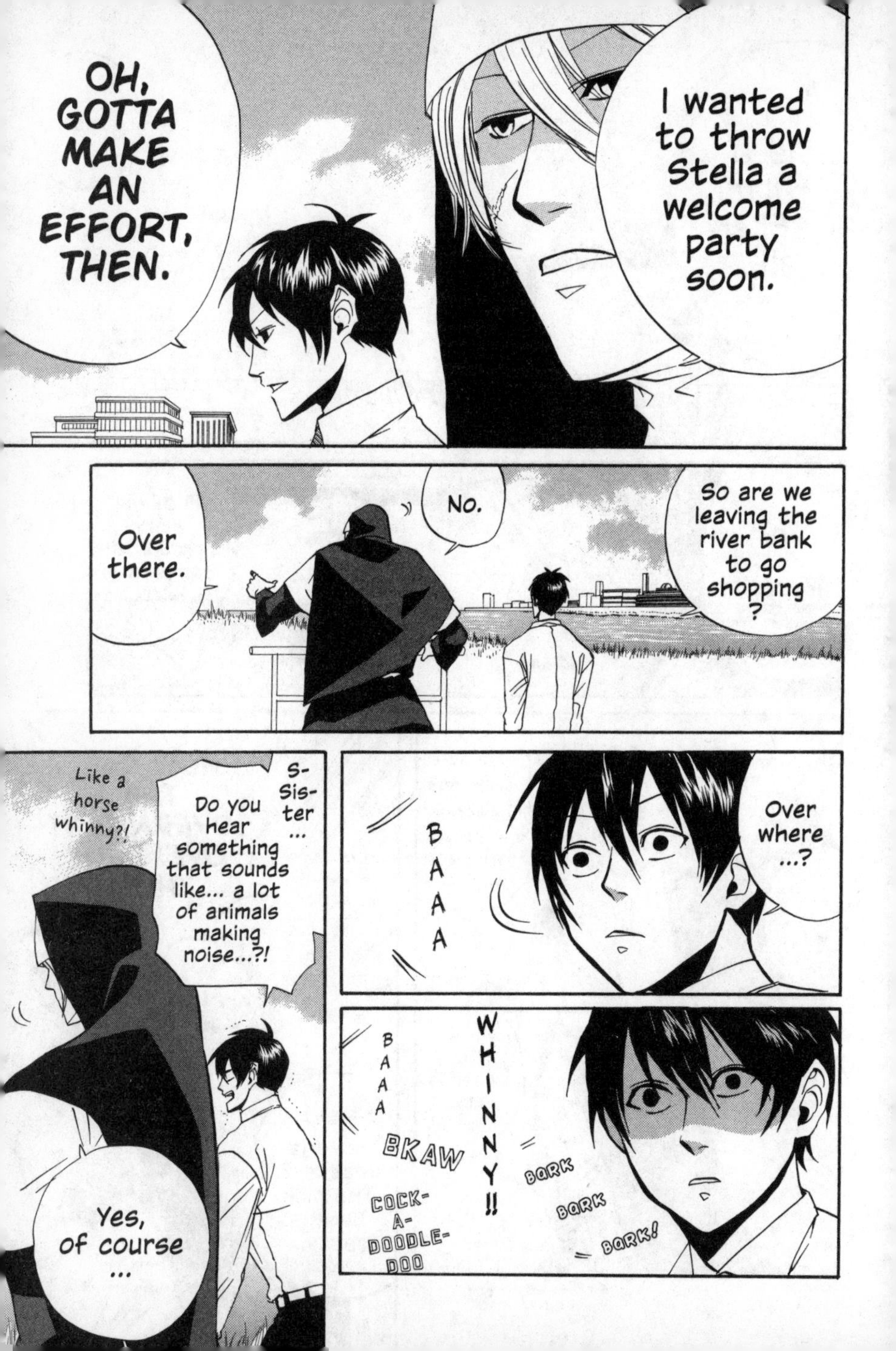
I wanted to throw Stella a welcome party soon.
OH, GOTTA MAKE AN EFFORT, THEN.
So are we leaving the river bank to go shopping?
No.
Over there.
Over where ...?
BAAA
WHINNY!!
BAAA
BKAW
COCK-A-DOODLE-DOO
BARK
BARK
BARK!
S-Sister ...
Do you hear something that sounds like... a lot of animals making noise...?!
Like a horse whinny?!
Yes, of course ...

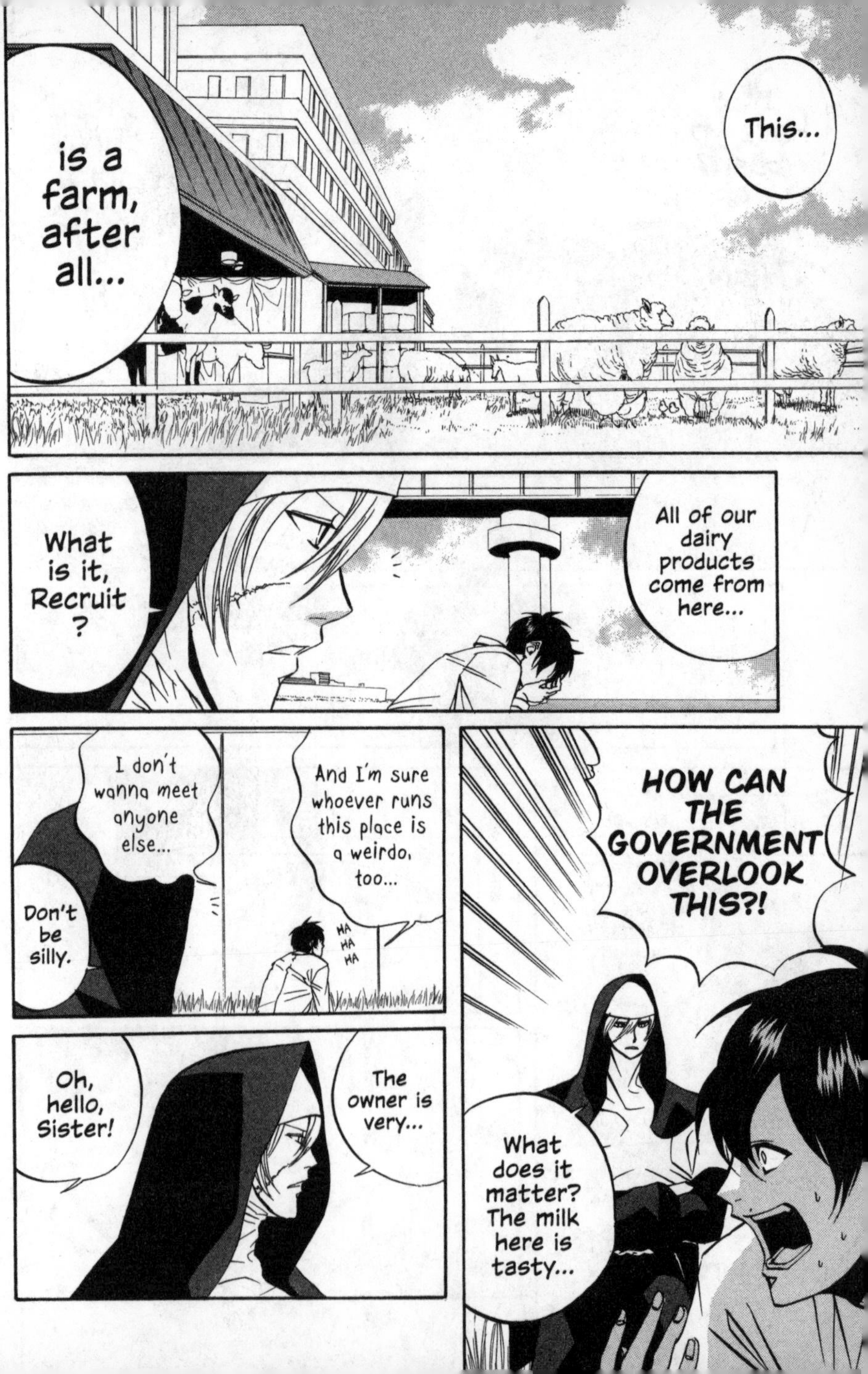
This...
is a farm, after all...
All of our dairy products come from here...
What is it, Recruit?
HOW CAN THE GOVERNMENT OVERLOOK THIS?!
What does it matter? The milk here is tasty...
And I'm sure whoever runs this place is a weirdo, too...
HA HA HA
I don't wanna meet anyone else...
Don't be silly.
The owner is very...
Oh, hello, Sister!

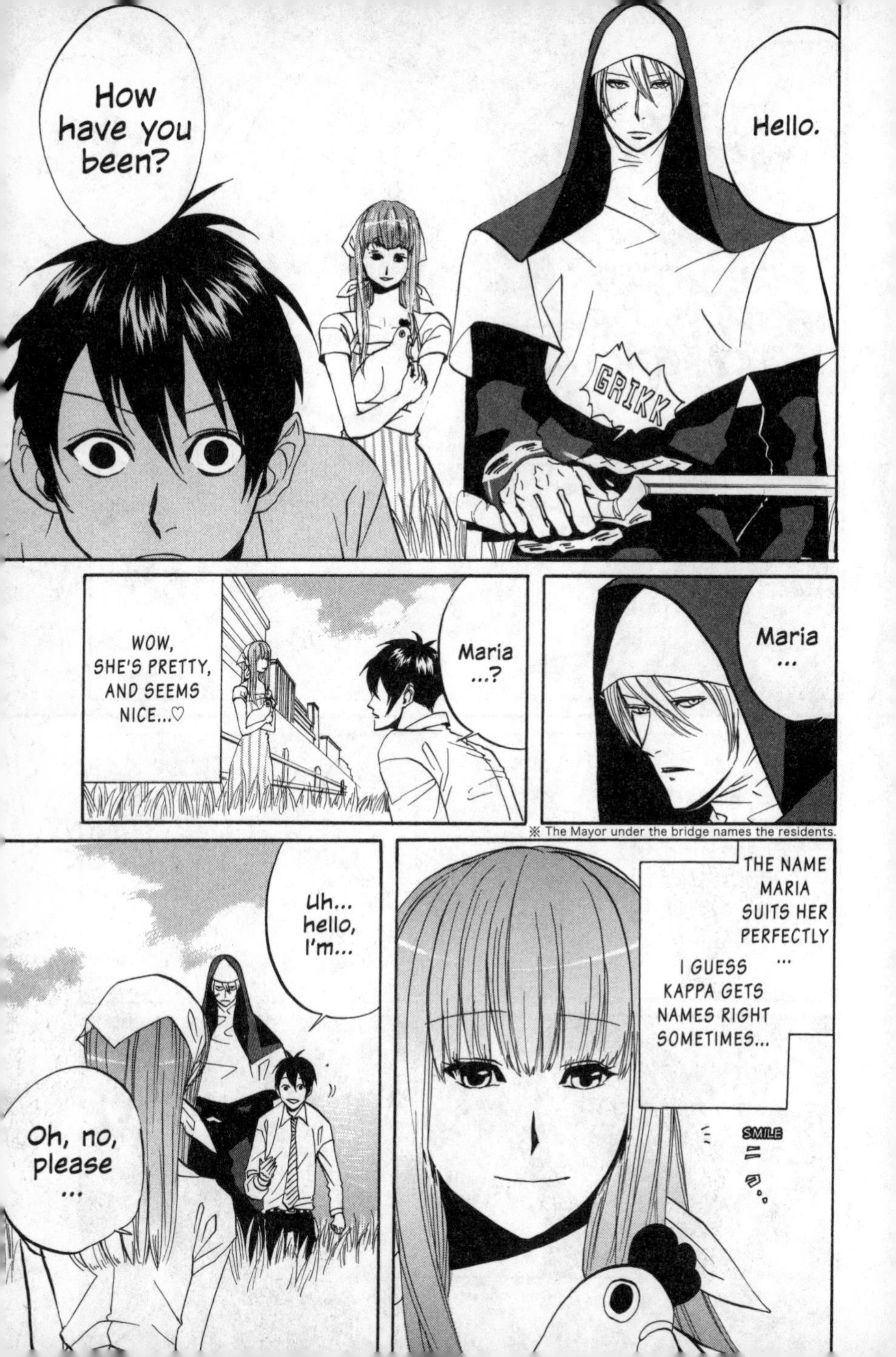
Hello.
How have you been?
GRIKK
Maria ...
Maria ...?
WOW, SHE'S PRETTY, AND SEEMS NICE...♡
※ The Mayor under the bridge names the residents.
THE NAME MARIA SUITS HER PERFECTLY ...
I GUESS KAPPA GETS NAMES RIGHT SOMETIMES...
SMILE
Uh... hello, I'm...
Oh, no, please ...

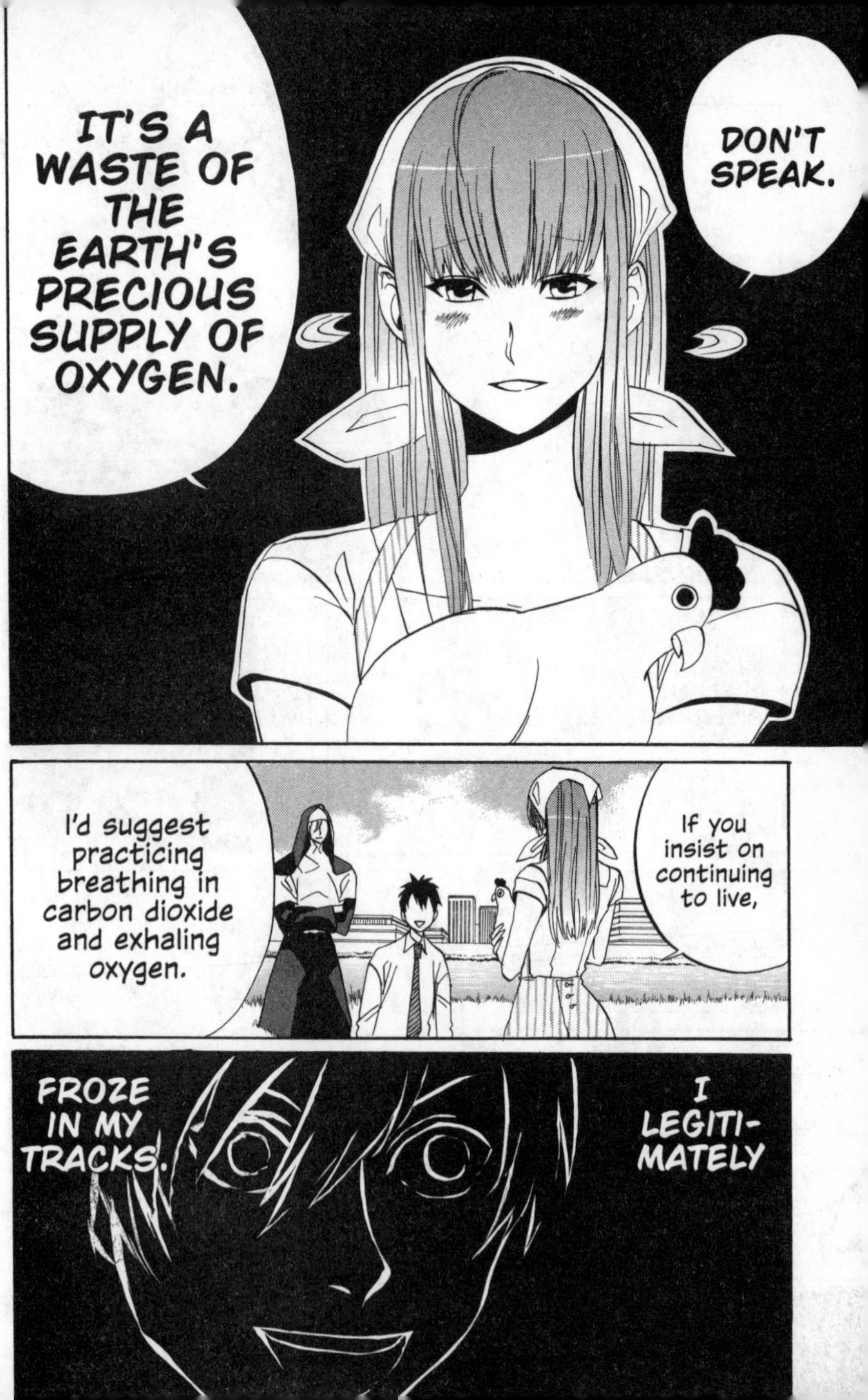
DON'T SPEAK.
IT'S A WASTE OF THE EARTH'S PRECIOUS SUPPLY OF OXYGEN.
If you insist on continuing to live,
I'd suggest practicing breathing in carbon dioxide and exhaling oxygen.
I LEGITI-MATELY
FROZE IN MY TRACKS.

Chapter 43: Fun with Projectile Bleeding

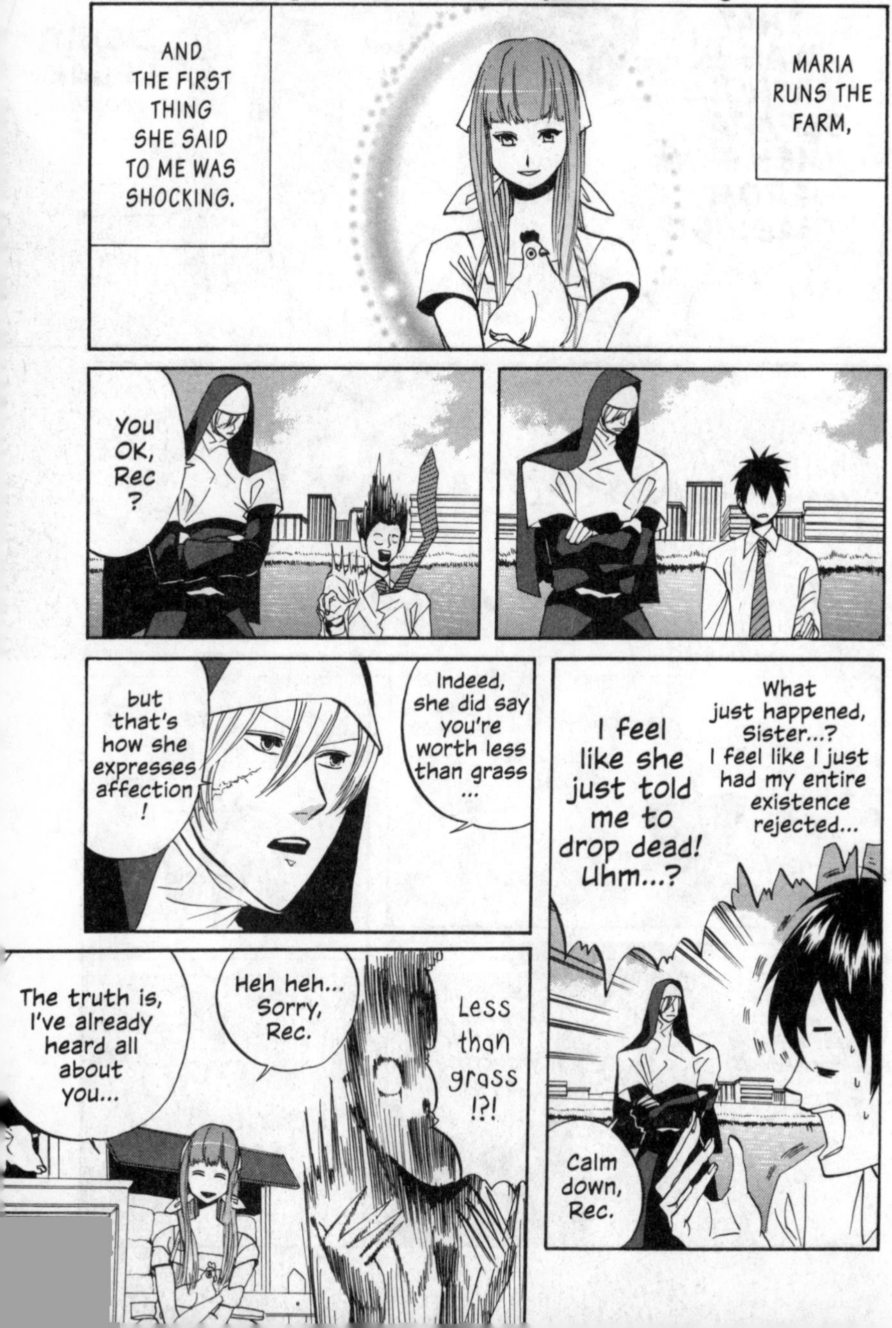
MARIA RUNS THE FARM,
AND THE FIRST THING SHE SAID TO ME WAS SHOCKING.
You OK, Rec?
What just happened, Sister...? I feel like I just had my entire existence rejected...
I feel like she just told me to drop dead! Uhm...?
Calm down, Rec.
Indeed, she did say you're worth less than grass...
but that's how she expresses affection!
Less than grass!?!
Heh heh... Sorry, Rec.
The truth is, I've already heard all about you...

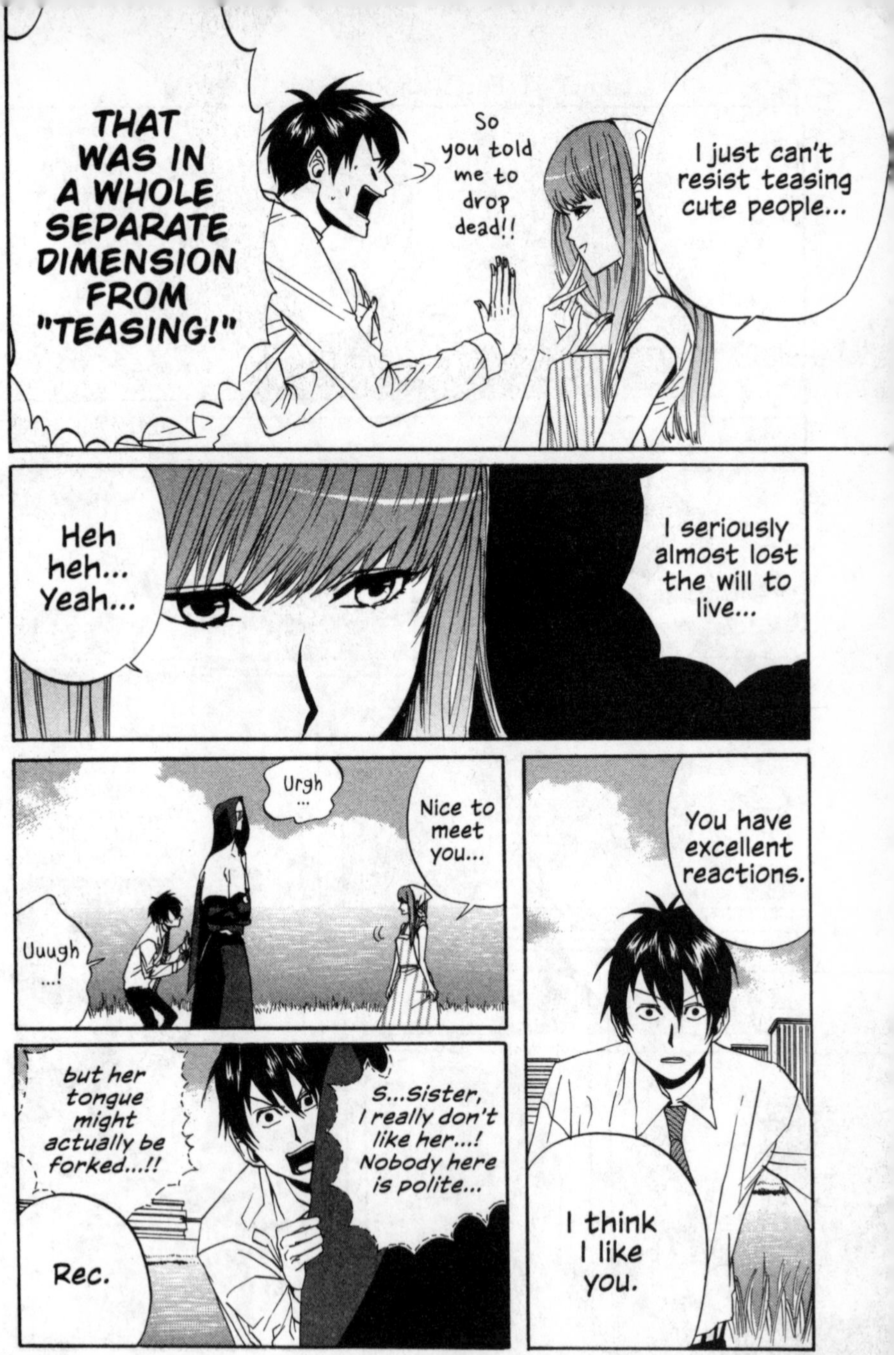
I just can't resist teasing cute people...
So you told me to drop dead!!
THAT WAS IN A WHOLE SEPARATE DIMENSION FROM "TEASING!"
I seriously almost lost the will to live...
Heh heh... Yeah...
You have excellent reactions.
I think I like you.
Nice to meet you...
Urgh...
Uuugh...!
S...Sister, I really don't like her...! Nobody here is polite...
but her tongue might actually be forked...!!
Rec.

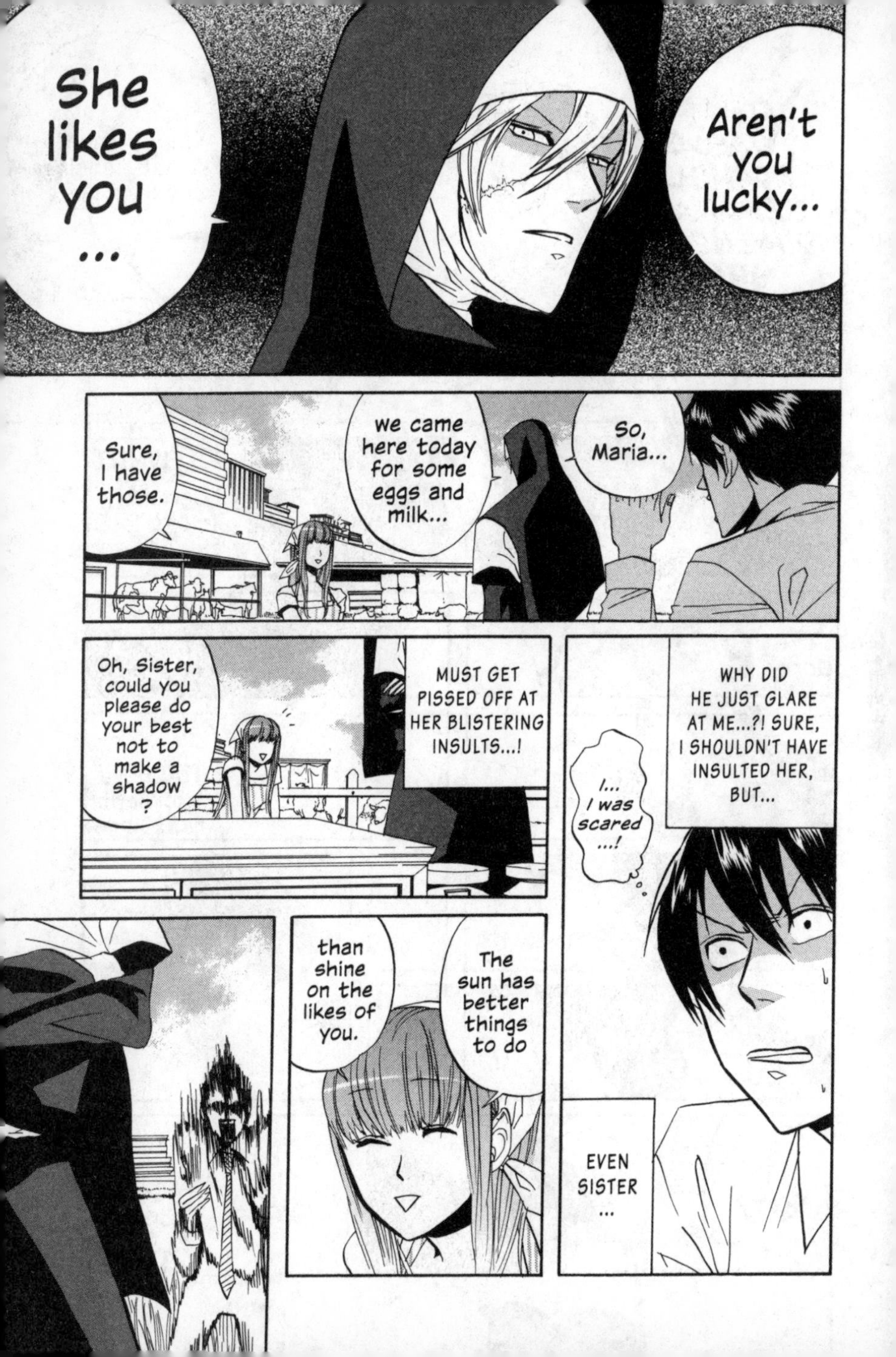

Aren't you lucky...
She likes you ...
So, Maria...
we came here today for some eggs and milk...
Sure, I have those.
WHY DID HE JUST GLARE AT ME...?! SURE, I SHOULDN'T HAVE INSULTED HER, BUT...
I... I was scared ...!
EVEN SISTER ...
MUST GET PISSED OFF AT HER BLISTERING INSULTS...!
Oh, Sister, could you please do your best not to make a shadow ?
The sun has better things to do
than shine on the likes of you.

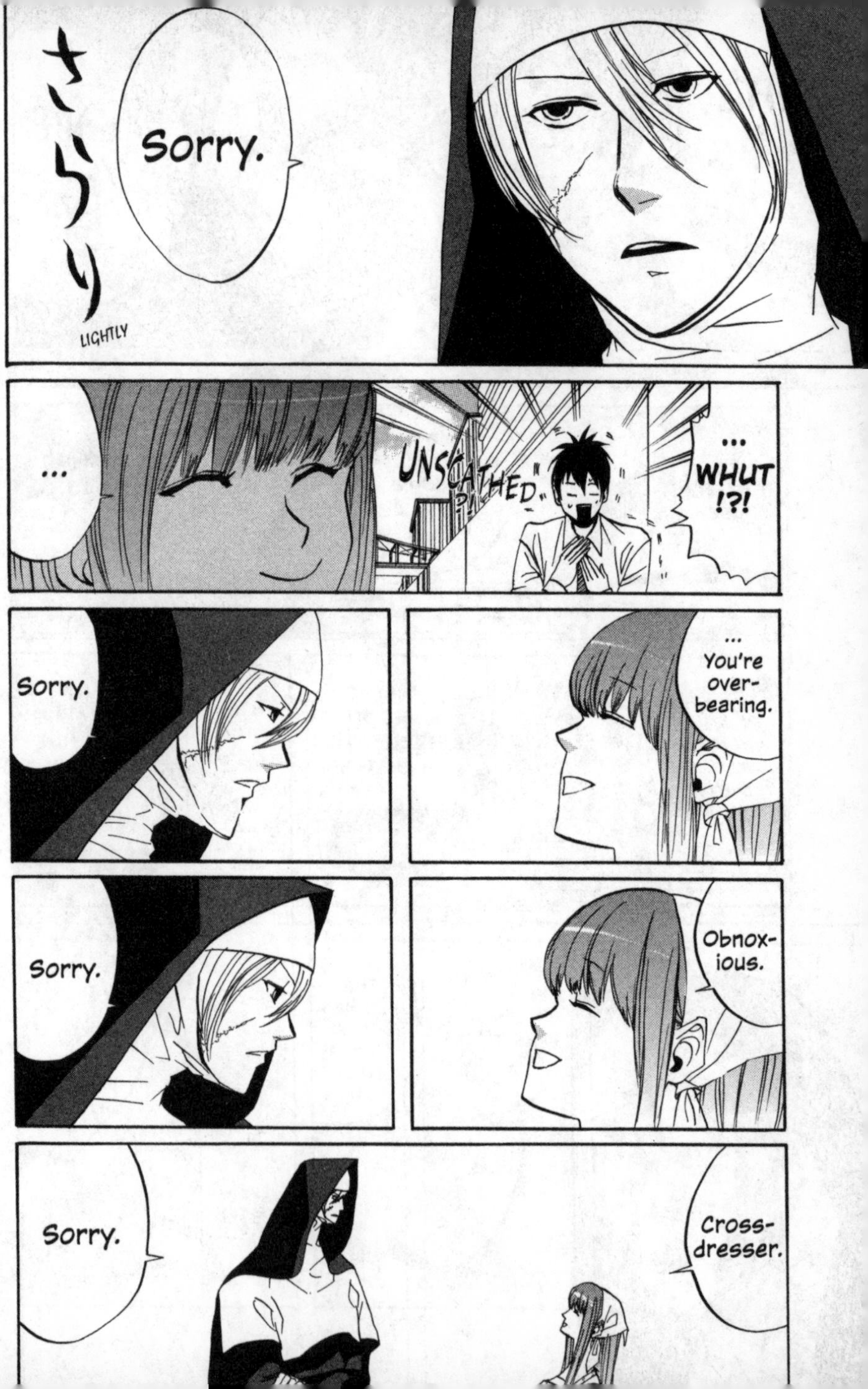
Sorry.
さらり
LIGHTLY
... WHUT !?!
UNSCATHED
?!
...
... You're over-bearing.
Sorry.
Obnox-ious.
Sorry.
Cross-dresser.
Sorry.

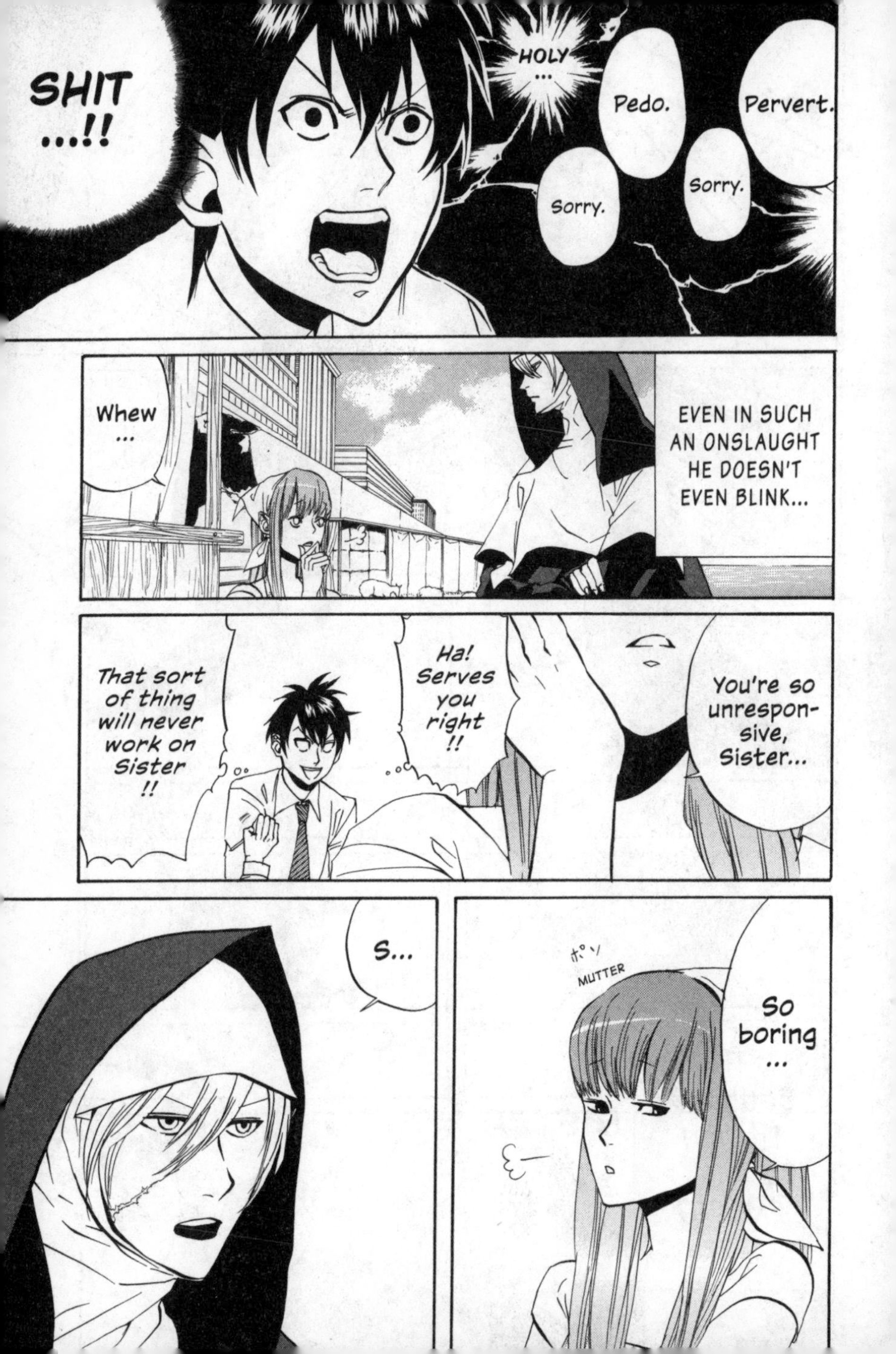
Pervert.
Pedo.
Sorry.
HOLY ...
Sorry.
SHIT ...!!
EVEN IN SUCH AN ONSLAUGHT HE DOESN'T EVEN BLINK...
Whew ...
You're so unrespon-sive, Sister...
Ha! Serves you right !!
That sort of thing will never work on Sister !!
So boring ...
ポソ
MUTTER
S...

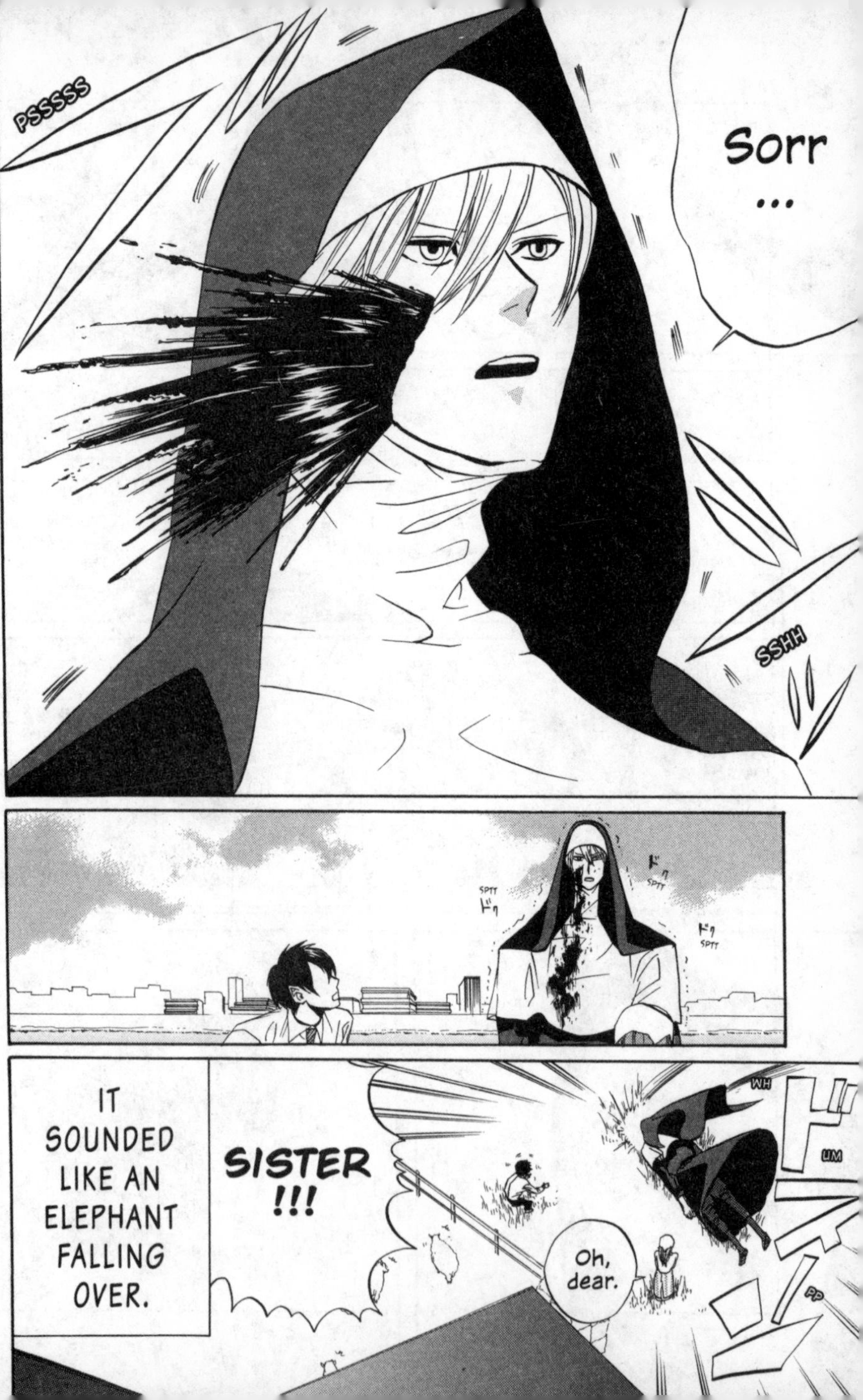
Sorr
...
PSSSSS
SSHH
ドク
SPTT
ドク
SPTT
ドク
SPTT
WH
UM
PP
Oh, dear.
SISTER !!!
IT SOUNDED LIKE AN ELEPHANT FALLING OVER.

☜ Chapter 44: Can't Hide My Feelings

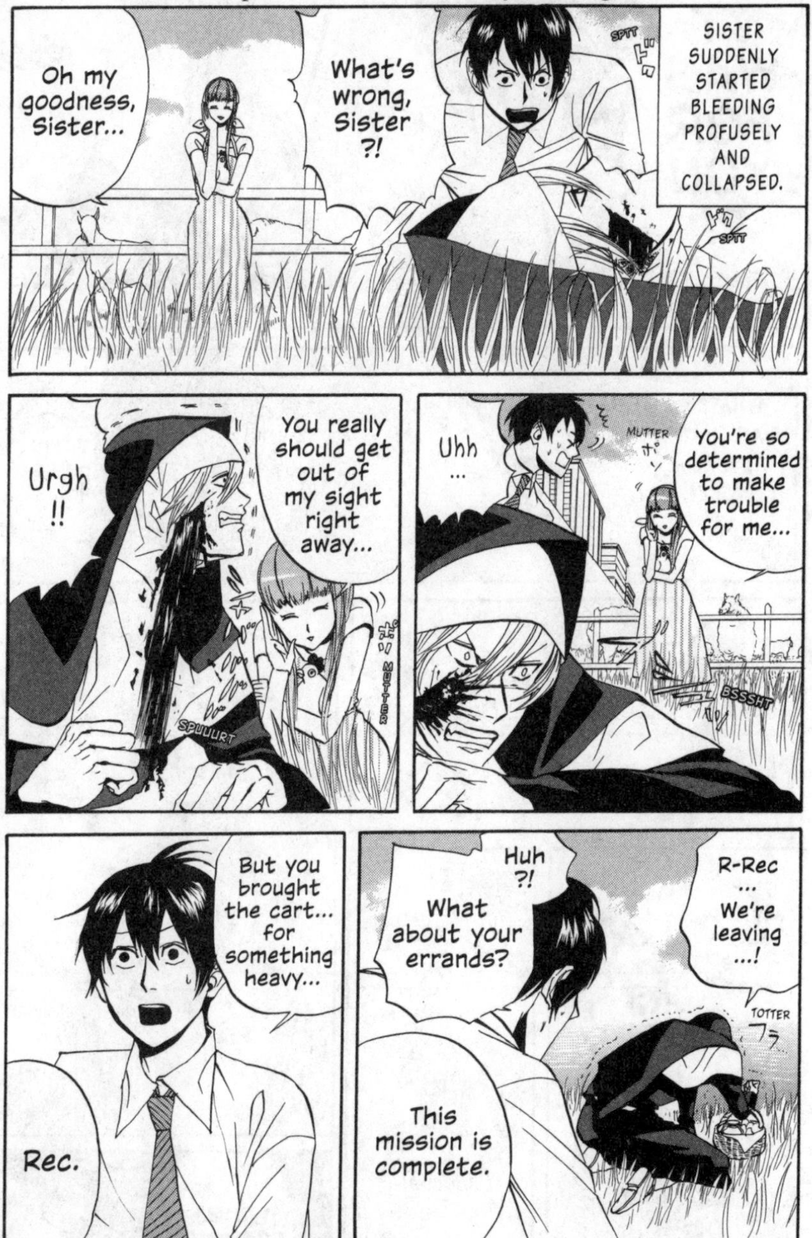
SISTER SUDDENLY STARTED BLEEDING PROFUSELY AND COLLAPSED.
SPTT
SPTT
What's wrong, Sister ?!
Oh my goodness, Sister...
You're so determined to make trouble for me...
MUTTER
Uhh ...
BSSSHT
You really should get out of my sight right away...
MUTTER
Urgh !!
SPUUURT
R-Rec ... We're leaving ...!
TOTTER
Huh ?! What about your errands?
This mission is complete.
But you brought the cart... for something heavy...
Rec.

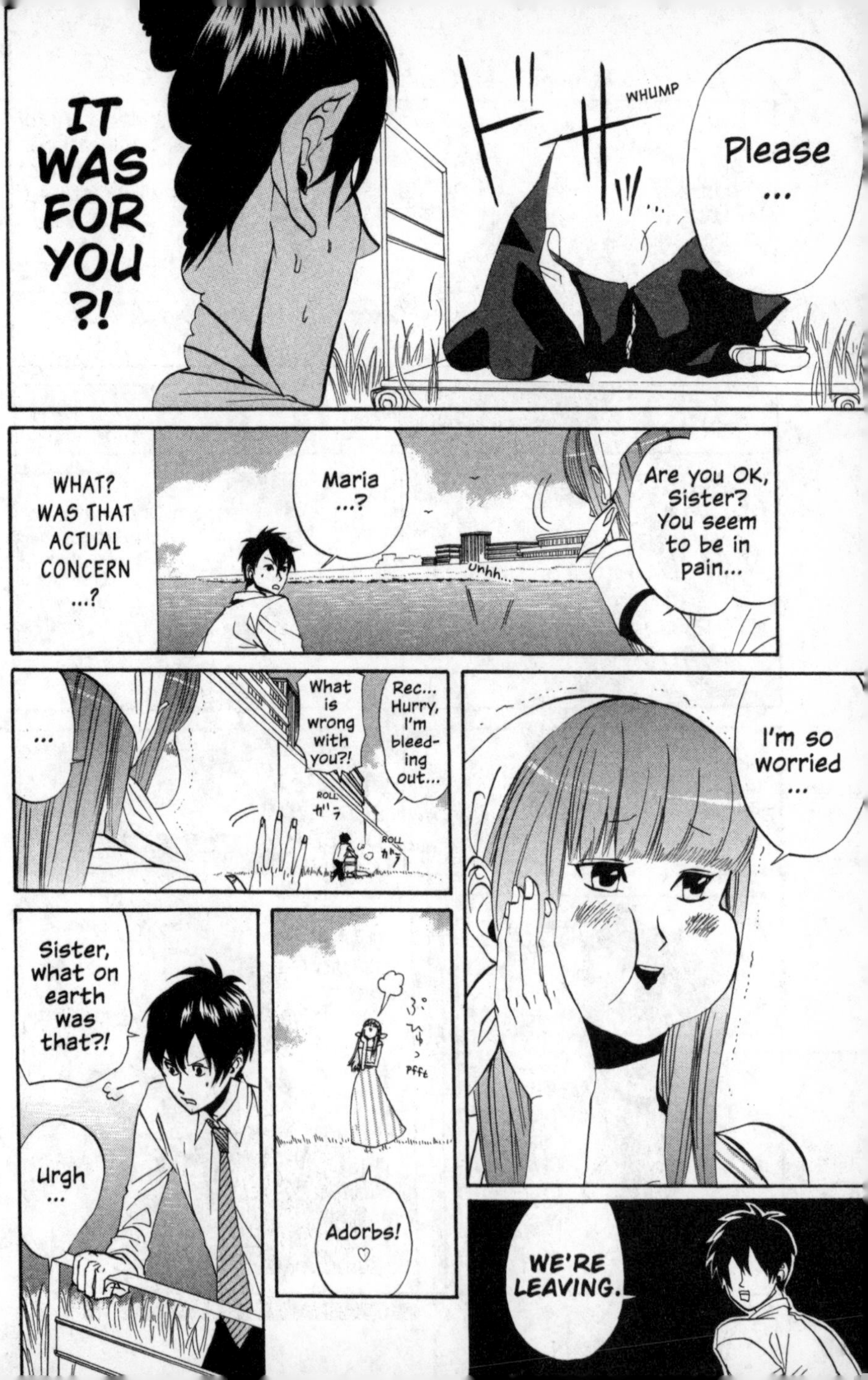
Please ...
WHUMP
IT WAS FOR YOU ?!
Are you OK, Sister? You seem to be in pain...
Unhh...
Maria ...?
WHAT? WAS THAT ACTUAL CONCERN ...?
I'm so worried ...
Rec... Hurry, I'm bleeding out...
What is wrong with you?!
ROLL
ROLL
...
pfft
Adorbs! ♡
Sister, what on earth was that?!
Urgh ...
WE'RE LEAVING.

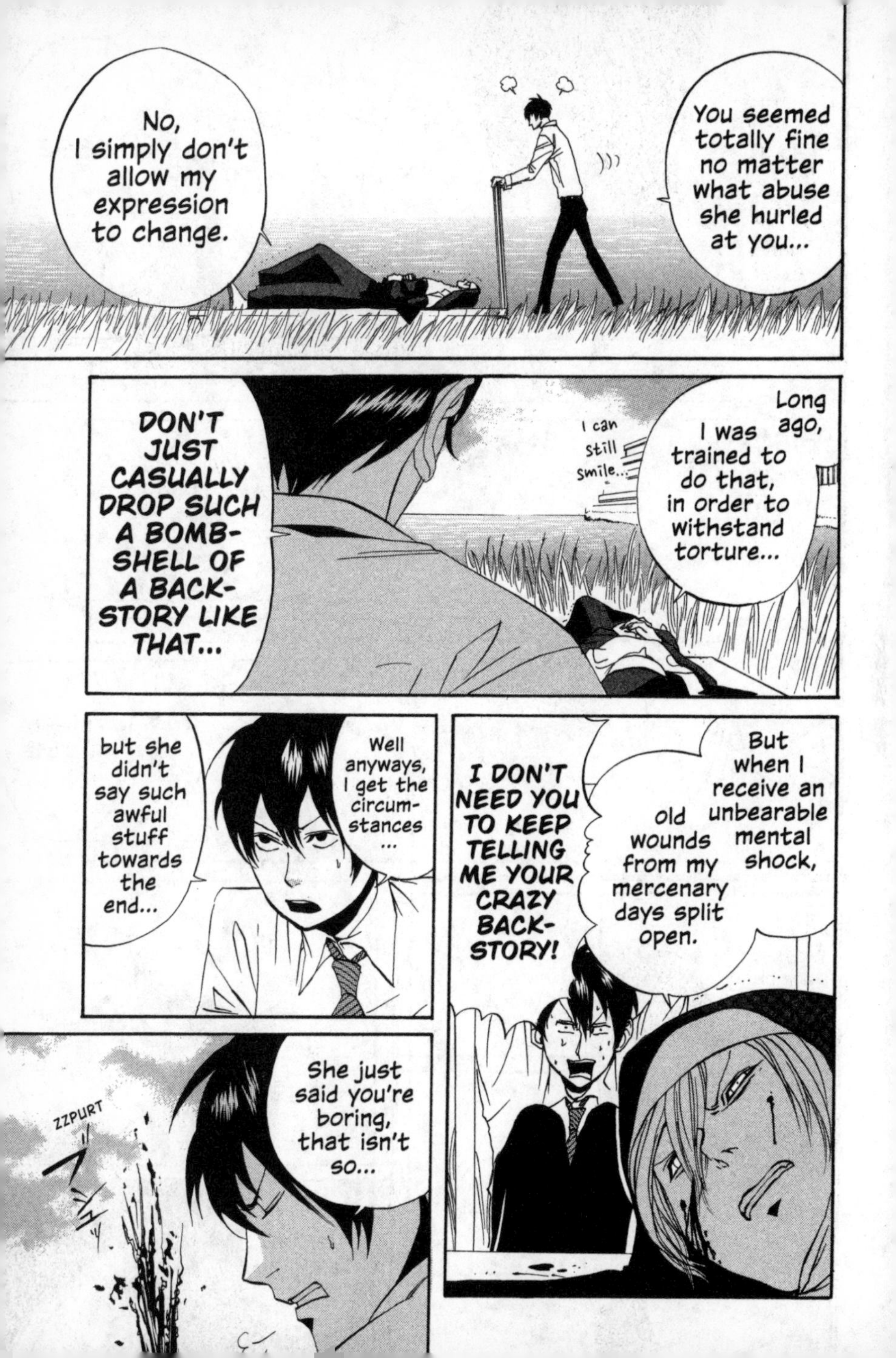
You seemed totally fine no matter what abuse she hurled at you...
No, I simply don't allow my expression to change.
Long ago, I was trained to do that, in order to withstand torture...
I can still smile...
DON'T JUST CASUALLY DROP SUCH A BOMB-SHELL OF A BACK-STORY LIKE THAT...
But when I receive an unbearable mental shock, old wounds from my mercenary days split open.
I DON'T NEED YOU TO KEEP TELLING ME YOUR CRAZY BACK-STORY!
...
Well anyways, I get the circum-stances ...
but she didn't say such awful stuff towards the end...
She just said you're boring, that isn't so...
ZZPURT

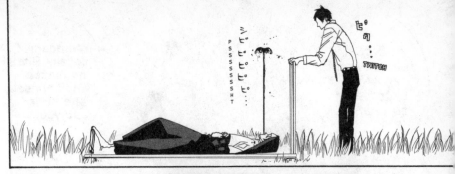

PSSSSSSSHT

ピ°…
TWITCH

S-Sister... Are you...

...

...

SPATTER

With Maria...

SNIK

Huh?

RISE

Uhm, Sister, was that...

TOSS

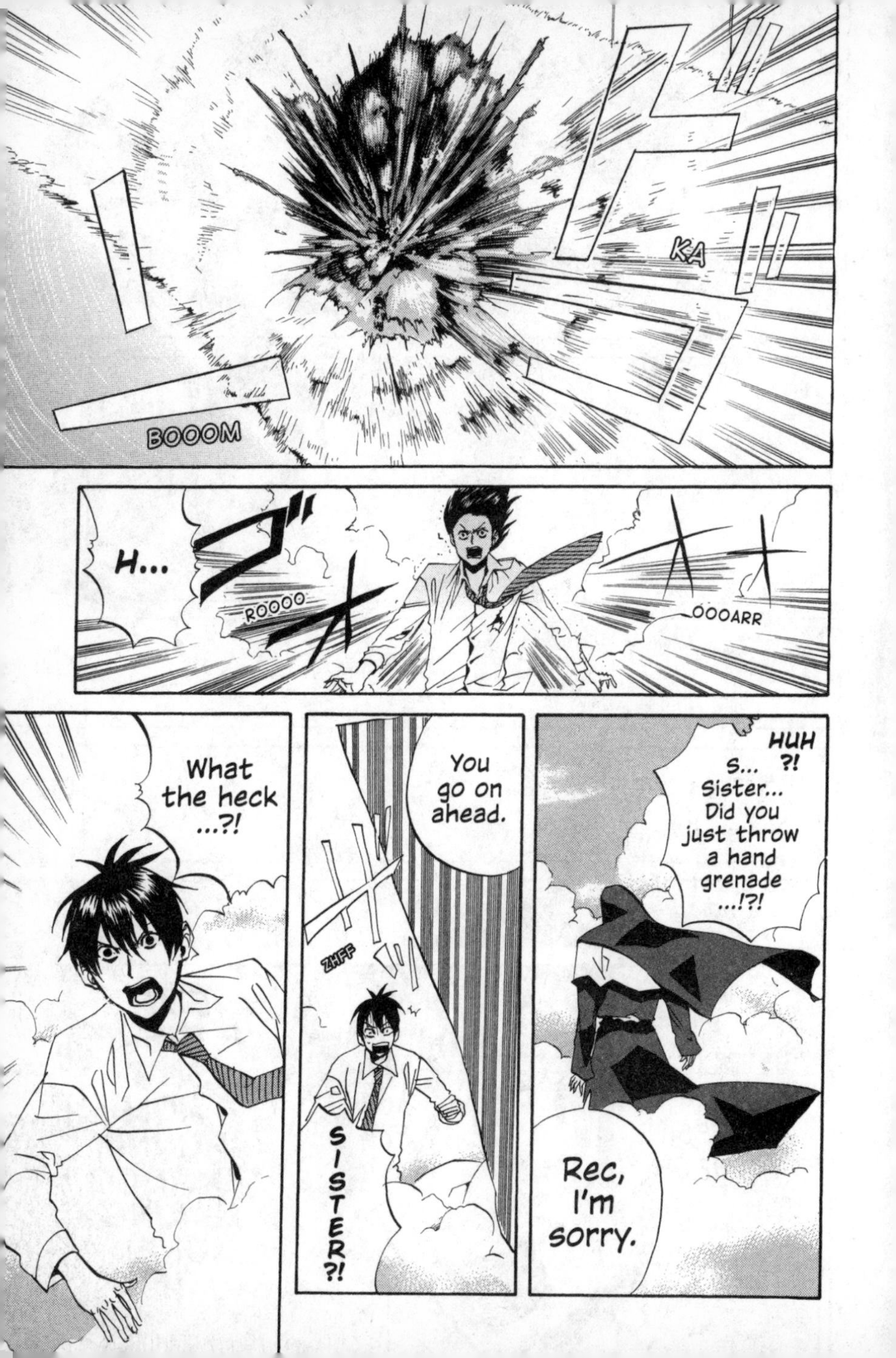
KA
BOOOM
H...
ROOOO
OOOARR
HUH ?!
S... Sister... Did you just throw a hand grenade ...!?!
Rec, I'm sorry.
You go on ahead.
ZHFF
SISTER?!
What the heck ...?!

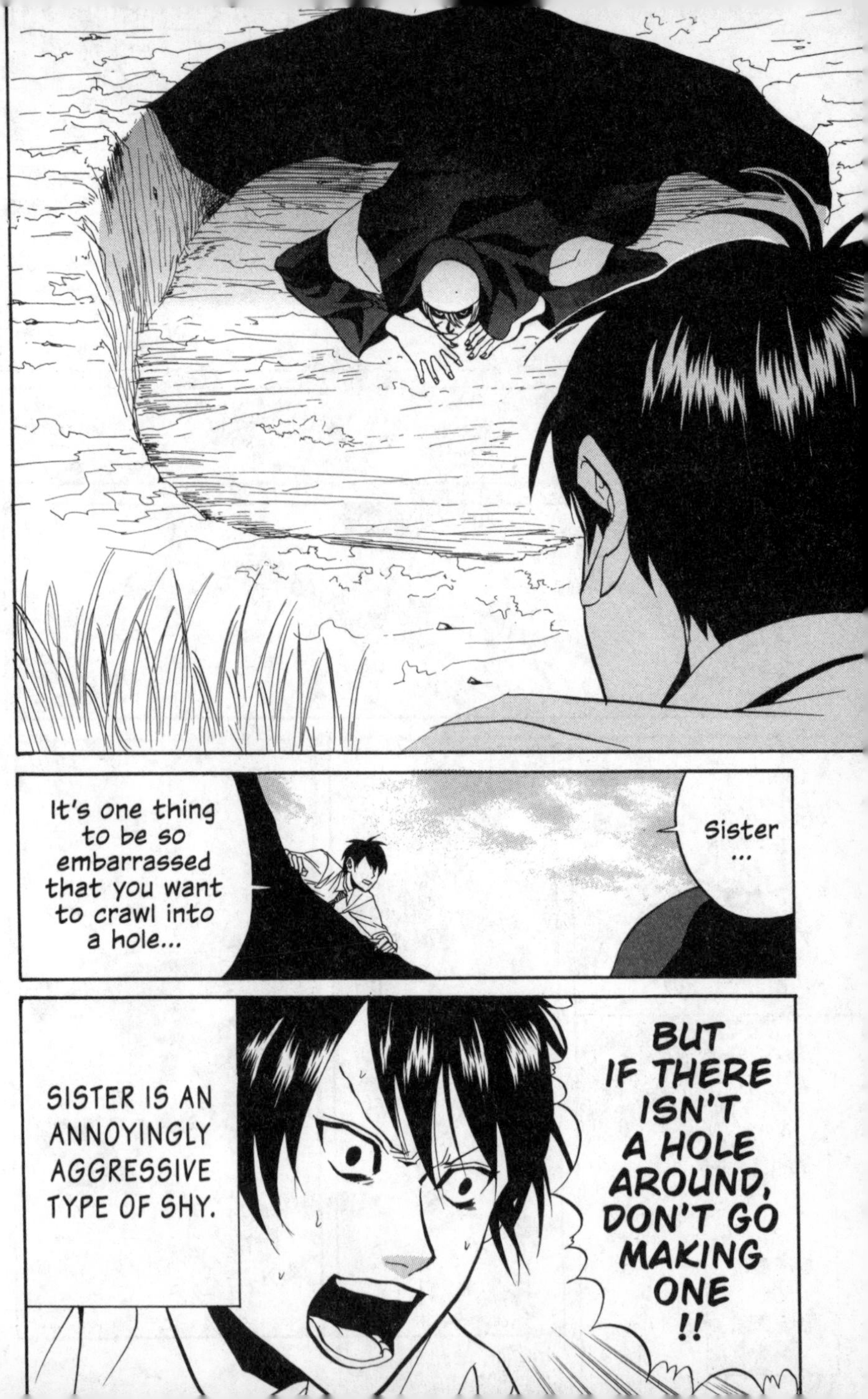
Sister ...
It's one thing to be so embarrassed that you want to crawl into a hole...
BUT IF THERE ISN'T A HOLE AROUND, DON'T GO MAKING ONE !!
SISTER IS AN ANNOYINGLY AGGRESSIVE TYPE OF SHY.

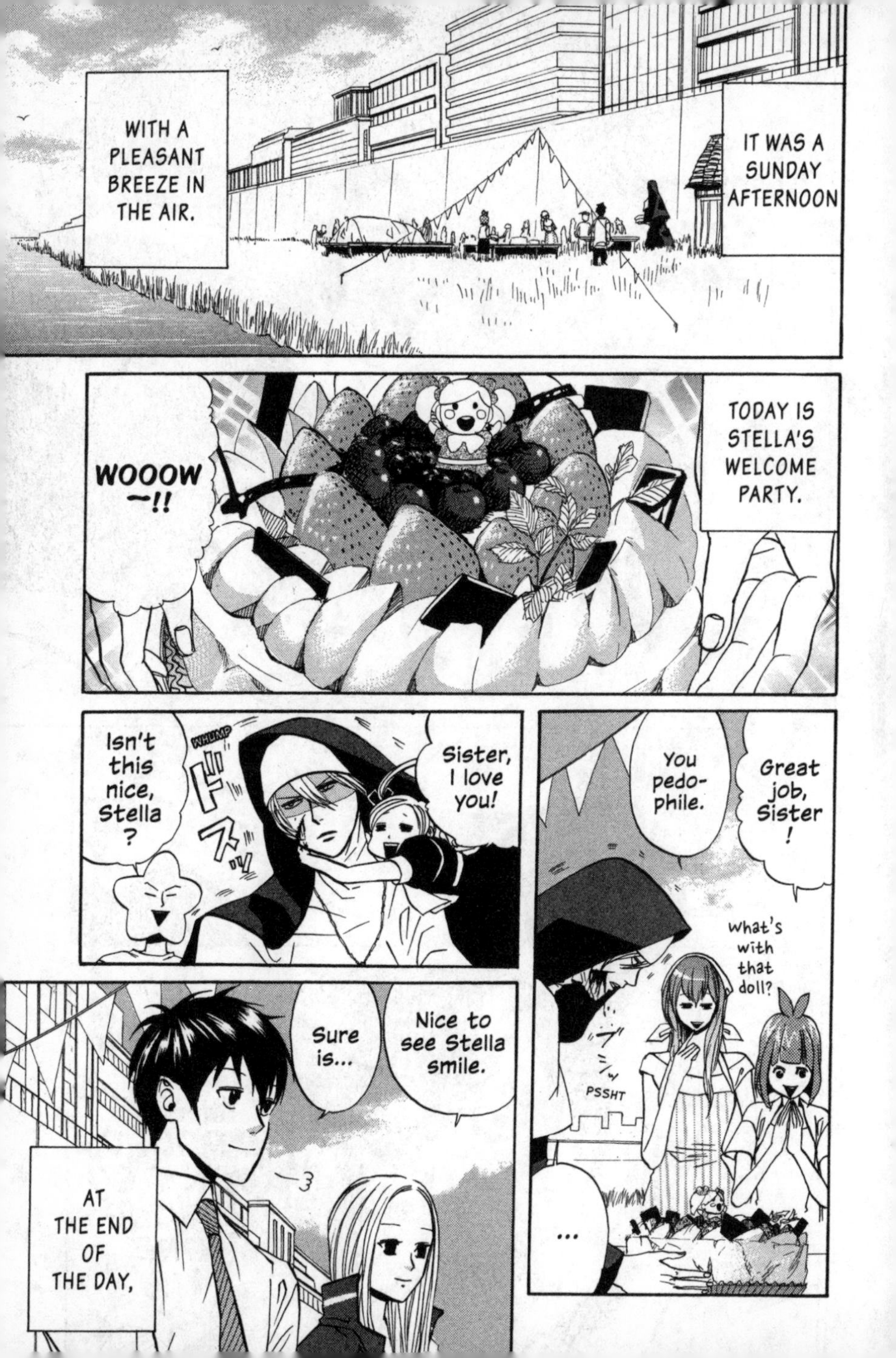
IT WAS A SUNDAY AFTERNOON
WITH A PLEASANT BREEZE IN THE AIR.
TODAY IS STELLA'S WELCOME PARTY.
WOOOW~!!
Great job, Sister!
You pedophile.
What's with that doll?
PSSHT
...
Sister, I love you!
WHUMP
Isn't this nice, Stella?
Nice to see Stella smile.
Sure is...
AT THE END OF THE DAY,

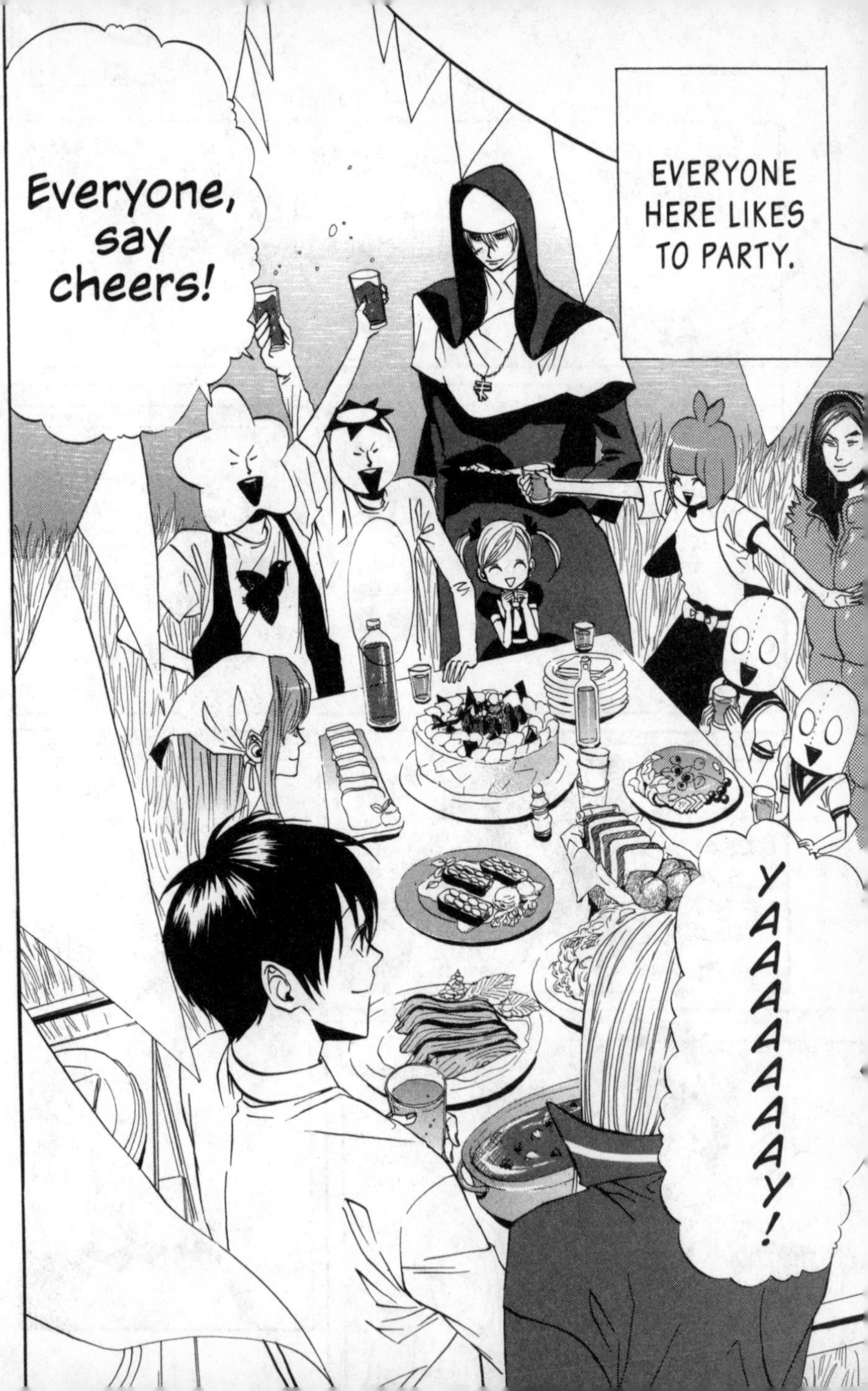
EVERYONE HERE LIKES TO PARTY.
Everyone, say cheers!
YAAAAAAAY!

Chapter 45: Family

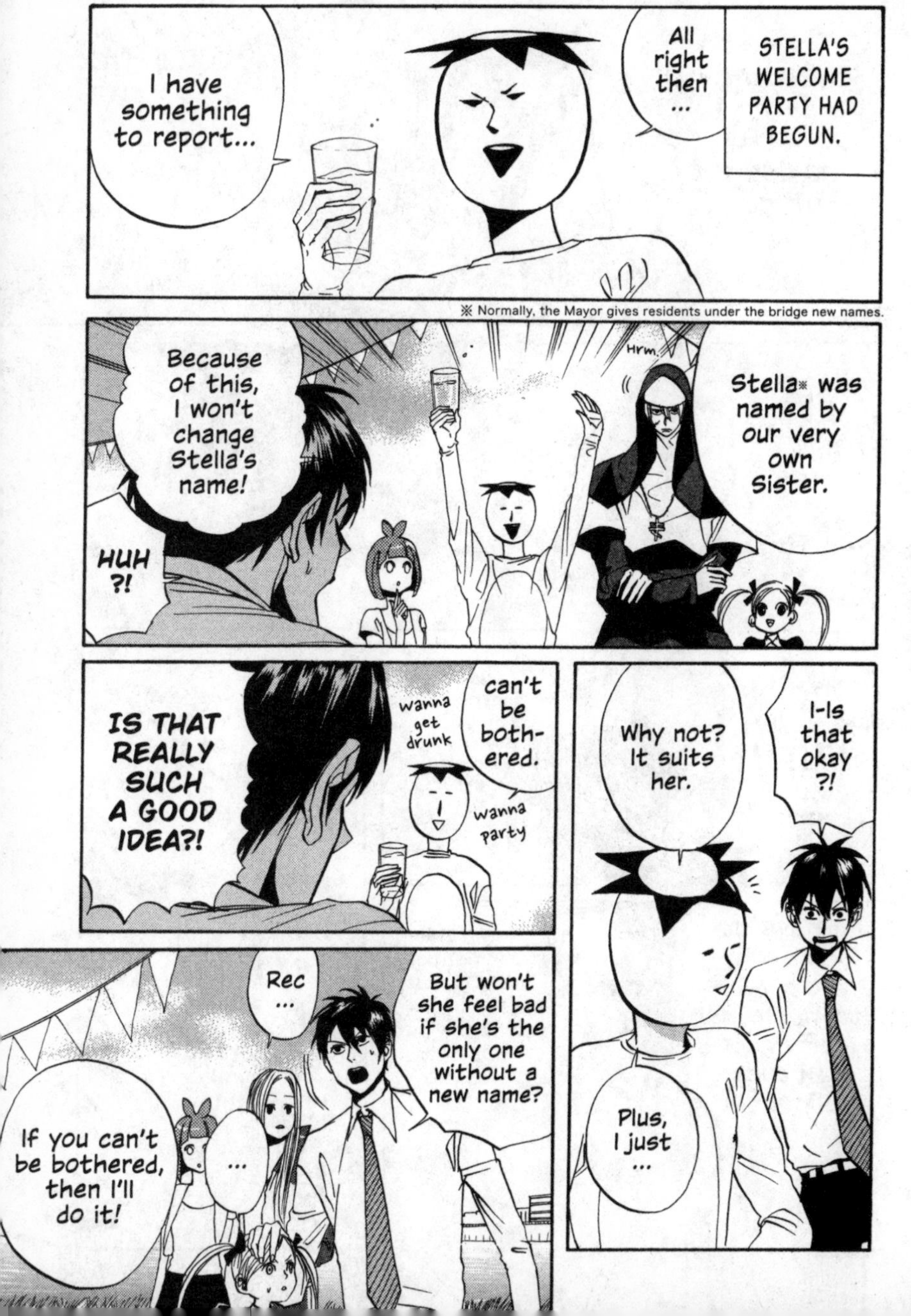

STELLA'S WELCOME PARTY HAD BEGUN.
All right then ...
I have something to report...
Stella※ was named by our very own Sister.
Hrm.
Because of this, I won't change Stella's name!
HUH ?!
I-Is that okay ?!
Why not? It suits her.
Plus, I just ...
can't be bothered.
wanna get drunk
wanna party
IS THAT REALLY SUCH A GOOD IDEA?!
But won't she feel bad if she's the only one without a new name?
Rec ...
...
If you can't be bothered, then I'll do it!

※ Normally, the Mayor gives residents under the bridge new names.

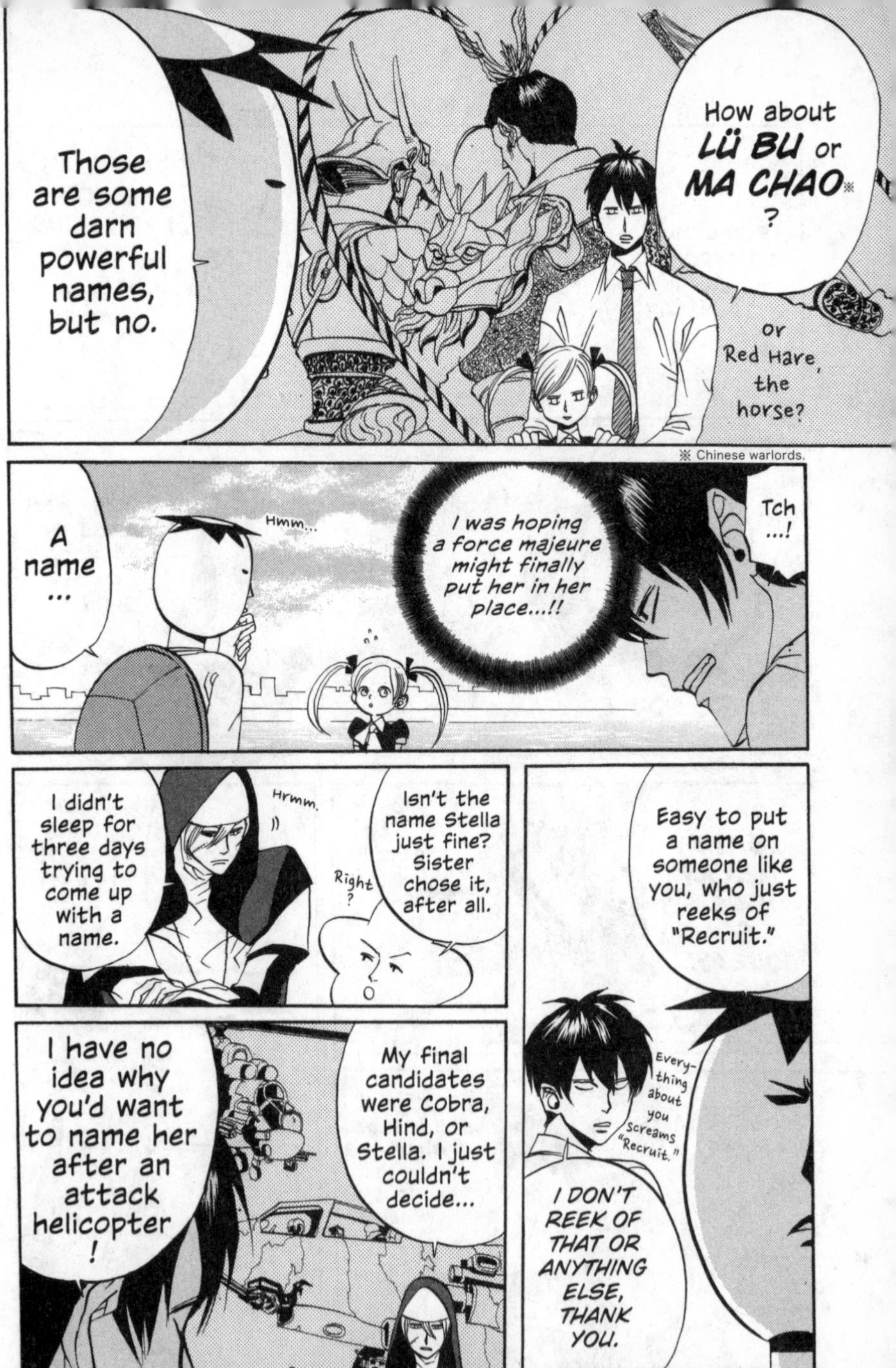
How about LÜ BU or MA CHAO※ ?
or Red Hare, the horse?
Those are some darn powerful names, but no.
Tch ...!
I was hoping a force majeure might finally put her in her place...!!
Hmm...
A name ...
Easy to put a name on someone like you, who just reeks of "Recruit."
Every-thing about you screams "Recruit."
I DON'T REEK OF THAT OR ANYTHING ELSE, THANK YOU.
Isn't the name Stella just fine? Sister chose it, after all.
Right ?
Hrmm.
I didn't sleep for three days trying to come up with a name.
My final candidates were Cobra, Hind, or Stella. I just couldn't decide...
I have no idea why you'd want to name her after an attack helicopter !

※ Chinese warlords.

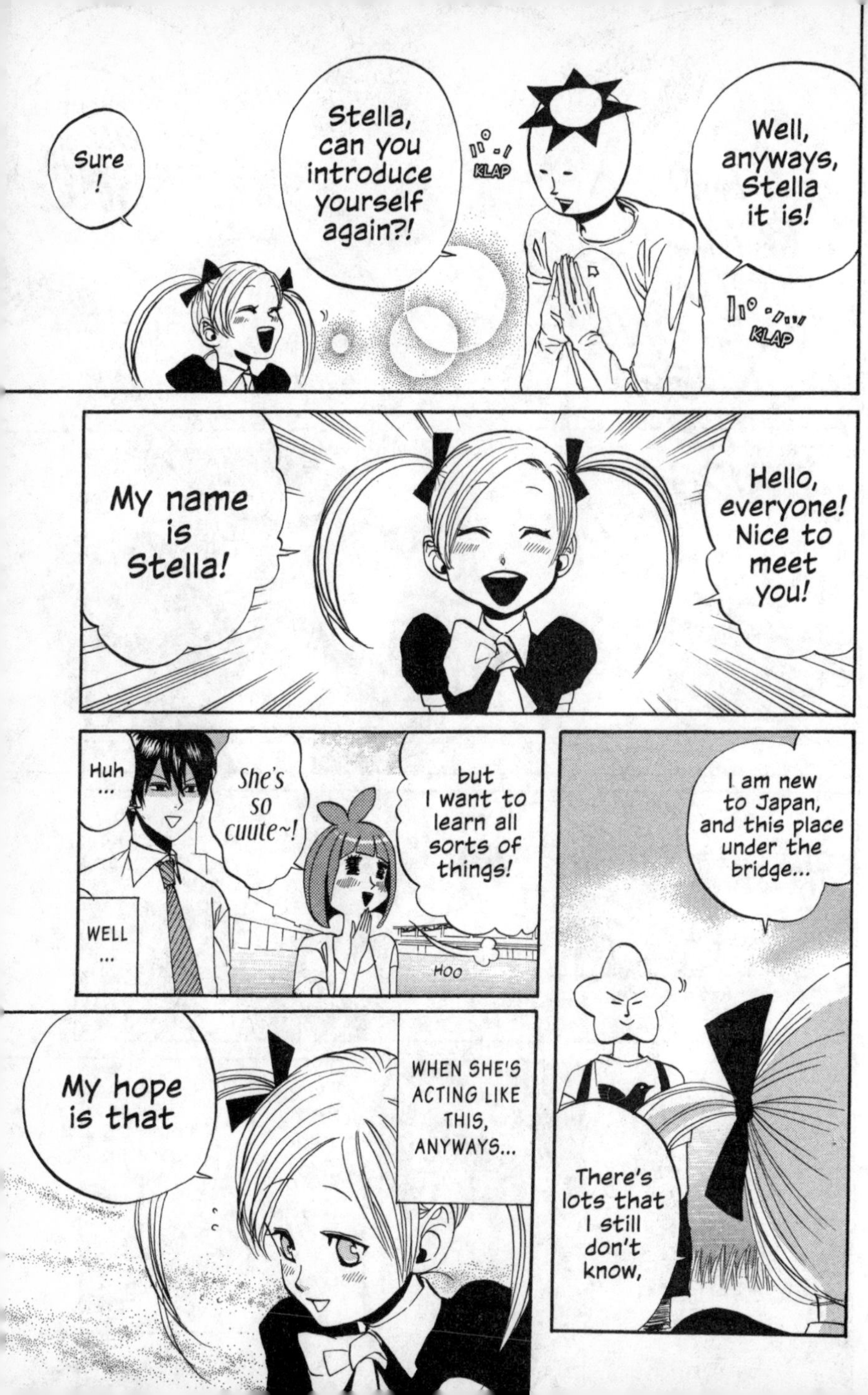
Well, anyways, Stella it is!
KLAP
KLAP
Stella, can you introduce yourself again?!
Sure!
Hello, everyone! Nice to meet you!
My name is Stella!
I am new to Japan, and this place under the bridge...
There's lots that I still don't know,
but I want to learn all sorts of things!
HOO
She's so cuute~!
Huh...
WELL...
WHEN SHE'S ACTING LIKE THIS, ANYWAYS...
My hope is that

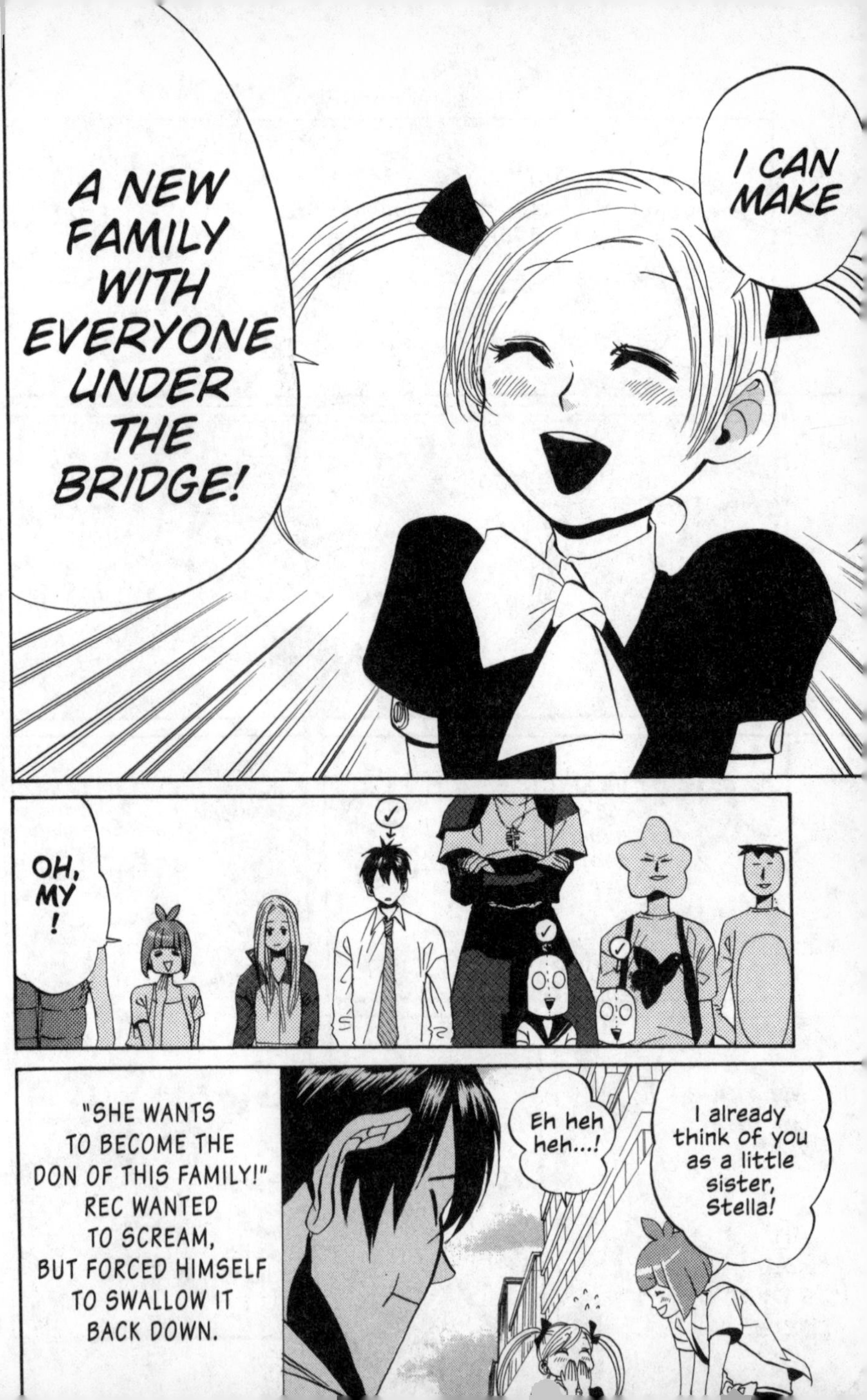
I CAN MAKE
A NEW FAMILY WITH EVERYONE UNDER THE BRIDGE!
OH, MY!
I already think of you as a little sister, Stella!
Eh heh heh...!
"SHE WANTS TO BECOME THE DON OF THIS FAMILY!" REC WANTED TO SCREAM, BUT FORCED HIMSELF TO SWALLOW IT BACK DOWN.

Chapter 46: Pimp

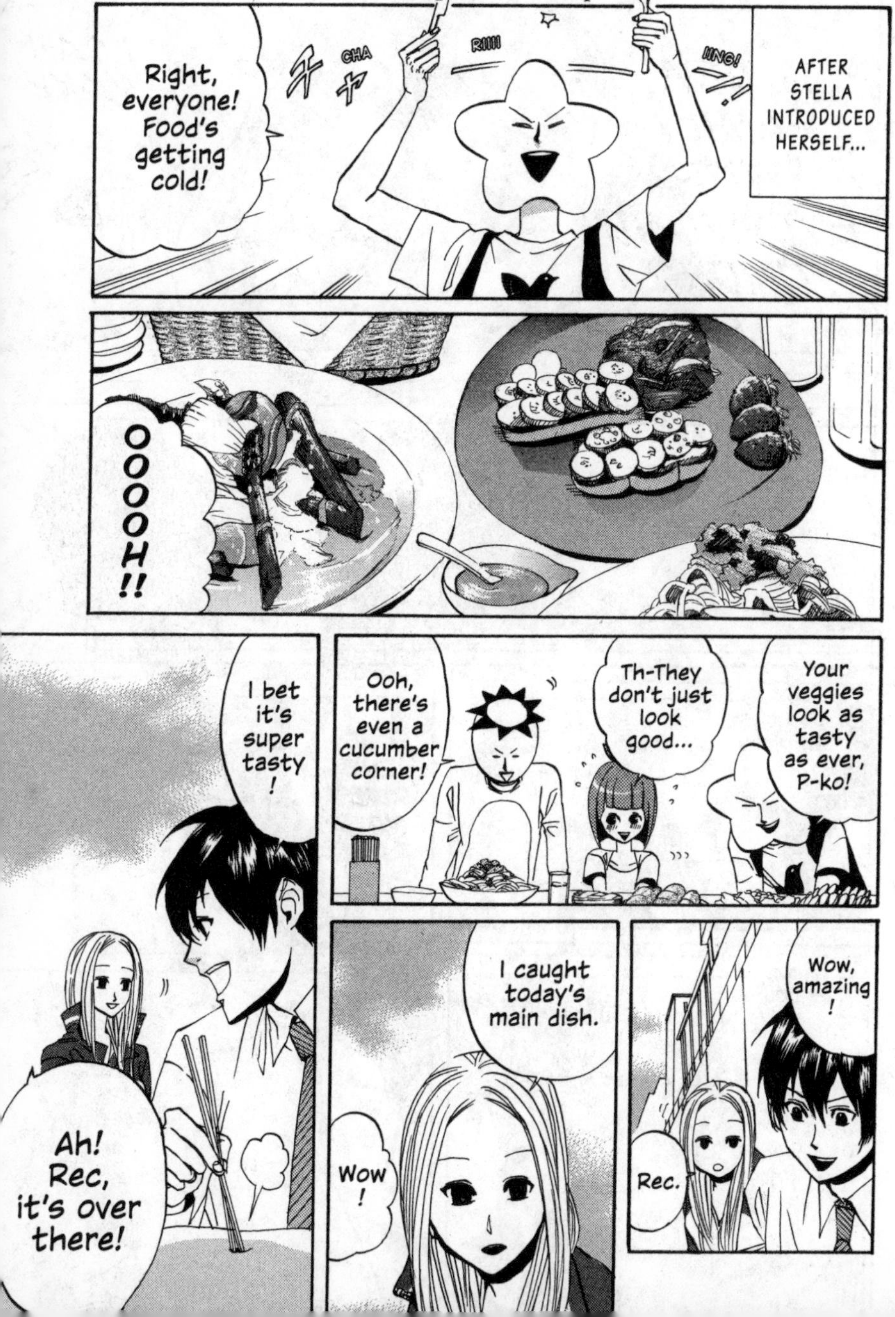
AFTER STELLA INTRODUCED HERSELF...
IING!
RIIII
CHA
Right, everyone! Food's getting cold!
OOOOOH!!
Your veggies look as tasty as ever, P-ko!
Th-They don't just look good...
Ooh, there's even a cucumber corner!
Wow, amazing!
Rec.
I caught today's main dish.
Wow!
I bet it's super tasty!
Ah! Rec, it's over there!

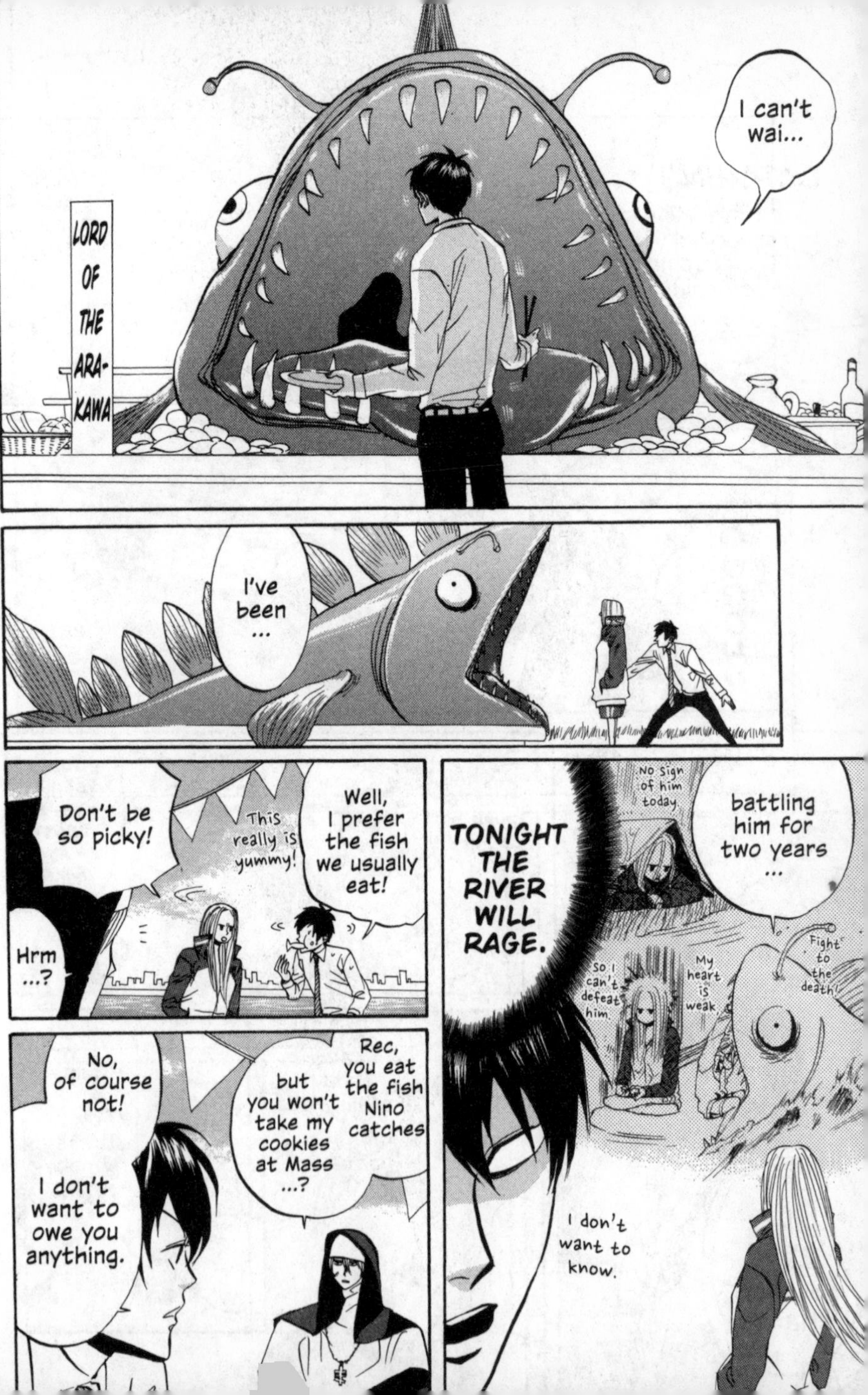
I can't wai...
LORD OF THE ARA-KAWA
I've been ...
battling him for two years ...
No sign of him today
TONIGHT THE RIVER WILL RAGE.
Fight to the death!
My heart is weak
So I can't defeat him.
I don't want to know.
Well, I prefer the fish we usually eat!
This really is yummy!
Don't be so picky!
Hrm ...?
Rec, you eat the fish Nino catches
but you won't take my cookies at Mass ...?
No, of course not!
I don't want to owe you anything.

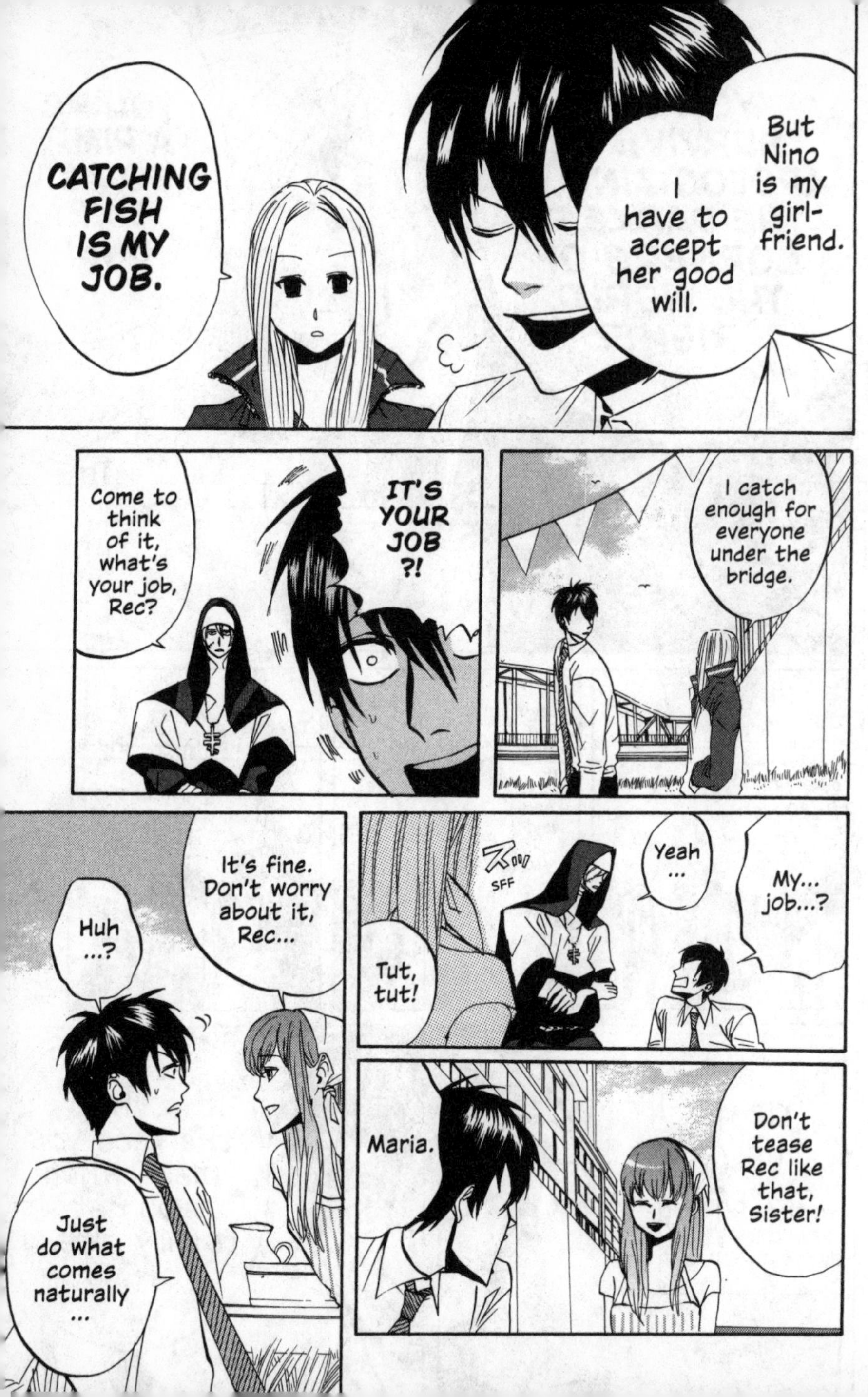
But Nino is my girl- friend.
I have to accept her good will.
CATCHING FISH IS MY JOB.
I catch enough for everyone under the bridge.
IT'S YOUR JOB ?!
Come to think of it, what's your job, Rec?
My... job...?
Yeah ...
SFF
Tut, tut!
Don't tease Rec like that, Sister!
Maria.
It's fine. Don't worry about it, Rec...
Huh ...?
Just do what comes naturally ...

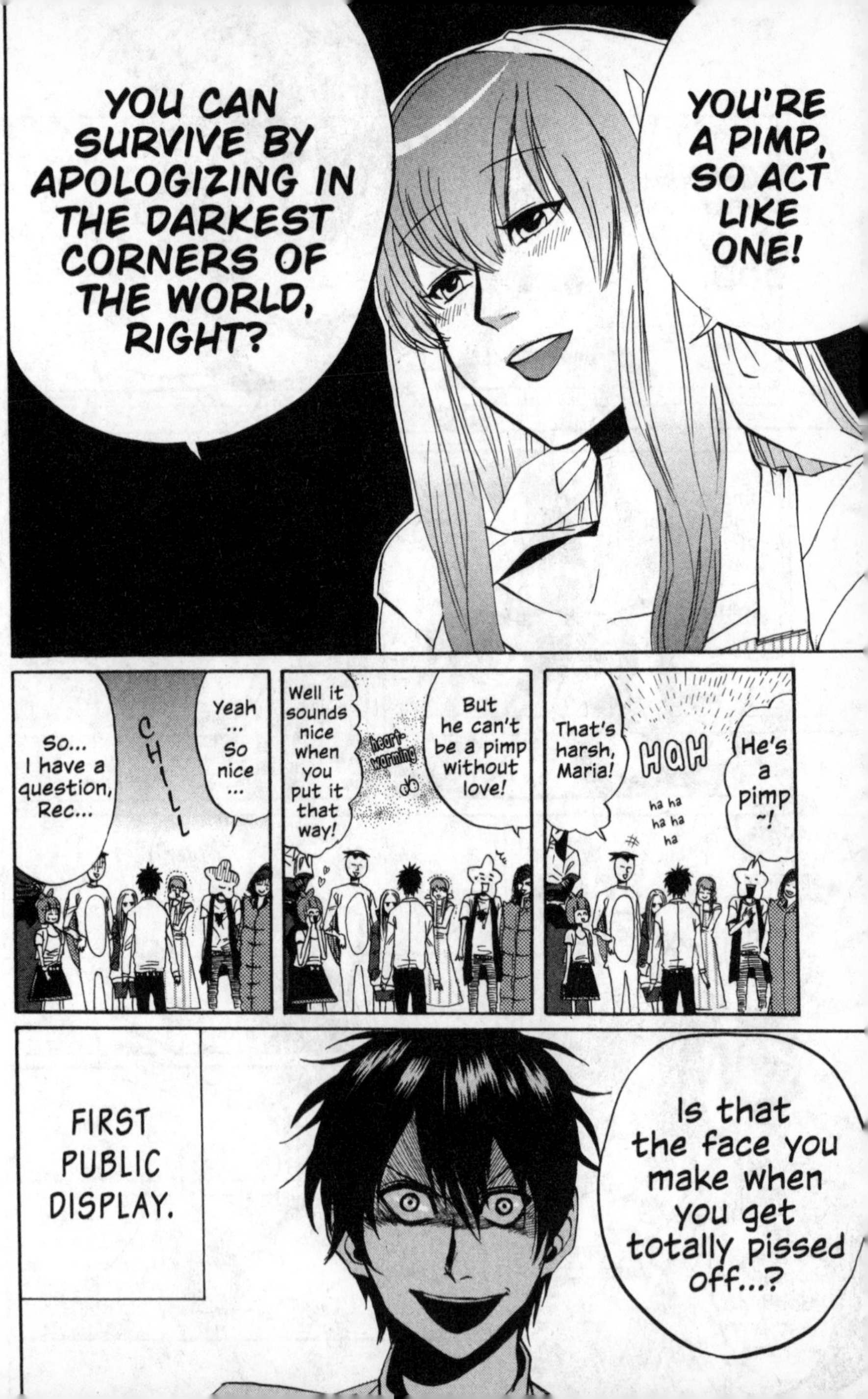
YOU'RE A PIMP, SO ACT LIKE ONE!
YOU CAN SURVIVE BY APOLOGIZING IN THE DARKEST CORNERS OF THE WORLD, RIGHT?
He's a pimp ~!
HAH
ha ha ha ha ha
That's harsh, Maria!
But he can't be a pimp without love!
heart-warming
Well it sounds nice when you put it that way!
Yeah ... So nice ...
CHILL
So... I have a question, Rec...
Is that the face you make when you get totally pissed off...?
FIRST PUBLIC DISPLAY.

Chapter 47: I'll Show You

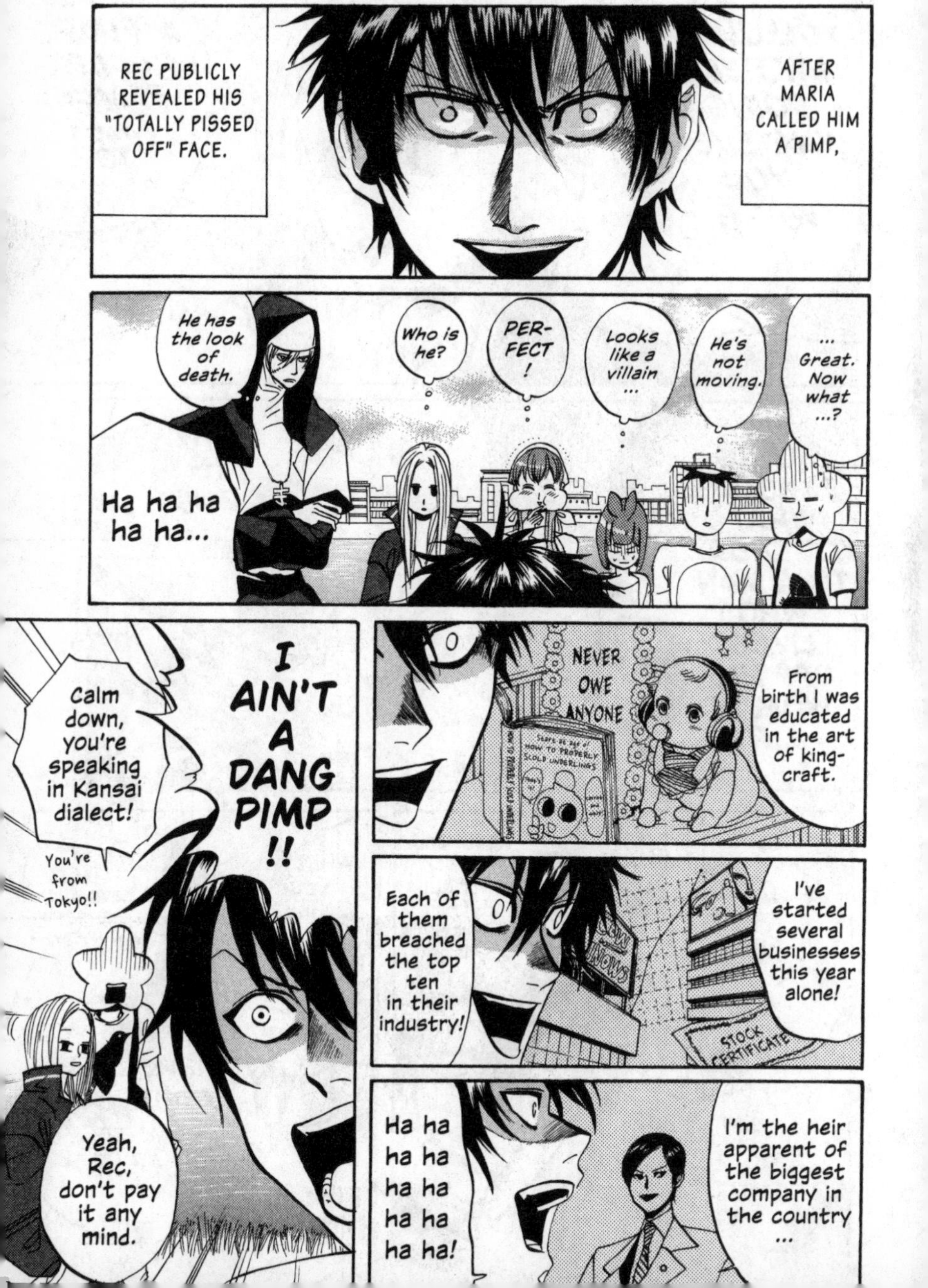
AFTER MARIA CALLED HIM A PIMP,
REC PUBLICLY REVEALED HIS "TOTALLY PISSED OFF" FACE.
... Great. Now what ...?
He's not moving.
Looks like a villain ...
PERFECT!
Who is he?
He has the look of death.
Ha ha ha ha ha...
From birth I was educated in the art of king-craft.
NEVER OWE ANYONE
HOW TO PROPERLY SCOLD UNDERLINGS
I've started several businesses this year alone!
Each of them breached the top ten in their industry!
STOCK CERTIFICATE
I'm the heir apparent of the biggest company in the country ...
Ha ha ha ha ha ha ha ha ha ha!
I AIN'T A DANG PIMP!!
Calm down, you're speaking in Kansai dialect!
You're from Tokyo!!
Yeah, Rec, don't pay it any mind.

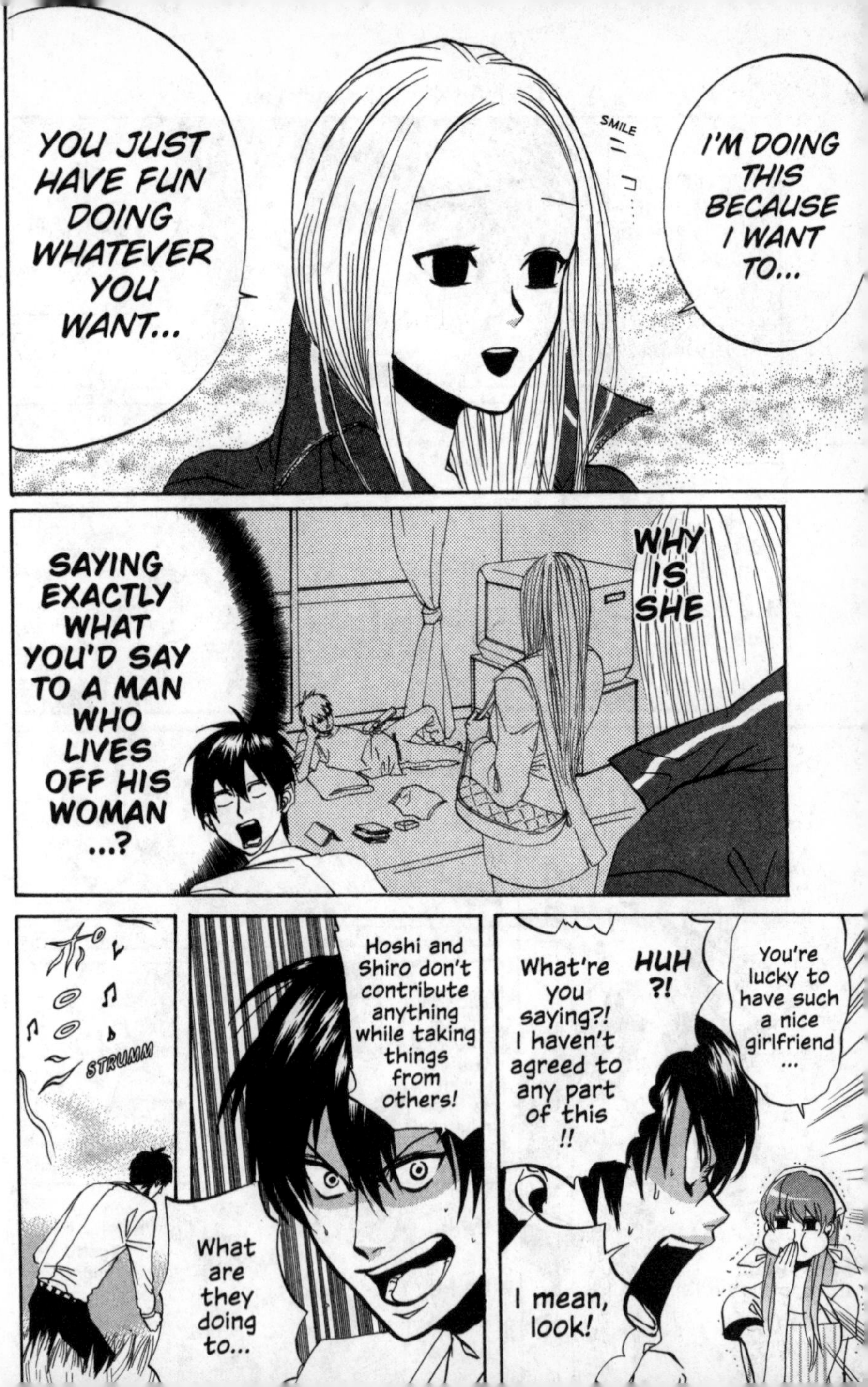
I'M DOING THIS BECAUSE I WANT TO...
SMILE
YOU JUST HAVE FUN DOING WHATEVER YOU WANT...
WHY IS SHE
SAYING EXACTLY WHAT YOU'D SAY TO A MAN WHO LIVES OFF HIS WOMAN ...?
You're lucky to have such a nice girlfriend ...
HUH ?!
What're you saying?! I haven't agreed to any part of this !!
I mean, look!
Hoshi and Shiro don't contribute anything while taking things from others!
What are they doing to...
STRUMM

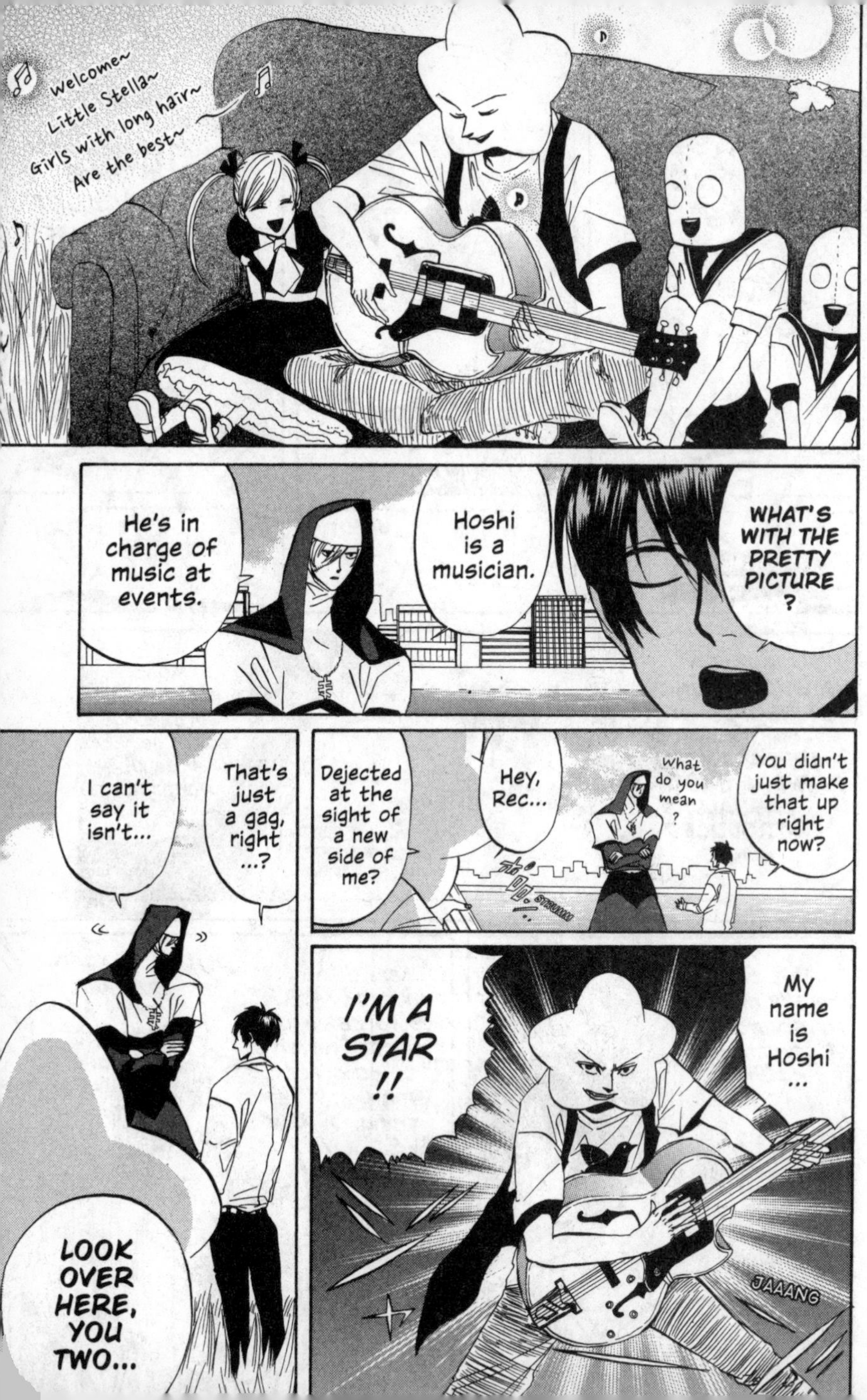

Welcome~
Little Stella~
Girls with long hair~
Are the best~
WHAT'S WITH THE PRETTY PICTURE?
Hoshi is a musician.
He's in charge of music at events.
You didn't just make that up right now?
What do you mean?
Hey, Rec...
Dejected at the sight of a new side of me?
STRUM
My name is Hoshi...
I'M A STAR!!
JAAANG
That's just a gag, right...?
I can't say it isn't...
LOOK OVER HERE, YOU TWO...

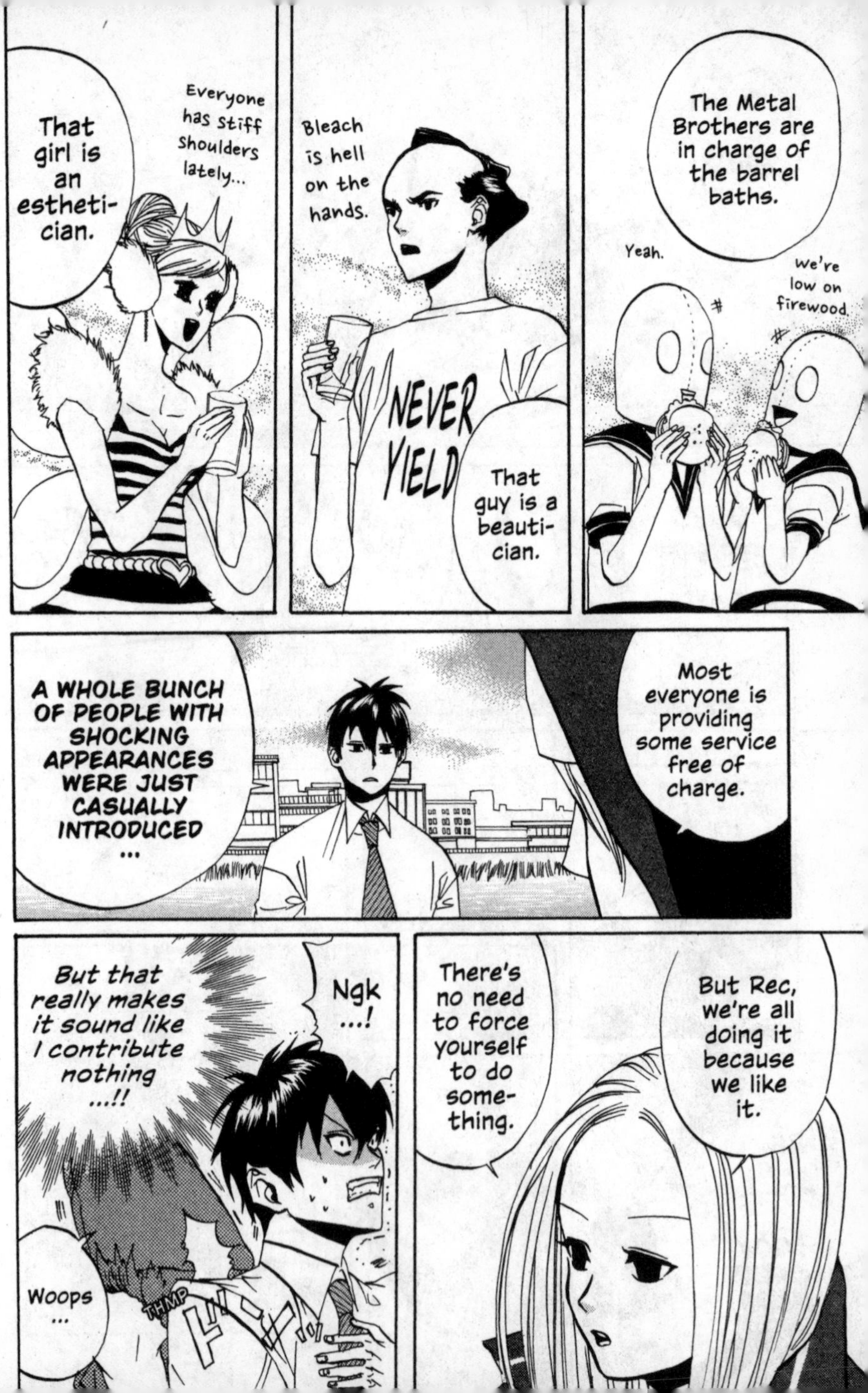
The Metal Brothers are in charge of the barrel baths.
We're low on firewood.
Yeah.
That guy is a beautician.
Bleach is hell on the hands.
NEVER YIELD
That girl is an esthetician.
Everyone has stiff Shoulders lately...
Most everyone is providing some service free of charge.
A WHOLE BUNCH OF PEOPLE WITH SHOCKING APPEARANCES WERE JUST CASUALLY INTRODUCED ...
But Rec, we're all doing it because we like it.
There's no need to force yourself to do something.
Ngk ...!
But that really makes it sound like I contribute nothing ...!!
Woops ...
THMP

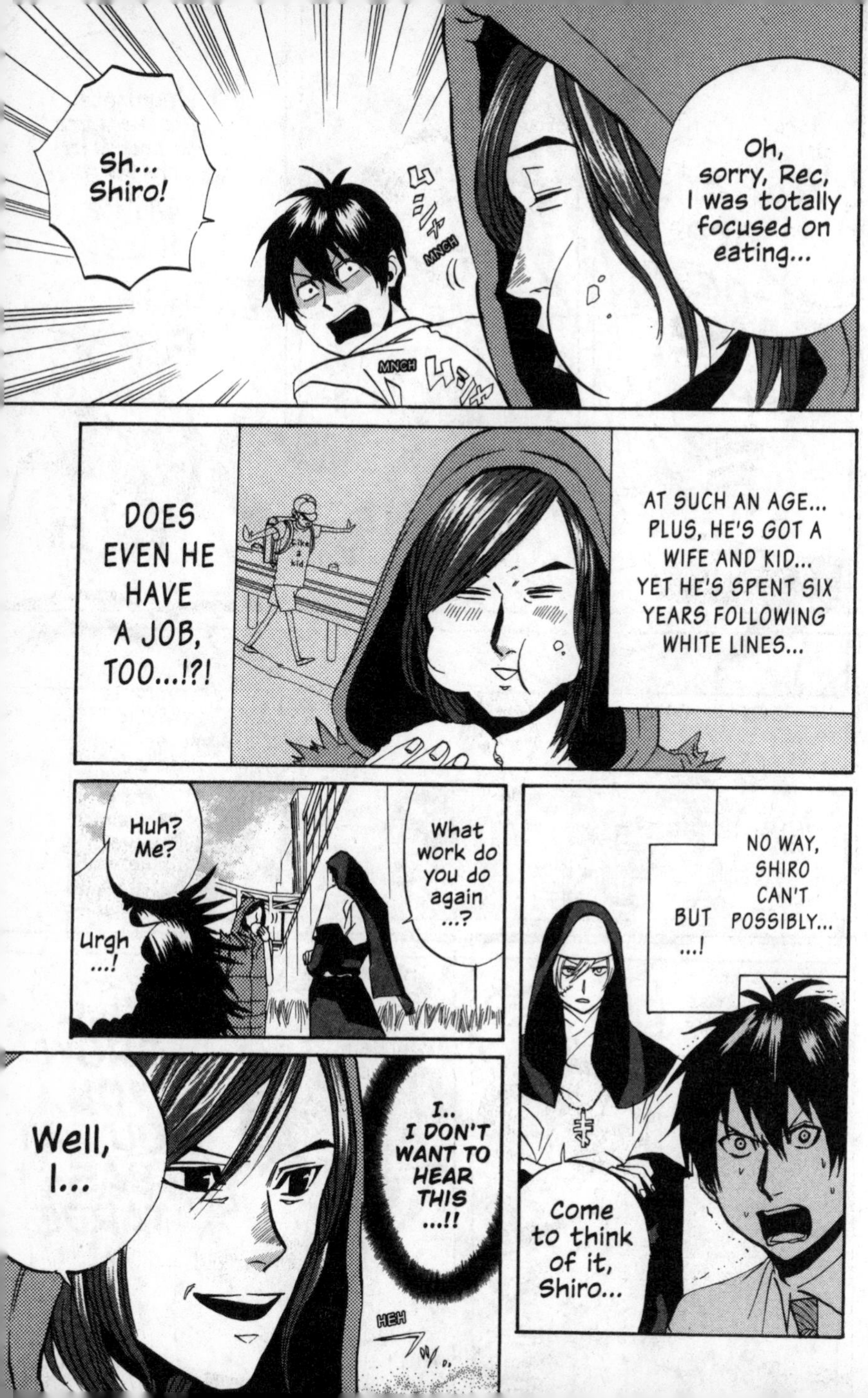

Oh, sorry, Rec, I was totally focused on eating...
MNCH
MNCH
Sh... Shiro!
AT SUCH AN AGE... PLUS, HE'S GOT A WIFE AND KID... YET HE'S SPENT SIX YEARS FOLLOWING WHITE LINES...
DOES EVEN HE HAVE A JOB, TOO...!?!
NO WAY, SHIRO CAN'T POSSIBLY...
BUT ...!
Come to think of it, Shiro...
What work do you do again ...?
Huh? Me?
Urgh ...!
I.. I DON'T WANT TO HEAR THIS ...!!
Well, I...
HEH

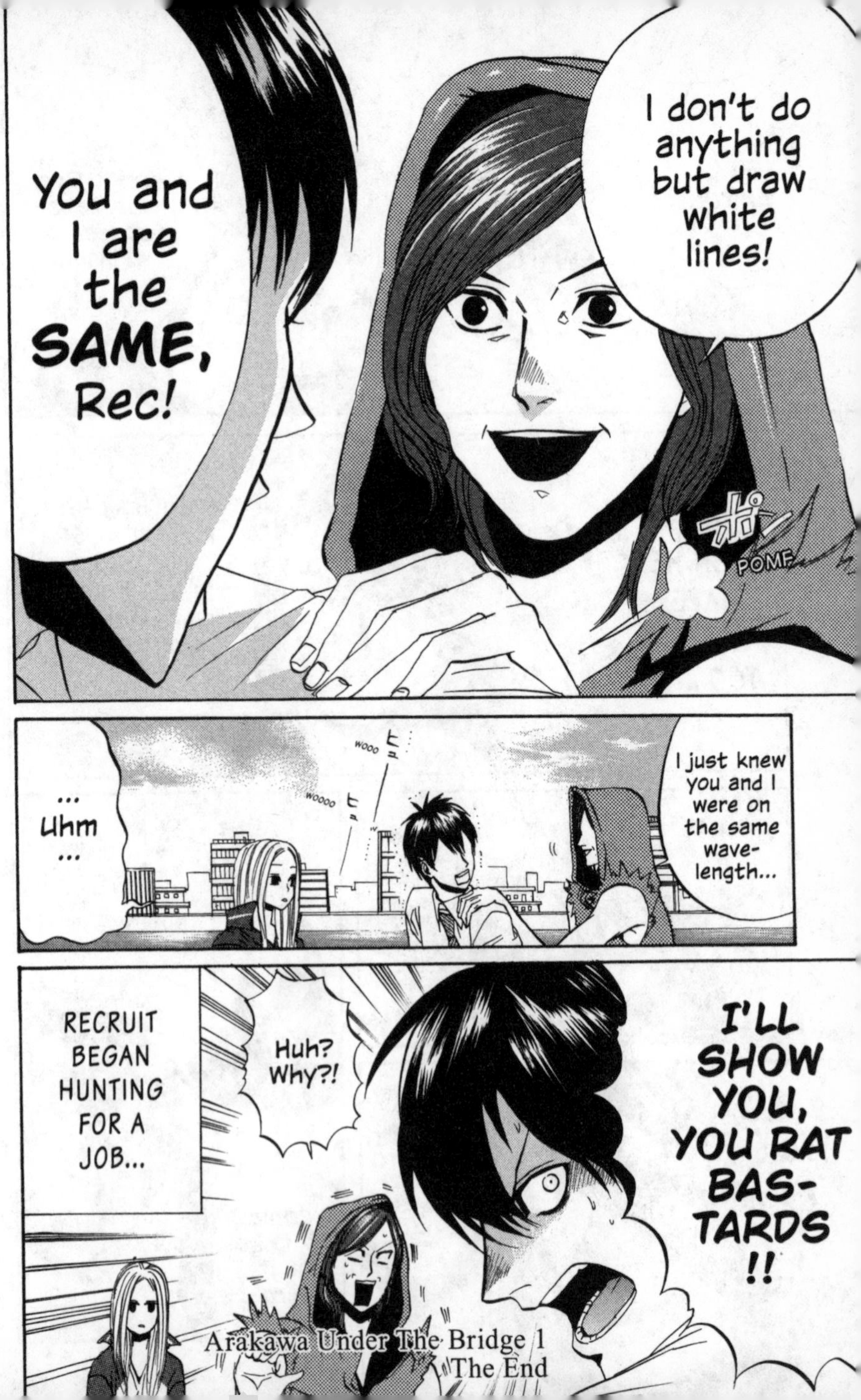
I don't do anything but draw white lines!
You and I are the SAME, Rec!
POMF
I just knew you and I were on the same wave-length...
WOOO
WOOOO
... Uhm ...
I'LL SHOW YOU, YOU RAT BAS-TARDS!!
Huh? Why?!
RECRUIT BEGAN HUNTING FOR A JOB...
Arakawa Under The Bridge 1
The End

NAKAMURA FACTORY RETURNS

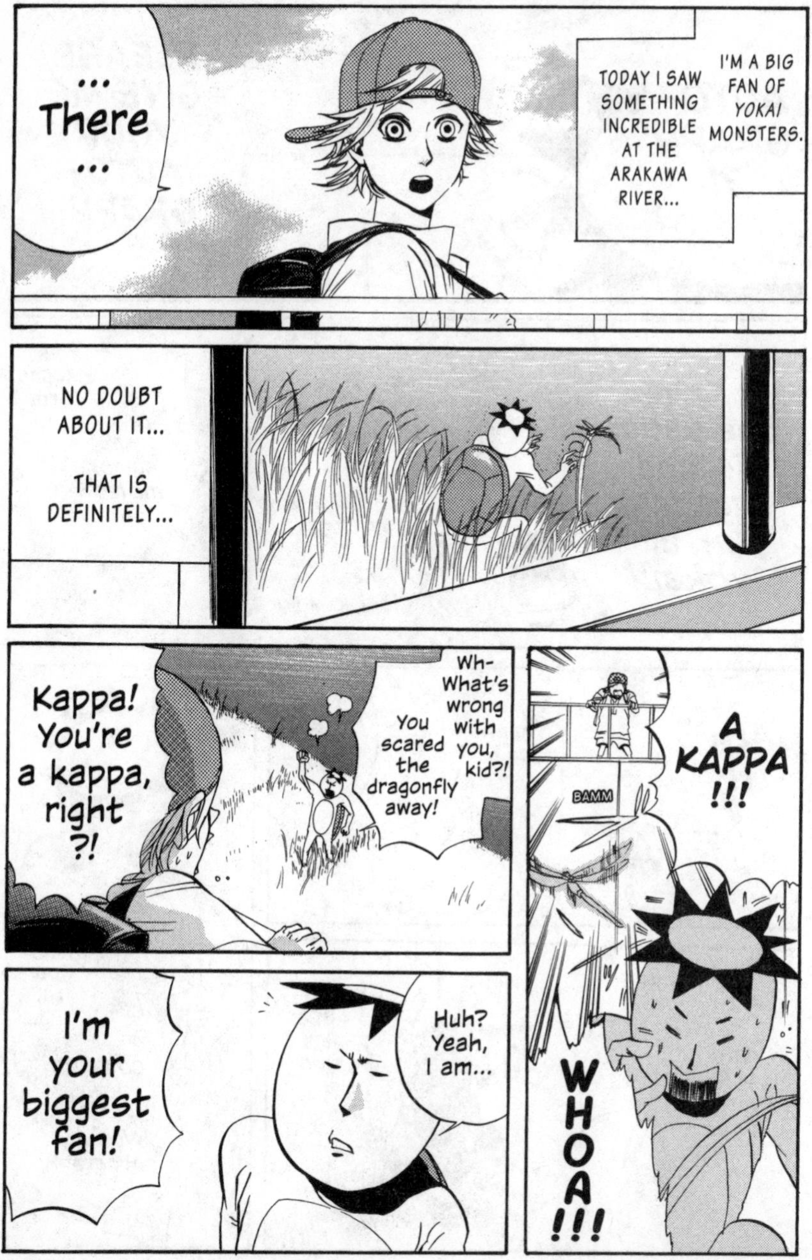
I'M A BIG FAN OF *YOKAI* MONSTERS.
TODAY I SAW SOMETHING INCREDIBLE AT THE ARAKAWA RIVER...
... There ...
NO DOUBT ABOUT IT...
THAT IS DEFINITELY...
A KAPPA !!!
BAMM
WHOA!!!
Wh- What's wrong with you, kid?!
You scared the dragonfly away!
Kappa! You're a kappa, right ?!
Huh? Yeah, I am...
I'm your biggest fan!

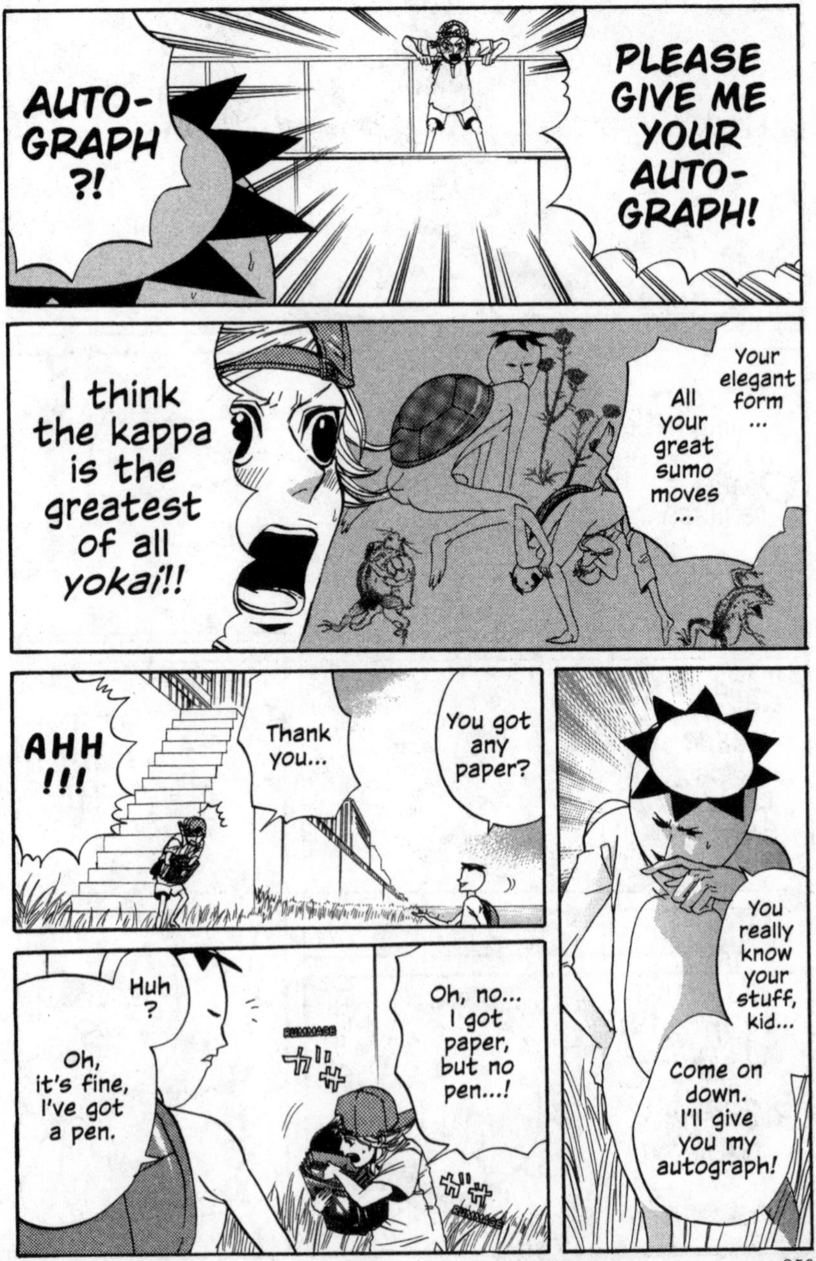
PLEASE GIVE ME YOUR AUTO-GRAPH!
AUTO-GRAPH ?!
Your elegant form ...
All your great sumo moves ...
I think the kappa is the greatest of all *yokai*!!
You really know your stuff, kid...
Come on down. I'll give you my autograph!
You got any paper?
Thank you...
AHH !!!
Oh, no... I got paper, but no pen...!
RUMMAGE
RUMMAGE
Huh ?
Oh, it's fine, I've got a pen.

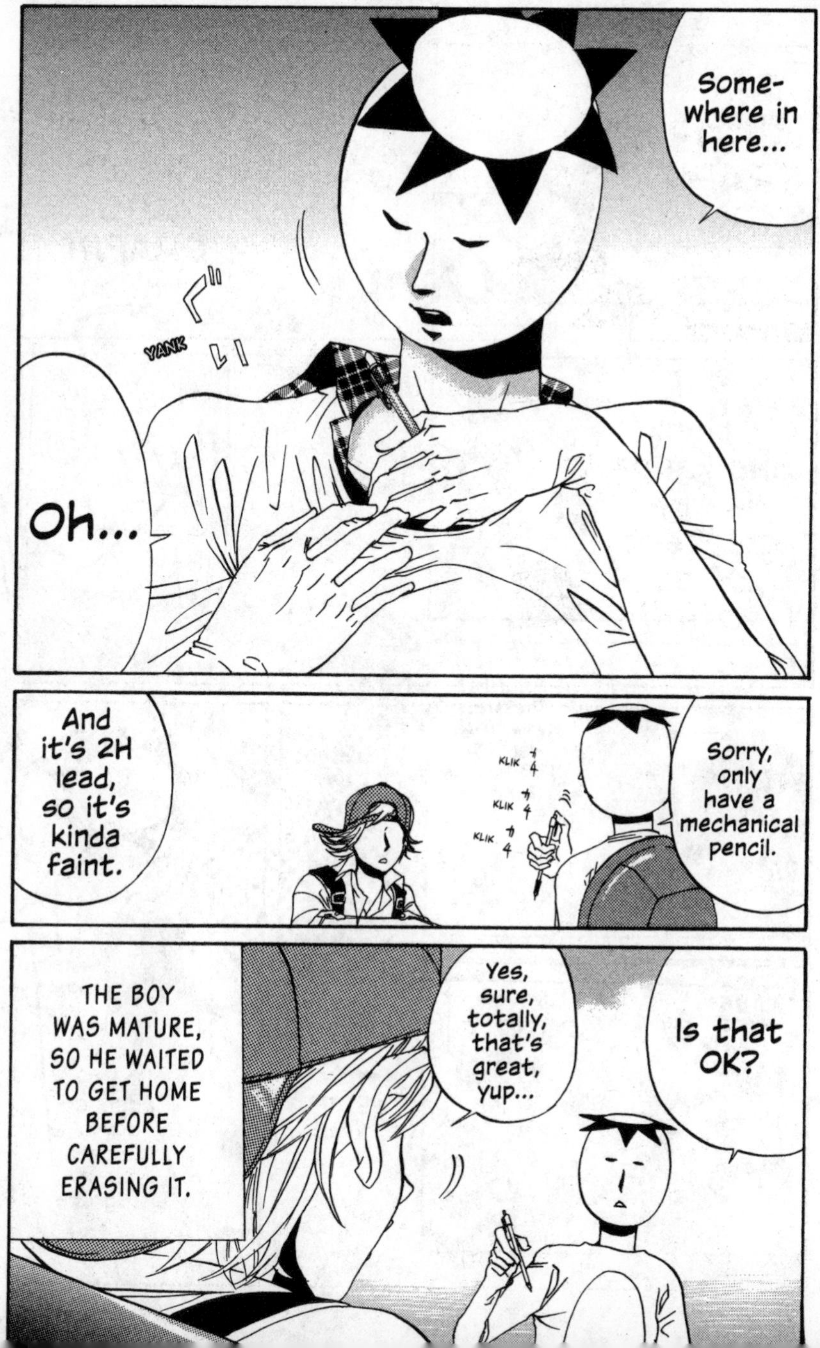
Some-where in here...
YANK
Oh...
Sorry, only have a mechanical pencil.
KLIK
KLIK
KLIK
And it's 2H lead, so it's kinda faint.
Is that OK?
Yes, sure, totally, that's great, yup...
THE BOY WAS MATURE, SO HE WAITED TO GET HOME BEFORE CAREFULLY ERASING IT.

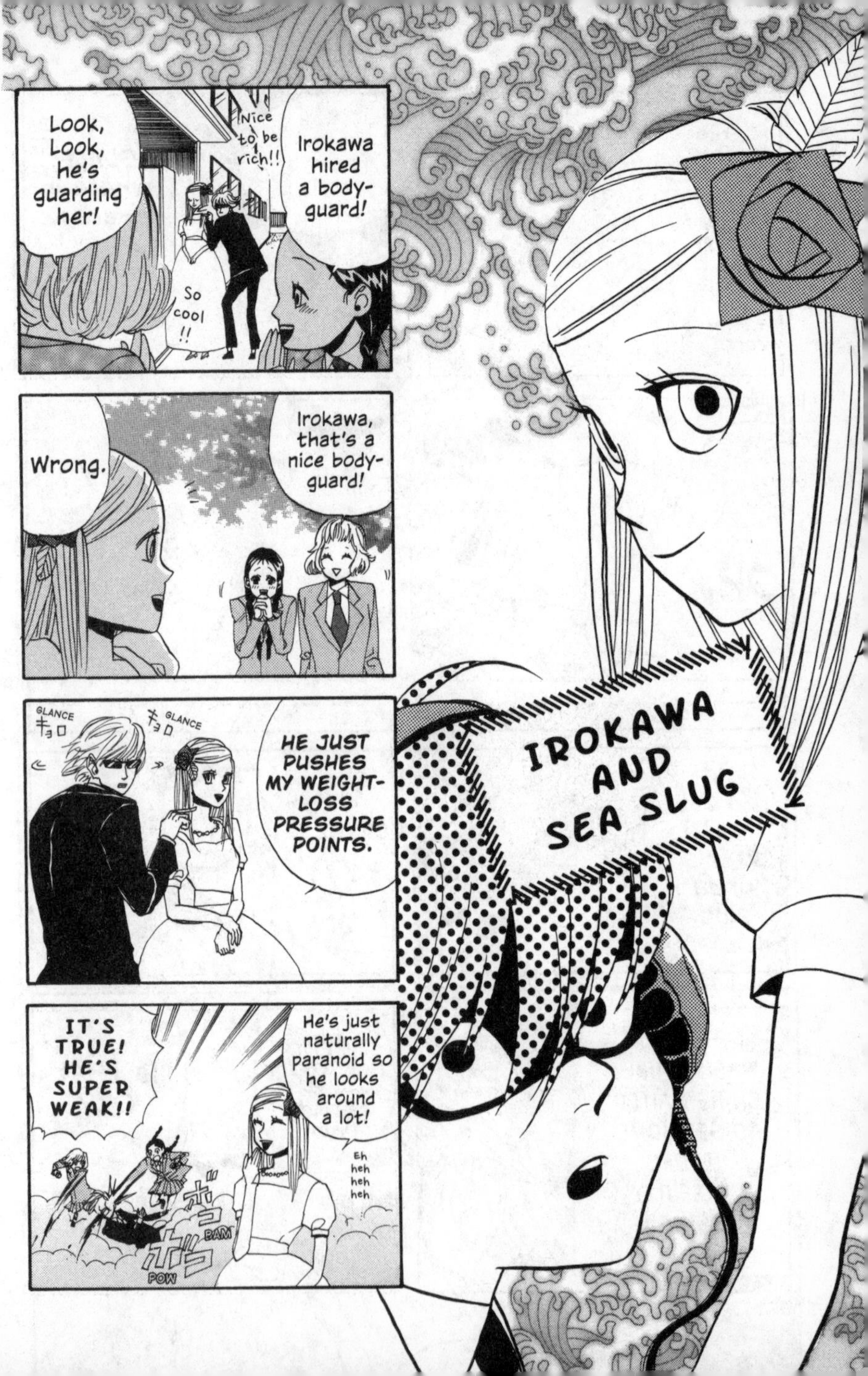
IROKAWA AND SEA SLUG
Irokawa hired a body-guard!
Nice to be rich!!
Look, Look, he's guarding her!
So cool !!
Irokawa, that's a nice body-guard!
Wrong.
HE JUST PUSHES MY WEIGHT-LOSS PRESSURE POINTS.
GLANCE キョロ
GLANCE キョロ
He's just naturally paranoid so he looks around a lot!
IT'S TRUE! HE'S SUPER WEAK!!
Eh heh heh heh
BAM
POW

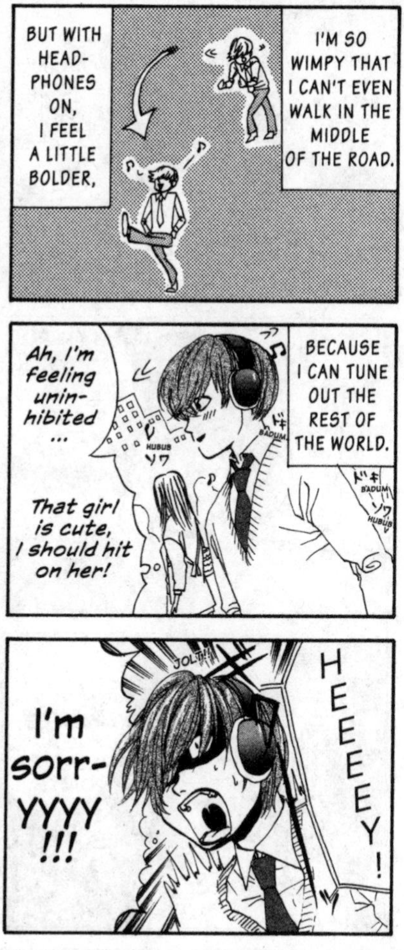

I'M SO WIMPY THAT I CAN'T EVEN WALK IN THE MIDDLE OF THE ROAD.
BUT WITH HEAD-PHONES ON, I FEEL A LITTLE BOLDER,
BECAUSE I CAN TUNE OUT THE REST OF THE WORLD.
BADUM ドキ
Ah, I'm feeling uninhibited ...
HUBUB ソワ
That girl is cute, I should hit on her!
HEEEEY!
JOLT!!
I'm sorr-YYYY!!!
SO I ADD IN TRACKS OF PEOPLE SCREAMING.
Know your place!
I'm sorry!
BECAUSE ONE TIME I GOT TOO CARRIED AWAY AND TRIED TO PUNCH A YAKUZA.
Say your nick-name!
Sea slug!

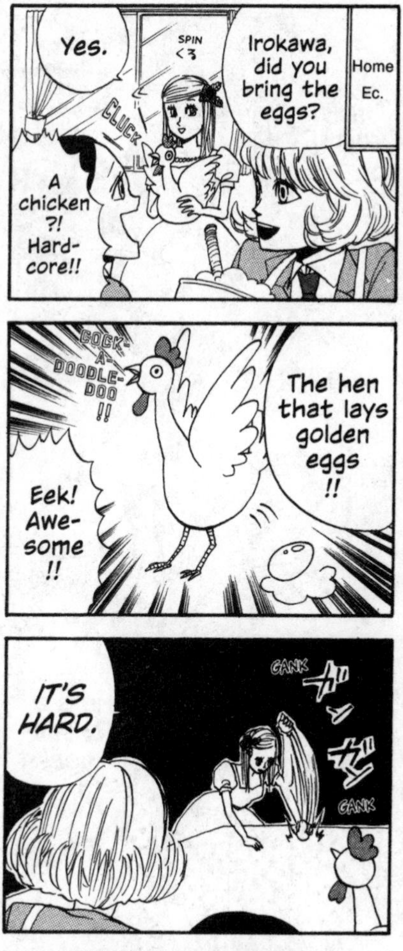

Home Ec.
Irokawa, did you bring the eggs?
SPIN くる
Yes.
CLUCK
A chicken?! Hard-core!!
The hen that lays golden eggs!!
COCK-A-DOODLE-DOO!!
Eek! Awe-some!!
GANK ガン
GANK ガッ
IT'S HARD.
BETTER CALL A STEAM-ROLLER.
BIP ピッ
Irokawa, when you make a mistake ...
Have the courage to admit it!

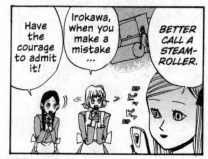

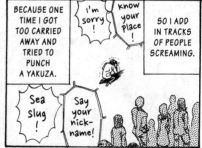

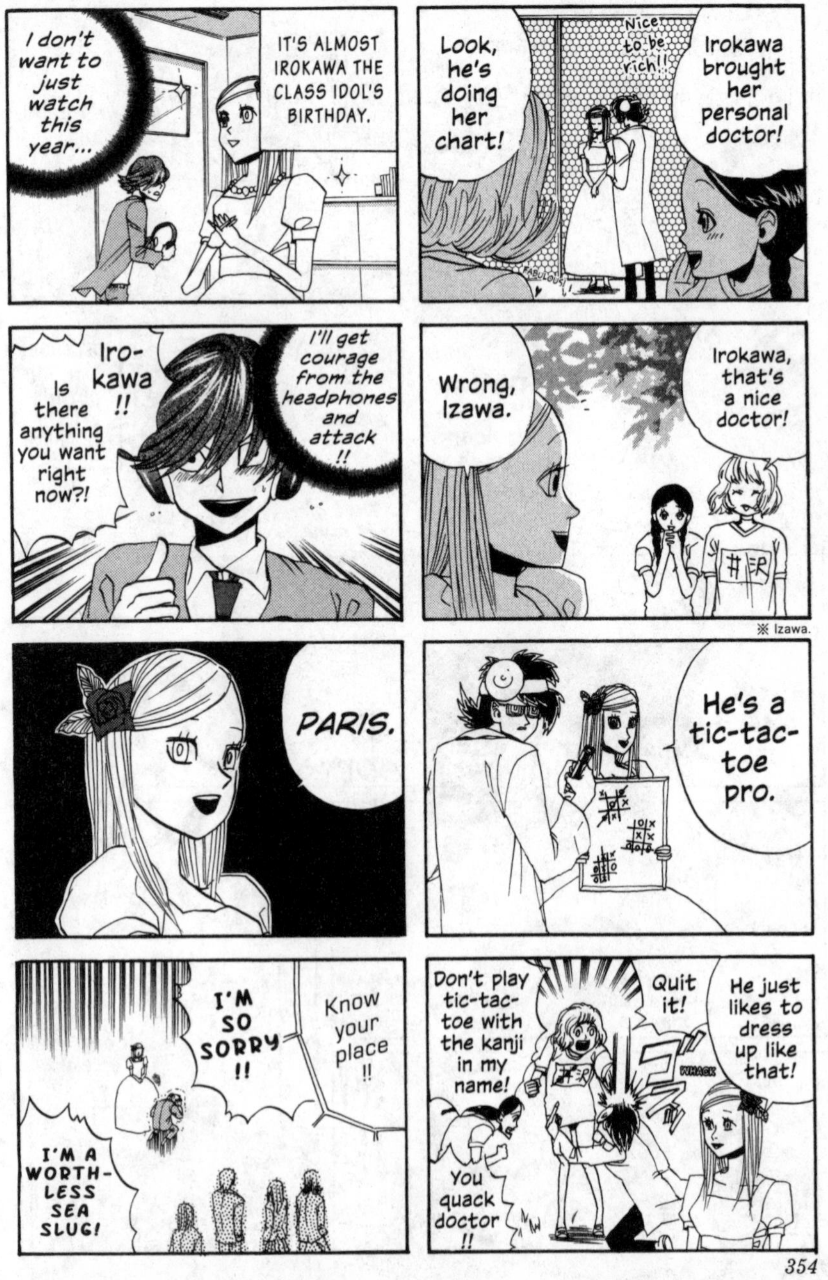
Irokawa brought her personal doctor!
Nice to be rich!!
Look, he's doing her chart!
FABULOUS!
IT'S ALMOST IROKAWA THE CLASS IDOL'S BIRTHDAY.
I don't want to just watch this year...
Irokawa, that's a nice doctor!
Wrong, Izawa.
I'll get courage from the headphones and attack !!
Iro-kawa !!
Is there anything you want right now?!
He's a tic-tac-toe pro.
PARIS.
He just likes to dress up like that!
Quit it!
Don't play tic-tac-toe with the kanji in my name!
WHACK
You quack doctor !!
Know your place !!
I'M SO SORRY !!
I'M A WORTHLESS SEA SLUG!

※ Izawa.

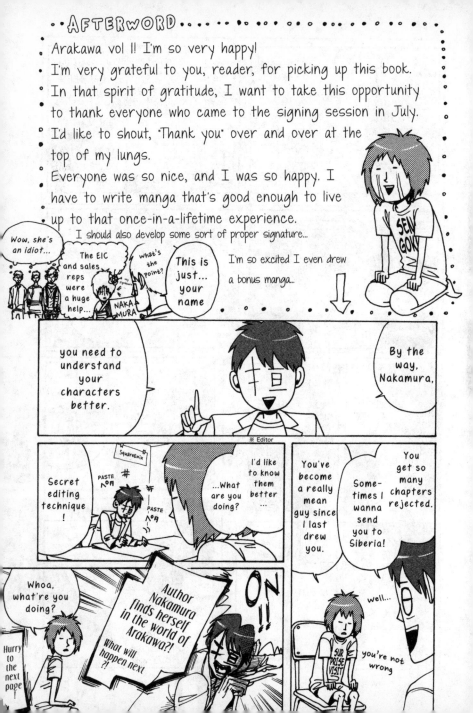

Afterword

Arakawa vol 1! I'm so very happy!
I'm very grateful to you, reader, for picking up this book.
In that spirit of gratitude, I want to take this opportunity to thank everyone who came to the signing session in July.
I'd like to shout, "Thank you" over and over at the top of my lungs.
Everyone was so nice, and I was so happy. I have to write manga that's good enough to live up to that once-in-a-lifetime experience.

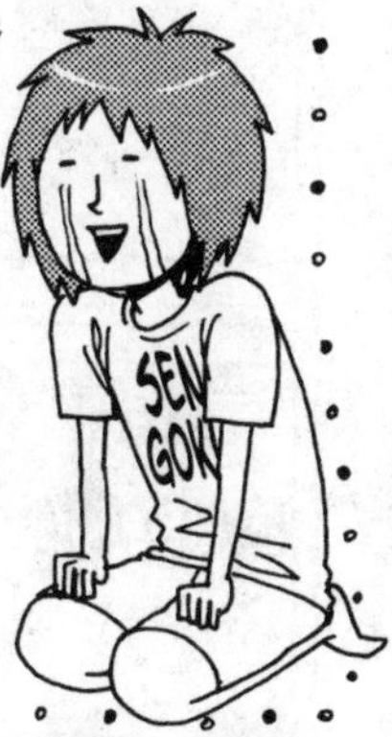
SEN
GOKU

I should also develop some sort of proper signature...

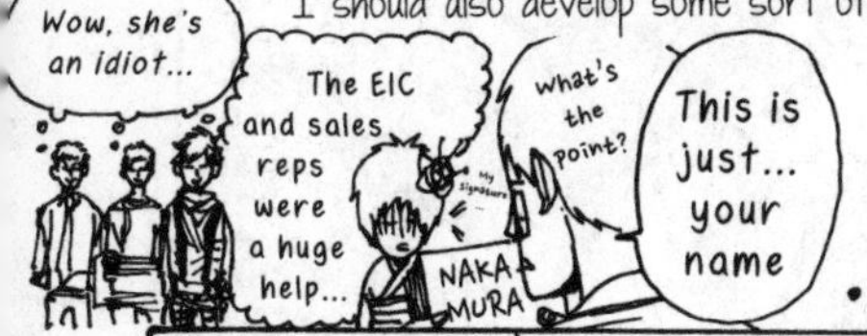
This is just... your name
what's the point?
NAKAMURA
The EIC and sales reps were a huge help...
Wow, she's an idiot...

I'm so excited I even drew a bonus manga...

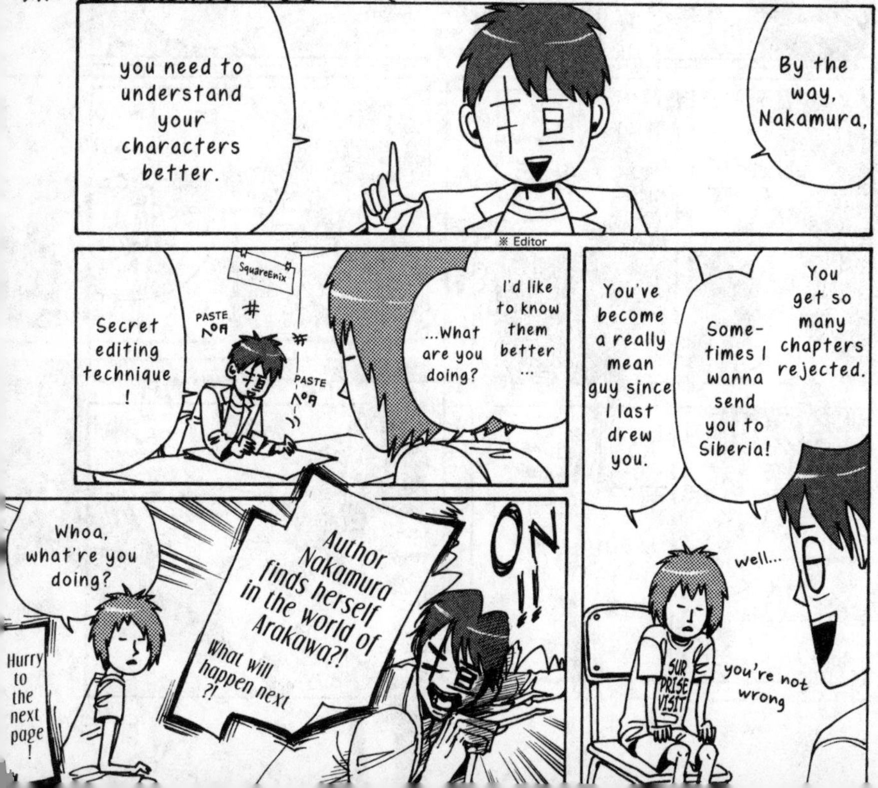
By the way, Nakamura,
you need to understand your characters better.
※ Editor
You get so many chapters rejected.
Sometimes I wanna send you to Siberia!
You've become a really mean guy since I last drew you.
well...
you're not wrong
SUR PRISE VISIT
I'd like to know them better...
...What are you doing?
SquareEnix
PASTE
PASTE
Secret editing technique!
ON!!
Author Nakamura finds herself in the world of Arakawa?! What will happen next?!
Whoa, what're you doing?
Hurry to the next page!

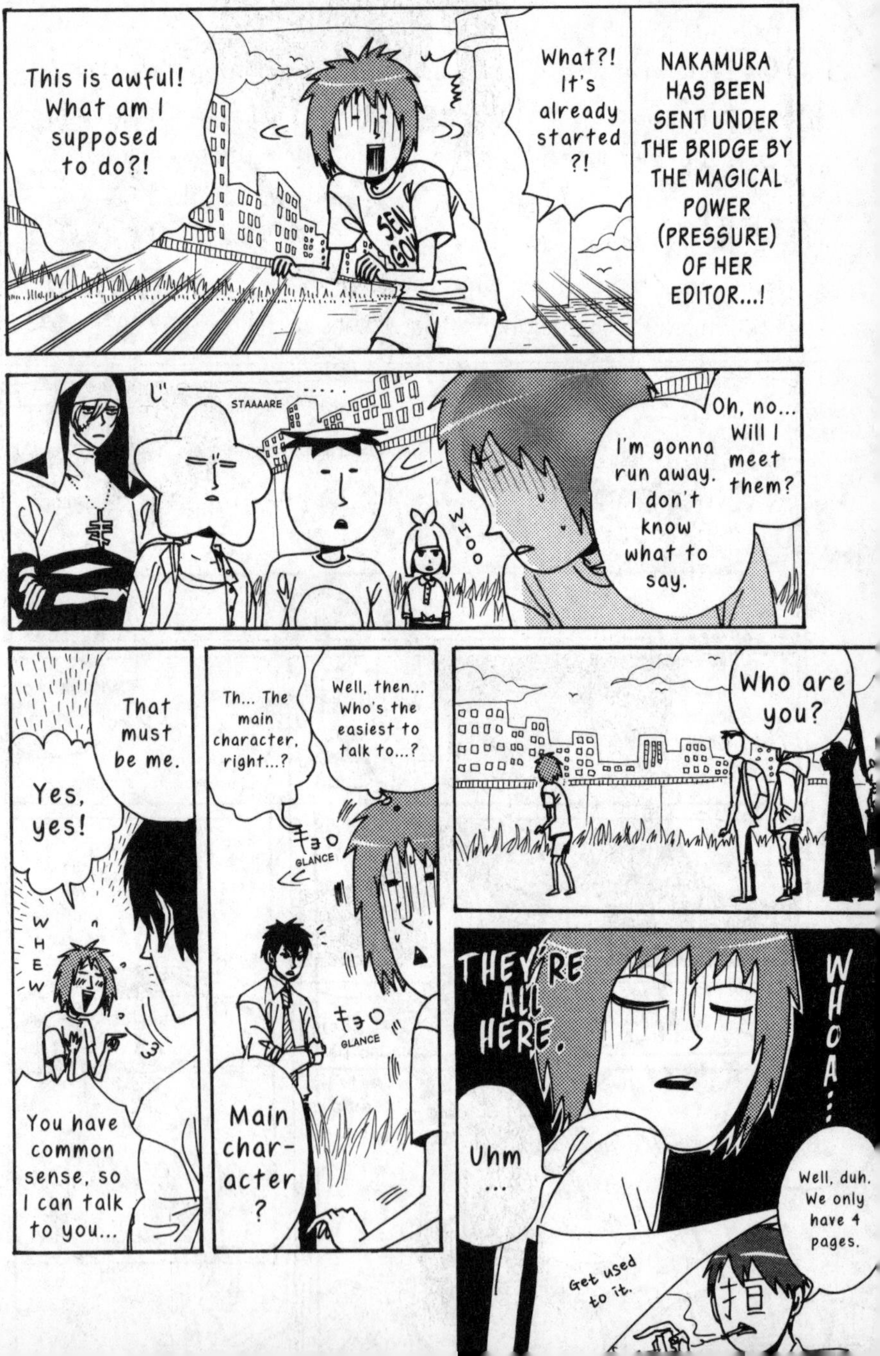

NAKAMURA HAS BEEN SENT UNDER THE BRIDGE BY THE MAGICAL POWER (PRESSURE) OF HER EDITOR...!
What?! It's already started?!
This is awful! What am I supposed to do?!
Oh, no... Will I meet them?
I'm gonna run away. I don't know what to say.
WHOO
じー.....
STAAAARE
Who are you?
WHOA...
THEY'RE ALL HERE.
Well, duh. We only have 4 pages.
Uhm ...
Get used to it.
Well, then... Who's the easiest to talk to...?
Th... The main character, right...?
キョロ
GLANCE
キョロ
GLANCE
Main character?
That must be me.
Yes, yes!
WHEW
You have common sense, so I can talk to you...

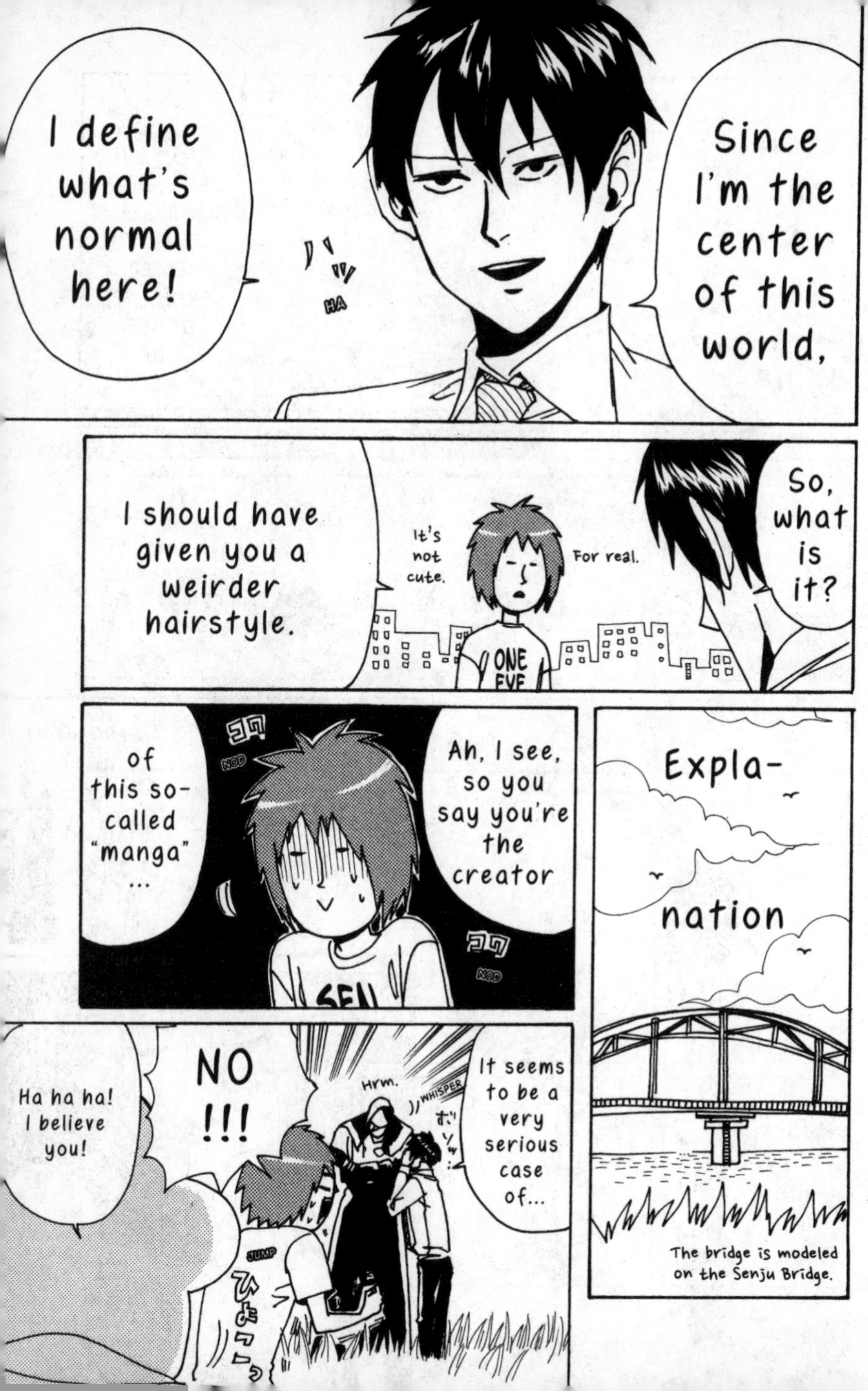
Since I'm the center of this world,
I define what's normal here!
HA
So, what is it?
For real.
It's not cute.
I should have given you a weirder hairstyle.
Expla-
nation
The bridge is modeled on the Senju Bridge.
Ah, I see, so you say you're the creator
NOD
of this so-called "manga" ...
NOD
It seems to be a very serious case of...
WHISPER
Hrm.
NO !!!
JUMP
Ha ha ha! I believe you!

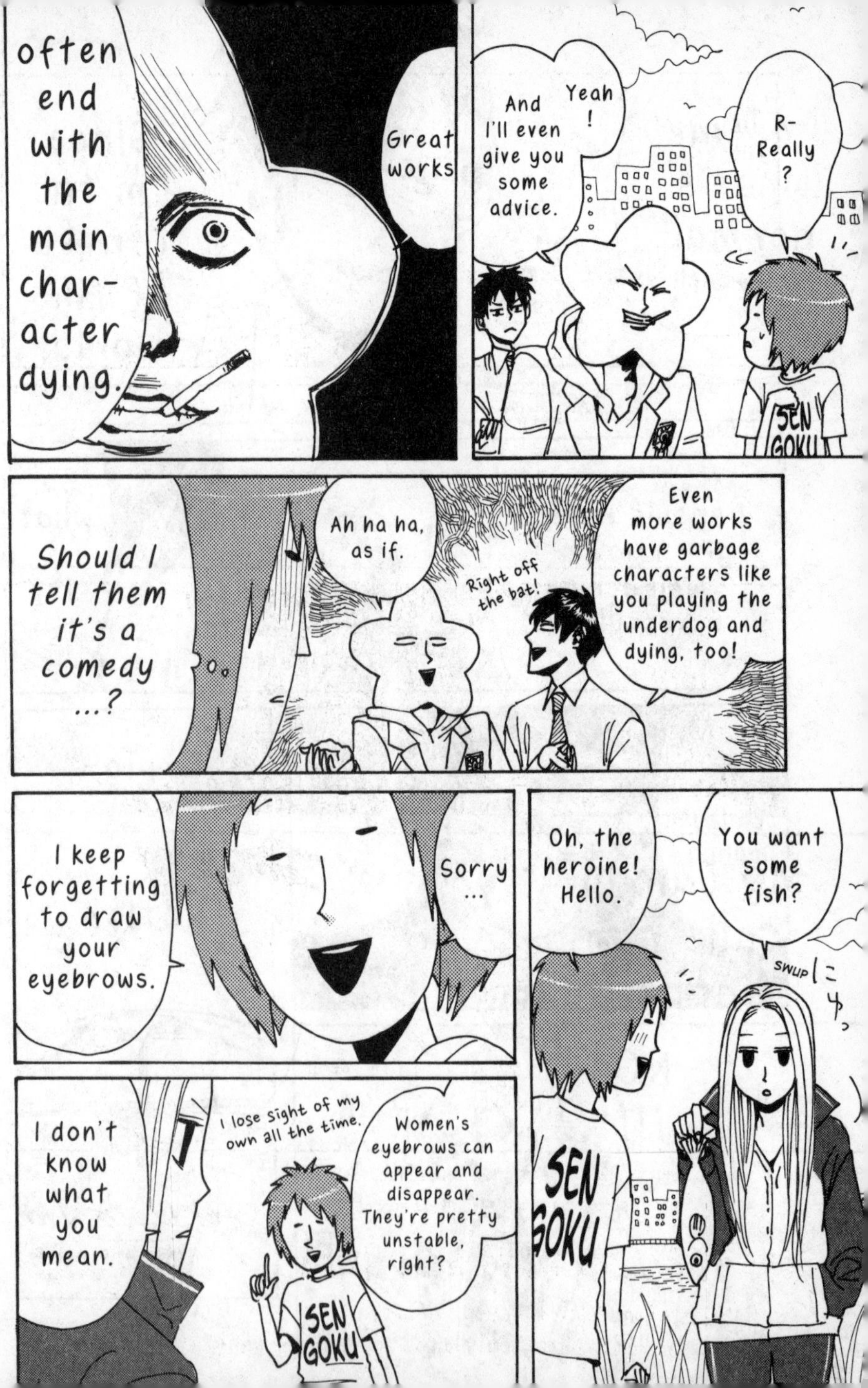

Yeah!
And I'll even give you some advice.
R-Really?
Great works
often end with the main character dying.
Even more works have garbage characters like you playing the underdog and dying, too!
Right off the bat!
Ah ha ha, as if.
Should I tell them it's a comedy...?
You want some fish?
SWUP
Oh, the heroine! Hello.
SEN GOKU
Sorry...
I keep forgetting to draw your eyebrows.
Women's eyebrows can appear and disappear. They're pretty unstable, right?
I lose sight of my own all the time.
SEN GOKU
I don't know what you mean.

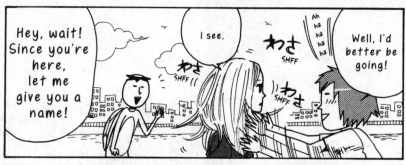

Well, I'd better be going!
Ah ha ha ha ha
わさ
SHFF
わさ
SHFF
I see.
わさ
SHFF
Hey, wait! Since you're here, let me give you a name!
But I don't live here...
You'll call me "Shut-in" or something. No thanks.
It's fine!
Hmm... Let me see...
... What?
STARE
STARE
Uhm...
Are we related ...?
we have the same face...
SEN GOKU
My family calls me "Kappa."

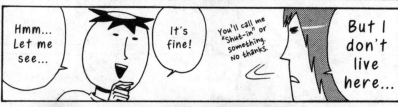

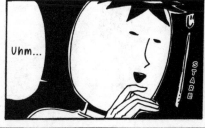

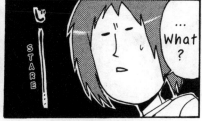

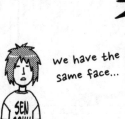

🡅 When I was in junior high, my brother started calling me Kappatsu (energetic) for some reason, and that gradually got shortened to kappa. I have no idea why...

KAPPATSU

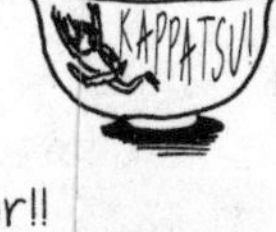

He even made a bowl for me, like this. Totally picking a fight.

SEE YOU NEXT VOLUME!

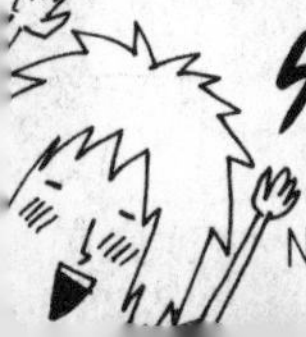

and special thanks
Naomi, Hara, Michi, Sugiyama, Ai, and my editor!!

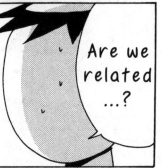

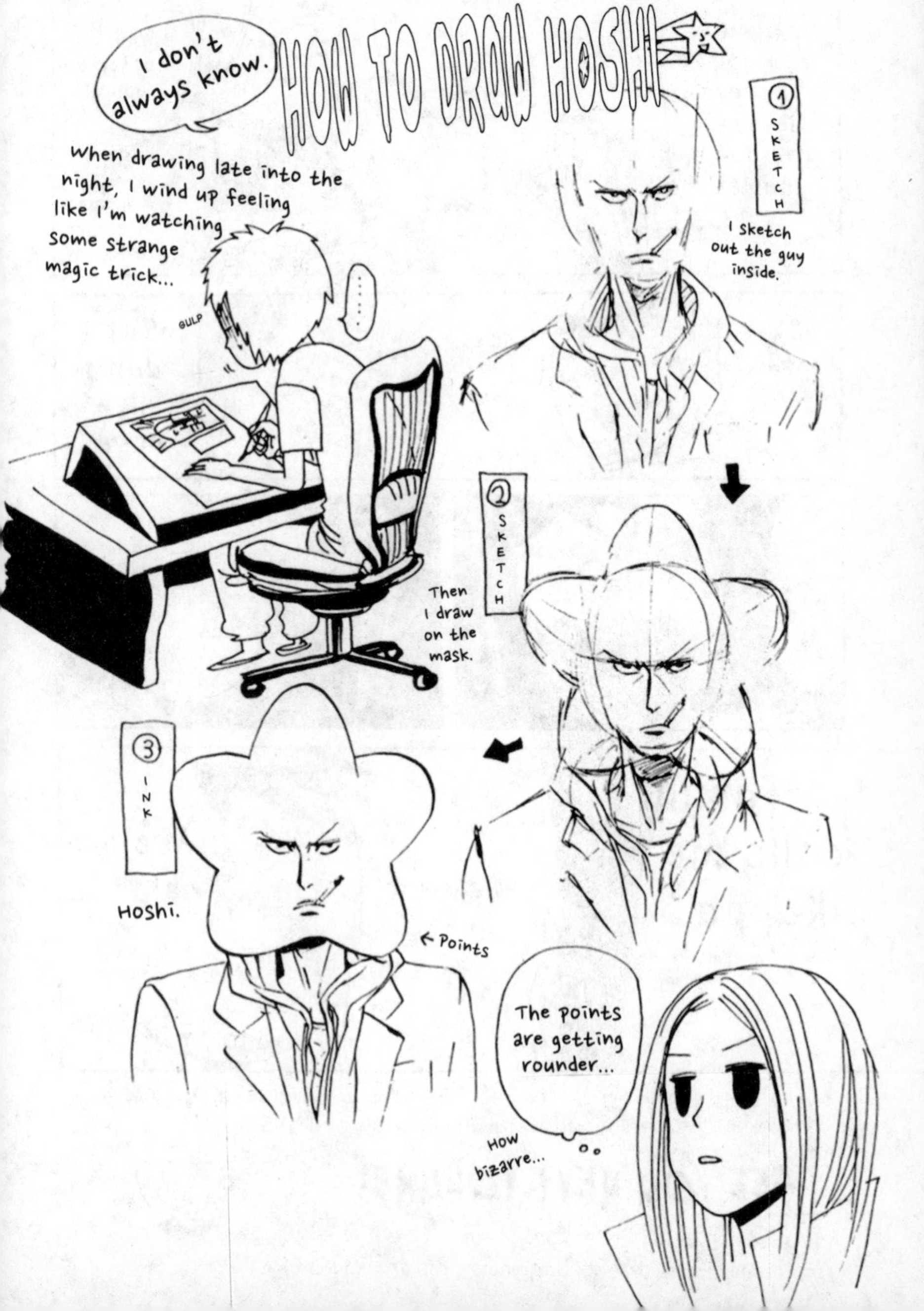

HOW TO DRAW HOSHI
1 SKETCH
I sketch out the guy inside.
I don't always know.
When drawing late into the night, I wind up feeling like I'm watching some strange magic trick...
GULP
......
2 SKETCH
Then I draw on the mask.
3 INK
HOSHI.
← Points
The points are getting rounder...
How bizarre...

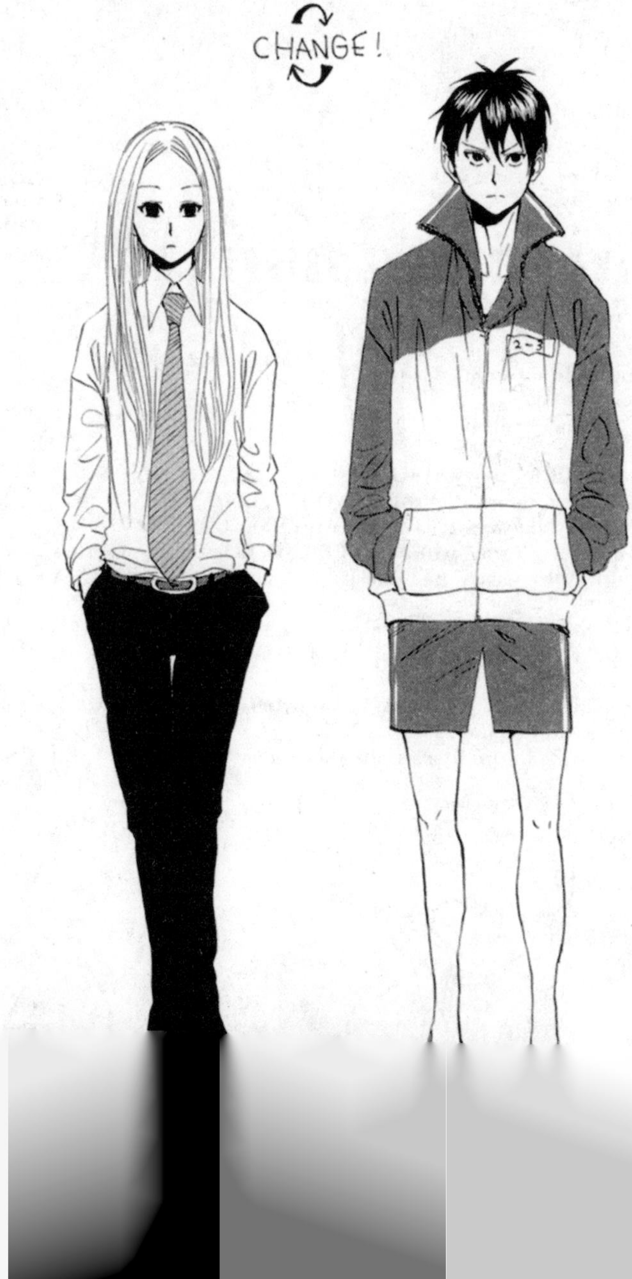
CHANGE!
2-3

ARAKAWA UNDER THE BRIDGE 1

Hikaru Nakamura

Translation: Andrew Cunningham
Production: Risa Cho
          Tomoe Tsutsumi

ARAKAWA UNDER THE BRIDGE Vol. 1 & 2
© 2005 Hikaru Nakamura / SQUARE ENIX CO., LTD.
First published in Japan in 2005 by SQUARE ENIX CO., LTD.
Translation rights arranged with SQUARE ENIX CO., LTD. and Vertical, Inc.
through Tuttle-Mori Agency, Inc. Translation © 2017 by SQUARE ENIX CO., LTD.

Translation provided by Vertical Comics, 2017
Published by Vertical Comics, an imprint of Vertical, Inc., New York

Originally published in Japanese as *Arakawa Andaa Za Burijji 1 & 2*
by SQUARE ENIX Co., Ltd., 2005
Arakawa Andaa Za Burijji first serialized in *Young Gangan*, SQUARE ENIX Co.,
Ltd., 2004-2015

This is a work of fiction.

ISBN: 978-1-945054-41-9

Manufactured in Canada

First Edition

Vertical, Inc.
451 Park Avenue
7th Floor
New York, NY 10(
www.vertical-co

Vertical books ar   ervices.

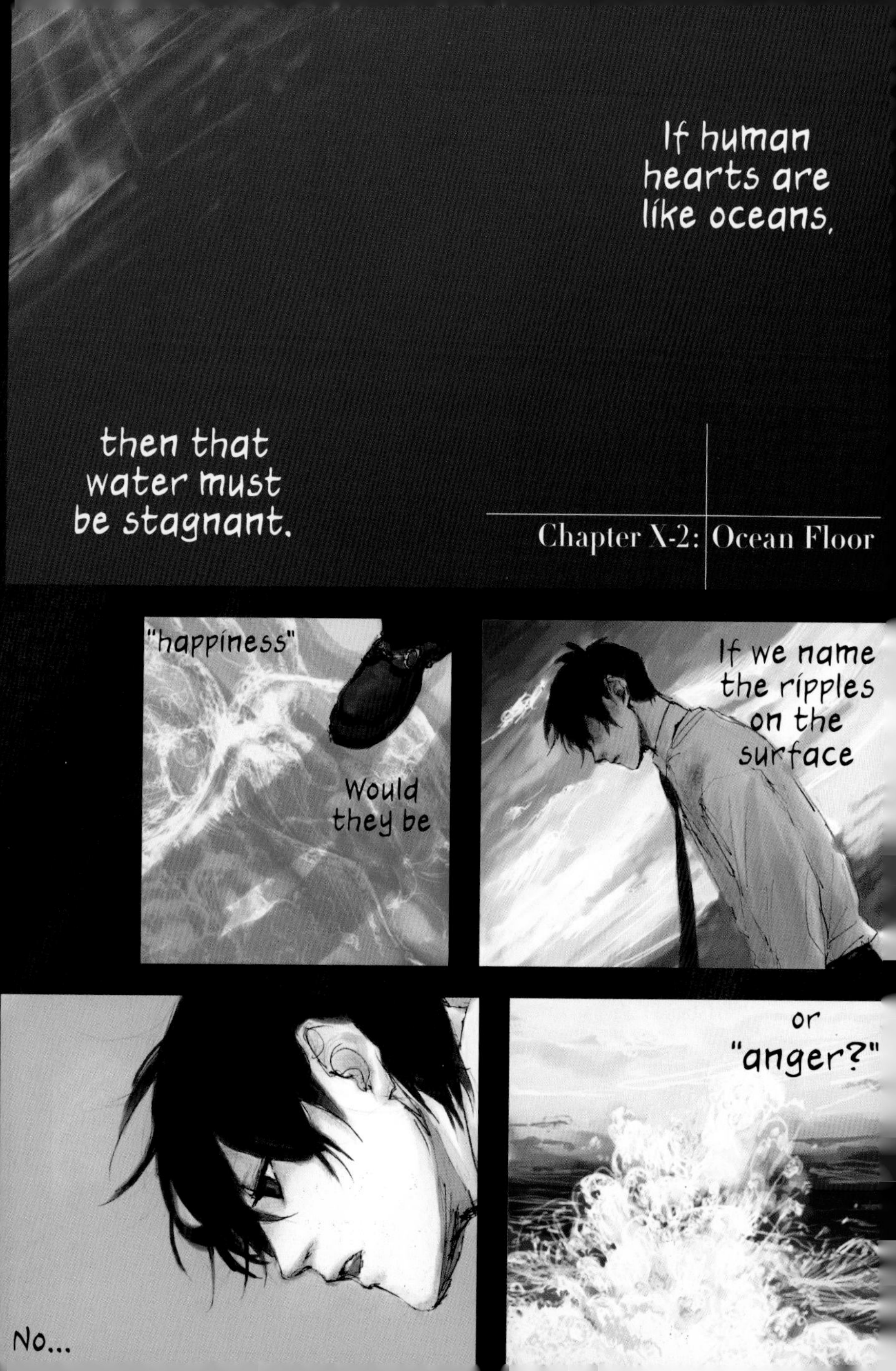
If human hearts are like oceans,
then that water must be stagnant.
Chapter X-2: Ocean Floor
If we name the ripples on the surface
Would they be
"happiness"
or "anger?"
No...

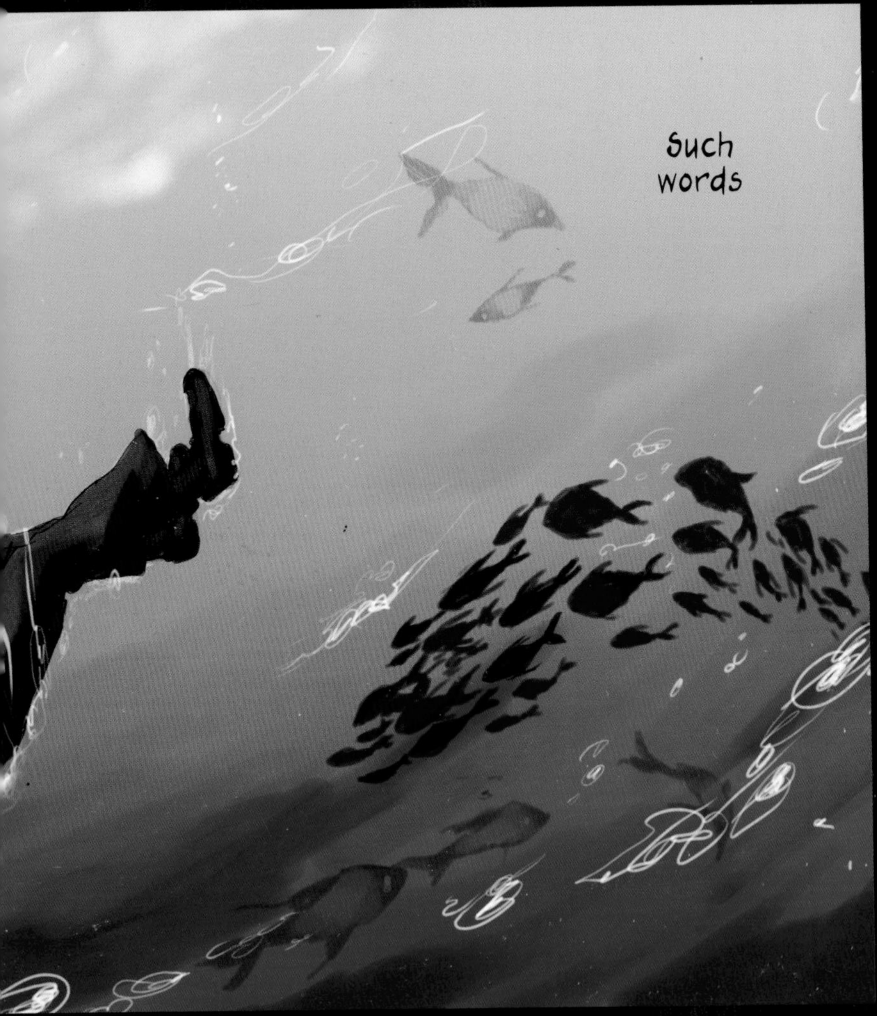
Such words
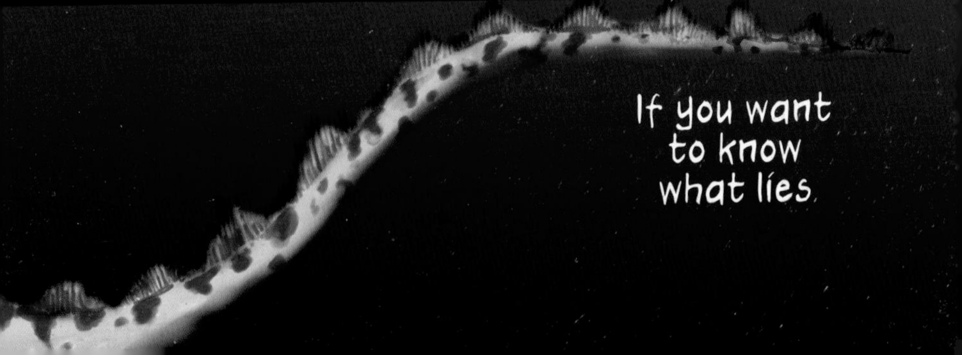
If you want to know what lies

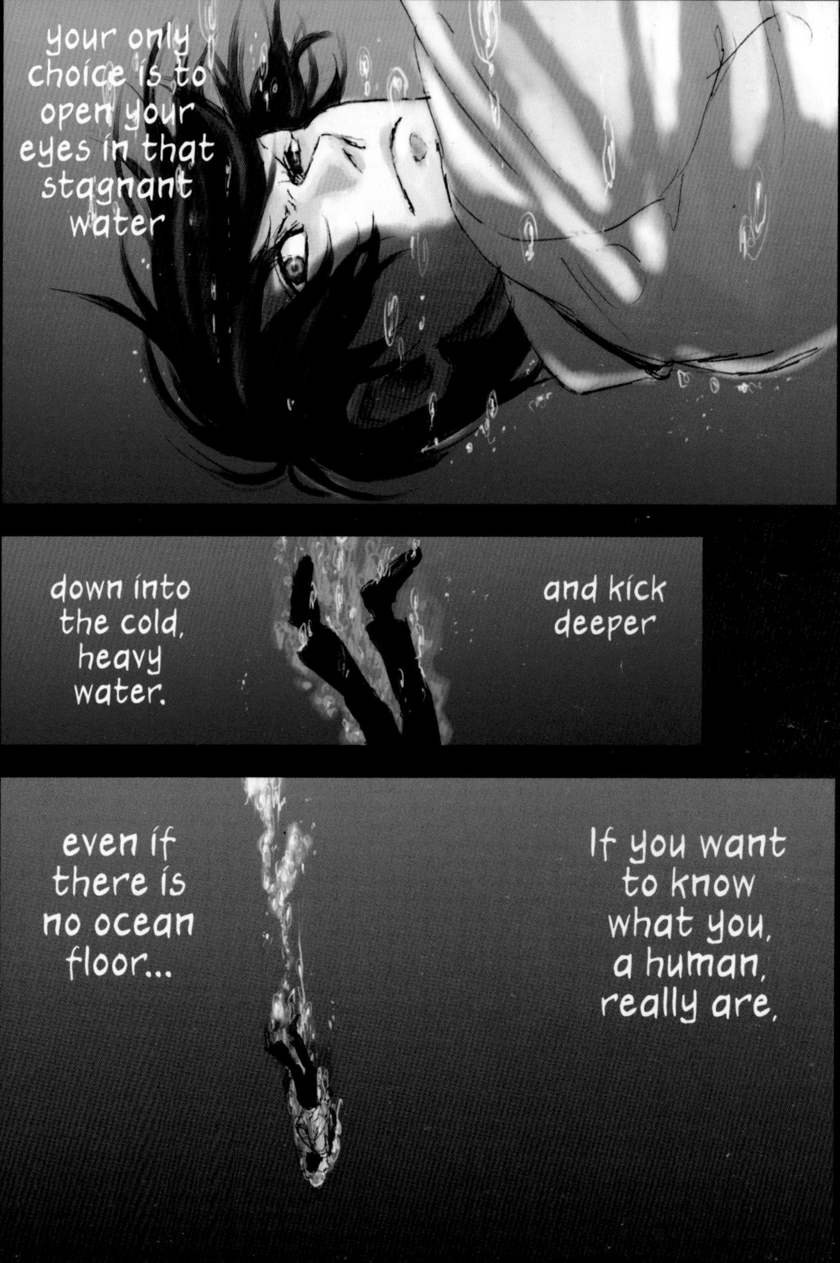
your only choice is to open your eyes in that stagnant water
and kick deeper
down into the cold, heavy water.
If you want to know what you, a human, really are,
even if there is no ocean floor...

There is a place where truth gathers... ARAKAWA UNDER THE BRIDGE

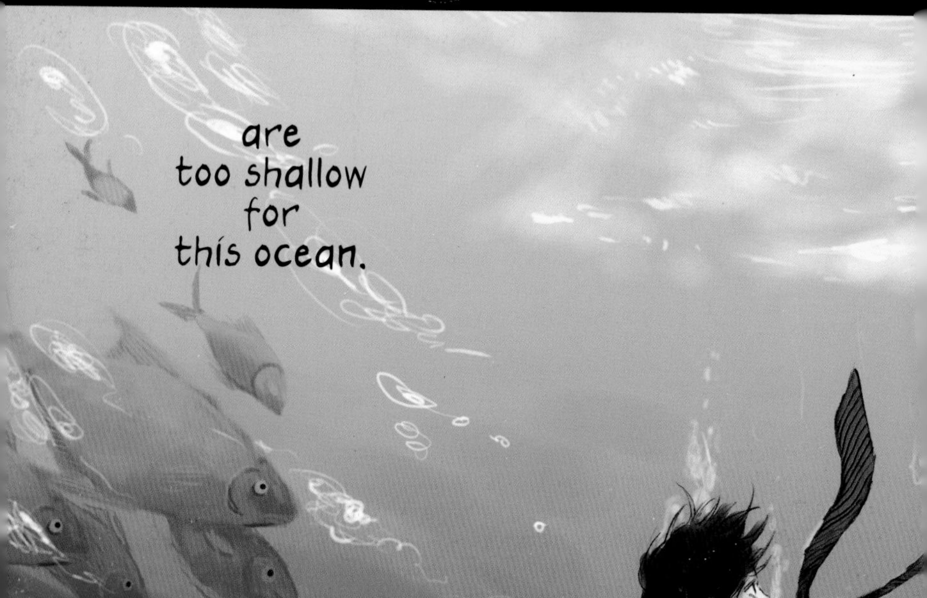
are too shallow for this ocean.
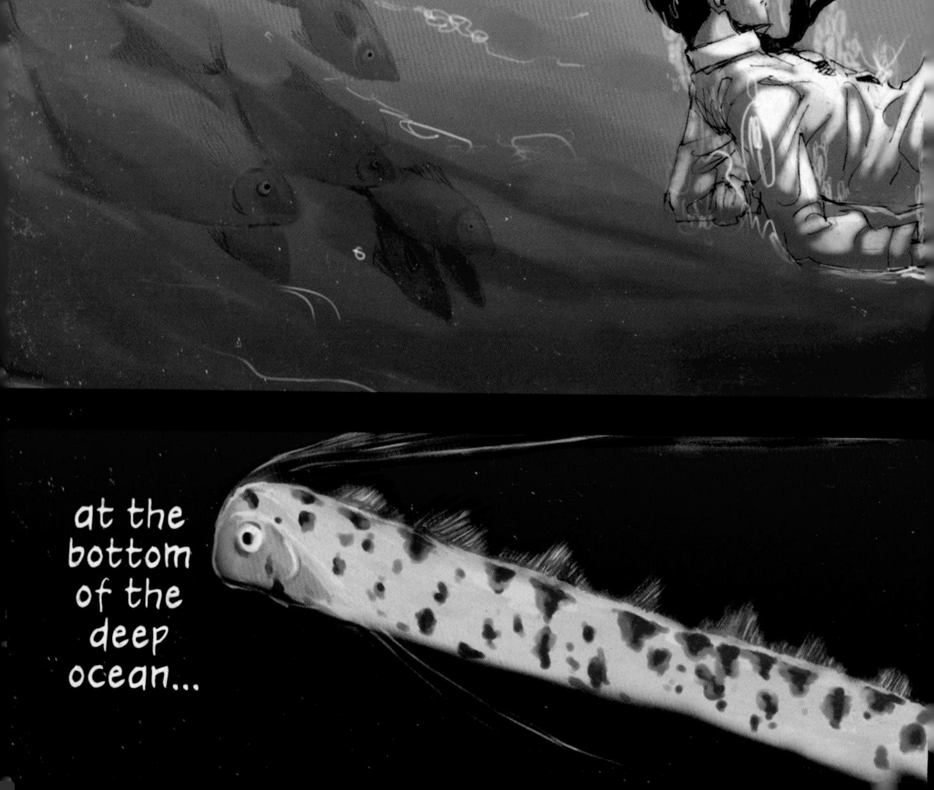
at the bottom of the deep ocean...